...

To our families
B. G.
J. S.
J.C.B.

Directory of Unpublished
Experimental Mental Measures

VOLUMES 1–3

BERT A. GOLDMAN

JOHN L. SAUNDERS

JOHN C. BUSCH

. . .

Series Editors: Bert A. Goldman and David F. Mitchell

American Psychological Association, Washington, DC

...

First printing February 1996
Second printing September 1996

Volume 1 was published in 1974 by Behavioral Publications, Volume 2 in 1978 by Human Sciences Press, and Volume 3 in 1982 by Human Sciences Press. Reissued in 1996 with a new Introduction.

Copies may be ordered from
APA Order Department
P.O. Box 92984
Washington, D.C. 20090-2984

In the United Kingdom and Europe, copies may be ordered from
American Psychological Association
3 Henrietta Street
Covent Garden
London, WC2E 8LU
England

Composition in Futura Bold and Bodoni Book by Jennifer Ruby, EDTEC Editorial Technologies, Arlington, VA.

Cover and Text Designer: Minker Design, Bethesda, MD
Printer: TechniGraphix, Reston, VA
Technical/Production Editor: Susan Bedford

ISBN: 1-55798-336-4

British Library Cataloguing-in-Publication Data
A CIP record is available from the British Library

Printed in the United States of America

Contents

(contents continue on next page)

VOLUME 3

Introduction

This combined *Directory of Unpublished Experimental Mental Measures* includes Volumes 1 through 3 and marks the second publication of these volumes. Now that the American Psychological Association (APA) has agreed to continue the series of *Directories* by publishing Volume 6, APA acquired the rights to the previously published first five volumes so that all volumes would be made available by one publisher. The authors and publisher believe that there is an ongoing need for directories such as these to enable researchers to determine what types of noncommercial experimental test instruments are currently in use. These reference books provide researchers with ready access to information about experimental measurement scales. The instruments are not evaluated, but the information given about each test should make it possible for researchers to make a preliminary judgment of its usefulness. The *Directories* do not provide all necessary information for researchers contemplating the use of a particular instrument. They do describe basic test properties and in most cases identify additional sources from which technical information concerning an instrument can be obtained.

Bert Arthur Goldman
David F. Mitchell

Directory of Unpublished
Experimental Mental Measures

VOLUME 1

BERT A. GOLDMAN, EDD
Dean, Academic Advising and Professor of Education
University of North Carolina at Greensboro

JOHN L. SAUNDERS, MED
Director, Institutional Research
University of North Carolina at Greensboro

Contents

A cumulative subject index to Volumes 1 through 3 appears at the end of this book.

Foreword

From the Original Printing of Volume 1, 1974

For over thirty-five years, users of published standardized tests have been able to turn to current and earlier editions of the *Mental Measurements Yearbooks* for detailed up-to-date information about the measures and for critiques of most of these tests by carefully selected reviewers. At times, Dr. Oscar Buros, editor of these yearbooks, has compiled indexes of all tests reviewed in a series of yearbooks, or all tests in an area of special interest—e.g., reading or personality measurement.

The *Directory of Unpublished Experimental Mental Measures: Volume I* proposes to supplement the *Mental Measurements Yearbooks* by publishing periodic surveys of tests not available commercially, using as sources those journals that carry studies and reports employing experimental instruments. The present volume is offered as the first in a series, this one based on the 1970 issues of 29 journals. Its orientation is predominantly educational, but it includes material related to psychology, sociology, and personnel work as well.

One is reminded of the bibliographies of standardized tests published by Buros in the years immediately preceding the first *Mental Measurements Yearbook* in 1938. The *Directory of Unpublished Experimental Mental Measures* will retain its relatively simple format.

The publication of a first *Directory of Unpublished Experimental Mental Measures* can thus best be viewed as an experimental effort to render a useful service to the test-using public. In turn, the test users are invited to make their contribution by indicating directions in which this projected series of periodic summaries might be developed in order to be maximally useful.

In these days of computer-assisted retrieval of references to topically organized areas and subareas, this series makes more efficient the search for those test instruments that have already been designed to meet the reader's purpose but have perhaps not yet come to his attention. It increases the likelihood that second and further users of a promising instrument will contribute to extension of its evaluation by systematic related research, thereby leading to the more rapid development of new standardized instruments to keep pace with the growing and changing demand for assessment in the several fields covered by the present summary.

One group to whom and through whose participation the present *Directory* may prove especially helpful is the multitude of doctoral students seeking to conduct logistically feasible studies on modest budgets. It is customary to deplore the one-shot nature of much of this research. If it could be geared to take advantage of current promising instrumentation, it might not only contribute to the systematic cumulative effect already cited, but might also further continued useful research by these often otherwise motivated products of our research training programs. There is, of course, a wide range of researchers between one-shot performers on the one hand, and seasoned investigators on the other; all will be served in varying degree by the *Directory,* which will enable them to be more systematic in their contributions to instrumentation.

The categories of tests summarized and their definitions by the compilers make good sense. Cross-referencing may be a refinement that readers will suggest for subsequent issues. Reference to current dissertations for other new instruments and their development may be another suggestion.

One is understandably hesitant to predict too boldly the success and usefulness of a new publication like the *Directory of Unpublished Experimental Mental Measures.* But, as President Kennedy once quoted an earlier source, "Every journey, however long, must begin with taking the first step." The compilers are to be commended for taking that first step in exploring the usefulness of this type of compilation. I am personally very hopeful that its refinement with time and constructive criticism will make it a regular addition to university, school district, and educational agency libraries; these libraries should certainly be encouraged to match the first step of the compilers by making this new publication available to their readers.

Warren G. Findley
University of Georgia

Preface

From the Original Printing of Volume 1, 1974

Purpose: This *Directory of Unpublished Experimental Mental Measures* is the first in a proposed series of annual publications designed to fill a distinct void in the publication of measurement research. The authors recognized the need for the publication of a directory of experimental test instruments, i.e., a compendium of experimental test instruments that are not currently produced commercially.[1] It is intended that this reference primarily serves to provide researchers ready access to sources of recently developed experimental mental measures. Also, it is anticipated that the directory may stimulate further use of the experimental instruments by providing researchers with relatively easy access to such information. In essence this directory is a reference to recently developed nonstandardized experimental mental measures. It is intended to point the way for the reader to locate information concerning these instruments.

Development: All available and relevant professional journals were examined by the authors. The following list includes those journals which, in the judgement of the authors, contained research involving instruments of value to researchers in education, psychology and sociology.

American Journal of Psychology
American Journal of Sociology
Behavioral Science
Child Development
Colorado Journal of Educational Research
Counselor Education and Supervision
Education
Educational and Psychological Measurement
Elementary School Guidance and Counseling
Gifted Child Quarterly
Improving College and University Teaching
Journal of College Student Personnel
Journal of Counseling Psychology
Journal of Educational Measurement
Journal of Educational Psychology
Journal of Educational Research
Journal of Educational Sociology
Journal of Experimental Education
Journal of Projective Techniques and Personality Assessment
Journal of Reading
Journal of School Psychology
Measurement and Evaluation in Guidance
NEA Research Bulletin
Personnel and Guidance Journal

---

[1]While this book was in production, several of the tests were published commercially. Those tests are marked with an asterisk.

Personnel Journal
Phi Delta Kappan
Reading Research Quarterly
Social Education
Sociology and Social Research

This directory lists all tests that were described in the 1970 issues of these journals which the present authors deemed of possible value to researchers in education, psychology and sociology. An attempt was made to omit commercially published standardized tests, task-type activities such as memory word lists used in serial learning research and achievement tests developed for a single, isolated course of study.

Organization: Following is a brief description of each of the twenty-two categories under which the authors chose to group the experimental mental measures:

Achievement: Measure Learning and/or Comprehension
Adjustment–Educational: Measure academic satisfaction
Adjustment–Psychological: Evaluate conditions and levels of adjustment along the psychological dimension
Adjustment--Social: Evaluate aspects of interactions with others
Aptitude: Predict success in given areas
Attitudes: Measure reaction to a variety of experiences and things
Communication: Evaluate information exchange
Concept meaning: Test one's understanding of words and other concepts
Creativity: Measure ability to reorganize data or information into unique configurations
Development: Measure emerging characteristics, primarily for preschool ages
Family: Measure intrafamily relations
Institutional Information: Evaluate institutions and their functioning
Interest: Identify selective attention to activities
Motivation: Measure goal strength
Personality: Measure personal attributes
Perception: Determine how one sees himself
Preference: Identify choices
Problem Solving: Test one's ability to select the most appropriate from a number of alternatives
Status: Identify one's hierarchy of acceptability
Trait Measurement: Identify and evaluate traits
Values: Measure worth one ascribes to an object or activity
Vocational Evaluation: Evaluate the person for the position

The choice of the category under which each test was grouped was determined by the purpose of the test and/or its apparent content. The authors attempted to include any of the following facts regarding each test, however in many cases only a few of these facts were provided in the journal article:

Test Name
Purpose
Description
      Number of items
      Time required
      Format

Statistics
> Reliability
> Validity

Source
> Author of the article in which the test was mentioned
> Title of the article
> Journal in which the article appeared, including date of publication, volume and page number

Related Research
> Identifying information of publications related to the source which was presented in the source.

The authors express their appreciation to their secretaries for the many evenings they spent in typing this manuscript.

Bert A. Goldman
John L. Saunders

CHAPTER 1
Achievement

1

Test Name: AUDIO-VISUAL PERCEPTION

Purpose: To discover whether sight–sound separation makes a difference in information acquisition and whether sight–sound separation or simultaneous sight sound is the best method.

Number of Items: 120

Format: Multiple-choice: 40 questions from audio information, 40 questions from visual information, and 40 questions from information presented by sight and sound.

Author: Galfo, A. J.

Article: Effects of audio and visual presentation sequences on pupil information acquisition.

Journal: *Journal of Educational Research,* December 1970, *64*(4), 172.

Related Research: Broadbent, D. E. (1958). *Perception and communications.* New York: Pergamon Press.

Lumsdaine, A. A. (1963). Instruments and media of instructions. In N. L. Gage (Ed.), *Handbook of research on teaching* (pp. 670–671). Chicago: Rand McNally.

...

2

Test Name: BOTEL READING INVENTORY*

Purpose: Provides two scores: (a) Instructional Level—represents grade level of achievement in mastery in word recognition and

word opposites (as read by the student) and (b) Achievement Level—represents mastery of word opposites as presented orally by the teacher and may be considered to some extent to be a measure of extensiveness of vocabulary.

Author: Goolsby, T. M., Jr., and Frary, R. B.

Article: Validity of the metropolitan readiness test for White and Black students in a southern city.

Journal: *Educational and Psychological Measurement,* Summer 1970, *30*(2), 443–450.

...

3

Test Name: COGNITION OF SEMANTIC UNITS TEST

Purpose: Measures verbal comprehension.

Format: Includes a multiple-choice vocabulary test and a completion test in which E unites definitions or synonyms for given words.

Validity: .32 to .69.

Author: Hoepfner, R., Guilford, J. P., and Bradley, P. A.

Article: Information–transformation abilities.

Journal: *Education and Psychological Measurement,* Winter 1970, *30*(4), 785–802.

...

4

Test Name: COMPREHENSIVE MATHEMATICS INVENTORY

Purpose: Assessing math abilities

of youngsters entering school.

Number of Items: 200

Time required: 35–40 minutes.

Format: Part I: 98 items on money, vocabulary, and numbers; Part II: 102 items on geometry, measurement, and recall—various pictorial presentations and manipulative objects.

Reliability: Ranges from .91 to .94 for Part I and from .83 to .87 for Part II.

Validity: Not reported in article.

Authors: Rea, R. E., and Reys, R. E.

Article: The comprehensive mathematics inventory.

Journal: *Journal of Educational Measurement,* Spring 1970, *7*(1), 45.

Related Research: Kaiser, H. F. (1958). The varimax criterion for analytic rotation in factor analysis. *Psychometrika, 23,* 187–200.

...

5

Test Name: COMPREHENSION SKILLS TEST

Purpose: Designed to test sentence comprehension, anaphora comprehension, and intersentence syntax.

Format: Includes 25 types of items testing sentence structure, 16 types testing anaphoric structures, and 14 types testing intersentence structures. Examples are provided.

Author: Bormuth, J. R., et al.

Article: Children's comprehension of between- and within-sentence syntactic structures.

Journal: *Journal of Educational Psychology*, October 1970, *61*(5), 349–357.

Related Research: Bormuth, J. R. (1970). *On the theory of achievement test items.* Chicago: University of Chicago Press.

Menzel, P. (1970). Linguistic bases of the theory of writing items for instruction stated in natural language. In J. R. Bormuth (Ed.), *On the theory of achievement test items.* Chicago: University of Chicago Press.

■ ■ ■

6

Test Name: DEVELOPED ABILITY PERFORMANCE

Purpose: To provide ability scores that have intrinsic meaning.

Number of Items: 18 subscales—items not listed.

Format: Paper and pencil.

Author: Jung, S.

Article: Guidance testing and the individualized program of studies.

Journal: *Education*, February–March 1970, *90*(3), 227–231.

Related Research: J. C. Flanagan. The implications of project talent and related research for guidance. *Measurement and Evaluation in Guidance*, 1969, *2*, 133–136.

■ ■ ■

7

Test Name: ECHOIC RESPONSE INVENTORY FOR CHILDREN

Purpose: Measure range of sentence complexity.

Number of Items: 20 sentences.

Reliability: .89–.91 (Intraform).

.91 (Test–retest).

Author: Stern, C., and Gupta, W.

Article: Echoic responding of disadvantaged pre-school children as a function of type of speech modeled.

Journal: *Journal of School Psychology*, 1970, *8*(1), 24–27.

Related Research: Stern, C., & Keislar, E. (1968). Effects of dialect and instructional procedures on children's oral language production and concept acquisition. *Urban Education, 3,* 169–176.

■ ■ ■

8

Test Name: HIGHER ORDER AND MEMORY LEVEL TEST

Purpose: To measure the subject's ability to recognize or recall information and to recall specific factual information where knowledge of that information may be attributable to higher order questions.

Number of Items: 36

Format: Includes memory learning of narrative material, memory learning of descriptive material, higher order learning of narrative material, higher order learning of descriptive material, higher questions on new material.

Author: Allan, D. I.

Article: Some effects of advance organizers and level of question in the learning and retention of written social studies material.

Journal: *Journal of Educational Psychology,* October 1970, *61*(5), 333–339.

■ ■ ■

9

Test Name: JUDGMENT TEST

Purpose: To measure effectiveness of judgment training.

Number of Items: 12

Format: Multiple-choice.

Author: Stratton, R. P., Parrott, G. L., and Johnson, D. M.

Article: Transfer of judgment training to production and judgment of solutions on a verbal problem.

Journal: *Journal of Educational Psychology*, February 1970, *61*(1), 16–23.

Related Research: Johnson, D. M., Parrott, G. L., & Stratton, R. P. (1968). Production and judgment of solutions to five problems. *Journal of Educational Psychology Monograph Supplement, 59*(6, Part 2).

■ ■ ■

10

Test Name: KNOWLEDGE TEST OF KUDER PREFERENCE RECORD, VOCATIONAL FORM C

Purpose: To measure clients' understanding of the Kuder Preference Record, Vocational Form C.

Number of Items: 18

Format: Multiple-choice.

Author: Miller, C. D., Morrill, W. H., and Uhlemann, M. R.

Article: Micro-counseling: An experimental study of pre-practicum training in communicating test results.

Journal: *Counselor Education and Supervision,* Spring 1970, *9*(3), 171–177.

■ ■ ■

11

Test Name: MEMORY FOR SEMANTIC TRANSFORMATIONS TESTS

Purpose: To measure the ability for remembering changes in meaning or redefinitions.

Format: Includes remembering the

transformation between pairs of words where the transformations are different meanings of the same word, homonyms, and ambiguous words.

Validity: .35 to .52.

Author: Hoepfner, R., Guilford, J. P., and Bradley, P. A.

Article: Information-transformation abilities.

Journal: *Educational and Psychological Measurement,* Winter 1970, *30*(4), 785–802.

■ ■ ■

12

Test Name: PRESCHOOL ACHIEVEMENT TEST IN READING, LETTER IDENTIFICATION, AND NUMERICAL IDENTIFICATION

Purpose: To identify achievement at the preschool level in reading, letter identification, numerical identification.

Number of Items: Reading, 37 words; Letter Identification, 52 letters; Numerical Identification, 21. Other correlations available.

Format: Individually administered.

Validity: Correlations with IQ range from .42 to .70 for first-year achievement.

Author: Durkin, D.

Article: A language arts program for pre-first-grade children: 2-year achievement report.

Journal: *Reading Research Quarterly,* Summer 1970, *5*(4), 534–565.

Related Research: Durkin, D. (1966). *Children who read early.* New York: Teachers College Press (Columbia University).

13

Test Name: RECONSTRUCTION TEST

Purpose: Measures ability to reconstruct part–whole configurations from memory.

Number of Items: 2 pictures.

Author: Elkind, D., Anagnostopoulou, R., and Malone, S.

Article: Determinants of part–whole perception in children.

Journal: *Child Development,* June 1970, *41*(2), 391–397.

Related Research: Elkind, D., Koegler R. R., & Go, E. (1964). Studies in perceptual development. II: Whole–part perception. *Child Development, 35,* 81–90.

■ ■ ■

14

Test Name: READING COMPREHENSION TESTS

Purpose: Two tests to measure reading comprehension.

Number of Items: 37 in each test.

Format: 37 sentences randomly altered; for each sentence the three pictures were randomly ordered.

Author: Tatham, S. M.

Article: Reading comprehension of materials written with select oral language patterns: A study of grades two and four.

Journal: *Reading Research Quarterly,* Spring 1970, *5*(3), 402–426.

■ ■ ■

15

Test Name: READING TESTS OF FLEXIBILITY

Purpose: To evaluate flexibility of speed and comprehension.

Author: Sargent, E. E.

Article: College reading before college.

Journal: *Journal of Reading,* October 1970, *14*(2), 83–88.

Related Research: Braam, L. S., & Sheldon, W. D. (1959). *Developing efficient reading.* New York: Oxford University Press.

■ ■ ■

16

Test Name: REVISION OF THE INTELLECTUAL ACHIEVEMENT RESPONSIBILITY SCALE

Purpose: To measure intellectual achievement responsibility.

Number of Items: 28

Format: Two-choice items are used; one of the choices represents an internal ascription, and the other is an external attribution.

Author: Weiner, B., and Potepan, P. A.

Article: Personality characteristics and affective reactions toward exams of superior and failing college students.

Journal: *Journal of Educational Psychology,* April 1970, *61*(2), 144–151.

Related Research: Crandall, V. C., Katkovsky, W., & Crandall, V. J. (1965).Children's belief in their own control of reinforcements in intellectual–academic achievement situations. *Child Development, 36,* 91–109.

■ ■ ■

17

Test Name: REVISED MEASURE OF INFLECTIONAL PERFORMANCE

Purpose: To provide an assessment of children's learning of inflectional principles.

Number of Items: 35

Time required: 10 to 15 minutes.

Format: Individually administered on 30 picture cards. The examiner reads the textual material aloud. The child's responses are tape-recorded and written in phonetic notation.

Reliability: .91 to .95.

Author: Brittain, M. M.

Article: Inflectional performance and early reading achievement.

Journal: *Reading Research Quarterly,* Fall 1970, *6*(1), 34–48.

Related Research: Berko, J. (1961). The child's learning of English morphology. In S. Saporta (Ed.), *Psycho-linguistics: A book of reading* (pp. 359–375). New York: Holt, Rinehart & Winston.

■ ■ ■

18

Test Name: SHORT-TERM MEMORY TEST

Purpose: To measure short-term memory span.

Number of Items: 20

Format: Two-digit numbers and adjective–noun word combinations.

Author: Furukawo.

Article: Chunking method of determining size of step in programmed instruction.

Journal: *Journal of Educational Psychology,* June 1970, *61*(3), 247–254.

■ ■ ■

19

Test Name: TESTS OF LOGICAL ADDITIONS

Purpose: To assess subject's success on verbal and object tests of logical addition.

Format: Includes two verbal tests of logical addition and two tests of logical addition involving concrete objects.

Author: Elkind, D., Anagnostopoulou, R., and Malone, S.

Article: Determinants of part-whole perception in children.

Journal: *Child Development,* June 1970, *41*(2), 391–397.

■ ■ ■

20

Test Name: TWO CLOZE TESTS

Purpose: To measure reading comprehension.

Author: Summers, E. G.

Article: Doctoral dissertations in college and adult reading.

Journal: *Journal of Reading,* October 1970, *14*(1), 9–14.

Related Research: Cranney, A. G., Jr. (1968). A comparison of a free-response and multiple-choice Cloze reading test. (Doctoral dissertation, University of Minnesota). *Dissertation Abstracts, 29*(3), 811A.

■ ■ ■

21

Test Name: ZIP

Purpose: To place migrant children at elementary school age in proper grade level.

Number of Items: 3 sections.

Time required: 15–25 minutes.

Format: Language facility section: Tell all you can about each picture. Reading section: word recognition. Math section: identifying numerals, matching objects, and graduated problems.

Reliability: .93 for language facility, 97 for reading, .93 for math.

Validity: .89 for language facility section, .93 for reading, .94 for math.

Author: Scott, N. C.

Article: Zip Test: A quick locater test for migrant children.

Journal: *Journal of Educational Measurement,* Spring 1970, *7*(1), 49.

CHAPTER 2
Adjustment—Educational

22

Test Name: COLLEGE INVENTORY OF ACADEMIC ADJUSTMENT

Purpose: To measure the adjustment students make to six areas of college life.

Number of Items: 90

Author: Graft, R., and Coley, G.

Article: Adjustment of commuter and resident students.

Journal: *Journal of College Student Personnel,* January 1970, *11*(1), 54–57.

Related Research: Barow, H. (1951). *Manual for the college inventory of academic adjustment.* Stanford: Stanford University Press.

· · ·

23

Test Name: MODIFICATION OF THE SURVEY OF STUDY HABITS AND ATTITUDES

Purpose: To measure attitudes, study habits, need-achievement, and achievement anxiety.

Number of Items: 122

Validity: –.06 to .62.

Author: Khan, S. B.

Article: Affective correlates of academic achievement: A longitudinal study.

Journal: *Measurement and Evaluation in Guidance,* Summer 1970, *3*(2), 76–80.

Related Research: Holstzman,

W. H., Brown, W. F., & Farquhar, W. G. (1954). The survey of study habits and attitudes: A new instrument for the prediction of academic success. *Educational and Psychological Measurement, 14,* 726–732.

McGuire, C., et al. (1961). Dimensions of talented behavior. *Educational and Psychological Measurement, 21,* 3–38.

· · ·

24

Test Name: RATING SCALE FOR TEACHERS OF STUDENTS

Purpose: Reflects teacher perceptions of student persistence, attention, liking school, sociability and cooperation.

Format: 7-point rating scale.

Authors: Bednar, R. L., Zelhart, P. F., Greathause, L., and Weinberg, S.

Article: Operant conditioning principles in the treatment of learning and behavior problems with delinquent boys.

Journal: *Journal of Counseling Psychology,* November 1970, *17*(6, Part 1), 492–497.

· · ·

25

Test Name: TEST ANXIETY SCALE FOR CHILDREN

Purpose: To measure school anxiety.

Reliability: .61 and .71.

Author: Mayer, G. R., et al.

Article: The use of public commitment and counseling with elementary school children: An evaluation.

Journal: *Elementary School Guidance and Counseling,* October 1970, *5*(1), 22–34.

Related Research: Sarason, S. B., Hill, K. T., & Zimbardo, P. G. (1964). A longitudinal study of the relation of test anxiety to performance on intelligence and achievement tests. *Monographs of the Society for Research in Child Development, 29*(Serial No. 98, 7), 1–51.

· · ·

26

Test Name: TEST ANXIETY QUESTIONNAIRE

Purpose: A self-report inventory of situationally aroused anxiety.

Format: Responses are recorded on a Likert scale.

Validity: .02 to –.75 with other scales.

Author: Weiner, B., and Potepan, P. A.

Article: Personality characteristics and affective reactions toward exams of superior and failing college students.

Journal: *Journal of Educational Psychology,* April 1970, *61*(2), 144–151.

Related Research: Mandler, G., & Sarason, S. B. (1952). A study of anxiety and learning. *Journal of Abnormal and Social Psychology, 47,* 166–173.

27

Test Name: TRAINEE ADJUSTMENT SCALE

Purpose: To measure changes in trainee adjustment for three conditions.

Number of Items: 14

Author: Hoffnung, R. J., and Mills, R. B.

Article: Situational group counseling with disadvantaged youth.

Journal: *Personnel and Guidance Journal,* February 1970, *48*(6), 458–464.

CHAPTER 3
Adjustment—Psychological

28

Test Name: CHILD BEHAVIOR RATING SCALE

Purpose: To identify behavior problems.

Number of Items: 15

Format: A list of 15 behavior problems.

Reliability: .63.

Author: Mayer, G. R., et al.

Article: The use of public commitment and counseling with elementary school children: An evaluation.

Journal: *Elementary School Guidance and Counseling,* October 1970, 5(1), 22–34.

Related Research: Mayer, G. R., & Beggs, D. L. (1969). *Pre-educationally disadvantaged elementary school child: Anxiety reduction and behavioral change through public commitment and counseling* (Cooperative Research Project No. 8–E-088). Southern Illinois University.

• • •

29

Test Name: CHILDREN'S FORM OF THE MANIFEST ANXIETY SCALE

Purpose: To measure anxiety level; fear of failure.

Number of Items: 53

Format: Low reading level, 11 of the items provide a lie score.

Author: Tseng, M. S.

Article: Locus of control as a determinant of job proficiency, employability, and training satisfaction of vocational rehabilitation clients.

Journal: *Journal of Counseling Psychology,* November 1970, 17(6, Part 1), 487–491.

Related Research: Castaneda, A., McCandless, B. R., & Palermo, D. S. (1956). The children's form of the manifest anxiety scale. *Child Development, 27,* 317–326.

• • •

30

Test Name: THE DREAM INCIDENT TECHNIQUE

Purpose: Uses dream associations to measure level of tension in 12 personality areas.

Format: Subject records dream on awakening. Asked to think of real incidents suggested by the dream. These incidents are rated by subject.

Reliability: "Scores … have shown moderate stability over two dreams."

Author: Tanck, R. H., and Robbins, P. R.

Journal: *Journal of Projective Techniques and Personality Assessment,* August 1970, 34(4), 277–282.

Related Research: Robbins, P. R. (1966). An approach to measuring psychological tensions by means of dream associations. *Psychological Reports, 18,* 959–971.

• • •

31

Test Name: GUIDANCE NEEDS QUESTIONNAIRE

Purpose: To determine guidance needs of elementary school pupils.

Number of Items: 20

Format: Subject responds to each question by indicating one of three responses: *very much, sometimes, rarely,* or *never.*

Author: Bedrosian, O., Sara, N., and Pearlman, J.

Article: A pilot study to determine the effectiveness of guidance classes in developing self-understanding in elementary school children.

Journal: *Elementary School Guidance and Counseling,* December 1970, 5(2), 124–134.

Related Research: Pearlman, J. (1966). *The place and value of group guidance classes in the intermediate grades of elementary school.* Unpublished master's thesis, National College of Education, Evanston, IL.

• • •

32

Test Name: HUMAN FIGURE DRAWING PROJECTIVE TEST

Purpose: Measure of anxiety.

Author: Engle, P., and Suppes, J. S.

Article: The relation between human figure drawing and test anxiety in children.

Journal: *Journal of Projective Techniques and Personality Assessment,* June 1970, 34(3), 223–231.

• • •

33

Test Name: LIFE SATISFACTION RATING SCALE

Purpose: Solicits information concerning the subjects' feelings of happiness and satisfaction with their life as such, provides an "inner" or psychological measure of successful aging.

Author: Gray, R. M., and Kasteler, J. M.

Article: An evaluation of the effectiveness of a foster grandparent project.

Journal: *Sociology and Social Research,* January 1970, *54*(2), 181–189.

Related Research: Neugarten, B. L., Havinghurst, R. S., & Tobin, S. S. (1961). The measurement of life satisfaction. *Journal of Gerontology, 16*(2), 134–143.

■ ■ ■

34

Test Name: MODIFIED VERSION OF THE DYMOND ADJUSTMENT INDEX

Purpose: To assess client adjustment as well as change in a noncognitive area.

Number of Items: 74 self-reference items.

Author: Edwards, B. C., and Edgerly, J. W.

Article: Effects of counselor-client cognitive congruence on counseling outcome in brief counseling.

Journal: *Journal of Counseling Psychology,* July 1970, *17*(4), 313–318.

Related Research: Rogers, C. S., & Dymond, R. (Eds.). (1954). *Psychotherapy and personality change.* Chicago: University of Chicago Press.

■ ■ ■

35

Test Name: THE MOST UNPLEASANT CONCEPT TEST

Purpose: To determine levels of psychological distress.

Format: Subject thinks of the most unpleasant thing he or she can, then draws it.

Reliability: Interrater reliability, .85.

Validity: Comparison of drawings of four groups of subjects at different levels of psychological distress, shows overall significance > .01.

Author: McAleer, C., and Tipton, R.

Article: The most unpleasant concept test: A validity study.

Journal: *Journal of Projective Techniques and Personality Assessment,* April 1970, *34*(2), 131–137.

■ ■ ■

36

Test Name: NEUROTIC MANIFESTATIONS

Purpose: To determine whether there have been any nervous conditions.

Number of Items: 3

Format: The three questions are presented.

Validity: .22.

Author: Taft, R., and Gilchrist, M. B.

Article: Creative attitudes and creative productivity: A comparison of two aspects of creativity among students.

Journal: *Journal of Educational Psychology,* April 1970, *61*(2), 136–143.

■ ■ ■

37

Test Name: PERSONAL ADJUSTMENT BEHAVIOR RATING SCALES

Purpose: To evaluate personal stability.

Number of Items: 98

Format: Consisted of three scales: (a) items that consistently reflected poor adjustment, (b) items that consistently reflected good adjustment, and (c) neutral items.

Author: Rotter, G. S., and Tinkleman, V.

Article: Anchor effects in the development of behavior rating scales.

Journal: *Educational and Psychological Measurement,* Summer 1970, *30*(2), 311–318.

■ ■ ■

38

Test Name: STANDARD HELPEE STIMULUS EXPRESSIONS AND ALTERNATE RESPONSES

Purpose: Stimulus expressions were designed to cross different affect areas (depression–distress, anger–hostility, elation–excitement) with different problem areas (social–interpersonal, education–vocational; child-rearing, sexual–marital) plus silence. Alternate responses were designed to cross level of facilitation or responsiveness with level of action orientation or initiative in random combinations.

Number of Items: 16

Validity: Correlations from −.71 to .73 with other measures.

Author: Carkhuff, R. R., and Bierman, R.

Article: Training as a preferred mode of treatment of parents of emotionally disturbed children.

Journal: *Journal of Counseling Psychology,* March 1970, *17*(2), 157–161.

■ ■ ■

39

Test Name: SUPER NEUROTICISM SCALE

Purpose: Measure of neuroticism.

Author: Shaffer, W. F.

Article: Experiment which casts doubt on the findings of the Stanford Mobility Study.

Journal: *Journal of Counseling Psychology,* July 1970, *17*(4), 299–305.

Related Research: Super, D. E., Heyde, M. B., & Atkins, W. R. (1965). *The biographical inventory form CX-1*(An unpublished instrument on file at the Career Pattern Study). Teachers College, Columbia University.

■ ■ ■

40

Test Name: TRANSCENDENCE INDEX

Purpose: To measure richness of fantasy.

Author: Pulaski, M. A. S.

Article: Play as a function of toy structure and fantasy predisposition.

Journal: *Child Development,* June 1970, *41*(2), 531–537.

Related Research: Weisskopf, E. (1950). A transcendence index as a

proposed measure in the TAT. *Journal of Psychology, 29,* 379–390.

■ ■ ■

41

Test Name: TRANSCENDENCE INDEX

Purpose: To measure amount of projection elicited.

Reliability: Interjudge and test–retest reliability judged to be "adequate."

Related Research: Weisskopf, E. (1950). A transcendence index as a proposed measure of the TAT. *Journal of Psychology, 29,* 407–416.

■ ■ ■

42

Test Name: TWENTY-TWO ITEM SCREENING SCORE

Purpose: An index of mental health.

Number of Items: 22

Author: Gallessich, J.

Article: An investigation of correlates of academic success of freshmen engineering students.

Journal: *Journal of Counseling*

Psychology, March 1970, *17*(2), 173–176.

Related Research: Langner, T. S. (1962). A twenty-two item screening score of psychiatric symptoms indicating impairment. *Journal of Health and Human Behavior, 3,* 269–275.

■ ■ ■

43

Test Name: WILLOUGHBY PERSONALITY SCHEDULE

Purpose: A rough measure of neuroticism or of general manifest anxiety contemporaneously providing a description of nondaters in terms of certain social behaviors.

Author: Martinson, W. D., and Zerface, J. P.

Article: Comparison of individual counseling and a social program with nondaters.

Journal: *Journal of Counseling Psychology,* January 1970, *17*(1), 36–40.

Related Research: Willoughby, R. R. (1932). Some properties of the Thurstone Personality Schedule and a suggested revision. *Journal of Social Psychology, 3,* 401–424.

CHAPTER 4
Adjustment—Social

44

Test Name: AFFILIATIVE TENDENCY SCALE

Purpose: Measures an individual's general expectation of the positive reinforcing quality of others.

Number of Items: 31

Format: Subject responds to all items using a 9-point scale.

Reliability: .89.

Validity: .13 with social desirability.

Author: Mehrabian, A.

Article: The development and validation of measures of affiliative tendency and sensitivity to rejection.

Journal: *Educational and Psychological Measurement,* Summer 1970, *30*(2), 417–428.

Related Research: Mehrabian, A., & Ksionsky, S. (in press). Models for affiliative and conformity behavior. *Psychological Bulletin, 74,* 110–126.

* * *

45

Test Name: ALIENATION SCALE

Purpose: To measure distrust and disengagement.

Number of Items: 8

Format: A raw score range of 8 to 30 with a high score indicating distrust and lack of confidence in other people.

Author: Egeland, B., Hunt, D. E., and Hardt, R. H.

Article: College enrollment of upward bound students as a function of attitude and motivation.

Journal: *Journal of Educational Psychology,* October 1970, *61*(5), 375–379.

Related Research: Srole, L. (1956). Integration and certain corollaries. *American Sociological Review, 21,* 709–716.

Rosenberg, M. (1965). *Society and the adolescent self-image.* Princeton: Princeton University Press.

* * *

46

Test Name: ANTI-WHITE AND ANTI-NEGRO SCALES

Purpose: To measure anti-White and anti-Negro ideology.

Number of Items: 34

Reliability: .84, .88, .90.

Validity: .46, .11 with *F* scale.

Author: Banks, W. M.

Article: The changing attitudes of Negro students.

Journal: *Personnel and Guidance Journal,* April 1970, *48*(9), 739–745.

Related Research: Steckler, G. (1957). Authoritarian ideology in Negro college students. *Journal of Abnormal and Social Psychology, 54,* 396–399.

* * *

47

Test Name: BIERI'S MODIFICATION OF KELLY'S ROLE CONSTRUCT REPERTORY TEST

Purpose: A measure of cognitive complexity in the interpersonal realm (interpersonal complexity).

Format: A grid (10 × 10) format with 10 personal role titles and 10 bipolar construct dimensions that the subject uses to rate the role titles.

Author: Bodden, J. L.

Article: Cognitive complexity as a factor in appropriate vocational choice.

Journal: *Journal of Counseling Psychology,* July 1970, *17*(4), 364–368.

Related Research: Bieri, J. A., Briar, S., Leaman, R., Miller, H., & Tripodi, T. (1966). *Clinical and social judgment: The discrimination of behavioral information.* New York: Wiley.

* * *

48

Test Name: CROWNE-MARLOWE SOCIAL DESIRABILITY SCALE

Purpose: A measure of the need for social approval.

Number of Items: 33

Author: Rotter, G. S., and Tinkleman, V.

Article: Anchor effects in the development of behavior rating scales.

Journal: *Educational and Psychological Measurement,* Summer 1970, *30*(2), 311–318.

Related Research: Crowne, D. P., & Marlowe, D. (1964). *The approval motive.* New York: Wiley.

49

Test Name: CROWNE & MARLOWE SOCIAL DESIRABILITY SCALE

Purpose: Measure of social desirability.

Number of Items: 33

Author: Eisenman, R., and Townsend, T.

Article: Studies in acquiescence: I. Social desirability, II. Self esteem, III. Creativity, and IV. Prejudice.

Journal: *Journal of Projective Techniques and Personality Assessment,* February 1970, *34*(1), 45–54.

■ ■ ■

50

Test Name: FUNDAMENTAL INTERPERSONAL RELATIONS ORIENTATION BEHAVIOR*

Purpose: Assessment of psychological distance or social withdrawal.

Author: Tolor, A., Brannigin, G. G., and Murphy, V. M.

Article: Psychological distance, future time perspective, and internal–external expectancy.

Journal: *Journal of Projective Techniques and Personality Assessment,* August 1970, *34*(4), 283–294.

Related Research: Schutz, W. C. (1958). *FIRO: A three-dimensional theory of interpersonal behavior.* New York: Holt, Rinehart & Winston.

■ ■ ■

51

Test Name: FUNDAMENTAL INTERPERSONAL RELATIONS ORIENTATION TEST*

Purpose: Measure of three interpersonal need areas

(inclusion, control, and affection).

Number of Items: 54 multiple-choice items that form six 9-item Guttman scales.

Format: For 24 the responses are in a 6-step continuum from *nobody* to *most people.* The remaining 30 are on a 6-step continuum from *never* to *usually.*

Validity: From .80 to .91 on six scales for the structural component.

Author: Ryan, B. A., Maguire, T. O., and Ryan, T. M.

Article: An examination of the construct validity of the FIRO-B.

Journal: *Journal of Projective Techniques and Personality Assessment,* October 1970, *34*(5), 419–425.

Related Research: Schutz, W. C. (1958). *FIRO: A three-dimensional theory of interpersonal behavior.* New York: Holt, Rinehart & Winston.

■ ■ ■

52

Test Name: BASES OF POWER QUESTIONNAIRE

Purpose: To measure social control.

Format: Included items in the following: coercive power, reward power, referent power, legitimate power, and expert power.

Author: Slocum, J. W., Jr.

Article: Supervisory influence and the professional employee.

Journal: *Personnel Journal,* June 1970, *49*(6), 484–488.

Related Research: French, J. R. P., & Raven, B. H. (1959). The bases of social power. In D. Cartwright (Ed.), *Studies in social power.* Ann Arbor: Institute for Social Research, University of Michigan.

53

Test Name: GROUP PARTICIPATION RATING SCALE

Purpose: To rate the degree and type of member participation.

Number of Items: 20

Author: Hoffnung, R. J., and Mills, R. B.

Article: Situational group counseling with disadvantaged youth.

Journal: *Personnel and Guidance Journal,* February 1970, *48*(6), 458–464.

■ ■ ■

54

Test Name: INTERPERSONAL ORIENTATION SCALE

Purpose: To measure interpersonal orientation.

Author: Bost, D. L.

Article: Changes in altruistic orientations and theory preferences of beginning counselors.

Journal: *Counselor Education and Supervision,* Winter 1970, *9*(2), 116–121.

Related Research: Alcorn, J. D., & Erb, E. D. (1965). *The interpersonal orientation scale.* Unpublished test instrument, Commerce, Texas.

■ ■ ■

55

Test Name: LIKING SCALE

Purpose: To measure one's preference for others.

Format: Composed of 15 steps represented graphically in a descending order from maximum to minimum liking.

Author: Lott, A. J., and Lott, B. E.

Article: Some indirect measures of interpersonal attraction among children.

Journal: *Journal of Educational Psychology*, April 1970, *61*(2), 124–135.

• • •

56

Test Name: MAKE A PICTURE STORY

Purpose: Assessment of psychological distance, social withdrawal.

Author: Tolor, A., Brannigan, G. G., and Murphy, V. M.

Article: Psychological distance, future time perspective and internal–external expectancy.

Journal: *Journal of Projective Techniques and Personality Assessment*, August 1970, *34*(4), 283–294.

Related Research: Neuringer, C. (1969). Clinical psychologists' ratings of MAPS figures along a social withdrawal scale. *Journal of Projective Techniques and Personality Assessment, 33*(1), 30–33.

• • •

57

Test Name: MARLOWE-CROWNE SOCIAL DESIRABILITY SCALE

Purpose: To measure social desirability.

Reliability: .88.

Author: MacGuffie, R. A., Jorgensen, G. Q., and Janzen, F. V.

Article: Need for approval and counseling outcomes.

Journal: *Personnel and Guidance Journal*, April 1970, *48*(8), 653–656.

Related Research: Horton, D. L., Marlowe, D., & Crowne, D. P.

(1963). The effect of instrumental set and need for social approval on commonality of word association. *Journal of Abnormal and Social Psychology, 66*, 67–72.

• • •

58

Test Name: MISCHEL'S ADAPTATION OF HARRIS' SCALE FOR SOCIAL RESPONSIBILITY IN CHILDREN

Purpose: To measure social responsibility in children.

Number of Items: 18

Format: Example: "At school, it is easy to find things to do when the teacher doesn't give us enough work."

Validity: .44.

Author: Walls, R. T., and Smith, T. S.

Article: Development of preference for delayed reinforcement in disadvantaged children.

Journal: *Journal of Educational Psychology*, April 1970, *61*(2), 118–123.

Related Research: Mischel, W. (1961). Preference for delayed reinforcement and social responsibility. *Journal of Abnormal and Social Psychology, 62*, 1–7.

• • •

59

Test Name: MOTOR INHIBITION TEST

Purpose: Designed to test possible consequences associated with restricted experience in receiving verbal requests for behavior control among the disadvantaged.

Author: Mumbauer, C. C., and Miller, J. O.

Article: Socioeconomic background

and cognitive functioning in preschool children.

Journal: *Child Development*, June 1970, *41*(2), 471–480.

Related Research: Maccoby, E. E., et al. (1965). Activity level and intellectual functioning in normal preschool children. *Child Development, 36*, 761–770.

• • •

60

Test Name: OBEDIENCE TEST

Purpose: To determine degree to which children comply with directions from mother and other adult women.

Format: Interactive session scored in accordance with how exactly child follows directions.

Author: Landauer, T. K., Carlsmith, J. M., and Lepper, M.

Article: Experimental analysis of the factors determining obedience of four-year-old children to adult females.

Journal: *Child Development*, September 1970, *41*(3), 601–611.

• • •

61

Test Name: THE PLAY REPORT

Purpose: To describe the degree of children's play socialization.

Number of Items: 5 items, two responses each.

Reliability: For ratings, .76–.99. For responses, .24–.88.

Validity: .64–.75.

Author: Seagal, M.

Article: An instrument for the analysis of children's play as an index of degree of socialization.

Journal: *Journal of School Psychology*, 1970, *8*(2), 139–144.

Related Research: Seagal, M., & Marakami, K. (1961). A

comparative study of children's play in America and Japan. *California Journal of Educational Research, 11,* 124–130.

Consulting Psychology, 29, 27–36.

. . .

62

Test Name: REVISED SOCIAL DESIRABILITY SCALE

Purpose: To measure the child's need for approval.

Validity: −.22 to −.44.

Author: Staub, E., and Sherk, L.

Article: Need for approval, children's sharing behavior and reciprocity in sharing.

Journal: *Child Development,* March 1970, *41*(1), 243–252.

Related Research: Crandall, B. D., et al. (1965). A children's social desirability questionnaire. *Journal of Consulting Psychology, 29,* 27–36.

. . .

63

Test Name: REVISED SOCIAL DISTANCE SCALE

Purpose: To measure social distance.

Author: Maw, W. H., and Maw, E. W.

Article: Self-concepts of high- and low-curiosity boys.

Journal: *Child Development,* March 1970, *41*(1), 123–129.

Related Research: Maw, W. H., & Maw, E. W. (1965). *Personal and social variables differentiating children with high and low curiosity* (Cooperative Research Project 1511). University of Delaware.

Bogardus, E. S. (1926). *The new social research.* Los Angeles: Miller.

64

Test Name: SCALE OF ALIENATION

Purpose: To identify alienated students.

Number of Items: 24

Format: Subjects respond to each statement on a 5-point scale.

Reliability: .73 to .83.

Author: Warner, R. W., Jr., and Hansen, J. C.

Article: Verbal-reinforcement and model-reinforcement group counseling with alienated students.

Journal: *Journal of Counseling Psychology,* March 1970, *17*(2), 168–172.

Related Research: Dean, D. G. (1961). Alienation: Its meaning and measurement. *American Sociological Review, 26,* 753–758.

. . .

65

Test Name: SCALE OF GENERAL ALIENATION

Purpose: To measure the general alienation tapping the components of "meaninglessness, normlessness, estrangement and powerlessness."

Number of Items: 8 (provided in the article).

Format: Likert items.

Reliability: .71.

Validity: Average interitem correlation, .24.

Author: Armer, M.

Article: Formal education and psychological malaise in an African society.

Journal: *Sociology of Education,* Spring 1970, *43*(2), 143–158.

. . .

66

Test Name: SCHOOL ATTITUDE RESEARCH INSTRUMENT

Purpose: Concerned with identification of the subject with his or her mother, father, teachers, peers; with the subject's estimate of the academic achievement values; and with characteristics of popular peers, peer attitudes toward scholars, and perceived teacher characterization of model-pupil behavior.

Number of Items: 59

Format: Likert items. Sample items are presented.

Reliability: .53 to .99.

Author: Ringness, T. A.

Article: Identifying figures, their achievement values, and children's values as related to actual and predicted achievement.

Journal: *Journal of Educational Psychology,* June 1970, *61*(3), 174–185.

. . .

67

Test Name: SCHUTZ' FUNDAMENTAL INTERPERSONAL ORIENTATIONS TEST FORM B

Purpose: A measure of interpersonal orientation; designed to measure components of the way in which a person characteristically interacts with others.

Number of Items: 54

Format: Six Guttman-type scales.

Author: Adinolfi, A. A.

Article: Characteristics of highly accepted, highly rejected and relatively unknown university freshmen.

Journal: *Journal of Counseling Psychology,* September 1970, *17*(5), 456–464.

Related Research: Schutz, W. C. (1960). *FIRO: A three-dimensional theory of interpersonal behavior.*

New York: Holt, Rinehart & Winston.

■ ■ ■

68

Test Name: SEMANTIC DIFFERENTIAL SCALES

Purpose: To measure reflection of attitude toward proxemic distance in interaction.

Number of Items: 12 bipolar adjective continua.

Author: Haase, R. F.

Article: The relationship of sex and instructional set to the regulation of interpersonal interaction distance in a counseling analogue.

Journal: *Journal of Counseling Psychology*, May 1970, *17*(3), 233–236.

Related Research: Osgood, C. E., Suci, G., & Tannenbaum, P. (1957). *The measurement of meaning.* Urbana: University of Illinois Press.

69

Test Name: SENSITIVITY TO REJECTION SCALE

Purpose: Measures an individual's general expectation of the negative reinforcing quality of others.

Number of Items: 38

Format: Subjects respond to all items using a 9-point scale.

Reliability: .92.

Validity: .04 with social desirability.

Author: Mehrabian, A.

Article: The development and validation of measures of affiliative tendency and sensitivity to rejection.

Journal: *Educational and Psychological Measurement,* Summer 1970, *30*(2), 417–428.

Related Research: Mehrabian, A., & Ksionsky, S. (in press). Models for affiliative and conformity behavior. *Psychological Bulletin, 74*, 110–126.

■ ■ ■

70

Test Name: SOCIOMETRIC TEST

Purpose: To evaluate peer relations.

Reliability: .72 to .92.

Author: Mayer, G. R., et al.

Article: The use of public commitment and counseling with elementary school children: An evaluation.

Journal: *Elementary School Guidance and Counseling,* October 1970, *5*(1), 22–34.

Related Research: Gronlund, N. E. (1959). *Sociometry in the classroom.* New York: Harper.

CHAPTER 5
Aptitude

71

Test Name: AYERS
PROGNOSTIC TEST FOR
EARLY CHILDHOOD
EDUCATION

Purpose: To determine how
successful a child who is just
entering school will be in later
schooling.

Number of Items: 35

Reliability: .80.

Validity: .29 to .71.

Author: Ayers, J. B., and
Johnson, C. E.

Article: A prognostic test for early
childhood.

Journal: *Educational and
Psychological Measurement.*
Winter 1970, *30*(4), 983–987.

Related Research: Ayers, J. B., &
Johnson, C. E. (1969). *The
development of a prognostic test
for early childhood.* Unpublished
manuscript, Research and
Development Center in
Educational Stimulation,
University of Georgia.

■ ■ ■

72

Test Name: DOVE TEST OF
MENTAL APTITUDE

Purpose: Intelligence test for
culturally disadvantaged
individuals.

Number of Items: 20

Reliability: .72.

Validity: "Reasonably valid."

Author: Frantz, T., and Gilbert, D.

Article: Characteristics of the Dove
test of mental aptitude.

Journal: *Education,* November–
December 1969, *90*(2), 112–114.

■ ■ ■

73

Test Name: PRE-EMPLOYMENT
CLERICAL TEST

Purpose: To predict success for
extremely low-level, routine
clerical jobs.

Time required: 15 minutes.

Format: Three parts: (a) rapid
matching of names and numbers;
(b) simulated filing activity; and
(c) grammar, spelling, and
vocabulary.

Author: Travaglio, R. F.

Article: Response differences
among employment applicants.

Journal: *Personnel Journal,* July
1970, *49*(7), 593–597.

■ ■ ■

74

Test Name: STRUCTURE OF
INTELLECT TESTS

Purpose: To predict scholastic
success.

Validity: .60.

Author: Caldwell, J. R., Schrader,
D. R., Michael, W. B., and
Meyers, C. E.

Article: Structure-of-intellect
measures and other tests as
predictors of success in
tenth-grade modern geometry.

Journal: *Educational and
Psychological Measurement,*
Summer 1970, *30* (2), 437–441.

■ ■ ■

75

Test Name: WASHINGTON
PRE-COLLEGE BATTERY

Purpose: Predicts both academic
and vocational-course grades for
community college students.

Format: Variables include age, sex,
six high school grade averages in
English, foreign language,
mathematics, natural science,
social studies, electives; and 10 test
scores: vocabulary, English usage,
spelling, reading speed, reading
comprehension, quantitative
skills, applied mathematics,
mathematics achievement, spatial
ability, and mechanical reasoning.

Validity: r^2 = .10 to .37.

Author: Lunneborg, P. W., et al.

Article: An attempt at predicting
long-term, nonintellective indices
of community college study.

Journal: *Educational and
Psychological Measurement,*
Summer 1970, *30*(2), 399–403.

Related Research: Cory, C. A.
(1968). *Comparison of fair models
for making predictions across
institutions.* Unpublished doctoral
dissertation, University of
Washington.

...

CHAPTER 6
Attitudes

76

Test Name: AN INDEX OF DISCRIMINATION

Purpose: To measure levels of discrimination.

Format: Index is based on ratings of alternative responses (crossing level of responsiveness of facilitation with initiative or action orientation). Training effectiveness was tested using ratings based on an index of communication and a second rating based on an index of discrimination.

Author: Carkhuff, R. R., and Banks, G.

Article: Training as a preferred mode of facilitating relations between races and generations.

Journal: *Journal of Counseling Psychology*, September 1970, *17*(5), 413–418.

Related Research: Carkhuff, R. R. (1969). *Helping and human relations: A primer for lay and professional helpers. 1: Selection and training. 2: Practice and research.* New York: Holt, Rinehart & Winston.

...

77

Test Name: ANTI-DEMOCRATIC ATTITUDE INSTRUMENT

Purpose: Measure of anti-democratic attitudes.

Author: Maw, W. H., and Maw, E. W.

Article: Self-concepts of high- and low-curiosity boys.

Journal: *Child Development*, March 1970, *41*(1), 123–129.

Related Research: Muuss, R. E. (1959, April). *A comparison of "high causally" and "low causally" oriented sixth-grade children on personality variables indicative of mental health.* Paper presented at the Iowa Academy of Science, Mount Pleasant, Iowa.

...

78

Test Name: ATTITUDES INTERVIEW (RACIAL)

Purpose: To measure attitudes toward racial issues. Also includes one personality variable and a personal-values variable.

Number of Items: 16 indices and items.

Time required: 75 minutes.

Format: (Exact questions can be obtained from the authors.)

Author: Schuman, H., and Gruenberg, B.

Article: The impact of city on racial attitudes.

Journal: *American Journal of Sociology*, September 1970, *76*(2), 213–261.

...

79

Test Name: ATTITUDE TOWARD NEGROES RATING SCALE

Purpose: Measures three components of attitude toward Negroes.

Number of Items: 45

Format: Includes the following three components: gradual versus rapid integration in segregated areas (gradualism); federal government intervention versus local governmental autonomy in desegregation (local autonomy); and minority group rights as contrasted with the rights of individuals (private rights).

Validity: .70, .82 with other scales.

Author: Brigham, J. C., and Cook, S. W.

Article: The influence of attitude on judgments of plausibility: A replication and extension.

Journal: *Educational and Psychological Measurement,* Summer 1970, *30*(2), 283–292.

Related Research: Woodmansee, J. J., & Cook, S. W. (1967). Dimensions of verbal racial attitudes: Their identification and measurement. *Journal of Personality and Social Psychology, 7,* 240–250.

Availability: Order Document No. 00876 from the National Auxiliary Publications Service of the American Society for Information Service, c/o CCM Information Sciences, Inc., 909 3rd Avenue, New York, NY 10022.

...

80

Test Name: ATTITUDE TOWARD THE CHURCH

Purpose: To obtain judgments of favorableness of the statements toward the church from which the stimulus scale is constructed, and to obtain choices of the statements closer to the subject's own point of view.

Number of Items: 6

Format: Statements were printed on cards and handed to the subjects in pairs. Each subject was tested individually and the complete method of paired comparisons was used. The item pairs were presented twice to each subject in each testing session. Following this the subject was given the items one at a time in the numbered order and instructed to indicate agreement or disagreement with the item.

Author: Hall, R. F.

Article: An application of unfolding theory to the measurement of attitudes.

Journal: *Educational and Psychological Measurement,* Autumn 1970, *30,* 621–637.

■ ■ ■

81

Test Name: ATTITUDES TOWARD MILITARY SERVICE

Purpose: To determine the attitudes of college students toward the war in Vietnam and military service.

Number of Items: Approximately 20 responses required.

Author: Hauck, R. J., and Stewart, M. A.

Article: College men and the draft: 1969.

Journal: *College Student Personnel,* November 1970, *11*(6), 439–444.

Related Research: Stewart, M., & Hauck, R. J. (1968). College men and the draft. *Journal of College Student Personnel, 9,* 371–377.

Suckman, E. A., Williams, R. M., & Goldsen, R. K. (1953). Student reaction to impending military service. *American Sociological Review, 18,* 293–304.

■ ■ ■

82

Test Name: ATTITUDE QUESTIONNAIRE

Purpose: Measured attitude in four domains: Institutional, professional, self-nonprofessional, professional-self.

Format: 8 concepts rated on nine 7-point scales. Scores range from 9 to 63.

Author: Salomon, G., and McDonald, F. J.

Article: Pretest and posttest reactions to self-viewing one's teaching performance on videotape.

Journal: *Journal of Educational Psychology,* August 1970, *61*(4, Part 1), 280–286.

■ ■ ■

83

Test Name: FIVE SCALES OF ATTITUDE

Purpose: To measure (a) attitudes toward the United States, (b) prior contact with the United States, (c) after-arrival contact with the United States, (d) alienation, and (e) authoritarianism.

Author: Basu, A. K., and Ames, R. G.

Article: Cross-cultural contact and attitude formation.

Journal: *Sociology and Social Research,* October 1970, *55*(1), 5–16.

■ ■ ■

84

Test Name: GENERAL ATTITUDE TOWARD BUSINESS SCALES

Purpose: To provide a quantitative measurement of each of five key dimensions of a general attitude toward business.

Number of Items: 100

Format: Five dimensions include: (a) basic economic convictions, (b) social responsibility of the business community, (c) ethical norms in the business world, (d) prestige of the business career, and (e) worth

and caliber of business education.

Author: Dawson, L. M.

Article: General attitude toward business as a job performance predictor.

Journal: *Personnel Journal,* January 1970, *49*(1), 52–56.

Related Research: Dawson, L. M. (1968). *Social and professional dimensions of the image of business: A study of the attitudes of college students and recent college graduates representing selected major fields of study.* Unpublished doctoral dissertation, Michigan State University.

■ ■ ■

85

Test Name: GUIDANCE TESTS AND COUNSELING ATTITUDE SCALE

Purpose: To measure attitudes toward guidance tests and counseling.

Number of Items: 54

Format: Likert format.

Author: Miller, C. D., Morrill, W. H., and Uhlemann, M. R.

Article: Micro-counseling: An experimental study of pre-practicum training in communicating test results.

Journal: *Counselor Education and Supervision,* Spring 1970, *9*(3), 171–177.

■ ■ ■

86

Test Name: INTELLECTUALISM–PRAGMATISM SCALE

Purpose: To measure varying degrees of intellectual and pragmatic attitudes.

Number of Items: 30

Reliability: "Sufficient reliability and validity for use with undergraduate and graduate college students."

Author: Polmantier, P., Ferguson, J., and Burton, R.

Article: Intellectual attitudes of graduate students in education.

Journal: *College Student Personnel*, January 1970, *11*(1), 33–34.

Related Research: Block, J. R., & Yuker, H. E. (1965). Correlates of an intellectual orientation among college students. In *Proceedings of the 73rd annual convention of the American Psychological Association* (pp. 315–316). Washington, DC: American Psychological Association.

■ ■ ■

87

Test Name: MULTIFACTOR RACIAL ATTITUDE INVENTORY

Purpose: Self-report inventory concerning attitudes toward Negroes.

Number of Items: 140

Validity: .78, .82 with other scales.

Author: Brigham, J. C., and Cook, S. W.

Article: The influence of attitude on judgments of plausibility: A replication and extension.

Journal: *Educational and Psychological Measurement,* Summer 1970, *30*(2), 283–292.

Related Research: Woodmansee, J. J., & Cook, S. W. (1967). Dimensions of verbal racial attitudes: Their identification and measurement. *Journal of Personality and Social Psychology, 7,* 240–250.

Availability: Order Document 00876 from the National Auxiliary Publications Service of the American Society for Information Service, c/o CCM Information Sciences, Inc., 909 3rd Avenue, New York, NY 10022.)

88

Test Name: OPINION OF NEGROES SCALE

Purpose: To assess White students' opinions of Negroes.

Number of Items: 13 sentences.

Author: Roth, R.

Article: The effects of "Black studies" on White fifth-grade students.

Journal: *Education,* April–May 1970, *90*(4), 328–331.

■ ■ ■

89

Test Name: PORTER TEST OF COUNSELOR ATTITUDES

Purpose: To measure counselor attitudes.

Author: Rochester, D. E.

Article: Persistence of attitudes and values of NDEA students–two years post institute.

Journal: *Counselor Education and Supervision,* Spring 1970, *9*(3), 205–207.

Related Research: Porter, E. H., Jr. (1949). A simple measure of counselor attitudes. In E. G. Williamson (Ed.), *Trends in student personnel work.* Minneapolis: University of Minnesota Press.

Hopke, W. E. (1955). The measurement of counselor attitudes. *Journal of Counseling Psychology, 2,* 212–216.

■ ■ ■

90

Test Name: RACIAL INTERMARRIAGE RATING SCALE

Purpose: Measures attitude toward racial intermarriage.

Number of Items: 55

Format: Items were labeled according to which side of the issue they supported, *for* or *against.*

Validity: .70, .78 with other scales.

Author: Brigham, J. C., and Cook, S. W.

Article: The influence of attitude on judgments of plausibility: A replication and extension.

Journal: *Educational and Psychological Measurement,* Summer 1970, *30*(2), 283–292.

Availability: Order Document No. 00876 from the National Auxiliary Publications Service of the American Society for Information Service, c/o CCM Information Sciences, Inc., 909 3rd Avenue, New York, NY 10022.

■ ■ ■

91

Test Name: ROOS TIME REFERENCE INVENTORY

Purpose: To explore affective attitudes toward the past, present, and future.

Number of Items: 30

Format: The subject assigns each item to the past, present, or future.

Reliability: Reported as being satisfactory.

Author: Megargee, E. I., Price, A. C., Frottwirth, R., and Levine, R.

Article: Time orientation of youthful prison inmates.

Journal: *Journal of Counseling Psychology,* January 1970, *17*(1), 8–14.

Related Research: Roos, P. (1964). Time reference inventory (mimeo, available from author). Austin State School, Austin, Texas.

■ ■ ■

92

Test Name: SCALE OF ATTITUDES TOWARD CHANGE

Purpose: To measure attitudes toward social, political, and economic change.

Number of Items: 40

Format: Five attitude-response categories from *strongly agree* to *strongly disagree* were used.

Author: Stewart, R. G.

Article: Some attitudes of college students toward certain aspects of social, political, and economic change.

Journal: *Educational and Psychological Measurement,* Spring 1970, *30*(1), 111–118.

. . .

93

Test Name: SEMANTIC DIFFERENTIAL FOR SECONDARY SCHOOL STUDENTS

Purpose: To assess attitude and attitude change among secondary and college students.

Number of Items: Three concepts, 35 pairs of opposed adjectives.

Time required: Not stated.

Format: Each of three concepts is evaluated on 35 pairs of opposed adjectives on a 7-step scale. Paper and pencil.

Reliability: Part scores from .421 to .610.

Author: Cassell, R. N.

Article: Development of a semantic differential to assess the attitudes of secondary and college students.

Journal: *Journal of Experimental Education,* Winter 1970, *39*(2), 10–14.

Related Research: Gough, H. G., & Heilbrun, A. B. (1965). *The Adjective Check List manual.* Palo Alto, CA: Consulting Psychologists Press.

94

Test Name: SOCIAL ATTITUDES SCALE

Purpose: To measure attitudes of social responsibility.

Author: Maw, W. H., and Maw, E. W.

Article: Self-concepts of high- and low-curiosity boys.

Journal: *Child Development,* March 1970, *41*(1), 123–129.

Related Research: Harris, D. B. (1957). A scale for measuring attitudes of social responsibility. *Journal of Abnormal and Social Psychology, 54,* 322–326.

. . .

95

Test Name: STUDENT OPINION SCALE

Purpose: A composite attitudinal inventory.

Format: Contains four scales: The Block & Yuker Intellectual–Pragmatism Scale, the Rokeach Dogmatism Scale, the conservatism–liberalism scale of the Minnesota Personality Test, and a college subcultural identification measure based on the typologies of Trow.

Author: Gallessich, J.

Article: An investigation of correlates of academic success of freshmen engineering students.

Journal: *Journal of Counseling Psychology,* March 1970, *17*(2), 173–176.

Related Research: Hill, A. (1966). A longitudinal study of attrition among high aptitude college students. *Journal of Educational Research, 60,* 166–173.

. . .

96

Test Name: THERAPIST ORIENTATION QUESTIONNAIRE

Purpose: To measure attitudinal differences between therapists.

Number of Items: 45 (presented in article).

Format: Likert items scored on a 5-point scale from *strongly agree* to *strongly disagree.*

Validity: –.29 to –.76 and .31 to .73.

Author: Howard, K. I., and Orlinsky, D. E.

Article: Therapist orientation and patient experience in psychotherapy.

Journal: *Journal of counseling Psychology,* May 1970, *17*(3), 263–270.

Related Research: Sundland, D. H., & Barker, E. N. (1962). The orientation of psychotherapists. *Journal of Consulting Psychology, 26,* 201–212.

. . .

97

Test Name: THREE SCALES FOR MEASURING ATTITUDES OF ARAB STUDENTS TOWARD AMERICANS

Purpose: To measure (a) interaction of Arab and American students, (b) perceived American attitudes toward the Arabs, and (c) the Arab students' attitudes toward Americans.

Number of Items: 30

Reliability: .89 to .94.

Author: Ibrahim, S. E. M.

Article: Interaction, perception, and attitudes of Arab students toward Americans.

Journal: *Sociology and Social Research,* October 1970, *55*(1), 29–46.

···
CHAPTER 7
Communication

98

Test Name: ADAPTATION OF THE AFFECTIVE SENSITIVITY SCALE

Purpose: To assess degree of direct, mutual communication.

Reliability: .89.

Author: Higgins, W. H., Ivey, A. E., and Uhlemann, M. R.

Article: Media therapy: A programmed approach to teaching behavioral skills.

Journal: *Journal of Counseling Psychology*, January 1970, *17*(1), 20–26.

Related Research: Kogan, N., & Krathwohl, D. (1967). Studies in human interaction (Research Report No. 20). Michigan State University, Educational Publication Services.

···

99

Test Name: AN INDEX OF COMMUNICATION

Purpose: To measure effectiveness of communication.

Number of Items: 16 standard helpee expressions and 5 racial relations items.

Format: Crosses different affects (depression–distress, anger–hostility, elation–excitement) with different problem areas (social–interpersonal, educational–vocational, child learning, sexual–marital, confrontation) and written responses to the five racial relations items.

Reliability: rs in the .80s and .90s.

Author: Carkhuff, R. R., and Banks, G.

Article: Training as a preferred mode of facilitating relations between races and generations.

Journal: *Journal of Counseling Psychology*, September 1970, *17*(5), 413–418.

Related Research: Carkhuff, R. R. (1969). Helper communication as a function of helpee affect and content. *Journal of Counseling Psychology, 16,* 126–131.

···

100

Test Name: CONSENSUAL INDEX

Purpose: To define consensual peer groups.

Number of Items: 7

Author: Warren, D. I.

Article: Variations on the theme of primary groups: Forms of social control within school staffs.

Journal: *Sociology of Education,* Summer 1970, *43*(3), 288–310.

···

101

Test Name: COUNSELOR VERBAL RESPONSE SCALE

Purpose: To describe counselors' responses to client communication in terms of several dimensions.

Reliability: .83.

Author: Mayer, G. R., et al.

Article: The use of public commitment and counseling with elementary school children: An evaluation.

Journal: *Elementary School Guidance and Counseling,* October 1970, *5*(1), 22–34.

Related Research: Kogan, N., & Krathwohl, D. R. (1967). Studies in human interaction (Project No. 5–0800). U.S. Department of Health, Education and Welfare, Office of Education, Bureau of Research.

···

102

Test Name: INTERACTION SCALE

Purpose: To measure the expressions and the perceptions of members in a dyad.

Number of Items: 40

Format: Composed of two subscales. One scale is a measure of the expression of feelings one member of a dyad has toward the partner (expression scale); the other scale measures the partner's perception of the other's feelings toward him or her (perception scale).

Author: MacGuffie, R. A., Janzen, F. V., and McPhee, W. M.

Article: The expression and perception of feelings between students and supervisors in a practicum setting.

Journal: *Counselor Education and Supervision,* Summer 1970, *9*(4), 263–271.

Related Research: Jorgensen, G. Q., Janzen, F. V., Samuelson, C. O., & McPhee, W. M. (1968).

Interpersonal relationships: Factors in job placement (University of Utah Regional Rehabilitation Research Institute, Bulletin No. 3). Salt Lake City: University of Utah Printing Service.

∎ ∎ ∎

103

Test Name: INTERGENERATION COMMUNICATION

Purpose: To expose communications between parents and children.

Number of Items: 65

Format: Three-part inventories for sons, complementary one for fathers, corresponding inventories for mothers and daughters.

Author: Berdie, R. F., Loeffler, D. R., and Rath, J. D.

Article: Intergenerational communication.

Journal: *Journal of College Student Personnel,* September 1970, *11*(5), 348–354.

∎ ∎ ∎

104

Test Name: SELF-DISCLOSURE QUESTIONNAIRE

Purpose: To determine what the subject is willing to disclose.

Number of Items: 40 self-disclosure topics.

Author: Jourard, S. M., and Jaffe, P. E.

Article: Influence of an interviewer's disclosure on the self-disclosing behavior of interviewers.

Journal: *Journal of Counseling Psychology,* May 1970, *17*(3), 252–257.

Related Research: Jourard, S. M. (1969). The effect of experimenters' disclosure on the behavior of subjects in psychological experiments. In C. Spielberger (Ed.), *Current topics in clinical and community psychology.* New York, Academic Press.

∎ ∎ ∎

105

Test Name: RYSTROM DIALECT TEST

Purpose: To evaluate dialect change attributable to dialect training.

Format: Covers six broad areas.

Author: Rystrom, R.

Article: Dialect training and reading: A further look.

Journal: *Reading Research Quarterly,* Summer 1970, *5*(4), 581–599.

Related Research: Rystrom, R. C. (1969). Testing Negro–standard English dialect differences. *Reading Research Quarterly, 4,* 500–511.

CHAPTER 8
Concept Meaning

106

Test Name: COGNITION OF SEMANTIC TRANSFORMATIONS TEST

Purpose: To measure the ability to see potential changes and interpretations of ideas.

Format: Subjects must indicate transformations of the meanings of cartoon pictures, see different meanings, and translate the given material into meaningful sentences or words.

Validity: .36 to .51.

Author: Hoepfner, R., Guilford, J. P., and Bradley, P. A.

Article: Information-transformation abilities.

Journal: *Educational and Psychological Measurement,* Winter 1970, *30*(4), 785–802.

Related Research: Hoepfner, R., Guilford, J. P., & Bradley, P. A. (1968). *Identification of transformation abilities in the structure-of-intellect model* (Report from the Psychological Laboratory No. 41). Los Angeles: University of Southern California Press.

• • •

107

Test Name: COGNITION OF SYMBOLIC TRANSFORMATIONS TEST

Purpose: To measure the ability to recognize that a specific transformation of symbolic information has occurred.

Format: Includes seeing letter changes, finding letter transformations, reading backwards, and reading confused words.

Validity: .45 to .58.

Author: Hoepfner, R., Guilford, J. P., and Bradley, P. A.

Article: Information-transformation abilities.

Journal: *Educational and Psychological Measurement,* Winter 1970, *30*(4), 785–802.

Related Research: Hoepfner, R., Guilford, J. P., & Bradley, P. A. (1968). *Identification of transformation abilities in the structure-of-intellect model* (Report from the Psychological Laboratory No. 41). Los Angeles: University of Southern California Press.

• • •

108

Test Name: COGNITION OF SYMBOLIC UNITS TEST

Purpose: To measure the ability to recognize symbolic units.

Format: Assesses subjects' ability to recognize whether given words are spelled correctly and to recognize words with the vowels removed.

Validity: .51, .52.

Author: Hoepfner, R., Guilford, J. P., and Bradley, P. A.

Article: Information-transformation abilities.

Journal: *Educational and*

Psychological Measurement, Winter 1970, *30*(4), 785–802.

• • •

109

Test Name: CONCEPTUAL PRE-STRUCTURING FOR DETAILED VERBAL PASSAGES

Purpose: To increase student's understanding of keypoints in a passage.

Number of Items: 20

Time required: 15 minutes.

Format: Multiple-choice and true–false.

Author: Proger, B. B., Taylor, R. G., Jr., and others.

Article: Conceptual prestructuring for detailed verbal passages.

Journal: *Journal of Educational Research,* September 1970, *64,* 28.

• • •

110

Test Name: DIVERGENT PRODUCTION OF SEMANTIC CLASSES TEST

Purpose: Measures semantic flexibility.

Format: Includes alternate uses and multiple grouping.

Validity: .33, .47.

Author: Hoepfner, R., Guilford, J. P., and Bradley, P. A.

Article: Information-transformation abilities.

Journal: *Educational and Psychological Measurement,* Winter 1970, *30*(4), 785–802.

111

Test Name: DIVERGENT PRODUCTION OF SYMBOLIC TRANSFORMATIONS

Purpose: Concerned with letters and words and the varied production of changes or alterations of them.

Format: Subjects must produce transformations by embedding a given word in different phrase contexts, by changing two or three letters of a given word to make new words, and by extracting small words that are embedded in two large words.

Validity: .39 to .48.

Author: Hoepfner, R., Guilford, J. P., and Bradley, P. A.

Article: Information-transformation abilities.

Journal: *Educational and Psychological Measurement,* Winter 1970, *30*(4), 785–802.

■ ■ ■

112

Test Name: EVALUATION OF SYMBOLIC TRANSFORMATIONS TEST

Purpose: Measures the ability to judge the adequacy of symbolic substitutions or reorderings.

Format: Includes codes, letter rearrangements in a word, and algebraic expressions.

Validity: .34 to .54.

Author: Hoepfner, R., Guilford, J. P., and Bradley, P. A.

Article: Information-transformation abilities.

Journal: *Educational and Psychological Measurement,* Winter 1970, *30*(4), 785–802.

113

Test Name: KINDNESS PICTURE-STORY MEASURE

Purpose: To measure the subject's understanding of the concept of kindness.

Number of Items: 10

Format: Ten pairs of stories are presented and the subject selects the one in each pair that he or she regards as a kinder situation.

Author: Baldwin, C. P., and Baldwin, A. L.

Article: Children's judgments of kindness.

Journal: *Child Development,* March 1970, *41*(1), 29–47.

Availability: The complete kindness picture-story measure has been deposited with the American Documentation Institute. Order NAPS Document 00653 from ASIS National Auxiliary Publications Service, c/o CCM Information Sciences, Inc., 22 West 34th Street, New York, NY 10001.

■ ■ ■

114

Test Name: MASCULINE–FEMININE SEMANTIC DIFFERENTIAL

Purpose: To test the meaning of sexually symbolic concepts.

Number of Items: 18 stimulus concepts rated on six scales.

Time required: Not given.

Format: Each of 18 stimulus concepts is rated on each of six scales; psychoanalytic theory posits 9 as masculine and 9 as feminine.

Author: Archer, G. S., and Burgess, I. S.

Article: A further investigation of sexually symbolic concepts using the semantic differential techniques.

Journal: *Journal of Projective Techniques and Personality Assessment,* October 1970, *34*(5), 369–372.

Related Research: Worthy, M., & Craddick, R. A. (1969). Semantic differential investigation of sexually symbolic concepts. *Journal of Projective Techniques and Personality Assessment, 33,* 78–80.

■ ■ ■

115

Test Name: MATHIS ET AL. SEMANTIC DIFFERENTIAL

Purpose: To measure attitudes toward the concept *computer* along with a control concept *automobile.*

Author: Mathis, A., Smith, T., and Hansen, D.

Article: College students' attitudes toward computer-assisted instruction.

Journal: *Journal of Educational Psychology,* February 1970, *61*(1), 46–51.

Related Research: Osgood, C. E., Suci, G. J., & Tannenbaum, P. H. (1957). *The measurement of meaning.* Urbana: University of Illinois Press.

■ ■ ■

116

Test Name: MEMORY FOR SYMBOLIC IMPLICATIONS TEST

Purpose: Measures the ability to remember arbitrary connections between symbols.

Format: Asks subjects to recall letters arbitrarily paired with numbers.

Validity: .49, .50.

Author: Hoepfner, R., Guilford, J. P., and Bradley, P. A.

Article: Information-transformation abilities.

Journal: *Educational and Psychological Measurement,* Winter 1970, *30*(4), 785–802.

■ ■ ■

117

Test Name: MEMORY FOR SYMBOLIC TRANSFORMATIONS TEST

Purpose: To measure the ability to remember rearrangements and regroupings of letters in words.

Format: Includes memory for misspelling, memory for hidden transformations, and memory for word transformations.

Validity: .54 to .67.

Author: Hoepfner, R., Guilford, J. P., and Bradley, P. A.

Article: Information-transformation abilities.

Journal: *Educational and Psychological Measurement,* Winter 1970, *30*(4), 785–802.

Related Research: Hoepfner, R., et al. (1968). *Identification of transformation abilities in the structure-of-intellect model* (Report from the Psychological Laboratory No. 41). Los Angeles: University of Southern California Press.

■ ■ ■

118

Test Name: MYRICK SEMANTIC DIFFERENTIAL

Purpose: To measure the psychological meaning of 9 concepts.

Format: A booklet containing 9

concepts separately presented along with 12 bipolar adjectives on a 7-point scale.

Author: Myrick, R. D.

Article: The counselor–consultant and the effeminate boy.

Journal: *Personnel and Guidance Journal,* January 1970, *48*(5), 355–361.

Related Research: Osgood, C., Suci, G., & Tannenbaum, P. (1957). *The measurement of meaning.* Urbana: University of Illinois Press.

■ ■ ■

119

Test Name: NEWTONIAN MECHANICS WORD-ASSOCIATION TEST

Purpose: To measure response to Newtonian mechanics' stimulus words.

Time required: 60 seconds.

Format: Each booklet contained one page for each stimulus word and the order of the 19 pages of each booklet was determined randomly. Stimulus words are presented in the text.

Validity: .81 to .83.

Author: Rothkopf, E. Z., and Thurner, R. D.

Article: Effect of written instructional material on the statistical structure of test essays.

Journal: *Journal of Educational Psychology,* February 1970, *61*(2), 83–89.

Related Research: Noble, C. E. An analysis of meaning. *Psychological Review,* 1952, *59*, 421–430.

■ ■ ■

120

Test Name: PARAGRAPH COMPLETION TEST

Purpose: Differentiates levels of conceptual complexity.

Author: Marx, D. J.

Article: Intentional and incidental concept formation as a function of conceptual complexity, intelligence, and task complexity.

Journal: *Journal of Educational Psychology,* August 1970, *61*(4, Part I), 207–304.

Related Research: Schroder, H. M., Driver, M. J., & Streufert, S. (1967). *Human information processing.* New York: Holt, Rinehart & Winston.

■ ■ ■

121

Test Name: A SEMANTIC DIFFERENTIAL INSTRUMENT

Purpose: To evaluate expressive data.

Format: Forty-six 7-point bipolar scales were used. Several scales are presented in the article.

Author: Sweeney, D. P., Tinling, D. C., and Schmale, A. H., Jr.

Article: Dimensions of affective expression in four expressive modes.

Journal: *Behavioral Science,* September 1970, *15*(5), 393–407.

■ ■ ■

122

Test Name: SENTENCE COMPLETION TEST

Purpose: Measures conceptual structure.

Number of Items: 6

Format: Semiprojective, requires subjects to respond to each of six paragraph stems by writing on each for 2 minutes.

Author: Stuempfig, D. W., and Maehr, M. L.

Article: Persistence as a function of conceptual structure and quality of feedback.

Journal: *Child Development,* December 1970, *41*(4), 1183–1190.

Related Research: Schroder, H. M., Driver, M. J., & Struefert, S. (1967). *Human information processing.* New York: Holt, Rinehart & Winston.

■ ■ ■

123

Test Name: TEST OF LOGICAL CONNECTIVES

Purpose: To assess the subject's understanding of class inclusion and exclusion, class intersection, and class union.

Number of Items: 16

Author: Neimark, E. D., and Slotnick, N. S.

Article: Development of the understanding of logical connectives.

Journal: *Journal of Educational Psychology,* December 1970, *61*(6, Part I), 451–460.

■ ■ ■

124

Test Name: VERBAL-FORMULAS TEST

Purpose: Assesses subject's verbal descriptions of simple fabricated objects.

Number of Items: 6

Author: Elkind, D., Anagnostopoulou, R., and Malone, S.

Article: Determinants of part-whole perception in children.

Journal: *Child Development,* June 1970, *41*(2), 391–397.

125

Test Name: WORD DEFINITION INVENTORY

Purpose: To measure change in ratings of word definitions and change in one's confidence in his ability to use the terms appropriately.

Number of Items: 6 psychological terms each with 5 synonyms.

Format: 13-point rating scales were employed.

Author: Sprafkin, R. P.

Article: Communicator expertness and changes in word meanings in psychological treatment.

Journal: *Journal of Counseling Psychology,* May 1970, *17*(3), 191–196.

···

CHAPTER 9
Creativity

126

Test Name: CONVERGENT PRODUCTION OF SYMBOLIC TRANSFORMATIONS TEST

Purpose: Measures the ability to break up or destroy symbolic items of information in order to produce new items.

Format: Involves three variations of the technique of embedded words: the subject converges upon one embedded word in a sentence, produces the most efficient overlapping of four words, or uses all the letters of a given word, and only those letters, to produce a new word.

Validity: .33 to .48.

Author: Hoepfner, R., Guilford, J. P., and Bradley, P. A.

Article: Information-transformation abilities.

Journal: *Educational and Psychological Measurement,* Winter 1970, *30*(4), 785–802.

■ ■ ■

127

Test Name: CONVERGENT PRODUCTION OF SEMANTIC TRANSFORMATIONS TEST

Purpose: Measures the ability to produce new uses for objects or parts of objects by redefining them in accordance with their new contexts.

Format: Involves redefinition of objects by requiring the subject to break down an object or to combine objects, and to redefine a word by producing a new and absurd use for it.

Validity: .36 to .57.

Author: Hoepfner, R., Guilford, J. P., and Bradley, P. A.

Article: Information-transformation abilities.

Journal: *Educational and Psychological Measurement,* Winter 1970, *30*(4), 785–802.

■ ■ ■

128

Test Name: DIVERGENT PRODUCTION OF SEMANTIC TRANSFORMATIONS

Purpose: Measures the ability to produce varied reinterpretations of some specified idea.

Format: Includes three types of tests to which responses are unusual, remote, and clever.

Validity: .33 to .56.

Author: Hoepfner, R., Guilford, J. P., and Bradley, P. A.

Article: Information-transformation abilities.

Journal: *Educational and Psychological Measurement,* Winter 1970, *30*(4), 785–802.

Related Research: Guilford, J. P. (1967). *The nature of human intelligence.* New York: McGraw-Hill.

■ ■ ■

129

Test Name: DIVERGENT PRODUCTION OF SYMBOLIC IMPLICATIONS TEST

Purpose: Measures the ability to

produce varied implications of symbolic information.

Validity: .35 to .67.

Author: Hoepfner, R., Guilford, J. P., & Bradley, P. A.

Article: Information-transformation abilities.

Journal: *Educational and Psychological Measurement,* Winter 1970, *30*(4), 785–802.

■ ■ ■

130

Test Name: EXPERIENCES QUESTIONNAIRE

Purpose: Inventory of peak experiences and other related phenomena.

Number of Items: 79

Format: Sample items are presented.

Author: Taft, R., and Gilchrist, M. B.

Article: Creative attitudes and creative productivity: A comparison of two aspects of creativity among students.

Journal: *Journal of Educational Psychology,* April 1970, *61*(2), 136–143.

Related Research: Taft, R. (1969). Peak experience and ego permissiveness: An exploratory factor study of their dimensions in normal persons. *Acta Psychologica, 29,* 35–64.

■ ■ ■

131

Test Name: PM SCALE

Purpose: Measure of flexibility of approach to educational problems.

Author: Felker, D. W., and Brown, D. F.

Article: Counselor candidates and graduate students in education: A comparison of characteristics.

Journal: *Counselor Education and Supervision,* Summer 1970, *9*(4), 286–291.

Related Research: Felker, D. W., & Smith, P. G. (1966). The measurement of philosophic-mindedness on the criterion of flexibility. *Bulletin of the School of Education* (Indiana University), *42*, 1–138.

■ ■ ■

132

Test Name: REMOTE ASSOCIATES TEST*

Purpose: Tests for individual differences in creativity.

Reliability: .81.

Validity: .07 to .48.

Author: Smith, I. L.

Article: Associational achievement, aptitudes, and creativity.

Journal: *Educational and Psychological Measurement,* Winter 1970, *30*(4), 999–1000.

Related Research: Mednick, S. A. (1962). The associative basis of the creative process. *Psychological Review, 69,* 220–232.

■ ■ ■

133

Test Name: WHAT KIND OF PERSON ARE YOU?

Purpose: Screening devices for identifying creatively gifted adolescents and adults.

Number of Items: 50

Time required: 5–10 minutes.

Format: Paper and pencil.

Reliability: Test–retest reliability; from 26 to 47 subjects; from 1-day to 1-month interval; values from .71 to .97.

Validity: From .26 to .75 in various studies cited—more above .50 than below.

Author: Torrence, E. P., and Khatena, J.

Article: What kind of person are you?

Journal: *The Gifted Child Quarterly,* Summer 1970, *14*(2), 71–75.

Related Research: Torrence, E. P. (1966). *Torrence tests of creative thinking, directions, manual and scoring guide: Verbal forms A and B.* Princeton, NJ: Personnel Press.

CHAPTER 10
Development

134

Test Name: BAYLEY MENTAL SCALE

Purpose: Involves sustained attention, manipulation of objects in a purposeful fashion, simple initiation and comprehension, simple vocalization and memory.

Author: Ireton, H., Thuing, E., and Graven, H.

Article: Infant mental development and neurological status, family socioeconomic status, and intelligence at age 4.

Journal: *Child Development,* December 1970, *41*(4), 937–945.

• • •

135

Test Name: CONCEPTUAL LEVEL QUESTIONNAIRE

Purpose: To assess the development of conceptual systems.

Number of Items: 6

Format: Included 6 stems to be completed by three or four sentences.

Reliability: .76.

Validity: With moral development, .62; with ego development, .56.

Author: Sullivan, E. V., McCullough, G., and Stager, M.

Article: A developmental study of the relationship between conceptual, ego, and moral development.

Journal: *Child Development,* June 1970, *41*(2), 399–411.

Related Research: Hunt, D. E., &

Halverson, C. (1964). Manual for scoring sentence completion responses for adolescents. Unpublished scoring manual, Syracuse University.

• • •

136

Test Name: EGO DEVELOPMENT TEST

Purpose: To assess the development of ego.

Number of Items: 36

Format: Includes 36 stems to be completed by a single sentence.

Reliability: .77, .85.

Validity: With moral development, .66; with conceptual development, .56.

Author: Sullivan, E. V., McCullough, G., and Stager, M.

Article: A developmental study of the relationship between conceptual, ego, and moral development.

Journal: *Child Development,* June 1970, *41*(2), 399–411.

Related Research: Loevinger, J., & Wessler, R. (1968, August). *Measuring ego development by sentence completions I: Theoretical and methodological issues.* Paper presented at the meeting of the American Psychological Association, San Francisco.

• • •

137

Test Name: IT SCALE FOR CHILDREN

Purpose: To assess sex-role development in children.

Number of Items: 16

Validity: With teacher ratings from .001 to .512.

Author: Thompson, N. L., Jr., and McCandless, B. R.

Article: IT score variations by instructional style.

Journal: *Child Development,* June 1970, *41*(2), 425–436.

Related Research: Brown, D. G. (1956). Sex-role preference in young children. *Psychological Monographs, 70*(14, Whole No. 421).

• • •

138

Test Name: LOWENFELD MOSAIC TEST

Purpose: Used as a diagnostic tool in clinical and hospital settings, in evaluation of emotional factors and mental ability in the schools, and in investigations in child development.

Format: Involves mosaic productions.

Validity: .03 to .74.

Author: Leiffer, A.

Article: Relation of mosaic patterns to spelling and reading in low achievers.

Journal: *Educational and Psychological Measurement,* Summer 1970, *30*(2), 463–467.

Related Research: Ames, L. B., & Ilg, F. L. (1962). *Mosaic patterns* *of American children.* New York: Harper.

• • •

139

Test Name: MORAL DEVELOPMENT TEST

Purpose: To assess the development of moral judgment.

Number of Items: 9

Format: Contains nine hypothetical conflict stories and corresponding sets of probing questions concerning such problems as stealing and mercy killing.

Reliability: .74.

Validity: With ego development, .66; with conceptual development, .62.

Author: Sullivan, E. V., McCullough, G., and Stager, M.

Article: A developmental study of the relationship between conceptual, ego, and moral development.

Journal: *Child Development,* June 1970, *41*(2), 399–411.

Related Research: Kohlberg, L. (1958). *The development of modes of moral thinking and choice in the years 10–16.* Unpublished doctoral dissertation, University of Chicago.

• • •

140

Test Name: OBJECT AND PERSON PERMANENCE SCALE

Purpose: To assess object and person permanence.

Format: A summarized account of the test is presented.

Author: Bell, S. M.

Article: The development of the concept of object as related to infant–mother attachment.

Journal: *Child Development,* June 1970, *41*(2), 291–311.

Availability: Order NAPS Document 00965 from ASIS National Auxiliary Publications Service, c/o CCM Information Sciences, Inc., 22 West 34th Street, New York, NY 10001.

...

CHAPTER 11
Family

141

Test Name: BENE-ANTHONY FAMILY RELATIONS TEST

Purpose: To assess the intensity and quality of a child's feelings toward family members and the child's perceptions of how they feel toward him or her.

Format: Child places cards (representing feelings) into boxes attached to ambiguously drawn figures.

Reliability: Odd–even reliabilities from .68 to .90.

Validity: Clouded values from .56 to .98, although author questions some methodology.

Author: Kauffman, J. M.

Article: Validation of the family relations test: A review of research.

Journal: *Journal of Projective Techniques and Personality Assessment,* April 1970, *34*(2), 186–189.

Related Research: Bene, E., & Anthony, J. (1957). *Manual for family relations test.* London: National Foundation for Educational Research in England and Wales.

...

142

Test Name: FAMILY RELATIONS INVENTORY

Purpose: To quantify interpersonal orientations.

Number of Items: 202 true–false.

Format: Items are distributed among six scales.

Author: Medvene, A. M.

Article: Person-oriented and non-person-oriented occupations in psychology.

Journal: *Journal of Counseling Psychology,* May 1970, *17*(3), 243–246.

Related Research: Brunkan, R. J., & Crites, J. O. (1964). An inventory to measure the parental attitude variables in Roe's theory of vocational choice. *Journal of Counseling Psychology, 1,* 3–12.

...

143

Test Name: IDENTIFICATION SCALE

Purpose: To determine the degree to which a student identifies with each parent.

Format: Paper and pencil.

Reliability: See Heilbrun, Related Research.

Validity: See Heilbrun, Related Research.

Author: Johnson, R. W.

Article: Parental identification and vocational interests of college women.

Journal: *Measurement and Evaluation in Guidance,* Fall 1970, *3*(3), 147–151.

Related Research: Heilbrun, A. B., Jr. (1965). The measurement of identification. *Child Development, 36,* 111–127.

Edwards, A. L. (1954). *Manual for the Edwards personal preference schedule.* New York: Psychological Comparing.

...

144

Test Name: PARENT ATTITUDE RESEARCH INSTRUMENT

Purpose: To measure perceived maternal childrearing behaviors.

Number of Items: 115

Format: Includes 23 five-item scales.

Author: Heilbrun, A. B., Jr.

Article: Perceived maternal child-rearing experience and the effects of vicarious and direct reinforcement on males.

Journal: *Child Development,* March 1970, *41*(1), 253–262.

Related Research: Schaefer, E. S., & Bell, R. G. (1958). Development of a parent attitude research instrument. *Child Development, 29,* 339–361.

...

145

Test Name: PARENTAL CONTROL QUESTIONNAIRE

Purpose: To learn how much control parents have been exerting over the daily life of their children in the years just preceding college, in what areas they have exerted these controls, and what kinds of controls they anticipate the university will exert.

Format: Three major sections; responses are made on a 5-point scale.

Author: Bordin, E. S., Shaevitz, M. H., and Lacher, M.

Article: Entering college students' preparation for self-regulation.

Journal: *Journal of Counseling Psychology,* July 1970, *17*(4), 291–298.

■ ■ ■

146

Test Name: PERCEPTION OF INTERPERSONAL HOSTILITY SCALE

Purpose: To measure a client's hostility toward his mate and to compare it with his mate's hostility toward himself.

Number of Items: 20

Author: Smith, J. R.

Article: Perception of self and other (mate) as motivation for marriage counseling: An interactionist approach.

Journal: *Sociology and Social Research,* July 1970, *54*(4), 466–476.

Related Research: Kotlar, S. L. (1961). *Middle-class roles—ideal and perceived—in relationship to*

adjustment in marriage. Unpublished doctoral dissertation, University of Southern California.

■ ■ ■

147

Test Name: POSTCOUNSELING QUESTIONNAIRE

Purpose: For use in premarital counseling of college students.

Format: Some items are presented.

Author: Meadows, M. E., and Taplin, J. F.

Article: Premarital counseling with college students.

Journal: *Journal of Counseling Psychology,* November 1970, *17*(6, Part I), 516–518.

■ ■ ■

148

Test Name: RELATIONSHIP INVENTORY

Purpose: To assess the level of communication of all responsive and initiative dimensions between parent and child.

Author: Carkhuff, R. R., and Bierman, R.

Article: Training as a preferred mode of treatment of parents of emotionally disturbed children.

Journal: *Journal of Counseling Psychology,* March 1970, *17*(2), 157–161.

■ ■ ■

149

Test Name: ROE-SIEGELMAN PARENT–CHILD RELATIONS QUESTIONNAIRE

Purpose: To measure loving-rejecting parental behaviors in child rearing.

Format: Includes 10 scales.

Validity: .13 to .53.

Author: Cox, S. H.

Article: Intrafamily comparison of loving–rejecting child-rearing practices.

Journal: *Child Development,* June 1970, *41*(2), 437–448.

Related Research: Roe, A., & Siegelman, M. A. (1963). A parent–child relations questionnaire. *Child Development, 34,* 355–359.

CHAPTER 12
Institutional Information

150

Test Name: ATTITUDE SURVEY

Purpose: To identify and define an industry's problem areas.

Time required: 30–40 minutes.

Author: Truell, G. F.

Article: Using mini-surveys to start problem-solving process.

Journal: *Personnel Journal*, July 1970, *49*(7), 552–558.

• • •

151

Test Name: ATTITUDES TOWARD COLLEGE COURSES

Purpose: A scale to measure attitudes toward college courses.

Reliability: .92.

Author: Mathis, A., Smith, T., and Hansen, D.

Article: College students' attitudes toward computer-assisted instruction.

Journal: *Journal of Educational Psychology*, February 1970, *61*(1), 46–51.

Related Research: Hand, J. A. (1953). Method of weighting attitude scale items from subject responses. *Journal of Clinical Psychology, 9,* 37–39.

• • •

152

Test Name: ATTITUDES TOWARD COMPUTER-ASSISTED INSTRUCTION

Purpose: To measure attitudes toward computer-assisted instruction.

Number of Items: 30

Format: Items are presented.

Reliability: .82.

Author: Mathis, A., Smith, T., and Hansen, D.

Article: College students' attitudes toward computer-assisted instruction.

Journal: *Journal of Educational Psychology*, February 1970, *61*(1), 46–51.

Related Research: Brown, B. R. (1966). An instrument for the measurement of expressed attitude toward computer-assisted instruction. In H. E. Mitzel & G. L. Brandon (Eds.), *Experimentation with computer-assisted instruction in technical education* (Semi-Annual Progress Report, Project No. OEC-5-85-074). University Park: Pennsylvania State University Press.

• • •

153

Test Name: ATTITUDES TOWARD MATHEMATICS

Purpose: To assess the extent to which subjects liked or disliked mathematics.

Author: Davis, R. H., Marzocco, F. N., and Denny, M. R.

Article: Interaction of individual differences with modes of presenting programmed instruction.

Journal: *Journal of Educational Psychology*, June 1970, *61*(3), 198–204.

Related Research: Aiken, L. R., Jr. (1960). *Mathemaphobia and mathemaphilia: An analysis of personal and social factors affecting performance in mathematics* (Doctoral dissertation, University of North Carolina, 1960). *Dissertaion Abstracts International, 21,* 1992. (University Microfilms No. 60-4822).

• • •

154

Test Name: ATTITUDES TOWARD PSYCHOLOGICAL REPORTS AND SERVICES

Purpose: To assess attitudes of psychologist and teachers of mentally retarded children toward psychological reports and services.

Format: Four sections: (a) psychological relation to special education program, (b) general information, (c) rating of psychological reports, and (d) data sheet.

Author: Lucas, M., and Jones, R.

Article: Attitudes of teachers of mentally retarded children toward psychological reports and services.

Journal: *Journal of School Psychology*, 1970, *8*(2), 122–130.

• • •

155

Test Name: ATTITUDE TOWARD SCHOOL QUESTIONNAIRE

Purpose: To measure 4th and 5th

grade children's attitude toward school.

Number of Items: 62

Format: 10 scales consisting of 5–18 items each.

Validity: Intercorrelations (socioeconomic status and IQ included) from .00 to .60.

Author: Beck, L. E., Rose, M. H., and Stewart, D.

Article: Attitudes of English and American children toward their school experience.

Journal: *Journal of Educational Psychology,* February 1970, *61*(1), 33–40.

Related Research: Lunn, J. C. B. (1969).The development of scales to measure junior school children's attitudes. *British Journal of Educational Psychology,* 39, 64–71.

■ ■ ■

156

Test Name: BANKING ATTITUDE QUESTIONNAIRE

Purpose: A survey of banking public relations and pervasive stereotypes.

Number of Items: 20

Format: A 4-point scale was used for all items.

Author: Jones, G. B., and Krumboltz, J. D.

Article: Stimulating vocational exploration through film-mediated problems.

Journal: *Journal of Counseling Psychology,* March 1970, *17*(2), 107–114.

Related Research: Maccoby, N. A. (1955). *A survey of banking public relations in two New England communities* (mimeo). Boston University of Research, School of Public Relations and Communications.

157

Test Name: BLACK HISTORY CURRICULUM PRIORITIES RATING

Purpose: To determine what objectives hold highest and lowest priorities for classroom teachers implementing the new Black history curriculum.

Format: Paper and pencil.

Author: Guenther, J., and Dumas, W.

Article: Black history for what?

Journal: *Social Education,* December 1970, *34*(8), 927–930.

■ ■ ■

158

Test Name: COLLEGE ALUMNI QUESTIONNAIRE

Purpose: To provide information on the careers of college alumni.

Author: Calvert, R., Jr.

Article: Liberal arts graduates: They would do it again.

Journal: *Personnel and Guidance Journal,* October 1970, *49*(2), 123–129.

■ ■ ■

159

Test Name: COLLEGE STUDENT SATISFACTION QUESTIONNAIRE

Purpose: To measure college student satisfaction as an analogue to job satisfaction.

Number of Items: 92.

Format: Measures six dimensions: (a) policies and procedures, (b) working conditions, (c) compensation, (d) quality of education, (e) social life, and (f) recognition.

Reliability: .85 to .91.

Validity: .36 to .80 (between scales correlations).

Author: Betz, E. L., Klingensmith, J. E., and Menne, J. W.

Article: The measurement and analysis of college student satisfaction.

Journal: *Measurement and Evaluation in Guidance,* Summer 1970, *3*(2), 110–118.

■ ■ ■

160

Test Name: COUNSELOR EDUCATION PROGRAM INNOVATION INDEX

Purpose: Part I: to elicit responses descriptive of the extent to which you and your department have used 35 specific innovations. Part II: Items of Part I are repeated with instruction to ignore feasibility and to estimate on a 5-point scale the importance of each of these innovations in an optimal counselor education program.

Author: Lauver, P. J., and Froehle, T. C.

Article: The CEPII: Respondent reaction.

Journal: *Counselor Education and Supervision,* Fall 1970, *10*(1), 46–50.

■ ■ ■

161

Test Name: CORRELATION OF ITEM–EXAMINEE SAMPLING PROCEDURES AND ESTIMATION OF TEST PARAMETERS

Purpose: To show that in estimating parameters by item–examinee sampling the variable of importance is not the item–examinee sampling procedure but is instead the number of observations obtained by that procedure.

Number of Items: 36-item examinee sampling procedures.

Format: Three levels of number of subtests (10, 5, 2), three levels of number of items per subtest (15, 10, 5), and four levels of number of examinees per subtest (120, 90) were manipulated systematically (60, 30).

Reliability: Norm for skewed distribution, .799; norm for normal distribution, .774.

Author: Shoemaker, D. M.

Article: Item–examinee sampling procedures and associated standard errors in estimating test parameters.

Journal: *Journal of Educational Measurement,* Winter 1970, *7*(4), 255.

Related Research: Lord, F. M. (1962). Estimating norms by item sampling. *Educational and Psychological Measurement, 22,* 259–267.

■ ■ ■

162

Test Name: CURRICULUM EVALUATION QUESTIONNAIRE IN SOCIAL WELFARE

Purpose: To determine whether the social welfare curriculum is meeting the need of the social welfare workers in the field, the client, and the agency.

Author: Sielski, L. M.

Article: The undergraduate social welfare curriculum.

Journal: *Improving College and University Teaching,* Spring 1970, *18*(2), 110–111.

■ ■ ■

163

Test Name: DIFFUSE PEER GROUP INDEX

Purpose: To rank schools by the proportion of staff giving particular responses.

Number of Items: 4

Reliability: .88.

Author: Warren, D. I.

Article: Variation on the theme of primary groups: Forms of social control with school staffs.

Journal: *Sociology of Education,* Summer 1970, *43*(3), 288–310.

■ ■ ■

164

Test Name: EMPLOYEE SATISFACTION QUESTIONNAIRE

Purpose: To measure the employee's perception of five environmental factors and the importance of the factors to the employee.

Number of Items: 50

Format: Factors include (a) the job content itself, (b) the supervisor, (c) the company and management, (d) the degree of job autonomy, and (e) the pay.

Validity: .45 to –.01.

Author: Slocum, J. W., Jr.

Article: Supervisory influence and the professional employee.

Journal: *Personnel Journal,* June 1970, *49*(6), 484–488.

Related Research: Slocum, J. W., Jr., & Misshauk, M. (1969). Operative employees' satisfaction with selected environmental work factors, *Personnel Journal, 48*(3), 205–209.

■ ■ ■

165

Test Name: ENVIRONMENTAL ASSESSMENT TECHNIQUE

Purpose: To measure characteristics of college environment by assessing the average or modal characteristics of the students at the institution.

Format: Based on eight measures of the student body.

Author: Astin, A. W.

Article: The methodology of research on college impact, part two.

Journal: *Sociology of Education,* Fall 1970, *43*(4), 437–450.

Related Research: Astin, A. W., & Holland, J. L. (1961). The environmental assessment technique: A way to measure college environments. *Journal of Educational Psychology, 52,* 308–316.

■ ■ ■

166

Test Name: GRADES AND GRADING PRACTICES QUESTIONNAIRE

Purpose: To assess student attitudes toward grades and grading practices.

Number of Items: 11

Format: Complete questionnaire is presented in the article.

Author: Stallings, W. M., and Leslie, E. K.

Article: Student attitudes toward grades and grading.

Journal: *Improving College and University Teaching,* Winter 1970, *18*(1), 66–68.

■ ■ ■

167

Test Name: HIGHER EDUCATION OPPORTUNITIES QUESTIONNAIRE

Purpose: To study higher education opportunities available to married women with unique job and/or family responsibilities.

Number of Items: Not indicated.

Format: Some items are presented.

Author: Cosper, W.

Article: Nepotism: Desirable or undesirable?

Journal: *Improving College and University Teaching,* Autumn 1970, *18*(4), 282–284.

∎ ∎ ∎

168

Test Name: THE ILLINOIS COURSE EVALUATION QUESTIONNAIRE*

Purpose: To elicit student opinions about a standardized set of statements relative to certain aspects of an instructional program or course. Six subscales are reported.

Number of Items: 50 statements.

Time required: 15–20 minutes.

Format: Student responds to 50 statements by indicating preference on a 4-point scale. Printed on DIGITEK answer sheet.

Reliability: Split-half reliability, .93; Kuder-Richardson Formula 21, .931.

Author: Spencer, R. E., and Aleamani, L. M.

Article: A student course evaluation questionnaire.

Journal: *Journal of Educational Measurement,* Fall 1970, *7*(3), 209–210.

Related comments: For further details see *The Illinois evaluation questionnaire, a description and a report of some of its results* (Research Report No. 292). (1969). Champaign, Illinois: Measurement and Research Division, Office of Instructional Resources.

∎ ∎ ∎

169

Test Name: INDIVIDUAL STUDY PRACTICES QUESTIONNAIRE

Purpose: To measure the extent to which a given collegiate institution tended to emphasize individual

study practices and to obtain specific data about the individual study programs concerned.

Author: Dixon, D. R.

Article: Independent study and institutional productivity.

Journal: *Improving College and University Teaching,* Spring 1970, *18*(2), 137–138.

∎ ∎ ∎

170

Test Name: INSTITUTIONAL FUNCTIONING INVENTORY*

Purpose: To measure faculty members' perceptions of their campus climates.

Number of Items: 132

Format: Yields scores on 11 dimensions or scales: intellectual–aesthetic, extracurriculum, freedom, human diversity, concern for improvement of society, democratic governance, meeting local needs, self-study and planning, concern for advising knowledge, concern for innovation, and institutional esprit.

Validity: .01 to .77, –.2 to –.75.

Author: Centra, J. A., et al.

Article: Faculty view of institutional functioning: A new measure of college environments.

Journal: *Educational and Psychological Measurement,* Summer 1970, *30*(2), 405–416.

∎ ∎ ∎

171

Test Name: INSTITUTIONAL INFORMATION QUESTIONNAIRE

Purpose: To collect comprehensive data on the characteristics of 2-year colleges.

Author: Hedlund, D. E., and Jones, J. T.

Article: Effect of student personnel services on completion rate in 2-year colleges.

Journal: *Journal of College Student Personnel,* May 1970, *11*(3), 196–199.

∎ ∎ ∎

172

Test Name: INVENTORY OF COLLEGE ACTIVITIES*

Purpose: Assesses college environment by means of the stimulus approach.

Format: Based on eight image factors.

Author: Astin, A. W.

Article: The methodology of research on college impact, part two.

Journal: *Sociology of Education,* Fall 1970, *43*(4), 437–450.

Related Research: Astin, A. W. (1968). *The college environment.* Washington, DC: American Council on Education.

∎ ∎ ∎

173

Test Name: ITEM DISTRACTOR EFFICACY TEST

Purpose: Find out which method of selecting item distractors for multiple-choice tests is best.

Number of Items: 17 items in each of three tests.

Time required: Each test takes 20 minutes.

Format: Multiple-choice, every third student had the same test, test developed from judgmental, frequency, and discrimination methods of selecting item distractors.

Reliability: Judgmental Method Test, .556; Frequency Method

Test, .620; Discrimination Method Test, .614.

Validity: Judgmental Method Test, .617; Frequency Method Test, .646; Discrimination Method Test, .647.

Author: Owens, R. E., Hanna, G. S., and Coppedge, F. L.

Article: Comparison of item distractor selection techniques.

Journal: *Journal of Educational Measurement*, Summer 1970, *7*(3), 87.

Related Research: Adams, G. S. (1964). *Measurement and evaluation in education, psychology, and guidance.* New York: Holt, Rinehart & Winston.

Hopkins, K. O. (1964). Extrinsic reliability; estimating and attenuating variance from response styles, chance, and other irrelevant sources. *Educational and Psychological Measurement, 24,* 271–281.

■ ■ ■

174

Test Name: JOB-SPECIFIC INDEX

Purpose: Ranking schools on basis of extent of policy making by faculty.

Reliability: Interitem reliability, .97.

Author: Warren, D. I.

Article: Variation on the theme of primary groups: Forms of social control within school staffs.

Journal: *Sociology of Education*, Summer 1970, *43*(3), 288–310.

■ ■ ■

175

Test Name: LEARNING INSTRUMENT

Purpose: Describes the student's perceptions of what he or she learned from the course.

Number of Items: 26

Format: Includes the following six scales: global course satisfaction, improved thinking and communication skills, increased enthusiasm about learning, increased personal understanding, change in career plans, cognitive learning. Items are presented.

Reliability: Subtest reliability, .64 to .84.

Validity: .52.

Author: Hall, D. T.

Article: The effect of teacher–student congruence upon student learning in college classes.

Journal: *Journal of Educational Psychology*, June 1970, *61*(3), 205–213.

■ ■ ■

176

Test Name: ORGANIZATION CLIMATE SURVEY INSTRUMENT

Purpose: To measure the normative expectations of individuals in organizations in any organizational role.

Number of Items: 90

Format: Items are included in five categories: (a) rules orientation, (b) nurturance of subordinates, (c) closeness of supervision, (d) universalism, and (e) promotion–achievement orientation. Items are presented in the article.

Author: Salemi, E. C., and Monahan, J. B.

Article: The psychological contract of employment: Do recruiters and students agree?

Journal: *Personnel Journal*, December 1970, *49*(12), 986–993.

Related Research: Kuhn, R. L., Wolfe, D. M., Quinn, R. P., & Snoek, J. D. (1964). *Organizational stress.* New York: Wiley.

177

Test Name: PERCEPTION OF COLLEGE ENVIRONMENT RATING SCALE

Purpose: To measure the student's perception of the college environment.

Number of Items: 21

Format: Five aspects of the college environment included were students, faculty, administration, faculty–student relations, and physical plant. Items were presented.

Author: Marks, E.

Article: Individual differences in perceptions of the college environment.

Journal: *Journal of Educational Psychology*, August 1970, *61*(4, Part I), 270–279.

Related Research: Stern, G. G. (1958). *College characteristics index: Preliminary manual.* Syracuse, NY: Psychological Research Center.

Webb, S. C. (1964). *Inventory of student characteristics.* Atlanta: Emory University Testing Service.

■ ■ ■

178

Test Name: PERSONNEL SATISFACTION QUESTIONNAIRE

Purpose: To measure several aspects of subordinate work satisfaction.

Validity: −.19 to −.48.

Author: Burke, R. J., Faber, F., and Bresver, B.

Article: Managing interpersonal differences.

Journal: *Personnel Journal*, May 1970, *49*(5), 408–413.

179

Test Name: QUESTIONNAIRE OF CHILDREN'S PERCEPTION OF THEIR ENVIRONMENT

Purpose: To assess children's own perception of their environment.

Number of Items: 72

Validity: .29, .35.

Author: Miller, G. W.

Article: Factors in school achievement and social class.

Journal: *Journal of Educational Psychology*, August 1970, *61*(4, Part I), 260–269.

Availability: Order NAPS Document 01016 from ASIS National Auxiliary Publications Service, c/o CCM Information Sciences, Inc., 909 Third Avenue, New York, NY 10022.

• • •

180

Test Name: QUESTIONNAIRE ON STUDENT AND COLLEGE CHARACTERISTICS

Purpose: To obtain general descriptions of colleges and their students and to help colleges interpret themselves to prospective students.

Author: Gentra, J. A.

Article: Black students at predominantly White colleges: A research description.

Journal: *Sociology of Education*, Summer 1970, *43*(3), 325–339.

Related Research: Centra, J. A. (1968). *Development of the questionnaire on student and college characteristics* (Research Memorandum 68-11). Princeton, NJ: Educational Testing Service.

• • •

181

Test Name: REACTIONS TO OFF-CAMPUS COHABITATION

Purpose: To obtain parents' reactions to several aspects of a university's responsibility toward students living off campus.

Number of Items: 65

Author: Smith, P. B., and Kimmel, K.

Article: Student–parent reactions to off-campus cohabitation.

Journal: *Journal of College Student Personnel*, May 1970, *11*(3), 188–193.

• • •

182

Test Name: REHABILITATION SERVICES SATISFACTION SURVEY

Purpose: To determine clients' satisfaction with rehabilitation services.

Format: Five factors of satisfaction are available.

Reliability: Agreement among clients on the client satisfaction with counselor factor was .77.

Author: Engelkes, J. R., and Roberts, R. R.

Article: Level of training and job performance.

Journal: *Journal of Counseling Psychology*, November 1970, *17*(6, Part I), 522–526.

• • •

183

Test Name: RELIGIOUS GROUPS QUESTIONNAIRE

Purpose: To provide information in 10 areas germane to the study of religious groups.

Format: Face sheet information and information in 10 areas.

Author: Shippey, F. A.

Article: Clique structure in religious youth groups.

Journal: *Sociology and Social Research,* April 1970, *54*(3), 371–377.

• • •

184

Test Name: REVISED ENVIRONMENTAL ASSESSMENT TECHNIQUE

Purpose: To assess the college environment.

Format: Classifies the faculty and curriculum according to six personal orientations.

Validity: −.59 to .94 (undergraduate school); .28 to .88 (graduate school).

Author: Richards, J. M., Seligman, R., and Jones, P. K.

Article: Faculty and curriculum as measures of college environment.

Journal: *Journal of Educational Psychology,* August 1970, *61*(4, Part I), 324–332.

Related Research: Holland, J. L. (1966). *The psychology of vocational choice: A theory of personality types and model environments.* Waltham, MA: Blaisdell.

• • •

185

Test Name: SCALE ON USE AND VALUE OF GUIDANCE PRACTICES

Purpose: To determine from teachers the use and value of guidance practices.

Number of Items: 75

Format: 5-point Likert rating scale.

Reliability: .87, .89.

Author: Witmer, J. M., and Cottingham, H. F.

Article: The teacher's role and guidance functions as reported by elementary teachers.

Journal: *Elementary School*

Guidance and Counseling, October 1970, *5*(1), 12–21.

• • •

186

Test Name: STAFF–STUDENT OPINION QUESTIONNAIRE

Purpose: To determine the felt effects of a staff–student sensitivity training group.

Number of Items: 23

Format: Likert items in which the subject responds on a 7-point scale ranging from *agree strongly* to *disagree strongly*.

Author: Reddy, W. B.

Article: Sensitivity training as an integral phase of counselor education.

Journal: *Counselor Education and Supervision,* Winter 1970, *9*(2), 110–115.

• • •

187

Test Name: STERN'S COLLEGE CHARACTERISTICS INDEX

Purpose: Measures students' perceptions of the prevailing atmosphere or climate of the campus.

Format: Yields scores on 11 environmental factors.

Author: Schoemer, J. R., and McConnell, W. A.

Article: Is there a case for the freshman women's residence hall?

Journal: *Personnel and Guidance Journal,* September 1970, *49*(1), 35–40.

Related Research: Stern, G. G. (1963). *Scoring instructions and college norms, activities index, college characteristics index.* Syracuse, NY: Psychological Research Center.

188

Test Name: SUPERVISION QUESTIONNAIRE

Purpose: To determine employee attitudes toward a bank's style of supervision.

Number of Items: 9

Format: Responses are made along a 7-point scale of disagreement–agreement.

Author: Gannon, M. J.

Article: Analysis of employee attitudes about supervisory behavior.

Journal: *Personnel Journal,* April 1970, *49*(4), 332–336.

• • •

189

Test Name: TEACHER ATTITUDE TOWARD COUNSELING AND GUIDANCE

Purpose: To evaluate elementary guidance demonstration projects.

Number of Items: 12

Format: One responds to each statement on a 5-point scale indicating how characteristic the statement is of one's feelings.

Author: Mayer, G. R., et al.

Article: The use of public commitment and counseling with elementary school children: An evaluation.

Journal: *Elementary School Guidance and Counseling,* October 1970, *5*(1), 22–34.

Related Research: Mayer, G. R., & Beggs, D. C. (1969). *The educationally disadvantaged elementary school child: Anxiety reduction and behavioral change through public commitment and counseling* (Cooperative Research Project No. 8–E–088). Southern Illinois University.

190

Test Name: TESTING PRACTICES QUESTIONNAIRE

Purpose: To determine testing practices in institutions of higher learning.

Author: Stallings, W. M.

Article: Some observations on testing practices.

Journal: *Improving College and University Teaching,* Spring 1970, *18*(2), 142–143.

• • •

191

Test Name: THERAPY SESSION REPORT

Purpose: Provides patient-experience factor scores.

Number of Items: 147

Format: Items cover eight topics and are in a fixed-response format.

Author: Howard, K. I., and Orlinsky, D. E.

Article: Therapist orientation and patient experience in psychotherapy.

Journal: *Journal of Counseling Psychology,* May (1970), *17*(3), 263–270.

Related Research: Orlinsky, D. E., & Howard, K. I. (1966). *Therapy session report (Form P).* Chicago: Institute for Juvenile Research.

Orlinsky, D. E., Howard, K. I., & Hill, J. A. (1970). The patient's concerns in psychotherapy. *Journal of Clinical Psychology, 26,* 104–111.

• • •

192

Test Name: TRANSFER QUESTIONNAIRE

Purpose: To identify six cognitive and goal variables related to within-university transfer.

Author: Marks, E.

Article: Cognitive and incentive factors involved in within-university transfer.

Journal: *Journal of Educational Psychology,* February 1970, *61*(l), 1–9.

Related Research: Marks, E., Webb, S. C., & Strickland, J. A. (1967, June). *Intra-institute transfer report: I. Educational and career goals and perceptions of choice of major* (Research memorandum 67-6). Georgia Institute of Technology, Evaluation Studies.

■ ■ ■

193

Test Name: WORK RELATIONS QUESTIONNAIRE

Purpose: To obtain the attitudes and opinions of the employees so as to provide for employee feedback and participation in improving their organization.

Number of Items: 21

Format: 18 structured questions each with 5 multiple-choice answers and 3 open-end questions soliciting suggestions for organizational improvements. Items are presented.

Author: Brianas, J. G.

Article: Between employees and supervisors: Three cases in point.

Journal: *Personnel Journal,* November 1970, *49*(11), 892–899.

CHAPTER 13
Interest

194

Test Name: HOLLAND VOCATIONAL PREFERENCE INVENTORY

Purpose: To measure vocational preference.

Format: Uses six personality dimensions: realistic, intellectual, social, conventional, enterprising, artistic.

Validity: Correctly classified 20 of 43 students who remained in an engineering major, correctly classified 15 of the 33 who changed major and 13 of those who left the university.

Author: Southworth, J. A., and Morningstar, M. E.

Article: Persistence of occupational choice and personality congruence.

Journal: *Journal of Counseling Psychology,* September 1970, *17*(5), 409–412.

Related Research: Holland, J. L. (1962). Some explorations of a theory of vocational choice: I. One and two-year longitudinal studies. *Psychological Monographs, 76*(26, Whole No. 545).

● ● ●

195

Test Name: HOLLAND'S VOCATIONAL PREFERENCE INVENTORY

Purpose: To determine vocational choice.

Author: Bodden, J. L.

Article: Cognitive complexity as a

factor in appropriate vocational choice.

Journal: *Journal of Counseling Psychology,* July 1970, *17*(4), 364–368.

Related Research: Holland, J. L. (1966). *The psychology of vocational choice.* Waltham, MA: Blaisdell.

● ● ●

196

Test Name: INTEREST SELF-RATING INVENTORY

Purpose: To determine whether a subject indicated high or low interest in each of 100 occupations.

Number of Items: 100

Format: The items were the first 100 items of the 1965 edition of the Strong Vocational Interest Blank.

Reliability: .31–.80.

Author: Sharf, R.

Article: Relative importance of interest and ability in vocational decision making.

Journal: *Journal of Counseling Psychology,* May 1970, *17*(3), 258–262.

● ● ●

197

Test Name: JOB INTERESTS LIST

Purpose: Subjects express their current occupational interests.

Author: Jones, G. B., and Krumboltz, J. D.

Article: Stimulating vocational exploration through film-mediated problems.

Journal: *Journal of Counseling Psychology,* March 1970, *17*(2), 107–114.

● ● ●

198

Test Name: LEISURE ACTIVITIES QUESTIONNAIRE

Purpose: To determine frequency of participation in leisure activities.

Number of Items: 32

Format: Response format was a 9-category scale with each category corresponding to a frequency or frequency range (0–354).

Author: Bishop, D. W.

Article: Status and role factors in the leisure behavior of different occupations.

Journal: *Sociology and Social Research,* January 1970, *54*(2), 190–208.

● ● ●

199

Test Name: OCCUPATIONAL INTEREST AREA INDICATOR

Purpose: To determine systematically each subject's most- and least-preferred occupational interest areas.

Format: The indicator lists 14 major occupational interest areas.

Author: Ziegler, D. J.

Article: Self-concept, occupational member concept, and occupational interest area relationships in male college students.

Journal: *Journal of Counseling Psychology,* March 1970, *17*(2), 133–136.

Related Research: Keat, D. B. (1967). *A cluster and factor analysis of the occupational interest of five hundred male college students.* Unpublished doctoral dissertation, Temple University.

■ ■ ■

200

Test Name: PREFERENCE EDUCATION QUESTIONNAIRE

Purpose: To measure the degree to which subjects favored broad- or career-oriented education.

Author: Vidmar, N., and McGrath, J. E.

Article: Forces affecting success in negotiation groups.

Journal: *Behavioral Science,* March 1970, *15*(2), 154–163.

■ ■ ■

201

Test Name: PROJECT TALENT INTEREST INVENTORY

Purpose: To measure interest in occupations and activities.

Number of Items: 205

Format: Degree of interest for each of the occupations and activities was recorded on a 5-point scale.

Author: Jones, G. B., and Krumboltz, J. D.

Article: Stimulating vocational exploration through film-mediated problems.

Journal: *Journal of Counseling Psychology,* March 1970, *17*(2), 107–114.

Related Research: Flanagan, J. C., et al. (1962). *Design for a study of American youth.* Boston: Houghton Mifflin.

Flanagan, J. C., et al. (1964). Project TALENT: *The American high school student* (Final report, Cooperative Research Project No. 635). Washington, DC: Government Printing Office.

■ ■ ■

202

Test Name: SURVEY OF CAREER PLANS AND EXPERIENCES

Purpose: To provide measures of the extensiveness and the effectiveness of vocational exploratory behavior.

Reliability: .63, .81, .88.

Author: Buck, C. W.

Article: Crystallization of

vocational interests as a function of vocational exploration in college.

Journal: *Journal of Counseling Psychology,* July 1970, *17*(4), 347–351.

■ ■ ■

203

Test Name: VOCATIONAL EXPLORATORY BEHAVIOR INVENTORY

Purpose: Provides an inventory representing the number of exploratory responses the subjects reported for which they could provide supportive information including specification of the dates during which the responses were made.

Author: Jones, G. B., and Krumboltz, J. D.

Article: Stimulating vocational exploration through film-mediated problems.

Journal: *Journal of Counseling Psychology,* March 1970, *17*(2), 107–114.

Related Research: Krumboltz, J. D., & Sheppard, L. E. (1966). *The effect of a vocational problem-solving experience on career exploration and interest* (mimeo). Unpublished manuscript, Stanford University.

CHAPTER 14
Motivation

204

Test Name: N ACH TAT

Purpose: To measure need achievement.

Number of Items: 4 pictures.

Reliability: .90.

Validity: Correlations from –.12 to –.24 with other scales.

Author: Tseng, M. S., and Carter, A. R.

Article: Achievement motivation and fear of failure as determinants of vocational choice, vocational aspiration, and perception of vocational prestige.

Journal: *Journal of Counseling Psychology,* March 1970, *17*(2), 150–156.

Related Research: McClelland, D. C., Atkinson, J. W., Clark, R. A., & Lowell, E. L. (1953). *The achievement motive.* New York: Appleton-Century-Crofts.

• • •

205

Test Name: AN EXPLORATORY STUDY OF TASK PREFERENCES

Purpose: A task-preference study resulting from efforts to improve employee motivation in a midwestern police department.

Number of Items: Sixteen items covering four areas.

Time required: Not given, probably 15–20 minutes maximum.

Format: Sixteen items in four areas

with five response options to each item.

Author: Olsen, B.

Article: An exploratory study of task preferences.

Journal: *Personnel Journal,* December 1970, *49*(12), 1015–1020.

• • •

206

Test Name: COMMITMENT TO COLLEGE QUESTIONNAIRE

Purpose: To measure the extent of one's commitment to obtaining a college education.

Author: Hackman, J. R., and Dysinger, W. S.

Article: Research notes: Commitment to college as a factor in student attraction.

Journal: *Sociology of Education,* Summer 1970, *43* (3), 311–324.

• • •

207

Test Name: FUTURE ORIENTATION SCALE

Purpose: Measures the degree to which a person is willing to postpone immediate gratification for future reward.

Number of Items: 9

Format: Eight items on a 4-point scale and an additional item in forced-choice form.

Author: Egeland, B., Hunt, D. E., and Hardt, R. H.

Article: College enrollment of upward bound students as a

function of attitude and motivation.

Journal: *Journal of Educational Psychology,* October 1970, *61*(5), 375–379.

Related Research: Strodtbeck, F. L. (1958). Family interaction, values and achievement. In D. C. McClelland, A. L. Baldwin, U. Bronfenbrenner, & F. L. Strodtbeck (Eds.), *Talent and society.* New York: Van Nostrand.

• • •

208

Test Name: SCALES OF MOTIVATION FOR COLLEGE

Purpose: Direct measures of motivation for college.

Format: Two scales: Importance of college graduation, possibility of college graduation. Students respond to the statement, "if graduation from college is:" with a 5-point rating scale ranging from 1 (*not possible*) to 5 (*extremely possible*).

Author: Egeland, B., Hunt, D. E., and Hardt, R. H.

Article: College enrollment of upward bound students as a function of attitude and motivation.

Journal: *Journal of Educational Psychology,* October 1970, *61*(5), 375–379.

• • •

209

Test Name: TEST ANXIETY QUESTIONNAIRE (SHORT FORM)

Purpose: To measure test anxiety and also to measure the strength of motive to avoid failure.

Number of Items: 32

Format: Graded on a 9-point scale with 1 representing *low-anxiety level* and 9 representing *high-anxiety level.*

Reliability: .95.

Validity: Correlations from −.22 to .26 with other scales.

Author: Tseng, M. S., and Carter, A. R.

Article: Achievement motivation and fear of failure as determinants of vocational choice, vocational aspiration, and perception of vocational prestige.

Journal: *Journal of Counseling Psychology,* March 1970, *17*(2), 150–156.

Related Research: Mandler, G., & Cowan, J. (1958). Test anxiety questionnaire. *Journal of Consulting Psychology, 22,* 228–229.

■ ■ ■

210

Test Name: THEMATIC APPERCEPTION TEST-TYPE PICTURES

Purpose: To measure need for achievement.

Number of Items: Six 5 × 7-inch cards.

Author: Lin, Y., and McKeachie, W. J.

Article: Aptitude, anxiety, study habits, and academic-achievement.

Journal: *Journal of Counseling Psychology,* July 1970, *17*(4), 306–309.

Related Research: Veroff, J., Atkinson, J. W., Feld, S. C., & Gurin, G. (1960). The use of thematic apperception to assess motivation in a nationwide interview study. *Psychological Monographs, 74*(12, Whole No. 499).

...

CHAPTER 15
Personality

211

Test Name: ADJECTIVE CHECK LIST*

Purpose: To derive personality scores based on the manifest needs catalogued by Murray (1938).

Number of Items: 300 behavioral adjectives.

Time required: 10 minutes.

Format: Paper and pencil check list.

Reliability: See Heilbrun, Related Research.

Validity: See Heilbrun, Related Research.

Author: Johnson, R. W.

Article: Parental identification and vocational interests of college women.

Journal: *Measurement and Evaluation in Guidance,* Fall 1970, *3*(3), 147–151.

Related Research: Heilbrun, A. B., Jr. (1965). The measurement of identification. *Child Development, 36,* 111–127.

Edwards, A. L. (1954). *Manual for the Edwards personal preference schedule.* New York: Psychological Corporation.

...

212

Test Name: BIOGRAPHICAL INFORMATION FORM

Purpose: To obtain demographic data as well as self-expectations, vocational identification, and satisfaction with the college environment.

Number of Items: 20

Author: Gallessich, J.

Article: An investigation of correlates of academic success of freshmen engineering students.

Journal: *Journal of Counseling Psychology,* March 1970, *17*(2), 173–176.

...

213

Test Name: BIOGRAPHICAL INVENTORY QUESTIONNAIRE

Purpose: To ascertain a number of attributes.

Format: Includes the following: age, parental income, college major and minor, grade-point average, extracurricular activities, expected career patterns, and for women, purposes in attending college, mother's working pattern, and information about certainty of career choice.

Author: Resnick, H., Fauble, M. L., and Osipow, S. H.

Article: Vocational crystallization and self-esteem in college students.

Journal: *Journal of Counseling Psychology,* September 1970, *17*(5), 465–467.

...

214

Test Name: EXPANDED SOCIOMETRIC DEVICE

Purpose: A personality test designed to measure behavior that deviates from statistical normalcy but in a positive or healthy direction.

Format: Factors measured include: (a) perceptual and task effectiveness, (b) autonomy and self-actualization, (c) commitment, and (d) openness.

Author: Wright, L., and Dunn, T.

Article: Factor structure of the expanded sociometric device: A measure of personal effectiveness.

Journal: *Educational and Psychological Measurement,* Summer 1970, *30*(2), 319–326.

Related Research: Wright, L., Bond, D., & Denison, J. W. An expanded sociometric device for measuring personal effectiveness. *Psychological Reports,* 1968, *23,* 263–269.

...

215

Test Name: FOUR EXAMPLE-ANCHORED DESCRIPTIVE RATING SCALES

Purpose: Assessed the following variables: (a) degree of coping adequacy or inadequacy, (b) degree of physical health or debility, (c) degree of informal social support available, and (d) degree of financial comfort or stress.

Format: All scales consisted of 100 points, with six case-history vignettes marking way points along the thermometerlike line, and all were designed so that higher scores indicated more adequate functioning or circumstances. Available by writing to senior author at the Menninger Foundation.

Reliability: .76 to .98.

Author: Taylor, J. B., et al.

Article: Rating scales as measures of clinical judgment: II. The reliability of example-anchored scales under conditions of rater heterogeneity and divergent behavior sampling.

Journal: *Educational and Psychological Measurement,* Summer 1970, *30*(2), 301–310.

Related Research: Taylor, J. B. (1968). Rating scales as measures of clinical judgment: A method for increasing scale reliability and sensitivity. *Educational and Psychological Measurement, 28,* 747–766.

■ ■ ■

216

Test Name: FOUR FACTOR-ANALYTIC SCALES OF THE EPPS

Purpose: Personality assessment.

Format: The four scales include (a) interpersonal orientation, (b) assertive aggressiveness, (c) persistence–dependence, and (d) thinking–doing.

Reliability: .83 to .92.

Validity: −.42 to .32.

Author: Sherman, R. C., and Poe, C. A.

Article: Factor-analytic scales of a normative form of the EPPS.

Journal: *Measurement and Evaluation in Guidance,* Winter 1970, *2*(4), 243–248.

■ ■ ■

217

Test Name: INTERPERSONAL FLEXIBILITY SCALE

Purpose: Reflects the degree to which one can take on other perspectives.

Number of Items: 21

Format: For each item the student responds to a 4-point agree–disagree scale resulting in a possible raw score range from 21 to 84.

Author: Egeland, B., Hunt, D. E., & Hardt, R. H.

Article: College enrollment of upward bound students as a function of attitude and motivation.

Journal: *Journal of Educational Psychology,* October 1970, *61*(5), 375–379.

Related Research: Hunt, D. E. (1964). *Personality patterns of adolescent boys* (National Institute of Mental Health Progress Report). Washington, DC: United States Government Printing Office.

■ ■ ■

218

Test Name: JACKSON'S PERSONALITY RESEARCH FORM

Purpose: Twenty-two scales for measuring personality.

Format: Use of 4 of the 22 scales was reported in this study: achievement, autonomy, change, and cognitive structure. These scales were felt to possess excellent convergent and discriminant validity.

Reliability: .68 to .78.

Author: Marks, E.

Article: Cognitive and incentive factors involved in within-university transfer.

Journal: *Journal of Educational Psychology,* February 1970, *61*(1), 1–9.

Related Research: Jackson, D. N., & Guthrie, G. M. (1968). Multitrait–multimethod evaluation of the Personality Research Form. *Proceedings of the 76th Annual Convention of the American Psychological Association, 3,* 177–178.

■ ■ ■

219

Test Name: KELLY ROLE CONSTRUCT REPERTORY TEST

Purpose: To elicit personal construct dimensions.

Format: Part I requires the subject to identify individuals in his or her life who fit each of 15 role titles. Part II arranges these role titles in 15 triads and asks that the subjects identify an important way in which two persons are alike and yet different from the third. The subject then indicates what he or she considers to be the exact opposite of this similarity.

Reliability: .80.

Author: Bailey, S. T.

Article: Independence and factor structure of self-concept metadimensions.

Journal: *Journal of Counseling Psychology,* September 1970, *17*(5), 425–430.

Related Research: Kelly, G. A. (1955). *The psychology of personal constructs: 1. A theory of personality.* New York: Norton.

■ ■ ■

220

Test Name: RELATIONSHIP INVENTORY

Purpose: To measure the extent to which one person perceives another as having positive regard, empathy, congruence, and unconditionality of positive regard.

Number of Items: 64

Format: A questionnaire yielding four scores plus a total score.

Author: Reddy, B. W.

Article: Sensitivity training as an integral phase of counselor education.

Journal: *Counselor Education and Supervision*, Winter 1970, *9*(2), 110–115.

Related Research: Barrett-Lennard, G. T. (1962). Dimensions of therapist response as causal factors in therapeutic change. *Psychological Monographs, 76*(43, Whole No. 562).

• • •

221

Test Name: ROTTER'S INTERNAL–EXTERNAL LOCUS OF CONTROL SCALE

Purpose: To measure personality.

Number of Items: 29

Format: Items are of a forced-choice nature.

Author: Adinolfi, A. A.

Article: Characteristics of highly accepted, highly rejected, and relatively unknown university freshmen.

Journal: *Journal of Counseling Psychology*, September 1970, *17*(5), 456–464.

Related Research: Rotter, J. (1966). Generalized expectancies for internal versus external control of reinforcement. *Psychological Monographs, 88*(1, Whole No. 609).

• • •

222

Test Name: RUNNER STUDIES OF ATTITUDE PATTERNS— COLLEGE FORM

Purpose: A personality measure used to discriminate among students majoring in various academic curricula.

Format: Measures 10 variables.

Author: Baggaly, A. R., Isard, E. S., and Sherwood, E. J.

Article: Discrimination of academic curricula by the runner studies of attitude patterns—college form.

Journal: *Measurement and Evaluation in Guidance,* Spring 1970, *3*(1), 41–44.

Related Research: For further information write to Dr. Eleanore S. Isard, Temple University, Philadelphia.

• • •

223

Test Name: SAGE'S DEVELOPMENTAL SCALE

Purpose: To measure personality.

Format: A true–false test developed on a longitudinal sample in a cross-validation design. Separate forms for each sex.

Validity: $r = .71$ for female form with age over high school and college; $r = .73$ for male form with age over high school and college.

Author: Adinolfi, A. A.

Article: Characteristics of highly accepted, highly rejected, and relatively unknown university freshmen.

Journal: *Journal of Counseling Psychology*, September 1970, *17*(5), 456–464.

Related Research: Sage, E. (1968). Developmental scales for college freshmen. *Journal of Counseling Psychology, 15,* 381–385.

• • •

224

Test Name: STRUCTURED OBJECTIVE RORSCHACH TEST*

Purpose: Measures personality as revealed on 15 scoring categories.

Author: Jansen, D. G., Robb, G. P., and Bonk, E. C.

Article: Characteristics of high-rated and low-rated master's degree candidates in counseling and guidance.

Journal: *Counselor Education and Supervision,* Winter 1970, *9*(3), 162–170.

• • •

225

Test Name: STUDENT INFORMATION BLANK

Purpose: To obtain biodata.

Number of Items: 394

Author: Prediger, D.

Article: Biographical data differentiating college attenders from nonattenders at various ability levels.

Journal: *Measurement and Evaluation in Guidance,* Winter 1970, *2*(4), 217–224.

Related Research: Flanagan, J. C., et al. (1964). *The American high school student.* Pittsburgh, PA: University of Pittsburgh, Project TALENT Office.

• • •

226

Test Name: TEACHER QUESTIONNAIRE REGARDING MOONLIGHTING

Purpose: To identify specific teacher characteristics pertaining to moonlighting activities.

Author: Campbell, L. P.

Article: A study of moonlighting activities of male Jefferson County teachers.

Journal: *Colorado Journal of Educational Research,* Winter 1970, *9*(2), 2–5.

⋯

CHAPTER 16

Perception

227

Test Name:
BARRETT-LENNARD
RELATIONSHIP INVENTORY

Purpose: Client perceptions of the relationships with the counselor.

Format: Yields four relationship components—empathy, unconditional positive regard, level of regard, and congruence—plus a total rating from each client.

Reliability: .82.

Author: Tosi, D. J.

Article: Dogmatism within the counselor–client dyad.

Journal: *Journal of Counseling Psychology*, May 1970, *17*(3), 284–288.

Related Research:
Barrett-Lennard, G. T. (1962). Dimensions of therapist response as causal factors in therapeutic change. *Psychological Monographs, 76*(43, Whole No. 562).

■ ■ ■

228

Test Name: BEHAVIOR ORIENTATION CARD SORT

Purpose: Assessment of subjects' statements of ways they typically behave.

Number of Items: 80

Format: Dimensions included are academic achievement orientation, independence, peer affiliation, and nonconformity orientation. Sample items are presented.

Reliability: .51 to .93.

Author: Ringness, T. S.

Article: Identifying figures, their achievement values, and children's values as related to actual and predicted achievement.

Journal: *Journal of Educational Psychology*, June 1970, *61*(3), 174–185.

Related Research: Ringness, T. A. (1965). *Non-intellective variables related to academic achievement of bright junior high school boys* (Final Report, United States Office of Education Project S-036, mimeo). Madison: University of Wisconsin.

■ ■ ■

229

Test Name: BIOGRAPHICAL QUESTIONNAIRE

Purpose: Parental dominance as perceived by the subject.

Number of Items: 5 multiple-choice.

Author: Medvene, A. M.

Article: Person-oriented and non-person oriented occupations in psychology.

Journal: *Journal of Counseling Psychology*, May 1970 *17*(3), 243–246.

Related Research: Roe, A., & Siegelman, M. (1964). *The origin of interest.* Washington, DC: American Personnel and Guidance Association.

■ ■ ■

230

Test Name: CHILD'S SELF-CONCEPT

Purpose: To assess the child's self-concept.

Validity: With other measures, .13 to .53.

Author: Cox, S. H.

Article: Intrafamily comparison of loving-rejecting child-rearing practices.

Journal: *Child Development*, June 1970, *41*(2), 437–448.

Related Research: Piers, E. V., & Harris, D. B. (1963). Age and other correlates of self-concept in children. *Journal of Educational Psychology, 55*, 91–95.

■ ■ ■

231

Test Name: COLLEGE OPINION SURVEY

Purpose: To measure self-made academic predictions.

Number of Items: 16

Reliability: .77 to .80.

Validity: −.05 to .44.

Author: Biggs, D. A., Roth, J. D., and Strong, S. R.

Article: Self-made academic predictions and academic performance.

Journal: *Measurement and Evaluation in Guidance*, Summer 1970, *3*(2), 81–85.

Related Research: Brookover, W. B. (1962, December). *Self-concept of ability and school achievement I* (Cooperative Project No. 845). Michigan State University, Office of Research and Publications.

232

Test Name: COLLEGE OPINION SURVEY

Purpose: A measure of self-made academic predictions.

Number of Items: 16

Author: Biggs, D. A.

Article: Counseling interviews or counseling letters.

Journal: *Journal of Counseling Psychology*, May 1970, *17*(3), 224–227.

Related Research: Biggs, D. A. (1968, December). *Self-made predictions and college performance, measurement-therapeutic changes* (Technical Report I, Office of the Dean of Students, Staff Paper No. 41). Minneapolis: University of Minnesota.

Biggs, D. A., & Tinsley, D. J. (1970). Student-made academic predictions. *Journal of Educational Research, 63*(5), 195–197.

● ● ●

233

Test Name: CURIOSITY SCALE

Purpose: A self-appraisal of curiosity.

Author: Maw, W. H., and Maw, E. W.

Article: Self-concepts of high- and low-curiosity boys.

Journal: *Child Development*, March 1970, *41*(1), 123–129.

Related Research: Maw, W. H., & Maw, E. W. (1968). Self-appraisal of curiosity. *Journal of Educational Research, 61*, 462–466.

● ● ●

234

Test Name: DISTRIBUTIVE JUSTICE SCALE

Purpose: To measure "perceived deprivation of distributive justice."

Number of Items: 4 indices.

Author: Arnott, C., and Bengtson, V. L.

Article: "Only a homemaker" distributive justice and role choices among married women.

Journal: *Sociology and Social Research*, July 1970, *54*(4), 495–507.

● ● ●

235

Test Name: EMPATHY SCALE

Purpose: To tap the capacity to empathize with the characters in stories or plays and with people in face-to-face situations and to imagine oneself as a person different from oneself.

Number of Items: 10

Validity: .15, .22.

Author: Taft, R., and Gilchrist, M.

Article: Creative attitudes and creative productivity: A comparison of two aspects of creativity among students.

Journal: *Journal of Educational Psychology*, April 1970, *61*(2), 136–143.

Related Research: Elms, A. C. (1966). Influence of fantasy ability on attitude change through role playing. *Journal of Personality and Social Psychology, 4*, 36–43.

● ● ●

236

Test Name: IDEAS OF REFERENCE SCALE

Purpose: To measure hypersensitivity to other people's actions or presumed feelings toward self.

Number of Items: 18

Reliability: .76.

Author: Sears, R. R.

Article: Relation of early socialization experiences to self-concepts and gender role in middle childhood.

Journal: *Child Development*, June 1970, *41*(2), 267–289.

Related Research: Sears, R. R. (1937). Experimental studies of projection: II. Ideas of reference. *Journal of Social Psychology, 8*, 389–400.

● ● ●

237

Test Name: INTERACTION SCALE

Purpose: To measure feelings and the perceptions of feelings of each member in a dyad.

Format: Two scales: the Expression scale measures the expression of feelings a member of the dyad has toward a partner; the Perception scale measures that person's perception of the partner's feelings toward him. Yields four scores.

Author: MacGuffie, R. A.

Article: Relationship between the social vocabulary index and the interaction scale and rehabilitation success.

Journal: *Journal of Counseling Psychology*, May 1970, *17*(3), 289–290.

Related Research: Jorgensen, G. Q., Janzen, F. V., Samuelson, C. O., & McPhee, W. M. (1968). *Interpersonal relationships: Factors in job placement* (University of Utah Regional Rehabilitation Research Institute Bulletin No. 3). Salt Lake City: University of Utah Press.

● ● ●

238

Test Name: INTERNAL CONTROL SCALE

Purpose: Designed to reflect the degree to which subjects see themselves as controlling the outcome of their experience.

Number of Items: 13

Format: A forced-choice technique with a possible raw score ranging from 13 to 26.

Author: Egeland, B., Hunt, D. E., and Hardt, R. H.

Article: College enrollment of upward bound students as a function of attitude and motivation.

Journal: *Journal of Educational Psychology*, October 1970, *61*(5), 375–379.

Related Research: Rotter, J. B. (1966). Generalized expectancies for internal versus external control of reinforcement. *Psychological Monographs, 80*(1, Whole No. 609).

239

Test Name: LOCUS OF CONTROL SCALE FOR CHILDREN

Purpose: To measure the child's perception of control.

Number of Items: 23

Format: Yes–no items such as "Can you do anything about what is going to happen tomorrow?"

Validity: .21 to .34.

Author: Walls, R. T., and Smith, T. S.

Article: Development of preference for delayed reinforcement in disadvantaged children.

Journal: *Journal of Educational Psychology*, April 1970, *61*(2), 118–123.

Related Research: Bailer, I. (1961). Conceptualization of success and failure in mentally retarded and normal children. *Journal of Personality, 29,* 303–320.

240

Test Name: PERCEPTION OF MARITAL INTERACTION SCALE

Purpose: To measure the individual and married pair's perceptions of the present relationship.

Number of Items: 20

Author: Smith, J. P.

Article: Perception of self and other (mate) as motivation for marriage counseling: An Interactionist approach.

Journal: *Sociology and Social Research,* July 1970, *54*(4), 466–476.

■ ■ ■

241

Test Name: PRE-EMPLOYMENT QUESTIONNAIRE

Purpose: To permit the applicant to predict his or her own employment success.

Number of Items: 4

Format: Each question is rated on a 5-point continuum scale.

Author: Travaglio, R. F.

Article: Response differences among employment applicants.

Journal: *Personnel Journal,* July 1970, *49*(7), 593–597.

■ ■ ■

242

Test Name: SELF-AGGRESSION SCALE

Purpose: Measures hostility toward self.

Number of Items: 5

Format: Items are presented in article.

Author: Sears, R. R.

Article: Relation of early socialization experiences to

self-concepts and gender role in middle childhood.

Journal: *Child Development,* June 1970, *41*(2), 267–289.

Related Research: Sears, R. R. (1961). Relation of early socialization experiences to aggression in middle childhood. *Journal of Abnormal and Social Psychology, 63,* 466–492.

■ ■ ■

243

Test Name: SELF-CONCEPT INVENTORY—REVISED

Purpose: To measure a child's feelings and judgments about his own effectiveness and competence.

Number of Items: 40

Format: 10 general categories.

Reliability: .92.

Author: Sears, R. R.

Article: Relation of early socialization experiences to self-concepts and gender role in middle childhood.

Journal: *Child Development,* June 1970, *41*(2), 267–289.

Related Research: Sears, P. S. (1963). *The effect of classroom conditions on the strength of achievement motive and work output of elementary school children.* Washington, DC: U.S. Office of Education Cooperative Research Project No. 873.

■ ■ ■

244

Test Name: SELF-CRITICISM SCALE

Purpose: To measure self-criticism of physical abilities, achievements in school, or social relations.

Number of Items: 20

Reliability: .84.

Author: Sears, R. R.

Article: Relation of early socialization experiences to self-concepts and gender role in middle childhood.

Journal: *Child Development*, June 1970, *41*(2), 267–289.

Related Research: Sears, R. R. (1937). Experimental studies of projection: II. Ideas of reference. *Journal of Social Psychology, 8*, 389–400.

■ ■ ■

245

Test Name: SELF-DESCRIPTION QUESTIONNAIRE

Purpose: Used to investigate certain aspects of Erikson's eight stages of man.

Number of Items: 160

Reliability: Test–retest for 16 scales ranged from high 40s to upper 80s with 12 above .70.

Validity: At or beyond .05 level of significance.

Author: Boyd, R. D., and Kaskela, R. N.

Article: A test of Erikson's theory of ego–stage development by means of a self-report instrument.

Journal: *Experimental Research*, Spring 1970, *38*(3), 1–14.

■ ■ ■

246

Test Name: SELF-ESTEEM SCALE

Purpose: Indexes a person's present feelings of self-adequacy.

Number of Items: 10

Format: Each item has four alternatives from *strongly agree* to *strongly disagree*, which results in a possible raw score ranging from 10 to 40.

Author: Egeland, B., Hunt, D. E., and Hardt, R. H.

Article: College enrollment of upward bound students as a function of attitude and motivation.

Journal: *Journal of Educational Psychology*, October 1970, *60*(5), 375–379.

Related Research: Rosenberg, M. (1965). *Society and the adolescent self-image*. Princeton, NJ: Princeton University Press.

■ ■ ■

247

Test Name: SELF-EVALUATED INTELLIGENCE SCALE

Purpose: A self-evaluation of one's intelligence.

Format: Rating of self on a 7-point scale in semantic differential form ranging from 1 (*dumb*) to 7 (*smart*).

Author: Egeland, B., Hunt, D. E., and Hardt, R. H.

Article: College enrollment of upward bound students as a function of attitude and motivation.

Journal: *Journal of Educational Psychology*, October 1970, *61*(5), 375–379.

■ ■ ■

248

Test Name: SELF-RATING SCALE

Purpose: To assess achievement orientation. Items tap, in part, the kind of affect (hope or fear), the direction of behavior (approach or avoidance), and the preference for risk (intermediate versus easy or difficult) elicited in achievement contexts.

Format: Responses range from strong agreement (+3) to strong disagreement (−3). Sample items are provided.

Validity: −.13 to .75 with other scales.

Author: Weiner, B., and Potepan, P. A.

Article: Personality characteristics and affective reactions toward exams of superior and failing college students.

Journal: *Journal of Educational Psychology*, April 1970, *61*(2), 144–151.

Related Research: Mehrabian, A. (1968). Male and female scales of the tendency to achieve. *Educational and Psychological Measurement, 28*, 493–502.

■ ■ ■

249

Test Name: SELF SOCIAL SYMBOLS TASK

Purpose: Includes scales to measure self-esteem, self-centrality, social interest, and marginality.

Format: A projective test.

Author: Alper, T. C., and Kranzler, G. D.

Article: A comparison of the effectiveness of behavioral and client-centered approaches for the behavior problems of elementary school children.

Journal: *Elementary School Guidance and Counseling*, October 1970, *5*(1), 35–43.

Related Research: Ziller, R. (1969). *Self–other orientation: Theory and tasks*. Unpublished manuscript, University of Oregon.

■ ■ ■

250

Test Name: SEMANTIC DIFFERENTIAL SCHEDULE

Purpose: To measure the semantic meaning of self.

Number of Items: Nine bipolar adjective scales identified by Osgood, et al.

Format: Adjective pairs are presented in article.

Author: Pallone, N. J., Rickard, F. S., Hurley, R. B., and Tirman, R. J.

Article: Work values and self meaning.

Journal: *Journal of Counseling Psychology,* July 1970, *17*(4), 376–377.

Related Research: Osgood, C. E., Suci, G. J., & Tannenbaum, P. H. (1957). *The measurement of meaning.* Urbana: University of Illinois Press.

● ● ●

251

Test Name: SOCIAL DESIRABILITY QUESTIONNAIRE

Purpose: To measure how well one thinks others think of one.

Number of Items: 48

Format: True–false items.

Reliability: .80, .88.

Validity: .10 to –.55.

Author: LaHáderne, H. M., and Jackson, P. W.

Article: Withdrawal in the classroom: A note on some educational correlates of social desirability among school children.

Journal: *Journal of Educational Psychology,* April 1970, *61*(2), 97–101.

Related Research: Crandall, V. C., Crandall, V. J., & Katkovsky, W. (1965). Children's social desirability questionnaire. *Journal of Consulting Psychology, 29,* 27–36.

252

Test Name: SOCIAL VOCABULARY INDEX

Purpose: Measures the self-concept system.

Format: Consists of five subscales: self-concept scale, self-acceptance scale, ideal self scale, concept of others scale, and the Marlowe-Crowne social desirability scale.

Validity: .25 with interaction scale and rehabilitation success.

Author: MacGuffie, R. A.

Article: Relationship between the social vocabulary index and the interaction scale and rehabilitation success.

Journal: *Journal of Counseling Psychology,* May 1970, *17*(3), 289–290.

Related Research: Jorgensen, G. Q., Janzen, F. V., Samuelson, C. O., & McPhee, W. M. (1968). *Interpersonal relationships: Factors in job placement* (University of Utah Regional Rehabilitation Research Institute Bulletin No. 3). Salt Lake City: University of Utah Press.

● ● ●

253

Test Name: SPECIFIC FEAR INDEX

Purpose: A measure of a subject's perceived fear of a situation considered fundamental to dating behavior.

Format: A 9-integral-graphic rating scale.

Author: Martinson, W. D., and Zerface, J. P.

Article: Comparison of individual counseling and a social program with nondaters.

Journal: *Journal of Counseling*

Psychology, January 1970, *17*(1), 36–40.

● ● ●

254

Test Name: SQUIRES EMPATHY TEST

Purpose: To measure aesthetic perception of televised drama.

Author: Gellen, M. I.

Article: Finger blood volume responses of counselors, counselor trainees and non-counselors to stimuli from an empathy test.

Journal: *Counselor Education and Supervision,* Fall 1970, *10*(1), 64–74.

Related Research: Squires, S. I. (1956). The construction and evaluation of a test designed to measure aesthetic perception of televised drama. *Dissertation Abstracts International, 17,* 307. (University Microfilms No. 57-485.)

● ● ●

255

Test Name: TENNESSEE SELF-CONCEPT SCALE*

Purpose: A measure of the subject's self-concept strength and degree of defensiveness.

Author: Martin, F. C., and Gazda, G. M.

Article: A method of self-evaluation for counselor education utilizing the measurement of facilitative conditions.

Journal: *Counselor Education and Supervision,* Winter 1970, *9*(2), 87–92.

● ● ●

256

Test Name: TEACHER–PUPIL RELATIONSHIP INVENTORY

Purpose: To determine differences

in peer perceptions of teacher–pupil relations.

Format: A 5-point scale for ranking how well each of a student's classmates gets along with the teacher.

Reliability: .72.

Author: Mayer, G. R., et al.

Article: The use of public commitment and counseling with elementary school children: An evaluation.

Journal: *Elementary School Guidance and Counseling,* October 1970, *5*(1), 22–34.

Related Research: Mayer, G. R.,

Kranzler, G. D., & Matthes, W. A. (1967). The elementary school counselor and teacher–pupil relations. *Elementary School Guidance and Counseling, 2,* 3–14.

CHAPTER 17
Preference

257

Test Name: PATROLMAN'S WORK ROLE QUESTIONNAIRE

Purpose: To measure the degree to which respondents report they enjoy performing sixteen police tasks.

Number of Items: 16

Format: Consists of four categories (criminal apprehension, traffic, crime prevention, and public service), each with four items. Items are presented in the article.

Author: Olson, B.

Article: An exploratory study of task preferences.

Journal: *Personnel Journal,* December 1970, *49*(12), 1015–1020.

■ ■ ■

258

Test Name: POLAND'S MODIFICATION OF THE EDWARDS PERSONAL PREFERENCE SCHEDULE

Purpose: Permits an individual to compare his liking to engage in certain behaviors with college men in general.

Author: Strong, S. R., and Schmidt, L. D.

Article: Trustworthiness and influence in counseling.

Journal: *Journal of Counseling Psychology,* May 1970, *17*(3), 197–204.

Related Research: Poland, W. D. (1963). *An exploration of the relationship between self-estimated and measured personality characteristics in the open and closed mind.* Unpublished doctoral dissertation, Ohio State University.

■ ■ ■

259

Test Name: PREFERENCE FOR TYPES OF ORGANIZATIONS SCALE

Purpose: To acquire information concerning the students' preferences among organization types.

Format: Utilizes a forced-choice format in which the subject is required to select the type of organization in each pair which he or she would prefer as a place to work upon completion of a college degree.

Author: Sheard, J. L.

Article: College student preferences for types of work organizations.

Journal: *Research Journal,* April 1970, *49*(4), 299–304.

■ ■ ■

260

Test Name: REACTIVE OBJECT CURIOSITY TEST

Purpose: To measure children's exploratory behavior.

Format: Observations are made of the exploratory activities of children placed in a room with hidden toys.

Author: Mumbauer, C. C., and Miller, J. O.

Article: Socioeconomic background and cognitive functioning in preschool children.

Journal: *Child Development,* June 1970, *41*(2), 471–480.

■ ■ ■

261

Test Name: REWARD PREFERENCE INVENTORY

Purpose: A method of assessing preferences as an index of the attractiveness of various positive rewards.

Number of Items: 60

Format: Paired-comparison items including rewards sampled from the following categories: (a) adult approval, (b) competition, (c) peer approval, (d) independence, and (e) consumable.

Author: Cartwright, C. A.

Article: Efficacy of preferential incentives with elementary school children.

Journal: *Journal of Educational Psychology,* April 1970, *61*(2), 152–158.

Related Research: King, F. J., & Dunn-Rankin, P. (1965). *Reward preference inventory.* Unpublished inventory, Florida State University.

Cartwright, C. (1968). *The efficacy of preferential incentives with elementary school children.* Unpublished doctoral dissertation, University of Pittsburgh.

■ ■ ■

262

Test Name: ROOMMATE CHECKLIST

Purpose: For measuring different

residence hall roommate preferences.

Number of Items: 60

Author: Pace, T.

Article: Roommate dissatisfaction in residence halls.

Journal: *Journal of College Student Personnel,* May 1970, *11*(2), 144–147.

Related Research: Nudd, T. R. (1962). *A study of roommate compatibility.* Unpublished doctoral dissertation, University of California at Los Angeles.

263

Test Name: STUDENT PREFERENCE SCHEDULE

Purpose: To provide a profile of role orientations.

Format: Contains eight role orientations as follows: vocational, instrumental collegiate, intellectual, consummatory collegiate, social development, ritualistic, academic, Greek or fraternity and sorority system.

Author: Savicki, V., Schumer, H., and Stanfield, R. E.

Article: Student role orientations and college dropouts.

Journal: *Journal of Counseling Psychology,* November 1970, *17*(6, Part 1), 559–566.

Related Research: Schumer, H., & Stanfield, R. E. (1966). Assessment of the student role orientation in college. *Proceedings of the American Psychological Association, 21*(7), 285–286.

CHAPTER 18
Problem Solving

264

Test Name: CHILDREN'S ASSOCIATIVE RESPONDING TEST

Purpose: To identify children who rely on free association rather than on reasoning processes which may be available to them.

Number of Items: 68

Format: A multiple-choice analogy test. Grades 5–8.

Reliability: .90, .83, .77.

Validity: With Otis and Binet, *r*s = −.66 to −.74.

Author: Achenbach, T. M.

Article: The children's associative responding test: A possible alternative to group IQ tests.

Journal: *Journal of Educational Psychology,* October 1970, *61*(5), 340–348.

Related Research: Achenbach, T. M. (1970). Standardization of a research instrument for identifying associative responding in children. *Developmental Psychology, 2,* 283–291.

· · ·

265

Test Name: COGNITIVE PROCESS INVENTORY

Purpose: To determine rate of frequency of visual imagery (thinking in pictures).

Number of Items: 14

Author: Cooper, L., and Caston, J.

Article: Physical activity and increases in M response.

Journal: *Journal of Projective Techniques and Personality Assessment,* August 1970, *34*(4), 295–301.

Related Research: Article states "Questionnaire and details are available from J. Caston, M. D." at Mount Zion Hospital & Medical Center, San Francisco, CA 94115.

· · ·

266

Test Name: COGNITION OF SEMANTIC IMPLICATIONS TEST

Purpose: Measures the ability to anticipate or be sensitive to the needs or consequences of situations.

Format: Subject is required to (a) suggest two improvements in each of several common appliances, (b) write as many as four different questions that need to be considered in making everyday decisions and (c) to state as many as three different problems that might be associated with each given common object.

Validity: .30 to .52.

Author: Hoepfner, R., Guilford, J. P., and Bradley, P. A.

Article: Information-transformation abilities.

Journal: *Educational and Psychological Measurement,* Winter 1970, *30*(4) 785–802.

· · ·

267

Test Name: EVALUATION OF SEMANTIC TRANSFORMATION TEST

Purpose: Measure subjects' ability to choose one of three objects that best completes a task where all three could possibly be used, to choose the one most ingenious use of a given object and to choose the better of pairs of punch lines for a cartoon.

Validity: .45, .47.

Author: Hoepfner, R., Guilford, J. P., and Bradley, P. A.

Article: Information-transformation abilities.

Journal: *Educational and Psychological Measurement,* Winter 1970, *30*(4) 785–802.

CHAPTER 19
Status

268

Test Name: FIVE SCALES OF SOCIAL STRATIFICATION IN CZECHOSLOVAKIA

Purpose: To give a description of Czechoslovak society in terms of an "average" multidimensional general index of social status.

Format: The five scales include: complexity of work, cultural level of leisure activities and consumption (life style), participation in management (power), education, and income. Description of each scale is included.

Author: Machonin, P.

Article: Social stratification in contemporary Czechoslovakia.

Journal: *American Journal of Sociology,* March 1970, *75*(5), 725–741.

● ● ●

269

Test Name: HALLER OCCUPATIONAL ASPIRATION SCALE

Purpose: A relative indicator of the prestige level on the occupational hierarchy that an individual views as a goal.

Number of Items: 8

Format: Multiple-choice test for use among male high school students.

Reliability: .80.

Validity: Correlations of −.60 to .22.

Author: Tseng, M. S., and Carter, A. R.

Article: Achievement motivation and fear of failure as determinants of vocational choice, vocational aspiration, and perception of vocational prestige.

Journal: *Journal of Counseling Psychology,* March 1970, *17*(2), 150–156.

Related Research: Haller, A. O., & Miller, I. W. (1957). *The occupational aspiration scale: Theory, structure and correlates.* University of Wisconsin, Department of Rural Sociology.

● ● ●

270

Test Name: HIERONYMUS SCALE VALUES

Purpose: Rating students' socioeconomic status.

Format: Includes 140 occupations.

Author: Banducci, R.

Article: Accuracy of occupational stereotypes of grade-twelve boys.

Journal: *Journal of Counseling Psychology,* November 1970, *17*(6, Part 1), 534–539.

Related Research: Hieronymus, A. N. (1948). *Relationship between anxiety for education and certain socioeconomic variables.* Unpublished doctoral dissertation, University of Iowa.

● ● ●

271

Test Name: IDENTITY ACHIEVEMENT STATUS SCALE

Purpose: To measure objectively an individual's status with regard to identity achievement.

Number of Items: 24

Reliability: Test–retest, .76.

Validity: Some supporting evidence of adequate validity for predictive purposes.

Author: Simmons, D.

Article: Development of an objective measure of identity achievement status.

Journal: *Journal of Projective Techniques and Personality Assessment,* June 1970, *34*(3), 241–244.

Related Research: Erikson, E. H. (1956). The problem of ego identity. *Journal of the American Psychoanalytic Association, 4,* 56–121.

● ● ●

272

Test Name: LOW SELF-ESTEEM SCALE

Purpose: To measure self-esteem and middle-class inclusion.

Format: Modification of the Kelly role construct repertory test.

Reliability: Reported to be "acceptable."

Author: Shaffer, W. F.

Article: Experiment that casts doubt on the findings of the Stanford mobility study.

Journal: *Journal of Counseling Psychology,* July 1970, *17*(4), 299–305.

Related Research: Shaffer, W. F. (1968). *Tests of hypotheses relating psychopathology to*

extreme upward mobility.
Unpublished doctoral dissertation, Teachers College, Columbia University.

■ ■ ■

273

Test Name: MODIFICATION OF THE NORTH-HATT-NORC OCCUPATIONAL PRESTIGE QUESTIONNAIRE

Purpose: To rate the relative prestige of 102 job occupations.

Format: Ratings utilize a 5-point scale from *excellent* to *poor.*

Author: Delbecq, A. L., and Vigen, J.

Article: Prestige ratings of business and other occupations.

Journal: *Personnel Journal,* February 1970, *49*(2), 111–116.

Related Research: Hodge, R. W., Siegal, P. M., & Rossi, P. H. (1964). Occupational prestige in the United States, 1925–1963. *American Sociological Review, 70*(3), 286–302.

■ ■ ■

274

Test Name: OCCUPATIONAL PRESTIGE SCALE

Purpose: The score represents the deviation or accuracy of the subject's perception of occupational prestige in relation to the social norm.

Number of Items: 20 occupations.

Format: Subjects rank the occupations on the basis of their

opinion as to which occupation has the most prestige.

Validity: Correlations of –.50 to .72 with other measures.

Author: Tseng, M. S., and Carter, A. R.

Article: Achievement motivation and fear of failure as determinants of vocational choice, vocational aspiration, and perception of vocational prestige.

Journal: *Journal of Counseling Psychology,* March 1970, *17*(2), 150–156.

Related Research: North, C. C., & Hatt, P. K. (1961). The NORC scale. In A. J. Reiss, Jr., et al. (Eds.), *Occupations and social status.* Glencoe, IL: The Free Press.

■ ■ ■

275

Test Name: OCCUPATIONAL PRESTIGE QUESTIONNAIRE

Purpose: To measure occupational prestige.

Number of Items: 32

Format: A copy of the questionnaire is presented.

Reliability: .92.

Author: Hicks, R. E.

Article: A note on the test–retest reliability of a Zambian occupational prestige questionnaire.

Journal: *Measurement and Evaluation in Guidance,* Summer 1970, *3*(2), 97–101.

276

Test Name: SEVEN-LEVEL OCCUPATIONAL STATUS SCALE

Purpose: For measuring occupational rank.

Format: Occupational Level 1 is the highest occupational status level and 7 is the lowest.

Author: Burma, J. H., Cretser, G. A., and Seacrest, T.

Article: A comparison of the occupational status of intramarrying and intermarrying couples: A research note.

Journal: *Sociology and Social Research,* July 1970, *54*(4), 508–519.

Related Research: Hollingshead, A. B., & Redlick, F. C. (1958). *Social class and mental illness.* New York: Wiley.

■ ■ ■

277

Test Name: WARNER'S INDEX OF SOCIAL CLASS

Purpose: To determine socioeconomic level.

Author: Durkin, D.

Article: A language arts program for pre-first-grade children: Two-year achievement report.

Journal: *Reading Research Quarterly,* Summer 1970, *5*(4), 534–565.

Related Research: Warner, W. L., Meeker, M., & Eels, K. (1949). *Social class in America.* Chicago: Science Research Associates.

...

CHAPTER 20
Trait Measurement

278

Test Name: ACQUIESCENT TEST

Purpose: To identify potentially acquiescent respondents.

Number of Items: 3 (presented in article).

Format: Likert items.

Author: Armer, M.

Article: Formal education and psychological malaise in an African society.

Journal: *Sociology of Education,* Spring 1970, *43*(2), 143–158.

...

279

Test Name: BARBER SUGGESTIBILITY SCALE

Purpose: To measure degree of suggestibility.

Author: Sweeney, D. R., Tinling, D. C., and Schmal, A. H., Jr.

Article: Dimensions of affective expression in four expressive modes.

Journal: *Behavioral Science,* September 1970, *15*(5), 393–407.

Related Research: Barber, T. X. (1965). Measuring "hypnotic-like" suggestibility with and without hypnotic induction, psychometric properties, norms, and variables influencing response to the Barber Suggestibility Scale (BSS). *Psychological Reports, 16,* 809–844.

280

Test Name: CONSERVATISM–RADICALISM OPINIONNAIRE

Purpose: Identification of liberal and conservative persons.

Number of Items: 60

Format: Paper-and-pencil response to 60 items with responses graded from *liberal* to *radical.*

Author: Gezi, K. I., and Kruschke, E. R.

Article: Law abidingness among conservative and liberal students.

Journal: *Education,* November–December 1970, *91*(2), 97–102.

Related Research: Shaw, M., & Wright, J. (1967). *Scales for the measurement of attitudes.* New York: McGraw-Hill.

...

281

Test Name: COUCH-KINISTON AGREEMENT-RESPONSE TEST

Purpose: To measure agreeing response tendency.

Number of Items: 15

Author: Eisenman, R., and Townsend, T.

Article: Studies in acquiescence: I. Social desirability. II. Self-esteem. III. Creativity. IV. Prejudice.

Journal: *Journal of Projective Techniques and Personality Assessment,* February 1970, *34*(1), 45–54.

282

Test Name: DEPENDENCE–INDEPENDENCE SCALES

Purpose: To measure frequency with which the subject seeks proximity, attention, and help (dependence), and the frequency with which the subject takes initiative, persists, and wants to do things alone (independence).

Format: Six 7-point independence scales and three 7-point dependence scales.

Reliability: .85 (mean reliability coefficient).

Validity: .64 mean coefficient between scales.

Author: Todd, J., and Nakamura, C. Y.

Article: Interactive effects of informational and affective components of social and nonsocial reinforcers on independent and dependent children.

Journal: *Child Development,* June 1970, *41*(2), 365–376.

Related Research: Beller, E. K. (1955). Dependency and independency in young children. *Journal of Genetic Psychology, 87,* 25–35.

...

283

Test Name: EVALUATION SENSITIVITY SCALE

Purpose: Designed to deal with consistencies in the degree to which concern or anxiety may be expressed by an individual in situations where he or she is being appraised or evaluated.

Number of Items: 88. 44 were positively keyed and 44 negatively keyed.

Reliability: Kuder-Richardson Formula 20 reliability for two samples used was .91 and .93.

Author: Neill, J. A., and Jackson, D. N.

Article: An evaluation of item selection strategies in personality scale construction.

Journal: *Educational and Psychological Measurement,* Autumn 1970, *30,* 647–661.

■ ■ ■

284

Test Name: FEMININE RATING SCALE

Purpose: To measure sex-role adoption.

Number of Items: 16

Format: The teacher rates the child on a scale ranging from *very frequently* to *never* for each item of behavior.

Validity: With It scale for children from .001 to –.489.

Author: Thompson, N. L., Jr., and McCandless, B. R.

Article: It score variations by instructional style.

Journal: *Child Development,* June 1970, *41*(2), 425–436.

■ ■ ■

285

Test Name: HAPTIC VISUAL MATCHING TEST

Purpose: To measure reflection–impulsivity.

Number of Items: 20

Format: Subjects individually

explore with their fingers a wooden form about 3 inches square, to which they have no visual access. After exploring the form for as long as they like, they are presented with a visual array of five stimuli from which they have to choose the one that corresponds to the form explored.

Validity: Correlations with Matching Familiar Figures Test, .32, –.32, –.43, .33.

Author: Messer, S.

Article: Reflection–impulsivity: Stability and school failure.

Journal: *Journal of Educational Psychology,* December 1970, *61*(6 Part 1), 487–490.

■ ■ ■

286

Test Name: HEDQUIST AND WEINHOLD REVISION OF S-R INVENTORY OF ANXIOUSNESS

Purpose: A measure of anxiety.

Format: Provides an anxiety score for each situation and a total score across all situations.

Author: Hedquist, F. J., and Weinhold, B. K.

Article: Behavioral group counseling with socially anxious and unassertive college students.

Journal: *Journal of Counseling Psychology,* May 1970, *17*(3), 237–242.

■ ■ ■

287

Test Name: LAW-ABIDINGNESS SCALE

Purpose: To determine the frequency and degree of conformity to certain laws.

Number of Items: 14

Format: Paper and pencil.

Author: Gezi, K. I., and Kruschke, E. R.

Article: Law abidingness among conservative and liberal students.

Journal: *Education,* November–December 1970, *91*(2), 97–102.

Related Research: Shaw, M., & Wright, J. (1967). *Scales for the measurement of attitudes.* New York: McGraw-Hill.

■ ■ ■

288

Test Name: MASCULINE RATING SCALE

Purpose: To measure sex-role adoption.

Number of Items: 16

Format: The teacher rates the child on a scale ranging from *very frequently* to *never* for each item of behavior.

Validity: With It scale for children from .004 to .512.

Author: Thompson, N. L., Jr., and McCandless, B. R.

Article: It score variations by instructional style.

Journal: *Child Development,* June 1970, *41*(2), 425–436.

Related Research: Biller, H. B. (1969). Father dominance and sex-role development in kindergarten age boys. *Developmental Psychology, 1,* 87–94.

■ ■ ■

289

Test Name: MASHER GUILT SCALE

Purpose: To measure personality predisposition to guilt.

Format: Three subscales plus total guilt scale.

Reliability: "Reliable and has shown convergent, discriminant and construct validity."

Author: Persons, R. W.

Article: The Masher guilt scale: Theoretical formulation, research review, and normative data.

Journal: *Journal of Projective Techniques and Personality Assessment*, August 1970, *34*(4), 266–269.

Related Research: Masher, D. L. (1966). The development and multi-trait multi-method matrix analysis of three measures of three aspects of guilt. *Journal of Consulting Psychology, 30,* 25–29.

■ ■ ■

290

Test Name: MATCHING FAMILIAR FIGURES TEST

Purpose: To assess the degree of reflection-impulsivity.

Number of Items: 10

Reliability: .48, .50, .62.

Validity: −.40 to −.65.

Author: Messer, S.

Article: Reflection–impulsivity.

Journal: *Journal of Educational Psychology,* December 1970, *61*(6, Part 1), 487–490.

■ ■ ■

291

Test Name: MATCHING FAMILY FIGURES TEST

Purpose: To measure the children's tendency to be impulsive or reflective.

Author: Mumbauer, C. C., and Miller, J. O.

Article: Socioeconomic background and cognitive functioning in preschool children.

Journal: *Child Development,* June 1970, *41*(2), 471–480.

Related Research: Kagan, J. (1965). Impulsive and reflective children: The significance of conceptual tempo. In J. D.

Krumboltz (Ed.), *Learning and the educational process.* Chicago: Rand McNally.

■ ■ ■

292

Test Name: OCCUPATIONAL INTROVERSION–EXTROVERSION

Purpose: To measure a dimension of occupational introversion–extroversion for the Strong Vocational Interest Blank.

Number of Items: 69

Reliability: rs =.91, .72, .64.

Validity: rs = .51, and .58 with Si scale of the Minnesota Multiphasic Personality Inventory.

Author: Johansson, C. B.

Article: Strong vocational interest blank introversion–extroversion and occupational membership.

Journal: *Journal of Counseling Psychology,* September 1970, *17*(5), 451–455.

■ ■ ■

293

Test Name: REPRESSION–SENSITIZATION SCALE

Purpose: To measure a dimension apparently characterized by openness to one's own feelings and experiences and defensiveness.

Author: Tanck, R., and Robbins, P. R.

Article: Pupillary reactions to sexual, aggressive, and other stimuli as a function of personality.

Journal: *Journal of Projective Techniques and Personality Assessment,* August 1970, *34*(4), 277–282.

Related Research: Byrne, D. The repression-sensitization scale: Rationale, reliability, and validity.

Journal of Personality, 1961, *29,* 334–349.

■ ■ ■

294

Test Name: ROKEACH DOGMATISM SCALE

Purpose: Measures degrees of client dogmatism.

Reliability: .68 to .85.

Validity: −.19 to −.37 with Barrett-Lennard Relationship Inventory.

Author: Tosi, D. J., and Carlson, W. A.

Article: Client dogmatism and perceived counselor attitudes.

Journal: *Personnel and Guidance Journal,* April 1970, *48*(8), 657–660.

Related Research: Rokeach, M. (1960). *The open and closed mind.* New York: Basic Books.

■ ■ ■

295

Test Name: ROMANTIC LOVE COMPLEX SCALES

Purpose: To analyze the romantic love complex of Americans.

Number of Items: 23

Author: Spaulding, C. B.

Article: The romantic love complex in American culture.

Journal: *Sociology and Social Research,* October 1970, *55*(1), 82–100.

■ ■ ■

296

Test Name: RUDIN'S RATIONAL AUTHORITY SCALE

Purpose: Measure of "rational authoritarianism."

Number of Items: 19

Author: Eisenman, R., and Townsend, T.

Article: Studies in acquiesence: I. Social desirability. II. Self-esteem. III. Creativity. IV. Prejudice.

Journal: *Journal of Projective Techniques and Personality Assessment,* Fall 1970, *34*(1), 95–154.

■ ■ ■

297

Test Name: TEACHERS RATE PUPILS

Purpose: Evaluation of pupils on 7 characteristics related to work habits.

Number of Items: 7 items, scaled 0–100.

Author: Dixon, P. W., Fukuda, N. K., and Berens, A. B.

Article: Two-factor explanation of post-high school destinations in Hawaii.

Journal: *Journal of Experimental Education,* Fall 1970, *39*(1), 24–35.

■ ■ ■

298

Test Name: TEACHER RATINGS OF PUPILS

Purpose: Permits the teacher to rate each pupil on 24 traits.

Number of Items: 24

Format: Pupils rated for each trait on a 7-point scale.

Validity: Intercorrelations range from .22 through .68.

Author: Cox, S. H.

Article: Intrafamily comparison of loving–rejecting child-rearing practices.

Journal: *Child Development,* June 1970, *41*(2), 437–448.

Related Research: Cattell, R. B. (1963). Teachers' personality descriptions of six-year-olds: A check on structure. *British Journal of Educational Psychology, 33,* 219–235.

■ ■ ■

299

Test Name: THREATENING-DEFENSIVENESS QUESTIONNAIRE

Purpose: To measure defensiveness and degree of being threatened.

Number of Items: 33

Format: 11 items were intended to be threatening, 11 were neutral, and 11 were designed to elicit defensiveness.

Author: Koson, D., Kitchen, C., Kochen, M., and Stodolosky, D.

Article: Psychological testing by computer: Effect on response bias.

Journal: *Journal of Educational and Psychological Measurement,* Winter 1970, *30*(4), 803–810.

⋯

CHAPTER 21
Values

300

Test Name: BILLS INDEX OF ADJUSTMENT AND VALUES

Purpose: To ascertain a measure of adjustment and values.

Number of Items: 99 trait words.

Author: Hountras, P., and Pederson, L.

Article: Self-concept of fraternity members and independents.

Journal: *Journal of College Student Personnel,* January 1970, *11*(1), 46–49.

Related Research: Bills, R. E., Vance, E. L., & McLean, O. S. (1951). An index of adjustment and values. *Journal of Consulting Psychology, 15,* 257–261.

■ ■ ■

301

Test Name: GENERAL MODERNITY SCALE

Purpose: A measurement of modern vs. traditional value-orientations.

Number of Items: 22

Format: Includes six dimensions: independence, ethnic equality, empiricism, mastery, receptivity to change, future-orientation.

Reliability: .90 for 6 dimensions, .88 for the 22 items.

Validity: Interdimension correlation = .60; inferred average interitem correlation = .25.

Author: Armer, M.

Article: Formal education and psychological malaise in an African society.

Journal: *Sociology of Education,* Spring 1970, *43*(2), 143–158.

Related Research: Smith, D. H., & Inkeles, A. (1966). The OM scale: A comparative sociopsychological measure of individual modernity. *Sociometry, 29,* 353–377.

Kahl, J. A. (1968). *The measurement of modernism: A study of values in Brazil and Mexico.* Austin: University of Texas Press.

■ ■ ■

302

Test Name: MODERNISM INDEX

Purpose: To measure various dimensions of modernism.

Number of Items: 46

Format: Six indexes, each representing one of the modernism dimensions: mass media, extended-family ties, nuclear-family role structure, religiosity, environmental orientation, and production/consumption behavior. Items are included.

Reliability: Intercorrelations from .13 to .66, from .26 to .83.

Author: Schnaiberg, A.

Article: Measuring modernism: Theoretical and empirical explorations.

Journal: *American Journal of Sociology,* November 1970, *76*(3), 399–425.

303

Test Name: PIERCE'S MEASURE OF VALUES

Purpose: To measure values.

Number of Items: 134 phrases (reduced to 94 items for this study).

Format: Likert scale describing situations of various potential value. Eleven factors for men and 12 for women have been extracted.

Author: Adinolfi, A. A.

Article: Characteristics of highly accepted, highly rejected, and relatively unknown university freshmen.

Journal: *Journal of Counseling Psychology,* September 1970, *17*(5), 456–464.

■ ■ ■

304

Test Name: VALUES INVENTORY

Purpose: The subject indicates the importance of various aims in his or her university studies.

Number of Items: 13

Author: Taft, R., and Gilchrist, M. B.

Article: Creative attitudes and creative productivity: A comparison of two aspects of creativity among students.

Journal: *Journal of Educational Psychology,* April 1970, *61*(2), 136–143.

CHAPTER 22
Vocational Evaluation

305

Test Name: ABILITY SELF-RATING INVENTORY

Purpose: To elicit a subject's estimate of his or her ability for each of 100 different occupations.

Number of Items: 100

Format: The items were the first 100 items of the 1965 edition of the Strong Vocational Interest Blank.

Reliability: .28–.78.

Author: Sharf, R.

Article: Relative importance of interest and ability in vocational decision-making.

Journal: *Journal of Counseling Psychology,* May 1970, *17*(3), 258–262.

...

306

Test Name: AB SCALE

Purpose: To discriminate between psychotherapists according to their ability to achieve improvement with schizophrenic patients.

Number of Items: 19

Format: Scored in the A direction and treated as a continuous measure, departing from the usual procedure of dichotomizing into types.

Author: Howard, K. I., et al.

Article: Therapist orientation and patient experience in psychotherapy.

Journal: *Journal of Counseling Psychology,* May 1970, *17*(3), 263–270.

Related Research: Schiffman, H., & Carson, R. C. (1969). *A psychometric analysis of the Whitehorn-Betz A-B Scale.* Unpublished manuscript, Duke University.

...

307

Test Name: ADAPTATION OF THE COUNSELOR EFFECTIVENESS SCALE

Purpose: For couples to evaluate the effectiveness of their relationship.

Number of Items: 25

Format: A semantic differential scale.

Author: Higgins, W. H., Ivey, A. E., and Uhlemann, M. R.

Article: Media therapy: A programmed approach to teaching behavioral skills.

Journal: *Journal of Counseling Psychology,* January 1970, *17*(1), 20–26.

Related Research: Ivey, A. E., Miller, C. D., Morrill, W. H., & Norrington, C. J. (1967). *The counselor effectiveness scale* (mimeo). Unpublished report, Colorado State University.

...

308

Test Name: ATTITUDE SCALE OF THE VOCATIONAL DEVELOPMENT INVENTORY (J.O. CRITES)

Purpose: To measure vocational maturity.

Format: Grades 5–12. Each statement is related to one of the following dimensions of vocational maturity: (a) involvement in the choice process, (b) orientation to work, (c) independence in decision-making, (d) basis for choice, and (e) conception of the choice process. Total possible vocational maturity score of 50.

Validity: $r = .47$ with intelligence (Otis-Lennon Intelligence Test and Lorge-Thorndike Intelligence Test).

Author: Maynard, P. E., and Hansen, J. C.

Article: Vocational maturity among inner-city youths.

Journal: *Journal of Counseling Psychology,* September 1970, *17*(5), 400–404.

Related Research: Crites, J. O. (1965). Measurement of vocational maturity in adolescence: I. Attitude test of the vocational development inventory. *Psychological Monographs, 79*(2, Whole No. 595).

...

309

Test Name: BARRETT-LENNARD RELATIONSHIP INVENTORY

Purpose: To measure client perceptions of counselor's empathy, unconditional positive regard, level of regard, and congruence.

Reliability: .82 to .95.

Validity: −.19 to −.37 with Rokeach Dogmatism Scale.

Author: Tosi, D. J., and Carlson, W. A.

Article: Client dogmatism and perceived counselor attitudes.

Journal: *Personnel and Guidance Journal*, April 1970, *48*(8), 657–660.

Related Research: Barrett-Lennard, G. T. (1962). Dimensions of therapist response as casual factors in therapeutic change. *Psychological Monographs, 76*(43, Whole No. 562).

• • •

310

Test Name: CLIENT'S SELF-RATING SCALE

Purpose: To measure training satisfaction and client's own assessment of training success and employability.

Number of Items: 11

Format: First 9 items are designed to yield a composite score on training satisfaction, and the remaining 2 items are used to measure the subject's own predictions of training success and employability; also provides five rating categories from *strongly agree* to *strongly disagree*.

Author: Tseng, M. S.

Article: Locus of control as a determinant of job proficiency, employability, and training satisfaction of vocational rehabilitation clients.

Journal: *Journal of Counseling Psychology*, November 1970, *17*(6, Part I), 487–491.

• • •

311

Test Name: COUNSELING REACTION QUESTIONNAIRE

Purpose: To obtain information

about the client's reactions toward educational–vocational counseling.

Number of Items: 29

Format: Consisted of three parts.

Author: Graff, R. W., and Maclean, G. D.

Article: Evaluating educational–vocational counseling: A model for change.

Journal: *Personnel and Guidance Journal*, March 1970, *48*(7), 568–574.

• • •

312

Test Name: COUNSELOR EFFECTIVENESS SCALE

Purpose: To measure counselor effectiveness.

Number of Items: 25

Format: Paired adjectives presented in a semantic differential format.

Author: Miller, C. D., Morrill, W. H., and Uhlemann, M. R.

Article: Micro-counseling: An experimental study of pre-practicum training in communicating test results.

Journal: *Counselor Education and Supervision*, Spring 1970, *9*(3), 171–177.

Related Research: Ivey, A. E., Miller, C. D., Morrill, W. H., & Norrington, C. J. (1967). *The counselor effectiveness scale* (Mimeographed report). Colorado State University.

• • •

313

Test Name: COUNSELOR ROLE CONCEPTS ANALYSIS

Purpose: To assess the actual, ideal, and expected counselor role concepts.

Number of Items: 50

Format: Checklist, paper and pencil.

Author: Dahlem, G.

Article: Actual, ideal and expected counselor role concepts of local elected public officials.

Journal: *Colorado Journal of Educational Research*, Fall 1970, *10*(1), 38–40.

• • •

314

Test Name: COUNSELOR ROLE QUESTIONNAIRE

Purpose: To reflect duties or responsibilities commonly assigned to school counselors.

Number of Items: 25

Format: 9 factors were identified.

Author: Hart, D. H., and Prince, D. J.

Article: Role conflict for school counselors: Training versus job demands.

Journal: *Personnel and Guidance Journal*, January 1970, *48*(5), 374–380.

• • •

315

Test Name: CRITERION GROUP ELEMENTARY GUIDANCE OPINIONNAIRE

Purpose: To measure the teachers' perceptions of the counselor's role and function.

Number of Items: 71

Author: Kornick, J.

Article: An analysis: Impact of an elementary school counselor on teachers' perceptions of the counselor's role and functions.

Journal: *Elementary School Guidance and Counseling*, March 1970, *4*(3), 188–196.

316

Test Name: ELEMENTARY GUIDANCE WORKERS' EFFECTIVENESS QUESTIONNAIRE

Purpose: To determine from teachers the elementary guidance worker's effectiveness in the developmental guidance role and in the consulting role.

Author: Bender, D.

Article: Counseling, consulting, or developmental guidance? Toward an answer.

Journal: *Elementary School Guidance and Counseling,* May 1970, *4*(4), 245–252.

■ ■ ■

317

Test Name: GLOBAL RATING BLANK

Purpose: A rating scale for supervisors to rate their counselors.

Format: Provides for ratings on five dimensions: caseload management, evaluation as a worker, evaluation as a counselor, likableness, and overall effectiveness as a counselor.

Author: Engelkes, J. R., and Roberts, R. R.

Article: Level of training and job performance.

Journal: *Journal of Counseling Psychology,* November 1970, *17*(6, Part I), 522–526.

■ ■ ■

318

Test Name: GUIDANCE DIRECTORS' AND SUPERVISORS' QUESTIONNAIRE

Purpose: To determine the role of the state director of guidance.

Number of Items: 59

Format: Responses were recorded on a Likert scale.

Author: Duncan, J. A.

Article: A role study of the state director of guidance.

Journal: *Counselor Education and Supervision,* Spring 1970, *9*(3), 225–233.

■ ■ ■

319

Test Name: HOUSING ISSUES QUESTIONNAIRE

Purpose: To assess the negotiator's role force by determining the subject's attitude toward his own reference group, his perception of his own reference group's attitudes about itself, and his attitude toward the other reference group.

Number of Items: 28

Format: Each item was accompanied by a 7-point Likert scale ranging from *not at all true* to *very true.*

Validity: .23 to −.73.

Author: Vidmar, N., and McGruth, J. E.

Article: Forces affecting success in negotiation groups.

Journal: *Behavioral Science,* March 1970, *15*(2), 154–163.

■ ■ ■

320

Test Name: INSTRUCTOR'S RATING SCALE

Purpose: For the training instructor to rate the subject's personal quality, job proficiency, and employability.

Number of Items: 18

Format: Each item is rated on a 5-point scale. Yields 11 scores in the personal quality dimension, 6 scores in the job proficiency dimension, and a score on employability.

Author: Tseng, M. S.

Article: Locus of control as a determinant of job proficiency, employability, and training satisfaction of vocational rehabilitation clients.

Journal: *Journal of Counseling Psychology,* November 1970, *17*(6, Part 1), 487–491.

■ ■ ■

321

Test Name: JOB VALUES QUESTIONNAIRE

Purpose: To measure job values.

Number of Items: 11 job value statements.

Format: Subjects are directed to rank the statements in order of preference (the highest rank is 1 and the lowest 11).

Reliability: ρs = .95, .82.

Author: Masih, L. K., and Kushel, G.

Article: A comparison of the job values of prospective teachers and counselors.

Journal: *Counselor Education and Supervision,* Fall 1970, *10*(1), 75–79.

Related Research: Kuhlen, R. G., & Dipboyle, W. J. (1959). *Motivational and personality factors in the selection of elementary and secondary school teaching as a career.* Syracuse, NY: Syracuse University Institute of Research.

Masih, L. K. (1967). Career saliency and its relation to certain needs, interests, and job values. *Personnel and Guidance Journal, 45,* 653–658.

■ ■ ■

322

Test Name: TUTOR OBSERVATION SCALE

Purpose: To assess instructional behavior of student tutors.

Format: Printed grid with activities on left margin and boxes to record observed activity along horizontal axis. Numbers entered in boxes indicate sequence of activities.

Author: Niedermeyer, F. C.

Article: Effect of training on the instructional behavior of student tutors.

Journal: *Journal of Educational Research,* November 1970, *64*(3), 119–123.

Related Research: *The development of a tutorial program for kindergarten reading instructors.* (1970 May). Southwest Regional Laboratory for Educational Research and Development, 11300 La Cienega Boulevard, Inglewood, CA 90304.

• • •

323

Test Name: MINNESOTA IMPORTANCE QUESTIONNAIRE (MIQ)*

Purpose: Measures vocational needs.

Number of Items: 190

Format: A complete pair-comparison of 20 statements measuring vocational needs. Scale scores used in the analyses were derived by counting, for each of the stimulus variables, the number of times it was chosen over the other 19 stimuli. The maximum score on any scale was 19, the minimum score, 0. For each individual, the sum of the 20 scale scores was 190.

Reliability: .62 to .91.

Author: Hendel, D., and Weiss, D. J.

Article: Individual inconsistency and reliability of measurement.

Journal: *Educational and*

Psychological Measurement, Autumn 1970, *30*, 579–593.

Related Research: Reported in Weiss, D. J., Davis, R. V., England, G. W., & Lofquist, L. H. (1966). Instrumentation for the theory of work adjustment. *Minnesota Studies in Vocational Rehabilitation, 21*, 11–26.

• • •

324

Test Name: OTHER ESTEEM QUESTIONNAIRE

Purpose: To assess the negotiator's role force by having each subject describe his or her partner.

Number of Items: 21

Format: 8-point rating items of the semantic differential type.

Author: Vidmar, N., and McGrath, J. E.

Article: Forces affecting success in negotiation groups.

Journal: *Behavioral Science,* March 1970, *15*(2), 154–163.

• • •

325

Test Name: PERFORMANCE OF GUIDANCE FUNCTIONS RATING SCALE

Purpose: To assess perceptions of effectiveness of guidance functions for practicing counselors.

Author: Hopper, G., Brown, D., and Pfister, S.

Article: Ratings by counselors without teaching experience and their principals regarding performance of guidance functions.

Journal: *Counselor Education and Supervision,* Winter 1970, *9*(2), 99–105.

• • •

326

Test Name: PROFESSIONALISM QUESTIONNAIRE

Purpose: To distinguish between individuals who are locally oriented (company-oriented) and cosmopolitan oriented (professionally oriented).

Number of Items: 17

Author: Slocum, J. W., Jr.

Article: Supervisory influence and the professional employee.

Journal: *Personnel Journal,* June 1970, *4*, 484–488.

Related Research: House, R., & Wigdor, L. (1969, August). *Cosmopolitans and locals: Some differential correlations between leader, behavior, satisfaction, and performance.* Paper presented to Academy of Management, Cincinnati, Ohio.

• • •

327

Test Name: PROFESSIONAL-SUPERVISORY RATING SCALE

Purpose: To offer an objective approach to the task of employee rating.

Number of Items: 15

Format: Management rates the individual and the individual then rates himself or herself. All items are presented in the article.

Author: Cangemi, J. P.

Article: Personnel evaluation rating scale.

Journal: *Personnel Journal,* August 1970, *49*(8), 665–667.

• • •

328

Test Name: PSYCHOTHERAPEUTIC INTERACTION SCALES

Purpose: To evaluate and to self-evaluate counseling performance.

Format: The four scales include: non-possessive warmth, accurate empathy, intensity and intimacy of interpersonal contact, and therapist genuineness or self-congruence.

Validity: From .61 to .75.

Author: Martin, D. C., and Gazda, G. M.

Article: A method of self-evaluation for counselor education utilizing the measurement of facilitative condition.

Journal: *Counselor Education and Supervision,* Winter 1970, *9*(2), 87–92.

Related Research: Truax, C. B. (1961-1962). *Therapeutic conditions* (Discussion papers No. 13, 1961; Research Report No. 56, 1962; Research Report No. 25, 1962). University of Wisconsin, Wisconsin Psychiatric Institute.

■ ■ ■

329

Test Name: QUESTIONNAIRE FOR INSTRUCTOR RATING

Purpose: To evaluate instructors.

Number of Items: 21

Format: Each item is accompanied by a 0 through 10 rating scale, a scale value of 5 indicating a relatively neutral or intermediate rating. (All items are presented.)

Validity: .25 to .93.

Author: Harvey, J. N., and Barker, D. G.

Article: Student evaluation of teaching effectiveness.

Journal: *Improving College and University Teaching,* Autumn 1970, *18*(4), 275–278.

■ ■ ■

330

Test Name: RELATIONSHIP QUESTIONNAIRE

Purpose: A measure of the therapeutic relationship as perceived by the client and therapist.

Format: A single score which is a composite of empathy, warmth, genuineness, interpersonal intimacy, and concreteness.

Author: Bednar, R. L.

Article: Therapeutic relationship of A-B therapists as perceived by client and therapist.

Journal: *Journal of Counseling Psychology,* March 1970, *17*(2), 119–122.

Related Research: Truax, C. B. (1962). *Relationship questionnaire* (Test and manual, mimeo). University of Wisconsin.

Truax, C. B., & Carkhuff, R. R. (1967). *Toward effective counseling and psychotherapy: Training and practice.* Chicago: Aldine.

■ ■ ■

331

Test Name: ROLE-TYPE IDENTIFICATION QUESTIONNAIRE

Purpose: To determine amount of time faculty wives spent outside the home as volunteer workers, students, or employees. Also requested the rating of the "general standing" (status) of women in 20 occupations, including homemaker. Further, asked to select the three occupations most attractive to them.

Author: Arnott, C., and Bengtson, V. L.

Article: "Only a homemaker" distributive justice and role choices among married women.

Journal: *Sociology and Social Research,* July 1970, *54*(4), 495–507.

332

Test Name: TEACHERS' ELEMENTARY GUIDANCE OPINIONNAIRE

Purpose: To measure the teachers' perceptions of the counselor's role and functions.

Number of Items: 53 activities.

Format: Six categories of activities. Subjects respond to each activity on a 4-point scale.

Reliability: .77.

Author: Kornick, J.

Article: An analysis: Impact of an elementary school counselor on teachers' perceptions of the counselor's role and functions.

Journal: *Elementary School Guidance and Counseling,* March 1970, *4*(3), 188–196.

Related Research: Raines, B. G. (1966). *A study of the role of the counselor in the elementary schools of Ohio. Dissertation Abstracts International, 25,* 1666. (University Microfilms No. 64-8570)

■ ■ ■

333

Test Name: TEACHER STYLE INSTRUMENT

Purpose: To measure teacher behaviors.

Number of Items: 35

Format: Includes seven factors: interaction facilitation, willingness to change, student autonomy, feedback on student work, personal rapport with students, instructor's contribution, and task concern. Items are presented.

Reliability: Subtest reliability .19 to .85.

Validity: .27 to .73.

Author: Hall, D. T.

Article: The effect of teacher–

student congruence upon student learning in college classes.

Journal: *Journal of Educational Psychology,* June 1970, *61*(3), 205–213.

Related Research: Fleishman, E. A. (1953). The measurement of leadership attitudes in industry. *Journal of Applied Psychology, 37,* 153–158.

■ ■ ■

334

Test Name: TEAM TEACHING ATTITUDE QUESTIONNAIRE

Purpose: To identify students' and professors' perceptions of team teaching.

Number of Items: 14

Format: Open-ended questionnaire for recording viewpoints.

Author: Johnson, J. C., II, and Geoffroy, K. E.

Article: A subjective appraisal of team teaching.

Journal: *Improving College and University Teaching,* Summer 1970, *18*(3), 227–228.

■ ■ ■

335

Test Name: UNIVERSITY OF ILLINOIS COURSE EVALUATION QUESTIONNAIRE*

Purpose: To obtain a measure of teaching effectiveness.

Author: Stallings, W. M., and Leslie, E. K.

Article: Student attitudes toward grades and grading.

Journal: *Improving College and University Teaching,* Winter 1970, *18*(1), 66–68.

336

Test Name: VOCATIONAL COMPLEXITY INSTRUMENT

Purpose: To measure vocational complexity.

Format: A grid format with 12 occupational titles of both professional and blue collar occupations plus 12 vocationally relevant construct dimensions. Subjects rated each role title on all 12 construct dimensions by using a 6-point Likert scale.

Reliability: .82.

Author: Bodden, J. L.

Article: Cognitive complexity as a factor in appropriate vocational choice.

Journal: *Journal of Counseling Psychology,* July 1970, *17*(4), 364–368.

Related Research: Bodden, J. L. (1969). *Cognitive complexity as a factor in appropriate vocational choice.* Unpublished doctoral dissertation, Ohio State University.

Roe, A. (1956). *The psychology of occupations.* New York: Wiley.

■ ■ ■

337

Test Name: WORK ADJUSTMENT RATING FORM

Purpose: A rating scale used to measure work readiness in rehabilitation.

Number of Items: 40

Format: Eight subscales of five items each.

Reliability: .91, .94.

Validity: .36 to .60.

Author: Bitter, J. A.

Article: Bias effect on validity and reliability of a rating scale.

Journal: *Measurement and Evaluation in Guidance,* Summer 1970, *3*(2), 70–75.

Related Research: Bitter, J. A., & Bolanovich, D. J. (1969). WARF: A scale for measuring job readiness behaviors. *American Journal of Mental Deficiency, 74,* 616–621.

■ ■ ■

338

Test Name: WORK TRAINER RATING SCALE

Purpose: To evaluate five major areas of on-the-job behavior for trainees participating in urban construction work crews.

Format: The 5 areas rated were: (a) work skill, quality, and quantity; (b) cooperativeness and willingness to accept supervision; (c) self-confidence; (d) responsibility, leadership qualities, and success potential; and (e) motivation for training.

Author: Hoffnung, R. J., and Mills, R. B.

Article: Situational group counseling with disadvantaged youth.

Journal: *Personnel and Guidance Journal,* February 1970, *48*(6), 458–464.

■ ■ ■

339

Test Name: WORKER TRAITS INVENTORY

Purpose: To obtain ratings on 12 occupations to assess the accuracy of stereotypes.

Author: Banducci, R.

Article: Accuracy of occupational stereotypes of grade-twelve boys.

Journal: *Journal of Counseling Psychology,* November 1970, *17*(6), 534–539.

Directory of Unpublished

Experimental Mental Measures

VOLUME 2

BERT A. GOLDMAN, EDD
Dean, Academic Advising and Professor of Education
University of North Carolina at Greensboro

JOHN CHRISTIAN BUSCH, EDD
Associate Professor of Education
University of North Carolina at Greensboro

Contents

_____

A cumulative subject index to Volumes 1 through 3 appears at the end of this book.

...

Preface

From the Original Printing of Volume 2, 1978

Purpose: This *Directory of Unpublished Experimental Mental Measures* marks the second in a series of publications designed to fill a distinct void in the publication of measurement research. The authors recognized the need for the publication of a directory of experimental test instruments, i.e., a compendium of experimental test instruments that are not currently produced commercially. It is intended that this reference primarily serve to provide researchers ready access to sources of recently developed experimental mental measures. Also, it is anticipated that the directory may stimulate further use of the experimental instruments by providing researchers with relatively easy access to such information. In essence this directory is a reference to recently developed nonstandardized experimental mental measures. The directory is not intended to provide all necessary information for the researcher contemplating the use of a particular instrument. Rather it should serve as a reference point to enable the reader to identify potentially useful measures and other sources from which this information can be obtained.

Development: All available and relevant professional journals were examined by the authors. The following list includes those journals that, in the judgment of the authors, contained research involving instruments of value to researchers in education, psychology, and sociology. This list is similar to that of Volume 1 with the exception that it includes sixteen additional journals that were found to contain relevant information; and three from Volume 1 were deleted for lack of appropriate instruments. In general, foreign journals were not surveyed for use in this directory. However, one exception was the British journal *Occupational Psychology*. Measures identified in dissertations were excluded as a matter of expediency and because the microfilm abstracts contain minimal information.

American Journal of Psychology
American Journal of Sociology
American Sociologist
American Vocational Journal
Behavioral Science
California Journal of Educational Research
Child Development
Colorado Journal of Educational Research
Counseling Psychologist
Counselor Education and Supervision
Developmental Psychology
Education
Educational and Psychological Measurement

Educational Leadership
Elementary School Guidance and Counseling
Gifted Child Quarterly
Human Development
Improving College and University Teaching
Journal of College Student Personnel
Journal of Counseling Psychology
Journal of Creative Behavior
Journal of Education
Journal of Educational Measurement
Journal of Educational Psychology
Journal of Educational Research
Journal of Experimental Education
Journal of General Education
Journal of Personality Assessment
Journal of School Psychology
Measurement and Evaluation in Guidance
NEA Research Bulletin
Occupational Psychology
Peabody Journal of Education
Perceptual and Motor Skills
Personnel and Guidance Journal
Personnel Journal
Phi Delta Kappan
Psychological Reports
Reading Research Quarterly
Social Education
Sociology and Social Research
Sociology of Education

This directory lists all tests that were described in the 1971-1972 issue of these journals that the present authors deemed of possible value to researchers in education, psychology, and sociology. An attempt was made to omit commercially published standardized tests; task-type activities, such as memory word lists used in serial learning research; and achievement tests developed for a single, isolated course of study. Obviously the reader should not assume that the instruments described herein form a representative sample of the universe of unpublished experimental measures.

Organization: The authors found the need to include in this Volume 2 a category entitled Behavior and the former category of Problem-Solving contained in Volume 1 was expanded to Problem-Solving and Reasoning. These additions to the list of categories and revisions of some of the definitions of the categories mark further differences between Volumes 1 and 2. Following is a brief description of each of the twenty-three categories under which the authors chose to group the experimental mental measures of Volume 2:

Achievement: Measure learning and/or comprehension. Category also includes tests of memory and tests of drug knowledge.

Adjustment—Educational: Measure academic satisfaction. Category also includes tests of school anxiety.

Adjustment—Psychological: Evaluate conditions and levels of adjustment along the psychological dimension.

Adjustment—Social: Evaluate aspects of interactions with others. Category also includes tests of alienation, conformity, need for social approval, social desirability, and instruments for assessing interpersonal attraction, perception, and sensitivity.

Aptitude: Predict success in given areas.

Attitude: Measure reaction to a variety of experiences and things.

Behavior: Measure general and specific types of activities, such as classroom behavior and drug-use behavior.

Communication: Evaluate information exchange. Category also includes tests of self-disclosure and counselor-client interaction.

Concept Meaning: Test one's understanding of words and other concepts. Category also includes tests of conceptual structure, style, and information processing.

Creativity: Measure ability to reorganize data or information into unique configurations. Category also includes tests of divergent thinking.

Development: Measure emerging characteristics, primarily for preschool ages. Category also includes tests of cognitive and moral development.

Family: Measure intrafamily relations. Category also includes tests of marital satisfaction, nurturance, parental interest, and warmth.

Institutional Information: Evaluate institutions and their functioning.

Interest: Identify selective attention to activities. Category also includes tests measuring interest in specific occupations and vocations.

Motivation: Measure goal strength. Category also includes measures of curiosity.

Perception: Determine how one sees himself. Category also includes tests dealing with empathy, imagery, locus of control, self concept, and time.

Personality: Measure personal attributes. Category also includes biographical information and defense mechanisms.

Preference: Identify choices. Category also includes tests of preference for objects, taste preference, and sex role preference.

Problem-Solving and Reasoning: Test one's ability to select the most appropriate from a number of alternatives.

Status: Identify one's hierarchy of acceptability.

Trait Measurement: Identify and evaluate traits. Category also includes tests of anger, anxiety, authoritarianism, blame, and cheating.

Values: Measure worth one ascribes to an object or activity. Category also includes tests or moral, philosophical, political, and religious values.

Vocational Evaluation: Evaluate the person for the position.

The choice of the category under which each test was grouped was determined by the purpose of the test and/or its apparent content. The authors attempted to include any of the following facts regarding each test; however, in many cases only a few of these facts were provided in the journal article:

Test Name
Purpose
Description
> Number of items
> Time required
> Format

Statistics
> Reliability
> Validity (In many cases this refers to correlation with other tests rather than with specific validation data.)

Source
> Author of the article in which the test was mentioned
> Title of the article
> Journal in which the article appeared, including date of publication, volume, and page number

Related research
> Identifying information of publications related to the source that was presented in the source

In instances where additional information may be found in Volume 1 of the *Directory of Unpublished Experimental Mental Measures,* the reader is referred to D.U.E.M.M. with specific reference following.

Further, the reader is alerted to the fact that the numbers within the index of Volume 2 refer to test numbers rather than to page numbers, which was the procedure followed for Volume 1. As a convenience to the reader, the authors have incorporated the Volume 1 indexing to the Volume 2 index, and in so doing they converted all page numbers to test numbers. Thus, numbers 1 through 339 refer to tests of Volume 1 and numbers 340 through 1034 refer to the tests of Volume 2.

The authors express their appreciation to Mrs. Jo O'Keefe for editing and typing the manuscript.

Bert Arthur Goldman
John Christian Busch

CHAPTER 1
Achievement

340

Test Name: BEAN SYMBOL SUBSTITUTION TEST

Purpose: To determine source of reading difficulty.

Format: Similar to the Wechsler Intelligence Scale for Children (WISC) coding subtest. It involves pairing geometric symbols with those letters commonly reversed by retarded readers.

Author: Bell, B. D., et al.

Article: Some personality and motivational factors in reading retardation.

Journal: *Journal of Educational Research,* January 1972, *65*(5), 229–233.

Related Research: Bean, W. J. (1967). *The isolation of some psychometric indices of severe reading disabilities.* Unpublished doctoral dissertation, Texas Tech University.

•••

341

Test Name: BEHAVIORAL OBJECTIVE WRITING SKILLS TEST

Purpose: To assess elementary teachers' abilities to write behavioral objectives.

Number of Items: Four hypothetical class settings.

Time Required: Approximately 55 minutes.

Format: Subjects develop three behavioral objectives for each of the four settings. Maximum number of points is 36. Forms A and B. An outline of the test is presented.

Reliability: Interrater correlations from .96 to .99+. No significant differences between Forms A and B.

Validity: Two content validation studies were conducted.

Author: Lapp, D.

Article: Behavioral objectives writing skills test.

Journal: *Journal of Education,* February 1972, *154*(3), 13–24.

•••

342

Test Name: DANIELS WORD RECOGNITION TEST

Purpose: To assess knowledge of words.

Validity: Correlations with Peabody Picture Vocabulary were .41 and .46 (*p* < .01).

Author: Hall, J., and Chansky, N.

Article: Relationships between selected ability and achievement tests in an economically disadvantaged Negro sample.

Journal: *Psychological Reports,* June 1971, *28*(3), 741–742.

•••

343

Test Name: DRUG KNOWLEDGE SCALE

Purpose: To measure knowledge about drugs in five areas including narcotics, marijuana, LSD, amphetamines, and barbiturates.

Number of Items: 30

Format: Provides a single score based on correct answers. Multiple choice items. Examples are presented.

Reliability: Split-half coefficient was .69.

Validity: Correlations with Drug Abuse Attitude Scale were .17 and .40.

Author: Swisher, J. D., et al.

Article: Drug education: Pushing or preventing?

Journal: *Peabody Journal of Education,* October 1971, *49*(1), 68–75.

•••

344

Test Name: DRUG KNOWLEDGE TEST

Purpose: To measure the level of knowledge a subject has of drugs that have been abused.

Number of Items: 41

Reliability: Split-half (original form 50 items) *r* = .83; 30 items, *r* = .56.

Validity: Correlation with grade average of 11th graders = .27.

Author: Swisher, J., et al.

Article: Experimental comparison of four approaches to drug abuse prevention among ninth and eleventh graders.

Journal: *Journal of Counseling Psychology,* July 1972, *19*(4), 328–332.

Related Research: Swisher, J., & Horman, R. (1968). *Evaluation of Temple University's drug abuse* *prevention program* (Research Report, Contract J-68–50). Washington, DC: U.S. Department of Justice.

■ ■ ■

345

Test Name: EARLY MATHEMATICS BEHAVIORS TESTS

Purpose: To assess ability to perform specific tasks involving counting, use of numerals, or comparison of set size.

Format: A battery of tests designed for oral, individual administration. Each consisted of 1–5 items.

Author: Wang, M. C., et al.

Article: The sequence of development of some early mathematics behaviors.

Journal: *Child Development,* December 1971, *42*(6), 1767–1778.

Related Research: Wang, M. C., et al. (1971). *The sequence of development of some early mathematics behaviors* (Working Paper 6). Pittsburgh, PA: University of Pittsburgh, Learning Research and Development Center.

■ ■ ■

346

Test Name: HARVEY'S "THIS I BELIEVE" TEST

Purpose: To assess a subject's ability to recall factual material and reaction to threat.

Format: Sentence completion.

Author: Greaves, G.

Article: Differences in reaction to threatening factual material.

Journal: *Psychological Reports,* August 1971, *29*(1), 330.

Related Research: Greaves, G. (1971). Harvey's "This I Believe" Test: Studies of reliability.

Psychological Reports, 28, 387–390.

■ ■ ■

347

Test Name: HIGHER LEARNING TEST

Purpose: To measure the acquisition of the ability to use geographic materials in new situations.

Number of Items: 67

Format: Multiple choice items designed to meet Bloom's criteria for intellectual skills and abilities.

Author: Grieve, T. D., and Davis, J. K.

Article: The relationship of cognitive style and method of instruction to performance in ninth grade geography.

Journal: *Journal of Educational Research,* November 1971, *65*(3), 137–141.

■ ■ ■

348

Test Name: HOLBROOK–OSERETSKY SCALE

Purpose: To evaluate motor proficiency.

Number of Items: 44

Format: Includes five subcategories: speed, general static coordination, dynamic coordination, general dynamic coordination, and simultaneous movement. Item descriptions are provided.

Author: Finkenbinder, R. L.

Article: A comparison of two American adaptations of the Oseretsky Test of Motor Proficiency.

Journal: *Journal of School Psychology,* 1972, *10*(1), 17–24.

Related Research: Holbrook, S. F. (1953). *A study of the development*

of motor abilities between the ages of 4 and 12, using a modification of the Oseretsky scale. Unpublished doctoral dissertation, University of Minnesota.

■ ■ ■

349

Test Name: IMITATION AND COMPREHENSION TEST

Purpose: To measure speech imitation and comprehension abilities.

Number of Items: 26

Format: Includes 26 sentences representing 13 standard English syntactical structures and sets of three pictures constructed for each sentence, from which the child picks the one representing the meaning of each sentence. The sentences and one set of pictures are presented.

Reliability: Estimates ranged from .49 to .87.

Author: Hall, V. C., and Turner, R. R.

Article: Comparison of imitation and comprehension scores between two lower-class groups and the effects of two warm-up conditions on imitation of the same groups.

Journal: *Child Development,* December 1971, *42*(6), 1735–1750.

Related Research: Osser, H., et al. (1969). The young child's ability to imitate and comprehend speech: A comparison of two subcultural groups. *Child Development,* 40, 1063–1076.

■ ■ ■

350

Test Name: INFORMAL READING INVENTORY

Purpose: To assess reading achievement.

Validity: Correlations with Peabody Picture Vocabulary were .45, and .57 ($p < .01$).

Author: Hall, J., and Chansky, N.

Article: Relationships between selected ability and achievement tests in an economically disadvantaged Negro sample.

Journal: *Psychological Reports,* June 1971, *28*(3), 741–742.

Related Research: *Informal Reading Invention* (SIC). (1953). Unpublished manuscript, Temple University Reading Clinic.

■ ■ ■

351

Test Name: JAPAN KNOWLEDGE TEST

Purpose: To measure acquisition of knowledge of Japan's geography.

Number of Items: 57

Format: Multiple choice items based on the High School Geography Project Team, Japan: *A Unit with Geography in an Urban Age,* Association of American Geographers, Boulder, CO, 1968.

Author: Grieve, T. D., and Davis, J. K.

Article: The relationship of cognitive style and method of instruction to performance in ninth grade geography.

Journal: *Journal of Educational Research,* November 1971, *65*(3), 137–141.

■ ■ ■

352

Test Name: KINDERGARTEN READING QUESTIONNAIRE

Purpose: To assess pre-reading and reading activities on the kindergarten level.

Format: Three parts: I is concerned with obtaining general background information about the community, the school, and the individual teacher; II is concerned

with reading readiness; and III is concerned with the formal reading program.

Author: Ching, D. C.

Article: The teaching of reading in kindergarten.

Journal: *California Journal of Educational Research,* September 1972, *23*(4), 156–162.

■ ■ ■

353

Test Name: KNOWLEDGE OF MARIJUANA TEST

Purpose: To measure students' knowledge of marijuana.

Number of Items: 30 items each in two parallel forms.

Format: Multiple choice: four homogeneous options and a "don't know" option.

Reliability: On 372 college freshmen, internal consistency coefficient = .75.

Validity: Test content chosen on basis of detailed study of 70 popular and technical articles.

Author: Taylor, H.

Article: A test for measuring students' knowledge of marijuana.

Journal: *Measurement and Evaluation in Guidance,* July 1971, *4*(2), 116.

■ ■ ■

354

Test Name: KNOWN-WORD VOCABULARY TEST

Purpose: To measure the quality or maturity level of definition.

Number of Items: 30

Format: Within each of three groups of 10 words, each word corresponded in meaning to one of the first 10 words of the Stanford-Binet vocabulary test.

Author: Levinson, E. J.

Article: The modification of intelligence by training in the verbalization of word definitions and simple concepts.

Journal: *Child Development,* November 1971, *42*(5), 1361–1380.

■ ■ ■

355

Test Name: LANGUAGE COMPREHENSION TEST

Purpose: To measure comprehension of the possessive, negative, passive, and negative–passive syntactic structures.

Reliability: Test–retest $r = .94$ (3-week interval).

Author: Elardo, R.

Article: The experimental facilitation of children's comprehension and production of four syntactic structures.

Journal: *Child Development,* December 1971, *42*(6), 2101–2104.

Related Research: Fraser, C., et al. (1963). Control of grammar in imitation, comprehension, and production. *Journal of Verbal Learning and Verbal Behavior, 2,* 121–135.

■ ■ ■

356

Test Name: LETTER-LIKE FORMS VISUAL DISCRIMINATION TEST

Purpose: To evaluate the word discrimination ability of kindergarten children.

Number of Items: 30

Format: Pupils are required to select the one simulated word of five presented in each item that is different. Scores range from 1 to 30.

Author: Pryzwansky, W. B.

Article: Effects of perceptual-motor training and manuscript writing on reading readiness skills in kindergarten.

Journal: *Journal of Educational Psychology*, April 1972, *63*(2), 110–115.

Related Research: Gibson, E. J., et al. (1962). *Journal of Comparative and Physiological Psychology, 55,* 897–906.

• • •

357

Test Name: MAKING VISUAL DISCRIMINATIONS TEST— MODIFIED

Purpose: To evaluate the word discrimination ability of kindergarten children.

Number of Items: 30

Format: Pupils are required to identify the one of four stimulus words that match the sample word provided for each item. Scores range from 1 to 30.

Author: Pryzwansky, W. B.

Article: Effects of perceptual-motor training and manuscript writing on reading readiness skills in kindergarten.

Journal: *Journal of Educational Psychology*, April 1972, *63*(2), 110–115.

• • •

358

Test Name: MEMORY FOR SEMANTIC CLASSES

Purpose: To evaluate one's memory for semantic classes.

Format: Includes sets of three words with common attributes that subjects must recall in order to recognize whether new sets of three words have the same common attributes as sets previously studied.

Reliability: Spearman-Brown estimated *r* = .42.

Author: Blaine, D. D., and Dunham, J. L.

Article: Effect of availability on the relationship of memory abilities to performance in multiple-category concept tasks.

Journal: *Journal of Educational Psychology*, August 1971, *62*(4), 333–338.

Related Research: Guilford, J. P. (1967). *The nature of human intelligence.* New York: McGraw-Hill.

Guilford, J. P., & Hoepfner, R. (1966). *Structure-of-intellect tests and factors* (Reports from the Psychological Laboratory, No. 36). Los Angeles: University of Southern California Press.

• • •

359

Test Name: MEMORY FOR SEMANTIC IMPLICATIONS

Purpose: To evaluate one's memory for semantic implication.

Format: Includes pairs of meaningful words presented on a study page and the first word of each pair presented on the test page. The subject must recall the word that is associated with each word presented.

Reliability: Spearman-Brown estimated *r* = .82.

Author: Blaine, D. D., and Dunham, J. L.

Article: Effect of availability on the relationship of memory abilities to performance in multiple category concept tasks.

Journal: *Journal of Educational Psychology*, August 1971, *62*(4), 333–338.

Related Research: Guilford, J. P. (1967). *The nature of human intelligence.* New York: McGraw-Hill.

Guilford, J. P., & Hoepfner, R.

(1966). *Structure-of-intellect tests and factors* (Reports from the Psychological Laboratory, No. 36). Los Angeles: University of Southern California Press.

• • •

360

Test Name: MEMORY FOR SEMANTIC UNITS

Purpose: To evaluate one's memory for semantic units.

Number of Items: 20

Format: Involves recall of meaningful words.

Reliability: Spearman-Brown estimated *r* = .71.

Author: Blaine, D. D., and Dunham, J. L.

Article: Effect of availability on the relationship of memory abilities to performance in multiple-category concept tasks.

Journal: *Journal of Educational Psychology*, August 1971, *62*(4), 333–338.

Related Research: Guilford, J. P. (1967). *The nature of human intelligence.* New York: McGraw-Hill.

Guilford, J. P., & Hoepfner, R. (1966). *Structure-of-intellect tests and factors* (Reports from the Psychological Laboratory, No. 36). Los Angeles: University of Southern California Press.

• • •

361

Test Name: MEMORY FOR SYMBOLIC CLASSES

Purpose: To evaluate one's memory for symbolic classes.

Number of Items: 10

Format: Each item consists of three trigrams with common attributes that the subject must recall in order to recognize which one of four trigrams in several sets of four belong with a set previously studied.

Reliability: Spearman-Brown estimated $r = .83$.

Author: Blaine, D. D., and Dunham, J. L.

Article: Effect of availability on the relationship of memory abilities to performance in multiple-category concept tasks.

Journal: *Journal of Educational Psychology*, August 1971, *62*(4), 333–338.

Related Research: Guilford, J. P. (1967). *The nature of human intelligence.* New York: McGraw-Hill.

Guilford, J. P., & Hoepfner, R. (1966). *Structure-of-intellect tests and factors* (Reports from the Psychological Laboratory, No. 36). Los Angeles: University of Southern California Press.

■ ■ ■

362

Test Name: MEMORY FOR SYMBOLIC IMPLICATIONS

Purpose: To evaluate one's memory for symbolic implications.

Format: Includes a study page of two digit numbers with a letter associated with each. On a test page, the two-digit numbers are presented in random order, and subjects must recall the letter associated with each.

Reliability: Spearman-Brown estimated $r = .73$.

Author: Blaine, D. D., and Dunham, J. L.

Article: Effect of availability on the relationship of abilities to performance in multiple-category concept tasks.

Journal: *Journal of Educational Psychology*, August 1971, *62*(4), 333–338.

Related Research: Guilford, J. P. (1967). *The nature of human intelligence.* New York: McGraw-Hill.

Guilford, J. P., & Hoepfner, R. (1966). *Structure-of-intellect tests and factors* (Reports from the Psychological Laboratory, No. 36). Los Angeles: University of Southern California Press.

■ ■ ■

363

Test Name: MEMORY FOR SYMBOLIC UNITS

Purpose: To evaluate one's memory for symbolic units.

Number of Items: 15

Format: Involves recognition of nonsense trigrams.

Reliability: Spearman-Brown estimated $r = .65$.

Author: Blaine, D. D., and Dunham, J. L.

Article: Effect of availability on the relationship of memory abilities to performance in multiple-category concept tasks.

Journal: *Journal of Educational Psychology*, August 1971, *62*(4), 333–338.

Related Research: Guilford, J. P. (1967). *The nature of human intelligence.* New York: McGraw-Hill.

Guilford, J. P., & Hoepfner, R. (1966). *Structure-of-intellect tests and factors* (Reports from the Psychological Laboratory, No. 36). Los Angeles: University of Southern California Press.

■ ■ ■

364

Test Name: MISSOURI COLLEGE ENGLISH TEST

Purpose: To measure basic writing

skills and concepts relevant to a freshman writing course and accessible through an object test.

Reliability: See related research.

Validity: See related research.

Author: Di Russo, L., and Aven, S. D.

Article: Does remedial English help for college freshmen?

Journal: *California Journal of Educational Research,* January 1971, *22*(1), 5–8.

Related Research: Willis, C. G., & Kopf, C. J. (1967, June). 1967–68 Official norms, sectioning procedures and trend data for the freshman placement test battery (mimeo). Columbia, Mo., *Testing and Counseling Service Report, 21*(5), 1–3.

■ ■ ■

365

Test Name: ORAL MULTIPLE CHOICE VOCABULARY COMPREHENSION TEST

Purpose: To assess vocabulary comprehension.

Number of Items: 50

Format: Three forms each with change of vowel, consonant sounds, and truncation of words. Test 1 had standard English stem and dialect distractors; Test 2 had dialect stem with standard English distractors; Test 3 was composed of all dialect.

Reliability: Kuder-Richardson Formula 21: Test 1 = .89; Test 2 = .54; Test 3 = .78.

Author: Hooper, P., and Powell, E.

Article: Note on oral comprehension in standard and non-standard English.

Journal: *Perceptual and Motor Skills*, August 1971, *33*(1), 34.

366

Test Name: PHONEME–GRAPHEME AND GRAPHEME–PHONEME TESTS

Purpose: To assess knowledge of English sound symbol relationship.

Number of Items: 33 per test.

Format: One test involved the recognition of the appropriate grapheme, given a phoneme as a stimulus, and the second test required the child to judge whether a given grapheme could be used to produce a particular phoneme.

Author: Hardy, M., et al.

Article: Developmental patterns in elemental reading skills: Phoneme–grapheme and grapheme–phoneme correspondences.

Journal: *Journal of Educational Psychology*, October 1972, *63*(5), 433–436.

• • •

367

Test Name: PLURAL FORMATION PATTERNS TEST

Purpose: To study primary grade children's ability to produce orally appropriate noun plural forms for real and nonsense words.

Number of Items: 34

Format: Includes six types of plural formations patterns, all of which are monosyllabic and end with a constant sound. All items are presented.

Author: Graves, M. F., and Koziol, S.

Article: Noun plural development in primary grade children.

Journal: *Child Development,* October 1971, *42*(4), 1165–1173.

Related Research: Berko, J. (1958). The child's learning of

English morphology. *Word, 14,* 150–177.

• • •

368

Test Name: POLITICAL KNOWLEDGE TEST

Purpose: To assess secondary student performance with respect to the "American Political Behavior Course."

Format: Maximum numerical score = 55; measured student memory of information from course and ability to interpret cases.

Reliability: Kuder-Richardson formula = .80.

Author: Patrick, J.

Article: The impact of an experimental course "American Political Behavior" on the knowledge, skills and attitudes of secondary school students.

Journal: *Social Education,* February 1972, *36*(2), 168–179.

• • •

369

Test Name: POLITICAL SCIENCES SKILLS TEST

Purpose: To assess secondary students' ability to critically evaluate and interpret statements and questions.

Format: Total number points = 25; subjects interpreted tables, sampling techniques, and deduced.

Reliability: Kuder-Richardson formula = .69 (mean).

Author: Patrick, J.

Article: The impact of an experimental course "American Political Behavior" on the knowledge, skills and attitudes of secondary school students.

Journal: *Social Education,* February 1972, *36*(2), 168–179.

370

Test Name: PRIMARY ESSAY TESTS

Purpose: To measure composition ability in young children.

Number of Items: A single topic description for each form.

Time Required: 30 minutes.

Format: Product scaled instrument; the child's written composition is compared to previously rated models of high to low performance; measure is a single score from 1–7: Five separate test forms available. Used at 2nd and 3rd grade level.

Reliability: Interrater reliability for models was .87 for 4 raters; interrater reliability on test group was in the .70s and .80s for each form; intraclass correlation coefficient ranged from .63 for 1 rater to .89 for 5 raters. Test–retest reliability was .58 to .89.

Validity: Correlation with teachers' estimates of composition skill = .52; Ki = .79 when ratings based on comparisons with models correlated with a rating made by reference to the original set of criteria.

Author: Veal, L. R., and Biesbrock, E. F.

Article: Primary Essay Tests.

Journal: *Journal of Educational Measurement,* Spring 1971, *8*(1), 45.

Availability: Order NAPS Document 01235, ASIS National Auxiliary Publication Services, c/o CCM Information Sciences Inc., 22 W. 34th St., New York, NY 10001; $2.00 microfilm, $5.10 photocopy.

• • •

371

Test Name: PRONUNCIATION TEST

Purpose: To determine first graders' ability to use phonetic generalizations and to produce words.

Number of Items: 40

Format: 20 items were real monosyllabic words and 20 items were pronounceable nonsense monosyllabic units.

Reliability: Internal reliability coefficient alpha rs= .90, .91.

Author: Hartley, R. N.

Article: A method of increasing the ability of first grade pupils to use phonetic generalizations.

Journal: *California Journal of Educational Research,* January 1971, *22*(1), 9–16.

■ ■ ■

372

Test Name: READING-INPUT TEST

Purpose: To indicate reading input performance.

Number of Items: 20

Format: Subject selects one of two words to complete each sentence of three paragraphs. All items are presented.

Author: Carver, R. P.

Article: A computer model of reading and its implications for measurement and research.

Journal: *Reading Research Quarterly,* Summer 1971, *6*(4), 449–471.

■ ■ ■

373

Test Name: READING-STORAGE TEST

Purpose: To measure the degree to which the verbal information has been stored during reading.

Number of Items: 20

Format: Subject selects one of two

words to complete each sentence of three paragraphs. The words on either side of the choice point have been deleted. All items are presented.

Author: Carver, R. P.

Article: A computer model of reading and its implications for measurement and research.

Journal: *Reading Research Quarterly,* Summer 1971, *6*(4), 449–471.

■ ■ ■

374

Test Name: RECOGNITION TEST

Purpose: To determine first graders' ability to use phonetic generalizations and to recognize a word when an auditory cue is given.

Number of Items: 40

Format: 20 items were real monosyllabic words and 20 items were pronounceable nonsense monosyllabic units.

Reliability: Alpha coefficients ranged from .77 to .95.

Author: Hartley, R. N.

Article: A method of increasing the ability of first grade pupils to use phonetic generalization.

Journal: *California Journal of Educational Research.* January 1971, *22*(1), 9–16.

■ ■ ■

375

Test Name: SAN DIEGO QUICK ASSESSMENT CHECK

Purpose: To establish prevailing reading levels.

Format: Provides general error patterns including omission, word analysis skills, and reversals.

Author: Kimble, R. L., and Davison, R. G.

Article: Reading improvement for disadvantaged American Indian youth.

Journal: *Journal of Reading,* February 1972, *15*(5), 342–346.

■ ■ ■

376

Test Name: SENTENCE-IMITATION TEST

Purpose: To determine language proficiency in economically disadvantaged Negro children.

Number of Items: 30

Format: Includes 15 sentences in standard English and the nonstandard translation of each.

Author: Foreit, K. G., and Donaldson, P. L.

Article: Dialect, race, and language proficiency: Another dead heat on the merry-go-round.

Journal: *Child Development,* November 1971, *42*(5), 1572–1574.

Related Research: Baratz, J. C. (1969). A bi-dialectal task for determining language proficiency in economically disadvantaged Negro children. *Child Development, 40,* 889–901.

■ ■ ■

377

Test Name: SENTENCE IMITATION TEST

Purpose: To assess a child's control of several elaborative sentence elements.

Number of Items: 50

Format: Test includes the following elaborative sentence elements: prenominal adjectives and possessive nouns, locative prepositional phrases, relative clauses, and adverbial clauses.

Reliability: Test–retest reliability ranged from r = .81 to r = .90.

Author: Ammon, P. R., and Ammon, M. S.

Article: Effects of training Black preschool children in vocabulary versus sentence construction.

Journal: *Journal of Educational Psychology,* October 1971, *62*(5), 421–426.

• • •

378

Test Name: SLANG TEST

Purpose: To assess knowledge of "street language" or informal language.

Number of Items: 28

Format: Multiple choice format (5 choices).

Reliability: Spearman-Brown = .88.

Validity: Significantly differentiated between delinquent and nondelinquent subjects; correlation with self-report delinquent activities = .22 (*p* < .01).

Author: Kulik, J., et al.

Article: Language, socialization, and delinquency.

Journal: *Developmental Psychology,* May 1971, *4*(3), 434–439.

• • •

379

Test Name: TAPED NOTETAKING TEST

Purpose: To evaluate the quality of student notes.

Number of Items: 30

Format: Includes a 10-minute tape-recorded lecture followed by 30 comprehensive questions covering the lecture material. Scoring includes three ratios representing completeness, clarity, and conciseness, and a total that is the quality-of-notes score.

Author: Palmatier, R. A.

Article: Comparison of four note-taking procedures.

Journal: *Journal of Reading,* January 1971, *14*(4), 235–240.

• • •

380

Test Name: TEST OF BASIC LANGUAGE COMPETENCE IN ENGLISH AND SPANISH (Level I)

Purpose: To assess basic language competence of children who speak English or Spanish, or who are bilingual in these two languages.

Format: Consists of nine English and nine parallel Spanish subtests that include: oral vocabulary, comprehension of commands and directions, recognition of interrogative patterns, phonemic discrimination at word level, production of grammatical structures, assimilation of meaning, phonemic discrimination at sentence level, grammatical sensitivity, and grammatical discrimination.

Reliability: .93 and .87.

Author: Stedman, J. M., and Adams, R. L.

Article: Achievement as a function of language competence, behavior adjustment, and sex in young, disadvantaged Mexican-American children.

Journal: *Journal of Educational Psychology,* October 1972, *63*(5), 411–417.

• • •

381

Test Name: TEST OF CONCEPTIONS OF JUSTICE FOR YOUNG CHILDREN

Purpose: To assess levels of understanding of social justice.

Number of Items: 21 stories.

Format: Child was read three training and 18 test stories (six each related to guilt–innocence, apology–restitution, intent–accidental.) Child selected one of two possible endings for story. Responses scored 1 or 0.

Author: Irwin, D., and Moore, S.

Article: The young child's understanding of social justice.

Journal: *Developmental Psychology,* November 1971, *5*(3), 406–410.

• • •

382

Test Name: TEST OF MEMORY PERFORMANCE

Purpose: To assess memory performance in children 5–10 years old.

Format: Eight cards exposed momentarily in sequence; child had to recall where the match to the ninth card lay.

Author: Hagen, J.

Article: Some thoughts on how children learn to remember.

Journal: *Human Development,* 1971, *14*(4), 262–271.

Related Research: Atkinson, R., et al. (1964). Short term memory with young children. *Psychonomic Science, 1,* 255–256.

• • •

383

Test Name: TEST OF SYNTACTIC COMPREHENSION

Purpose: To assess the "ability to choose between alternatives representing syntactic contrasts."

Number of Items: 80

Format: Individually administered. The subject is presented a sentence and two pictures. The task is to choose the picture that corresponds to the sentence. Correct choice of the appropriate picture is based on correct understanding of a syntactic principle.

Author: Parisi, D.

Article: Development of Syntactic Comprehension in preschool children as a function of socioeconomic level.

Journal: *Developmental Psychology,* September 1971, *5*(2), 186–189.

Related Research: Fraser, C., et al. (1963). Control of grammar in imitation, comprehension, and production. *Journal of Verbal Learning and Verbal Behavior, 2,* 121–135.

■ ■ ■

384

Test Name: TESTS OF BASIC LANGUAGE COMPETENCE: LEVEL I

Purpose: To assess language ability.

Format: Includes four parallel English and Spanish subtests: oral vocabulary, comprehension of commands and directions, recognition of interrogative patterns, and phonemic discrimination at work level.

Reliability: Spearman split-half for English was .93.

Spearman split-half for Spanish was .87.

Author: Stedman, J. M., and McKenzie, R. E.

Article: Family factors related to competence in young disadvantaged Mexican-American children.

Journal: *Child Development,* November 1971, *42*(5), 1602–1607.

Related Research: Cervenka, E. (1967, August). *The measurement of bilingualism and bicultural socialization of the child in the school setting: Development of instruments* (Report to the Institute for Educational Development). Washington, DC: U.S. Office of Economic Opportunity.

■ ■ ■

385

Test Name: TEST WISENESS SCALE

Purpose: To measure the ability to respond to multiple choice items using extraneous clues.

Number of Items: 34

Format: Four option multiple choice: instrument contained five subscales: association, use of specific determiners, use of correct alternatives, use of grammatical clues, use of overlapping distractors.

Reliability: Kuder-Richardson Formula 20 for 5 subscales was .22 to .80; total score Kuder-Richardson Formula 20 = .72.

Validity: Total Lorge Thorndike and total test wise score = .49.

Author: Diamond, J., and Evans, W.

Article: An investigation of the cognitive correlates of test-wiseness.

Journal: *Journal of Educational Measurement,* Summer 1972, *9*(2), 145–150.

■ ■ ■

386

Test Name: WALK A LINE SLOWLY TEST

Purpose: To assess motor impulse control.

Format: Assesses ability to inhibit an impulse when situation calls for it.

Author: Bucky, S., and Banta, T.

Article: Racial factors in test performance.

Journal: *Developmental Psychology,* January 1972, *6*(1), 7–13.

Related Research: Maccoby, E., et al. (1965). Activity level and intellectual functioning in normal preschool children. *Child Development, 36,* 761–769.

CHAPTER 2
Adjustment—Educational

387

Test Name: ALPERT-HABER ANXIETY TEST

Purpose: To identify test-anxious students.

Format: Includes a scale for measuring the presence and intensity of responses that facilitate performance and for measuring the presence and intensity of responses that debilitate performance.

Validity: Correlations of facilitating scale and examination performance .23 to .37.

Correlations of debilitating scale and examination performance −.25 to −.28.

Author: Wittmaier, B. C.

Article: Test anxiety and study habits.

Journal: *Journal of Educational Research,* April 1972, *65*(8), 352–354.

Related Research: Alpert, R., & Haber, R. N. (1960). Anxiety in academic achievement situations. *Journal of Abnormal and Social Psychology, 61,* 207–215.

■ ■ ■

388

Test Name: BEHAVIOR DESCRIPTION REFERRAL FORM

Purpose: To provide performance related descriptions of school problems for the behaviorally oriented school psychologist.

Format: Includes six areas: management, work habits, speech,

social behavior, academics, and other. A copy of the form is presented.

Author: Alper, T. G., and White, O. R.

Article: The behavior description referral form: A tool for the school psychologist in the elementary school.

Journal: *Journal of School Psychology,* 1971, *9*(2), 177–181.

■ ■ ■

389

Test Name: BEHAVIOR PROBLEMS QUESTIONNAIRE

Purpose: To identify behavior problems in the elementary school.

Number of Items: 50

Format: Each item is responded to on a 7-point rating scale with four calibrations. The behavior problems are listed.

Author: Rajpal, P. L.

Article: Seriousness of behavior problems of elementary school boys.

Journal: *Education,* February–March 1972, *92*(3), 46–51.

Related Research: Wickman, E. K. (1928). *Children's behavior problems and teachers' attitudes.* New York: The Commonwealth Fund.

■ ■ ■

390

Test Name: CLASSROOM BEHAVIOR INVENTORY, PRESCHOOL TO PRIMARY

Purpose: To assess adjustment.

Format: The teacher rates each child on a 4-point scale ranging from *very much like* to *very little like.* Includes three factors: introversion, extroversion, positive–negative task orientation, and positive–negative social behavior.

Reliability: Test–retest Pearson product–moment correlation was .88.

Author: Stedman, J. M., and McKenzie, R. E.

Article: Family factors related to competence in young disadvantaged Mexican-American children.

Journal: *Child Development,* November 1971, *42*(5), 1602–1607.

Related Research: Schaefer, E. S., et al. (1965, March). *Development of a classroom behavior checklist and factor analysis of children's school behavior in the United States and the Netherlands.* Paper delivered at the annual meeting of the Society for Research in Child Development, Minneapolis, MN.

■ ■ ■

391

Test Name: COTTLE SCHOOL INTEREST INVENTORY

Purpose: To measure dropout potential.

Number of Items: 150

Format: A true–false test battery. The higher the score, the higher the dropout potential.

Author: Dauw, E. G.

Article: Separate schools for potential dropouts.

Journal: *Educational Leadership*, January 1972, *29*(4), 333–340.

■ ■ ■

392

Test Name:
MANDLER-COWAN'S TEST ANXIETY QUESTIONNAIRE FOR HIGH SCHOOL STUDENTS—SHORT FORM

Purpose: To measure fear of failure.

Number of Items: 32

Format: Each item was graded on a 9-point scale with 1 representing *low anxiety level* and 9 representing *high anxiety level*.

Validity: With the full version of 48 items: .94. Haller's Occupational Apiration Scale: .26. NORC Occupational Prestige Scale: .25. McClelland's Need Achievement Thematic Apperception Test: .10.

Author: Tseng, M. S.

Article: Social class, occupational aspiration, and other variables.

Journal: *Journal of Experimental Education*, Summer 1971, *39*(4), 88–92.

Related Research: Maudler, G., & Cowan, J. (1958). Text anxiety questionnaires. *Journal of Consulting Psychology, 22*, 228–229.

Entwisle, D., & Greenberger, E. (1972). Questions about social class, internality–externality, and test anxiety. *Developmental Psychology, 6*(2), 218.

■ ■ ■

393

Test Name: MANN TEST ANXIETY SCALE

Purpose: To assess self reported test anxiety.

Validity: Measures of test anxiety varied by experimental procedures.

Author: Mann, J.

Article: Vicarious desensitization of test anxiety through observation of videotaped treatment.

Journal: *Journal of Counseling Psychology*, January 1972, *19*(1), 1–7.

Related Research: Mann, J. (1969). *A comparison of the effects of direct versus vicarious individual and group desensitization of test anxious students.* Unpublished masters thesis, University of Arizona.

■ ■ ■

394

Test Name: MATHEMATICS ANXIETY RATING SCALE

Purpose: To assess anxiety towards mathematics.

Number of Items: 98

Format: Brief descriptions of behavioral situations are given and the subject is requested to check the level of anxiety on a 1–5 scale.

Reliability: Test–retest (7 weeks) reliability was .85. Alpha coefficient was .97.

Validity: Pre to post therapy drops in scores were reported in several studies; correlation with Differential Aptitude test was .64 ($p < .01$).

Author: Richardson, F., and Suinn, R.

Article: The Mathematics anxiety rating scale: Psychometric data.

Journal: *Journal of Counseling Psychology*, November 1972, *19*(6), 551–554.

■ ■ ■

395

Test Name: OSTERHOUSE TEST ANXIETY INVENTORY

Purpose: To assess: (a) physiological reactions to examination taking and (b) worry over test performance.

Number of Items: 16

Format: 1–5 Likert Scale.

Reliability: Judges were reliable in assigning items to either worry or physiological categories. Split-half $r = .92$; test–retest reliabilities were .68 and .72 over 7 weeks.

Author: Osterhouse, R.

Article: Desensitization and study-skills training as treatment for two types of test-anxious students.

Journal: *Journal of Counseling Psychology*, July 1972, *19*(4), 301–307.

Related Research: Osterhouse, R. (1969). *A comparison of desensitization and study-skills training for the treatment of two kinds of text-anxious students.* Unpublished doctoral dissertation, Ohio State University.

Osipow, S., & Kreinbring, I. (1971). Temporal stability of an inventory to measure test anxiety. *Journal of Counseling Psychology, 18*, 152–154.

McMillan, J., & Osterhouse, R. (1972). Specific and generalized anxiety as determinants of outcome with desensitization of test anxiety. *Journal of Counseling Psychology*, November, *19*(6), 518–521.

■ ■ ■

396

Test Name: OSTERHOUSE TEST ANXIETY INSTRUMENT (MODIFIED)

Purpose: To assess test anxiety.

Number of Items: 21

Format: Subjects responded true–false to each of statements describing test anxiety situations.

Reliability: Test–retest (10 days) reliabilities were all significant: range (emotionality subscale) .47–.72 and (worry subscale) .65–.84.

Author: Osipow, S., and Kreinbring, I.

Article: Temporal stability of an inventory to measure test anxiety.

Journal: *Journal of Counseling Psychology*, March 1971, *18*(2), 152–154.

• • •

397

Test Name: PERSONAL–SOCIAL ADJUSTMENT RATING SCALES

Purpose: To permit teachers to rate the personal–social adjustment of their preschool pupils.

Format: Includes 17 scales: quality of speech; peer relationships; independence; restraint of motor activity; cooperation; aggression; active vs. passive speech; verbal skills; the silent child; child with separation problems; fearful or tearful child; the isolated child; the child who doesn't learn; the provocative child; the unhappy child; the disruptive child; the hyperactive child.

Reliability: Interjudge reliabilities ranged from .46 to .89.

Author: Richards, H. C., and McCandless, B. R.

Article: Socialization dimensions among 5-year-old slum children.

Journal: *Journal of Educational Psychology*, February 1972, *63*(1), 44–55.

Related Research: Goldstein, K. M., & Chorost, S. B. (1966). *A preliminary evaluation of nursery school experience on the later school adjustment of culturally disadvantaged children* (Final Report, United States Office of Education, S-323). Staten Island, NY: Wakoff Research Center.

• • •

398

Test Name: SARASON TEST ANXIETY QUESTIONNAIRE

Purpose: To assess test anxiety.

Reliability: Test–retest reliability was .82 (Alpert-Huber, 1960).

Validity: Correlation with Taylor MAS = .35 ($p < .01$).

Author: Reiter, H.

Article: Relationships among four measures of anxiety.

Journal: *Psychological Reports*, June 1971, *28*(3), 761–762.

Related Research: Sarason, I. (1960). Empirical findings and theoretical problems in the use of anxiety scales. *Psychological Bulletin, 57,* 407–415.

Alpert, R., & Haber, R. (1960). Anxiety in an academic achievement situation. *Journal of Abnormal and Social Psychology, 61,* 207–215.

• • •

399

Test Name: SARASON TEST ANXIETY SCALE

Purpose: To assess the level of test anxiety.

Author: Graff, R., et al.

Article: Group reactive inhibition and reciprocal inhibitions therapies with anxious college students.

Journal: *Journal of Counseling Psychology*, September 1971, *18*(5), 431–436.

Related Research: Sarason, I. (1961). Interrelationships among individual difference variables, behavior in psychotherapy and verbal conditioning. *Journal of*

Abnormal and Social Psychology, 52, 201–206.

• • •

400

Test Name: SPECIAL INCOMPLETE SENTENCE TESTS

Purpose: To assess psychological and behavior attributes in underachievers.

Format: Areas assessed are academic anxiety, self-value, authority relations, independence–dependence, activity patterns, goal orientation, academic skills.

Validity: Differentiated significantly in 617 areas between underachievers and high achievers; correlation with scale factors and Manifest Anxiety Scale ranged .007 to .410 ($p < .05$).

Author: Riedel, R., et al.

Article: Special incomplete sentences test for underachievers: Further research.

Journal: *Psychological Reports*, August 1971, *29*(1), 251–257.

401

Test Name: TEST ANXIETY QUESTIONNAIRE—SHORT FORM

Purpose: To measure degree of anxiety.

Number of Items: 32

Format: Each item is graded on a 9-point scale with 1 representing *low anxiety* and 9 representing *high anxiety.*

Validity: Correlation with the long form is .95.

Author: Tseng, M. S.

Article: Comparisons of selected familial, personality, and vocational variables of high school students and dropouts.

Journal: *Journal of Educational*

Research, July–August 1972, *65*(10), 462–466.

Related Research: See *D.U.E.M.M., 1,* 1974: 17–18.

■ ■ ■

402

Test Name: TEST ANXIETY SCALE FOR CHILDREN

Purpose: A measure of test anxiety.

Format: A high score on the test reflects anxiety reactions in a variety of testlike situations.

Author: Doyal, G. T., & Forsyth, R. A.

Article: The effect of test anxiety, intelligence, and sex on children's problem solving ability.

Journal: *Journal of Experimental Education,* Winter 1972, *41*(2), 23–26.

Related Research: Sarason, S. B., et al. (1960). *Anxiety in elementary school children.* New York: Wiley.

Greenberger, E., et al. (1971). Personality, cognitive and academic correlates of problem solving flexibility. *Developmental Psychology,* May, *4*(3), 416–424.

See *D.U.E.M.M., 1,* 1974: 16–17.

CHAPTER 3
Adjustment—Psychological

403

Test Name: ADJUSTMENT RATING SCALE

Purpose: To identify children with adjustment difficulties.

Number of Items: 7

Format: Includes three factors describing behavior control problems: delay, emotionality, aggression.

Author: Shure, M. B., et al.

Article: Problem-solving thinking and adjustment among disadvantaged preschool children.

Journal: Child Development, December 1971, 42(6), 1791–1803.

Related Research: Spivack, G., & Spotts, J. (1965). The Devereux Child Behavior Scale: Symptom behaviors in latency age children. American Journal of Mental Deficiency, 69, 839–853.

• • •

404

Test Name: AFFECT–COGNITION SCALE

Purpose: To evaluate statements about emotion.

Format: Based on TAT responses; there are four categories of response: affect content, attributed affect, defined affect dimension, developed affect. Rating done on a 4-point scale.

Reliability: Test–retest reliability was .78. Significant interjudge and intrajudge reliabilities;. Cohen's coefficients of agreement = .51, .59.

Validity: Correlations with 6

variables, 4 were significant (e.g., with dogmatism = −.32, p < .05).

Author: Gerber, L.

Article: Measurement of statements made about emotion: An investigation of the affect-cognition scale.

Journal: Psychological Reports, February 1972, 30(1), 231–235.

Related Research: Rachman, A. Changes in cognitive dimensions of affective responses as a result of psychotherapy. Unpublished doctoral dissertation, University of Chicago.

• • •

405

Test Name: BRIEF PSYCHIATRIC RATING SCALE

Purpose: To provide a method of rating patients on 23 scales and three factors.

Number of Items: 26

Format: Items deal with somatic concern, anxiety, emotional withdrawl. Factors include: neuroticism, retardation, personality disorder. Intended to be used by clinical personnel in rating patients.

Author: Hoffman, H., and Wefring, L.

Article: Sex and age differences in psychiatric symptoms of alcoholics.

Journal: Psychological Reports, June 1972, 30(3), 877–889.

Related Research: Overall, J., & Gorham, D. (1962). The brief psychiatric rating scale.

Psychological Reports, 10, 799–812.

• • •

406

Test Name: COLLETT-LESTER FEAR OF DYING SCALE

Purpose: To assess fear of death.

Validity: Only one of 8 correlations with number of jumps made by skydivers was significant (r = .70, p < .005).

Author: Alexander, M., and Lester, D.

Article: Fear of death in parachute jumpers.

Journal: Perceptual and Motor Skills, February 1972, 34(1), 338.

Related Research: Collett, L., & Lester, D. (1969). The fear of death and the fear of dying. Journal of Psychology, 72, 179–181.

Lester, D. (1967). Fear of death of suicidal persons. Psychological Reports, 20, 1077–1078.

Lester, D. (1971, April). Attitudes toward death held by staff of a suicide prevention center. Psychological Reports, 28(2), 650.

• • •

407

Test Name: COMMON AILMENTS

Purpose: To identify an individual's common ailments.

Number of Items: 32

Format: Each subject is asked whether he or she had each ailment and responds *yes* or *no* for each ailment.

Author: Poorkaj, H.

Article: Social-psychological factors and successful aging.

Journal: *Sociology and Social Research*, April 1972, *56*(3), 289–300.

• • •

408

Test Name: CONSTRICTION SCALE

Purpose: To assess nonassertive behavior.

Number of Items: 43 long forms, 29 short forms.

Format: Yes–no response mode.

Reliability: Spearman-Brown coefficients were .78 and .77 for men and women, respectively. Kuder-Richardson formula coefficients were .81 and .80 for men and women, respectively. Test–retest coefficients were .79 and .91 for 1 month.

Validity: Correlations with MMPI fear scale = .26 (men) and .34 (*p* < .05, women); correlation with neuroticism scale = .36 (*p* < 01, men) .33 (*p* < .05, women).

Author: Bates. H., and Zimmerman, S.

Article: Toward the development of a screening scale for assertive training.

Journal: *Psychological Reports,* February 1971, *28*(1), 99–107.

• • •

409

Test Name: COUNSELING APPROPRIATENESS CHECK LIST

Purpose: To identify problems that students feel are appropriate to discuss with a counselor at the counseling center.

Number of Items: 66

Format: Includes three factors: college routine, vocational choice, and adjustment to self and others. Responses are made on a 5-point scale ranging from 1 (*definitely inappropriate*) to 5 (*most appropriate*).

Author: Gelso, C. J., et al.

Article: Perceptions of the role of a university counseling center.

Journal: *Journal of College Student Personnel,* September 1972, *13*(5), 441–447.

Related Research: Warman, R. E. Differential perceptions of counseling role. *Journal of Counseling Psychology,* 1960, 7, 269–274.

• • •

410

Test Name: DEATH ANXIETY SCALE

Purpose: To measure the extent of anxiety about death.

Author: Templer, D., and Ruff, C.

Article: Death anxiety scale means, standard deviations, and embedding.

Journal: *Psychological Reports,* August 1971, *29*(1), 173–174.

Related Research: Templer, D. (1969). Death Anxiety Scale. *Proceedings of the 77th Annual Convention of the American Psychological Association, 4,* 737–738.

• • •

411

Test Name: DEATH CONCERN SCALE

Purpose: To assess subjects' concern about and ability to confront death.

Number of Items: 30

Format: Statements (e.g., "I think about my own death") to which subjects respond *often* to *never* or *strongly disagree* to *strongly agree*.

Reliability: Split-half reliabilities for four administrations ranged .86 to .88.

Validity: *r* with Manifest Anxiety Scale = .36 (men), .30 (women), .34 (total group), *p* < .05.

Author: Dickstein, L.

Article: Death concern: Measurement and correlates.

Journal: *Psychological Reports.* April 1972, *30*(3), 563–571.

Related Research: Dickstein, L., & Blatt, S. (1966). Death concern, futurity, and anticipation. *Journal of Counseling Psychology, 30,* 11–17.

• • •

412

Test Name: DIMENSIONS OF PSYCHOPATHOLOGY IN MIDDLE CHILDHOOD

Purpose: To assess symptoms of psychopathology.

Number of Items: 58 from the Peterson Problems Checklist (PPC), 55 items from the Wichita Guidance Center Checklist (WGCC), and 36 items from the Institute for Juvenile Research Symptom Checklist (IJRC).

Format: For PPC, the mother identified which symptom(s) described her child; for the WGCC, she responded to single sentence descriptions; for the IJRC, the examining psychiatrist coded following interview.

Validity: Factor analysis accounted for less than 50% of the variance by three or four factors originally rotated. Four factors from the PPC and the WGCC and three from the IJRC.

Author: Lessing, E., and Zagorin, S.

Article: Dimensions of psychopathology in middle childhood as evaluated by three symptom checklists.

Journal: *Educational and Psychological Measurement*, 1971, *31*, 175–198.

Related Research: Peterson, D. (1961). Behavior problems of middle childhood. *Journal of Consulting Psychology, 25,* 205–209.

Engel, M. (1955). The development of a scale to be used in play therapy research. *Transactions of the Kansas Academy of Science, 58,* 561–565.

Lessing, E., & Shilling, F. (1966). Relationship between treatment selection variables and treatment outcome in a child guidance clinic: An application of data processing methods. *Journal of the Academy of Child Psychiatry, 5,* 313–348.

■ ■ ■

413

Test Name: ELMORE PSYCHOLOGICAL ANOMIE SCALE

Purpose: To assess feeling of anomie.

Format: Contains scales: meaninglessness, valuelessness, hopelessness, powerlessness, aloneness, close-mindedness.

Author: Woody, R.

Article: Self understanding seminars: The effects of group psychotherapy in counselor training.

Journal: *Counselor Education and Supervision, Winter,* 1971, *10*(2), 112–119.

Related Research: Elmore, T. (1962). *The development of a scale to measure psychological anomie.* Unpublished doctoral dissertation, Ohio State University.

414

Test Name: GEER'S SPECIFIC FEAR RATING SHEET

Purpose: To assess level of fear associated with physical contact with the opposite sex.

Format: Seven-point scale in which subject indicated the degree of fear he or she felt toward various levels of contact with a person of the opposite sex.

Author: Dua, P. S.

Article: Group densitization of a phobia with three massing procedures.

Journal: *Journal of Counseling Psychology,* March 1972, *19*(2), 125–129.

■ ■ ■

415

Test Name: LIFE SATISFACTION SCALE

Purpose: To measure morale.

Number of Items: 13

Author: Poorkaj, H.

Article: Social-psychological factors and successful aging.

Journal: *Sociology and Social Research,* April 1972, *56*(3), 289–300.

■ ■ ■

416

Test Name: MOOD SCALE

Purpose: To assess immediate emotional state.

Number of Items: 52

Format: Adjective checklist; eight factors have been identified. High scores associated with dysphoric feeling.

Validity: r with Daily Activities List = .53 ($p < .05$).

Author: Stanfiel, J., et al.

Article: A daily activites list and its

relation to measures of adjustment and early environment.

Journal: *Psychological Reports,* June 1971, *28*(3), 691–699.

Related Research: Raskin, A., et al. (1969). Replication of factors of psychopathology in interview, ward behavior and self report ratings of hospitalized depressives. *Journal of Nervous and Mental Disease,* 148, 87–98.

■ ■ ■

417

Test Name: NOWLIS-GREEN MOOD ADJECTIVE CHECKLIST

Purpose: To measure suffering.

Format: Includes factors that relate to suffering (anxiety, depression, deactivation, and aggression) and those that do not (egotism, activation, social affection, pleasantness).

Author: Grand, S.

Article: Reactions to unfavorable evaluations of the self as a function of acceptance of disability: A test of Dembo, Leviton, and Wright's misfortune hypothesis.

Journal: *Journal of Counseling Psychology,* March 1972, *19*(2), 87–93.

Related Research: Nowlis, V., & Green, R. (1957). *A factor analytic study of the domain of mood* (Technical Report No. 4, Program on mood and attitude change, Research Project No. NR171–342, Contract NONR-668.12). Rochester, NY: University of Rochester Press.

■ ■ ■

418

Test Name: PATIENT ADJUSTMENT Q SORT TECHNIQUE

Purpose: To provide adjustment ratings.

Format: Subjects were rated on a 9-point sort-rating scale.

Reliability: Interrater reliability for hospital adjustment rating ranged .39–.84.

Validity: Correlation for hospital adjustment and intelligence = .24. Correlation for amount of education and intelligence = .31.

Author: Nickerson, E.

Article: Some correlates of adjustment by paraplegics.

Journal: *Perceptual and Motor Skills,* February 1971, *32*(1), 11–23.

• • •

419

Test Name: PERSONAL QUESTIONNAIRE

Purpose: To identify social and personal problems.

Number of Items: 77

Format: Self-report: a high score is associated with "feelings of dissatisfaction, discomfort or worry in regard to himself and his relations with others." Most items drawn from Wright and Remmers scale.

Validity: Correlation with Daily Activities List = .50 ($p < .05$).

Author: Stanfiel, J., et al.

Article: A daily activities list and its relation to measures of adjustment and early environment.

Journal: *Psychological Reports,* June 1971, *28*(3), 691–699.

Related Research: Wright, G., & Remmers, H. (1960). *Manual for the Handicap Problems Inventory.* Lafayette, IN: University Book Store.

420

Test Name: PRAGMATIC CLASSIFICATION OF DEPRESSION SCALE

Purpose: To classify depressive patients.

Number of Items: 57

Format: Each item (rated on 1–4 scale) associated with a specific trait, based on patient interview.

Reliability: Interrater reliability = .78.

Validity: Found four factors.

Author: Vath, R., et al.

Article: Attempted validation of a "Pragmatic Classification of Depression."

Journal: *Psychological Reports,* February 1972, *30*(1), 287–290.

• • •

421

Test Name: PROCESS-REACTIVE SCALE

Purpose: To measure psychological adjustment.

Validity: Low correlations with various attention measures.

Author: Haley, G.

Article: Relations among chronicity, diagnosis, pre-morbid adjustment, defensiveness and two measures of preceptual scanning.

Journal: *Perceptual and Motor Skills,* December 1971. *33*(13), 1163–1170.

Related Research: Ullman, L., & Giovannoni, J. (1964). The development of a self-report measure of the process-reactive continiuum. *Journal of Nervous and Mental Disease, 138,* 38–42.

• • •

422

Test Name: Q-ADJUSTMENT SCORE

Purpose: To provide an external criterion of adjustment level.

Format: A Q-sort whereby the subject chooses from among a set of cards those most descriptive to him, those least descriptive, and those about which he is indifferent. The subject's distribution is compared to the "ideal" well-adjusted person to provide the adjustment score.

Author: Garfield, S. V., et al.

Article: Effects of group counseling on creativity.

Journal: *Journal of Educational Research,* January 1971, *64*(5), 235–237.

Related Research: Rogers, C. R., & Dymond, R. F. (Eds.). (1954). *Psychotherapy and personality changes Coordinated studies in the client-centered approach.* Chicago: University of Chicago Press.

• • •

423

Test Name: SCALE OF PSYCHOSOMATIC SYMPTOMS OF STRESS

Purpose: To obtain a "global psychiatric rating."

Number of Items: 22

Format: Scored *well* (three or less symptoms) or *impaired* (four or more symptoms); interview format.

Author: Yancey, W., et al.

Article: Social position and self evaluation: The relative importance of race.

Journal: *American Journal of Sociology,* September 1972, *78*(2), 338–359.

Related Research: Langner, T. (1962). A twenty-two item screening score of psychiatric symptoms indicating impairment.

Journal of Health and Human Behavior, 3, 269–276.

■ ■ ■

424

Test Name: SROLE ANOMIA SCALE

Purpose: To assess a feeling of meaninglessness.

Format: Subject responds to statements on scale: *strongly agree* to *strongly disagree* (5 points).

Validity: Item-total correlations ranged .85–.98.

Author: Bolton, C.

Article: Alienation and action: A study of peace group members.

Journal: *American Journal of Sociology,* November 1972, *78*(3), 537–561.

Related Research: Srole, L. (1956). Social integration and certain corolaries: An exploratory study. *American Sociological Review, 21,* 709–16.

■ ■ ■

425

Test Name: SYMPTOM CHECKLIST

Purpose: To assess preschool childrens' functioning.

Number of Items: 58

Format: Teacher rating: includes list of major symptoms of clinical disturbance found in preschool children.

Reliability: Spearman-Brown was .73 for both sets of factors.

Validity: Correlation between two factors on Social Competence Scale = .75, .79.

Author: Kohn, M., and Rosman, B.

Article: Social competence scale and symptom checklist for the preschool child: Factor dimensions, their cross instrument generalization, and longitudinal persistance.

Journal: *Developmental Psychology,* May 1972, *6*(3), 430–444.

CHAPTER 4
Adjustment—Social

426

Test Name: ABRIDGED BYRNE ATTRACTION SCALE

Purpose: To measure interpersonal attraction.

Number of Items: 3

Format: Subject responds on a 7-point scale to such questions as, "How well do you think you would like this person?"

Author: Hogan, R., et al.

Article: An extension of the similarity–attraction hypothesis to the study of vocational behavior.

Journal: *Journal of Counseling Psychology,* May 1972, *19*(3), 238–240.

Related Research: Byrne, D. (1961). Interpersonal attraction and attitude similarity. *Journal of Abnormal and Social Psychology, 62,* 713–715.

· · ·

427

Test Name: ADAPTATION OF BALES INTERACTION ANALYSIS

Purpose: To assess counselor and counselee behavior.

Time Required: 35 minute spans per interview.

Format: Adapted original 12 categories: for example Positive Reactions: Leading behavior (clients), and directed behavior (therapists).

Reliability: Fourth and eleventh interview chosen and analyzed a second time. Chi square used to establish reliability between two

interviews; nonsignificant difference was interpreted to indicate no change in behavior.

Validity: Significant differences were found in directive behavior between impulsive and constricted counselors.

Author: Smith, W., and Martinson, W.

Article: Counselor's and Counselee's learning style on interview behavior.

Journal: *Journal of Counseling Psychology,* March 1971, *18*(2), 138–141.

Related Research: Bales, R. F. (1951). *Interaction process analysis: A method for the study of small groups.* Cambridge, MA: Addison-Wesley Press.

· · ·

428

Test Name: AFFECTIVE SENSITIVITY MEASURE

Purpose: To assess interpersonal sensitivity.

Number of Items: 41 scenes involving 11 clients and counselors.

Format: Videotape situational test: Following each scene the subject answers several multiple-choice items describing the affective state of the client.

Validity: Significant increases pre to post, a T-Group laboratory experience.

Author: Danish, S., and Kagan, N.

Article: Measurement of affective sensitivity: Toward a valid

measure of interpersonal perception.

Journal: *Journal of Counseling Psychology,* 1971, *18*(1), 51–54.

Related Research: Campbell, R. C. (1967). *Development and validation of a multiple-choice scale to measure affective sensitivity (empathy).* Unpublished doctoral dissertation, Michigan State University.

Kagan, N., et al. (1967). *Studies in human interaction: Inter-personal process recall stimulated by videotape.* Ann Arbor: Michigan State University, Educational Publication Services.

· · ·

429

Test Name: AFFECTIVE SENSITIVITY SCALE FORM C

Purpose: To measure the ability to detect the immediate affective response of another person.

Time Required: 1 hour.

Format: By means of videotape.

Validity: Correlation between pre–post change score and the initial affective sensitivity scores ranged .18 to .36 under four different conditions.

Author: Danish, S.

Article: Factors influencing changes in empathy following a group experience.

Journal: *Journal of Counseling Psychology,* May 1971, *18*(3), 262–267.

Related Research: Kagan, N., et al. (1968). *The affective sensitivity* *scale.* Unpublished manuscript, Michigan State University.

■ ■ ■

430

Test Name: ALIENATION AND SELF-ESTRANGEMENT QUESTIONNAIRE

Purpose: To identify alienating conditions and feelings of self-estrangement among white-collar workers.

Number of Items: 57

Format: Subject responds to a series of statements by circling the response that most accurately describes the objective features of his or her job. Subject indicates whether certain features are present *all of the time, most of the time, part of the time,* or *never.* One or more statements were given for each alienating condition.

Author: Kirsch, B. A., and Lengermann, J. J.

Article: An empirical test of Robert Blauner's ideas on alienation in work as applied to different type jobs in a white-collar setting.

Journal: *Sociology and Social Research,* January 1972, *56*(2), 180–194.

Related Research: Blauner, R. *Alienation and freedom.* Chicago: University of Chicago Press, 1964.

■ ■ ■

431

Test Name: BARRETT-LENNARD RELATIONSHIP INVENTORY

Purpose: To assess perception of an interpersonal relationship.

Format: Developed to measure four relationship conditions: level of regard, congruence, unconditional positive regard, empathic understanding.

Reliability: Internal consistency = .82–.95. Stability = .93–.95.

Author: Lanning, W.

Article: A study of the relationship between groups and individual counseling supervision and three relationship measures.

Journal: *Journal of Counseling Psychology,* September 1971, *18*(5), 401–406.

Related Research: Barrett-Lennard, G. (1962). Dimensions of therapists' responses as causal factors in therapeutic change. *Psychological Monographs, 76,* 21–44.

■ ■ ■

432

Test Name: BEHAVIORAL INVENTORY OF INTERPERSONAL SKILLS

Purpose: To assess the amount of competency behavior, relatedness behavior, and innovative and facilitative behaviors demonstrated by a person in social interactions.

Format: Includes two parts: Part I is the subject's self-rating and Part II is used by raters other than the subjects.

Author: Thorman, J. H.

Article: Relative effectiveness of four methods of training prospective teachers in interpersonal skills.

Journal: *Journal of Educational Research,* September 1971, *65*(1), 19–22.

■ ■ ■

433

Test Name: BIERI COGNITIVE COMPLEXITY–SIMPLICITY SCALE

Purpose: To assess information processing style as it relates to interpersonal perception.

Format: Self-rating paper-and-pencil instrument.

Validity: Correlation with years of counseling experience = .38 (*p* < .05).

Author: Baldwin, B.

Article: Change in interpersonal cognitive complexity as a function of training group experience.

Journal: *Psychological Reports,* June 1972, *30*(3), 935–940.

Related Research: Bieri, J., et al. (1966). *Clinical and social judgment: The discrimination of behavioral information.* New York: Wiley.

■ ■ ■

434

Test Name: CHILDREN'S SELF-SOCIAL CONSTRUCT TEST

Purpose: To measure self-esteem, social dependency, identification with and preference for mother, father, teacher, and friend; realism as to size; and minority identification.

Format: An individually administered, paper-and-pencil, nonverbal instrument with all directions oral and all responses nonverbal.

Reliability: Esteem: split-half corrected for length, $r = .65$. Social dependency: split-half corrected for length, $r = .65$. Identification: split-half corrected for length, $rs = .64$ to .83. Realism: split-half corrected for length, $r = .71$.

Validity: With IQ, rs ranged from .17 to .21.

Author: Henderson, E. H., and Long, B. H.

Article: Personal-social correlates of academic success among disadvantaged school beginners.

Journal: *Journal of School Psychology,* 1971, *9*(2), 101–113.

Related Research: Richards, H. C., & McCandless, B. R. (1972). Socialization dimensions among five-year-old slum children. *Journal of Educational Psychology,* February, *63*(1), 44–55.

■ ■ ■

435

Test Name: CHILDREN'S SOCIAL DESIRABILITY SCALE

Purpose: To assess social desirability in grade school.

Format: Orally and individually administered.

Reliability: .43 for boys; .19 for girls.

Author: Allaman, J. D., et al.

Article: The antecedents of social desirability response tendencies of children and young adults.

Journal: *Child Development,* December 1972, *43*(4), 1135–1160.

Related Research: Crandall, V. C., et al. (1965). A children's social desirability questionnaire. *Journal of Consulting Psychology, 29,* 27–36.

■ ■ ■

436

Test Name: COMFORTABLE INTERPERSONAL DISTANCE SCALE

Purpose: To measure "comfortable" distance at which a subject would place a stimulus person.

Format: Paper and pencil; distances measured in mm.

Author: Nowicki, S., and Duke, M.

Article: Use of comfortable interpersonal distance scale in high school students: Replication.

Journal: *Psychological Reports,* February 1972, *30*(1), 182.

437

Test Name: DEAN'S ALIENATION SCALE

Purpose: To measure alienation.

Number of Items: 24

Format: Includes three subscales: powerlessness, normlessness, and social isolation. Employs a 5-point Likert scale ranging from 1 (*strongly agree*) to 5 (*strongly disagree*).

Validity: Correlations with achievement ranged from .16 to .21.

Author: Pulvino, C., and Mickelson, D.

Article: Alienated feelings of normlessness and discrepant academic achievement.

Journal: *Journal of Educational Research,* January 1972, *65*(5), 216–218.

Related Research: Dean, D. G. (1961). Alienation, its meaning and measurement. *American Sociological Review, 26,* 753–758.

Pulvino, C. J., & Hansen, J. C. (1972). Relevance of "needs" and press to anxiety, alienation, and GPA. *Journal of Experimental Education,* Spring, *40*(3), 70–75.

Burbach, H., & Thompson, M. (1971). Alienation among college freshmen: A comparison of Puerto Rican, Black and White students. *Journal of College Student Personnel,* July, *12*(4), 248–252.

■ ■ ■

438

Test Name: EDWARDS SOCIAL DESIRABILITY SCALE

Purpose: To measure social desirability.

Reliability: Test–retest (2 weeks) *r* = .98.

Author: Bernhardson, C.

Article: Social desirability,

endorsement and judged frequency of occurrence on the items from four social desirability scales.

Journal: *Perceptual and Motor Skills,* December 1971, *33*(3), 1007–1012.

Related Research: Edwards, A. (1957). *The social desirability variable in personality assessment and research.* New York: Dryden.

■ ■ ■

439

Test Name: ENVY QUESTIONNAIRE

Purpose: To assess interpersonal envy.

Number of Items: 24

Format: Administered in groups of 4–6. Subjects are given 24 stories describing inequity for two individuals and are asked to report each individual's reaction.

Validity: When content and intensity of satisfaction were manipulated, changes in the level of envy occurred.

Author: Lieblich, A.

Article: Antecedents of envy reaction.

Journal: *Journal of Personality Assessment, 1971, 35*(1), 92–98.

■ ■ ■

440

Test Name: FELT FIGURE REPLACEMENT TECHNIQUE

Purpose: To assess social schemas.

Format: Subject is asked to first study the position of cut-out felt figures on a 9 x 6-ft rectangle of felt, then after they are removed, to replace them in the same position. The distance between the figures is measured.

Author: Berman, A.

Article: Social schemas: An

investigation of age and socialization variables.

Journal: *Psychological Reports,* April 1971, *28*(2), 343–348.

Related Research: Kuethe, J. (1962). Social schemas. *Journal of Abnormal and Social Psychology, 64,* 31–38.

● ● ●

441

Test Name: FORD SOCIAL DESIRABILITY SCALE

Purpose: To assess social desirability.

Validity: Correlation with College Expectation Questionnaire was nonsignificant.

Author: Waterman, A.

Article: Relationship between the psychosocial maturity of entering college freshmen and their expectations about college.

Journal: *Journal of Counseling Psychology,* January 1971, *19*(1), 42–46.

Related Research: Ford, L. (1964). A forced-choice acquiescence free social desireability (defensiveness) scale. *Journal of Consulting Psychology, 28,* 475.

● ● ●

442

Test Name: GENERAL ALIENATION SCALE

Purpose: To measure degree of feeling alienated.

Reliability: Hoyt reliability was .72.

Author: Biggs, D. A., et al.

Article: Parents of university students.

Journal: *Journal of College Student Personnel,* November 1972, *13*(6), 538–545.

Related Research: Srole, L. (1956).

Social integration and certain corollaries: An explanatory study. *American Sociological Review, 21,* 709–716.

● ● ●

443

Test Name: GOULD MANIFEST ALIENATION MEASURE

Purpose: To assess individual differences in alienation.

Validity: Correlation with Niederhoffers Cynicism measure was .44 (*p* < .01).

Author: Zacker, J.

Article: Understanding one's clients: An attempt to improve sensitivity and morale in police recruits.

Journal: *Psychological Reports,* December 1972, *31*(3), 999–1008.

Related Research: Gould, L. (1964). *The alienation syndrome: Psychosocial correlates and behavioral consequences.* Unpublished doctoral dissertation, University of Connecticut.

● ● ●

444

Test Name: GROSSMAN INTERPERSONAL SENSITIVITY MEASURE

Purpose: To assess differences in sensitivity to individuals.

Format: Subjects are presented typescripts of interviews of individuals and are asked to predict how the individual would respond to a personality inventory.

Validity: Correlation with feeling identification measure = .29 (*p* < .05).

Author: Zacker, J.

Article: Understanding one's clients: An attempt to improve sensitivity and morale in police recruits.

Journal: *Psychological Reports,* December 1972, *31*(3), 999–1008.

Related Research: Grossman, B. (1967). Evaluation of a training program to improve the ability to differentiate between individuals. Doctoral dissertation, Michigan State University. *Dissertation Abstracts International, 28*(03A), 1127. (University Microfilms No. 67–10524).

● ● ●

445

Test Name: GROUP CONFORMITY MEASURE

Purpose: To assess conformity of an individual to a simulated group majority.

Number of Items: 44 trials.

Format: Subjects are required to make perceptual judgments under various conditions of pressure to conform; requires apparatus.

Reliability: Kuder-Richardson Formula 20 under three levels of pressure were: .49, .54, .69, and .78 (total).

Author: Mock, R., and Tuddenham, R.

Article: Race and conformity among children.

Journal: *Developmental Psychology,* May 1971, *4*(3), 349–365.

● ● ●

446

Test Name: INTERPERSONAL COMPETENCY SCALE

Purpose: To poll the subjects for factors conducive to interpersonal competence.

Number of Items: 20

Author: Schmidt, M. R.

Article: Relationship between sorority membership and changes in selected personality variables and attitudes.

Journal: *Journal of College Student Personnel,* May 1971, *12*(3), 208–213.

Related Research: Foote, N. N., & Cottrell, L. S. (1955). *Identity and interpersonal competencies.* Chicago: University of Chicago Press.

■ ■ ■

447

Test Name: INTERPERSONAL INDEX

Purpose: To measure the individual's relationship to others and views of friendship.

Number of Items: 25

Format: One item is presented.

Reliability: Test–retest, .06, .17.

Author: Athanasiou, R.

Article: Selection and socialization: A study of engineering student attrition.

Journal: *Journal of Educational Psychology,* April 1971, *62*(2), 157–166.

■ ■ ■

448

Test Name: INTERPERSONAL INTERACTION ANALYSIS

Purpose: To analyze interpersonal interaction (between therapist and client).

Time Required: To train to reliability was 40 hours.

Format: Each communication unit is scored in terms of one or more of 16 interpersonal reflexes.

Reliability: Dittmann's R = .68; agreement = 75%.

Author: Crowder, J.

Article: Relationship between

therapist and client interpersonal behaviors and psychotherapy outcome.

Journal: *Journal of Counseling Psychology,* January 1972, *19*(1), 68–75.

Related Research: Freedman, M., et al. (1951). The interpersonal dimensions of personality. *Journal of Personality,* 20, 143–162.

■ ■ ■

449

Test Name: MARLOWE-CROWNE SOCIAL DESIRABILITY SCALE

Purpose: To assess need for social approval; that is, whether the subject attempts to place himself or herself in a socially approved manner.

Number of Items: 33

Format: True–false.

Validity: Correlation with Shimkunas Uncertainty Anxiety Scale was .30, ($p < .01$).

Author: Daster, J., and Slaymaker, J.

Article: Need approval, uncertainty anxiety, and expectancies of interview behavior.

Journal: *Journal of Counseling Psychology,* November 1972, *19*(6), 522–528.

Related Research: Crowne, D., & Marlowe, D. (1964). *The approval motive: Studies in evaluative dependence.* New York: Wiley.

Bernhardson, C. (1971). Social desirability endorsement and judged frequency of occurrence on the items from four social desirability scales. *Perceptual and Motor Skills,* December, *33*(3), 1007–1012.

See *D.U.E.M.M. 1*, 1974: 30–31, 35.

450

Test Name: MARLOWE-CROWNE SOCIAL DESIRABILITY TEST—ADAPTED

Purpose: To measure subjects' need for approval.

Number of Items: 10

Format: Consists of Items 2, 3, 4, 6, 9, 10, 14, 15, 19, and 31 of the Marlowe-Crowne Social Desirability Test.

Reliability: Split-half coefficient of .479.

Author: Turner, C.

Article: Effects of race of tester and need for approval on children's learning.

Journal: *Journal of Educational Psychology,* June 1971, *62*(3), 240–244.

Related Research: Marlowe, D., & Crowne, D. (1960). New scale of social desirability. *Journal of Consulting Psychology, 24,* 349–354.

■ ■ ■

451

Test Name: MOTTOLA HISTORY OF INTERPERSONAL DISTANCE SCALE

Purpose: To assess the reported closeness–distance of subject to significant others in history.

Number of Items: 18

Format: Forced-choice with five alternatives.

Validity: Correlation of father and sons scores = .03 (*ns*). Correlation of mother and daughter scores = .01 (*ns*).

Author: Tolor, A., et al.

Article: Relation between parental interpersonal styles and their children's psychological distance.

Journal: *Psychological Reports,*

December 1971, *29*(3), 1263–1275.

Related Research: Mottola, W. (1969). *History of interpersonal distance: A new dimension of personality.* Paper presented at the meeting of the Southeastern Psychological Association, New Orleans.

■ ■ ■

452

Test Name: NEGRO-WHITE STUDENT FRIENDSHIP QUESTIONNAIRE

Purpose: To measure the development of friendships between Negro and White students.

Number of Items: 6

Format: Each question is answered on a 4-point scale by circling one of the following responses: *many* (1), *some* (2), *not very many* (3), *none* (4). All six items are presented.

Author: Sachdeva, D.

Article: Friendships among students in desegrated schools.

Journal: *California Journal of Educational Research,* January 1972, *23*(1), 45–51.

■ ■ ■

453

Test Name: NETTLER'S ALIENATION SCALE

Purpose: To assess extent of perceived isolation.

Number of Items: 17

Validity: Total score correlations for 17 items ranged from .26 to .90.

Author: Bolton, C.

Article: Alienation and action: A study of peace group members.

Journal: *American Journal of Sociology,* November 1972, *78*(3), 537–561.

454

Test Name: NORMLESSNESS SCALE

Purpose: To measure alienation from norms of American society.

Number of Items: 6

Validity: Item total correlations for six items: .65, .64, .68, .47, .74, .67.

Author: Bolton, C.

Article: Alienation and action: A study of peace group members.

Journal: *American Journal of Sociology,* November 1972, *78*(3), 537–561.

Related Research: Seeman, M. (1959). On the meaning of alienation. *American Sociological Review, 24,* 783–791.

■ ■ ■

455

Test Name: PUPIL ATTITUDE QUESTIONNAIRE

Purpose: To assess various dimensions of student alienation.

Number of Items: 60

Format: Likert items in five subtests with each subtest measuring one of Seaman's five alienation components. Responses are made on a 5-point scale from *strongly agree* to *strongly disagree.*

Author: Hartley, M. C., and Hoy, W. K.

Article: "Openness" of school climate and alienation of high school students.

Journal: *California Journal of Educational Research,* January 1972, *23*(1), 17–24.

Related Research: Kolesar, H. (1967). *An empirical study of client alienation in the bureaucratic organization.* Unpublished doctoral dissertation,

University of Alberta, Edmonton, Canada.

■ ■ ■

456

Test Name: RUSSELL SAGE SOCIAL RELATIONS TEST

Purpose: To evaluate the nature and quality of elementary school children's skill in cooperative group planning and group action.

Format: Test material consists of a construction problem involving 36 interlocking blocks of two shapes and three colors. Administration requires an examiner and an observer.

Author: Vogel, F. X., and Bowers, N. D.

Article: Pupil behavior in a multi-age nongraded school.

Journal: *Journal of Experimental Education,* Winter 1972, *41*(2), 78–86.

Related Research: Damrin, D. C. (1969). The Russell Sage Social Relations Test: A technique for measuring group problem solving skills in elementary school children. *Journal of Experimental Education, 38*(1), 72–73.

■ ■ ■

457

Test Name: SELF-ESTRANGEMENT SCALE

Purpose: To measure self-estrangement.

Number of Items: 9

Format: Likert items. Respondents respond in terms of their own feelings about their jobs.

Reliability: Cronbach alpha is .92.

Validity: Item to total scale correlations ranged from .64 to .85.

Author: Kirsch, B. A., and Lengermann, J. J.

Article: An empirical test of Robert

Blauner's ideas on alienation in work as applied to different type jobs in a white-collar setting.

Journal: *Sociology and Social Research,* January 1972, *56*(2), 180–194.

458

Test Name: SELF-PERCEIVED POPULARITY MEASURE

Purpose: To assess how children perceive their popularity with a peer group.

Format: Subjects wrote down names of all children they thought would choose them as preferred classmate.

Validity: High self-esteem children (by Coopersmith's Inventory) were significantly different in popularity index than low self-esteem children.

Author: Simon, W.

Article: Some sociometric evidence for validity of Coopersmith's self-esteem inventory.

Journal: *Perceptual and Motor Skills,* February 1972, *34*(1), 93–94.

■ ■ ■

459

Test Name: SOCIAL COMPETENCE SCALE

Purpose: To assess preschool children's functioning.

Number of Items: 90

Format: Teacher rating; Items rated on 7-point frequency scale: Two major factors. I: use of opportunity in the classroom. II: conforming to rules of a classroom.

Reliability: Interrater correlation = .62 (Factor I), .66 (Factor II).

Validity: For Factors I and II, correlations with the same factors on the symptom checklist were .75 and .79.

Author: Kohn, M., and Rosman, B.

Article: A social competence scale and symptom checklist for the preschool child: Factor dimensions, their cross instrument generalization, and longitudinal persistence.

Journal: *Developmental Psychology,* May 1972, *6*(3), 430–444.

■ ■ ■

460

Test Name: SOCIAL DIFFUSION QUESTIONNAIRE

Purpose: To measure the extent of social diffusion along the three dimensions of liking, school competence, and social power.

Number of Items: 6

Format: First three items require selection of others along the dimensions of liking, school competence, and social power. The last three items ask the student to indicate those who he or she thought had selected him or her.

Validity: Item correlations with class size range from .02 to .76.

Author: O'Reilly, R. P., and Illenberg, G. J.

Article: Relationship of classroom grouping practices to diffusion of students' sociometric choices and diffusion of students' perception of sociometric choice.

Journal: *California Journal of Educational Research,* May 1971, *22*(3), 104–114.

■ ■ ■

461

Test Name: SOCIAL ROLES INSTRUMENT

Purpose: To provide a frequency count on the extent to which each child is perceived by classmates as being "good at" the 18 social roles.

Number of Items: 18

Format: The subject writes under each item the names of others in the class whom he or she considers to be "one of the best" in this particular kind of group functioning.

Author: Bonney, M. E.

Article: Assessment of efforts to aid socially isolated elementary school pupils.

Journal: *Journal of Educational Research,* April 1971, *64*(8), 359–364.

■ ■ ■

462

Test Name: SOCIAL WELFARE CONCERN SCALE

Purpose: To measure a dimension of social responsibility.

Number of Items: 22

Format: Items rated on 4-point Likert scales.

Reliability: Kuder-Richardson Formula 20 = .78 to .82.

Author: Mueller, D. J.

Article: A technique for the utilization of items with highly skewed response distributions in personality scaling.

Journal: *Journal of Experimental Education,* Summer 1972, *40*(4), 62–64.

Related Research: Mueller, D. J. (1969). *Differences in social responsibility among various groups of college students.* Unpublished doctoral dissertation, University of Illinois.

■ ■ ■

463

Test Name: STANFORD PARENT QUESTIONNAIRE

Purpose: To classify delinquent girls as either social or individual delinquents.

Format: A checklist that included material taken from social history data, institutional behavior reports, a psychiatric interview, and the Minnesota Counseling Inventory.

Reliability: Interjudge reliability was .86.

Author: Duncan, P.

Article: Parental attitudes and interactions in delinquency.

Journal: *Child Development,* December 1971, *42*(6), 1751–1765.

Related Research: Duncan, P. (1968). *Parental attitudes and interactions in delinquency.* Unpublished doctoral dissertation, University of Wisconsin.

Winder, C. L., & Rau, L. (1962). Parental attitudes associated with social deviance in preadolescent boys. *Journal of Abnormal and Social Psychology, 64,* 418–424.

● ● ●

464

Test Name: SYRACUSE SCALES OF SOCIAL RELATIONS— REVISED

Purpose: To assess pupils' interpersonal relationships within the classroom.

Format: Each pupil is scored in terms of the average rating he or she made of other same- and opposite-sex pupils and the average rating received from other same-sex and opposite-sex pupils on a need succorance criterion.

Author: Glick, O.

Article: Some social–emotional consequences of early inadequate acquisition of reading skills.

Journal: *Journal of Educational Psychology,* June 1972, *63*(3), 253–257.

Related Research: de Jung, J., & Haring, N. (1962). *The measurement of social relations of mentally retarded and young elementary school children using a modification of the Syracuse Scales of Social Relations* (mimeo). University of Kansas, School of Education.

● ● ●

465

Test Name: UNIVERSITY ALIENATION SCALE

Purpose: To measure the student's feeling of alienation from the university.

Number of Items: 7

Format: Likert scale. Examples are presented.

Reliability: Test–retest correlation was .92.

Author: Vaughan, C. E.

Article: The relationship between student alienation and participation in extracurricular activities.

Journal: *Journal of College Student Personnel,* January 1971, *13*(1), 31–38.

Related Research: Vaughan, C. E. (1968). *An empirical study of the relationship between participation in university extracurricular activities and student alienation.* Unpublished doctoral dissertation, University of Minnesota.

● ● ●

466

Test Name: ZIEGLER SOCIAL DEPRIVATION SCALE

Purpose: To assess social history with respect to social deprivation.

Format: Yields 13 indexes and four orthogonal factors: (a) continuity of residence, (b) parent attitude, (c) familial richness, (d) familial harmony. Two other scores are obtained: overall subjective score, overall objective score. Rater used the scales.

Validity: For retarded subjects: For Vacation with Parents and Subjective score, $r = .55$ ($p < .001$); Objective score, $r = .47$ ($p < .01$); Continuity score, $r = .30$ ($p < .05$); Harmony score, $r = .48$ ($p < .01$).

Author: Ziegler, E., and Balla, D.

Article: Developmental course of responsiveness to social reinforcement in normal children and institutionalized retarded children.

Journal: *Developmental Psychology,* January 1972, *6*(1), 66–73.

Related Research: Ziegler, E., et al. (1966). A measure of pre-institutional social deprivation for institutionalized retardates. *American Journal of Mental Deficiency, 70,* 873–885.

...
CHAPTER 5
Aptitude

467

Test Name: ACADEMIC ACHIEVEMENT ACCOUNTABILITY QUESTIONNAIRE

Purpose: To assess internal versus external control as it relates to school performance. To predict achievement.

Number of Items: 15

Format: Student answers *yes* or *no* to each question.

Reliability: Estimated Kuder-Richardson Formula 20 coefficients of .66 and .67.

Validity: .43 with IQ and .43 with total performance.

Author: Clifford, M. M., and Cleary, T. A.

Article: The relationship between children's academic performance and achievement accountability.

Journal: *Child Development*, June 1972, *43*(2), 647–655.

...

468

Test Name: CULTURE FAIR INTELLIGENCE TEST

Purpose: To measure intelligence.

Author: Barton, K., et al.

Article: Personality and IQ measures as predictors of school achievement.

Journal: *Journal of Educational Psychology*, August 1972, *63*(4), 398–404.

Related Research: Correlations with personality measures may be obtained by ordering document

NAPS01794 from ASIS National Auxiliary Publications Service, c/o CCM-Information Corporation, 866 Third Avenue, New York, NY 10022.

...

469

Test Name: GESELL SCHOOL READINESS TESTS

Purpose: To predict first-grade achievement.

Time Required: 20 minutes.

Format: Predominantly perceptual-motor. Includes five subtests that have been divided into 11 tasks.

Reliability: .84.

Validity: Correlates .50 with Lorge-Thorndike IQ and .61 with MA, also .64 with the Stanford Achievement Tests.

Author: Kaufman, A. S., and Kaufman, N. L.

Article: Tests built from Piaget's and Gesell's tasks as predictors of first-grade achievement.

Journal: *Child Development*, June 1972, *43*(2), 521–535.

Related Research: Ilg, F. L., & Ames, L. B. (1965). *School readiness*. New York: Harper & Row.

...

470

Test Name: GRIBBONS-LOHNES READINESS FOR VOCATIONAL PLANNING

Purpose: To assess dimensions of readiness for vocational planning.

Number of Items: 22

Format: Factors in curriculum choice, occupational choice, verbalized strengths and weaknesses, accuracy of self-appraisal, evidence for self-rating, interests, values, and independence of choice; a questionnaire answered in an interview with a counselor; responses rated 0–2.

Author: Ansell, E. H., and Hansen, J.

Article: Patterns in vocational development in urban youth.

Journal: *Journal of Counseling Psychology*, November 1971, *18*(6), 505–508.

Related Research: Gribbons, W., & Lohnes, P. (1967). Predicting five years of development in adolescents from readiness for Vocational Planning Scales, *Journal of Educational Psychology, 56,* 244–253.

...

471

Test Name: INTERVIEW SCHEDULE FOR PREDICTING HIGH SCHOOL GRADES

Purpose: To act as a selection device to predict academic performance.

Number of Items: 14

Format: Individual is rated on a 9-point scale (A to F) after he or she responds to each question (e.g., "Do you ever use a library? How often? Why?").

Reliability: Interrater reliability was .80.

Validity: Correlation with previous grade point average = .48.

Author: Asher, J., et al.

Article: Interview as a predictor of high school grades.

Journal: *Psychological Reports,* April 1972, *30*(2), 588.

■ ■ ■

472

Test Name: INVENTORY OF SELF-APPRAISAL

Purpose: To identify the multiple correlates of academic achievement and nonachievement among junior and senior high school students.

Number of Items: 150

Format: The items are divided into six subgroups: authority relationships, peer relationships, moral and social values, school related experiences and aspirations, self-concept, and interest patterns. A separate form with identical items is available for Mexican-Americans.

Author: Hall, L. H.

Article: Personality variables of achieving and nonachieving Mexican-American and other community college freshmen.

Journal: *Journal of Educational Research,* January 1972, *65*(5), 224–228.

■ ■ ■

473

Test Name: LEARNING ENVIRONMENT INVENTORY

Purpose: To predict achievement in the high school curriculum.

Number of Items: 105

Format: Includes 15 scales. Each item within the scales is descriptive of high school classes.

Respondents express agreement or disagreement with each item on a 4-point scale.

Reliability: Alpha reliabilities range from .50 to .80.

Validity: Correlations with school courses from .90 to +.93. Correlations with IQ from .62 to +.90.

Author: Walberg, H. J., and Anderson, G. J.

Article: Properties of the achieving urban classes.

Journal: *Journal of Educational Psychology,* August 1972, *63*(4), 381–385.

Related Research: Walberg, H. J. (1969). Social environment as a mediator of learning. *Journal of Educational Psychology, 60,* 443–448.

■ ■ ■

474

Test Name: PIAGET BATTERY

Purpose: To predict first-grade achievement.

Time Required: 20–25 minutes.

Format: Includes items from the areas of number, logic, space, and geometry.

Reliability: .80

Validity: Correlates .55 with Lorge-Thorndike and .62 with MA; also .64 with the Stanford Achievement Tests.

Author: Kaufman, A. S., and Kaufman, N. L.

Article: Tests built from Piaget's and Gesell's tasks as predictors of first-grade achievement.

Journal: *Child Development,* June 1972, *43*(2), 521–535.

Related Research: Piaget, J. (1965). *The child's conception of number.* New York: Norton.

Piaget, J., & Inhelder, B. (1967).

The child's conception of space. New York: Norton.

Piaget, J., et al. (1964). *The child's conception of geometry.* New York: Harper & Row.

■ ■ ■

475

Test Name: PREDICTIVE INDEX TEST

Purpose: To identify possible reading failures.

Format: Contains nine subtests.

Author: Weintraub, S., et al.

Article: Summary of investigations relating to reading.

Journal: *Reading Research Quarterly,* Winter 1971, *6*(2), 249–250.

Related Research: Trimble, A. C. (1970). Can remedial reading be eliminated? *Academic Therapy, 5,* 207–213.

■ ■ ■

476

Test Name: SCHOOL DROP OUT PREDICTION SCALE

Purpose: To discriminate between Appalachian students who will and those who will not drop out of school.

Number of Items: 34

Format: Forced choice items selected on the basis of the research literature.

Validity: Retrospective differentiation between drop outs and seniors (significant chi square on 18 of 34 items).

Author: Smith, J. E., et al.

Article: Prediction of school drop outs in Appalachia: Validation of a drop out scale.

Journal: *Measurement and Evaluation in Guidance.* April 1971, *4*(1), 31–37.

477

Test Name: SHAPE-O BALL TEST

Purpose: To assess perceptual motor development and predict academic achievement.

Format: Subject inserts pieces into corresponding holes in ball.

Validity: Correlation with Frostig (Total) = .70 ($p < .01$). Correlation with teacher rating = .67.

Author: Thomas, J., et al.

Article: Investigation of the shape-o ball test as a perceptual-motor task for pre-schoolers.

Journal: *Perceptual and Motor Skills,* October 1972, *35*(2), 447–450.

Related Research: Thomas, J., & Chissom, B. (1972). Relationships as assessed by canonical correlation between perceptual-motor and intellectual abilities for pre-school and early elementary age children. *Journal of Motor Behavior, 4,* 23–29.

• • •

478

Test Name: TSAI NUMBER JOINING TEST

Purpose: To predict success of air cadets, pilot accidents, and auto driving skills—a test of serial discrimination reaction; in general a special aptitude test.

Number of Items: Either 50 or 100.

Time Required: 8 minutes.

Format: Subject required to join numbers.

Validity: Correlation with the Wechsler Adult Intelligence Scale Perf. IQ = .31 (*ns*); Verbal IQ, *r* = .00 (*ns*); Full Scale, *r* = .13 (*ns*); DAT Spelling, *r* = .65 ($p < .01$).

Verbal Reasoning, *r* = .61 ($p < .01$).

Author: Tsai, L., and Haines, R.

Article: Tsai number joining test scores correlated with college students' performance on WAIS and DAT.

Journal: *Perceptual and Motor Skills,* August 1971, *33*(1), 35–44.

Related Research: Tsai, L., & Newbold, J. (1970). Nature, reliability and administration of the TSAI number joining test. *Perceptual and Motor Skills, 31,* 3–9.

• • •

479

Test Name: VOCATIONAL (SPATIAL) APTITUDE TEST FOR RETARDED

Purpose: To measure vocational aptitude of retarded subjects; specifically to assess spatial ability that would be important to jobs such as packing materials, and so forth.

Number of Items: 32

Time Required: 20 minutes.

Format: Format recorded on tape; does not require reading ability. Questions evenly divided to general reasoning and spatial abilities.

Reliability: Split-half reliabilities uncorrected for two parts were .74 and .79.

Validity: Total score with WAIS *r* = .34. Total score with assembly task, *r* = .29. Total score with packing task, *r* = .33. Total score with folding and packing task, *r* = .38.

Author: Hartlage, L.

Article: Measuring spatial aptitudes of the retarded.

Journal: *Perceptual and Motor*

Skills, December 1971, *33*(3), 1107–1110.

• • •

480

Test Name: WASHINGTON PRE-COLLEGE (WPC) TESTING PROGRAM

Purpose: To predict college achievement of minority groups.

Format: An aptitude-achievement battery yielding 12 scores.

Validity: WPC used by itself and with high school grades to predict grade point average; correlation not reported.

Author: Jensema, C. J., and Lunneborg, C. E.

Article: A preliminary investigation of a special education program for minority group university students.

Journal: *Measurement and Evaluation in Guidance,* 1972, *5*(2), 326–331.

Related Research: Austin, M. (1969). *Revalidation of WPC predictor weights and predictor and course statistics* (Project 1068-11, mimeo). University of Washington, Bureau of Testing.

• • •

481

Test Name: WEBSTER DEVELOPMENTAL STATUS SCALE

Purpose: To identify selected attitudes held by college students.

Format: Identifies rebellious independence that includes impulsivity, openness to expression, anti-authoritarianism, independence, flexibility, nonconformity, tolerance for ambiguity, introspection, freedom from cynicism, impunitive attitudes. Scores range from 0 to 72 with a higher score indicating a greater degree of the factors listed.

Author: Lange, A. J.

Article: An analysis of Clark-Trow subtypes.

Journal: *Journal of College Student Personnel,* July 1972, *13*(4), 347–351.

Related Research: Webster, H. (1966). Some quantitative results. *Journal of Social Issues, 12*(4), 29–43.

482

Test Name:
WOODMANSEE-COOK
MULTIFACTOR RACIAL
ATTITUDE INVENTORY

Purpose: To assess racial attitude.

Author: Buys, C., and Bebeau, C.

Article: Prejudice, socio-economic status and public attitudes toward riots and demonstrations.

Journal: *Psychological Reports,* October 1971, *29*(2), 451–458.

Related Research: Woodmansee, J., & Cook, S. (1967). Dimensions of verbal racial attitudes: Their identification and measurement. *Journal of Personality and Social Psychology, 7,* 240–250.

CHAPTER 6
Attitudes

483

Test Name: AGREEMENT/
DISAGREEMENT TEST

Purpose: To explore the extent to which teachers agree with generalizations based on educational research results.

Number of Items: 34, four forms.

Format: Teachers mark whether they agree or disagree with each statement and then complete an open-ended sentence to explain the basis for their response. Some examples are presented.

Reliability: Test–retest reliability ranged from .79 to .95.

Author: Rumstein, R.

Article: Teachers' evaluation of research findings in educational psychology.

Journal: *California Journal of Educational Research,* March 1972, *23*(2), 71–82.

. . .

484

Test Name: ATTITUDE TOWARD CHANGE AND DISSENT INSTRUMENT

Purpose: To survey teacher, counselor, and principal attitudes toward change and dissent.

Number of Items: 40

Format: A 5-point Likert scale was used to indicate how desirable/undesirable each item was (e.g., peaceful demonstrations, establishment of Students for a Democratic Society chapters, etc.).

Author: Morgan, L., and Wicas, E.

Article: The short unhappy life of student dissent.

Journal: *Personnel and Guidance Journal,* September 1972, *51*(1), 33–38.

. . .

485

Test Name: ATTITUDE TOWARD CONTEMPORARY ISSUES QUESTIONNAIRE

Purpose: To assess attitude toward police authority, power, sexual behavior, religion, drug use.

Number of Items: 29

Format: Items rated on a 7-point Likert scale.

Author: Lerner, R., et al.

Article: Attitudes of adolescents and adults toward contemporary issues.

Journal: *Psychological Reports,* February 1971, *28*(1), 139–145.

. . .

486

Test Name: ATTITUDES TOWARD FRATERNITY ACTIVITIES QUESTIONNAIRE

Purpose: To measure attitudes toward selected activities of social fraternities.

Format: Includes three parts covering six factors. Samples are presented.

Author: Gordon, S. E.

Article: An instrument to measure attitudes toward selected fraternity activities.

Journal: *Journal of College*

Student Personnel, May 1972, *13*(3), 229–232.

. . .

487

Test Name: ATTITUDES TOWARD GRADING QUESTIONNAIRE

Purpose: To measure attitudes toward 3-point and 5-point grading systems.

Number of Items: 64

Format: Items were designed to reflect eight dimensions of concern: amount of feedback, motivation to work well, anxiety and pressure, encouraging creativity, true learning versus learning for grades, general evaluation, ease of entering graduate school, and fairness of the system.

Author: Goldstein, K. M., and Tilker, H. A.

Article: Attitudes toward A-B-C-D-F and Honors-Pass-Fail grading systems.

Journal: *Journal of Educational Research,* November 1971, *65*(3), 99–100.

. . .

488

Test Name: ATTITUDE TOWARD INSTRUCTIONAL TELEVISION SCALE

Purpose: To assess elementary teachers' attitudes toward instructional television.

Number of Items: 25

Format: Teachers replied to items on 5-point scales.

Validity: Four factors were found: teaching process, threat of instruction, problems in the use of instructional television, and learning process.

Author: Ayers, J.

Article: Elementary school teachers' attitudes toward instructional television.

Journal: *Journal of Experimental Education*, Fall 1972, *41*(1), 1–4.

■ ■ ■

489

Test Name: ATTITUDE TOWARD PSYCHIATRIC PATIENTS SCALE

Purpose: To assess attitude toward psychiatric patients.

Number of Items: 26

Format: Likert scale.

Author: Smyth, V., and Thomas, D.

Article: Effects of nursing training on attitudes toward psychiatric patients.

Journal: *Psychological Reports,* February 1971, *28*(1), 34.

Related Research: Pryer, M., et al. (1969). Attitude changes in psychiatric attendants following experience and training. *Mental Hygiene, 53,* 253–257.

■ ■ ■

490

Test Name: ATTITUDE TOWARD REARING ADOLESCENTS—Q SORT

Purpose: To rank behavior problems associated with parenting an adolescent.

Reliability: Test–retest (pre–post a course in adolescent psychology) = .93 (for ranking of the 50 items).

Author: Treichel, B., and Nance, D.

Article: Attitudes of young adults

toward rearing adolescents; test–retest.

Journal: *Psychological Reports,* August 1971, *29*(1), 111–114.

■ ■ ■

491

Test Name: ATTITUDE TOWARD SCHOOL SCALE

Purpose: To identify attitudes toward school.

Number of Items: 47

Format: The scale is scored for different degrees of positive and negative attitudes toward the school.

Reliability: Details on the test–retest reliability, internal consistency, and scoring procedures may be obtained from the author at North Texas State University.

Author: Bonney, M. E.

Article: Assessment of efforts to aid socially isolated elementary school pupils.

Journal: *Journal of Educational Research,* April 1971, *64*(8), 359–364.

■ ■ ■

492

Test Name: ATTITUDE TOWARD TEACHING QUESTIONNAIRE

Purpose: To assess teachers' attitude toward teaching.

Number of Items: 1

Format: Teachers are asked whether teaching today versus 5 years ago is *getting better, staying the same, getting worse, no opinion, not a teacher five years ago.*

Article: Teachers' view of teaching.

Journal: *NEA Research Bulletin,* December 1971, *49*(4), 102–103.

493

Test Name: ATTITUDE TOWARD TRADITIONAL/ NONTRADITIONAL VALUES SEMANTIC DIFFERENTIAL

Purpose: To assess extent of favorability toward tradition congruent and nontradition congruent concepts.

Number of Items: 16 concepts.

Format: Each concept rated on 14 seven-point bipolar semantic differential scales.

Author: Rappaport, J., et al.

Article: Fraternal and communal living: Values and behavior on the campus.

Journal: *Journal of Counseling Psychology,* July 1972, *19*(4), 296–300.

■ ■ ■

494

Test Name: ATTITUDES QUESTIONNAIRE

Purpose: To measure attitudes toward school, teacher, self, learning, and school last year.

Number of Items: 21

Format: A semantic differential that included six concepts and a 7-point scale. The 21 items are presented.

Author: Wilson, F. S., et al.

Article: Are pupils in the open plan school different?

Journal: *Journal of Educational Research,* November 1972, *66*(3), 115–118.

■ ■ ■

495

Test Name: BEHAVIORAL PROBLEMS INVENTORY AND TREATMENT SHEET

Purpose: To measure the attitudes and practices of elementary school student teachers toward behavioral problems of their pupils.

Number of Items: 59

Format: Includes 37 behavioral problems and the subject rates the seriousness of each as being high, medium, or low. Also included is a list of 22 treatments from which the subject selects treatment for each problem. Most of the items are presented.

Reliability: Split-half coefficient of .70.

Author: Dobson, R., et al.

Article: The effect of intensive human relations laboratory experiences upon student teacher perception and treatment of behavioral problems of elementary school children.

Journal: *Educational Leadership,* November 1971, *29*(2), 159–164.

Related Research: Dobson, R. L. (1966). *The perception and treatment by teachers of the behavioral problems of elementary school children in culturally deprived middle-class neighborhoods.* Unpublished doctoral dissertation, University of Oklahoma.

■ ■ ■

496

Test Name: CHILD BEHAVIOR INVENTORY

Purpose: To assess child-rearing attitudes.

Number of Items: 179

Format: Includes manifest rejection items, overprotection, achievement pressure items.

Reliability: Over 6 years for 3 scales reliability coefficients were .37, .19, and .43.

Author: Hurley, J., and Hohn, R.

Article: Shifts in child-rearing attitudes linked with parenthood and occupation.

Journal: *Developmental Psychology,* May 1971, *4*(3), 324–328.

Related Research: Hurley, J., & Laffey, J. (1957). Influence of a conventional child psychology course upon attitude toward children. *Collected papers of the Michigan Academy of Science, Arts & Letters, 42,* 299–306.

Mark, J. (1953). The attitudes of mothers of male schizophrenics toward child behavior. *Journal of Abnormal and Social Psychology, 48,* 185–190.

Shoben, E. (1949). Measurement of parental attitudes in relation to child adjustment. *Genetic Psychology Monographs, 39,* 101–148.

■ ■ ■

497

Test Name: CHILDREN'S ATTITUDINAL RANGE INDICATOR

Purpose: To assess the child's positive and negative attitudes toward peers, home, school, and society.

Number of Items: 32

Format: The items consist of eight picture-stories in each of the four areas of school, home, peers, and society. The cartoon figures are ambiguous to facilitate identification regardless of ethnic or racial backgrounds. Each item is scored from 1 to 3 to reflect *negative, neutral,* and *positive* attitudes. Examples are presented.

Reliability: Internal consistency (Cronbach's alpha) was .88 for total score and .66, .59, .68, .70 for subgroups. Test–retest reliability after 2 weeks was .65 for total score and .57, .45, .52, and .49 for subgroups.

Author: Cicirelli, V. G., et al.

Article: Measures of self-concept, attitudes, and achievement

motivation of primary grade children.

Journal: *Journal of School Psychology,* 1971, *9*(4), 383–392.

■ ■ ■

498

Test Name: CONTEMPORARY TOPICS QUESTIONNAIRE (CTQ)

Purpose: To assess attitudes toward current issues.

Author: Lerner, R., and Weinstock, A.

Article: Note on the generation gap.

Journal: *Psychological Reports,* October 1972, *31*(2), 457–458.

Related Research: Weinstock, A., & Lerner, R. (1972). Attitudes of late adolescents and their parents toward contemporary issues. *Psychological Reports, 30,* 239–244.

■ ■ ■

499

Test Name: COOPERSMITH SELF-ESTEEM INVENTORY

Purpose: To assess attitudes toward self.

Number of Items: 58

Format: Five factors were identified: self-rejection, parental approval, rejection by authority, lie scale, social and self-acceptance. The subject indicates whether or not each statement describes how he or she feels about himself or herself. All items are presented.

Validity: With Peer Ratings Semantic Differential, $r = .325$.

Author: Richmond, B. O., and White, W. F.

Article: Sociometric predictors of the self-concept among fifth and sixth grade children.

Journal: *Journal of Educational Research,* May–June 1971, *64*(9), 425–429.

Related Research: Coopersmith, S. (1967). *The antecedents of self-esteem.* San Francisco: Freeman.

■ ■ ■

500

Test Name: COUNSELING OUTCOME SEMANTIC DIFFERENTIAL

Purpose: To assess attitude toward concepts related to a treatment, "The General Relationship Improvement Program."

Number of Items: 6

Format: Concepts assessed were open expression of feelings, needing approval and acceptance, sensitivity to personal feelings, offering approval and acceptance, open expression is more important than rational understanding of feelings, sensitivity to feelings is more important than sensitivity to rational thinking.

Author: Kaul, T., and Parker, C.

Article: Suggestibility and expectancy in a counseling analogue.

Journal: *Journal of Counseling Psychology,* November 1971, *18*(6), 536–541.

■ ■ ■

501

Test Name: CURRICULUM ATTITUDE INVENTORY

Purpose: To discriminate between teachers with positive and negative attitudes toward curriculum use and planning.

Number of Items: 50

Format: Respondents decide whether they agree or disagree with each statement by indicating

the intensity of their decision on a 6-point scale.

Reliability: .54 and .66.

Author: Langenbach, M.

Article: Development of an instrument to measure teachers' attitudes toward curriculum use and planning.

Journal: *Journal of Educational Research,* September 1972, *66*(1), 35–38.

Availability: The inventory, manual, and scoring key may be obtained from Michael Langenbach, 820 Van Vleet Oval, College of Education, University of Oklahoma, Norman, OK 73069. Enclose $1.00 for handling.

■ ■ ■

502

Test Name: CURRICULUM-PEOPLE SEMANTIC DIFFERENTIAL SCALES

Purpose: To measure attitudes toward curriculum and people concepts.

Number of Items: 17 scales. All scales are presented.

Format: People concepts include nine 7-point, bipolar scales and the curriculum concepts include eight scales. Three people factors (movement, security, and merit) and two curriculum factors (vigor and certainty) were identified.

Author: Thomas, E. C., and Yamamoto, K.

Article: Minority children and their school-related perceptions.

Journal: *Journal of Experimental Education,* Fall 1971, *40*(1), 89–96.

Related Research: Yamamoto, K., et al. (1969). Dimensions of school-related attitudes in middle-school age students.

Psychology in the Schools, 6, 375–378.

■ ■ ■

503

Test Name: DATING-MARRIAGE SCALE

Purpose: To measure Jewish college students' attitudes toward dating and marrying members of other religions.

Format: Like a social distance scale, six categories: not date, marry if mate converts, marry if rear children as Jews, no requirement, Jew would convert. Attitudes ranged toward Reform and Conservative, Protestant and Catholic.

Author: Cavan, R.

Article: Jewish student attitudes toward interreligious and intra-Jewish marriage.

Journal: *American Journal of Sociology,* May 1971, *76*(6), 1064–1071.

■ ■ ■

504

Test Name: DREWS PARENTAL ATTITUDE SCALE

Purpose: To assess parent attitudes.

Format: Scales include possessing, ignoring, dominating attitudes.

Validity: Correlation of IQ and three scales, all nonsignificant.

Author: Willis, J.

Article: Parental attitudes and academic achievement in a sample of emotionally disturbed children.

Journal: *Psychological Reports,* December 1971, *29*(3), 866.

Related Research: Drews, E., & Teahan, J. (1957). Parental attitudes and academic achievement. *Journal of Clinical Psychology, 13,* 328–332.

505

Test Name: DRUG ABUSE ATTITUDE SCALE

Purpose: To measure opinions about issues related to drug abuse.

Number of Items: 14

Format: Multiple choice items that provide a single score based on seven items worded positively and seven worded negatively. Examples are presented.

Reliability: Split half coefficient, .84.

Validity: With Drug Knowledge Scale correlations of .17 and .40.

Author: Swisher, J. D., et al.

Article: Drug education: Pushing or preventing?

Journal: *Peabody Journal of Education,* October 1971, *49*(1), 68–75.

■ ■ ■

506

Test Name: DRUG ISSUES ATTITUDE SCALE

Purpose: To assess student attitude toward current issues regarding drugs.

Number of Items: 14

Reliability: Alpha reliability ranged .73 to .81.

Validity: Correlated .47 with reported drug use (11th graders).

Author: Swisher, J. D., et al.

Journal: *Journal of Counseling Psychology,* July 1972, *19*(4), 328–332.

■ ■ ■

507

Test Name: DRUG USE ATTITUDE QUESTIONNAIRE

Purpose: To elicit information about attitudes toward drug use, family, various national issues,

and other sociological, demographic, and academic information.

Number of Items: 119

Format: Short answer questions. Some items are presented.

Author: Chipman, D. A., & Parker, C. A.

Article: Characteristics of liberal arts college student marijuana users.

Journal: *Journal of College Student Personnel,* November 1972, *13*(6), 511–517.

■ ■ ■

508

Test Name: DUTTON ATTITUDE TEST

Purpose: To measure attitude toward mathematics.

Validity: Correlations with Sex = .02; Work status = .06; Class hours = .07; High school average = .08; Reading = .26; Sentences = .25; Mathematics = .07; Math Interest = .50; Credit hours in remedial math = .02; Grades in remedial math course = .07.

Author: Edwards, R. R.

Article: The prediction of success in remedial mathematics courses in the public community junior college.

Journal: *Journal of Educational Research,* December 1972, *66*(4), 157–160.

Related Research: Dutton, W. H. (1954). Measuring attitudes toward arithmetic. *The Elementary School Journal,* September, *55*, 22–31.

■ ■ ■

509

Test Name: FACULTY ROLES RATING SCALE

Purpose: To identify attitudes

toward faculty roles within the university.

Format: Includes brief descriptions of teaching, research, and character-building roles. Respondents rate each role on a 7-point continuum from 1 (*very important*) to 7 (*not important*).

Author: Kelly, R., and Hart, B. D.

Article: Role preferences of faculty in different age groups and academic disciplines.

Journal: *Sociology of Education,* Summer 1971, *44*(3), 351–357.

Related Research: Kelly, R., & Hart, B. D. (1969). Professor role preferences of entering college students and their parents. *Journal of Educational Research,* December, *63*, 150–151.

■ ■ ■

510

Test Name: FOREIGN POLICY ATTITUDE SCALE

Purpose: To assess attitude toward various foreign policies.

Number of Items: 9

Format: Items rated on a 5-point scale, *strongly agree* to *strongly disagree.*

Validity: Item total correlations on 4 items: .90, .94, .57, .63.

Author: Bolton, C.

Article: Alienation and action: A study of peace group members.

Journal: *American Journal of Sociology,* November 1972, *78*(3), 537–561.

■ ■ ■

511

Test Name: FOUR-YEAR TO TWO-YEAR COLLEGE STUDENT TRANSFER QUESTIONNAIRE

Purpose: To identify goals and attitudes of students transferring from four-year to two-year colleges.

Format: Includes items dealing with educational goals (past and present), vocational goals (past and present), the decision-making process of transfer students, and the transfer students' feelings about their 2-year and 4-year college experience.

Author: Kuznik, A.

Article: Reverse transfers: Students who transfer from four-year to two-year colleges.

Journal: *Journal of College Student Personnel*, September 1972, *13*(5), 425–428.

■ ■ ■

512

Test Name: GOUGH AND DI PALMA ATTITUDE MEASURE

Purpose: To measure attitude toward colonialism, political independence, and political dependence of underdeveloped countries.

Validity: *r* with Rokeach left and right opinionation scales .56 and .33.

Author: Alker, H.

Article: A quasi-paranoid feature of students' extreme attitudes against colonialism.

Journal: *Behavioral Science*, May 1971, *16*(3), 218–227.

Related Research: Gough, H., & di Palma, G. (1965). Attitudes toward colonialism, political dependence, and independence. *Journal of Psychology*, *60*(2), 155–163.

■ ■ ■

513

Test Name: GRADE CONTRACT ATTITUDE SCALE

Purpose: To measure attitude toward the grade contract system.

Number of Items: 14

Format: Items rated on a 6-point Likert scale from *strongly agree* through *neutral* to *strongly disagree* with a minimum score of 14 and a maximum score of 84. Each item is presented.

Author: Taylor, H.

Article: Student reaction to the grade contract.

Journal: *Journal of Educational Research*, March 1971, *64*(7), 311–314.

■ ■ ■

514

Test Name: HOMOPHOBIC SCALE

Purpose: To assess negative attitude toward homosexuals.

Number of Items: 24 total; nine comprised the Homophobia Scale.

Format: Homophobic scale composed of statements of opinion about homosexuals to which respondent answered *yes* or *no*.

Validity: Scores related to status consciousness and authoritarianism.

Author: Smith, K.

Article: Homophobia: A tentative personality profile.

Journal: *Psychological Reports*, December 1971, *29*(3), 1091–1094.

■ ■ ■

515

Test Name: I SCALE

Purpose: To assess a composite of attitudes—including feelings of inferiority, insecurity, and inadequacy as well as lack of confidence and loss of self-respect and self-esteem—as responses to unemployment and disablement.

Number of Items: 44

Format: The subject responds on a 5-point scale from *strongly agree*

through *uncertain* to *strongly disagree*.

Reliability: Split-half reliability was .81. Test–retest reliability was .81.

Validity: .41

Author: Hartmann, P.

Article: A study of attitudes in industrial rehabilitation.

Journal: *Occupational Psychology*, 1972, *46*(2), 87–97.

■ ■ ■

516

Test Name: IMAGINATIVE REACTIONS TO PICTURES TEST OF ATTITUDE TOWARD READING

Purpose: To assess attitudes toward reading by means of a projective test.

Number of Items: Nine pictures and 109 statements; subject responds *agree* or *disagree*.

Format: Pictures drawn to assess the influences of the home, peers, cultural values, and school on attitudes toward reading. Subject is shown picture and asked to make up a story telling how the story began, ended, and so forth.

Reliability: Five judges classified 194 statements as positive or negative attitudes on two occasions: 415 judges agreed on 165/194. Test–retest by judge over 4 weeks, *r* = .89.

Validity: Subjects were classified as high or low on an IQ and Reading Achievement test. Subjects were presented with pictures and asked to agree or disagree with positive and negative statements drawn from an earlier sample. Significant differences were found between high and low groups for all nine pictures.

Author: Lipsky, J. A.

Article: Students' imaginative

reactions to pictures: A means for studying their attitudes toward reading.

Journal: *Elementary School Guidance and Counseling,* May 1971, *5*(4), 266–272.

■ ■ ■

517

Test Name: INTERRACIAL ATTITUDES QUESTIONNAIRE

Purpose: To elicit responses that indicate existing interracial attitudes.

Number of Items: 22

Format: Subjects answer *yes* or *no* to each question by gridding their responses on IBM cards.

Author: Mastroianni, M., and Khatena, J.

Article: The attitudes of Black and White high school seniors toward integration.

Journal: *Sociology and Social Research,* January 1972, *56*(2), 221–227.

Related Research: Khatena, J. (1970). Relative integration of selected ethnic groups in Singapore. *Sociology and Social Research, 54,* 460–464.

■ ■ ■

518

Test Name: JOB RECRUITERS' EVALUATION OF MILITARY EXPERIENCE QUESTIONNAIRE

Purpose: To assess recruiters' attitude toward military experience as a factor in selection.

Author: Luthans, F., and Hodgetts, R.

Article: How do recruiters view military experience?

Journal: *Personnel Journal,* July 1971, *50*(7), 530–534.

519

Test Name: JUVENILE DELINQUENCY ATTITUDE SCALE

Purpose: To assess attitudes toward juvenile delinquency.

Number of Items: 23

Format: Respondents classified on an authoritarian-supportive dimension.

Reliability: Test–retest (6 months) was .782.

Author: Zelhart, P.

Article: RPM correlates of attitudes toward delinquency: Before and after contact with delinquents.

Journal: *Psychological Reports,* August 1971, *29*(1), 293–294.

Related Research: Alberts, W. (1963). Personality and attitude toward juvenile delinquency: A study of Protestant ministers. *Journal of Social Psychology, 60,* 71–83.

■ ■ ■

520

Test Name: KATZ & BRALY RACIAL STEREOTYPE INVENTORY

Purpose: To assess racial attitudes.

Number of Items: 84 adjectives.

Format: Subjects instructed to choose 5 adjectives to describe Whites, Blacks, and Japanese-Americans.

Author: Maykovich, M.

Article: Reciprocity in racial stereotypes: White, Black, and Yellow.

Journal: *American Journal of Sociology,* March 1971, *77*(5), 876–897.

Related Research: Katz, D., & Braly, K. (1933). Racial stereotypes of 100 college students.

Journal of Abnormal and Social Psychology, 28, 280–290.

■ ■ ■

521

Test Name: LEARNING AND KNOWLEDGE ATTITUDES QUESTIONNAIRE

Purpose: To identify attitudes about children's learning and knowledge.

Number of Items: 29

Format: Each item requires a response on a 5-point scale from *strongly agree* to *strongly disagree.* All items are presented.

Author: Barth, R. S.

Article: So you want to change to an open class-room.

Journal: *Phi Delta Kappan,* October 1971, *53*(2), 97–99.

Related Research: Barth, R. S. (1970). *Open education.* Unpublished doctoral dissertation, Harvard Graduate School of Education.

■ ■ ■

522

Test Name: MACDONALD'S POVERTY SCALE

Purpose: To assess attitudes toward the poor.

Format: Responses made to statements on a 10–point scale (*strongly agree* to *strongly disagree*).

Author: MacDonald, A., and Majumder, R.

Article: Do the poor know how we see them? Preliminary study.

Journal: *Perceptual and Motor Skills,* February 1972, *34*(1), 47–49.

Related Research: MacDonald, A. (1971). Relation of birth order to morality types and attitudes toward the poor. *Psychological Reports, 29*, 732.

■ ■ ■

523

Test Name: MANAGERIAL ATTITUDES SCALE

Purpose: To measure select managerial attitudes.

Number of Items: 30

Format: A Likert scale that includes 6 dimensions: staff, communication, peers, group processes, change, interpersonal conflict.

Author: Viano, E., and Wildeman, J.

Article: Organizational size and managerial attitudes of probation administrators.

Journal: *Sociology and Social Research,* July 1972, *56*(4), 480–493.

■ ■ ■

524

Test Name: MATHEMATICS ATTITUDE SCALE

Purpose: To measure attitude toward mathematics.

Number of Items: 20. A few of the items are presented.

Format: An opinionnaire that makes use of a 5-point Likert scale ranging from *strongly disagree* to *strongly agree.*

Reliability: Test–retest, *r* = .94.

Validity: Predictive validity-mathematics achievement = .67 (for male subjects), .63 (for female subjects).

Author: McCallon, E. L., and Brown, J. D.

Article: A semantic differential instrument for measuring attitude toward mathematics.

Journal: *Journal of Experimental Education,* Summer 1971, *39*(4), 69–72.

Related Research: Aiken, L. R., & Dreger, R. M. (1957). The identification of number anxiety in college populations. *Journal of Educational Research,* December, *68*, 344–351.

Aiken, L. R., & Dreger, R. M. (1961). The effects of attitude on performance in mathematics. *Journal of Educational Psychology, 52*, 19–24.

■ ■ ■

525

Test Name: MATHEMATICS SEMANTIC DIFFERENTIAL SCALES

Purpose: To measure attitude toward mathematics.

Number of Items: 15. All items are presented.

Format: Each item consisted of bipolar adjectives placed at opposite ends of a 7-point continuum.

Validity: Correlations with the Mathematics Attitude Scale: .87, .90.

Author: McCallon, E. L., and Brown, J. D.

Article: A semantic differential instrument for measuring attitude toward mathematics.

Journal: *Journal of Experimental Education,* Summer 1971, *39*(4), 69–72.

■ ■ ■

526

Test Name: McREYNOLDS SUCCESS FAILURE INVENTORY

Purpose: To measure attitude toward success and failure.

Number of Items: 22

Format: True–false.

Validity: Test significantly differentiated schizophrenics and alcoholics from normals.

Author: Page, R., and Ollendick, J.

Article: Cross-validation of the success-failure inventory.

Journal: *Psychological Reports,* February 1972, *30*(1), 165–166.

Related Research: McReynolds, P., & Guevara, C. (1967). Attitudes of schizophrenics and normals toward success and failure. *Journal of Abnormal and Social Psychology, 72*, 303–310.

Weinstein, D. (1972). Social desirability as related to the success-failure inventory. *Psychological Reports,* October, *31*(2), 674.

■ ■ ■

527

Test Name: MEICHENBAUM— INSTRUMENT TO ASSESS ATTITUDE TOWARD ACADEMIC FACTORS

Purpose: To assess attitude toward courses, instructors, curriculum, and own capabilities.

Number of Items: 30

Format: Included 30 attitude items plus report on school related behaviors, and prediction of final grade.

Author: Meichenbaum, D., & Smart, I.

Article: Use of direct expectancy to modify academic performance and attitudes of college students.

Journal: *Journal of Counseling Psychology,* November 1971, *18*(6), 531–535.

■ ■ ■

528

Test Name: NEGATIVE ADMINISTRATIVE STEREOTYPES QUESTIONNAIRE

Purpose: To ascertain the extent to which graduate students in educational administration hold negative attitudes toward school administrators.

Number of Items: 20

Format: Includes declarative statements to which the respondent indicates agreement or disagreement on a 5-point scale from 1 (*strong agreement*) to 5 (*strong disagreement*) with the stereotype. Examples are provided.

Reliability: Spearman-Brown coefficients of .86 and .88.

Author: Spencer, R. L., and Walters, D. L.

Article: A study of attitudes toward negative administrative stereotypes.

Journal: *Journal of Educational Research,* September 1971, *65*(1), 31–34.

■ ■ ■

529

Test Name: OLIVER & BUTCHER SURVEY OF OPINIONS ABOUT EDUCATION

Purpose: To measure attitude toward education.

Number of Items: 33

Format: Summating rating type items: Yields three scores: naturalism, radicalism, tendermindedness.

Reliability: Split-half reliabilities for the three scales were .69, .84, .86. Test–retest reliabilities for the three scales were .90, .87, and .88.

Validity: Correlations with Kerlinger's Educational Attitudes

Scale: Naturalism and Kerlinger Traditionalism = .624. Radicalism and Kerlinger Progressivism = .486. Tendermindedness and Kerlinger Traditionalism = .642.

Author: Sontag, M., and Pedhazur, E.

Article: Dimensions of educational

attitudes: Factorial congruence of two scales.

Journal: *Journal of Educational Measurement,* Fall 1972, *9*(3), 189–198.

Related Research: Oliver, R., & Butcher, H. (1968). Teachers' attitudes to education. *British Journal of Educational Psychology, 38,* 38–44.

■ ■ ■

530

Test Name: OPENNESS ABOUT MENTAL ILLNESS SCALE

Purpose: To assess attitude toward mental illness.

Format: Five factors measured: Authoritarianism, Benevolence, Mental Health Ideology, Social Restrictiveness, Interpersonal Etiology.

Author: Fracchia, J., et al.

Article: Comparison of intercorrelations of scale scores from the Opinions About Mental Illness Scale.

Journal: *Psychological Reports:* February 1972, *30*(1), 149–150.

Related Research: Cohen, J., & Struening, J. (1962). Opinions about mental illness in the personnel of two large mental hospitals. *Journal of Abnormal and Social Psychology, 64,* 349–360.

■ ■ ■

531

Test Name: OPINION QUESTIONNAIRE ON CULTURALLY AND ECONOMICALLY DISADVANTAGED CHILDREN & YOUTH

Purpose: To measure the realism and positive aspects of teacher attitude toward disadvantaged children and youth.

Number of Items: 130

Author: Torrence, E.

Article: Training teachers and leaders to recognize and acknowledge creative behavior among disadvantaged children.

Journal: *Gifted Child Quarterly,* Spring 1971, *16*(1), 3–10.

Related Research: Torrence, E. (1971). *Preliminary manual for opinion questionnaire: Culturally and Economically Disadvantaged Children & Youth (Form S-1).* Athens, Georgia: Georgia Studies of Creative Behavior.

■ ■ ■

532

Test Name: PARENT ATTITUDE QUESTIONNAIRE

Purpose: To measure the attitude of parents toward the school and toward their child's classroom experience.

Number of Items: 29

Format: Likert opinion questionnaire. Respondents expressed their opinion regarding each statement on a six-category scale from +3 (*strongly agree*) to –3 (*strongly disagree*). 0 (*neutral*) responses were not permitted.

Author: Rhodes, F.

Article: Team teaching compared with traditional instruction in grades kindergarten through six.

Journal: *Journal of Educational Psychology,* April 1971, *62*(2), 110–116.

■ ■ ■

533

Test Name: PARENT ATTITUDE RESEARCH INSTRUMENT

Purpose: To assess adults' perceptions and recall of their own parents' attitudes toward child rearing.

Number of Items: 115

Format: Includes 23 attitude subscales.

Author: Paulson, M. J., et al.

Article: Family harmony: An etiologic factor in alienation.

Journal: *Child Development,* June 1972, *43*(2), 591–603.

Related Research: Radin, N. (1972, December). Three degrees of maternal involvement in a pre-school program: Impact on mothers and children. *Child Development, 43*(4), 1355–1364.

Schaefer, E. S., & Bell, R. Q. (1958). Development of Parental Attitude Research Instrument. *Child Development, 29,* 339–361.

See *D.U.E.M.M.,* 1, 1974: 92.

■ ■ ■

534

Test Name: PEER GROUP ORIENTATION SCALE

Purpose: To survey school orientation attitude.

Number of Items: 8

Format: Student responds to each statement on a 4-point Likert scale from *strongly agree or agree* to *disagree or strongly disagree.* All items are presented.

Reliability: Internal consistency measured through coefficient alpha was .52.

Validity: With self-esteem, $r = .18$. With amount of children a child chose to work with, $r = .16$.

Author: Larkin, R. W.

Article: Class, race, sex, and preadolescent attitudes.

Journal: *California Journal of Educational Research,* November 1972, *23*(5), 213–223.

■ ■ ■

535

Test Name: PEOPLE TEST

Purpose: To measure children's

normative beliefs and personal attitudes concerning the social distance between different types of people.

Format: One set of judgments requires the child to judge the distance between self and others. The other set requires the child to judge the distance between pairs of people who differ by race, by sex, or both. The test employs simple line sketches of children as the stimulus figures. The datum from each item is the centimeter distance between the two figures, which range from 3 to 24 cm.

Author: Koslin, S., et al.

Article: Classroom racial balance and students' inter-racial attitudes.

Journal: *Sociology of Education,* Fall 1972, *45*(4), 386–407.

■ ■ ■

536

Test Name: POLITICAL ATTITUDE SCALE

Purpose: To assess political attitudes.

Number of Items: 7

Format: Items are rated on a 5-point scale from *strongly agree* to *strongly disagree.*

Validity: Item total correlation on four items: .84, .65, .63, .85.

Author: Bolton, C.

Article: Alienation and action: A study of peace-group members.

Journal: *American Journal of Sociology,* November 1972, *78*(3), 537–561.

■ ■ ■

537

Test Name: POLITICAL ATTITUDE SCALES

Purpose: To assess secondary level students' political attitudes.

Format: Measure of attitudes: political tolerance, political interest, sense of political efficacy, equalitarianism, political trust, political cynicism.

Author: Patrick, J.

Article: The impact of an experimental course "American Political Behavior" on the knowledge, skills and attitudes of secondary school students.

Journal: *Social Education,* February 1972, *36*(2), 168–179.

■ ■ ■

538

Test Name: PRINCIPAL'S ROLE IN COLLECTIVE NEGOTIATIONS Q-SORT

Purpose: To identify administrators' attitudes toward collective negotiations and the principal's role in this process.

Number of Items: 60

Time Required: 45 minutes.

Format: Each card of the Q-Sort is placed in rank order with a range of one to nine.

Author: Urich, T., and Turbegen, N. V.

Article: The role of the principal in collective negotiations.

Journal: *Journal of Educational Research,* May-June 1972, *65*(9), 401–404.

■ ■ ■

539

Test Name: PROFESSIONAL ORIENTATION SCALE

Purpose: To measure professional role orientation.

Number of Items: 16

Format: Likert scale scored from 7 (*agree strongly*) to 1 (*disagree strongly*). The higher the total score, the more positive the orientation. Examples are presented.

Author: Helsel, A. R., and Krchniak, S. P.

Article: Socialization in a heteronomous profession: Public school teaching.

Journal: *Journal of Educational Research,* October 1972, *66*(2), 89–93.

Related Research: Corwin, R. G. (1970). *Militant professionalism.* New York: Appleton-Century-Crofts.

■ ■ ■

540

Test Name: PUPIL ATTITUDE CHECKLIST

Purpose: To assess favorability of each child's attitude toward school and learning.

Number of Items: 45

Format: A weighted checklist containing descriptive examples of various pupil behaviors reflecting different degrees of enthusiasm toward school and learning.

Author: Rhodes, F.

Article: Team teaching compared with traditional instruction in grades kindergarten through six.

Journal: *Journal of Educational Psychology,* April 1971, *62*(2), 110–116.

■ ■ ■

541

Test Name: PUPIL OPINION QUESTIONNAIRE

Purpose: To assess pupil attitudes toward school.

Number of Items: 60

Format: Likert-type scale measuring attitude toward teachers, school work, peers, and school in general. Responses are recorded on a 5-point scale ranging from *strongly agree* to *strongly disagree.* Examples are presented.

Author: Glick, O.

Article: Some social-emotional consequences of early inadequate acquisition of reading skills.

Journal: *Journal of Educational Psychology,* June 1972, *63*(3), 253–257.

Related Research: Glick, O. (1967). *An assessment of the effects of the Youth Development teacher training program on pupil attitudes toward school* (mimeo). Institute for Community Studies, Kansas City, Missouri.

■ ■ ■

542

Test Name: RACIAL ATTITUDES QUESTIONNAIRE

Purpose: To identify attitudes toward discrimination, Whites, and the Black movement.

Number of Items: 14

Format: Direct questions. All items are presented.

Author: Edwards, O. L.

Article: Intergenerational variation in racial attitudes.

Journal: *Sociology and Social Research,* October 1971, *57*(1), 22–31.

Related Research: Campbell, A., & Schuman, H. (1968). *Racial attitudes in fifteen American cities.* Ann Arbor: University of Michigan, Institute for Social Research, Survey Research Center.

■ ■ ■

543

Test Name: READING ATTITUDE SCALE

Purpose: To measure attitudes toward reading.

Number of Items: 20

Format: A Likert scale where each item is answered on a 5-point scale from *I strongly agree* to *I strongly disagree.* Each item is presented.

Reliability: Based upon original 28 items, split-half method produced correlations from .92 to .96.

Author: Estes, T. H.

Article: A scale to measure attitudes toward reading.

Journal: *Journal of Reading,* November 1971, *15*(2), 135–138.

■ ■ ■

544

Test Name: READING CLASS ATTITUDE INVENTORY

Purpose: To measure pupil attitude toward reading.

Number of Items: 11

Format: All items are presented.

Author: Eberwein, L.

Article: A comparison of a flexible grouping plan with a three-group achievement plan in fourth grade reading instruction.

Journal: *Journal of Educational Research,* December 1972, *66*(4), 169–174.

■ ■ ■

545

Test Name: READING TEACHER SURVEY, REVISED EDITION

Purpose: To measure teachers' attitudes toward individualizing reading instruction.

Number of Items: 61

Time Required: Not timed but 20 minutes is sufficient.

Format: The items or scales are grouped under 11 examples of classroom situations. Teachers respond to each item on a 7-point scale. All items are presented.

Reliability: Internal consistency (Hoyt reliability coefficient) = .93.

Validity: Two validation studies are presented.

Author: Askov, E. N.

Article: An instrument for assessing teachers' attitudes toward individualizing reading instruction.

Journal: *Journal of Experimental Education,* Spring 1971, *39*(3), 5–10.

• • •

546

Test Name: RESIDENCE HALL VIEWPOINTS INVENTORY

Purpose: To measure job viewpoints and interpersonal attitudes of candidates for residence counseling positions.

Number of Items: 120

Format: Half of the items cover such topics as objectives for residence counseling, differences between residence and nonresidence counseling, conducting interviews with residents, advising residence hall groups, and methods of disciplining residents. Responses are made on a 5-point scale from *strongly agree* to *strongly disagree.* The remaining 60 items cover interpersonal relations. Several items are presented.

Validity: Correlation with total job performance rating was .61.

Author: Biggs, D. A.

Article: Selecting residence counselors—Job viewpoints and interpersonal attitudes.

Journal: *Journal of College Student Personnel,* March 1971, *12*(2), 111–115.

• • •

547

Test Name: SCHOOL ORIENTATION SCALE

Purpose: To survey school orientation attitude.

Number of Items: 7

Format: Student responds to each statement on a 4-point Likert scale

from *strongly agree or agree* to *disagree to strongly disagree.* All items are presented.

Reliability: Internal consistency measured through coefficient alpha = .68.

Validity: With family authority orientation, $r = .19$. With friends chosen from classmates, $r = .20$.

Author: Larkin, R. W.

Article: Class, race, sex, and preadolescent attitudes.

Journal: *California Journal of Educational Research,* November 1972, *23*(5), 213–223.

• • •

548

Test Name: SCHOOL RATING SCALE

Purpose: To determine attitude of high school juniors toward the 2-year, 4-year, and ideal college.

Number of Items: 40

Format: Utilized a 7-point semantic differential format, with each of 40 dimensions identified with reasonably bipolar descriptive phrases. Items are presented.

Author: Birnbaum, R.

Article: Student attitudes toward 2– and 4–year colleges.

Journal: *Journal of Educational Research,* April 1972, *65*(8), 369–374.

• • •

549

Test Name: SECONDARY STUDENT ATTITUDE TOWARD EDUCATION MEASURE

Purpose: To assess attitudes toward teachers and education.

Number of Items: 62

Format: Subjects responded on 7-point scale ranging from *agree very much* to *disagree very much.*

Author: Ramirez, M., et al.

Article: Mexican-American cultural membership and adjustment to school.

Journal: *Developmental Psychology,* March 1971, *4*(2), 141–148.

• • •

550

Test Name: SELF RATING SCALE

Purpose: To identify the teachers' general orientation toward research findings in educational psychology and factors that contributed to that orientation.

Format: Teachers indicate feelings toward research in educational psychology and factors that influenced such research. Teachers respond with a positive or negative check mark.

Reliability: Test–retest reliabilities ranged from .79 to .95.

Author: Rumstein, R.

Article: Teachers' evaluation of research findings in educational psychology.

Journal: *California Journal of Educational Research,* March 1972, *23*(2), 71–82.

• • •

551

Test Name: SELF REPORT INVENTORY

Purpose: To permit the respondent to describe his or her attitudes toward various aspects of his or her phenomenological world.

Format: Scales represent attitudes toward self, others, and authority, in addition to the total score.

Author: Austad, C. A.

Article: Personality correlates of teacher performance in a micro-teaching laboratory.

Journal: *Journal of Experimental*

Education, Spring 1972, *40*(3), 1–5.

Related Research: Bown, O. H. (1961). The development of self-report inventory and its function in a mental health assessment battery. *American Psychologist, 16,* 402.

▪ ▪ ▪

552

Test Name: SEX ROLE QUESTIONNAIRE

Purpose: To assess attitudes toward sex roles.

Number of Items: 16

Format: True–false response to each statement (e.g., "Men should be evaluated in terms of their sexual attractiveness and expertise.")

Author: Joesting, J., and Joesting, R.

Article: Attitudes about sex roles, sex and marital status of anti-war demonstrators.

Journal: *Psychological Reports,* October 1972, *31*(2), 413–414.

▪ ▪ ▪

553

Test Name: SITUATIONAL CASE QUESTIONNAIRE TO ASSESS DAMAGING INFORMATION ON APPLICATION

Purpose: To determine the attitudes and admission practices of deans toward potential students with personality and behavioral disturbances.

Number of Items: 20

Format: Twenty "cases" are given and the dean is asked to judge whether information would affect admission, whether college would want information, and whether counseling would be provided if student was admitted.

Author: Noland, R.

Article: Damaging information and the college application.

Journal: *Personnel and Guidance Journal,* March 1971, *49*(7), 544–554.

▪ ▪ ▪

554

Test Name: SOCIAL ATTITUDE Q SORT

Purpose: To measure social attitude.

Number of Items: 60

Format: Subject directed to do a Q sort on 30 conservative and 30 liberal items.

Reliability: Intraclass correlation coefficients: Liberals (.56) and conservatives (.08).

Author: Kerlinger, F.

Article: A Q validation of the structure of social attitudes.

Journal: *Educational and Psychological Measurement,* Winter 1972, *32*(4), 987–995.

Related Research: Smith, I. (1963). The invariance of educational attitudes and their relation to social attitudes: An inverse factor analytic study. Doctoral dissertation, New York University. *Dissertation Abstracts International, 24* (07), 3004. (University Microfilms)

▪ ▪ ▪

555

Test Name: SOCIAL ATTITUDE REFERENTS SCALE

Purpose: To assess social attitudes using attitude referents (objects).

Number of Items: 50

Format: 50 single words and short phrases on a 7-point Likert scale: 25 liberalism and 25 conservatism referents. Subject asked to express degrees of positive/negative feelings.

Reliability: Alpha coefficients were

.83–.90 for L (Liberalism) and C (Conservatism). Test–retest reliability was .73–.88.

Validity: Correlation of L and C subscales = .21 to .01.

Author: Kerlinger, F.

Article: The structure and content of social attitude referents: A preliminary study.

Journal: *Educational and Psychological Measurement,* Autumn 1972, *32*(3), 613–630.

▪ ▪ ▪

556

Test Name: STUDENT ATTITUDES AND BELIEFS QUESTIONNAIRE

Purpose: To assess student attitudes and beliefs in the following areas: scholastic activities and attitudes, popularity, peer influence on behavior, and self-regard.

Author: Jones, J. C., et al.

Article: Coeducation and adolescent values.

Journal: *Journal of Educational Psychology,* August 1972, *63*(4), 334–341.

Related Research: Coleman, J. S. (1961). *The adolescent society.* New York: The Free Press of Glencoe.

▪ ▪ ▪

557

Test Name: TEACHER ATTITUDE QUESTIONNAIRE

Purpose: To measure the attitude of teachers toward their job.

Number of Items: 28

Format: Likert opinion questionnaire. Respondents expressed their opinion regarding each statement on a 6-point scale from +3 (*strongly agree*) to –3 (*strongly disagree*). 0 (*neutral*) responses were not permitted.

Author: Rhodes, R.

Article: Team teaching compared with traditional instruction in grades kindergarten through six.

Journal: *Journal of Educational Psychology*, April 1971, *62*(2), 110–116.

▪ ▪ ▪

558

Test Name: TEACHER ATTITUDE TOWARD GIFTED CHILDREN INSTRUMENT

Purpose: To measure teacher attitude toward gifted children.

Number of Items: 18

Format: Forced choice.

Reliability: Test–retest (3 weeks) reliability was .74.

Author: Jacobs, J.

Article: Teacher attitude toward gifted children.

Journal: *Gifted Child Quarterly*, September 1972, *16*(1), 23–26.

▪ ▪ ▪

559

Test Name: TEACHERS ATTITUDE INVENTORY

Purpose: To assess the direction and intensity of teachers' attitudes toward the teaching of reading in the content areas.

Number of Items: 14

Format: Equal number of positive and negative items in a Likert scale format.

Author: Weintraub, S., et al.

Article: Summary of investigations relating to reading.

Journal: *Reading Research Quarterly*, Winter 1971, *6*(2), 142.

Related Research: Otto, W. (1969). Junior and senior high school teachers' attitudes toward reading in the content areas. *Yearbook of the National Reading Conference, 18*, 49–54.

▪ ▪ ▪

560

Test Name: TEST OF COUNSELOR ATTITUDES

Purpose: To evaluate counselors' attitudes.

Author: Rochester, D.

Article: Sex and age as factors relating to counselor attitude

change.

Journal: *Counselor Education and Supervision*, March 1972, *11*(3), 214–221.

Related Research: Hopke, W. (1955). The measurement of counselor attitudes. *Journal of Counseling Psychology, 2*, 212–216.

▪ ▪ ▪

561

Test Name: VERBAL CHECKLIST

Purpose: To gain an understanding of certain dimensions of body-build stereotyping.

Number of Items: 56 (28 item pairs).

Format: A list of adjectives to reflect physical attributes, social attributes, and personal attributes.

Author: Lerner, R. M., and Korn, S. J.

Article: The development of body-build stereotypes in males.

Journal: *Child Development*, September 1972, *43*(3), 908–920.

CHAPTER 7
Behavior

562

Test Name: ADOLESCENT DRUG USE QUESTIONNAIRE

Purpose: To assess the patterns of adolescent drug use of White students in grades 8–12 of a nonmetropolitan community in the Midwest.

Number of Items: 190

Format: Group administered, forced choice.

Reliability: Less than 2% of answer sheets were discarded due to lack of completion or clarity.

Author: Hager, D., et al.

Article: Patterns of adolescent drug use in Middle America.

Journal: *Journal of Counseling Psychology,* July 1971, *18*(4), 292–297.

■ ■ ■

563

Test Name: ALCOHOL AND DRUG USE QUESTIONNAIRE

Purpose: To describe use of alcohol and drugs.

Number of Items: 31

Format: Six-point and 7-point scales completed by respondent.

Author: Eisenthal, S., and Odin, H.

Article: Psychological factors associated with drug and alcohol usage among neighborhood youth corps enrollees.

Journal: *Developmental Psychology,* September 1972, *7*(2), 119–123.

564

Test Name: BEHAVIORAL STYLE RATING SCALE

Purpose: To classify child's response to new classroom activities.

Format: Four categories: Plungers, Go Alongers, Sideliners, Non Participators. Teacher uses experience with child to classify.

Validity: Correlation with estimated intelligence = .40 ($p < .01$).

Correlation with measured intelligence = .62 ($p < .01$).

Author: Lerner, R., and Miller, R.

Article: Relation of students' behavioral style to estimated and measured intelligence.

Journal: *Perceptual and Motor Skills,* August 1971, *33*(1), 11–14.

Related Research: Gordon, E., & Thomas A. (1967). Children's behavioral style and the teachers' appraisal of their intelligence. *Journal of School Psychology, 5,* 292–300.

■ ■ ■

565

Test Name: CLASSROOM BEHAVIOR INVENTORY
Purpose: To permit teachers to rate their students' behavior.

Number of Items: 60

Format: Teachers describe students' behavior using a 4-point scale. The items were equally divided among 12 scales.

Reliability: Internal consistency

coefficients for boys were in the .80s.

Internal consistency coefficients for girls were in the .70s.

Internal consistency coefficients for individuals scales were as high as the .90s.

Author: Price, E., and Rosemier, R.

Article: Some cognitive and affective outcomes of same-sex versus coeducational grouping in first grade.

Journal: *Journal of Experimental Education,* Summer 1970, *40*(4), 70–77.

Related Research: Schaefer, E. S., & Droppleman, L. (1970). *Development of a classroom behavior check list and factor analyses of children's school behavior in the United States and the Netherlands* (mimeo). National Institute of Mental Health.

Stedman, J. M., & Adams, R. L. (1972). Achievement as a function of language competence, behavior adjustment, and sex in young disadvantaged Mexican-American children. *Journal of Educational Psychology,* October, *63*(5), 411–417.

■ ■ ■

566

Test Name: CLASSROOM BEHAVIOR RATING SCALES

Purpose: To permit teachers to describe classroom behavior.

Number of Items: 24

Format: The teacher rates each child on each of the 24 items using a 7-point scale. All items are presented.

Reliability: Split-half reliability was .95.

Validity: Correlations with promotion were .42 and .14; with Metropolitan Readiness, .32 and .47; with Otis IQ, .36 and .30.

Author: Long, B. H., and Henderson, E. H.

Article: Teachers' judgments of Black and White school beginners.

Journal: *Sociology of Education*, Summer 1971, *44*(3), 358–368.

Related Research: Medinnus, G. R. (1961). The development of a first grade adjustment scale. *Journal of Experimental Education, 30,* 243–248.

■ ■ ■

567

Test Name: DAILY ACTIVITY LIST

Purpose: To record normal daily activities.

Number of Items: 33

Format: Self report format: Subject checks items representing activities in which he engaged on the previous day.

Reliability: Test–retest (1 week) reliability was .64 ($p < .01$). Test–retest (4 weeks) was .88 ($p < .001$).

Validity: Correlation with Mood Scale = .53 ($p < .05$).

Author: Stanfiel, J., et al.

Article: A daily activities list and its relation to measures of adjustment and early environment.

Journal: *Psychological Reports,* June 1971, *28*(3), 691–699.

Related Research: Katz, M., & Lyerly, S. (1963). Methods for measuring adjustment and social behavior in the community: I. Rationale, description, discriminative validity and scale

development. *Psychological Reports, 13,* 503–535.

■ ■ ■

568

Test Name: DESCRIPTION OF STUDENT PERFORMANCE ASPECTS

Purpose: To evaluate student affective and cognitive behavior.

Number of Items: 26.

Format: Two concepts of behavior: willingness and ability. Behaviors assessed were communication, thinking, and acting scored on high, medium, and low scales.

Author: Cox, C.

Article: Behavior as objective in education.

Journal: *Social Education,* May 1971, *35*(5), 435–449.

Related Research: Leppert, E., & Payette, R. (1970–1971). *Description of student performance aspects* (mimeo). University of Illinois.

■ ■ ■

569

Test Name: DRUG BEHAVIOR SCALE

Purpose: To assess the extent of drug use, sources of drugs, and reasons for using drugs.

Number of Items: 35

Author: Swisher, J., et al.

Article: Experimental comparison of four approaches to drug abuse prevention among ninth and eleventh graders.

Journal: *Counseling Psychology,* July 1972, *19*(4), 328–332.

■ ■ ■

570

Test Name: FREE-TIME ACTIVITIES

Purpose: To measure the amount

of energy an individual has available for his tasks as well as the pace that an individual sets.

Number of Items: 26

Format: Each activity is answered on a 5-point scale: *never, less than once a week, once a week, two-three times a week, once a day.*

Author: Poorkaj, H.

Article: Social-psychological factors and successful aging.

Journal: *Sociology and Social Research,* April 1972, *56*(3), 289–300.

■ ■ ■

571

Test Name: GENERAL HIGH ALTITUDE QUESTIONNAIRE (GHAQ)

Purpose: To measure acute mountain sickness.

Format: Yields clusters: arousal level, somatic discomfort, mood, and tiredness.

Reliability: Alpha reliability ranged .91–.98.

Author: Stamper, D., et al.

Article: Symptomatology subscales for the measurement of acute mountain sickness.

Journal: *Perceptual and Motor Skills,* December 1971, *33*(3), 735–742.

■ ■ ■

572

Test Name: HOME ECONOMICS BEHAVIORAL CHANGE QUESTIONNAIRE

Purpose: To identify cognitive and affective behavioral changes of vocational home economics teachers.

Number of Items: 90

Format: Contains 24 cognitive

items and 66 affective items. Each item is answered on a 5-point scale from 1 (*strongly agree*) to 5 (*strongly disagree*).

Author: Ridley, A. F.

Article: Inservice teacher education and the affective domain.

Journal: *American Vocational Journal*, January 1971, *46*(1), 46–48.

• • •

573

Test Name: LOUISVILLE BEHAVIOR CHECKLIST

Purpose: To assess deviant behavior.

Number of Items: 163 statements.

Format: Parents observe and rate children; includes two anxiety scales: fear, sensitivity.

Reliability: Split-half = .80.

Related Research: Stamper, D., et al. (1970). Subjective symptomatology and cognitive performance at high altitudes. *Perceptual and Motor Skills, 31*, 247–261.

Author: Miller, L., et al.

Article: Revised anxiety scales for the Louisville Behavior Check List.

Journal: *Psychological Reports*, October 1971, *29*(2), 503–511.

Availability: Document NAPS-01581, ASIS. National Auxiliary Publications Service, c/o CCM Information Corporation, 909 Third Ave., 21st floor, New York, NY 10022.

• • •

574

Test Name: OBSERVATION SCHEDULE AND RECORD

Purpose: To provide a technique for measuring classroom behavior.

Time Required: 30 minutes.

Format: An observer records specific classroom behavior with the activities scored as *contributing* or *noncontributing*.

Author: Vogel, F. X., and Bowers, N. D.

Article: Pupil behavior in a multi-age nongraded school.

Journal: *Journal of Experimental Education*, Winter 1972, *41*(2), 78–86.

Related Research: Medley, D. M., & Mitzel, H. E. (1958). A technique for measuring classroom behavior. *Journal of Educational Psychology, 86*(2), 325.

• • •

575

Test Name: PEER CLASSROOM PERFORMANCE RATING SCALE

Purpose: To obtain ratings of individual performance from peers.

Number of Items: 4 scales.

Format: Each of four scales provides definitions of behavior, the anchor points, and midpoint. Scales consist of: coordination and organization; ideas, information, and resources; effort; interpersonal relations.

Reliability: Intraclass correlation coefficients reported for different time periods vary considerably (36 are reported).

Author: Prien, E., and Woodley, K.

Article: Note on reliability of peer ratings of classroom performance.

Journal: *Psychological Reports*, February 1971, *28*(1), 89–90.

Related Research: Prien, E., & Lee, R. (1965). Peer ratings and leaderless group discussions for evaluation of classroom performance. *Psychological Reports, 16*, 59–64.

576

Test Name: POLITICAL ACTIVITY SCALE

Purpose: To assess extent of political activity.

Number of Items: 10

Format: Subject asked to respond (*yes–no*) whether he or she participated in each of 10 activities; maximum score = 10.

Reliability: Kuder-Richardson formula = .76.

Validity: Correlation with I-E Scale = .57 ($\pi < .001$).

Author: Rosen, B., and Salling, R.

Article: Political participation as a function of internal-external locus of control.

Journal: *Psychological Reports*, December 1971, *29*(3), 880–882.

• • •

577

Test Name: PROCESS ACTIVITY FORM

Purpose: To assess aide–child interactions.

Format: Includes two parts. Part I includes eight interaction categories, each describing an activity in which aides engage with children during contact sessions. Part II requests the aide to indicate her specific goals for a child during a session. There are 11 goals.

Author: McWilliams, S. A.

Article: A process analysis of nonprofessional intervention with children.

Journal: *Journal of School Psychology*. 1972, *10*(4), 367–377.

Related Research: McWilliams, S. A. (1971). *A process analysis of a school-based mental health program*. Unpublished doctoral dissertation, University of Rochester.

Availability: May be ordered by requesting McWilliams (1971) from University Microfilms, Ann Arbor, Michigan. Order No. 72–18, 825 submitting $4 for microfilm or $10 for xerography.

• • •

578

Test Name: PUPIL BEHAVIOR INVENTORY—REVISED

Purpose: To evaluate classroom behavior.

Format: A teacher rating form containing eight factors: creative inquisitiveness, academic motivation, good student behavior, classroom misconduct, teacher independence, anti-social behavior, poor physical condition, and problematic socio-emotional state.

Author: Radin, N.

Article: Three degrees of maternal involvement in a preschool program: Impact on mothers and children.

Journal: *Child Development,* December 1972, *43*(4), 1355–1364.

Related Research: Sarri, R., & Radin, N. (1970). *The development of a pupil behavior assessment inventory for pre-school and early elementary students: A preliminary report.* Unpublished manuscript, University of Michigan School of Social Work.

Vinter, R., et al. (1966). *Pupil behavior inventory: A manual for administration and scoring.* University of Michigan, Ann Arbor.

• • •

579

Test Name: ROLE-TAKING TEST

Purpose: To measure role taking behavior as manifested in fantasy projections.

Number of Items: Five backgrounds and 17 figures taken from the Make A Picture Story Test.

Format: Responses are evaluated in terms of subjects' ability to project into various social roles, simultaneously maintaining continuity between characterizations.

Reliability: Interjudge scoring reliability, .86.

Author: Weinheimer, S.

Article: Egocentrism and social influence in children.

Journal: *Child Development,* June 1972, *43*(2), 567–578.

Related Research: Feffer, M., & Gourevitch, V. (1960). Cognitive aspects of role-taking in children. *Journal of Personality, 28,* 383–396.

• • •

580

Test Name: SCALE FOR MEASURING ATTITUDES TOWARD ANY TEACHER

Purpose: To permit pupils to report their perceptions of teacher behavior characteristics.

Number of Items: Forms A and B, 45 items each.

Format: Pupils respond by placing a plus sign before each statement with which they agree with reference to their teacher.

Author: Bledsoe, J. C., et al.

Article: Factors related to pupil observation reports of teachers and attitudes toward their teacher.

Journal: *Journal of Educational Research,* November 1971, *65*(3), 119–126.

Related Research: Hoshaw, L. D. (1936). The construction and evaluation of a scale for measuring attitude toward any teacher.

Studies in Higher Education, Bulletin of Purdue University, 37(4), 238–251.

• • •

581

Test Name: SURVEY OF CLASSROOM BEHAVIOR

Purpose: To permit students to identify types of classroom behavior performed by students and teacher.

Number of Items: 30

Format: Students responded on a 5-point scale to each item (i.e., *almost always, often, occasionally, not usually, almost never*). Half the items represented teacher-centered characteristics and the other half reflected student-centered characteristics. Examples are presented.

Author: Costin, F.

Article: Empirical test of the "teacher-centered" versus "student-centered" dichotomy.

Journal: *Journal of Educational Psychology,* October 1971, *62*(5), 410–412.

• • •

582

Test Name: TEACHER'S BEHAVIOR RATING SCALE

Purpose: To record teacher behavior.

Number of Items: 15 behavioral categories.

Format: Scales run from inappropriate to appropriate behavior.

Reliability: $r = .39$, between two teachers on the same student.

Author: Warner, R.

Article: Alienated students: Six months after receiving behavioral group counseling.

Journal: *Journal of Counseling Psychology,* 1971, *18*(5), 426–430.

Related Research: Cowen, E., et al. (1961). *Adjustment to visual disability in adolescence.* New York: American Foundation for the Blind.

■ ■ ■

583

Test Name: WITHALL'S SOCIO-EMOTIONAL CLIMATE INDEX-REVISED

Purpose: To provide systematic observation of teacher verbal behavior.

Format: Includes the following categories: acceptance, rejection, problem centeredness, and directiveness.

Author: Hunter, C. P., and Meyers, C. F.

Article: Classroom climate and pupil characteristics in special classes for educationally handicapped.

Journal: *Journal of School Psychology,* 1972, *10*(1), 25–32.

Related Research: Withall, J. (1949). Development of a technique for the measurement of socio-emotional climate in classrooms. *Journal of Experimental Education, 17,* 347–361.

■ ■ ■

584

Test Name: WITMER COUNSELOR ACTIVITY PROFILE

Purpose: To assess counselor interview behavior.

Number of Items: 16 behavior categories.

Format: Raters record off video tape.

Reliability: Interrater reliability ranged .76 to .94.

Author: Witmer, J., and Lister, J.

Article: Rehabilitation and non-rehabilitation counselor candidates: Comparison of interview behavior and personality techniques.

Journal: *Counselor Education and Supervision,* Summer 1971, *10*(4), 324–329.

Related Research: Witmer, J. (1971). An objective scale for content analysis of the counselor's interview behavior. *Counselor Education and Supervision, 10,* 283–290.

CHAPTER 8
Communication

585

Test Name: BEHAVIORAL INTERACTION MEASURE

Purpose: To assess three behavioral measures: latency, verbal rejection, and verbal incorporation.

Format: Assessed by coders from a tape recording of triad interaction.

Reliability: 92% agreement by two raters on verbal rejection.

Author: Feshbach, N., and Sones, G.

Article: Sex differences in adolescent reactions toward newcomers.

Journal: *Developmental Psychology*, May 1971, *4*(3), 381–386.

586

Test Name: CAMPUS FREEDOM-OF-EXPRESSION SCALE

Purpose: To identify freedom of students and faculty to express their opinions and to sponsor controversial lectures on campus.

Reliability: Hoyt reliability was .75.

Author: Biggs, D. A., et al.

Article: Parents of university students.

Journal: *Journal of College Student Personnel*, November 1972, *13*(6), 538–545.

Related Research: Biggs, D. A., & Vaughan, C. E. (1971). Some parents' attitudes toward campus

dissent. *Journal of College Student Personnel, 12*, 347–352.

587

Test Name: CLIENT VERBAL INFORMATION SEEKING BEHAVIOR SYSTEM

Purpose: To determine the extent of information seeking behavior exhibited by a client during an interview.

Format: Measure was the frequency of defined behavior determined by raters of tapes.

Reliability: Interrater agreement .88 to .96 (proportion of agreement).

Author: Mickelson, D., and Stevic, R.

Article: Differential effects of facilitative and nonfacilitative behavioral counselors.

Journal: *Journal of Counseling Psychology*, July, 1971, *18*(4), 314–319.

588

Test Name: COUNSELOR VERBAL RESPONSE SCALE

Purpose: To record counselor verbal response.

Format: Verbal response system to be used by trained raters.

Reliability: Interrater reliability range .93–.99.

Author: Spivack, J.

Article: Laboratory to classroom: The practical application of IPR in a Master's Level Prepracticum Counselor Education Program.

Journal: *Counselor Education and Supervision*, September 1972, *12*(1), 3–16.

Related Research: Kagan, N. (1967). *Studies in human interaction* (Final Report, Grant No. DE 7-32-0410-270). Michigan State University, East Lansing, Educational Publication Services.

See *D.U.E.M.M., 1*, 1974: 64.

589

Test Name: INTERVIEW REACTION QUESTIONNAIRE

Purpose: To assess client reaction to an interview.

Format: True–false; all verbs were in the past tense.

Author: Murphy, K., and Strong, S.

Article: Some effects of similarity self disclosure.

Journal: *Journal of Counseling Psychology*, March 1972, *19*(2), 121–124.

Related Research: Strong, S. R., & Dixon, D. (1971). Expertness, attractiveness and influence in counseling. *Journal of Counseling Psychology, 10*, 562–570.

590

Test Name: JOURARD LEVEL OF VERBAL SELF DISCLOSURE SCALE

Purpose: To assess the extent of self disclosure by the individual.

Format: Based on self-report; two orientations of verbal self-disclosure: to students, to best friend.

Validity: Correlation with criterion of teacher effectiveness: disclosure to student ($r = .50$, $p < .01$) and to best friend ($r = .32$, ns).

Author: Usher, R., and Hanke, J.

Article: The third force in psychology and college teacher effectiveness research at the University of Northern Colorado.

Journal: *Colorado Journal of Educational Research,* Winter 1971, *10*(2), 2–9.

Related Research: Jourard, S. (1968). *Disclosing man to himself.* New York: Van Nostrand.

■ ■ ■

591

Test Name: JOURARD SELF DISCLOSURE QUESTIONNAIRE

Purpose: To assess the way in which individuals become known to others.

Number of Items: 60

Format: Subjects were asked to indicate how much they had disclosed about themselves on 60 topics using a 6-point scale.

Reliability: Split-half $rs = .91$ and .93. Test–retest (6 months) $r = .91$.

Author: Panyard, C.

Article: Method to improve the reliability of the Jourard Self Disclosure Questionnaire.

Journal: *Journal of Counseling Psychology,* November 1971, *18*(6), 606.

Related Research: Jourard, S., & Landsman, M. (1960). Cognition, cathexis and the dyadic effect in men's self disclosing behavior. *Merrill Palmer Quarterly, 6,* 178–186.

See *D.U.E.M.M., 1,* 1974: 66.

592

Test Name: JOURARD TACTILE BODY ACCESSIBILITY SCALE

Purpose: To assess level of tactile body accessibility.

Format: Based on self-report; two orientations of accessibility: to students, best friends.

Validity: Correlation with criterion of teacher effectiveness: students accessibility ($r = .43$, $p < .05$), best friend ($r = .48$, $p < .05$).

Author: Usher, R., and Hanke, J.

Article: The third force in psychology and college teacher effectiveness at the University of Northern Colorado.

Journal: *Colorado Journal of Educational Research,* Winter 1971, *10*(2), 2–9.

Related Research: Jourard, S. (1968). *Disclosing man to himself.* New York: Van Nostrand.

■ ■ ■

593

Test Name: MARSHALL SELF-DISCLOSURE QUESTIONNAIRE

Purpose: To assess degree of self-disclosure.

Number of Items: 144

Format: Different content areas tapped: religion; dating and sex; parental family; own marriage and family; physical condition and appearance; money and property; government and politics; emotions and feelings; interests, hobbies, and habits; relations with other people; personal attitude; school work.

Validity: Total score correlated with Interpersonal Trust Scale = .01.

Author: Vondracek, F., and Marshall, M.

Article: Self-disclosure and

interpersonal trust: An exploratory study.

Journal: *Psychological Reports,* February 1971, *28*(1), 235–240.

Related Research: Marshall, M. (1970). *The effects of two interviewer variables on self-disclosure in an experimental interview situation.* Unpublished master's thesis, Pennsylvania State University.

■ ■ ■

594

Test Name: MIST TEST (MOTORIC IDEATIONAL SENSORY TEST)

Purpose: To assess expressive dimensions.

Format: Likert scale items.

Author: Stein, K., et al.

Article: Motoric, ideational and sensory expressive styles: Further validation of the Stein and Lenrow types.

Journal: *Psychological Reports,* August 1972, *31*(1), 335–338.

Related Research: Stein, K., & Lenrow, P. (1970). Expressive styles and their measurement. *Journal of Personality and Social Psychology, 16,* 656–664.

■ ■ ■

595

Test Name: PRINCIPAL'S DATA SHEET

Purpose: To obtain the frequency of various types of oral and written communications between a principal and faculty.

Reliability: Odd–even = .82.

Author: Helwig, C.

Article: Organizational climate and frequency of principal–teacher communications in selected Ohio elementary schools.

Journal: *Journal of Experimental*

Education, Summer 1971, *39*(4), 52–55.

Related Research: Helwig, C. (1969). *Organizational climate and principal–teacher communications in selected Ohio elementary schools.* Unpublished doctoral dissertation, University of Akron.

■ ■ ■

596

Test Name: RANK BEHAVIORAL INTERACTION DESCRIPTION SYSTEM (REVISED)

Purpose: To assess verbal interaction in a small group.

Format: Observers rate verbal interaction on five dimensions (total nine subcategories). Four dimensions analyzed in present study were: delivery, content, process, and focus.

Reliability: Trained graduate counselor interrater Hoyt reliabilities for delivery = .71, content = .97, process = .76, focus = .87.

Author: Rank, R., et al.

Article: Encouraging counselor trainee affective group behavior by social modeling.

Journal: *Counselor Education and Supervision,* June 1972, *11*(4), 270–278.

Related Research: Rank, R. (1966). Counseling competence and perceptions. *Personnel and Guidance Journal, 45,* 359–365.

■ ■ ■

597

Test Name: RISKIN-FAUNCE FAMILY INTERACTION SCALES

Purpose: To record patterns of communication.

Number of Items: Seven scales.

Author: Lowe, R., and Murphy, J.

Article: Communication patterns in engaged couples.

Journal: *Psychological Reports,* October 1972, *31*(2), 655–658.

Related Research: Riskin, J., & Faunce, E. (1970). Family interaction scales. *Archives of General Psychiatry, 22,* 504–512.

■ ■ ■

598

Test Name: SELF DISCLOSURE QUESTIONNAIRE—ADAPTED

Purpose: To assess the extent to which individuals have discussed certain data about themselves with important people in their life and to identify the need for new disclosures and toward whom this need is directed.

Number of Items: Varies from 10 to 15.

Format: Useful in group work. For each group a separate self-disclosure questionnaire is constructed to focus on the particular group situation or problem. An example is presented.

Author: Danish, S. J., and Zelenski, J. F., Jr.

Article: Structured group interaction.

Journal: *Journal of College Student Personnel,* January 1971, *13*(1), 53–56.

Related Research: Jourard, S. (1964). *The transparent self: Self disclosure and well-being.* Princeton, NJ: Van Nostrand.

■ ■ ■

599

Test Name: SINHA SELF DISCLOSURE INVENTORY

Purpose: To assess extent of self disclosure.

Format: Self-rating scale; measures self-disclosure in eight areas of self and to six target figures.

Author: Sinha, V.

Article: Age differences in self disclosure.

Journal: *Developmental Psychology,* November 1972, *7*(3), 257–258.

Related Research: Sinha, V. (1972). A tool for self disclosure: Reliability and validity. *Indian Journal of Applied Psychology,* in press.

■ ■ ■

600

Test Name: TEACHER-PUPIL QUESTION INVENTORY

Purpose: To classify classroom questions.

Format: Includes nine categories: memory, translation, interpretation, application, analysis, synthesis, evaluation, affectivity, and procedure.

Reliability: .976.

Author: Tinsley, D.C., et al.

Article: Cognitive objectives in process-oriented and content-oriented secondary social studies programs.

Journal: *Educational Leadership,* December 1972, *30*(3), 245–248.

Related Research: Davis, O. L, Jr., & Tinsley, D. C. (1968). Cognitive objectives revealed by classroom questions asked by social studies student teachers. In R. T. Hyman (Ed.), *Teaching: Vantage points for study.* Philadelphia: Lippincott.

■ ■ ■

601

Test Name: WATSON ANALYSIS SCHEDULE

Purpose: To measure selected aspects of the communication of expectations, need disposition, and actual behaviors.

Number of Items: 213

Format: 71 items are repeated with different directions for each of the following three parts: purposes, behaviors, and affective characteristics.

Reliability: Test–retest estimates were .525 to .561.

Author: Marshall, J. C., et al.

Article: Dimensions of teacher expectations and student behavior in high school social studies classes.

Journal: *Journal of Educational Research,* October 1972, *66*(2), 61–67.

Related Research: Watson, E. P. (1969). *Inventoried perceptions of expectations for students in three social studies programs.* Unpublished doctoral dissertation, Indiana University.

...

CHAPTER 9
Concept Meaning

602

Test Name: AURAL WORD REPRESENTATION TEST

Purpose: To evaluate the ability to make word boundary discriminations or word segmentations.

Number of Items: 15

Format: The examinee is required to represent each spoken word in a stimuli utterance with a single one inch foam rubber cube.

Reliability: Kuder-Richardson Formula 20 coefficient is .71.

Validity: With SRA Total Reading .66.

Author: McNinck, G.

Article: Auditory perceptual factors and measured first-grade reading achievement.

Journal: *Reading Research Quarterly,* Summer 1971, *6*(4), 472–492.

...

603

Test Name: CONCEPTUAL STYLE TEST (CST)

Purpose: To assess whether the child's conceptual style is either "relational" or "analytic."

Number of Items: 15

Format: Two forms available (A & B). Subjects are presented three line drawings and are asked to choose the two that go together. Choice indicates either relational or analytical response.

Author: Denney, D.

Article: Modeling effects upon conceptual style and cognitive tempo.

Journal: *Child Development,* March 1972, *43*(1), 105–119.

Related Research: Denney, D. (1971). The assessment of differences in conceptual style. *Child Study Journal, 1,* 142–155.

...

604

Test Name: HUNT TEST OF CONCEPTUAL STRUCTURE

Purpose: To classify individuals on an abstract–concrete dimension.

Number of Items: 6

Format: Paragraph completion test: protocols scored by judges on a 0–3 scale.

Reliability: 70% agreement by judges.

Author: Wolfe, R., et al.

Article: Conceptual structure and conceptual tempo.

Journal: *Perceptual and Motor Skills,* August 1972, *35*(1), 331–337.

Related Research: Hunt, D., et al. (1968). *Manual for coding paragraph completion responses for adolescents.* Unpublished manuscript, Syracuse University, Youth Development Center.

...

605

Test Name: TAGATZ INFORMATION PROCESSING TEST

Purpose: To measure cognitive functioning of adolescents.

Number of Items: 60

Format: Divided into two subtests of 30 items each.

Author: Tagatz, G. E., et al.

Article: Effects of ethnic background, response option, task complexity and sex on information processing in concept attainment.

Journal: *Journal of Experimental Education,* Spring 1971, *39*(3), 69–72.

Related Research: Lemke, E. A., et al. (1969). The relationship between conceptual learning and curricular achievement. *Journal of Experimental Education, 38,* 70–75.

Tagatz, G. E., & Meinke, D. L. (1966). Information processing concept attainment tasks. *Teacher College Journal, 37,* 182–186.

CHAPTER 10
Creativity

606

Test Name: ADAPTIVE REGRESSION SCALE

Purpose: To assess creativity.

Format: Scale "tapped capacity for temporarily loosened ego boundaries."

Validity: Correlation with Wallach Kogan creativity measure = .17 (*ns*). Correlation with SAT = .16 (*ns*).

Author: Singer, D., and Berkowitz, L.

Article: Differing "creativities" in the wit and the clown.

Journal: *Perceptual and Motor Skills,* August 1972, *35*(1), 3–6.

Related Research: Child, I. (1964). Personality correlates of esthetic judgment in college students. *Journal of Personality, 33,* 476–511.

●●●

607

Test Name: CREATIVE MOTIVATION SCALE

Purpose: To assess creativity.

Number of Items: 30

Format: True–false items.

Validity: Significantly differed between research workers rated high or low in creativity.

Author: Torrence, E.

Article: Some validity studies of two brief screening devices for studying the creative personality.

Journal: *Journal of Creative Behavior,* 1971, *5*(2), 94–103.

Related Research: Torrence, E. (1958). *Preliminary manual for Personal-Social Motivation Inventory.* Minneapolis: University of Minnesota, Bureau of Educational Research. (Original out of print; revised edition available from author.)

●●●

608

Test Name: DIVERGENT THINKING TEST

Purpose: To assess divergent thinking.

Number of Items: 7

Format: Includes verbal and nonverbal factors. Items were pattern meanings, line meanings, similarities, and alternate uses.

Validity: With intelligence correlations ranged from .32 to .76.

Author: Nicholls, J. G.

Article: Some effects of testing procedure on divergent thinking.

Journal: *Child Development,* November 1971, *42*(5), 1647–1651.

Related Research: Wallach, M. A., & Kogan, N. (1965). *Modes of thinking in young children.* New York: Holt, Rinehart & Winston.

●●●

609

Test Name: EISENMAN-CHERRY CREATIVITY TEST

Purpose: To measure creativity.

Validity: Correlation with directionality (Time Metaphors Test) = .26 ($p < .10$) for female subjects.

Author: Platt, J., et al.

Article: Temporal perspective as a personality dimension in college students: A re-evaluation.

Journal: *Perceptual and Motor Skills,* August 1971, *33*(1), 103–109.

Related Research: Eisenman, R., & Cherry, H. (1968, April). *Creativity and authoritarianism.* Paper presented at the meeting of the Southeastern Psychological Association, Roanoke, VA.

●●●

610

Test Name: FUNCTIONALLY REMOTE ASSOCIATES TEST (FRAT)

Purpose: To measure remote associational ability (based on Mednick's theory of creativity).

Number of Items: 38

Format: Revised Mednick's Remote Associate Test (RAT), which consisted of three words from mutually distant associative clusters. Subject's task was to find a word that relates in some way with the three words. Same responses were used but new stems based on functional association were written.

Reliability: Kuder-Richardson Formula 21 estimates ranged from .38 to .76 with 5 out of 6 greater than .64.

Validity: Three studies relating RAT and FRAT to various measures (Quick Word Test,

Estimated GPA, Word Fluency, Instructor Rating, Peer Rating); correlations for FRAT and RAT generally similiar; in one substudy authors maintained that FRAT measures divergent or creative ability, and is less related to intelligence than RAT.

Author: Worthen, B., and Clark, P.

Article: Toward an improved measure of remote associational ability.

Journal: *Journal of Educational Measurement,* Summer 1971, *8*(2), 113–123.

Availability: Order NAPS Document No. 01284. ASIA National Auxiliary. Publication Service, c/o CCM Information Sciences Inc., 909 Third Avenue, New York, NY 10022. ($2 microfiche, $5 photocopy)

■ ■ ■

611

Test Name: MOSAIC CONSTRUCTION TEST

Purpose: To assess creativity.

Format: Subjects assessed individually. Subject is presented with a variety of one-inch squares of various colors and is asked to construct an 8 x 10 rectangle. Product is evaluated on (a) overall artistic merit, (b) use of color, (c) use of form, (d) originality, (e) warmth-vitality, (f) pleasingness.

Reliability: Interrater reliabilities were .64, .77, .70, .73, .70, and .73.

Validity: Significantly discriminated between those rated as high and low in creativity.

Author: Hall, W.

Article: A technique for assessing aesthetic predispositions: Mosaic Construction Test.

Journal: *Journal of Creative Behavior,* 1972, *6*(4), 225–235.

612

Test Name: PERSONAL OPINION SURVEY

Purpose: To measure creativity.

Number of Items: 30

Format: Five short form subtests taken from Child (1965): tolerance for complexity, tolerance for ambiguity, scanning, independence of judgment, repression.

Author: Dua, P.

Article: Development in creativity: A study of high school counselors.

Journal: *Journal of Counseling Psychology,* January 1972, *19*(1),53–57.

Related Research: Child, I. L. (1965). Personality correlates of esthetic judgement in college students. *Journal of Personality, 33,* 476–511.

■ ■ ■

613

Test Name: PUN TEST

Purpose: To assess creativity.

Number of Items: 50

Format: Subject is given a word and asked to make up a definition that is a pun (e.g., "bulldoze—a sleeping animal").

Author: Karlins, M.

Article: A note on a new test of creativity.

Journal: *Journal of Creative Behavior,* 1972, *6*(2), 95–101.

■ ■ ■

614

Test Name: SEMANTIC DIFFERENTIAL CREATIVITY

Purpose: A semantic differential test of complexity and independence of judgment.

Validity: .028 to .396.

Author: Bruch, C. B., and Morse, J. A.

Article: Initial study of creative (productive) women under the Bruch-Morse model.

Journal: *The Gifted Child Quarterly,* Winter 1972, *16*(4), 282–289.

■ ■ ■

615

Test Name: "SOMETHING ABOUT MYSELF" CHECK LIST

Purpose: To identify creatively gifted children and adults.

Number of Items: 50

Format: Items represented three categories of creative functioning: personality traits, use of creative thinking strategies, and creative productions.

Reliability: Interrater reliability = .99 ($p < .01$). Split-half = .92 (adolescent), .95 (adult), .94 (combined), corrected. Test–retest (1 day to 4 weeks) .98 (adolescent), .77 (adult).

Author: Khatena, J.

Article: Something About Myself: A brief screening device for identifying creative gifted children and adults.

Journal: *The Gifted Child Quarterly,* Winter 1971, *15*(4), 262–266.

■ ■ ■

616

Test Name: STARKWEATHER FORM BOARDS TEST

Purpose: To assess creativity in pre-school children.

Number of Items: 80 choices.

Format: Two sessions: an individually administered test that assesses conformity to a model.

Author: Starkweather, E.

Article: Creativity research

instruments designed for use with pre-school children.

Journal: *Journal of Creative Behavior,* 1971, *5*(4), 245–255.

■ ■ ■

617

Test Name: STARKWEATHER ORIGINALITY TEST

Purpose: To assess creativity in pre-school children.

Number of Items: 40 responses.

Format: Individually administered; child is given foam pieces and asked what they might be.

Validity: Significant agreement with teacher ratings of originality.

Author: Starkweather, E.

Article: Creativity research instruments designed for use with pre-school children.

Journal: *Journal of Creative Behavior,* 1971, *5*(4), 245–255.

■ ■ ■

618

Test Name: STARKWEATHER TARGET GAME

Purpose: To assess creativity in pre-school children.

Format: Assesses subjects' willingness to attempt a difficult task. Individually administered.

Author: Starkweather, E.

Article: Creativity research instruments designed for use with pre-school children.

Journal: *Journal of Creative Behavior,* 1971, *5*(4), 245–255.

■ ■ ■

619

Test Name: WALLACH & KOGAN CREATIVITY MEASURES (SHORT FORM)

Purpose: To assess ideational creativity.

Number of Items: Four "uses" items; four "similarities" items.

Format: Scored for uniqueness and fluency of response.

Reliability: Internal consistency was .78 ($p < .01$).

Validity: Correlation with adaptive regression (Child, 1964) was .17 (*ns*). Correlation with SAT was .05 (*ns*).

Author: Singer, D., and Berkowitz, L.

Article: Differing "creativities" in the wit and the clown.

Journal: *Perceptual and Motor Skills,* August 1972, *35*(1), 3–6.

Related Research: Wallach, M., & Kogan, N. (1965). *Modes of thinking in young children.* New York: Holt, Rinehart & Winston.

Child, I. (1964). Personality correlates of esthetic judgement in college students. *Journal of Personality, 33,* 476–511.

■ ■ ■

620

Test Name: "WHAT KIND OF PERSON ARE YOU" TEST

Purpose: To assess creativity.

Number of Items: 50

Time Required: 5–10 minutes.

Format: Subject is asked to choose the most descriptive characteristic of a pair of either two desirable or two socially undesirable attributes.

Reliability: Test–retest (1 week to 1 month) reliabilities were .91, .97, .71, and .73.

Validity: Correlation with Sounds and Images Test = .75.

Author: Torrance, E.

Article: Some validity studies of two brief screening devices for studying the creative personality.

Journal: *Journal of Creative Behavior,* 1971, *5*(2), 94–103.

Related Research: Khatena, J. (1971). Evaluation and the creative potential in music. *Gifted Child Quarterly,* Spring, *15*(1), 19–22.

See *D.U.E.M.M., 1,* 1974: 84.

...

CHAPTER 11
Development

621

Test Name: BEHAVIOR MATURITY SCALE

Purpose: To assess maturity of children.

Format: Used by teacher to rate children; three scales: academic, interpersonal, emotional maturity.

Validity: Correlation with Self Social Constructs subscales: academic maturity and social esteem, .26; interpersonal maturity and dependency, .12, and emotional maturity and self realism, .06.

Author: White, W., and Bashaw, W.

Article: High self-esteem and identification with adult models among economically deprived children.

Journal: *Perceptual and Motor Skills,* December 1971, *33*(3), 1127–1130.

Related Research: Kim, Y. (1968). *Behavior Maturity Scale.* Athens: University of Georgia, Research and Development Center.

...

622

Test Name: BREZNITZ AND KUGELMASS INTENTIONALITY QUESTIONNAIRE

Purpose: To measure children's development of moral judgments concerning naughtiness.

Format: Includes five parts.

Author: Hebble, P. W.

Article: The development of elementary school children's judgment of intent.

Journal: *Child Development,* October 1971, *42*(4), 1203–1215.

Related Research: Breznitz, S., & Kugelmass, S. (1967). Intentionality in moral judgment: Developmental stages. *Child Development, 38,* 469–479.

...

623

Test Name: CATEGORIZATION BEHAVIOR TEST

Purpose: To assess cognitive development in infancy and early childhood.

Number of Items: 10 tasks.

Format: 10 sorting tasks included 2 of size, color, texture contrasts and 1 each of form and complexity. Objects were presented on a tray. A coding system was used to analyze the results.

Author: Brockman, L., and Ricciuti, H.

Article: Severe protein-calorie malnutrition and cognitive development in infancy and early childhood.

Journal: *Developmental Psychology,* May 1971, *4*(3), 312–319.

Related Research: Brockman, L. (1966). *The effects of severe malnutrition on cognitive development in infants.* Unpublished doctoral dissertation, Cornell University.

624

Test Name: CHANGE SCALE

Purpose: To identify changes that take place in college-age students.

Number of Items: 64

Format: Includes five factors: intellectual, social, moralism, traditional, and altruism.

Reliability: .74 to .95 for main scales; .61 to .80 for changes toward main scale; .45 to .66 for changes away from main scale.

Author: Frantz, T. T.

Article: Student and non-student change.

Journal: *Journal of College Student Personnel,* January 1971, *12*(1), 49–53.

...

625

Test Name: CHILD DEVELOPMENT QUESTIONNAIRE

Purpose: To assess variables in the childhood of a respondent.

Number of Items: 94

Format: Generally fixed response in six categories: school history and adjustment, family background and infant development, dissention and discipline, early traumas, interpersonal, and moral development.

Author: Fretz, B.

Article: Predicting career preference from pre-adolescent development.

Journal: *Journal of Counseling Psychology,* July 1972, *19*(4), 286–291.

• • •

626

Test Name: CHILDREN'S INTENT JUDGMENT RATING SCALE

Purpose: To measure children's development of moral judgment concerning naughtiness.

Format: Includes seven stories varied in four ways corresponding to the combinations of two intent levels and two consequence levels.

Reliability: Mean intrasubject reliability coefficients over a 1-month interval ranged from .54 to .76.

Author: Hebble, P. W.

Article: The development of elementary school children's judgment of intent.

Journal: *Child Development,* October 1971, *42*(4), 1203–1215.

Related Research: Breznitz, S., & Kugelmass, S. (1967). Intentionality in moral judgment: Developmental stages. *Child Development, 38,* 469–479.

• • •

627

Test Name: CLASSIFICATION SKILLS DEVELOPMENT TEST

Purpose: To measure cognitive development as reflected by classification skills.

Format: Includes the ability to correctly manipulate a set of geometric blocks whose plane surfaces are either square, circular, or triangular and whose colors are red, blue, green, or yellow.

Author: Rardin, D. R., and Moan, C. E.

Article: Peer interaction and cognitive development.

Journal: *Child Development,* December 1971, *42*(6), 1685–1699.

Related Research: Kofsky, E. A. (1966). A scalogram study of classificatory development. *Child Development, 37,* 191–204.

• • •

628

Test Name: EGO IDENTITY STATUS MEASURE

Purpose: To assess the status of ego identity (Erikson's theory) development.

Time Required: 15–30 minutes.

Format: Interview (semistructured) included questions designed to determine presence or absence of crises in several life areas. Taped interviews are scored. Yields judgment that subject is at one of four status points: identity achievement, moratorium, foreclosure, or identity diffusion.

Reliability: Average interjudge agreement was .72.

Author: Waterman, A., and Waterman, C.

Article: A longitudinal study of changes in ego identity status during the freshman year in college.

Journal: *Developmental Psychology,* July 1971, *5*(1), 167–173.

Related Research: Marcia, J. (1966). Development and validation of ego-identity status. *Journal of Personality and Social Psychology, 3,* 551–558.

• • •

629

Test Name: ERIKSON EGO EPIGENESIS TEST

Purpose: To assess the degree of ego development in an Eriksonian theoretical framework.

Format: Projective test: subjects are presented a picture as in a Thematic Apperception Test. A coding procedure is utilized.

Reliability: Test–retest (2 weeks) reliability was .78 (average); test–retest (5 months) reliability was .69 (average). Intercoder analysis ranged from .45 to .88.

Validity: A relationship between ego strength progression and increasing age.

Author: Ciaccio, N.

Article: A test of Erikson's theory of ego epigenesis.

Journal: *Developmental Psychology,* May 1971, *4*(3), 306–311.

Related Research: Boyd, R. (1964). Analysis of the ego-stage development of school-age children. *Journal of Experimental Education, 32,* 249–257.

• • •

630

Test Name: GENDER IDENTITY PROCEDURE

Purpose: To assess development of gender identity.

Format: Children asked to write a story about two pictures (male and female trapeze artists, bullfighter); scored by raters.

Reliability: Interscorer reliability was .89.

Validity: Significant sex differences reported ($p < .05$).

Author: May, R.

Article: A method for studying the development of gender identity.

Journal: *Developmental Psychology,* November 1971, *5*(3), 484–487.

631

Test Name: INFANT PSYCHOLOGICAL DEVELOPMENT SCALE

Purpose: To assess infant psychological development.

Author: Roberts, G. C., and Black, K. N.

Article: The effect of naming and object permanence on toy preferences.

Journal: *Child Development,* September 1972, *43*(3), 858–868.

Related Research: Uzgiris, I., & Hunt, J. McV. (1966). *An instrument for assessing infant psychological development* (mimeo). University of Illinois.

• • •

632

Test Name: INVENTORY OF PSYCHOSOCIAL DEVELOPMENT

Purpose: To assess level of psychosocial development through measurement of six personality components thought to develop within the first six of Erikson's stages of development.

Number of Items: 60

Format: Six scales comprised of 10 items each.

Validity: Correlation with College Expectations Questionnaire: 22 of 24 correlations were positive and 18 were significant; range was .19 to +.36.

Author: Waterman, A.

Article: Relationship between the psychosocial maturity of entering college freshmen and their expectations about college.

Journal: *Journal of Counseling Psychology,* January 1972, *19*(1), 42–46.

Related Research: Constantinople,

A. (1969). An Eriksonian measure of personality development in college students. *Developmental Psychology, 1,* 357–372.

• • •

633

Test Name: KOHLBERG'S MORAL JUDGMENT SCALE

Purpose: To assess each child's developmental level of moral judgment.

Author: Selman, R. L.

Article: The relation of role taking to the development of moral judgment in children.

Journal: *Child Development,* March 1971, *42*(1), 79–91.

Related Research: Kohlberg, L. (1963). The development of children's orientation toward a moral order: I. Sequence in the development of moral thought. *Vita Humana, 6,* 11–33.

• • •

634

Test Name: LINCOLN-OSERETSKY MOTOR DEVELOPMENT SCALE

Purpose: To measure motor proficiency.

Validity: With verbal intelligence, $r = .427$. With reading, $r = .216$.

Author: Bell, D. B., et al.

Article: Some personality and motivational factors in reading retardation.

Journal: *Journal of Educational Research,* January 1972, *65*(5), 229–233.

Related Research: Sinks, T. A., & Thurston, J. F. (1972). The effect of typing on school achievement in elementary grades. *Educational Leadership,* January, *29*(4), 344–348.

Sloan, W. (1955). The Lincoln-Oseretsky Motor Development Scale, *General Psychological Monographs, 51,* 183–252.

• • •

635

Test Name: OBJECT SCALE

Purpose: To measure cognitive development.

Format: The scale is based upon the work of Piaget.

Author: Golden, M., et al.

Article: Social-class differentiation in cognitive development among Black pre-school children.

Journal: *Child Development,* March 1971, *42*(1), 37–45.

• • •

636

Test Name: PERFORMANCE INDEX

Purpose: To measure developmental changes in general social competence, vocational maturity, and self esteem.

Number of Items: 150

Format: 50 items for each of three factors (vocational maturity, personal maturity, and social maturity) requiring true–false response to attitude, opinion, or course of action statements; four forms.

Reliability: Test–retest reliability on total score was greater than .80.

Validity: Established on basis of test content; items differentiating between less and more mature groups retained (primarily armed service groups). The three factors were not independent on the basis of a factor analysis.

Author: Edgerton, H. A., et al.

Article: The performance index: A

measure of maturity of young adult males.

Journal: *Measurement and Evaluation in Guidance,* Winter 1971, *3*(4), 213–219.

■ ■ ■

637

Test Name: PUPIL DEVELOPMENT SURVEY

Purpose: To rate pupils on intellectual, social, emotional, physical, and motor development, language arts, and arithmetic skills.

Number of Items: 25

Format: Teachers respond to each item on a 1 (*poor or low*) through 9 (*good or high*) scale. All items are presented.

Author: Ross, R. F.

Article: Pupil development survey of Project Head Start participants.

Journal: *Education,* April–May 1972, *92*(4), 99–107.

638

Test Name: TEST OF INTERNAL MORAL JUDGMENT

Purpose: To assess the level of development used as the bases for various moral judgments.

Format: Subject is given a moral dilemma story and is asked to judge the morality of the hero's decision and give reasons for the choice. Scores summed to obtain internal moral development score.

Author: Hoffman, M.

Article: Father absence and conscience development.

Journal: *Developmental Psychology,* May 1971, *4*(3), 400–406.

Related Research: Kohlberg, L. (1958). *The development of modes of moral thinking and choice in the years 10 to 16.* Unpublished doctoral dissertation. University of Chicago.

639

Test Name: VOCATIONAL MATURITY SCALE

Purpose: To provide an objective measure of an individual's general level of vocational maturity.

Number of Items: 200 original, reduced to 50 on each of two forms.

Format: Multiple choice for 16 variables (e.g., related occupations, duties); two forms.

Reliability: Kuder-Richardson Formula 20: .77 (Form A), .85 (Form B). Forms A and B correlated .65 over 2-week period.

Validity: Correlations with mental ability on original forms were .60 (A) and .59 (B); correlation with a vocational maturity instrument was .76.

Author: Westbrook, B., et al.

Article: The development of a measure of vocational maturity.

Journal: *Educational and Psychological Measurement,* 1971, *31*(2), 541–543.

CHAPTER 12
Family

640

Test Name: ADOLESCENT–PARENT INTERACTION QUESTIONNAIRE

Purpose: A self-report measure of parent–adolescent interaction.

Format: Dimensions of family behavior: "Parental authority, communication between parent and child, parental support, affective quality of relationship and identification."

Author: Kandel, D.

Article: Race, maternal authority, and adolescent aspiration.

Journal: *American Journal of Sociology*, May 1971, *76*(6), 999–1020.

• • •

641

Test Name: AFI-65 SCALE

Purpose: To assess extent of authoritarianism in a family.

Author: Jordan, T., and Spaner, S.

Article: Biological and ecological influences on development at 24 and 36 months of age.

Journal: *Psychological Reports,* August 1972, *31*(1), 319–332.

Related Research: Ernhart, C., & Loevinger, J. (1969). Authoritarian family ideology: A measure, its correlates and its robustness. *Multivariate Behavioral Research Monographs, 69*(1).

642

Test Name: COGNITIVE HOME ENVIRONMENT SCALE

Purpose: To assess stimulation present in the home.

Format: A questionnaire.

Author: Radin, N.

Article: Three degrees of material involvement in a preschool program: Impact on mothers and children.

Journal: *Child Development,* December 1972, *43*(4), 1355–1364.

Related Research: Radin, N. (1969). The impact of a kindergarten home counseling program. *Exceptional Children, 36,* 251–256.

• • •

643

Test Name: CORNELL PARENT BEHAVIOR DESCRIPTION

Purpose: To provide parent rating by children.

Format: Nine variables; used a 5-point scale of frequency of occurrence (never to very often).

Author: Rodgers, R.

Article: Changes in parental behavior reported by children in West Germany and the United States.

Journal: *Human Development,* 1971, *14*(3), 208–224.

Related Research: Devereux, E., et al. (1969). Childrearing in England and the United States: A cross-national comparison. *Journal of Marriage and the Family, 31,* 257–270.

• • •

644

Test Name: FAMILY AUTHORITY ORIENTATION SCALE

Purpose: To survey family authority orientation attitude.

Number of Items: 8

Format: Student responds to each statement on a 4-point Likert scale from *strongly agree or agree* to *disagree or strongly disagree.* All items are presented.

Reliability: Internal consistency measured through coefficient alpha was .48.

Validity: With peer group status, $r = .14$. With self-esteem, $r = .14$. With school orientation, $r = .19$.

Author: Larkin, R. W.

Article: Class, race, sex, and preadolescent attitudes.

Journal: *California Journal of Educational Research,* November 1972, *23*(5), 213–223.

• • •

645

Test Name: FAMILY RELATION INVENTORY—FATHER

Purpose: To measure perception of the father's attitudes toward the subject in terms of acceptance, avoidance, and concentration.

Number of Items: 18

Format: Includes three subscales of father acceptance, avoidance, and concentration.

Reliability: Test–retest coefficients were .97, .93, and .73.

Author: Tseng, M. S.

Article: Comparisons of selected familial, personality, and vocational variables of high school students and dropouts.

Journal: *Journal of Educational Research,* July-August 1972, *65*(10), 462–466.

■ ■ ■

646

Test Name: HEILBRUN PARENT–CHILD INTERACTION RATING SCALES

Purpose: To measure perceived maternal nurturance.

Format: Five-point anchored scales.

Author: Heilbrun, A.

Article: Tolerance for ambiguity in late adolescent males: Implications for a developmental model of paranoid behavior.

Journal: *Developmental Psychology,* November 1972, *7*(3), 288–294.

Related Research: Heilbrun, A. (1964). Parent model attributes, nurturant reinforcement and consistency of behavior in adolescents. *Child Development, 35,* 151–167.

■ ■ ■

647

Test Name: HOME INTERVIEW SCHEDULE

Purpose: To gain a measure of the learning environment of the home.

Number of Items: 188

Format: Semi-structured: includes 8 scales: press for achievement,

press for activeness, press for intellectuality, press for independence, press for English, father dominance, mother dominance, and press for ethlanguage.

Reliability: Coefficient alpha range from .66 to .98.

Validity: Correlation with Science Research Associates Primary Mental Abilities subtests ranged from .04 to .66.

Author: Marjoribanks, K.

Article: Environmental correlates of diverse mental abilities.

Journal: *Journal of Experimental Education,* Summer 1971, *39*(4), 64–68.

■ ■ ■

648

Test Name: MARRIAGE ADJUSTMENT SCALE

Purpose: To assess marital satisfaction.

Format: Completed by married couples.

Author: Cone, J.

Article: Social desirability, marital satisfaction, and concomitant perceptions of self and spouse.

Journal: *Psychological Reports,* February 1971, *28*(1), 173–174.

Related Research: Locke, H. (1951). *Predicting adjustment in marriage.* New York: Holt.

■ ■ ■

649

Test Name: MOTHER–CHILD INTERACTION SCALE

Purpose: To record mother–child interaction behavior for 1-year-old children.

Format: Behavioral Observation System; some of the behaviors are physical contact, prohibitions,

maternal vocalization.

Author: Tulkin, S., and Kagan, J.

Article: Mother–child interaction in the first year of life.

Journal: *Child Development,* March 1972, *43*(1), 31–41.

■ ■ ■

650

Test Name: PARENTAL INTEREST SCALE

Purpose: To measure perceived parental interest.

Number of Items: 7

Format: A high score indicates a high perceived parental interest.

Author: Tseng, M. S.

Article: Comparisons of selected familial, personality, and vocational variables of high school students and dropouts.

Journal: *Journal of Educational Research,* July–August 1972, *65*(10), 462–466.

■ ■ ■

651

Test Name: PERCEIVED MATERNAL ENCOURAGEMENT MEASURE

Purpose: To assess degree of maternal encouragement of aggressive and independent behavior.

Number of Items: 14

Format: Q Sort technique. (1951).

Author: Biller, H., and Bahm, R.

Article: Father absence, perceived maternal behavior, and masculinity of self concept among junior high boys.

Journal: *Developmental Psychology,* March 1971, *4*(2), 178–181.

Related Research: Block, J., & Christiansen, B. (1966). A test of

Henden's hypothesis relating suicide in Scandinavia to child rearing orientations. *Scandinavian Journal of Psychology, 7,* 267–288.

∎ ∎ ∎

652

Test Name: PERCEIVED MATERNAL WARMTH QUESTIONNAIRE

Purpose: To assess subjects' judgment of role of mother (controlling or warm).

Number of Items: 12

Format: Items drawn to reflect two dimensions: affectionate–nurturant and punitive–controlling.

Author: Berman, A.

Article: Social schemas: An investigation of age on socialization variables.

Journal: *Psychological Reports,* April 1971, *28*(4), 343–348.

∎ ∎ ∎

653

Test Name: RELATIONSHIP WITH FATHER SCALE

Purpose: To determine degree of relationship with father.

Number of Items: 6

Format: The score identifies positive responses; the higher the score, the more positive relationship the subject has with the father.

Author: Tseng, M. S.

Article: Comparisons of selected familial, personality, and vocational variables of high school students and dropouts.

Journal: *Journal of Educational*

Research, July-August 1972, *65*(10), 462–466.

654

Test Name: ROE-SIEGELMAN PARENT CHILD RELATIONS QUESTIONNAIRE

Purpose: To assess subject's perception of parent–child relations.

Format: Four scales are: symbolic love reward, direct object reward, symbolic love punishment, direct object punishment.

Author: McKinney, J.

Article: The development of values—Prescriptive or proscriptive?

Journal: *Human Development,* 1971, *14*(1), 71–80.

Related Research: Roe, A., & Siegelman, M. (1963). A parent-child relations questionnaire. *Child Development, 34,* 355–369.

See *D.U.E.M.M., 1,* 1974: 94–95.

∎ ∎ ∎

655

Test Name: SCHAEFER PARENT BEHAVIOR INVENTORY

Purpose: To assess parent behavior as reported by children.

Format: Includes the following among scales: acceptance, child centeredness, possessiveness, control, positive involvement, intrusiveness, inconsistent discipline.

Validity: Control and intrusiveness scales significantly ($p < .05$, and one tailed) differentiated between supervised and unsupervised fifth graders.

Author: Woods, M.

Article: The unsupervised child of the working mother.

Journal: *Developmental Psychology,* January 1972, *6*(1), 14–25.

Related Research: Schaefer, E. (1965). Children's reports of parental behavior: An inventory. *Child Development, 36,* 413–424.

∎ ∎ ∎

656

Test Name: STRUCTURED SITUATIONAL TEST

Purpose: To identify attitudes and interactions of parents of delinquent and normal adolescent girls.

Number of Items: 10

Format: Each parent is interviewed by means of the 10 statements. Ratings are made of a number of characteristics of parental behavior and attitudes from the parents' content and manner of responding. The 10 statements are presented.

Reliability: Interjudge reliability was .88.

Author: Duncan, P.

Article: Parental attitudes and interactions in delinquency.

Journal: *Child Development,* December 1971, *42*(6), 1751–1765.

Related Research: Farina, A. (1960). Patterns of role dominance and conflict in parents of schizophrenic patients. *Journal of Abnormal and Social Psychology, 61,* 31–38.

Farina, A., & Dunham, R. M. (1963). Measurements of family relationships and their effects. *Archives of Genetic Psychiatry, 9,* 64–73.

CHAPTER 13
Institutional Information

657

Test Name: CHAIRMANSHIP FUNCTIONS QUESTIONNAIRE

Purpose: To reflect characteristics of effective departmental chairmen.

Number of Items: 36

Format: Items are divided among three functions: professional activities, direct administrative responsibilities, personal characteristics. All items are presented in brief form.

Reliability: Test–retest rank order correlation was .94. Test–retest product-moment correlations were .27 to .86. Median test–retest rank order correlation was .70.

Author: Siever, R. G., et al.

Article: Role perceptions of department chairmen in two land grant universities.

Journal: *Journal of Educational Research,* May–June 1972, *65*(9), 405–410.

• • •

658

Test Name: CINCINNATI AUTONOMY TEST BATTERY

Purpose: A battery of tests used to evaluate early childhood education.

Format: Includes several tests: Draw a Line Slowly Test, Childhood Matching Familiar Figures, Early Childhood Embedded Figures, Dog and Bone Test, and Curiosity Box Test.

Author: Bucky, S., and Banta, T.

Article: Racial factors in test performance.

Journal: *Developmental Psychology,* January 1972, *6*(1), 7–13.

Related Research: Banta, T. (1970). Tests for the evaluation of early childhood education: The Cincinnati Autonomy Battery (CATB). In J. Hellmuth (Ed.), *Cognitive studies.* New York: Brunner & Mazel.

• • •

659

Test Name: CLASSROOM STATUS AND TEACHER APPROVAL-DISAPPROVAL QUESTIONNAIRE

Purpose: To measure acceptance, competence, power, teacher approval, and disapproval.

Number of Items: 25

Time Required: 30 minutes.

Format: Includes three standard sociometric items (acceptance items) and 22 "guess who" items.

Author: Herrmann, R. W.

Article: Classroom status and teacher approval and disapproval-study of children's perceptions.

Journal: *Journal of Experimental Education,* Winter 1972, *41*(2), 32–39.

Related Research: DeGwat, A. F., & Thompson, G. G. (1949). A study of the distribution of teacher approval and disapproval among sixth-grade pupils. *Journal of Experimental Education, 18,* 57–75.

660

Test Name: COLLEGE ADMISSIONS ASSISTANCE QUESTIONNAIRE

Purpose: To describe assistance given to students before being admitted to a university.

Number of Items: 26

Format: Items dealt with: timing of decisions, sources of information, ratings of high school counselor.

Author: Fredrickson, R., and Fonda, T.

Article: College admissions assistance by secondary school counselors.

Journal: *Personnel and Guidance Journal,* January 1971, *49*(5), 383–389.

Related Research: Kerr, W. (1962). Student perceptions of counselor role in the college decision. *Personnel and Guidance Journal, 41,* 337–342.

• • •

661

Test Name: COLLEGE BUSINESS MAJOR CURRICULUM OBJECTIVES SURVEY

Purpose: To assess what training and skills are desired in graduates of business programs.

Number of Items: 11 objectives.

Format: Objectives were rated on a 5-point scale (*very important* to *no opinion*) and included "training in business principles," "training to develop analytic abilities," and so forth.

Author: No author given.

Article: As you were saying—Executives can agree on student training.

Journal: *Personnel Journal,* May 1971, *50*(5), 405–406.

Related Research: Bond, F., et al. (1964). *Preparation for business leadership* (Michigan Business Report No. 43). The Graduate School of Business, Ann Arbor, Michigan: The University of Michigan, *61,* 35–36.

■ ■ ■

662

Test Name: COLLEGE EXPECTATIONS QUESTIONNAIRE—ADAPTED

Purpose: To assess student expectations regarding the campus environment.

Number of Items: 40

Format: Likert items yielding four scores related to faculty, major field, students, and administration.

Validity: Correlation with Inventory of Psychosocial Development: 22 of 24 correlations were positive and 18 significant; range was .19 to +.36.

Author: Waterman, A.

Article: Relationship between the psychosocial maturity of entering college freshmen and their expectations about college.

Journal: *Journal of Counseling Psychology,* January 1971, *19*(1), 42–46.

Related Research: Peterson, R. (1968). *College student questionnaires.* Princeton, NJ: Educational Testing Service.

■ ■ ■

663

Test Name: COLLEGE STUDENT SATISFACTION QUESTIONNAIRE

Purpose: To measure six dimensions of college student satisfaction.

Format: Involves five-choice Likert responses ranging from *very satisfied* through *satisfied* to *very unsatisfied.* Overall satisfaction is measured by the sum of the scale scores. The six dimensions are policies and procedures, working conditions, compensation, quality of education, social life, and recognition.

Author: Sturtz, S. A.

Article: Age differences in college student satisfaction.

Journal: *Journal of College Student Personnel,* May 1971, *12*(3), 220–222.

Related Research: Betz, E. L., et al. (1970). The measurement and analysis of college student satisfaction. *Measurement and Evaluation in Guidance, 3*(2)110–118.

See *D.U.E.M.M., 1,* 1974: 101.

■ ■ ■

664

Test Name: COMMUNITY COLLEGE COUNSELOR TRAINING QUESTIONNAIRE

Purpose: To determine curriculum content for training community college counselors.

Number of Items: 52

Format: Includes 31 course descriptions that are ranked on a 5-point scale ranging from *full course absolutely essential* to *subject of no value for professional training.* Also includes 21 pairs of statements dealing with the curriculum itself as well as certain attitudes and functions of community college counselors that have relevance for training programs. Respondents divide 9 points between the two statements. Items are presented.

Author: Schoenmaker, A., and Hood, A. B.

Article: How should community college counselors be trained?

Journal: *Journal of College Student Personnel,* March 1972, *13*(2), 129–135.

■ ■ ■

665

Test Name: COUNSELOR APPRAISAL OF POSITION SCALE

Purpose: To collect data related to the number and nature of student-counselor contacts.

Number of Items: 10

Format: Multiple choice items regarding the amount of time spent on supervisory and clerical duties.

Author: Van Riper, B. W.

Article: Toward a separate professional identity.

Journal: *Journal of Counseling Psychology,* March 1972, *19*(2), 117–120.

■ ■ ■

666

Test Name: COURSE EVALUATION FORM

Purpose: To permit student evaluation of courses.

Format: Includes seven scales: preparation, explanation, responsiveness, stimulation, examinations, text recommended. Scales are printed on IBM data card-size forms.

Author: Grant, C. W.

Article: Faculty allocation of effort and student course evaluations.

Journal: *Journal of Educational Research,* May–June 1971, *64*(9), 405–410.

Related Research: A.S.U.U. (1969). University of Utah, Faculty-Course Evaluation Survey Report, Fall Quarter, 1968–69. *Desert News Press.*

667

Test Name: COURSE EVALUATION INSTRUMENT

Purpose: To evaluate course and instructor.

Number of Items: 29

Format: The items covered course workload, text quality, instructor quality, and course structure. A 5-point bipolar scale was used for each item.

Reliability: Spearman-Brown reliability estimate was .94.

Author: Bausell, R. B., and Magoon, J.

Article: Instructional methods and college student ratings of courses and instructors.

Journal: *Journal of Experimental Education,* Summer 1972, *40*(4), 29–33.

● ● ●

668

Test Name: COURSE EVALUATION QUESTIONNAIRE

Purpose: To permit students to evaluate a high school sex education course.

Format: An open-ended questionnaire directed toward the following: (a) interest in specific topics; (b) suitability of class activities; (c) freedom of discussion; (d) ease of understanding; (e) value of the course; and (f) suggestions for improvement.

Author: Juhasz, A. M.

Article: Student evaluation of a high school sex education program.

Journal: *California Journal of Educational Research,* September 1971, *22*(4), 144–155.

669

Test Name: EARLY RETIREMENT QUESTIONNAIRE

Purpose: To assess reasons why employees retire early.

Author: Manion, U.

Article: Why employees retire early.

Journal: *Personnel Journal,* March 1972, *51*(3), 183–187, 207.

● ● ●

670

Test Name: EDUCATIONAL VOCATIONAL COUNSELING SURVEY

Purpose: To assess areas in which the client felt he or she needed help, and a rating by the client of the help actually received.

Number of Items: 14

Format: Subjects responded *yes–no* on Part I indicating the areas in which they needed help; in Part II they rated (on a 5-point Likert scale) the help they received.

Author: Graff, R., et al.

Article: Reactions to three kinds of vocational-educational counseling.

Journal: *Journal of Counseling Psychology,* May 1972, *19*(3), 224–228.

● ● ●

671

Test Name: ELEMENTARY SCHOOL COUNSELING SURVEY FORM

Purpose: To examine status of elementary counseling in two high schools.

Number of Items: 5 major questions.

Author: Hoose, W., and Carlson, J.

Article: Counselors in the elementary school: 1970–71.

Journal: *Personnel and Guidance Journal,* April 1972, *50*(8), 679–682.

● ● ●

672

Test Name: ENVIRONMENTAL ASSESSMENT TECHNIQUE

Purpose: To define college environments in terms of eight characteristics of the student body.

Format: Includes these student body characteristics: average intelligence, enrollment size, and proportions of students enrolled in six broad areas of study called realistic, scientific, social, conventional, enterprising, and artistic.

Author: Chickering, A. W.

Article: Undergraduate academic experience.

Journal: *Journal of Educational Psychology,* April 1972, *63*(2), 134–143.

Related Research: Astin, A. W., & Holland, J. L. (1961). The environmental assessment technique: A way to measure college environments. *Journal of Educational Psychology, 52,* 308–316.

See *D.U.E.M.M., 1,* 1974: 104–105.

● ● ●

673

Test Name: ENVIRONMENTAL FORCES SCHEDULE

Purpose: To measure the intensity of the present learning environment and to measure the cumulative nature of the learning environment over time.

Format: Includes the following forces: press for achievement, press for activeness, press for intellectuality, press for independence, press for English, press for ethlanguage, father dominance, mother dominance. A set of alternate responses was supplied for each item and a 6-point rating scale was developed in order to score each item.

Reliability: Reliability ranged from .66 to .94.

Validity: Relationships with mental ability ranged from .04 to .69.

Author: Marjoribanks, K.

Article: Environment, social class, and mental abilities.

Journal: *Journal of Educational Psychology,* April 1972, *63*(2), 103–109.

Related Research: Marjoribanks, K. (1972). Ethnic and environmental influences on mental abilities. *American Journal of Sociology,* September, *78*(2), 323–337.

■ ■ ■

674

Test Name: EVALUATION OF STUDENTS WHO MAJOR IN SOCIAL WORK

Purpose: To provide personal-demographic data on students at schools in which community organization concentrations exist.

Author: Lauffer, A.

Article: A new breed of social actionist comes to social work: The community organization student.

Journal: *Journal of Education for Social Work,* Winter 1971, *7*(1), 43–53.

■ ■ ■

675

Test Name: EXPERIENCE OF COLLEGE QUESTIONNAIRE

Purpose: To permit students to

assess their college environment.

Format: Students are asked to report their concrete experiences and behaviors in several general areas: academics, extracurricular activities, relationships with peers, student faculty relations, and religious experiences and activities.

Author: Chickering, A. W.

Article: Undergraduate academic experience.

Journal: *Journal of Educational Psychology,* April 1972, *63*(2), 134–143.

Related Research: McDowell, J., & Chickering, A. W. (1967). (mimeo). Plainfield, VT: Project on student development.

■ ■ ■

676

Test Name: GLENN-VILLEMEZ INDEX OF PRODUCTIVITY

Purpose: To assess productivity of departments of sociology.

Format: Yields: comprehensive index; per person index.

Validity: Correlation with Knudsen-Vaughn Index for 1968 were .828 and .574.

Author: Solomon, W.

Article: Correlates of prestige rating of graduate programs in sociology.

Journal: *American Sociologist,* May 1972, *7*(5), 13–14.

Related Research: Glenn, N., & Villemez, W. (1970). The productivity of sociologists at 45 American universities. *American Sociologist,* 5, 244–252.

■ ■ ■

677

Test Name: GUIDANCE ADMINISTRATOR QUESTIONNAIRE

Purpose: To obtain information on the work of the guidance administrator.

Format: Four Parts: I. Information about respondent. II. Information about the guidance program in the school system. III. List of 40 duties that respondents checked if they performed them and rated criticality of duty. IV. Open ended questions regarding additional duties, and so forth.

Author: Biggers, J., and Mangusso, D.

Article: The work of the guidance administrator.

Journal: *Counselor Education and Supervision,* December 1972, *12*(2), 130–136.

■ ■ ■

678

Test Name: GUIDELINES FOR ANALYSIS OF EARLY CHILDHOOD EDUCATION PROGRAMS

Purpose: To identify the main ways in which early childhood education programs may differ from one another and to gain increased insight into the consequences for children that might follow the choice of one program rather than another.

Format: Five parts, each with a variety of items. The entire set of guidelines is presented in the article.

Author: Elliott, D. L.

Article: Guidelines for the analysis and description of early childhood education programs.

Journal: *Educational Leadership,* May 1971, *28*(8), 812–820.

■ ■ ■

679

Test Name: IDEAL TEACHER Q-SORT

Purpose: To identify the characteristics of desirable teachers.

Number of Items: 50 statements.

Format: Five factors: knowledge and organization of subject matter, relations with students, plans and procedures in class, enthusiasm, teaching method.

Author: Bybee, R., and Chaloupka, D.

Article: Students' perceptions of the teacher they like best, a comparison including advantaged-average and disadvantaged students.

Journal: *Colorado Journal of Educational Research,* Summer 1971, *10*(4), 31–35.

Related Research: Cosgrove, D. (1959). Diagnostic rating of teacher performance. *Journal of Education and Psychology, 50*(5), 200–204.

■ ■ ■

680

Test Name: IMPRESSIONS OF UNIVERSITY SETTING QUESTIONNAIRE

Purpose: To secure reactions to a series of statements about university instructors, students, and classroom environments.

Number of Items: 18

Format: Subjects respond to each item on a 5-point scale, indicating agreement or disagreement with each statement. All items are presented.

Author: Atkinson, D. R., et al.

Article: The effect of a class visitation on superior students' concepts of a university class.

Journal: *Journal of College Student Personnel,* September 1971, *12*(5), 353–358.

681

Test Name: INDICATORS OF QUALITY

Purpose: To assess a school system's classroom processes on four criteria: individualization, interpersonal regard, group activity, and creativity.

Format: Provides a quantitative score for each situation observed. Observation data consist of both positive and negative teacher and student classroom behavior as related to the four categories.

Author: Olson, M. N.

Article: Ways to achieve quality in school classrooms: Some definitive answers.

Journal: *Phi Delta Kappan,* September 1971, *53*(1), 63–65.

Related Research: IAR Research Bulletin, Teachers College, Columbia University, *7*(3); *8*(3), *9*(3).

Indicators of quality: A brochure. (1968). New York: Columbia University, Institute of Administrative Research, Teachers College.

■ ■ ■

682

Test Name: INSTITUTIONAL PROCEDURES IN COLLEGES AND UNIVERSITIES

Purpose: To measure student perceptions of campus discipline.

Number of Items: 45

Format: Includes two parts: Part I seeks information on the goals, objectives, and procedures employed in the discipline program; Part II contains statements descriptive of student behavior that might result in disciplinary action by the institution.

Author: Seligman, R.

Article: An instrument to measure institutional stance on matters of student conduct.

Journal: *Journal of College Student Personnel,* November 1971, *12*(6), 417–421.

Related Research: Seligman, R. (1969). *Student and administrator perceptions of campus discipline.* Unpublished doctoral dissertation, University of California at Los Angeles.

■ ■ ■

683

Test Name: INVENTORY OF COLLEGE ACTIVITIES

Purpose: To permit students to assess their college environment.

Format: Includes 27 stimulus factors and eight "image factors."

Author: Chickering, A. W.

Article: Undergraduate academic experience.

Journal: *Journal of Educational Psychology,* April 1972, *63*(2), 134–143.

Related Research: Astin, A. W. (1968). *The college environment.* Washington, DC: American Council on Education.

See *D.U.E.M.M., 1,* 1974: 108–109.

■ ■ ■

684

Test Name: INVENTORY OF TEACHER CHARACTERISTICS

Purpose: To identify teacher characteristics such as age, grade taught, occupational commitment, educational experience, and travel experience.

Format: The instrument is in the form of a questionnaire.

Reliability: Test–retest reliability ranged from .79 to .95.

Author: Rumstein, R.

Article: Teachers' evaluation of research findings in educational psychology.

Journal: *California Journal of Educational Research,* March 1972, *23*(2), 71–82.

• • •

685

Test Name: KNUDSEN-VAUGHN INDEX

Purpose: To index the quality of graduate education in sociology departments.

Validity: Correlations with Glenn-Villemez Indexes were .828 and .574.

Author: Solomon, W.

Article: Correlates of prestige ranking of graduate programs in sociology.

Journal: *American Sociologist,* May 1972, *7*(5), 13–14.

Related Research: Knudsen, D., & Vaughn, T. (1969). Quality in graduate education: A re-evaluation of the rankings of the Carter report. *American Sociologist, 4,* 1279.

• • •

686

Test Name: LEARNING ENVIRONMENT INVENTORY

Purpose: To permit assessment of students' perceptions of their classroom environments.

Number of Items: 98

Format: The items form 14 dimensions. Students indicate on a 4-point scale agreement or disagreement that each item describes their class.

Reliability: Internal consistencies range from .58 to .86.

Author: Walberg, H. J.

Article: Social environment and individual learning: A test of the Bloom model.

Journal: *Journal of Educational Psychology,* February 1972, *63*(1), 69–73.

Related Research: Walberg, H. J. (1969). Social environment as a mediator of classroom learning. *Journal of Educational Psychology, 60,* 443–448.

• • •

687

Test Name: MILWAUKEE SCHOOL GUIDANCE EVALUATION SCALE

Purpose: To provide assessment in five specific areas of the educational guidance effort.

Number of Items: 85

Format: Includes the five areas motivational structure, guidance process, student outcomes, counselor qualifications, and guidance assessment. Each item is rated on a 5-point scale. Each item is presented.

Author: Cassell, R. N., and Thurner, A.

Article: Counselors' self-evaluation of the guidance and counseling activities in the Milwaukee Public Schools.

Journal: *Education,* February–March 1972, *92*(3), 21–30.

• • •

688

Test Name: ORGANIZATIONAL CLIMATE DESCRIPTION QUESTIONNAIRE

Purpose: To identify the school's organizational climate through eight subdimensions.

Format: A summated, equal interval Likert scale. Contains eight subdimensions or subtests: disengagement, hindrance, esprit, intimacy, aloofness, production emphasis, thrust, and consideration.

Reliability: Estimates of internal consistency and of equivalence for the eight subdivisions range from .26 to .84. Test–retest reliability ranged from .19 to .80; odd–even reliability ranged from .54 to .79.

Validity: Subtest esprit correlates .21 with frequency of total principal–teacher communications; .28 with frequency of principal downward communications to the faculty; and .31 with frequency of teacher upward communications to the principal.

Author: Helwig, C.

Article: Organizational climate and frequency of principal–teacher communications in selected Ohio elementary schools.

Journal: *Journal of Experimental Education,* Summer 1971, *39*(4), 52–55.

Related Research: Halpin, A. (1966). *Theory and research in administration.* New York: Macmillan.

Hartley, M. C., & Hoy, W. K. (1972). Openness of school climate and alienation of high school students. *California Journal of Educational Research,* January, *23*(1), 17–24.

Nuil, E. J. (1971, April). Relationships between personal variables of teachers and their perception of the behavior of school personnel. *Journal of Educational Research, 64*(8), 351–354.

• • •

689

Test Name: PORTER COUNSELING INVENTORY

Purpose: To evaluate effects of counseling.

Format: Subscales for evaluative,

interpretive, supportive, probing understanding, content, shallow or partial, reflection, and interpretive.

Author: Woody, R.

Article: Self understanding seminars: The effects of group psychotherapy in counselor training.

Journal: *Counselor Education and Supervision,* Winter 1971, *10*(2), 112–119.

Related Research: Porter, E. (1950). *An introduction to therapeutic counseling.* Boston: Houghton Mifflin.

■ ■ ■

690

Test Name: PRACTICE TEACHING QUESTIONNAIRE

Purpose: To determine the nature and effectiveness of practice teaching.

Number of Items: 35

Format: 30 questions are concerned with student experience with the supervising teacher, the principal, and other staff; physical arrangements within the school; and contacts with fellow students. Five questions elicited a rating from students of the value of the practice experience as they saw it.

Author: Poole, C.

Article: The influence of experience in the schools on students' evaluation of teaching practice.

Journal: *Journal of Educational Research,* December 1972, *66*(4), 161–164.

■ ■ ■

691

Test Name: REAGLES MEASURE OF REHABILITATION GAIN

Purpose: To assess the degree of client change following vocational rehabilitation.

Number of Items: 20

Format: Completed by client pretherapy and posttherapy to obtain gain score: includes earnings, hours worked, work status.

Validity: Item analysis performed.

Author: Reagles, K., et al.

Article: Rehabilitation gain: Relationship with client characteristics, and counselor intervention.

Journal: *Journal of Counseling Psychology,* September 1971, *18*(5), 490–495.

Related Research: Reagles, K. (1969). *Rehabilitation gain of clients in an expanded vocational rehabilitation program.* Doctoral dissertation, University of Wisconsin. (University Microfilms No. 69-22460)

■ ■ ■

692

Test Name: REHABILITATION COUNSELING, PERSONAL ATTRIBUTES, WORK PREFERENCES AND EMPLOYABILITY RATING SCALE

Purpose: To assess the three named factors during rehabilitation counseling; gives objective reality, self, and perceived reality data.

Number of Items: 18, 17, and 17 on Forms A, B, and C, respectively.

Format: Each item is rated on a 5-point scale filled in by the client and instructor in a vocational rehabilitation class.

Author: Tseng, M.

Article: Self perception and employability: A vocational rehabilitation problem.

Journal: *Journal of Counseling Psychology,* July 1972, *19*(4), 314–317.

693

Test Name: RESEARCH ARTICLE RATING SCALE

Purpose: To rate research articles.

Number of Items: 25

Format: Eight factors: method of analysis, design, sampling, rigor, significance, hypotheses, exposition, objectivity.

Author: Shay, C., et al.

Article: The factorial validity of a rating scale for the evaluation of research articles.

Journal: *Educational and Psychological Measurement,* Spring 1972, *32*(2), 453–457.

■ ■ ■

694

Test Name: SCHOOL OF NURSING EVALUATIVE Q-SORT

Purpose: To measure the degree of agreement and diversity of student perceptions of the curriculum.

Number of Items: 72

Format: Includes four categories of program features: curriculum objectives, opportunities, and experiences; program planning, scheduling, and evaluation; teaching styles, methods, and procedures; and student–faculty roles and relationships.

Author: Stone, J. C., and Green, J. L.

Article: The double Q-sort as a research tool.

Journal: *Journal of Experimental Education,* Fall 1971, *40*(1), 81–88.

Related Research: Whiting, J. F. (1955, October). Q-sort: A technique for evaluation perceptions of interpersonal relationships. *Nursing Research, 4,* 70–73.

695

Test Name: SCHOOL ORGANIZATION INVENTORY

Purpose: To assess school bureaucratic structure.

Number of Items: 48

Format: Items are rated on Likert scales. Six dimensions are measured: hierarchy, rules, procedures, impersonality, division of labor, and technical competence.

Validity: Two factors identified: "Organizational Control-Role" and "Organizational Control Methods."

Author: Isherwood, G., and Hoy, W.

Article: Bureaucratic structure reconsidered.

Journal: *Journal of Experimental Education,* Fall 1972, *41*(1), 47–50.

Related Research: Robinson, N. (1966). *A study of the professional role orientations of teachers and principals and their relationship to bureaucratic characteristics of school organization.* Unpublished doctoral dissertation, University of Alberta.

696

Test Name: SIGNIFICANCE SCALE

Purpose: To learn the degree of practical significance teachers assign to each statement as the statements relate to importance or implications for educational practices in the elementary grades 3, 4, 5, and 6.

Number of Items: 30, four forms.

Format: Teachers respond to each item on a 30-point scale ranging from *low significance* to *high significance.*

Reliability: Test–retest reliability ranged from .79 to .95.

Author: Rumstein, R.

Article: Teachers' evaluation of research findings in educational psychology.

Journal: *California Journal of Educational Research,* March 1972, *23*(2), 71–82.

697

Test Name: STATE GUIDANCE OFFICE FUNCTION QUESTIONNAIRE

Purpose: To define the responsibilities and functions of state guidance offices.

Number of Items: 36

Format: Consisted of administrative, regulatory, and developmental functions.

Author: Herr, E.

Article: National perspectives on state guidance office functions.

Journal: *Counselor Education and Supervision,* Spring 1971, *10*(3), 209–218.

698

Test Name: STUDENT COURSE EVALUATION QUESTIONNAIRE

Purpose: To permit student course evaluation.

Number of Items: 50

Format: Includes four parts: general, instructor, student, and method. Each item is rated on a 5-point ordinal scale. All items are presented.

Reliability: .88.

Author: Cassel, R. N.

Article: A student course evaluation questionnaire.

Journal: *Improving College and University Teaching,* Summer 1971, *19*(3), 204–206.

699

Test Name: STUDENT RATING OF COUNSELING INTERVIEW QUESTIONNAIRE

Purpose: To evaluate counseling sessions.

Number of Items: 44

Format: Five-point scale (*not helpful* to *very helpful*).

Author: Gilbert, W., and Ewing, T.

Article: Programmed vs. face to face counseling.

Journal: *Journal of Counseling Psychology,* September 1971, *18*(5), 413–421.

700

Test Name: STUDENT SURVEY OF SCHOOL SITUATIONS

Purpose: To collect data regarding perception of various aspects of the school.

Number of Items: 100

Format: Multiple choice items about junior high school environment (school in general, teachers, skills, classroom methods and atmosphere, students, subjects, grading, and materials and facilities).

Validity: Teachers, principals, and counselors were accurate in predicting student choices that were most and least often selected on the instrument.

Author: Van Riper, B.W.

Article: Toward a separate professional identity.

Journal: *Journal of Counseling Psychology,* March 1972, *19*(2), 117–120.

701

Test Name: STUDENT TEACHER CONCERNS RATING SCALE

Purpose: To identify basic dimensions of elementary school student teacher concerns.

Number of Items: 122

Format: Each item is answered by selecting the most applicable of the following: *causes me no concern; causes me slight concern; causes me moderate concern; causes me great concern; causes me such great concern that it has led me to consider leaving the teaching profession.*

Reliability: Kuder-Richardson reliability was .98.

Author: Cohen, M. W., et al.

Article: Dimensions of elementary school student teacher concerns.

Journal: *Journal of Experimental Education,* Winter 1972, *41*(2), 6–10.

Availability: The questionnaire may be obtained from Mark W. Cohen, Department of Psychology, The Ohio State University, 1945 N. High Street, Columbus, Ohio 43210.

■ ■ ■

702

Test Name: TEACHING REQUIREMENTS FOR COUNSELOR CERTIFICATION QUESTIONNAIRE

Purpose: To determine whether states required teaching experience for certification of school counselors.

Number of Items: 3

Author: Boller, J.

Article: Counselor certification: Who still needs teaching experience?

Journal: *Personnel and Guidance*

Journal, January 1972, *50*(5), 388–391.

■ ■ ■

703

Test Name: UNIVERSITY COUNSELING CENTER USE QUESTIONNAIRE

Purpose: To determine why students do not use a university counseling center.

Format: Four sections: (a) biographical information; (b) 70 Likert items about counseling in general, the counseling center, and so forth; (c) 13 hypothethical problems in which students responded with source of help they would use; (d) subjects asked to check which of the 13 problems they had experienced.

Reliability: Cronbach alphas were all above .58 and were near .80 for longer scales.

Validity: Item analyses revealed five subscales from Part 2.

Author: Snyder, J., et al.

Article: Why some students do not use university counseling facilities.

Journal: *Journal of Counseling Psychology,* July 1972, *19*(4), 263–268.

■ ■ ■

704

Test Name: UNIVERSITY RESIDENCE ENVIRONMENT SCALES

Purpose: To measure the consensual perception of the press of the immediate environment.

Number of Items: 96

Format: True–false items grouped into 10 subscales: involvement, emotional support, independence, traditional social orientation, competition, academic achievement, intellectuality, order and organization, innovation,

student influence. These subscales were grouped into four categories: interpersonal relationships, personal growth, intellectual growth, and systematic change and maintenance.

Reliability: Subscale internal consistency Kuder-Richardson formula 20 correlations ranged from .76 to .87. Test–retest correlations ranged from .67 to .75 after 1 week and .59 to .74 after 1 month. Estimates of profile stability were .96 after 1 week and .86 and .98 after 1 month.

Author: Gerst, M. S., and Moos, R. H.

Article: Social ecology of university student residences.

Journal: *Journal of Educational Psychology,* December 1972, *63*(6), 513–525.

■ ■ ■

705

Test Name: UNIVERSITY STUDENT CENSUS

Purpose: To identify activities and attitudes.

Number of Items: 17

Format: Responses are made on a 6-point scale: *strongly agree, agree, neutral, disagree, strongly disagree, other.* Examples are presented.

Author: Schmidt, D. M. K., and Sedlacek, W. E.

Article: Variables related to university student satisfaction.

Journal: *Journal of College Student Personnel,* May 1972, *13*(3), 233–238.

■ ■ ■

706

Test Name: WORD ASSOCIATION STUDY

Purpose: Permits subjects to rate two kinds of college components:

people (parent, professor, academic dean, and dean of students) and curricula (natural sciences, social-behavioral sciences, educational methods, and student teaching).

Number of Items: 24 scales.

Format: Seven-point

semantic-differential scales were used. A total of 12 scales for people were distributed among four dimensions and 12 scales for curricula were distributed among three dimensions. The scales are presented.

Author: Yamamoto, K., and Wiersma, J.

Article: Typology and college-related perceptions in education students.

Journal: *Journal of Educational Research,* November 1971, *65*(3), 113–118.

CHAPTER 14
Interest

707

Test Name: BODDEN MEASURE OF VOCATIONAL COGNITIVE COMPLEXITY

Purpose: To measure vocational cognitive complexity and used to make predictions with respect to relations with appropriate vocational choice.

Number of Items: 12 occupational titles and 12 vocationally relevant construct dimensions.

Format: Subject uses construct dimensions to rate each occupation.

Author: Bodden, J., and Klein, A.

Article: Cognitive complexity and appropriate vocational choice: Another look.

Journal: *Journal of Counseling Psychology*, May 1972, *19*(3), 257–258.

708

Test Name: CAREER PATTERN STUDY WORK VALUES INVENTORY—ADAPTED

Purpose: To ascertain work preferences.

Number of Items: 13

Format: Items are arranged in 13 groups of four statements per group. Each statement appears four times but only once in conjunction with each of the remaining statements. All statements are presented.

Author: Underwood, K. L.

Article: Work values of university entrants.

Journal: *Journal of College Student Personnel,* November 1971, *12*(6), 455–459.

Related Research: Super, D. E. (1962). The structure of work values in relation to status, achievement, interests, and adjustment. *Journal of Applied Psychology, 46,* 231–239.

709

Test Name: JOB SATISFACTION INVENTORY

Purpose: To assess occupational satisfaction in eight areas.

Number of Items: 70

Format: Items are rated on a 5-point Likert scale that assesses satisfaction in eight areas: physical and mental exertion, relations with associates, relations with employers, security and so forth, interest in job, job information and training, physical surroundings, and future goals.

Reliability: Split-half reliability was .88 (corrected) for total score. Individual subpart coefficients ranged from .47 to .89.

Validity: Inventory successfully discriminated between counselors who terminated and those who were retained on the job.

Author: Smits, S.

Article: Counselor job satisfaction and employment turnover in the state rehabilitation agencies.

Journal: *Journal of Counseling Psychology,* November 1972, *19*(6), 512–517.

Related Research: Muthard, J., & Miller, L. (1966). *The criteria problem in rehabilitation counseling.* Iowa City: University of Iowa.

710

Test Name: MALE INFLUENCE ON FEMALE CAREER CHOICE SCALE

Purpose: To assess the effects on women of the influence of male views for appropriate female career choice.

Number of Items: 35

Format: Six-point scale in which women were asked to respond as they thought significant men in their life would respond. Factor analysis resulted in five constructs or subscales.

Reliability: Alpha coefficients for five subscales were .75, .73, .77, .83, .80.

Author: Hawley, P.

Article: What women think men think: Does it affect their career choice?

Journal: *Journal of Counseling Psychology,* May 1971, *18*(3), 192–199.

711

Test Name: OCCUPATIONAL INVENTORY

Purpose: To measure seventh graders' knowledge of the world of work.

Number of Items: 31

Format: Items based on Dictionary of Occupational Titles (3rd ed., 1965) with emphasis on worker traits of occupations.

Reliability: Kuder-Richardson Formula 20 was .828.

Validity: Average item total correlation was .497.

Author: Reardon, F., et al.

Article: The development and evaluation of an occupational inventory.

Journal: *Journal of Educational Measurement,* Summer 1972, *9*(2), 151–153.

CHAPTER 15
Motivation

712

Test Name: ACHIEVEMENT MOTIVE QUESTIONNAIRE

Purpose: To measure achievement motive.

Number of Items: 15

Format: A multiple-choice test. The score is the number of hope-of-success responses minus the number of fear-of-failure responses.

Reliability: .76, .73, .63.

Author: Epps, E. G., et al.

Article: Effect of race of comparison referent and motives on the Negro cognitive performance.

Journal: *Journal of Educational Psychology*, June 1971, *62*(3), 201–208.

Related Research: French, E. G. (1958). Development of a measure of complex motivation. In J. W. Atkinson (Ed.), *Motives in fantasy, action, and society.* Princeton, NJ: Van Nostrand.

Willerman, B., et al. (1960). Seeking and avoiding self-evaluation by working individually or in groups. In D. Willner (Ed.), *Decisions, values and groups.* London: Pergamon Press.

• • •

713

Test Name: ACHIEVEMENT-ORIENTATION QUESTIONNAIRE

Purpose: To assess achievement orientation.

Number of Items: 160

Format: All items are answered true or false depending on whether the subjects consider the statement descriptive of themselves. Includes 10 factors: test anxiety, threat of failure, parental encouragement, unwillingness to risk failing, dislike of those who do better than oneself, concern about primary roles, desire to excel, sensitivity to others' knowing of one's failure, exerting effort to do well, valuation of competition.

Reliability: Cronbach's alpha ranged from .71 to .84. Test–retest reliability ranged from .78 to .88.

Validity: Cumulative multiple correlations of demographic-personal characteristics with test score ranged from .10 to .25.

Author: Herrenkohl, R. C.

Article: Factor-analytic and criterion study of achievement orientation.

Journal: *Journal of Educational Psychology*, August 1972, *63*(4), 314–326.

• • •

714

Test Name: ATTAINMENT-SATISFACTION SCALE

Purpose: To measure students' perceptions of attainment of selected educational, vocation, social, and personal goals.

Number of Items: 12

Format: Includes 12 educational, vocational, social, and personal

goals. Scores range from 0 to 3 on the first 11 variables, and from 0 to 9 on the 12th. A higher score indicates a greater perceived attainment of the goal.

Author: Lange, A. J.

Article: An analysis of Clark-Trow subtypes.

Journal: *Journal of College Student Personnel*, July 1972, *13*(4), 347–351.

Related Research: Pace, C. R., & Baird, L. (1966). Attainment patterns in the environmental press of college subcultures. In T. M. Newcomb & E. K. Wilson (Eds.), *College peer groups: Problems and prospects for research* (pp. 215–243). Chicago: Aldine.

• • •

715

Test Name: ARONSON GRAPHIC EXPRESSION SCALE

Purpose: To assess need achievement.

Validity: Correlation with children's locus of control = .29 ($p < .05$).

Author: Pedhazur, L., and Wheeler, L.

Article: Locus of perceived control and need achievement.

Journal: *Perceptual and Motor Skills*, December 1971, *33*(3), 1281–1282.

Related Research: Aronson, E. (1958). The need for achievement as measured by graphic expression. In J. W. Atkinson (Ed.), *Motives in fantasy, action* *and society.* Princeton, NJ: Van Nostrand.

●●●

716

Test Name: BEHAVIOR PROFILE

Purpose: To assess curiosity and achievement striving.

Validity: Correlation of curiosity subscale with problem solving flexibility was .38 ($p < .01$).

Author: Greenberger, E., et al.

Article: Personality, cognitive and academic correlates of problem solving flexibility.

Journal: *Developmental Psychology,* May 1971, *4*(3), 416–424.

Related Research: Greenberger, E. (1969). *The development of a new measure for curiosity for children* (Report No. 56). Baltimore, MD: Johns Hopkins University, Center for the Study of Sound Organization of Schools.

●●●

717

Test Name: CHANGE SEEKER INDEX

Purpose: To assess a subject's motivation to seek novelty.

Author: McReynolds, P.

Article: Behavioral choice as a function of novelty seeking and anxiety-avoidance motivations.

Journal: *Psychological Reports,* August 1971, *29*(1), 3–6.

Related Research: Garlington, W., & Shimota, H. (1964). The change seeker index: A measure of the need for variable stimulus imput. *Psychological Reports, 14,* 919–924.

Zuckerman, M., et al. (1964). Development of a sensation-seeking scale. *Journal of*

Consulting Psychology, 28, 477–482.

●●●

718

Test Name: CLASSROOM BEHAVIOR INVENTORY

Purpose: To assess children's motivation to achieve in school learning.

Number of Items: 22

Format: Each item consists of a question and a 5-point, temporally oriented scale with the descriptives *never, rarely, half of the time, often,* and *almost always,* as well as *unable to observe.* Examples are presented.

Reliability: Internal consistency reliability (Cronbach's alpha) was .95. The coefficient of concordance used as an estimate of interrater reliability after correction for ties was .65.

Validity: Correlations with the California Achievement Test were reading vocabulary, .63; reading comprehension, .51; mathematical reasoning, .60; mathematical fundamentals, .51; mechanics of language, .56; and spelling, .45.

Author: Cicirelli, V. G., et al.

Article: Measures of self-concept, attitudes, and achievement motivation of primary grade children.

Journal: *Journal of School Psychology,* 1971, *9*(4), 383–392.

●●●

719

Test Name: EXPECTATION SURVEY

Purpose: To measure purposes and goals for attending college, educational aspirations, and occupational choices.

Number of Items: 58

Format: Divided into three sections: Section 1 includes intellectual, vocational, hedonistic, personal, and social service scales; Section 2 measures educational aspirations; and Section 3 identifies occupational choices.

Reliability: Correlations ranged from .49 to .64.

Author: Braskamp, L. A., and Flessner, D.

Article: The congruency between parental and entering freshman expectations.

Journal: *Journal of College Student Personnel,* May 1971, *12*(3), 179–185.

●●●

720

Test Name: EXPRESSED MOTIVATIONS QUESTIONNAIRE

Purpose: To identify expressed motivations for curricular choice.

Number of Items: 289

Format: Includes a 5-point intensity scale in order to enable the subjects to indicate how strong a motivation an item was in their choice. Four factors were identified. Several items are presented.

Author: Cohen, D.

Article: Differentiating motivations underlying vocational choice.

Journal: *Journal of Educational Research,* January 1971, *64*(5), 229–234.

●●●

721

Test Name: HERMAN'S NEED ACHIEVEMENT TEST

Purpose: To assess achievement motivation.

Author: Higgs, S.

Article: Personality traits and motor ability associated with observed competitiveness in women physical education majors.

Journal: *Perceptual and Motor Skills,* February 1972, *34*(4), 219–222.

Related Research: Hermans, H. (1970). A questionnaire measure of achievement motivation. *Journal of Applied Psychology, 54,* 353–363.

■ ■ ■

722

Test Name: HERRENKOHL FEELINGS ABOUT SUCCESS AND FAILURE SCALE

Purpose: To assess need for achievement.

Number of Items: 140

Format: True–false questionnaire.

Author: Dispenzieri, A., et al.

Article: College performance of disadvantaged students as a function of ability and personality.

Journal: *Journal of Counseling Psychology,* July 1971, *18*(4), 298–305.

Related Research: Herrenkohl, R. (1966). *Motivation in social comparison.* Unpublished doctoral dissertation, New York University.

■ ■ ■

723

Test Name:
HOGAN-GREENBERGER ADJECTIVE CHECKLIST

Purpose: To measure teacher assessed curiosity in children.

Format: Adjective checklist: yields scores that correlate positively and negatively with curiosity.

Validity: Correlation with problem solving flexibility was .22 ($p < .01$.

Author: Greenberger, E., et al.

Article: Personality, cognitive and

academic correlates of problem-solving flexibility.

Journal: *Developmental Psychology,* May 1971, *4*(3), 416–424.

Related Research: Hogan, R., & Greenberger, E. (1968). *Development of a curiosity scale* (Report No. 32). Baltimore, MD: Johns Hopkins University, Center for the Study of Social Organization of Schools.

■ ■ ■

724

Test Name: INVESTIGATORY ACTIVITIES INVENTORY (REVISED)

Purpose: To assess curiosity.

Format: Illustrated items asked children what they would do if confronted with a novel happening.

Validity: Correlation with problem solving flexibility was .28 ($p < .01$), boys.

Author: Greenberger, E., et al.

Article: Personality, cognitive and academic correlates of problem solving flexibility.

Journal: *Developmental Psychology,* May 1971, *4*(3), 416–424.

Related Research: Maw, W., & Maw, E. (1965). Differences in preference for investigatory activities by school children who differ in curiosity level. *Psychology in the Schools, 2,* 263–266.

■ ■ ■

725

Test Name: MARBLE IN THE HOLE GAME

Purpose: To assess extent of responsiveness to social reinforcement.

Time Required: 30 minutes maximum.

Format: Individually administered. Subject is reinforced (socially) for a boring task (dropping marbles in a hole).

Author: Zigler, E., and Balla, D.

Article: Developmental course of responsiveness to social reinforcement in normal children and institutionalized retarded children.

Journal: *Developmental Psychology,* January 1972, *6*(1), 66–73.

Related Research: Zigler, E. (1961). Social deprivation and rigidity in the performance of feeble-minded children. *Journal of Abnormal and Social Psychology, 62,* 413–421.

■ ■ ■

726

Test Name: MCCLELLAND THEMATIC APPERCEPTION TEST OF n-ACHIEVEMENT (n-ACH)

Purpose: To measure need to achieve.

Number of Items: 10

Format: Two pictures selected from the Murray Thematic Apperception Test and the Symonds Picture-Story Test.

Author: Hall, L. H.

Article: Personality variables of achieving and non-achieving Mexican-American and other community college freshmen.

Journal: *Journal of Educational Research,* January 1972, *65*(5), 224–228.

■ ■ ■

727

Test Name: MCCLELLAND'S NEED ACHIEVEMENT THEMATIC APPERCEPTION TEST

Purpose: To measure achievement motivation.

Number of Items: 4

Format: Four pictures are presented in a neutral classroom situation.

Reliability: Interrater reliability was .90.

Validity: Haller's Occupational Aspiration Scale: .22. NORC Occupational Prestige Scale: .26. Mandler-Cowan's Test Anxiety Questionnaire for High School Students: .10.

Author: Tseng, M. S.

Article: Social class, occupational aspiration, and other variables.

Journal: *Journal of Experimental Education,* Summer 1971, *39*(4), 88–92.

Related Research: Atkinson, J. W. (1958). *Motives in fantasy, action, and society.* Princeton, NJ: Van Nostrand.

■ ■ ■

728

Test Name: MEHRABIAN RESULTANT ACHIEVEMENT MOTIVATION SCALES

Purpose: To measure need-achievement.

Number of Items: 26

Format: Each item requires the subject to indicate extent of agreement with a preference statement ("I prefer A to B") on a 7-point Likert scale. Higher scores indicate that a person's motive to achieve success is stronger than motive to avoid failure, while low scores indicate that the opposite is true. Separate male and female scales.

Author: Raffini, J., and Rosemier, R. A.

Article: Effect of resultant achievement motivation on

postexam error-correcting performance.

Journal: *Journal of Educational Psychology,* June 1972, *63*(3), 281–286.

Related Research: Mehrabian, A. (1968). Male and female scales of the tendency to achieve. *Educational and Psychological Measurement, 28,* 493–502.

DuCette, J., & Wolk, S. (1971). The limitations of the interaction hypothesis in regard to ability grouping. *Journal of Experimental Education,* Fall, *40*(1), 23–27.

Wolk, S., & DuCette, J. (1971, December). Locus of control and achievement motivation: Theoretical overlap and methodological divergence. *Psychological Reports, 29*(3–1), 755–758.

■ ■ ■

729

Test Name: MYERS ACHIEVEMENT MOTIVATION SCALE

Purpose: To measure motivation to achieve in junior and senior high school students.

Validity: Correlation with grade point average = .29 ($p < .05$) at grade 9; nonsignificant for grades 7, 8, 10, 11; correlations with IQ or School and College Ability Tests all nonsignificant.

Author: Stewin, L., and Nyberg, V.

Article: Myers achievement motivation scale: A validation study.

Journal: *Educational and Psychological Measurement,* Winter 1972, *32*(4), 1103–1106.

Related Research: Myers, A. (1965). Risk taking and academic success and their relation to an objective measure of achievement motivation. *Educational and*

Psychological Measurement, 25, 355–363.

■ ■ ■

730

Test Name: ONTARIO TEST OF INTRINSIC MOTIVATION

Purpose: To assess subject curiosity.

Format: Includes scales: consultation, observation, and thinking.

Validity: Correlation of consultation with thinking was .63 ($p < .01$).

Author: Evans, D.

Article: The Ontario test of intrinsic motivation, question asking, and autistic thinking.

Journal: *Psychological Reports,* August 1971, *29*(1), 154.

Related Research: Day, H. (1970, June). *The measurement of specific curiosity.* Paper presented at the Symposium on Intrinsic Motivation in Education, Toronto.

■ ■ ■

731

Test Name: PHILLIPS SCHOOL MOTIVATION SCALE

Purpose: To assess children's school related motivation.

Format: Completed by teacher, the scale (1–5) is forced choice. Eight dimensions assessed: attentive to tasks, pleasure in good work, enjoys working with others, concerned with lessons, seeks social recognition, energetic, helpful to others with problems, tries to be accepted.

Author: Adams, R., and Phillips, B.

Article: Motivational and achievement differences among children of various ordinal birth positions.

Journal: *Child Development,*

March 1972, *43*(1), 155–164.

Related Research: Phillips, B. (1966, August). *An analysis of causes of anxiety among children in school* (Final Report, Project No. 2616, Grant No. OE-5–10–012). Washington, DC: U.S. Department of Health, Education and Welfare.

• • •

732

Test Name: POWER MOTIVATION SCALE

Purpose: To measure need for socialized power activities.

Number of Items: 26

Format: True–false.

Reliability: Kuder-Richardson Formula 20 was .89.

Author: Good, L., and Good, K.

Article: An objective measure of the motive to attain social power.

Journal: *Psychological Reports,* February 1972, *30*(1), 247–251.

• • •

733

Test Name: REACTIVE CURIOSITY QUESTIONNAIRE

Purpose: To assess curiosity.

Number of Items: 100

Format: True–false test with built-in lie or validity scale.

Author: Wilson, F. S., et al.

Article: Are pupils in the open plan school different?

Journal: *Journal of Educational Research,* November 1972, *66*(3), 115–118.

Related Research: Penney, R., & McCann, B. (1964). The children's reactive curiosity scale. *Psychological Reports, 15,* 323–334.

734

Test Name: REINFORCEMENT INVENTORY

Purpose: To predict reinforcer effectiveness of 15 stimuli.

Number of Items: 15

Format: Three categories of written descriptions of types of stimulation: verbal and social; tangible and manipulatable; and knowledge of progress. The descriptive statements were presented in pairs; each statement was paired with every other. All items presented.

Reliability: .57 to .77.

Validity: With "time on task" .21, .18. With "problems solved per minute" .29, .14.

Author: Runyon, H. L., and Williams, R. L.

Article: Differentiating reinforcement priorities of junior high school students.

Journal: *Journal of Experimental Education,* Spring 1972, *40*(3), 76–80.

• • •

735

Test Name: REINFORCEMENT SURVEY SCHEDULE

Purpose: To identify potential reinforcers to be used in therapy.

Number of Items: 54 major items (total 139 responses).

Format: In general, subject identifies objects, activities, situations that would be enjoyable and reinforcing.

Author: Cautela, J.

Article: Reinforcement survey schedule: Evaluation and current applications.

Journal: *Psychological Reports,* June 1972, *30*(3), 683–690.

Related Research: Cautela, J., and

Kastenbaum, R. (1967). A reinforcement survey schedule for use in therapy, training, and research. *Psychological Reports, 20,* 1115–1130.

Keehm, J., et al. (1970). Uses of the reinforcement survey schedule with alcoholics. *Quarterly Journal of Studies on Alcohol, 31,* 602–615.

• • •

736

Test Name: REINFORCING BEHAVIORS OF TEACHERS QUESTIONNAIRE

Purpose: To identify typical positive and negative reinforcing behaviors of teachers.

Number of Items: 20

Format: Subjects indicated their feelings about the reinforcement by choosing from among five statements ranging from *highly favorable* to *highly unfavorable.* An example is presented.

Author: Davison, D.C.

Article: Perceived reward value of teacher reinforcement and attitude toward teacher: An application of Newcomb's balance theory.

Journal: *Journal of Educational Psychology,* October 1972, *63*(5), 418–422.

Related Research: Davison, D. C. (1967). *Some demographic and attitudinal concomitants of the perceived reward value of classroom reinforcement: An application of Newcomb's balance theory.* Doctoral dissertation, University of Illinois. (University Microfilms No. 68-1739)

• • •

737

Test Name: SCHOOL MOTIVATION SCALE

Purpose: To measure persistent and consistent behavior over the school year as observed by the classroom teacher.

Format: Behavior of students is rated on a forced-distribution form containing eight school-related motivational dimensions.

Reliability: Test–retest reliabilities were .88 and .92; others ranged from .50 to .67.

Author: Adams, R. L., and Phillips, B. N.

Article: Motivational and achievement differences among children of various ordinal birth positions.

Journal: *Child Development,* March 1972, *43*(1), 155–164.

Related Research: Phillips, B. N. (1966, August). *An analysis of causes of anxiety among children in school* (Final Report, Project No. 2616, Grant No. OE-5–10–012). Washington, DC: U.S. Department of Health, Education and Welfare.

■ ■ ■

738

Test Name: SCHOOL SITUATIONS PICTURE STORIES TEST

Purpose: To assess n achievement, n affiliation, n power, and n rejection.

Format: Projective test administered individually. Ten pictures depicting school situations shown under instructions of the Thematic Apperception Test. Each story received points by rater for each need.

Reliability: Interscorer reliabilities were n achievement, .94; n affiliation, .89; n power, .86; n rejection, .85.

Author: Ramirez, M., et al.

Article: Mexican American cultural membership and adjustment to school.

Journal: *Developmental Psychology,* March 1971, *4*(2), 141–148.

■ ■ ■

739

Test Name: SELF-REPORT REINFORCEMENT INSTRUMENT

Purpose: To ascertain reinforcement preferences of individual subjects.

Number of Items: Nine items forming 36 pairs.

Format: Nine types of pictorial stimuli: three social, three tangible, and three knowledge of progress.

Reliability: .49 to .74.

Validity: .02, .01, .04.

Author: Atkins, J. W., and Williams, R. L.

Article: The utility of self-report in determining reinforcement priorities of primary school children.

Journal: *Journal of Educational Research,* March 1972, *65*(7), 324–328.

■ ■ ■

740

Test Name: SELLTIZ EXPECTATIONS ABOUT COLLEGE PERFORMANCE QUESTIONNAIRE

Purpose: To assess reality of aspiration level; in this study, the closer aspiration level to actual high school average the more realistic was the aspiration level.

Author: Dispenzieri, A., et al.

Article: College performance of disadvantaged students as a function of ability and personality.

Journal: *Journal of Counseling Psychology,* July 1971, *18*(4), 298–305.

Related Research: Selltiz, C. (1966). *Expectations about College Performance Questionnaire.* New York: City University, Social Dynamics Institute.

■ ■ ■

741

Test Name: SENSATION SEEKING SCALE

Purpose: To measure stimulation seeking.

Number of Items: 22

Validity: Correlation with Study of Values scales ranged social ($r = .02$) to economic ($r = .40$, $\pi < .02$).

Author: Farley, F., and Dionne, M.

Article: Value orientations of sensation-seekers.

Journal: *Perceptual and Motor Skills,* April 1972, *34*(2), 509–510.

Related Research: Zuckerman, M., et al. (1964). Development of a sensation seeking scale. *Journal of Consulting Psychology, 28,* 477–482.

McReynolds, P. (1971, August). Behavioral choice as a function of novelty-seeking and anxiety-avoidance motivation. *Psychological Reports, 29*(1), 3–6.

■ ■ ■

742

Test Name: SPECIFIC CURIOSITY QUESTIONNAIRE

Purpose: To assess curiosity.

Number of Items: 36

Format: True–false test.

Author: Wilson, F. S., et al.

Article: Are pupils in the open plan school different?

Journal: *Journal of Educational Research,* November 1972, *66*(3), 115–118.

Related Research: Day, H. (1968).

The role of specific curiosity in school achievement. *Journal of Educational Psychology, 59,* 37–43.

• • •

743

Test Name: STUDENT MOTIVATION AND ATTITUDES QUESTIONNAIRE

Purpose: To elicit a variety of information concerning the student's motivation to achieve the traditional goals of the academic system as well as attitudes toward specific reforms.

Number of Items: 98

Time Required: Approximately 35 minutes.

Format: Includes 6 sections. Some items are presented.

Reliability: From .27 to .80. Estimated reliabilities from .72 to .90.

Author: Priest, R. F.

Article: Why college students favor grading reforms.

Journal: *Journal of College Student Personnel,* March 1971, *12*(2), 120–125.

• • •

744

Test Name: VIDEBECK NEED ACHIEVEMENT SCALE

Purpose: To measure need achievement; that is, "having goals," "striving to accomplish tasks as quickly as possible," "attempting to exert one's best efforts."

Number of Items: 7

Format: Forced choice (*agree–disagree*).

Reliability: Kuder-Richardson Formula 20 was .53.

Validity: Correlation with impulsiveness was .260. Correlation with planfulness was .201.

Author: Friis, R., and Knox, A.

Article: A validity study of scales to measure need achievement, need affiliation, impulsiveness and intellectuality.

Journal: *Educational and Psychological Measurement,* Spring 1972, *32*(1), 147–154.

• • •

745

Test Name: VIDEBECK NEED AFFILIATION

Purpose: To assess the desire to be with other people.

Number of Items: 7

Format: Forced choice (*agree–disagree*).

Reliability: Kuder-Richardson Formula 20 was .43.

Validity: Correlation with need achievement, $r = .136$ ($p < .001$); with intellectual interest, $r = .149$ ($p < .001$); with organizational participation, $r = .130$ ($p < .01$).

Author: Friis, R., and Knox, A.

Article: A validity study of scales to measure need achievement, need affiliation, impulsiveness and intellectuality.

Journal: *Educational and Psychological Measurement,* Spring 1972, *32*(1), 147–154.

• • •

746

Test Name: VINDICATION MOTIVATION MEASURE

Purpose: To assess inclination to justify self and to seek opportunity to impose views on others.

Number of Items: 30

Format: True–false.

Reliability: Kuder-Richardson formula was .81.

Author: Good, L., and Good, K.

Article: An objective measure of the vindication motive.

Journal: *Psychological Reports,* December 1971, *29*(3), 983–986.

• • •

747

Test Name: W SCALE

Purpose: To measure keenness for work.

Number of Items: 42

Format: The subject responds on a 5-point scale from *strongly agree* through *uncertain* to *strongly disagree.*

Reliability: Split-half reliability was .73. Test–retest reliability was .75.

Validity: .33.

Author: Hartmann, P.

Article: A study of attitudes in industrial rehabilitation.

Journal: *Occupational Psychology,* 1972, *46*(2), 87–97.

CHAPTER 16
Perception

748

Test Name: ACTUAL–IDEAL SELF SEMANTIC DIFFERENTIAL

Purpose: To assess individual self perception, both actual and ideal.

Format: Seven-point scales for 21 bipolar adjectives on the two concepts: actual and ideal self.

Validity: Correlation between ideal and actual increased from .065 to .48 from before group encounter to after.

Author: Weissman, H., et al.

Article: Changes in self regard, creativity, and interpersonal behaviors as a function of audio tape encounter group experiences.

Journal: *Psychological Reports*, December 1972, *31*(3), 975–981.

Related Research: Jenkins, J., et al. (1958). An atlas of semantic differential profiles on a set of 360 words. *American Journal of Psychology, 71*, 688–699.

● ● ●

749

Test Name: ADJECTIVE RATING SCALE FOR SELF DESCRIPTION

Purpose: To permit the respondent to rate himself on descriptive adjectives.

Format: Factors included are: social warmth, social abrasiveness, ego organization, introversion–extraversion, neurotic anxiety, and attractiveness.

Author: Austad, C. A.

Article: Personality correlates of

teacher performance in a micro-teaching laboratory.

Journal: *Journal of Experimental Education*, Spring 1972, *40*(3), 1–5.

Related Research: Parker, G. V. C., & Veldman, D. J. (1969). Item factor structure of the adjective check list. *Educational Psychological Measurement, 29*, 605–614.

● ● ●

750

Test Name: AUDITORY-VISUAL RHYTHM PERCEPTION TEST

Purpose: To evaluate the ability to make cross-modal equivalence judgments.

Number of Items: 11

Format: Requires that a spoken language pattern, composed of varying combinations of juncture, be associated with a visual array representing this language pattern. The examinee must select the correct pattern from a group of three presented choices.

Reliability: Test–retest coefficient was .71. Kuder-Richardson Formula 20 coefficient was .79.

Validity: With SRA Total Reading, $r = .65$.

Author: McNinch, G.

Article: Auditory perceptual factors and measured first-grade reading achievement.

Journal: *Reading Research Quarterly*, Summer 1971, *6*(4), 472–492.

Related Research: Birch, H. G., & Belmont, L. (1964).

Auditory-visual integration in normal and retarded readers. *American Journal of Orthopsychiatry, 34*, 852–861.

Birch, H. G., & Belmont, L. (1965). Auditory-visual integration, intelligence and reading ability in school children. *Perceptual and Motor Skills, 20*, 295–305.

● ● ●

751

Test Name: BEAUTY RATING SCALE

Purpose: To assess perception of facial beauty.

Time Required: 15–30 minutes.

Format: 72 portrait photographs rated on a 7-point scale; individually administered for individuals 7 years old to adult.

Author: Cross, J., and Cross, J.

Article: Age, sex, race and the perception of facial beauty.

Journal: *Developmental Psychology*, November 1971, *5*(3), 433–439.

● ● ●

752

Test Name: BERGER SENTENCE COMPLETION TEST

Purpose: To assess a disabled person's attitude toward himself.

Number of Items: 25

Format: Specifically designed for physically disabled population.

Author: Grand, S.

Article: Reactions to unfavorable evaluations of the self as a function of acceptance of disability: A test of Dembo, Leviton, and Wright's misfortune hypothesis.

Journal: *Journal of Counseling Psychology,* March 1972, *19*(2), 87–93.

Related Research: Berger, S. (1951). *The role of sexual impotence in the concept of self in male paraplegics.* Unpublished doctoral dissertation, New York University.

■ ■ ■

753

Test Name: BETTS QMI VIVIDNESS OF IMAGERY SCALE

Purpose: To assess imagery.

Format: Self report.

Reliability: Odd–even: .95 (undergrads), .99 (professors).

Author: Juhasz, J.

Article: On the reliability of two measures of imagery.

Journal: *Perceptual and Motor Skills,* December 1972, *35*(3), 874.

Related Research: Richardson, A. (1969). *Mental Imagery.* New York: Springer.

Sheehan, P. (1967). Reliability of a short test of imagery. *Perceptual and Motor Skills, 25,* 744.

■ ■ ■

754

Test Name: BIALER-CROMWELL CHILDREN'S LOCUS OF CONTROL SCALE

Purpose: To measure degree of internal-external control in children.

Number of Items: 23

Format: A *yes* or *no* response is required for each item. A *yes* response indicates internal control

on some items and external control on other items. The sum of the external responses equals the external control score.

Reliability: .43 and .49.

Author: Shaw, R. L., and Uhl, N. P.

Article: Control of reinforcement and academic achievement.

Journal: *Journal of Educational Research,* January 1971, *64*(5), 226–228.

Related Research: Shaffer, S., et al. (1969, February). *The relationship of individual difference measures to socioeconomic level and to discrimination learning.* Paper presented at the annual convention of the Southeastern Psychological Association, New Orleans.

Milgram, N. (1971, October). Locus of control in Negro and White children at four age levels. *Psychological Reports, 29*(2), 459–465.

Pedhazur, L., & Wheeler, L. (1971, December). Locus of perceived control and need achievement. *Perceptual and Motor Skills, 33*(3), 1281–1282.

Powell, A. (1971, August). Alternative measures of locus control and the prediction of academic performance. *Psychological Reports, 29*(1), 47–50.

■ ■ ■

755

Test Name: BI-POLAR TRAITS INVENTORY

Purpose: To measure five dimensions of self-perceptions.

Number of Items: 40

Format: Each bi-polar trait is expressed in sentence form with a rating scale between each pair of traits indicating four spaces of

distance. Scores range from +40 to –40. The five dimensions of self-perception include: self concept, ideal concept, reflected self in the eyes of their classmates, reflected self with teachers, and reflected self with parents. An example is given.

Author: Soares, A. T., and Soares, L. M.

Article: Comparative differences in the self-perceptions of disadvantaged and advantaged students.

Journal: *Journal of School Psychology,* 1971, *9*(4), 424–429.

Related Research: Soares, A. T., & Soares, L. M. (1969). Self-perceptions of culturally disadvantaged children. *American Educational Research Journal, 6,* 31–45.

■ ■ ■

756

Test Name: BODY AND SELF SATISFACTION TEST

Purpose: To assess satisfaction with self in general and body in particular.

Number of Items: 45, body satisfaction; 30, self-satisfaction.

Format: Subjects rated self on 5-point scale.

Validity: Correlation with IQ and body satisfaction = -.09 women (*ns*); .44 men (*p* < .01).

Author: Clifford, E.

Article: Body satisfaction in adolescence.

Journal: *Perceptual and Motor Skills,* August 1971, *33*(1), 119–125.

Related Research: Secord, P., & Jourard, S. (1953). The appraisal of body-cathexis: Body cathexis and the self. *Journal of Consulting Psychology, 17,* 343–347.

757

Test Name:
CAMPBELL-KAGAN-KRATHWOHL
EMPATHY SCALE (FORM B)

Purpose: To measure an individual's ability to detect the immediate affective state of another.

Number of Items: 89

Format: Multiple choice (one correct and two distractors) given following viewing of video tape of counseling session.

Reliability: Test–retest (1 week), r = .75; (6 months), rs= .58 and .67. Kuder-Richardson Formula 20 was .74.

Validity: Correlation with therapist ranking (average r = .53).

Author: Campbell, R., et al.

Article: The development and validation of a scale to measure affective sensitivity (empathy).

Journal: *Journal of Counseling Psychology,* September 1971, *18*(5), 407–412.

● ● ●

758

Test Name: CANTRIL TIME PERSPECTIVE SCALE

Purpose: To assess personal time perspective.

Format: 11-point scale on which subject responds (best to worst possible life) for present, past, and future status.

Author: Bortner, R., and Hultsch, D.

Article: Personal time perspective in adulthood.

Journal: *Developmental Psychology,* September 1972, *7*(2), 98–103.

Related Research: Cantril, H. (1965). *The pattern of human concerns.* New Brunswick, NJ: Rutgers, The State University Press.

● ● ●

759

Test Name:
CATTERALL-REECE, IPSATIVE, TRUE-IDEAL, Q-SORT, UPPER ELEMENTARY TEST–REVISED

Purpose: To assess self-concept, ideal-self, self-acceptance, perceived maternal attitude, and perceived maternal acceptance.

Number of Items: 50 Q-deck cards.

Format: Included the following four sorts: first sort, self-concept or true-self sort, ideal-self sort, and maternal-attitude sort. The test was administered individually.

Author: Wechsler, J. D.

Article: Improving the self-concepts of academic underachievers through maternal group counseling.

Journal: *California Journal of Educational Research,* May 1971, *22*(3), 96–103.

● ● ●

760

Test Name: CHABASSOL ADOLESCENT STRUCTURE INVENTORY

Purpose: To measure the extent to which adolescents want structure and also perceive themselves as having such structure.

Number of Items: 47 (sample items are presented).

Format: Includes two scales of 20 items each plus 7 additional items dealing with parent and peer relations. The two scales are labeled the HAS Structure (HS) and the WANTS Structure (WS). Responses to each item are in the form of a 4-point Likert scale from *strongly agree* to *strongly disagree.*

Reliability: Split-half coefficients for the two scales range from .80 to .86.

Author: Chabassol, D. J.

Article: A scale for the evaluation of structure needs and perceptions in adolescence.

Journal: *Journal of Experimental Education,* Fall 1971, *40*(1), 12–16.

Related Research: Chabassol, D. J. (1971). *Structure needs and perceptions of adolescents in an unstructured school situation.* Paper read at the A.E.R.A. annual meeting, New York.

● ● ●

761

Test Name: CHILD'S REPORT OF PARENTAL BEHAVIOR— REVISED

Purpose: To assess perceptions of mother's behavior.

Format: Includes the following dimensions: acceptance, child centeredness, possessiveness, rejection, control and enforcement, positive involvement, intrusiveness, control through guilt, hostile control, inconsistent discipline, nonenforcement, lax discipline and extreme autonomy, acceptance of individuation, instilling persistent anxiety, hostile detachment, and withdrawal of relations.

Author: Glick, O.

Article: Some social-emotional consequences of early inadequate acquisition of reading skills.

Journal: *Journal of Educational Psychology,* June 1972, *63*(3), 253–257.

Related Research: Schaefer, E. (1965). Children's reports of parental behavior: An inventory. *Child Development, 36,* 413–424.

762

Test Name: CHILDREN'S RESPONSIBILITY INVENTORY

Purpose: To measure children's perception of development of responsibility.

Number of Items: 25

Format: Children asked to respond at what age the child could wash hands and so forth. Six areas of responsibility: care of clothing, children's relationships, cleanliness, household tasks, performance of activities alone, playing alone.

Author: Zunich, M.

Article: Perceptions of Indian, Mexican, Negro, and White children concerning the development of responsibility.

Journal: *Perceptual and Motor Skills,* June 1971, *32*(3), 796–798.

■ ■ ■

763

Test Name: CHILDREN'S SELF-CONCEPT INDEX

Purpose: To assess the degree of positive self-concept of children in the primary grades.

Number of Items: 26

Format: Each item consists of two sentences pertaining to stick figures of a socially desirable and an undesirable child. The child places an X in a small box under the child most like himself or herself. Undesirable responses receive a score of 1 and neutral or desirable responses receive a score of 2. Scores range from 26 to 52. A sample item is presented.

Reliability: Internal consistency reliability (Kuder-Richardson Formula 20) was .80, .87. Test–retest reliability after 2 weeks was .66.

Validity: Rank order correlations with teacher ratings of the child's

self-concept were .41, .60, .20, and .40. With Gumpcookies test of motivation to achieve, $r = .43$.

Author: Cicirelli, V., et al.

Article: Measures of self-concept, attitudes, and achievement motivation of primary grade children.

Journal: *Journal of School Psychology,* 1971, *9*(4), 383–392.

Related Research: Meyerowitz, J. (1961). Self-derogations in young retardates and special class placement. *Child Development, 33,* 443–451.

■ ■ ■

764

Test Name: CLIENT AND THERAPIST PERCEPTIONS OF OWN AND OTHERS PROBLEM SOLVING ADEQUACY

Purpose: To provide a measure by which the client and therapist rate their own and the other's adequacy in solving problems in their own personal lives.

Number of Items: 8

Format: Items rated on Likert scales; adapted from the Missouri Diagnostic Classification Plan. Respondent rated own and the other's adequacy on a scale of 1 (*completely incapable*) to 7 (*completely capable*).

Author: Jorgensen, G., and Hurst, J.

Article: Empirical investigation of two presuppositions in counseling and psychotherapy.

Journal: *Journal of Counseling Psychology,* May 1972, *19*(3), 259–261.

■ ■ ■

765

Test Name: CLINE INTERPERSONAL FILM TESTS

Purpose: To assess subject's ability

to attend to auditory and visual stimuli, as well as accurate perception of individuals in film.

Format: Four tests: 1. Behavior Postdiction Test; 2. Adjective Check List; 3. Opinion and Attitude Test; and 4. Physical and Behavioral Attribute Test.

Validity: Correlation with Barron Complexity Scale: Cline 1 = 11; Cline 2 = .18; Cline 3 = .27 ($p < .05$); Cline 4 = .28 ($p < .05$).

Author: Altmann, H., and Conklin, R.

Article: Further correlates of the Barron Complexity Scale.

Journal: *Perceptual and Motor Skills,* February 1972, *34*(1), 83–86.

Related Research: Cline, V. (1964). Interpersonal perception. In B. Maher (Ed.), *Progress in experimental personality research.* New York: Academic Press.

Sawatzky, D. (1968). *The relationship between open-mindedness and accurate interpersonal perception.* Unpublished master's thesis, University of Alberta.

■ ■ ■

766

Test Name: COLLEGE OPINION SURVEY

Purpose: To measure self-made academic predictions.

Number of Items: 16

Format: Eight items ask students to estimate their abilities compared with those of different reference groups—that is, friends, high school students, college students, and so forth. Eight items ask students to indicate the importance they give to getting high grades, having a high academic standing, and doing better than others.

Validity: Correlations with past performance ranged from .02 to .38. Correlations with future performance ranged from .13 to .28. Correlations with scholastic aptitude ranged from .04 to .38.

Author: Biggs, D. A., and Johnson, J.

Article: Self-made academic predictions of junior college students.

Journal: *Journal of Educational Research,* October 1972, *66*(2), 85–88.

Related Research: Brookover, W. B. (1962, December). *Self-concept of ability and school achievement I* (Cooperative Research Project No. 845). Michigan State University, Office of Research and Publications.

Brookover, W. B. (1965, October). *Self-concept of ability and school achievement II* (Cooperative Research Project No. 1636). Michigan State University, Office of Research and Publications.

See *D.U.E.M.M., 1,* 1974, 145–146.

• • •

767

Test Name: COMPETENCY SCALE

Purpose: To obtain a scale score for self-evaluations of competence.

Number of Items: 10

Format: Subjects rate themselves as above average, about average, or below average on each item. Points are awarded each item and a total obtained. Scores range from 0 (*low self-evaluation of competence*) to 10 (*high self-evaluation of competence*). All items are presented.

Author: Weidman, J., et al.

Article: The influence of

educational attainment on self-evaluations of competence.

Journal: *Sociology of Education,* Summer 1972, *45*(3), 303–312.

• • •

768

Test Name: COMPLEXITY SCALE

Purpose: To assess complexity of a subject's environmental perceptions.

Format: Score based on the number of times any of 17 constructs appeared in any of 5 Thematic Apperception Test card stories. Score ranged 1–17.

Reliability: Percentage agreement between 2 judges scoring 10 protocols = 92.6.

Author: Nawas, M.

Article: Change in efficiency of ego functioning and complexity from adolescence to young adulthood.

Journal: *Developmental Psychology,* May 1971, *4*(3), 412–415.

Related Research: Kelly, G. (1955). *The psychology of personal constructs.* New York: Norton.

• • •

769

Test Name: COUNSELORS' SELF RATING SCALE

Purpose: To enable the counselor to rate himself.

Number of Items: 18

Format: Five-point scale from *strongly agree* to *strongly disagree.* Scores on personal quality, job proficiency, observance of ethical principles, level of professional goals. The item stem read "If I were an employer, I would hire a person such as myself."

Validity: Levels of positive self rating were positively related to

number of years as a counselor.

Author: Dua, P.

Article: Development in creativity: A study of high school counselors.

Journal: *Journal of Counseling Psychology,* January 1972, *19*(1), 53–57.

• • •

770

Test Name: EMBEDDED FIGURES TEST

Purpose: A measure of perceptual field dependence and achievement.

Format: Requires close stimulus scanning, sorting out of relevant from irrelevant stimulus information, and retention and reproduction of that information in order to demonstrate competent performance.

Author: Crandall, V. C., and Lacey, B. W.

Article: Children's perceptions of internal-external control in intellectual-academic situations and their embedded figures test performance.

Journal: *Child Development,* December 1972, *43*(4), 1123–1134.

Related Research: Witkin, H., et al. (1954). *Personality through perception.* New York: Harper.

• • •

771

Test Name: EMPATHY SCALE (CHAPMAN)

Purpose: To assess the ability of a person to identify the emotion expressed by another.

Format: Four to seven descriptive adjectives were given to the subject to rate on a 4-point scale following viewing of videotaped counseling interviews.

Reliability: Kuder-Richardson Formula 20 was .44.

Validity: Only 65 of 280 items met criterion for purpose of validation and 9 met criterion for cross validation.

Author: Chapman, J.

Article: Development and validation of a scale to measure empathy.

Journal: *Journal of Counseling Psychology,* May 1971, *18*(3), 281–282.

• • •

772

Test Name: EVENTS TEST

Purpose: To assess length of future time perspective.

Number of Items: 20

Format: Subject chooses 11 of 20 events on a list that he would like to plan for now. The measure is the difference between current age and the culturally determined age for the events.

Author: Lessing, E.

Article: Extension of personal future time perspective, age, and life satisfaction of children and adolescents.

Journal: *Developmental Psychology,* May 1972, *6*(3), 457–468.

Related Research: Wallace, M. (1956). Future time perspective in schizophrenia. *Journal of Abnormal and Social Psychology, 52,* 240–245.

• • •

773

Test Name: FITZGIBBONS PATIENTS SELF PERCEIVED TREATMENT NEED SCALE

Purpose: To describe complaints of psychiatric patients.

Format: 11 major factors: anxiety depression, superego complaints,

gross psychotic symptoms, physical symptoms, feelings of inadequacy, economic–vocational problems, marital difficulties.

Author: Fitzgibbons, D.

Article: Social class differences in patients' self-perceived treatment needs.

Journal: *Psychological Reports,* December 1972, *31*(3), 987–997.

Related Research: Fitzgibbons, D., et al. (1971). Patients' self-perceived treatment needs and their relation to background variables. *Journal of Clinical and Consulting Psychology, 37,* 253.

• • •

774

Test Name: FRESHMAN CAMPS EXPECTATION AND EXPERIENCES QUESTIONNAIRE

Purpose: To assess the expectations and experiences of students toward camps.

Number of Items: Three sections, discussion topics (22); possible activities (16); statements about how faculty, upper class counselors, and so forth might behave (32).

Format: Sections 1 and 2 on a 5-point scale; Section 3 on a 4-point scale. Completed by 616 (78%) of 780 freshmen attending camp.

Validity: Correlations between expectations and satisfaction scores were low. Factor analysis on each of the scales revealed several factors.

Author: Biggs, D., and Harrold, R.

Article: The dynamics of freshman camps.

Journal: *Measurement and Evaluation in Guidance,* 1972, *4*(4), 242–248.

775

Test Name: FUTURE TIME PERSPECTIVE INVENTORY

Purpose: To measure future time perspective.

Number of Items: 25

Format: Subjects respond on 7-point scale (*complete disagree* to *complete agree*) to statements such as "The future seems very vague and uncertain to me."

Author: Lessing, E.

Article: Extension of personal future time perspective, age, and life satisfaction of children and adolescents.

Journal: *Developmental Psychology,* May 1972, *6*(3), 457–468.

Related Research: Heimberg, L. (1963). *The measurement of future time perspective.* Unpublished doctoral dissertation, Vanderbilt University.

• • •

776

Test Name: GERARD ROD AND FRAME TEST

Purpose: To measure field dependence.

Format: Subject was required to set the rod in perpendicular position despite the influence of a tilted frame.

Reliability: Split-half reliability was .92.

Author: Ruble, D., and Nakamura, C.

Article: Task orientation versus social orientation in young children and their attention to relevent social cues.

Journal: *Child Development,* June 1972, *43*(2), 471–480.

Related Research: Gerard, H. (1969). *Factors contributing to*

adjustment and achievement
(Progress Report, Grant No. PHS
HD-02863).California University,
Los Angeles, Department of
Psychology, Public Health
Service, DHEW, Washington, DC.
(ERIC Document Reproduction
Service No. ED 0355).

• • •

777

Test Name: GORDON TEST OF
VISUAL IMAGERY CONTROL

Purpose: To assess imagery.

Format: Self-report.

Reliability: Odd–even reliabilities
were .88 (undergrads) and .95
(professors).

Author: Juhasz, J.

Article: On the reliability of two
measures of imagery.

Journal: *Perceptual and Motor
Skills,* December 1972, *35*(3), 874.

Related Research: Sheenhan, P.
(1967). A shortened form of Betts'
questionnaire upon mental
imagery. *Journal of Clinical
Psychology, 23,* 386–389.

• • •

778

Test Name: GROUP BEHAVIOR
RATING SCALE

Purpose: To measure
self-perceptions.

Number of Items: 40

Format: Yields two scores:
Reinforcer and Idea Seeker.
Subjects are instructed to recall
their behavior with peer groups
and rate themselves on a 10–point
scale. Some examples are given.

Reliability: Spearman-Brown
split-half reliabilities of .93 and
.96.

Author: Rezler, A. G., and
Anderson, A. S.

Article: Focused and unfocused

feedback and self-perception.

Journal: *Journal of Educational
Research,* October 1971, *65*(2),
61–64.

Related Research: Bales, R. F.
(1950). *Interaction process
analysis: A method for the study of
small groups.* Cambridge, MA:
Addison-Wesley.

• • •

779

Test Name: HEALTH
PERCEPTION

Purpose: To elicit respondents'
self-health evaluation.

Number of Items: 7

Author: Poorkaj, H.

Article: Social-psychological
factors and successful aging.

Journal: *Sociology and Social
Research,* April 1972, *56*(3), 289–
300.

• • •

780

Test Name: HIPPLE
INTERPERSONAL
RELATIONSHIP SCALE

Purpose: To assess self-perception
and perception of interaction with
others.

Number of Items: 26

Format: Subjects rated items on a
7-point scale.

Author: Whittlesey, R., et al.

Article: The use of human relations
techniques in the training of
counselors: Course evaluation.

Journal: *Counselor Education and
Supervision,* December 1971,
11(2), 137–146.

Related Research: Hipple, J.
(1970). *Effects of differential
human relations laboratory
designs on the interpersonal
behavior of college students.*
Unpublished doctoral dissertation,

University of Iowa.

781

Test Name: HOGAN EMPATHY
SCALE

Purpose: To assess the ability to
understand another's feelings.

Validity: Correlation with
interpersonal sensitivity
(Grossman) was .22.

Author: Zacker, J.

Article: Understanding one's
clients: An attempt to improve
sensitivity and morale in police
recruits.

Journal: *Psychological Reports,*
December 1972, *31*(3), 999–1008.

Related Research: Hogan, R.
(1969). Development of an
empathy scale. *Journal of
Consulting and Clinical
Psychology, 33,* 307–316.

• • •

782

Test Name: IMPERSONAL
FUTURE EXTENSION SCALE

Purpose: To measure temporal
perspective.

Author: Platt, J., et al.

Article: Temporal perspective as a
personality dimension in college
students: A re-evaluation.

Journal: *Perceptual and Motor
Skills,* August 1971, *33*(1), 103–
109.

Related Research: Thor, D.
(1962). "Time perspective" and
time of day. *Psychological Record,
12,* 417–422.

• • •

783

Test Name: IMPERSONAL PAST
EXTENSION TEST

Purpose: To measure temporal
perspective.

Validity: Correlation with Fear of

Failure (Famous Sayings Test) = .31 ($p < .02$), women.

Author: Platt, J., et al.

Article: Temporal perspective as a personality dimension in college students: A re-evaluation.

Journal: *Perceptual and Motor Skills,* August 1971, *33*(1), 103–109.

Related Research: Thor, D. (1962). "Time perspective" and time of day. *Psychological Record, 12,* 417–422.

■ ■ ■

784

Test Name: INDIVIDUAL IMAGERY TEST

Purpose: To measure the imagery response of a subject, to whom a stimulus has been presented.

Number of Items: 34 stimulus words.

Format: Subject is given 40 words and asked to classify image into category (see, hear, touch, taste–smell, movement, or discard). Subjects were able to classify a primary, secondary, or third choice modality or a subset of these.

Author: Leibovitz, M., et al.

■ ■ ■

785

Test Name: INFERRED COLLEGE TEACHER PERCEPTIONS OF PERSONAL ADEQUACY CLASSROOM OBSERVATION SCALE

Purpose: To assess four inferred perceptual dimensions of a healthy personality.

Format: Four dimensions inferred by trained observers in the classroom including positive self and identification with others.

Validity: Correlation with total criterion of teacher effectiveness of

four dimensions: .61 ($p < .01$); .62 ($p < .01$); .59 ($p < .01$); .59 ($p < .01$).

Author: Usher, R., and Hanke, J.

Article: The third force in psychology and college teacher effectiveness research at the University of Northern Colorado.

Journal: *Colorado Journal of Educational Research,* Winter 1971, *10*(2), 2–9.

Related Research: Combs, A. (1963). A perceptual view of the adequate personality. In *Perceiving, behaving, becoming* (pp. 50–64). Washington, DC: Association for Supervision and Curriculum Development.

Doyle, E. (1969). *The relationship between college and teacher effectiveness and inferred characteristics of the adequate personality.* Unpublished doctoral dissertation, University of Northern Colorado.

■ ■ ■

786

Test Name: INTELLECTUAL ACHIEVEMENT RESPONSIBILITY QUESTIONNAIRE

Purpose: To measure locus of control.

Format: Includes two subscores: one for internal responsibility for success and one for internal responsibility for failures.

Validity: Correlations with Piers-Harris Self-Concept Scale ranged from .32 to .57.

Author: Felker, D. W., and Thomas, S. B.

Article: Self-initiated verbal reinforcement and positive self-concept.

Journal: *Child Development,* October 1971, *42*(4), 1285–1287.

Related Research: Buck, M., &

Austrin, H. (1971, December). Factors related to school achievement in an economically disadvantaged group. *Child Development, 42*(6), 1813–1826.

Clifford, M., & Cleary, T. (1972, June). The relationship between children's academic performance and achievement accountability. *Child Development, 43*(2), 647–655.

Crandall, V. C., et al. (1965). Children's beliefs in their own control of reinforcements in intellectual-academic achievement situations. *Child Development, 36,* 91–109.

Epstein, R., & Komorita, S. (1971, January). Self-esteem, success-failure, and locus of control in Negro children. *Developmental Psychology, 4*(1), 2–8.

Johnson, C., & Gormley, J. (1972, March). Academic cheating: The contribution of sex, personality, and situational variables. *Developmental Psychology, 6*(2), 320–325.

Messer, S. (1972, December). The relation of internal-external control to academic performance. *Child Development, 43*(4), 1456–1462.

Powell, A. (1971, August). Alternative measures of locus of control and the prediction of academic performance. *Psychological Reports, 29*(2), 47–50.

■ ■ ■

787

Test Name: INTERPERSONAL CHECKLIST

Purpose: To obtain measures of subject's self-concept.

Number of Items: 128

Format: Adjectives and adjective phrases grouped into eight categories, each referring to a major personality type: managerial–autocratic, competitive–narcissistic, aggressive–sadistic, rebellious–distrustful, self-effacing–masochistic, docile–dependent, cooperative–over-conventional, responsible–hypernormal. Two factor scores are provided: Dominance and Love.

Validity: Correlation of Dominance with performance in a psychology course: men, .17 and .02; women, .25 and .28. Correlation of Love with performance in a psychology course: men, .036 and .16; women, .11 and .17.

Author: Albott, W. L., and Haney, J. N.

Article: Self-concept, choice of study plan, and performance in an introductory psychology course.

Journal: *Journal of Educational Research*, April 1972, *65*(8), 339–342.

Related Research: Leary, T. (1957). *Interpersonal diagnosis of personality*. New York: Ronald Press.

• • •

788

Test Name: INTERPERSONAL DIFFERENTIATION TEST

Purpose: To assess esteem.

Number of Items: 10

Format: 10 bipolar adjectives using a 6-point scale were used in present study to assess self, mother, and father esteem.

Author: Bruch, M., et al.

Article: Parental devaluation: A protection of self esteem?

Journal: *Journal of Counseling Psychology*, November 1972, *19*(6), 555–558.

Related Research: Bieri, J., et al.

(1966). *Clinical and social judgement.* New York: Wiley.

• • •

789

Test Name: KASSARJIAN I-O SOCIAL PREFERENCE SCALE

Purpose: Measures inner–outward directedness.

Number of Items: 36

Format: Forced choice items scored on continuum.

Reliability: Test–retest reliability was .85.

Author: White, B., and Kernaleguen, A.

Article: Comparison of selected perceptual and personality variables among college women deviant and nondeviant in their appearance.

Journal: *Perceptual and Motor Skills*, February 1971, *32*(1), 87–92.

Related Research: Kassarjian, W. (1960). *A study of Riesman's Theory of Social Character.* Unpublished doctoral dissertation, University of California.

• • •

790

Test Name: KASTENBAUM FUTURE DENSITY TEST

Purpose: To measure temporal perspective.

Format: Has two forms.

Validity: Correlation with response acquiescence = .32 ($p - .05$), for male subjects (Form 1). Correlation with creativity = .28 ($p < .05$), for females (Form 1).

Author: Platt, J., et al.

Article: Temporal perspective as a personality dimension in college students: A re-evaluation.

Journal: *Perceptual and Motor*

Skills, August 1971, *33*(1), 103–109.

Related Research: Kastenbaum, R. (1961). The dimensions of future time perspective: An experimental analysis. *Journal of General Psychology, 65,* 203–218.

• • •

791

Test Name: KENYON ATTITUDE TOWARD PHYSICAL ACTIVITY SCALE

Purpose: To assess how an individual perceives physical activity.

Format: Six scales: activity perceived as (a) aesthetic experience; (b) catharsis; (c) physical fitness; (d) social experience; (e) vertigo; and (f) aescetic experience.

Author: Higgs, S.

Article: Personality traits and motor ability associated with observed competitiveness in women physical education majors.

Journal: *Perceptual and Motor Skills,* February 1972, *34*(1), 219–222.

Related Research: Kenyon, G. (1968). Six scales for assessing attitude toward physical activity. *Research Quarterly, 39,* 566–574.

• • •

792

Test Name: LEE-LYON SELF-ESTEEM Q-SORT

Purpose: To measure student self-esteem.

Number of Items: 25

Format: A statement describing student behavior or characteristic is printed on each colored IBM card. A few examples are presented.

Author: Lee, W. S.

Article: The measurement of

self-esteem for program evaluation.

Journal: *Journal of School Psychology,* 1972, *10*(1), 61–68.

Related Research: Lee, W. S., & Lyon, J. M. (1969). *The Lee-Lyon Self-esteem Q-Sort.* Tamalpais Union High School District, Larkspur, CA.

• • •

793

Test Name: LOCUS OF CONTROL SCALE

Purpose: To assess degree of externality–internality.

Number of Items: 14

Format: Four-point scale ranging from *very much agree* to *very much disagree.*

Reliability: Split-half (corrected) reliabilities were .79 and .70.

Author: Epstein, R., and Komorita, S.

Article: Self esteem, success failure, and locus of control in Negro children.

Journal: *Developmental Psychology,* January 1971, *4*(1), 2–8.

• • •

794

Test Name: LONDON-ROBINSON IMAGERY TEST

Purpose: To measure retention of images.

Number of Items: 20 line drawings (10 familiar, 10 unfamiliar).

Format: Subjects were presented drawings, then asked to select correct designs from 2 charts each with 50 drawings.

Author: Leibovitz, M., et al.

Article: Dominance in mental imagery.

Journal: *Educational and*

Psychological Measurement, Autumn 1972, *32*(3), 679–703.

Related Research: London, P., & Robinson, J. (1968). Imagination in learning and retention. *Child Development, 39,* 803–815.

• • •

795

Test Name: MASCULINITY/ FEMININITY OF SELF CONCEPT MEASURE

Purpose: To assess sex role of self concept.

Number of Items: 56

Format: Subject checked items that applied to him.

Author: Biller, H., and Bahm, R.

Article: Father absence, perceived maternal behavior, and masculinity of self concept among junior high school boys.

Journal: *Developmental Psychology,* March 1971, *4*(2), 178–181.

• • •

796

Test Name: MCKINNEY SENTENCE COMPLETION BLANK

Purpose: To generate statements about the self; to elicit responses to frustrations, conflict, and personal identity, and allow the individual to explore indirectly and existentially various aspects of self-involvement.

Number of Items: 46

Format: Each item is a stem and all but five contain the first person pronoun. Responses are categorized as self-actualizing, defensive, immobilized, affective, or nonclassifiable.

Reliability: Intrasubject reliability after 3 days was .89. Intrasubject reliabilities after 14 weeks were .58

and .51. Intrajudge reliabilities were .92 and .95. Interjudge reliabilities were .88.

Validity: With personal adjustment and separate categories .26 to +.24.

Author: Weigel, R. G., and McKinney, F.

Article: Self-oriented sentence completion responses and reported personal biographical data.

Journal: *Journal of Educational Research,* January 1971, *64*(5), 201–202.

Related Research: McKinney, F. (1967). The Sentence Completion Blank in assessing student self-actualization. *Personnel and Guidance Journal, 45,* 709–713.

• • •

797

Test Name: MILLER'S LOCUS-OF-CONTROL SCALE

Purpose: To separate those children who feel their reinforcements are completely within their power from those who feel their reinforcements are controlled by factors that they cannot influence.

Number of Items: 20

Reliability: Internal consistency was .87, .89.

Author: Gorsuch, R. L., et al.

Article: Locus of control: An example of dangers in using children's scales with children.

Journal: *Child Development,* June 1972, *43*(2), 579–590.

Related Research: Miller, J. O. (1963). *Role perception and reinforcement conditions in discrimination learning among culturally deprived and non-deprived children.* Unpublished doctoral dissertation, George Peabody College.

798

Test Name: MOST LIKE QUESTIONNAIRE

Purpose: To measure self-concept.

Number of Items: Six forms each with 110 items.

Format: Includes the following 12 concepts arranged in triads: teachers, policemen, school principals, school counselors, social workers, soldiers, Negroes, White people, Puerto Ricans, my friends, I, school. An example is presented.

Author: Landis, D., et al.

Article: Multidimensional analysis procedures for measuring self-concept in poverty area classrooms.

Journal: *Journal of Educational Psychology,* April 1971, *62*(2), 95–103.

● ● ●

799

Test Name: NOWICKI-STRICKLAND LOCUS OF CONTROL SCALE

Purpose: To assess locus of control in children.

Number of Items: 40

Format: Subject responds *yes* or *no.*

Reliability: Test–retest reliability ranged from .67 to .81. Internal consistency reliability ranged from .63 to .79.

Validity: Nonsignificant correlation with Otis Intelligence Test Scores. Female students who are internally oriented engage in more extracurricular activities than external (secondary level students).

Author: Nowicki, S., and Roundtree, J.

Article: Correlates of locus of

control in a secondary school population.

Journal: *Developmental Psychology,* May 1971, *4*(3), 477–478.

Related Research: Nowicki, S., & Strickland, B. (1970). *A locus of control scale for children.* Unpublished manuscript, Emory University.

● ● ●

800

Test Name: OSGOOD-TANNEBAUM-SUICI SELF ESTEEM SCALE

Purpose: To measure self esteem.

Format: Self esteem score = "square root of sum of squared differences between corresponding factor scores on actual- and ideal-self scales."

Author: Kayset, B.

Article: Authoritarianism, self-esteem, emotionality and intelligence.

Journal: *Perceptual and Motor Skills,* April 1972, *34*(2), 367–370.

● ● ●

801

Test Name: PATTERN COPYING TEST

Purpose: To measure visual perception.

Number of Items: 36

Format: A power test containing pairs of geometric forms, one of which is completed while the other has some lines missing. The pupil's task is to complete the second picture to make it like the first one. Scores range from 0 to 36.

Validity: Correlated .52 with reading achievement.

Author: Robinson, H. M.

Article: Visual and auditory

modalities related to methods for beginning reading.

Journal: *Reading Research Quarterly,* Fall 1972, *8*(1), 7–39.

● ● ●

802

Test Name: PEER RATINGS SEMANTIC DIFFERENTIAL

Purpose: To rate several peer concepts in the classroom.

Number of Items: 12

Format: Bipolar adjectives that the evaluator rates on a 7-point scale. Three factors were identified: evaluation, potency, activity. All adjective pairs are presented.

Validity: With Coopersmith Self-Esteem Inventory, $r = .325$.

Author: Richmond, B. O., and White, W. F.

Article: Sociometric predictors of the self concept among fifth and sixth grade children.

Journal: *Journal of Educational Research,* May-June 1971, *64*(9), 425–429.

● ● ●

803

Test Name: PERCEPTION OF INTERVIEWER CREDIBILITY

Purpose: To assess an interviewee's perception of the credibility of an interviewer.

Number of Items: 18

Format: Items were 7-point semantic differentials designed to measure three dimensions of credibility: safety, qualification, and dynamism.

Author: Widgerly, R., and Stackpole, C.

Article: Desk position, interviewee anxiety, and interviewer credibility: An example of cognitive balance in a dyad.

Journal: *Journal of Counseling Psychology*, May 1972, *19*(3), 173–177.

Related Research: Berlo, D., et al. (1969–1970, Winter). Dimensions for evaluating the acceptability of message sources. *The Public Opinion Quarterly, 33*, 563–576.

■ ■ ■

804

Test Name: PERSONAL FEELINGS SCALES

Purpose: To assess self-reported affect states.

Format: Subject reports his immediate state.

Validity: *r* with Edwards Social Desirability Scale = .34 (*p* < .01).

Author: Wahehime, R., and Jones, D.

Article: Social-desirability responding and self report of immediate affect states.

Journal: *Perceptual and Motor Skills*, August 1972, *35*(1), 190.

Related Research: Wessman, A., & Ricks, D. (1966). *Mood and personality.* New York: Holt, Rinehart & Winston.

■ ■ ■

805

Test Name: PERSONAL FUTURE EXTENSION TEST

Purpose: To measure temporal perspective.

Validity: Correlation with Eisenman & Cherry Response Acquiescence Test was .36 (*p* < .01) for male subjects. Correlation with Fear of Failure (Famous Sayings Test) was .21 (*p* < .10) for female subjects.

Author: Platt, J., et al.

Article: Temporal perspective as a personality dimension in college students: A re-evaluation.

Journal: *Perceptual and Motor Skills*, August 1971, *33*(1), 103–109.

Related Research: Wallace, N. (1956). Future time perspective in schizophrenia. *Journal of Abnormal and Social Psychology, 52*, 240–245.

■ ■ ■

806

Test Name: PERSONAL FUTURE TIME PERSPECTIVE

Purpose: To assess future time perspective.

Number of Items: 9

Format: Incomplete sentences format.

Validity: Correlation with Social Political Time Perspective = .15 (Whites) and .07 (Blacks), both *ns*.

Author: Lessing, E.

Article: Comparative extension of personal and social-political future time perspective.

Journal: *Perceptual and Motor Skills*, October 1971, *33*(2), 415–422.

Related Research: Lessing, E. (1968). Demographic, developmental, and personality correlates of length of future time perspective (FTP). *Journal of Personality, 36*, 183–201.

■ ■ ■

807

Test Name: PICTORIAL SELF CONCEPT SCALE FOR CHILDREN IN GRADES K-4

Purpose: To measure self concept.

Number of Items: 50

Format: Fifty cartoon-picture cards designed to reflect Jersild's categories of self concept. Subject sorts cards into three piles (*like him, sometimes like him, not like him*).

Reliability: Split-half for 1,813 subjects was .85 (author cautions that may be spuriously high).

Validity: Scoring weights on cards determined by eight psychologists who ranked cards. A correlation of .42 with the Piers Harris measure reported scores significantly differentiated between groups based on teacher and principal judgment.

Author: Bolea, A., et al.

Article: A pictoral self concept scale for children in K-4.

Journal: *Journal of Educational Measurement*, Fall 1971, *8*(3), 223–224.

■ ■ ■

808

Test Name: PICTURE SQUARES TEST

Purpose: To measure visual perception.

Number of Items: 18

Time Required: 2 minutes.

Format: Includes four sets of nine practice pictures and 18 sets on which pupils secure scores from 0–18 correct. Pupil marks as many identical pairs of pictures as possible.

Author: Robinson, H. M.

Article: Visual and auditory modalities related to methods for beginning reading.

Journal: *Reading Research Quarterly*, Fall 1972, *8*(1), 7–39.

Related Research: Goins, J. T. (1958). *Visual perceptual abilities and early reading progress* (Supplementary Educational Monographs No. 87). Chicago: University of Chicago Press.

■ ■ ■

809

Test Name: POWERLESSNESS SCALE

Purpose: To assess the extent to which a person feels his or her behavior either influences or does not influence outcomes.

Number of Items: 8

Format: Items rated on a 5-point scale, *strongly agree* to *strongly disagree.*

Validity: Item-total correlations on 8 items were .78, .79, .84, .67, .85, .60, .77, and .76.

Author: Bolton, C.

Article: Alienation and action: A study of peace group members.

Journal: *American Journal of Sociology,* November 1972, *78*(3), 537–561.

Related Research: Seeman, M. (1959). On the meaning of alienation. *American Sociological Review, 24,* 783–791.

■ ■ ■

810

Test Name: PUPIL CONTROL IDEOLOGY FORM

Purpose: An operational measure for pupil control orientation.

Number of Items: 20

Format: Likert items scored from 5 (*strongly agree*) to 1 (*strongly disagree*). The higher the overall score, the more custodial the ideology of the respondent. A few examples are presented.

Reliability: Split-half coefficients with Spearman-Brown formula applied were .91 and .95.

Validity: Supported by principals' judgments of the ideology of certain of their teachers.

Author: Leppert, E., and Hoy, W. K.

Article: Teacher personality and pupil control ideology.

Journal: *Journal of Experimental Education,* Spring 1972, *40*(3), 57–59.

Related Research: Dobson, R., et al. (1972, October). Pupil control ideology and teacher influence in the classroom. *Journal of Educational Research, 66*(2), 76–78.

Rexford, G. E., et al. (1972, Summer). Teachers' pupil control ideology and classroom verbal behavior. *Journal of Experimental Education, 40*(4), 78–82.

Willower, D. J., et al. (1967). *The school and pupil control ideology* (Penn State Studies monograph No. 24). University Park, PA.

■ ■ ■

811

Test Name: PUPIL OBSERVATION REPORT

Purpose: To permit pupils to report their perceptions of teacher behavior characteristics.

Number of Items: 38

Format: Test consists of a questionnaire containing positively phrased statements about teacher behavior. Responses are made on a 4-point scale that includes the following points: *completely true, more true than false, more false than true, completely false.* Five factors have been extracted.

Reliability: Test–retest coefficients ranged from .66 to .84.

Author: Bledsoe, J. C., et al.

Article: Factors related to pupil observation reports of teachers and attitudes toward their teacher.

Journal: *Journal of Educational Research,* November 1971, *65*(3), 119–126.

Related Research: Schmidt, L., & Gallessich, J. (1971, August). Adjustment of Anglo-American and Mexican-American pupil in self-contained and team-teaching classrooms. *Journal of Educational Psychology, 62*(4), 328–332.

Veldman, D. J., & Peck, R. F. (1963). Student teacher characteristics from the pupil's viewpoint. *Journal of Educational Psychology, 54,* 346–355.

■ ■ ■

812

Test Name: REMINISCENCE MEASURES

Purpose: To obtain information about the remembered past.

Format: Four general areas each with various indices (importance of reminiscence, restructuring of memories, selection of memories, uses of the past); a total of 35 indices.

Reliability: Interjudge correlations: .88, .91, .72, .85.

Author: Lieberman, M., and Falk, J.

Article: The remembered past as a source of data for research on the life cycle.

Journal: *Human Development,* 1971, *14*(2), 132–141.

■ ■ ■

813

Test Name: REVERSALS TEST

Purpose: To measure visual perception.

Number of Items: 84

Format: A power test consisting of pairs of pictures, some of which are identical and others that have either all or some part of the picture reversed. Chance responses were minimized by subtracting the number of wrong from the number right and 100 was added to all scores to eliminate the possibility of negative scores.

Validity: Correlated .49 with reading test scores.

Author: Robinson, H. M.

Article: Visual and auditory

modalities related to methods for beginning reading.

Journal: *Reading Research Quarterly,* Fall 1972, *8*(1), 7–39.

■ ■ ■

814

Test Name: RIGHT-LEFT DISCRIMINATION TESTS

Purpose: To assess whether subject can discriminate right and left.

Number of Items: 16 trials.

Format: Performance test. Child is requested to "Raise right hand," "Point to right eye" as the tester points to own ear, "Which ear is this?" and so forth.

Author: Croxen, M., and Lytton, H.

Article: Reading disability and difficulties in finger localization and right–left discrimination.

Journal: *Developmental Psychology,* September 1971, *5*(2), 256–262.

Related Research: Belmont, L., & Birch, H. (1965). Lateral dominance, lateral awareness and reading disability. *Child Development, 36,* 57–72.

■ ■ ■

815

Test Name: ROD AND FRAME TEST

Purpose: To measure cognitive style (field dependence).

Format: Subject faces an illuminated apparatus in a darkened room and must make judgment of perpendicular.

Validity: Correlation with Embedded Figures Test was .43 (*p* < .05).

Author: Denmark, F., et al.

Article: Re-evaluation of some measures of cognitive styles.

Journal: *Perceptual and Motor Skills,* August 1971, *33*(1), 133–134.

Related Research: Witkin, H., et al. (1954). *Personality through perception.* New York: Harper.

■ ■ ■

816

Test Name: ROLE CONSTRUCT REPERTORY TEST

Purpose: To measure self-esteem.

Format: The subject creates 12 pairs of bipolar adjectives.

Validity: Discrepancy measure of self-esteem had high convergent validity with three other measures of the same trait: difference between self and social self, *r* = .81; global self-esteem, *r* = .67; and interview rating of self-esteem, *r* = .63.

Author: Edwards, K. J., and Tuckman, B. W.

Article: Effect of differential college experiences in developing the students' self- and other occupational concepts.

Journal: *Journal of Educational Psychology,* December 1972, *63*(6), 563–571.

Related Research: Kelly, G. A. (1955). *The psychology of personal constructs.* New York: Norton.

Silber, E., & Tippett, J. S. (1965). Self-esteem: Clinical assessment and measurement validation. *Psychological Reports, 16,* 1017–1071.

■ ■ ■

817

Test Name: ROSENBERG SELF ESTEEM SCALE

Purpose: To assess self-evaluation.

Format: Likert format with no neutral category; strong positive responses scored 4, strong negative, 1.

Validity: Point biserial correlation with psychosomatic symptoms of stress = –.269.

Author: Yancey, W., et al.

Article: Social position and self evaluation: The relative importance of race.

Journal: *American Journal of Sociology,* September 1972, *78*(2), 338–359.

Related Research: Rosenberg, M. (1965). *Society and the adolescent self image.* Princeton, NJ: Princeton University Press.

■ ■ ■

818

Test Name: ROTTER INTERNAL-EXTERNAL SCALE

Purpose: To assess locus of control.

Author: Harvey, J.

Article: Locus of control shift in administrators.

Journal: *Perceptual and Motor Skills,* December 1971, *33*(3 Part 1), 980–982.

Related Research: Rotter, J. (1966). Generalized expectancies for internal v. external control of reinforcement. *Psychological Monographs, 80*(1, Whole No. 609).

■ ■ ■

819

Test Name: SARBIN-ROSENBERG ADJECTIVE CHECK LIST

Purpose: To assess self-perception.

Number of Items: 200 adjectives.

Format: Subject checked traits which were most self-descriptive.

Author: Koenig, F.

Article: Sex attribution to hypothetical persons described by adjective trait lists.

Journal: *Perceptual and Motor Skills,* August 1972, *35*(1), 15–18.

Related Research: Sarbin, T., & Rosenberg, B. (1955). Contributions to role taking theory: IV. A method for the qualitative analysis of the self. *Journal of Social Psychology, 42,* 71–81.

■ ■ ■

820

Test Name: SCHOOL COUNSELORS' CHECKLIST

Purpose: To measure actual, ideal, and expected counselor role concepts.

Number of Items: 50

Format: Items represent five service areas; 25 items state "proper" counselor duties; and 25 state "improper" duties. Counselors indicate whether they do or do not, would or would not, and should or should not perform each of the 50 duties. All items are presented.

Author: Dahlem, G. G.

Article: Actual, ideal, and expected role concepts of secondary counselors.

Journal: *Journal of Educational Research,* January 1971, *64*(5), 205–208.

Related Research: Schmidt, L. D. (1962). Concepts of the role of secondary school counselors. *Personnel and Guidance Journal, 41,* 600–605.

■ ■ ■

821

Test Name: SEEKING OF NOETIC GOALS TEST (SONG)

Purpose: To measure amount of awareness by a subject that there is a lack of meaning in his or her life and extent of need for purpose in living.

Validity: For normal subjects:

correlation with 11 personality variables ranged .03 to .55 (Minnesota Multiphasic Personality Inventory Factor A, $p < .01$); 6 of 11 were significant.

Author: Yarnell, T.

Article: Validation of the Seeking of Noetic Goals Test with schizophrenic and normal subjects.

Journal: *Psychological Reports,* February 1972, *30*(1), 79–82.

■ ■ ■

822

Test Name: SELF AND IDEAL SELF Q SORT

Purpose: To assess congruence of self and ideal self; in this case the congruence of the self and perception of counselor's occupational role.

Number of Items: 45

Format: Statements typed on cards, subject sorts for self and ideal self separately. First set written in first person; second in terms of third person. Obtained old self and old ideal self beginning of quarter and new self and new ideal self at end of quarter.

Reliability: Test–retest reliability for self was .69. Test–retest reliability for ideal self was 76.

Author: Stoner, W., and Riese, H.

Article: A study of change in perception of self and ideal self.

Journal: *Counselor Education and Supervision,* December 1971, *11*(2), 115–118.

■ ■ ■

823

Test Name: SELF-CONCEPT OF ABILITY-REVISED

Purpose: To measure self-concept.

Number of Items: 16

Format: Includes assessment of

general attributes as well as academic ability.

Author: Glick, O.

Article: Some social-emotional consequences of early inadequate acquisition of reading skills.

Journal: *Journal of Educational Psychology,* June 1972, *63*(3), 253–257.

Related Research: Brookover, W. G., et al. (1967). *Self-concept of ability and school achievement, III.* East Lansing, Michigan: Human Learning Research Institute, Michigan State University.

■ ■ ■

824

Test Name: SELF-ESTEEM INVENTORY-REVISED

Purpose: To assess self-concept.

Number of Items: 42

Author: Dauw, E. G.

Article: Separate schools for potential dropouts.

Journal: *Educational Leadership,* January 1972, *29*(4), 333–340.

■ ■ ■

825

Test Name: SELF-ESTEEM SCALE

Purpose: To survey self-esteem attitude.

Number of Items: 9

Format: Student responds to each statement on a 4–point Likert scale from *strongly agree or agree* to *disagree or strongly disagree.* All items are presented.

Reliability: Internal consistency measured through coefficient alpha was .49.

Validity: With family authority orientation, $r = .14$. With peer group status, $r = .14$. With peer orientation, $r = .18$.

Author: Larkin, R. W.

Article: Class, race, sex, and preadolescent attitudes.

Journal: *California Journal of Educational Research*, November 1972, *23*(5), 213–223.

. . .

826

Test Name: SELF-ESTEEM SCALE

Purpose: To measure self-esteem.

Number of Items: 52

Format: True–false items. Five items are presented.

Reliability: Coefficient of reproducibility is .90.

Validity: With a variety of traits .17 to .48.

Author: Luck, P. W., and Heiss, J.

Article: Social determinants of self-esteem in adult males.

Journal: *Sociology and Social Research*, October 1972, *57*(1), 69–84.

. . .

827

Test Name: SELF-ESTEEM SCALE

Purpose: To measure the subject's self-esteem.

Number of Items: 10

Format: A Guttman scale including the subject's self-respect, self-satisfaction, and self-content.

Author: Tseng, M. S.

Article: Comparisons of selected familial, personality, and vocational variables of high school students and dropouts.

Journal: *Journal of Educational Research*, July–August 1972, *65*(10), 462–466.

828

Test Name: SELF EVALUATION QUESTIONNAIRE

Purpose: To assess subjects' evaluation of self.

Format: Subjects rated self on 40 characteristics (five content areas: achievement traits, intellectual skills, interpersonal skills, physical skills, social responsibility).

Author: Mullener, N., and Laird, J.

Article: Some developmental changes in the organization of self-evaluations.

Journal: *Developmental Psychology*, September 1971, *5*(2), 233–236.

Related Research: Katz, P., & Zigler, E. (1967). Self-image disparity: A developmental approach. *Journal of Personality and Social Psychology, 5,* 186–195.

. . .

829

Test Name: SELF-PERCEPTION INDEX

Purpose: To measure the individual's perception of himself and his personal goals.

Number of Items: 17

Format: One item is presented.

Reliability: Test–retest reliability was .54, .45.

Author: Athanasiou, R.

Article: Selection and socialization: A study of engineering student attrition.

Journal: *Journal of Educational Psychology*, April 1971, *62*(2), 157–166.

. . .

830

Test Name: SELF-SOCIAL CONSTRUCTS SCALE

Purpose: To assess several constructs related to the subject.

Format: Constructs assessed by the test were (a) self-esteem; (b) dependency; (c) identification with mother; (d) identification with father; (e) identification with friend; (f) identification with teacher; (g) realism color; and (h) realism size.

Validity: Correlations with Behavior Maturity Scale: Academic Maturity and Social Esteem, $r = .26$. Interpersonal Maturity and Self Realism, $r = .03$. Emotional Maturity and Dependency, $r = .07$.

Author: White, W., and Bashaw, W.

Article: High *self-esteem* and identification with adult models among economically deprived children.

Journal: *Perceptual and Motor Skills*, December 1971, *33*(3), 1127–1130.

Related Research: Henderson, E., et al. (1967). *The self-social constructs scale.* Newark: University of Delaware.

. . .

831

Test Name: SELF-SORT-IDEAL-SORT DISCREPANCY SCORE

Purpose: To provide an internal criterion of self-acceptance.

Format: A Q sort whereby the subject selects cards most like himself or herself (self-sort) and then selects cards describing the ideal person he or she wishes to be (ideal-sort). The discrepancy between the two sorts is believed to be an indication of self-esteem.

Author: Garfield, S. J.

Article: Effects of group counseling on creativity.

Journal: *Journal of Educational Research,* January 1971, *64*(5), 235–237.

Related Research: Garfield, S. J., & Cohen, H. A. (1967). *A simplified method of using the self ideal Q sort.* Unpublished research, Illinois Institute of Technology.

Rogers, C. R., & Dymond, R. F. (Eds.). (1954). *Psychotherapy and personality change: Coordinated studies in the client-centered approach.* Chicago: University of Chicago Press.

■ ■ ■

832

Test Name: SOCIAL-POLITICAL FUTURE TIME PERSPECTIVE

Purpose: To assess the number of years that subject felt it was necessary to accomplish certain social and political goals.

Number of Items: 19

Format: Subject indicated the number of years he needed to accomplish the 19 goals; summary score was median number of years.

Validity: Correlation with Personal Future Time: Perspective, $r = .15$ (Whites) and $-.07$ (Blacks), both *ns.*

Author: Lessing, E.

Article: Comparative extension of personal and social-political time perspective.

Journal: *Perceptual and Motor Skills,* October 1971, *33*(2), 415–422.

■ ■ ■

833

Test Name: SUBJECTIVE STRESS SCALE

Purpose: To assess reported perception of stress under various conditions.

Number of Items: 14 adjectives.

Format: Subject is asked to identify which objectives describe feelings in certain circumstances.

Author: Neufeld, R., and Davidson, P.

Article: Scaling of the subjective stress scale with a sample of university undergraduates.

Journal: *Psychological Reports,* December 1972, *31*(3), 821–822.

Related Research: Berkun, M., et al. (1962). Experimental studies of psychological stress in man. *Psychological Monographs, 76*(15, Whole No. 534).

■ ■ ■

834

Test Name: TIME METAPHORS TEST

Purpose: To measure temporal perspective (directionality).

Validity: Correlation with Famous Sayings Test (hostility) was .38 ($p < .01$) for male subjects. Correlation with Famous Sayings Test (fear-failure) was .26 ($p < .10$) for male subjects. Correlation with Famous Sayings Test (hostility) was .38 ($p < .01$) for female subjects. Correlation with Eisenman & Cherry Creativity was .26 ($p < .10$) for female subjects.

Author: Platt, J., et al.

Article: Temporal perspective as a personality dimension in college students: A re-evaluation.

Journal: *Perceptual and Motor Skills,* August 1971, *33*(1), 103–109.

Related Research: Knapp, R., & Garbutt, J. (1958). Time imagery and the achievement motive. *Journal of Personality, 26,* 426–434.

835

Test Name: U SCALE

Purpose: To assess self-perception.

Format: Used with pre-school and kindergarten; nonverbal format: child is presented 50 pairs of bipolar drawings in which he or she is to choose the end representing himself or herself.

Reliability: Kuder-Richardson formula was .67 for boys, .67 for girls.

Author: Ozehosky, R., and Clark, E.

Article: Dominance in mental imagery.

Journal: *Educational and Psychological Measurement,* Autumn 1972, *32*(3), 679–703.

Article: Verbal and non-verbal measures of self-concept among kindergarten boys and girls.

Journal: *Psychological Reports,* February 1971, *28*(1), 195–199.

Related Research: Clark, E., & Ozehosky, R. (1966). *Preliminary manual for the U-scale.* Unpublished manual, St. Johns University, Department of Psychology.

■ ■ ■

836

Test Name: VROOM INDEX

Purpose: To measure perceived participation in decision-making by teachers.

Number of Items: 4

Format: Scores for each item range from 1 (*low participation*) to 4 (*high participation*). Test scores range from 4 to 20.

Reliability: Test–retest reliability was .63. An estimate of reliability was .78.

Validity: With Nonauthoritarian personality, $r = -.004$.

Consideration, $r = .582$. Initiating structure = .504. Socio-economic background = .043. Formal education = .216. Length of time in present position = .221. Age = .435.

Author: Ambrosie, F., and Heller, R. W.

Article: The secondary school administrator and perceived teacher participation in the decision-making process.

Journal: *Journal of Experimental Education,* Summer 1972, *40*(4), 6–13.

Related Research: Vroom, V. H. (1960). *Some personality determinants of the effects of participation.* Englewood Cliffs, NJ: Prentice-Hall.

■ ■ ■

837

Test Name: WARMAN'S COUNSELING APPROPRIATENESS CHECKLIST

Purpose: To assess the perceived appropriateness of counselors working with various problems.

Number of Items: 66

Format: Items rated on a 5-point scale from 1 (*definitely inappropriate*) to 5 (*most appropriate*); includes three factors: college routine, vocational choice, adjustment to self and others.

Author: Resnick, H., and Gelso, C.

Article: Differential perceptions of counseling role: A re-examination.

Journal: *Journal of Counseling Psychology,* November 1971, *18*(6), 549–553.

Related Research: Warman, R. (1960). Differential perceptions of counseling role. *Journal of Counseling Psychology, 7,* 269–274.

■ ■ ■

838

Test Name: WATSON ANALYSIS SCHEDULE

Purpose: To measure the perceptions of learning behaviors of persons in process oriented and conventionally oriented classroom situations.

Number of Items: 213

Format: Includes three parts: explicit expectations, realized expectations, actual expectations. Subjects respond to each item on a 5-point scale.

Reliability: Test–retest reliability was .563.

Validity: A discussion of construct validity is included.

Author: Watson, E. P., et al.

Article: Students' role expectations as perceived by teachers and students in American studies and American history programs.

Journal: *Educational Leadership,* January 1971, *28*(4), 397–404.

CHAPTER 17
Personality

839

Test Name: BIOGRAPHICAL DATA INVENTORY

Purpose: To identify biographical information for use in predicting many kinds of complex criteria; i.e., predicting attendance at campus cultural events.

Number of Items: 136

Format: Contains not only factual, objective items, but also evaluative and subjective items; 72 items are of a continuous nature. Noncontinuous items include binary items with many options but only one response permitted, and items with many options and more than one response permitted. The 136 items yield 366 scorable responses.

Validity: For predicting attendance at campus cultural events, rs = .32, .34, and .36.

Author: Schmidt, F. J., et al.

Article: Correlates of student attendance at cultural events.

Journal: *Journal of College Student Personnel*, January 1971, *12*(1), 41–43.

840

Test Name: BIOGRAPHICAL INVENTORY, ADULT I

Purpose: A biographical instrument devised to examine questions related especially to the early adulthood period.

Validity: .007 to .267.

Author: Bruch, C. B., and Morse, J. A.

Article: Initial study of creative (productive) women under the Bruch-Morse Model.

Journal: *The Gifted Child Quarterly*, Winter 1972, *16*(4), 282–289.

841

Test Name: CATTELL-CURRAN PSYCHOLOGICAL STATE BATTERY

Purpose: To assess psychological state factors.

Number of Items: 194

Format: Factors measured are repression mobilization, fatigue, guilt, extroversion, general depression, anxiety, and stress. Uses four-response, multiple choice format.

Author: Long, T., et al.

Article: Fluctuation in psychological state during two encounter-group weekends.

Journal: *Psychological Reports*, August 1971, *29*(1), 267–274.

842

Test Name: CHILDREN'S MINIMAL SOCIAL BEHAVIOR SCALE (CMSBS)

Purpose: To assess personality in children.

Number of Items: 31

Format: Presented orally; motor, verbal-motor and verbal scores combined = performance score; performance score + time = total CMSBS score.

Author: Ulmer, R.

Article: Relationships between objective personality test scores, schizophrenics' history and behavior in a mental hospital token economy ward.

Journal: *Psychological Reports*, August 1971, *29*(1), 307–312.

Related Research: Ulmer, R., & Lieberman, M. (1968). The children's minimal social behavior scale (CMSBS): A short objective measure of personality functioning (10-year level). *Psychological Reports, 22*, 283–286.

843

Test Name: CHILDREN'S SCHOOL QUESTIONNAIRE

Purpose: To assess the following response styles: acquiescence–negativism, self-enhancement–self-derogation.

Number of Items: 37 factored from original 198 items.

Format: School related items.

Validity: Teacher (Motivation) and Peer Appraisals (Acceptance) differentiated between acquiescent and negativistic but not between self-enhancing and self-derogating subjects. Self-enhancing subjects have lower means on school achievement and ability measures than self-derogating subjects. None of the differences in negativistic and acquiescent subjects were significant.

Author: Phillips, B.

Article: School stress as a factor in

children's responses to tests and testing.

Journal: *Journal of Educational Measurement,* 1971, *8*(1), 21–26.

Related Research: Phillips, B. (1966). An analysis of the causes of anxiety among children in school. (Final Report, Project No. 2616). U.S. Office of Education, Austin: University of Texas.

■ ■ ■

844

Test Name: CSSB RATING SCALE

Purpose: To assess personality characteristics.

Number of Items: 10

Format: Each person is rated on 10 characteristics by means of a 7-point scale. The entire scale is presented along with a definition of each characteristic.

Author: Anstey, E.

Article: The civil service administrative class: Extended interview selection procedure.

Journal: *Occupational Psychology,* 1971, *45*(3 & 4), 199–208.

■ ■ ■

845

Test Name: DIFFERENTIAL PERSONALITY INVENTORY

Purpose: To assess personality.

Format: Has at least two subscales: impulsivity and defensiveness.

Validity: Low nonsignificant correlation between impulsivity scale and attention measure; defensiveness correlated with a measure of reaction time, $r = .33$ to $r = .37$ (all $ps< .05$).

Author: Haley, G.

Article: Relations among chronicity, diagnosis, pre-morbid

adjustments, defensiveness and two measures of perceptual scanning.

Journal: *Perceptual and Motor Skills,* December 1971, *33*(3), 1163–1170.

Related Research: Jackson, D., & Messick, S. (1964). *Differential personality inventory (Form L).* College Park, PA: Authors.

■ ■ ■

846

Test Name: DRAW-A-CAR TEST

Purpose: Projective test of personality.

Format: Subject is asked to draw a car, then a series of 24 questions is asked (open ended).

Validity: No quantitative data are presented. However clinical cases are cited.

Author: Loney, J.

Article: Clinical aspects of the Loney Draw-a-Car Test: Enuresis and encopresis.

Journal: *Journal of Personality Assessment,* 1971, *35*(3), 265–274.

■ ■ ■

847

Test Name: DUNCAN PERSONALITY INTEGRATION REPUTATION TEST (PIRT)

Purpose: To measure personality integration.

Number of Items: 6

Format: Within a group respondents nominate three individuals "capable of forming deeper and more profound relationships with others."

Reliability: Test–retest (4 months) reliability was .84.

Validity: With 15 Tennessee Self Concept Scales ranged .00 to .20.

Author: Wright, L.

Article: Comparison of two sociometric devices for measuring personality integration.

Journal: *Psychological Reports,* December 1971, *29*(3), 1035–1039.

Related Research: Banikiotes, P., et al. (1971). Social desirability, adjustment and effectiveness. *Psychological Reports,* October, *29*(2), 581–582.

Duncan, C. (1963). *Personality integration population test.* Nashville, TN: George Peabody College.

Duncan, C. (1966). A reputation test of personality integration. *Journal of Personality and Social Psychology, 3,* 516–524.

■ ■ ■

848

Test Name: EARLY MEMORIES TEST

Purpose: To be used as a projective (personality) technique.

Time Required: 1–1.5 hours.

Format: Subjects were asked to recall their three earliest memories. Coded to assess active–passive and happy–sad dimensions.

Reliability: Agreement in coding between two raters was 83%(activity) and 89%(on affective dimension).

Validity: Significant relations between the dimensions described above and figure drawing activity; differention of body concept and Thematic Apperception Test sense of separate identity were reported.

Author: Lord, M.

Article: Activity and affect in early memories of adolescent boys.

Journal: *Journal of Personality Assessment,* 1971, *35*(5), 449–456.

849

Test Name: EXPANDED SOCIOMETRIC DEVICE

Purpose: To measure personality integration.

Number of Items: 30

Format: Sociometric scale, asked respondents in a group to nominate three individuals "capable of forming deeper and more profound relationships with others."

Reliability: Test–retest (4 months) reliability was .74.

Validity: Correlation with self ratings on Personality Integration Population Test = .38 ($p < .05$). Correlation with Tennessee Self Concept Scales ranged .00 to .16.

Author: Wright, L.

Article: Comparisons of two sociometric devices for measuring personality integration.

Journal: *Psychological Reports,* December 1972, *29*(3), 1035–1039.

Related Research: Wright, L., et al. (in press). Factor structure of the expanded sociometric device: A measure of personal effectiveness. *Educational and Psychological Measurement, 30*(2), 319–326.

See *D.U.E.M.M., 1,* 1974: 134–135.

• • •

850

Test Name: GLESER-IHILEVICH DEFENSE MECHANISM INVENTORY

Purpose: To measure defense mechanisms.

Number of Items: 40

Format: Assess five major defense mechanisms: principalization, projection, reversal, turning against object, turning against self. Multiple choice format.

Reliability: Test–retest (17 days) reliabilities were .70, .61, .80, .84, and .73 for each scale.

Author: Weissman, H., et al.

Article: Reliability study of the defense mechanism inventory.

Journal: *Psychological Reports,* December 1971, *29*(3), 1237–1238.

Related Research: Gleser, G., & Ihilevich, D. (1969). An objective instrument for measuring defense mechanisms. *Journal of Consulting and Clinical Psychology, 33,* 51–60.

• • •

851

Test Name: HIGH SCHOOL PERSONALITY QUESTIONNAIRE

Purpose: To measure dimensions of personality.

Format: Includes a set of 14 factorially independent dimensions of personality.

Author: Barton, K, et al.

Article: Personality and IQ measures as predictors of school achievement.

Journal: *Journal of Educational Psychology,* August 1972, *63*(4), 398–404.

• • •

852

Test Name: MORAL JUDGMENTS IN MITIGATING CIRCUMSTANCE SCALE

Purpose: To describe personality.

Format: Possibly based on analysis of figure drawings.

Author: Platt, J., et al.

Article: Temporal perspective as a personality dimension in college students: A re-evaluation.

Journal: *Perceptual and Motor Skills,* August 1971, *33*(1), 103–109.

Related Research: Eisenman, R., & Smith, J. (1966). Moral judgments and effort in human figure drawings. *Perceptual and Motor Skills, 23,* 951–954.

• • •

853

Test Name: PERSONAL OPINION STUDY

Purpose: To assess personality characteristics.

Format: Contains neurotic, psychotic scales.

Author: Gutierrez, M., and Eisenman, R.

Article: Verbal conditioning of neurotic and psychopathic delinquents using verbal and nonverbal reinforcers.

Journal: *Psychological Reports,* August 1971, *29*(1), 7–10.

Related Research: Peterson, D., et al. (1959). Personality and background factors in juvenile delinquency as inferred from questionnaire responses. *Journal of Consulting Psychology, 23,* 395–399.

• • •

854

Test Name: PERSONALITY RATING SCALE

Purpose: To rate personality characteristics.

Number of Items: 28

Format: Statements were checked on 4-point scale (*I agree very much* to *I disagree very much*) by the person rating the subject. Assesses impression of intelligence, appearance, social desirability, social acceptance, and leadership.

Reliability: Split-half reliability was .97 ($N = 58$, adolescents).

Author: Feshbach, N., and Sones, G.

Article: Sex differences in

adolescent reactions toward newcomers.

Journal: *Developmental Psychology,* May 1971, *4*(3), 381–386.

■ ■ ■

855

Test Name: QUAY BEHAVIOR RATING SCALES

Purpose: To assess personality in delinquents.

Number of Items: 55

Format: Contains neurotic, psychopathic, socialized, and immature factors.

Reliability: Split-half reliabilities were .92, psychopathic; .81, neurotic; .26, immature.

Validity: Correlation with Eysenck Personality Inventory Neuroticism was .04.

Author: Schuck, S., et al.

Article: Delinquency, personality tests and relationships to measures of guilt and adjustment.

Journal: *Psychological Reports,* August 1972, *31*(4), 219–226.

Related Research: Mack, J. (1969). Behavior ratings of recidivist and nonrecidivist delinquent males. *Psychological Reports, 25,* 260.

Quay, H. (1964). Personality dimensions in delinquent males as inferred from the factor analysis of behavior ratings. *Journal of Research in Crime and Delinquency, 1,* 33–37.

Quay, H. (1966). Personality patterns in preadolescent delinquent boys. *Educational and Psychological Measurement, 26,* 99–110.

■ ■ ■

856

Test Name: QUAY CASE HISTORY SCALE

Purpose: To measure personality in delinquents.

Number of Items: 36

Format: The instrument has neurotic, psychopathic, socialized, and immature factors.

Validity: Correlation of neurotic factors with neuroticism scale of Eysenck Scale was .18 ($p < .05$).

Author: Schuck, S., et al.

Article: Delinquency, personality tests and relationships to measures of guilt and adjustment.

Journal: *Psychological Reports,* August 1972, *31*(1), 219–226.

Related Research: Quay, H. (1966). Personality patterns in pre-adolescent delinquent boys. *Educational and Psychological Measurement, 26,* 99–110.

■ ■ ■

857

Test Name: QUAY PERSONAL OPINION INVENTORY

Purpose: To assess personality of delinquents.

Number of Items: 100

Format: Self-rating questionnaire. Instrument has neurotic, psychopathic, and socialized factors.

Validity: Correlation of Socialized Factor with Neuroticism of Eysenck Personality Inventory was .32 ($p < .01$).

Author: Schuck, S., et al.

Article: Delinquency, personality tests and relationships to measures of guilt and adjustment.

Journal: *Psychological Reports,* August 1972, *31*(1), 219–226.

Related Research: Quay, H. (1966). Personality patterns in pre-adolescent delinquent boys. *Educational and Psychological Measurement, 26,* 99–110.

Quay, H., & Peterson, D. (1974).

The questionnaire measurement of personality dimensions associated with juvenile delinquency. Unpublished manuscript, University of Illinois.

■ ■ ■

858

Test Name: SCHOENFELD DAYDREAMS INVENTORY

Purpose: To assess personality.

Format: Nine scales: pessimism–optimism, movement toward–away from people, morbid content–nonmorbid content, self-orientation–other orientation, unpleasant–pleasant, unrealistic–realistic, positive social orientation–negative social orientation, past–future, physical interest–psychosocial interest.

Reliability: Test–retest (14 weeks) reliabilities ranged from .41 to .73.

Author: Thakur, G., and Schoenfeld, L.

Article: A cross-cultural reliability study of the Schoenfeld daydream inventory.

Journal: *Perceptual and Motor Skills,* December 1971, *33*(3), 1218.

Related Research: Schoenfeld, L. (1970). Construction of a personality inventory through Thurstone scaling of daydreams. *Perceptual and Motor Skills, 31,* 678.

■ ■ ■

859

Test Name: STUDENT PERSONNEL INVENTORY

Purpose: To identify background information about the student and to measure attitudes.

Format: Two sections: Section I includes educational experience, vocational experience, membership in professional organizations, vocational conferences attended during past 3 years, student personnel research conducted or planned, articles or books published, professional journals subscribed to, student activities participated in undergraduate college. Section II measured the student personnel point of view of the deans of men.

Author: Bailey, W. R., and Shappell, D. L.

Article: The dean of men: Relatedness of experience and attitudes.

Journal: *Journal of College Student Personnel,* May 1972, *13*(3), 255–261.

■ ■ ■

860

Test Name: TAYLOR MANIFEST ANXIETY SCALE

Purpose: To assess anxiety.

Reliability: Test–retest reliabilities were .82 and .89 (Taylor, 1953).

Validity: Correlation was .73 ($p <$ .01) with Cattell 16 PF Anxiety Score.

Author: Reiter, H.

Article: Relationships among four measures of anxiety.

Journal: *Psychological Reports,* June 1971, *28*(3), 761–762.

Related Research: Taylor, J. (1953). A personality test of manifest anxiety. *Journal of Abnormal and Social Psychology, 48,* 285–290.

■ ■ ■

861

Test Name: TORRANCE LIFE EXPERIENCES INVENTORY

Purpose: To acquire information on subject's current and past behavior and family.

Number of Items: 107

Format: Multiple-choice. Includes scales: creativity, elaboration, originality, achievement for excellence, and risk taking.

Validity: Significant differences between women's liberation and control group were found for 4 of 5 scales.

Author: Joesting, J.

Article: Comparison of women's liberation members with their nonmember peers.

Journal: *Psychological Reports,* December 1971, *29*(3), 1291–1294.

Related Research: Torrance, E., & Ziller, R. (1957, February). *Risk and life experiences: Development of a scale for measuring risk-taking tendencies* (Research Bulletin AFPTRC-TN-57–23 ASTIA Document No. 093926). Lackland Air Force Base, Texas: Air Force Personnel and Training Research Center.

■ ■ ■

862

Test Name: TRAIT SELF KNOWLEDGE, RATED IMPORTANCE AND DESIRABILITY SCALE

Purpose: To assess the knowledge about importance of and desirability of 15 personal traits.

Number of Items: 45

Format: Subject rates three 15–point bipolar scales with respect to different traits selected from

Edwards Personal Preference schedule.

Reliability: Test–retest reliabilities were self-knowledge, .56; rated importance, .48; and desirability, .49.

Author: Binderman, R., et al.

Article: Effects of interpreter credibility and discrepancy level of results on responses to test results.

Journal: *Journal of Counseling Psychology,* September 1972, *19*(5), 399–403.

■ ■ ■

863

Test Name: TWO-DIMENSIONAL SENTENCE COMPLETION TEST

Purpose: To assess personality.

Number of Items: 36

Format: Two dimensions: subject (first person or impersonal) and stem affect (positive, negative, neutral).

Validity: Neutral items revealed more projection. First-person stems yielded more projection than impersonal form. Positively toned-sentence and first-person stem yielded much better indices of adjustment than neutral or negative stems and impersonal stems.

Author: Murstein, B., et al.

Article: Influence of stimulus properties of the sentence-completion method on projection and adjustment.

Journal: *Journal of Personality Assessment,* 1972, *36*(3), 241–247.

CHAPTER 18
Preference

864

Test Name: CLARKE SCIENCE INTEREST CHECKLIST

Purpose: To measure science area preference.

Number of Items: 25

Format: Each item consisted of three concepts (a, b, c) representing three broad areas (biological, earth, physical). Children indicated the concept in each item they wanted to learn about the most and the concept they wanted to learn about the least.

Validity: Validation by a five-member jury of Science Education Experts.

Author: Clarke, C. O., and Nelson, P. A.

Article: Commonalities of science interests held by intermediate grade children.

Journal: *Journal of Education,* February 1972, *154*(3), 3–12.

• • •

865

Test Name: CLASSROOM PREFERENCE TEST

Purpose: To measure children's racial preferences for classmates and teachers.

Number of Items: 18

Format: Items consist of classroom scenes that vary systematically in the activity portrayed, in the race of teacher, and in the racial composition of pupils. Sketches are organized into nine pairs.

Author: Koslin, S., et al.

Article: Classroom racial balance and students' interracial attitudes.

Journal: *Sociology of Education,* Fall 1972, *45*(4), 386–407.

• • •

866

Test Name: EIGHT PROFESSORS SCALE

Purpose: To examine preferences towards different types of social science professors.

Number of Items: 8

Format: Likert (1–5) scale on which students ranked eight descriptions of professors (two scores, four types—researcher, teacher, socialite, administrator).

Reliability: Mean reliability for single student was .30.

Author: Yamamoto, K., et al.

Article: Student perceptions of "eight professors" in small colleges.

Journal: *Journal of Experimental Education,* Fall 1972, *41*(1), 91–96.

Related Research: Yamamoto, K., & Dizney, H. (1968). College students' preferences among four types of professors. *Journal of College Student Personnel, 9,* 259–264.

• • •

867

Test Name: HOUSING NEEDS AND PREFERENCES QUESTIONNAIRE

Purpose: To identify housing needs and preferences of college students.

Number of Items: 86

Format: Includes a range of questions from those dealing with physical requirements to those pertaining to social/living arrangements.

Author: Titus, C. R.

Article: Students express their housing needs and preferences.

Journal: *Journal of College Student Personnel,* May 1972, *13*(3), 202–204.

• • •

868

Test Name: INFORMATION SEEKING INTEREST MEASURE

Purpose: To assess the interest of students in information-seeking.

Number of Items: 23

Format: Items described information seeking tasks and subject rates his interest on one of five levels of the 23 scales.

Reliability: Hoyt reliability was .91.

Author: Lafleur, N., and Johnson, R.

Article: Separate effects of social modeling and reinforcement in counseling adolescents.

Journal: *Journal of Counseling Psychology,* July 1972, *19*(4), 292–295.

869

Test Name: KAMMEYER'S ROLE CHOICE QUESTIONNAIRE

Purpose: To assess role choice among women.

Number of Items: 5

Format: Likert style with a range of 5 to 25 points on total scale. Women could vary from nontraditional to traditional in their choice of roles.

Author: Maxwell, P., and Gonzalez, A.

Article: Traditional and non-traditional role choice and need for failure among college women.

Journal: *Psychological Reports,* October 1972, *31*(2), 545–546.

Related Research: Kammeyer, K. (1967). Sibling position and the female role. *Journal of Marriage and the Family, 29,* 494–499.

■ ■ ■

870

Test Name: LEISURE ACTIVITIES QUESTIONNAIRE

Purpose: To identify leisure activities.

Number of Items: 61

Format: Subjects are asked to check the leisure activities in which they participated and the frequency. Several items are presented.

Author: Aven, S. D., and Roderick, J.

Article: Comparing leisure activities of male and female teachers.

Journal: *Education,* September–October 1972, *93*(1), 82–83.

■ ■ ■

871

Test Name: MODIFIED YAMAMOTO WORD ASSOCIATION STUDY

Purpose: To permit students to rate four school subjects (science, social studies, mathematics, and English).

Format: Each school subject was rated on twelve 7-point bipolar scales. The two factors studied on these scales were Vigor and Certainty.

Author: Clarke, C. O., and Nelson, P. A.

Article: Commonalities of science interests held by intermediate grade children.

Journal: *Journal of Education,* February 1972, *154*(3), 3–12.

■ ■ ■

872

Test Name: MORROW COLLEGE MAJOR SATISFACTION QUESTIONNAIRE

Purpose: To assess satisfaction with choice of major.

Number of Items: Three items, each with multiple statements.

Format: Subject indicates which statement in each of the three items best describes his or her feelings.

Reliability: Test–retest (approx. 5 weeks) reliability was .89, total group.

Validity: Relation between satisfaction with major and personality type (by Vocational Preference Inventory).

Author: Morrow, J.

Article: A test of Holland's theory of vocational choice.

Journal: *Journal of Counseling Psychology,* September 1971, *18*(5), 422–425.

■ ■ ■

873

Test Name: MULTI-DIMENSIONAL SCALE OF POLITICAL PREFERENCE

Purpose: To assess political preference.

Format: Subjects rated 14 political personalities regarding preferences as president; also rated paired candidates on similarity of pair in appeal to the subject.

Validity: Cross validated multiple correlation was .808.

Author: Elster, R., and Capra, J.

Article: Multi-dimensional scaling of political preferences.

Journal: *Perceptual and Motor Skills,* December 1972, *35*(3), 987–991.

■ ■ ■

874

Test Name: OCCUPATIONAL PREFERENCE SEX ROLE SCALE

Purpose: To assess sex role orientation.

Format: Child named three occupations he preferred. Judges rated choice on a 5-point scale for feminine–masculine.

Reliability: Agreement by judge on 67% of ratings (54% within one scale point).

Author: Laosa, L., and Brophy, J.

Article: Effects of sex and birth order on sex-role development and intelligence among kindergarten children.

Journal: *Developmental Psychology,* May 1972, *6*(3), 409–415.

■ ■ ■

875

Test Name: ORIENTATION TO CLOTHING INDEX

Purpose: To measure the relative position of an individual on two continua.

Number of Items: 12

Format: Items rated on Likert

scales. Subject responds to choices such as *almost like me, never like me.* Two scores were obtained: "reward seeking–punishment avoidance," "dressing to be different–dressing to be the same."

Reliability: Test–retest reliabilities were .81, .86.

Author: White, B., and Kernaleguen, A.

Article: Comparison of selected perceptual and personality variables among college women deviant and non-deviant in their appearance.

Journal: *Perceptual and Motor Skills,* February 1971, *32*(1), 87–92.

Related Research: Kernaleguen, A. (1970). *Selected perceptual and personality variables related to orientation to dress and adornment* (Research Grant U-500). Unpublished research project, Utah State University.

• • •

876

Test Name: SATISFACTION WITH COLLEGE MAJOR INDEX

Purpose: To assess students' satisfaction with their majors.

Number of Items: 1

Format: Scale from 1 (*low*) to 6 (*high*) satisfaction.

Validity: Differences in flexibility between satisfied and unsatisfied students were found, which interacted with area of study.

Author: Sherrick, M., et al.

Article: Flexibility and satisfaction with college major.

Journal: *Journal of Counseling Psychology,* September 1971, *18*(5), 487–489.

877

Test Name: SEX ROLE ACHIEVEMENT STANDARDS MEASURE

Purpose: To assess the extent that standards for achievement are sex role related.

Number of Items: 42

Format: Areas of achievement were: mechanical, athletic, mathematics, reading, artistic, and social skills.

Reliability: Test–retest reliabilities ranged from .52 to .80.

Author: Stein, A.

Article: The effects of sex-role standards for achievement and sex-role preference on three determinants of achievement motivation.

Journal: *Developmental Psychology,* March 1971, *4*(2), 219–231.

Related Research: Stein, A., & Smithells, J. (1969). Age and sex differences in children's sex-role standards about achievement. *Developmental Psychology, 1,* 252–259.

• • •

878

Test Name: SEX ROLE RATING QUESTIONNAIRE

Purpose: To describe a child in terms of masculine or feminine characteristics.

Number of Items: 24

Format: Seventeen bipolar adjectives on a 6-point scale plus seven placebo items. The rater is instructed to describe the subject on the 6-point continuum by circling a point on the scale.

Author: Meyer, J., and Sobieszek, B.

Article: Effect of a child's sex on

adult interpretations of its behavior.

Journal: *Developmental Psychology,* January 1972, *6*(1), 42–48.

• • •

879

Test Name: STUDENT ORIENTATION SURVEY

Purpose: To measure student orientations to college.

Format: Includes academic, collegiate, nonconforming, and vocational scales.

Author: Schmidt, M. R.

Article: Relationship between sorority membership and changes in selected personality variables and attitudes.

Journal: *Journal of College Student Personnel,* May 1971, *12*(3), 208–213.

Related Research: Farber, I. E., & Goldstein, L. D. (1964). *Student orientation survey* (Preliminary Report, PHS Research Grant M-226).

Trow, M. (1960). The campus reviewed as a culture. In H. T. Sprague (Ed.), *Research on college students.* Boulder: Western Interstate Commission for Higher Education.

• • •

880

Test Name: TEACHER PREFERENCE FOR CLASSROOM MANAGEMENT STRATEGY

Purpose: To measure the strategy (developmental, traditional formal discipline, behavior modification, psychodynamic mental health, group process problem solving) preferred by teachers.

Number of Items: 16

Format: Each item proposed a

hypothetical classroom situation. Respondent was required to rank five alternative solutions in order of preference.

Reliability: Test–retest over approximately 5 months with training period, correlations not reported.

Validity: Intercorrelation of five pretest subscales ranged from −.01 (group process and developmental) to .58 (group process and behavior modification). Intercorrelation of 5 posttest subscales ranged from .00 to .52.

Author: Barclay, J., et al.

Article: Effectiveness of teacher training in social learning and behavior modification techniques.

Journal: *Measurement and Evaluation in Guidance*, July 1971, *4*(2), 79–89.

■ ■ ■

881

Test Name: TEACHER SEX ROLE ADOPTION RATINGS

Purpose: To assess children's sex role orientations.

Number of Items: 20

Format: Teachers rated children on 20 behaviors using a 5-point scale. Obtains 3 measures: male, female, and difference score.

Author: Laosa, L., and Brophy, J.

Article: Effects of sex and birth order on sex-role development and intelligence among kindergarten children.

Journal: *Developmental Psychology*, May 1972, *6*(3), 409–415.

Related Research: Biller, H. (1968). A multiaspect investigation of masculine development in kindergarten age boys. *Genetic Psychology Monographs*, *78*, 89–139.

■ ■ ■

882

Test Name: TEACHING STYLE INVENTORY

Purpose: To assess preference for and understanding of expository and discovery teaching styles.

Number of Items: 29

Time Required: Approximately 15 minutes.

Format: Consist of three parts: Part I assesses preference for expository and discovery teaching styles; Part II is a checklist of statements concerning the two styles; and Part III is a multiple-choice test to assess understanding of the two styles.

Author: Emmer, E. T., et al.

Article: Effect of feedback expectancy on choice of teaching styles.

Journal: *Journal of Educational Psychology*, December 1971, *62*(6), 451–455.

■ ■ ■

883

Test Name: TOY PREFERENCE TEST

Purpose: To assess sex role orientation.

Format: Child is presented with choices of toys. Behavior is scored on a masculine–feminine dimension.

Author: Laosa, L., and Brophy, J.

Article: Effects of sex and birth order on sex-role development and intelligence among kindergarten children.

Journal: *Developmental Psychology*, May 1972, *6*(3), 409–415.

Related Research: Biller, H. (1968). A multiaspect investigation of masculine development in kindergarten age boys. *Genetic Psychology Monographs*, *78*, 89–139.

CHAPTER 19
Problem Solving

884

Test Name: ABSTRACT REASONING TEST

Purpose: To measure abstract reasoning through ability to identify and utilize concepts and principles, ability to recognize patterns and relationships, and ability to use simple inductive and deductive logic.

Number of Items: 10

Time Required: 10 minutes.

Format: Forms A, B, and D. Each includes four types of problems: completion of a mathematical series; drawing the missing member of a pair of figures; magic squares; one problem utilizing a fictitious ancient number system. Some examples are presented.

Validity: With CTMM: verbal, .18 to .28. With CTMM: non-verbal .25 to .31. With end-of-year grades in mathematics .38 to .62.

Author: Gallor, G. M.

Article: Teaching methods and incentives in relation to junior high mathematics achievement.

Journal: *California Journal of Educational Research,* March 1972, *23*(2), 56–70.

. . .

885

Test Name: AWARENESS OF CONSEQUENCES TEST

Purpose: To measure consequential thinking.

Format: For each item the subject is given the solution to a problem and asked to tell what would happen next. The score consists of responses independently judged as a reaction by 0 in direct relationship to P's act. Examples are presented.

Validity: With Preschool Interpersonal Problem Solving Test, *r* = .42 and .53. With Causality Test, *r*s= .37 and .49. With Peabody Picture Vocabulary Test, *r* = .40.

Author: Shure, M. B., et al.

Article: Problem-solving thinking and adjustment among disadvantaged preschool children.

Journal: *Child Development,* December 1971, *42*(6), 1791–1803.

. . .

886

Test Name: CAUSALITY TEST

Purpose: To measure a child's general inclination to think of cause and effect when presented with a hypothetical event.

Number of Items: 10

Time Required: Approximately 15 minutes.

Format: The subject tells what the hypothetical child would be saying to his mother or his friend about a stated event. Examples are presented.

Reliability: Interrater reliability ranged from .89 to .96.

Validity: With Preschool Interpersonal Problem Solving Test, *r*s = .45 and .58. With Awareness of Consequences Test, *r*s = .37 and .49. With Peabody Picture Vocabulary Test, *r* = .48.

Author: Shure, M. B., et al.

Article: Problem-solving thinking and adjustment among disadvantaged preschool children.

Journal: *Child Development,* December 1971, *42*(6), 1791–1803.

Related Research: Biber, B., & Lewis, C. (1949). An experimental study of what young school children expect from their teachers. *Genetic Psychological Monographs, 40,* 3–97.

. . .

887

Test Name: DRUMCONDRA VERBAL REASONING TEST

Purpose: To assess general verbal intelligence.

Format: Sections include: analogies, opposites, concepts, identified as belonging to a single category, induction and deduction.

Author: Kellaghan, T., and MacNamara, J.

Article: Family correlates of verbal reasoning ability.

Journal: *Developmental Psychology,* July 1972, *7*(1), 49–53.

Related Research: Gorman, W. (1968). *The construction and standardization of a verbal reasoning test for age range 10 years 0 months to 12 years 11 months in an Irish population.* Unpublished doctoral dissertation, University College, Dublin.

888

Test Name: DUNN-LORGE FIGURE DRAWING SCALE

Purpose: To evaluate children's intellectual ability.

Format: Quality scales for evaluating. Each consists of 12 drawings illustrating equal appearing intervals.

Reliability: Interrater reliability was .90. Test–retest reliability was .84.

Author: Struempfer, D.

Article: Validation of two quality scales for children's figure drawings.

Journal: *Perceptual and Motor Skills*, June 1971, *32*(3), 887–893.

Related Research: Dunn, M., & Lorge, I. (1954). A Gestalt scale for the appraisal of human figure drawings (abstract). *American Psychologist, 9*, 357.

■ ■ ■

889

Test Name: FORMAL REASONING TESTS

Purpose: To test formal operational thought.

Number of Items: 30 each.

Time Required: 40 minutes each.

Format: Three paper-and-pencil tests assessing three content areas (biology, history, literature). Multiple choice format.

Validity: Concurrent validity with Piagetian tasks averaged correlations of .33 (13 years), .62 (16 years), and .57 (19 years).

Author: Bart, W.

Article: Construction and validation of formal reasoning instruments.

Journal: *Psychological Reports*, April 1972, *30*(2), 663–670.

890

Test Name: JUDGMENT ACCURACY TEST

Purpose: To assess judgment accuracy.

Number of Items: 10

Format: The subject selects the one title out of five for each item that most closely matches his criteria for a superior title for a given plot.

Author: Stratton, R. P., and Brown, R.

Article: Improving creative thinking by training in the production and/or judgment of solutions.

Journal: *Journal of Educational Psychology*, August 1972, *63*(4), 390–397.

Related Research: Johnson, D. M., et al. (1968). Production and judgment of solutions to five problems. *Journal of Educational Psychology, 59*(6, Pt. 2).

■ ■ ■

891

Test Name: PARAGRAPH COMPLETION TEST

Purpose: To measure ability of a subject to think in terms of multiple concepts when given information; that is, to measure complex integrative thinking.

Time Required: 130 seconds per paragraph.

Format: Projective-type format where subject completes a sentence and then writes at least three additional sentences.

Author: Gardiner, G., and Schroder, H.

Article: Reliability and validity of the Paragraph Completion Test: Theoretical and empirical notes.

Journal: *Psychological Reports*, December 1972, *31*(3), 959–962.

Related Research: Bottenberg, E. (1969). Instrumental characteristics and validity of the Paragraph Completion Test (PCT) as a measure of integrative complexity. *Psychological Reports, 24*, 437–438.

■ ■ ■

892

Test Name: PRESCHOOL INTERPERSONAL PROBLEM SOLVING TEST

Purpose: To measure the child's ability to conceptualize alternative solutions.

Time Required: Approximately 30 minutes.

Format: Includes two types of problems individually administered: ways for one child to obtain a toy from another and ways to avert the mother's anger that could result from damage to property. A child's score consisted of the total number of different relevant solutions and separately, the total number of different solution categories. A description is provided.

Validity: With Awareness of Consequences Test, rs = .42 and .53. With Causality Test, rs = .45 and .58. With Peabody Picture Vocabulary Test, r = .49.

Author: Shure, M. B., et al.

Article: Problem-solving thinking and adjustment among disadvantaged preschool children.

Journal: *Child Development*, December 1971, *42*(6), 1791–1803.

■ ■ ■

893

Test Name: PROBLEM SOLVING FLEXIBILITY SCALE

Purpose: To assess problem solving flexibility.

Number of Items: Seven problems.

Format: Subjects are tested individually. Child is given a description (e.g., "You saw a man walking on his hands.") and is asked to give as many explanations for the action as possible. Protocols scored by examiners.

Reliability: Interrater reliability was .90. Average Hoyt-type reliability coefficient was .42 for boys and .45 for girls.

Validity: Correlation with intelligence was .23 ($p < .01$) for boys and girls.

Author: Greenberger, E., et al.

Article: Personality, cognitive, and academic correlates of problem-solving flexibility.

Journal: *Developmental Psychology,* May 1971, *4*(3), 416–424.

Related Research: Guilford, J. P., et al. (1957). *A factor-analytic study of flexibility in thinking* (Report No. 18). Los Angeles: University of Southern California, Psychology Laboratory.

Schroder, H. (1971). Conceptual complexity and personality organization. In H. M. Schroder & P. Suedfeld (Eds.), *Personality theory and information processing.* New York: Ronald.

Schroder, H., et al. (1967). *Human information processing.*

New York: Holt, Rinehart & Winston.

● ● ●

894

Test Name: PURDUE ELEMENTARY PROBLEM SOLVING INVENTORY

Purpose: To measure general problem solving ability in disadvantaged children.

Number of Items: 49 problems.

Format: Subject is presented a cartoon problem via slide presentation and responds to alternatives presented on a tape by marking a test booklet. Abilities assessed: awareness of existence of problem, problem definition, asking questions, guessing causes, clarifying goal, judging when more information is needed, analysis of details, redefines for original uses, seeing implications, solving problems, verifying solutions.

Reliability: Kuder-Richardson Formula 20 was .79.

Validity: Correlation with logical thinking was .505, .448, .452 (Grades 2, 4, 6). Correlation with concept formation was .314, .402, .305 (grades 2, 4, 6).

Author: Feldhusen, J., et al.

Article: The Purdue Elementary Problem Solving Inventory.

Journal: *Psychological Reports,* December 1972, *31*(3), 891–901.

Related Research: Prof. John Feldhusen, Educational Psychology and Research Section, Purdue University, SCC-G, Lafayette, IN 47907.

● ● ●

895

Test Name: TEST OF VERBAL ABSURDITIES

Purpose: To measure the child's ability to recognize verbal absurdities.

Number of Items: 51

Format: Consisted of common absurdities and straightforward statements. The subject indicates which are absurd and which are correct. The entire test is presented.

Reliability: Estimated coefficient of .77 and if expanded to 100 items, coefficient estimated to be .87.

Author: Maw, W. H., and Maw, E. W.

Article: Differences between high- and low-curiosity fifth-grade children in their recognition of verbal absurdities.

Journal: *Journal of Educational Psychology,* December 1972, *63*(6), 558–562.

...

CHAPTER 20
Status

896

Test Name: COLLEGE MAJOR PRESTIGE QUESTIONNAIRE

Purpose: To assess the degree of prestige of various college majors.

Format: Subjects were asked to rate 30 majors on a 5-point (*very low* to *high*) prestige scale.

Author: Dudley, L., and Garbin, A.

Article: The prestige of sociology compared to other college majors.

Journal: *American Sociologist,* August 1972, *7*(7), 7–8.

...

897

Test Name: HALLER'S OCCUPATIONAL ASPIRATION SCALE

Purpose: To indicate the prestige level of the occupational hierarchy which an individual views as a goal; a measure of occupational aspiration.

Number of Items: 8

Format: Multiple-choice items designed primarily for use among male high school students.

Validity: NORC Occupational Prestige Scale: –.50. McClelland's Need Achievement Thematic Apperception Test: .22. Mandler-Cowan's Test Anxiety Questionnaire for High School Students: –.26.

Author: Tseng, M. S.

Article: Social class, occupational aspiration, and other variables.

Journal: *Journal of Experimental Education,* Summer 1971, *39*(4), 88–92.

Related Research: Haller, A. O., & Miller, I. W. (1967). *The occupational aspiration scale theory, structure, and correlates.* The University of Wisconsin, Madison, Department of Rural Sociology.

See *D.U.E.M.M., 1,* 1974: 168–169.

...

898

Test Name: HOLLINGSHEAD OCCUPATIONAL SCALE

Purpose: To determine socioeconomic status.

Format: Includes seven levels.

Author: Guthrie, J. T.

Article: Relationships of teaching method, socio-economic status, and intelligence in concept formation.

Journal: Journal of Educational Psychology, August 1971, *62*(4), 345–351.

Related Research: Hollingshead, A. B., & Redlich, F. E. (1958). *Social class and mental illness.* New York: Wiley.

...

899

Test Name: MCGUIRE AND WHITE SOCIO-ECONOMIC STATUS SCALE

Purpose: To obtain an estimate of the subject's socio-economic status.

Format: Provides an SES rating from 1 for professional occupations to 7 for unskilled labor and unemployed.

Author: Hermann, R. W.

Article: Classroom status and teacher approval and disapproval–study of children's perceptions.

Journal: *Journal of Experimental Education,* Winter 1972, *41*(2), 32–39.

Related Research: Bell, D. B., et al. (1972, January). Some personality and motivational factors in reading retardation. *Journal of Educational Research, 65*(5), 229–233.

Jordan, T., & Spaner, S. (1972, August). Biological and ecological influences on development at 24 and 36 months of age. *Psychological Reports, 31*(1), 319–322.

Kennedy, W. A. (1969). A follow-up normative study of Negro intelligence and achievement. *S.R.C.D. Monographs*(126, 34), Appendix 2.

...

900

Test Name: NORC OCCUPATIONAL PRESTIGE SCALE

Purpose: To measure perception of occupational prestige.

Number of Items: 20

Format: Subject ranks 20 occupations on the basis of his opinion as to which occupation had the most prestige.

Validity: Haller's Occupational Aspiration Scale: –.50. McClelland's Need Achievement Thematic Apperception Test: –.26. Mandler-Cowan's Test Anxiety Questionnaire for High School Students: .25.

Author: Tseng, M. S.

Article: Social class, occupational aspiration, and other variables.

Journal: *Journal of Experimental Education,* Summer 1971, *39*(4), 88–92.

Related Research: National Opinion Research Center. (1947). Jobs and occupations: A popular evaluation. *Opinion News, 9,* 3–13.

Tseng, M. S. (1972). Comparison of selected familial, personality, and vocational variables of high school students and dropouts. *Journal of Educational Research,* July-August, *65*(10), 462–466.

See *D.U.E.M.M., 1,* 1974: 171–172.

■ ■ ■

901

Test Name: OCCUPATIONAL ASPIRATION SCALE

Purpose: To provide a relative indicator of the prestige level on the occupational hierarchy which the subject views as a goal.

Number of Items: 8

Format: Designed primarily for use among male high school students.

Reliability: .80

Author: Tseng, M. S.

Article: Comparisons of selected familial, personality, and vocational variables of high school students and dropouts.

Journal: *Journal of Educational Research,* July–August 1972, *65*(10), 462–466.

Related Research: Haller, A. O., & Miller, I. W. (1957). *The Occupational Aspiration Scale: Theory, structure and correlates.* The University of Wisconsin, Department of Rural Sociology, Madison.

■ ■ ■

902

Test Name: PEARLIN-ROSENBERG STATUS DISTANCE SCALE-MODIFIED

Purpose: To measure status distance.

Number of Items: 6

Format: All items are presented.

Reliability: Coefficient of reproducibility is .95. Coefficient of scalability is .67.

Author: Perry, J. B., and Snyder, E. E.

Article: Opinions of farm employers toward welfare assistance for Mexican American migrant workers.

Journal: *Sociology and Social Research,* January 1971, *55*(2), 161–169.

Related Research: Pearlin, L. I. (1962, November). Sources of resistance to change in a mental hospital. *The American Journal of Sociology, 68,* 325–334.

Pearlin, L. I., & Rosenberg, M. (1962, February). Nurse-patient social distance and the structure

context of a mental hospital. *American Sociological Review, 27,* 56–65.

■ ■ ■

903

Test Name: PSYCHOLOGICAL OCCUPATIONS PRESTIGE QUESTIONNAIRE

Purpose: To ascertain occupational prestige hierarchies in the profession of psychology.

Number of Items: 20 Psychological Job Titles.

Validity: An occupational prestige hierarchy was found that was similar to that found by Granger (1959).

Author: Kondrasuk, J.

Article: Graduate students rankings of prestige among occupations in psychology.

Journal: *Journal of Counseling Psychology,* March 1971, *18*(2), 142–146.

Related Research: Granger, S. (1959). Psychologists' prestige rankings of 20 psychological occupations. *Journal of Counseling Psychology, 6,* 183–188.

■ ■ ■

904

Test Name: PSYCHOSOCIAL QUESTIONNAIRE

Purpose: To identify present academic status; socio-economic status; perceptions of the pre-university experience; perceptions of the university experience; and present values, aspirations, and pressures.

Number of Items: 50

Author: Smith, L.

Article: A 5-year follow-up study of

high ability achieving and nonachieving college freshmen.

Journal: *Journal of Educational Research,* January 1971, *64*(5), 220–222.

■ ■ ■

905

Test Name: QUESTIONNAIRE ON TEACHER ATTITUDE TOWARD THE PROFESSION

Purpose: To assess teachers' perceptions of a status system within the profession.

Number of Items: 34

Format: Each item was answered on a 4-point scale from *definitely agree* to *definitely disagree.*

Includes the following factors: status, training, salary, time, predictor, and graduate education.

Author: Hansen, L. H., et al.

Article: Teacher perceptions of intra-occupational status relationships among elementary, junior high, and senior high school teaching positions.

Journal: *Journal of Experimental Education,* Winter 1971, *40*(2), 51–56.

■ ■ ■

906

Test Name: SOCIOLOGICAL JOURNAL EVALUATIVE QUESTIONNAIRE

Purpose: To obtain prestige ratings of journals in sociology.

Number of Items: 63

Format: Sixty-three journals rated in comparison to the *American Sociological Review.* Unit of measurement was the average importance of articles.

Author: Glenn, N.

Article: American sociologists' evaluations of sixty-three journals.

Journal: *American Sociologist,* August 1971, *6*(3), 298–303.

. . .

CHAPTER 21
Trait Measurement

907

Test Name: ACCEPTANCE OF BLAME MEASURE

Purpose: To assess the extent to which a child will accept blame.

Format: Teacher rated scale regarding how children respond when they are caught doing something wrong.

Author: Hoffman, M.

Article: Father absence and conscience development.

Journal: *Developmental Psychology*, May 1971, *4*(3), 400–406.

. . .

908

Test Name: ACHIEVEMENT ANXIETY TEST

Purpose: To measure anxiety.

Format: Includes two subscales: a plus subscale that deals with the kind of anxiety that facilitates performance in achievement situations and a minus subscale that taps the debilitating effects of anxiety on performance in achievement situations.

Author: Tobias, S., and Abramson, T.

Article: Interaction among anxiety, stress, response, mode, and familiarity of subject matter on achievement from programmed instruction.

Journal: *Journal of Educational Psychology*, August 1971, *62*(4), 357–364.

Related Research: Alpert, R., & Haber, R. (1960). Anxiety in academic achievement situations. *Journal of Abnormal and Social Psychology, 61*, 207–215.

. . .

909

Test Name: ADORNO F SCALE

Purpose: To measure authoritarianism.

Number of Items: 28

Validity: Subjects could fake "bad" on items but not fake "good."

Author: Hogan, H.

Article: Fakability of the Adorno F Scale.

Journal: *Psychological Reports*, February 1972, *30*(1), 15–21.

Related Research: Adorno, T., et al. (1950). *The authoritarian personality*. New York: Harper & Row.

. . .

910

Test Name: ANHEDONIA SCALE

Purpose: To measure subjects' inability to experience pleasure.

Number of Items: 5

Reliability: Test–retest reliability (1 week) was .82. Cronbach's alpha was .76.

Validity: Correlations with 10 physiological stress measures all nonsignificant and low.

Author: Watson, C.

Article: Relationships of anhedonia to physiological reactivity and threshold.

Journal: *Psychological Reports,* August 1972, *31*(1), 43–46.

Related Research: Watson, C., et al. (1970). Toward an operational definition of anhedonia. *Psychological Reports, 26*, 371–376.

. . .

911

Test Name: ANXIETY SELF RATING SCALE

Purpose: To assess degree of anxiety.

Number of Items: 1

Format: Eight-point scale. Subject is asked to indicate present level of anxiety. Two end points are defined.

Validity: Correlation with Manifest Anxiety Scale = .56 ($p < . 01$).

Author: McReynolds, P.

Article: Behavioral choice as a function of novelty-seeking and anxiety-avoidance motivations.

Journal: *Psychological Reports,* August 1971, *29*(1), 3–6.

Related Research: McReynolds, P. (1958). Anxiety as related to incongruencies between values and feelings. *Psychological Record, 8,* 57–66.

. . .

912

Test Name: ATTITUDE-PERSONALITY QUESTIONNAIRE

Purpose: To measure authoritarianism.

Number of Items: 48

Format: Statements are answered as either true or false. Two examples are provided.

Reliability: Test–retest reliabilities were .32 and .62.

Author: Athansiou, R.

Article: Selection and socialization: A study of engineering student attrition.

Journal: *Journal of Educational Psychology,* April 1971, *62*(2), 157–166.

• • •

913

Test Name: AUTOKINETIC TEST

Purpose: To assess ego closeness–ego distance, a cognitive control measure.

Reliability: Test–retest (1 year) reliability was .77.

Author: Gardner, R.

Article: Reliability of group-test scores for cognitive controls and intellectual abilities over a one year period.

Journal: *Perceptual and Motor Skills,* June 1973, *36*(3), 753–754.

Related Research: Gardner, R., & Lohrenz, L. (1969). Some old and new tests of cognitive controls and intellectual abilities. *Perceptual and Motor Skills, 29,* 935–950.

• • •

914

Test Name: BARBER SUGGESTIBILITY SCALE

Purpose: To assess responsiveness to test suggestions.

Format: May be administered with and without formal hypnotic induction or task motivation instruction. It provides objective and subjective suggestibility scores.

Validity: Subjectively experienced suggestibility was more related to attitude change than was objective suggestibility.

Author: Kaul, T., and Parker, C.

Article: Suggestibility and expectancy in a counseling analogue.

Journal: *Journal of Counseling Psychology,* November 1971, *18*(6), 536–541.

Related Research: Barber, T. (1965). Measuring "hypnotic-like" suggestibility with and without hypnotic induction; psychometric properties, norms and variables influencing responses to the Barber Suggestibility Scale (BSS). *Psychological Reports, 16,* 809–844.

See *D.U.E.M.M., 1,* 1974: 75–76.

• • •

915

Test Name: BELIEF IN THE INTEGRITY OF MAN SCALE

Purpose: To measure a dimension of social responsibility.

Number of Items: 22

Format: Items rated on 4-point Likert scales.

Reliability: Kuder-Richardson Formula 20 = .72 to .76.

Author: Mueller, D. J.

Article: A technique for the utilization of items with highly skewed response distributions in personality scaling.

Journal: *Journal of Experimental Education,* Summer 1972, *40*(4), 62–64.

Related Research: Mueller, D. J. (1969). *Differences in social responsibility among various groups of college students.* Unpublished doctoral dissertation, University of Illinois.

916

Test Name: BORGOTTA ADHERENCE TO AUTHORITY SCALE

Purpose: To assess a subject's adherence to authority.

Validity: Correlation with Strodtbeck Fatalism was .320 ($p <$ .001).

Author: Friis, R., and Knox, A.

Article: A validity study of scales to measure need achievement, need affiliation, impulsiveness and intellectuality.

Journal: *Educational and Psychological Measurement,* Spring 1972, *32*(1), 147–154.

Related Research: Borgotta, E. (1967). The work components study: A set of measures for work motivation. *Journal of Psychological Studies, 16,* 1–11.

• • •

917

Test Name: BRESKIN RIGIDITY TEST

Purpose: To measure nonverbal rigidity.

Number of Items: 15

Format: Subject chooses between 15 pairs of stimulus figures. Responses scored on 0, 1 scale; maximum rigidity was 15 points.

Validity: Correlation with high school average was .07. Correlation with college grade point was .00.

Author: Primavera, L., and Simon, W.

Article: Nonverbal rigidity and academic achievement in high school and college.

Journal: *Perceptual and Motor Skills,* December 1971, *33*(3), 1178.

Related Research: Breskin, S.

(1968). Measurement of rigidity, a non-verbal test. *Perceptual and Motor Skills, 27,* 1203–1206.

■ ■ ■

918

Test Name: BUREAUCRATIC/ EMPLOYEE ORIENTATION SCALE

Purpose: To measure bureaucratic role orientation.

Number of Items: 29

Format: Likert scale scored from 7 (*agree strongly*) to 1 (*disagree strongly*). The higher the total score, the more positive the orientation. Examples are presented.

Author: Helsel, A. R., and Krchniak, S. P.

Article: Socialization in a heteronomous profession: Public school teaching.

Journal: *Journal of Educational Research,* October 1972, *66*(2), 89–93.

Related Research: Corwin, R. G. (1970). *Militant professionalism.* New York: Appleton-Century-Crofts.

■ ■ ■

919

Test Name: BUSS-DURKEE HOSTILITY SCALE

Purpose: To measure hostility.

Number of Items: 39

Format: Contains four hostility measures. Subjects respond yes/no to statements.

Author: Greenberg, R., and Fisher, S.

Article: Some differential effects of music on projective and structured psychological tests.

Journal: *Psychological Reports,* June 1971, *28*(3), 817–818.

Related Research: Buss, A. (1961). *The psychology of aggression.* New York: Wiley.

■ ■ ■

920

Test Name: BUSS-DURKEE INVENTORY

Purpose: To measure aggression.

Author: Hearn, M., and Evans, D.

Article: Anger and reciprocal inhibition therapy.

Journal: *Psychological Reports,* June 1972, *30*(3), 943–948.

Related Research: Buss, A. (1963). Physical aggression in relation to different frustrations. *Journal of Abnormal and Social Psychology, 67,* 1–7.

■ ■ ■

921

Test Name: BYRNE REPRESSION-SENSITIZATION SCALE

Purpose: To assess the defense mechanisms of repression and sensitization.

Number of Items: 182

Format: Selected from the M.M.P.I. scales (L, K, Hy, denial, D, Pt, Welsh Anxiety). High scores indicate sensitizing defense and low scores repressing defenses.

Author: Baldwin, B., and Cabianca, W.

Article: Defensive strategies of repressors and sensitizers in counseling.

Journal: *Journal of Counseling Psychology,* January 1972, *19*(1), 16–20.

Related Research: Byrne, D., et al. (1963). Relation of the revised repression-sensitization scale to measures of self description. *Psychological Reports, 13,* 323–334.

Lewinsohn, P., et al. (1972, December). The repression-sensitization dimension and emotional responses to stimuli. *Psychological Reports, 31*(3), 707–716.

Pellegrine, R. (1971, July). Repression-sensitization and perceived sensitivity of presenting problem of four hundred and forty-four counseling center clients. *Journal of Counseling Psychology, 18*(4), 332–336.

■ ■ ■

922

Test Name: CHEATING TEST

Purpose: To measure cheating.

Number of Items: 50

Format: Five-alternative, multiple-choice vocabulary test.

Author: Vitro, F. T., and Schoer, L. A.

Article: The effects of probability of test success, test importance, and risk of detection on the incidence of cheating.

Journal: *Journal of School Psychology,* 1972, *10*(3), 269–277.

■ ■ ■

923

Test Name: COGNITIVE FLEXIBILITY TEST

Purpose: To measure the ability to shift in three general areas: perceptual, conceptual, and spontaneous.

Format: Includes five tests: stencil design (the ability to shift figure–ground relationships); embedded figures (the ability to shift in terms of part-whole relationships); picture anomalies (the ability to shift set when confronted with dissonant information); object sorting (the ability to shift conceptual categories); and tell about this (the ability to shift in the rapid production of ideas).

Reliability: Test–retest reliabilities ranged from .72 to .90.

Internal consistencies ranged from .73 to .93.

Author: McKinney, J. D., and Corter, H. M.

Article: Flexibility training with educable retarded children.

Journal: *Journal of School Psychology,* 1971, *9*(4), 455–461.

Related Research: Corter, H. M., & McKinney, J. D. (1968). Flexibility training with educable retarded and bright normal children. *American Journal of Mental Deficiency, 72,* 603–609.

McKinney, J. D. (1966). *Cognitive flexibility training with educable retarded and bright normal children of the same mental age.* Unpublished master's thesis, Department of Psychology, North Carolina State University.

■ ■ ■

924

Test Name: WORD COLOR TEST

Purpose: Cognitive control measure; assesses constricted-flexibility control.

Reliability: Test–retest (1 year) $r = .38$.

Author: Gardner, R.

Article: Reliability of group-test scores for cognitive controls and intellectual abilities over a one year period.

Journal: *Perceptual and Motor Skills,* June 1973, *36*(3), 753–754.

Related Research: Gardner, R., & Lohrenz, L. (1969). Some old and new tests of cognitive controls and intellectual abilities. *Perceptual and Motor Skills, 29,* 935–950.

■ ■ ■

925

Test Name: COSTELLO-COMREY ANXIETY SCALE

Purpose: To assess predisposition to become anxious.

Reliability: Test–retest reliability was .73 ($p < .01$).

Validity: Correlation with Manifest Anxiety Scale was .50.

Author: Ogston, D., and Drakeford, G.

Article: Note on the Costello-Comrey Anxiety Scale.

Journal: *Psychological Reports,* February 1971, *28*(1), 287–289.

Related Research: Costello, C., & Comrey, A. (1967). Scale for measuring depression and anxiety. *Journal of Psychology, 66,* 303–313.

■ ■ ■

926

Test Name: DOGMATISM SCALE

Purpose: To provide an index of authoritarianism.

Number of Items: 40

Author: McQuarrie, D., and Grotelueschen, A.

Article: Effects of verbal warning upon misapplication of a rule of limited applicability.

Journal: *Journal of Educational Psychology,* October 1971, *62*(5), 432–438.

Related Research: Rokeach, M. (1960). *The open and closed mind.* New York: Basic Books.

■ ■ ■

927

Test Name: DOLL PLAY AND MATERNAL INTERVIEW TECHNIQUES

Purpose: To assess masculinity–feminity, aggression, dependency.

Format: In doll play technique child was presented with either forced choice pairs of pictures, or various doll play situations designed to elicit the behavior

being assessed. In maternal interview mother was asked 26 questions.

Reliability: Interrater reliabilities .82 to .87.

Validity: Correlation with maternal interview of .208 ($p < .05$) for masculinity-femininity; of .107 (*ns*) for aggression; of –.004 (*ns*) for dependency.

Author: Wohlford, P., et al.

Article: Older brothers' influence on sex-typed aggressive, and dependent behavior in father absent children.

Journal: *Developmental Psychology,* March 1971, *4*(2), 124–134.

Related Research: Santrock, J. (1970). Parental absence, sex typing, and identification. *Developmental Psychology, 2,* 264–272.

■ ■ ■

928

Test Name: DUA ANXIETY EXPRESSION SCALE

Purpose: To assess change in anxiety.

Reliability: Test–retest (two samples, 6 weeks) reliabilities were .75 and .78.

Validity: Significant correlation with Taylor Manifest Anxiety Scale, level of *r* not reported.

Author: Dua, P. S.

Article: Effects of laboratory training on anxiety.

Journal: *Journal of Counseling Psychology,* March 1972, *19*(2), 171–172.

■ ■ ■

929

Test Name: EGO SUFFICIENCY SCALE

Purpose: To assess subject's ability

to cope with emotional issues and the degree of mastery of problems.

Format: TAT scored for this construct; scored by trained raters.

Reliability: Intrajudge and interjudge reliability in the .90s.

Author: Newas, M.

Article: Change in efficiency of ego functioning and complexity from adolescence to young adulthood.

Journal: *Developmental Psychology,* May 1971, *4*(3), 412–415.

Related Research: Dana, R. (1959). Proposal for the objective scoring of the TAT. *Perceptual and Motor Skills, 9,* 23–43.

■ ■ ■

930

Test Name: EISENMAN-CHERRY RESPONSE ACQUIESCENCE SCALE

Purpose: To measure response acquiescence.

Validity: Correlation with directionality scale (Time Metaphors Test) was .26 (*p* < .10).

Author: Platt, J., et al.

Article: Temporal perspective as a personality dimension in college students: A re-evaluation.

Journal: *Perceptual and Motor Skills,* August 1971, *33*(1), 103–109.

Related Research: Eisenman, R., & Cherry, H. (1968, April). *Creativity and authoritarianism.* Paper presented at Southeastern Psychological Association, Roanoke, VA.

■ ■ ■

931

Test Name: EMOTIONAL DEPENDENCE SCALE

Purpose: To assess the extent to

which a worker attempts to gain the approval and attention of a superior.

Number of Items: 8

Format: Four categories of response (*strong agree* to *strong disagree*).

Reliability: Split-half (Spearman-Brown) reliability was .90.

Validity: Correlation with Work Dependence Scale was .28 (*p* < .05).

Author: Shivdasani, H.

Article: Construct of dependence need: Bi-dimensional proneness in work organization.

Journal: *Psychological Reports,* August 1971, *29*(1), 282.

■ ■ ■

932

Test Name: EVANS REACTION INVENTORY

Purpose: To measure anger.

Author: Hearn, M., and Evans, D.

Article: Anger and reciprocal inhibition therapy.

Journal: *Psychological Reports,* June 1972, *30*(2), 943–948.

Related Research: Evans, D., & Stangeland, M. (1971). The development of a reaction inventory to measure anger. *Psychological Reports, 29,* 412–414.

■ ■ ■

933

Test Name: GENERAL ANXIETY QUESTIONNAIRE

Purpose: To measure anxiety.

Number of Items: 50

Format: Includes an anxiety scale and a lie scale. Responses to each item are either *yes* or *no*. All items are presented.

Validity: With teacher ratings of

behavior correlations from .03 to .23 and +.11.

Author: Hawkes, T. H., and Furst, N. F.

Article: Research notes: race, socio-economic situation, achievement, IQ, and teacher ratings of students' behavior as factors relating to anxiety in upper elementary school children.

Journal: *Sociology of Education,* Summer 1971, *44*(3), 333–350.

Related Research: Hawkes, T. H., & Koff, R. H. (1970, July). Differences in anxiety of private school and inner city public elementary school children. *Psychology in the Schools, 7,* 250–259.

■ ■ ■

934

Test Name: GOTTHEIL'S ORAL TRAIT SCALE

Purpose: To measure oral traits in a psychoanalytic framework.

Number of Items: 40

Format: Open questions that can be answered *yes/no.*

Validity: 22 of 40 items correlated less than .3 with the total score.

Reliability: Kuder-Richardson Formula 20 was .558.

Author: Kline, P.

Article: The validity of Gottheil's Oral Trait Scale in Great Britain.

Journal: *Journal of Personality Assessment,* 1973, *37*(6), 551–554.

Related Research: Gottheil, E., & Stone, G. (1968). Factor-analytic study of orality and anality. *Journal of Nervous and Mental Disease, 146,* 1–17.

■ ■ ■

935

Test Name: HAIMAN OPEN-MINDEDNESS SCALE

Purpose: To assess open-mindedness.

Number of Items: 30

Format: Ten items from California F, Rokeach, and Measurement of Authoritarian Attitudes Scales.

Author: Altmann, H., and Conklin, R.

Article: Further correlates of the Barton Complexity Scale.

Journal: *Perceptual and Motor Skills*, February 1972, *34*(1), 83–86.

Related Research: Haiman, F. (1964). A revised scale for the measurement of open-mindedness. *Speech Monographs, 31*(97).

■ ■ ■

936

Test Name: H-SCALE OF DIRECTIVENESS

Purpose: To assess level of directiveness.

Number of Items: 4

Format: Each item consists of a description of a critical classroom incident followed by four responses from which teachers select the one that would have the most desirable effect on the pupil or pupils concerned. An example is presented.

Author: Dunkin, M. J.

Article: The nature and resolution of role conflicts among male primary school teachers.

Journal: *Sociology of Education*, Spring 1972, *45*(2), 167–185.

■ ■ ■

937

Test Name: H-SCALE OF WARMTH

Purpose: To assess level of warmth.

Number of Items: 5

Format: Each item consists of a description of a critical classroom incident followed by four responses from which teachers select the one which would have the most desirable effect on the pupil or pupils concerned. An example is presented.

Author: Dunkin, M. J.

Article: The nature and resolution of role conflicts among male primary school teachers.

Journal: *Sociology of Education*, Spring 1972, *45*(2), 167–185.

■ ■ ■

938

Test Name: INTERVIEWER TRUSTWORTHINESS SCALE

Purpose: To assess the trustworthiness of an interviewer.

Number of Items: 1

Format: Eight-point scale from *extremely untrustworthy* to *extremely trustworthy.*

Validity: Individuals exposed to a definition of trustworthiness rated taped interviews differently than those not exposed.

Author: Kaul, T., and Schmidt, K.

Article: Dimensions of interviewer trustworthiness.

Journal: *Journal of Counseling Psychology*, November 1971, *18*(6), 542–548.

Related Research: Strong, S., & Schmidt, L. (1970). Trustworthiness and influence in counseling. *Journal of Counseling Psychology, 17*, 81–87.

■ ■ ■

939

Test Name: KAGAN COGNITIVE STYLE TEST

Purpose: To identify flexibility and rigidity of cognitive styles.

Number of Items: 19

Time Required: 45 seconds/item.

Format: Cognitive style preference is identified on each item. Also flexibility is indicated by the number of times the subject changes his cognitive style and fluency is the sum of all responses on each item.

Author: Yeatts, P. P., and Strag, G. A.

Article: Flexibility of cognitive style and its relationship to academic achievement in fourth and sixth grades.

Journal: *Journal of Educational Research*, April 1971, *64*(8), 345–346.

Related Research: Kagan, J., et al. (1964). Information processing in the child, significance of analytic and reflective attitudes. *Psychological Monographs, 78*(1, Whole No. 578).

■ ■ ■

940

Test Name: LARSEN AGGRESSION SCALE

Purpose: To measure aggression.

Number of Items: 37 (20 Form A, 17 Form B).

Format: Subject is asked to agree or disagree to statements.

Reliability: Equivalent Forms $r = .42$. Test–retest $r = .60$.

Validity: Correlation with parental aggression training scale measure was .35 ($p < .01$) for total group; correlation with the Sampson & Smith Worldmindedness Scale was .22; correlation with Buss Hostility Scale was .04; and correlation with the Machiavellianism Scale was .20 ($p < .01$).

Author: Larsen, K.

Article: Aggression-altruism: A scale and some data on its reliability and validity.

Journal: *Journal of Personality Assessment*, 1971, *35*(3), 275–281.

941

Test Name: LEAST PREFERRED COWORKER SCALE (LPC)

Purpose: To assess leadership style.

Format: High scores are associated with a relationship oriented style; low scores with a task oriented style.

Author: Stinson, J.

Article: "Least Preferred Coworker" as a measure of leadership style.

Journal: *Psychological Reports*, June 1972, *30*(3), 930.

Related Research: Fiedler, F. (1967). *A theory of leadership effectiveness*. New York: McGraw Hill.

■ ■ ■

942

Test Name: MATCHING FAMILIAR FIGURES TEST

Purpose: To assess cognitive tempo.

Number of Items: 12 plus 2 samples.

Format: Subject is given a standard drawing and asked to match one of six alternatives to the standard; latency and error scores are used.

Author: Denney, D.

Article: Modeling effects upon conceptual styles and cognitive tempo.

Journal: *Child Development*, March 1972, *43*(1), 105–119.

Related Research: Heider, E. R. (1971, October). Information processing and the modification of an "implusive conceptual tempo." *Child Development, 42*(4), 1276–1281.

Kagan, J., et al. (1964). Information processing in the child: Significance of analytic and reflective attitudes. *Psychological Monographs, 78*(1, Whole No. 578).

Ridberg, E., et al. (1971). Modification of implusive and reflective cognitive styles through observation of film-mediated models. *Developmental Psychology, 5*(3), 369–377.

Wolfe, R., et al. (1972). Conceptual structure and conceptual tempo. *Perceptual and Motor Skills, 35*(1), 331–337.

■ ■ ■

943

Test Name: NIEDERHOFFER POLICE CYNICISM SCALE

Purpose: To assess cynicism among policemen.

Validity: Correlation with Gould alienation measure was .44 ($p < .01$).

Author: Zacker, J.

Article: Understanding one's clients: An attempt to improve sensitivity and morale in police recruits.

Journal: *Psychological Reports*, December 1972, *31*(3), 999–1008.

Related Research: Niederhoffer, A. (1967). *Behind the shield*. Garden City, NY: Doubleday.

■ ■ ■

944

Test Name: OSGOOD TANNENBAUM AND SUCI EMOTIONALITY SCALE

Purpose: To measure the strength of an affective response to a concept.

Author: Kayser, B.

Article: Authoritarianism, self-esteem, emotionality and intelligence.

Journal: *Perceptual and Motor Skills*, April 1972, *34*(2), 367–370.

■ ■ ■

945

Test Name: PAGE FANTASY SCALE (WORRY SCORE)

Purpose: To measure anxiety.

Validity: Correlation with Taylor MAS was .48 ($p < .01$).

Author: Reiter, H.

Article: Relationships among four measures of anxiety.

Journal: *Psychological Reports*, June 1971, *28*(3), 761–762.

Related Research: Page, H. (1953). *Description of the fantasy scale*. Unpublished manuscript, University of Wisconsin.

Page, H. (1960). A scale for the assessment of daydreaming behavior. *Perceptual and Motor Skills, 10*, 110.

■ ■ ■

946

Test Name: PEER RATING INDEX OF AGGRESSION

Purpose: To assess the degree of aggressiveness in a child.

Format: Members of a class are rated by their peers. Questions include: "Who does not obey the teacher?" and "Who pushes or shoves children?"

Author: Peterson, R.

Article: Aggression as a function of expected retaliation and aggression level of target and aggressor.

Journal: *Developmental Psychology*, July 1971, *5*(1), 161–166.

Related Research: Walder, L., et al. (1961). Development of a peer-rating measure of aggression. *Psychological Reports, 9*, 497–556.

947

Test Name: PHILLIPS ANXIETY TEST

Purpose: To measure anxiety of sixth graders.

Number of Items: 33

Format: Yes or no questions. Examples are provided.

Author: Schmidt, L., and Gallessich, J.

Article: Adjustment of Anglo-American and Mexican-American pupils in self-contained and team-teaching classrooms.

Journal: *Journal of Educational Psychology*, August 1971, *62*(4), 328–332.

Related Research: Phillips, B. (1966). *An analysis of causes of anxiety among children in school* (Final Report, United States Office of Education, Project No. 2616). Washington, DC: United States Government Printing Office.

■ ■ ■

948

Test Name: PICTURE ANXIETY TEST-REVISED

Purpose: To measure anxiety of first graders.

Number of Items: 22

Format: The items consist of children in potentially anxious situations at home and school.

Reliability: From the original version: 8-week test–retest Pearson's product moment correlation was .67; split-half corrected reliability was .95.

Validity: With teacher ratings of anxiety, *r* = .57.

Author: Schmidt, L., and Gallessich, J.

Article: Adjustment of Anglo-American and

Mexican-American pupils in self-contained and team-teaching classrooms.

Journal: *Journal of Educational Psychology*, August 1971, *62*(4), 328–332.

Related Research: Dorkey, M., & Amen, E. W. (1947). A continuation study of anxiety reactions in young children by means of a projective technique. *Genetic Psychological Monograph, 35*, 139–183.

Temple, R., & Amen, E. (1944). A study of anxiety reactions in young children by means of a projective technique. *Genetic Psychological Monograph, 30*, 59–114.

■ ■ ■

949

Test Name: RASMUSSEN'S EGO IDENTITY SCALE

Purpose: To assess extent of success of a subject in resolving psycho-social conflicts.

Number of Items: 72

Time Required: 30 minutes.

Format: Paper-and-pencil self-report. Total identity score is provided as well as scores for trust, autonomy, initiative, achievement, identity, and affiliation.

Validity: Significant differences in ego identity were found between high and low need affiliation and need achievement subjects.

Author: Bauer, R., and Snyder, R.

Article: Ego identity and motivation: An empirical study of achievement and affiliation in Erikson's theory.

Journal: *Psychological Reports*, June 1972, *30*(3), 951–955.

Related Research: Rasmussen, J. (1964). *An experimental approach to the concept of ego identity as*

related to character disorder. Unpublished doctoral dissertation, American University.

950

Test Name: REACTION INVENTORY

Purpose: To measure anger.

Number of Items: 76

Format: Factors measured were minor chance annoyances, destructive people, unnecessary delays, inconsiderate people, self-opinionated people, frustration in business, criticism, major chance annoyances, people being personal, authority.

Reliability: Internal consistency was .95.

Validity: Correlations with Buss-Durkee Inventory were .52 and .57 (*p* < .01).

Author: Evans, D., and Stangeland, M.

Article: Development of the reaction inventory to measure anger.

Journal: *Psychological Reports*, October 1971, *29*(1), 412–414.

■ ■ ■

951

Test Name: REPRESSION-SENSITIZATION SCALE

Purpose: To measure how subjects react to unpleasant stimuli repression (denial) or sensitization (confrontation).

Validity: Correlation with time attending to unpleasant slides was .12 (*ns*); with pleasant slides, .16 (*ns*); with interesting slides, .10 (*ns*); with boring slides, .11 (*ns*).

Author: Carroll, D.

Article: Repression-sensitization and duration of visual attention.

Journal: *Perceptual and Motor*

Skills, June 1972, *34*(3), 949–950.

Related Research: Byrne, D. (1961). The repression–sensitization scale: rationale, reliability, and validity. *Journal of Personality, 29,* 334–349.

See *D.U.E.M.M., 1,* 1974: 183.

• • •

952

Test Name: RESISTANCE TO DEVIATIONS TEST

Purpose: To determine whether a child will disobey directions.

Format: Situational test in which child is instructed not to touch a group of toys. The number of deviations from instruction, duration of deviation, and latency of first response in absence is recorded by observers.

Reliability: Interrater reliabilities of three measures were .99, .99, and .99.

Author: Slaby, R., and Parke, R.

Article: Effect on resistance to deviation of observing a model's affective reaction to response consequences.

Journal: *Developmental Psychology,* July 1971, *5*(1), 40–47.

• • •

953

Test Name: ROKEACH DOGMATISM SCALE

Purpose: To measure dogmatic, rigid thinking.

Number of Items: 40

Author: Schmidt, M. R.

Article: Relationship between sorority membership and changes in selected personality variables and attitudes.

Journal: *Journal of College Student Personnel,* May 1971, *12*(3), 208–213.

Related Research: Rokeach, M. (1956). Political and religious dogmatism and alternatives to the authoritarian personality. *Psychological Monographs, 70*(18, Whole No. 425).

See *D.U.E.M.M., 1,* 1974: 184.

• • •

954

Test Name: ROTTER INTERPERSONAL TRUST SCALE

Purpose: To assess degree of trust in the respondent.

Author: Vondracek, F., and Marshall, M.

Article: Self-disclosure and interpersonal trust: An exploratory study.

Journal: *Psychological Reports,* February–June 1971, *28,* 235–240.

Related Research: Rotter, J. (1967). A new scale for the measurement of interpersonal trust. *Journal of Personality, 35,* 651–665.

• • •

955

Test Name: RYDELL-ROSEN TOLERANCE OF AMBIGUITY SCALE

Purpose: To assess subjects' tolerance for ambiguous situations.

Validity: Correlation with Locus of Control Scale was .11 (*ns*).

Author: Pawlicki, R.

Article: Relationship between locus of control and tolerance of ambiguity.

Journal: *Psychological Reports,* August 1972, *31*(1), 102.

Related Research: McDonald, A. (1970). Revised scale for ambiguity tolerance: Reliability and validity.

Psychological Reports, 26, 791–798.

• • •

956

Test Name: SALIVARY RESPONSE TO LEMON JUICE INTROVERSION MEASURE

Purpose: To assess the degree of introversion-extroversion.

Time Required: 20 seconds.

Format: Lemon juice was rubbed on subject's tongue. The increase in salivation was ascertained by weighing a cotton dental roll that had been placed under the tongue.

Validity: Correlation with Junior Eysenck Personality Inventory Introversion Scale = .43 (*p* < .01) girls, = .19 (*ns*) boys.

Author: Casey, J., and McManis, D.

Article: Salivary response to lemon juice as a measure of introversion in children.

Journal: *Perceptual and Motor Skills,* December 1971, *33*(3), 1059–1065.

Related Research: Eysenck, H., & Eysenck, S. (1967). Salivary response to lemon juice as a measure of introversion. *Perceptual and Motor Skills, 24,* 1047–1053.

• • •

957

Test Name: SCHOOL ENVIRONMENT PREFERENCE SCHEDULE

Purpose: To measure the bureaucratic personality.

Number of Items: 24

Format: A Likert scale that includes the four categories of items: self-subordination, uncriticalness, rule conformity, and traditionalism. The five response categories are *strongly* *agree, agree, undecided, disagree,* and *strongly disagree.* Sample items are provided.

Reliability: Test–retest reliability for a 9-week interval was .75 and for a 1 year interval was .62.

Validity: Correlation with Work Environment Preference Schedule ranged from .50 to .78; with Survey of Interpersonal Values, from .54 to .37; with Survey of Personal Values, from .41 to .34; with Authoritarianism, .40 to .68; with Dogmatism, .39 to .59; with Acquiescence, .16 to .32; with Social Desirability, .07 to .24; with School Grades, .21 to .51; with Scholastic Aptitude, .11 to .37.

Author: Gordon, L. V.

Article: Weber in the Classroom.

Journal: *Journal of Educational Psychology,* February 1971, *62*(1), 60–66.

Related Research: Gordon, L. V. (1968). School Environment Preference Schedule (SEPS). Albany: State University of New York, Program for Behavioral Research.

■ ■ ■

958

Test Name: SELF REPORT TRUST SCALE

Purpose: To assess extent of trust maintained by a subject.

Number of Items: 10

Format: Likert scale: *strongly agree* to *strongly disagree.*

Reliability: Cronbach's alpha was .84.

Validity: Correlation with Rotters Interpersonal Trust was .56 ($p <$ .01).

Author: MacDonald, A., et al.

Article: Self disclosure and two kinds of trust.

Journal: *Psychological Reports,*

February 1972, *30*(1), 141–148.

■ ■ ■

959

Test Name: SIMILIES PREFERENCE INVENTORY

Purpose: To measure tendency toward variety.

Reliability: Test–retest reliability was .61. Test–retest reliabilities were .85, .27.

Validity: Correlation with competency rating .003 and –.38.

Author: Woody, R., and Dubner, M.

Article: British and commonwealth counselors: An investigation of counselor characteristics and theoretical views.

Journal: *Counselor Education and Supervision,* Spring 1971, *10*(3), 233–241.

Related Research: Pearson, P., & Maddi, S. (1966). The Similies preference inventory: Development of a structured measure of the tendency toward variety. *Journal of Consulting Psychology, 30,* 301–308.

■ ■ ■

960

Test Name: SHIMKUNAS UNCERTAINTY ANXIETY SCALE

Purpose: To assess anxiety about uncertainty of situations.

Number of Items: 42

Format: True–false items relating to both inter- and intrapersonal nature.

Validity: Correlation with Marlowe Crowne Test .30 ($p < .01$).

Author: Doster, J., and Slaymaker, J.

Article: Need approval, uncertainty anxiety, and

expectancies of interview behavior.

Journal: *Journal of Counseling Psychology,* November 1972, *19*(6), 522–528.

Related Research: Shimkunas, A. (1972). *A scale of anxiety about uncertainty.* Unpublished manuscript, University of Missouri.

■ ■ ■

961

Test Name: SMITH IMPULSIVITY-CONSTRICTED SCALE

Purpose: To understand the manner in which an individual approached learning situations.

Number of Items: 20

Format: Questionnaire.

Validity: Significant differences in directive behavior between impulsive and constricted counselors were found.

Author: Smith, W., and Martinson, W.

Article: Counselor's and counselee's learning style on interview behavior.

Journal: *Journal of Counseling Psychology,* March 1971, *18*(2), 138–141.

Related Research: Smith, D. P. (1961). *Learning to learn.* New York: Harcourt, Brace & World.

■ ■ ■

962

Test Name: TEACHER RATING FORM

Purpose: To measure altruism.

Number of Items: 18 behavior sketches.

Format: The sketches are arranged into nine bipolar pairs, with each end of the pole representing either an altruistic or egoistic behavior episode.

Author: Bond, N. D., and Phillips, B. N.

Article: Personality traits associated with altruistic behavior of children.

Journal: *Journal of School Psychology,* 1971, *9*(1), 24–34.

Related Research: Turner, W. (1948). Altruism and its measurement in children. *Journal of Abnormal and Social Psychology, 43,* 502–516.

■ ■ ■

963

Test Name: TEACHER RATING FORM

Purpose: To obtain trait ratings on a series of pro-social dimensions from the subject's teachers.

Number of Items: Eight bipolar dimensions.

Format: Includes the following dimensions: ability to recognize the need for help; ability to help others; general helpfulness; helpfulness with peers; helpfulness with adults; and—as discriminators—general competence, activity level, and likeability.

Reliability: .89 to 1.00.

Author: Severy, L. J., and Davis, K. E.

Article: Helping behavior among normal and retarded children.

Journal: *Child Development,* October 1971, *42*(4), 1017–1031.

■ ■ ■

964

Test Name: TEST OF GUILT REACTION

Purpose: To assess child's guilt reaction to transgressions.

Format: Subject was presented with story and asked to respond in similar manner as to the Thematic Apperception Test. Two guilt scores: maximum guilt experienced by story hero (early in the story) and terminal guilt.

Author: Hoffman, M.

Article: Father absence and conscience development.

Journal: *Developmental Psychology,* May 1971, *4*(3), 400–406.

Related Research: Allinsmith, W. (1960). Moral standards: II. The learning of moral standards. In D. R. Miller & G. E. Swanson (Eds.), *Inner conflict and defense.* New York: Holt.

■ ■ ■

965

Test Name: TOLERANCE FOR AMBIGUITY

Purpose: To assess tolerance for ambiguity.

Author: Crandall, J.

Article: Effects of intolerance of ambiguity upon interpersonal attraction.

Journal: *Psychological Reports,* April 1971, *28*(2), 550.

Related Research: Budner, S. (1962). Intolerance of ambiguity as personality variable. *Journal of Personality, 30,* 29–50.

■ ■ ■

966

Test Name: WIDGERY-STACKPOLE ANXIETY TEST

Purpose: To assess anxiety in subjects during an experimental situation.

Number of Items: 18

Format: Likert format.

Author: Widgery, R., and Stackpole, C.

Article: Desk position, interviewer anxiety, and interviewee credibility.

Journal: *Journal of Counseling Psychology,* May 1972, *19*(3), 173–177.

■ ■ ■

967

Test Name: WORK ENVIRONMENT PREFERENCE SCHEDULE

Purpose: To measure the bureaucratic personality.

Number of Items: 24

Format: A Likert scale that includes the four categories of items: self-subordination, impersonalization, rule conformity, and traditionalism. The 5 response categories are *strongly agree, agree, undecided, disagree,* and *strongly disagree.*

Validity: With School Environment Preference Schedule from .50 to .78.

Author: Gordon, L. V.

Article: Weber in the Classroom.

Journal: *Journal of Educational Psychology,* February 1971, *62*(1), 60–66.

Related Research: Gordon, L. V. (1968). *Work Environment Preference Schedule (WEPS).* Albany: State University of New York, Program for Behavioral Research.

CHAPTER 22
Values

968

Test Name: AMES PHILOSOPHICAL BELIEF INVENTORY

Purpose: To describe the philosophical orientation of counselors and counselor trainees (e.g., realism, idealism, pragmatism, phenomenology, and existentialism).

Number of Items: 250

Format: Forced choice paper and pencil.

Reliability: Test–Retest ($N = 41$; 75 days) scored on short and long form: long form, .41 to .70; short form, .34 to .67. (Short form contained 40% fewer items.)

Validity: Concurrent: with 9 selected psychometric variables range .26 to .21 intercorrelation of subscales of PBI range .00 to .53.

Author: Sawyer, R. N.

Article: The Ames Philosophical Belief Inventory: Reliability and validity.

Journal: *Measurement and Evaluation in Guidance,* Winter 1971, *3*(4), 203–208.

Related Research: Ames, K. A. (1965). *The development of an instrument for assessing the philosophical positions of school counselors.* Doctoral dissertation, University of Wyoming.

Ames, K. A. (1968). The development of an instrument for assessing the philosophical positions of school counselors. *Counselor Education and Supervision, 7,* 335–339.

Wise, D. E. (1966). *An initial study of the Ames Philosophical Belief Inventory with students in education.* Doctoral dissertation, University of Wyoming.

. . .

969

Test Name: CRITICAL INCIDENT COUNSELOR ETHICAL DISCRIMINATION ABILITY QUESTIONNAIRE

Purpose: To determine whether counselors would select an ethically appropriate response to a critical incident.

Number of Items: 12 ethical situations.

Format: Ethical situations were selected from APGA Ethical Standards Casebook. Subject read incident and selected the ethical response from a choice of five alternatives. Three sections: general, counseling, testing.

Reliability: Test–retest: general, .81; counseling, .72; testing, .77; total score, .90 ($p < .01$).

Author: Shertzer, B., and Morris, K.

Article: APGA members' ethical discriminary ability.

Journal: *Counselor Education and Supervision,* March 1972, *11*(3), 200–206.

. . .

970

Test Name: CULTURAL RATING SCALE FOR HOMICIDE REGULATION

Purpose: To assess relative amount of legal control of homicide.

Format: Rated on a scale of 1–10 (least to most lawful). Criteria for rating was the expected reaction to murder.

Author: Witucki, J.

Article: A language pattern co-occurring with violence permissiveness.

Journal: *Behavioral Science,* November 1971, *16*(6), 531–537.

. . .

971

Test Name: ETHICAL RISK QUESTIONNAIRE

Purpose: To assess the degree to which a subject would violate ethical behavior.

Number of Items: 16

Format: Subjects are given a hypothetical case in which they are assumed to be a bank employee. They are asked to rate the probability (0–7 scale) that they might steal money.

Author: Zimmerman, J., and Krauss, H.

Article: Source and magnitude of censure in predictions of unethical behavior.

Journal: *Psychological Reports,* June 1971, *28*(3), 727–732.

. . .

972

Test Name: FLORIDA SCALE OF CIVIC BELIEFS

Purpose: To measure the political

orientation of school superintendents.

Number of Items: 60

Format: Contains five subtests, each of which is arranged as a continuum with a high score indicating a liberal political orientation and a low score indicating a conservative political orientation.

Validity: Correlations of the total score with the Leader Behavior Description Questionnaire subtests range from .46 to –.05.

Author: Null, E. J., and Smead, W. H.

Article: Relationships between the political orientation of superintendents and their leader behavior as perceived by subordinates.

Journal: *Journal of Educational Research,* November 1971, *65*(3), 103–106.

■ ■ ■

973

Test Name: FREE SPEECH QUESTIONNAIRE

Purpose: To assess commitment to free speech.

Number of Items: 6

Format: One multiple choice item and five yes–no questions relating to degree of commitment to support of free speech.

Validity: Extent of commitment to position was related to need for social approval; subjects low in need for approval showed greater commitment to their position.

Author: Shimkunas, A., and Kime, R.

Article: Personality correlates of student commitment to social action.

Journal: *Journal of Personality Assessment,* 1973, *35*(6), 561–568.

974

Test Name: GARDNER-THOMPSON REFERENCE VALENCE TEST

Purpose: To assess prescriptive values in adolescence.

Number of Items: 10 situations.

Format: Nine scales: subject is given 10 conflict situations in which he must choose a solution (five alternatives). Classifies respondents as prescriptive (ought to) or proscriptive (ought not to) value orientation.

Author: McKinney, J.

Article: The development of values—Prescriptive or proscriptive?

Journal: *Human Development,* 1971, *14*(1), 71–80.

Related Research: Gardner, E. F., and Thompson, G. (1963). *Investigation and measurement of the social values governing interpersonal relations among adolescent youth and their teachers. Parts I and II* (Final report to the Cooperative Program of the United States Office of Education).

■ ■ ■

975

Test Name: GOLDBERG ARTICLES TEST

Purpose: To assess values of feminine professional competence.

Number of Items: Eight articles, each with seven ratings.

Format: Articles in several professional fields are presented for review with either male or female author name. Seven items followed asking the reviewer to assess the article on a 12-point rating scale.

Author: Baruch, G.

Article: Maternal influences upon college women's attitudes toward women and work.

Journal: *Developmental Psychology,* January 1972, *6*(1), 32–37.

Related Research: Goldberg, P. (1967, April). *Misogyny and the college girl.* Paper presented at the meeting of the Eastern Psychological Association, Boston.

■ ■ ■

976

Test Name: MODERN VALUE ORIENTATION INDEX

Purpose: To index modern or western values and beliefs.

Number of Items: 22

Format: Based on factor analysis; six dimensions: independence from family, ethnic equality, empiricism, efficacy, receptivity to change, future oriented.

Reliability: Kuder-Richardson formula consistency for 22 items was .88. Kuder-Richardson formula consistency for 6 dimensions was .90.

Author: Armer, M., and Youtz, R.

Article: Formal education and individual modernity in an African society.

Journal: *American Journal of Sociology,* January 1971, *76*(4), 604–626.

■ ■ ■

977

Test Name: MORAL INDEXES

Purpose: To tap different aspects of the child's moral structure.

Format: Includes measures of intensity of guilt following transgressions; use of moral judgments about others that are based on moral principles rather than external considerations; tendency to confess and accept responsibility for one's misdeeds; the extent to which one shows consideration for others, conforms to rules, and expresses moral values.

Author: Hoffman, M. L.

Article: Identification and conscience development.

Journal: *Child Development,* October 1971, *42*(4), 1071–1082.

■ ■ ■

978

Test Name: MORAL VALUES RATING SCALE

Purpose: To assess the extent of importance of moral values to a child.

Format: Subject rated 21 attributes as most important "in boys (girls) your age." Some of the attributes were moral; others were nonmoral. The three top-rated items are counted and those that are moral items were weighted to obtain a score.

Author: Hoffman, M.

Article: Father absence and conscience development.

Journal: *Developmental Psychology,* May 1971, *4*(3), 400–406.

■ ■ ■

979

Test Name: PERSONAL ORIENTATION INVENTORY

Purpose: To measure some of the values and behavioral patterns depicted by self-actualizing individuals; to measure the level of self-actualization of students studying to be educational administrators.

Format: Self-administered.

Author: Hamilton, J. T.

Article: Educational administrators and their level of self-actualization.

Journal: *Educational Leadership,* March 1971, *28*(6), 633–635.

Related Research: Shostrum, E. L. (1965). A test for the measurement of self-actualization. *Educational and Psychological Measurement, 24,* 207–218.

■ ■ ■

980

Test Name: PHILOSOPHIES OF HUMAN NATURE SCALE

Purpose: To measure person's belief about human nature.

Format: Likert scale with six dimensions measured trustworthiness–untrustworthiness, altruism–selfishness, strength of will and rationality versus lack of will power and irrationality, independence versus conformity, simplicity versus complexity, and similarity versus variability.

Author: Gardiner, H.

Article: Philosophies of human nature among Roman Catholic sisters.

Journal: *Psychological Reports,* April 1972, *30*(2), 369–370.

Related Research: Wrightsman, L. (1964). Measurement of philosophies of human nature. *Psychological Reports, 14,* 743–751.

■ ■ ■

981

Test Name: PROHIBITED MORAL CODES QUESTIONNAIRE

Purpose: To discern cultural differences and study changes in moral behavior through time.

Number of Items: 50

Format: Each item is evaluated in terms of "least wrong" and "most wrong" on a scale ranging from 1

to 10. All items are presented.

Author: Tomeh, A. K.

Article: Patterns of moral behavior in two social structures.

Journal: *Sociology and Social Research,* January 1971, *55*(2), 149–160.

Related Research: Crissman, P. (1942). Temporal changes and sexual differences in moral judgments. *Journal of Social Psychology, 16,* 29–38.

■ ■ ■

982

Test Name: RELIGIOUS COMMITMENT SCALE

Purpose: To assess degree of religious commitment.

Format: Questionnaire with 5-point Likert scale. Includes measures of devotionalism, associationalism, communalism (11 scales).

Validity: Correlations with Self Concept (Twenty Statements Test) ranged .172 to .488, median about .4.

Author: Johnson, W.

Article: The religious crusade: Revival or ritual.

Journal: *American Journal of Sociology,* March 1971, *76*(5), 873–890.

Related Research: Lenski, G. (1961). *The religious factor.* Garden City, NY: Doubleday.

■ ■ ■

983

Test Name: RELIGIOUS DOGMA SCALE

Purpose: To assess conservatism of religious beliefs.

Validity: Eta squared value was .32 of religious dogma scale and peak-experience ratings.

Author: Breed, G., and Fagan, J.

Article: Religious dogmatism and peak experiences: A test of Maslow's hypothesis.

Journal: *Psychological Reports,* December 1972, *31*(3), 866.

Related Research: Fagan, J., & Breed, G. (1970). A good, short measure of religious dogmatism. *Psychological Reports, 26,* 533–534.

● ● ●

984

Test Name: RELIGIOUS QUESTIONNAIRE

Purpose: To measure the significance of religion to the respondent.

Number of Items: 9

Validity: Correlation with Dogmatism Scale was .89 ($p < .01$).

Author: Di Giuseppe, R.

Article: Dogmatism correlation with strength of religious conviction.

Journal: *Psychological Reports,* February 1971, *28*(1), 64.

Related Research: Dr. John Aboud, Department of Organizational Behavior, Babson College, Babson Park, MA.

● ● ●

985

Test Name: STRODTBECK FATALISM SCALE

Purpose: To assess subject's values with respect to fatalism.

Validity: Correlation with Strodtbeck Thoughtfulness Scale was −.412 ($p < .001$).

Author: Friis, R., and Knox, A.

Article: A validity study of scales to measure need achievement, need affiliation, impulsiveness, and intellectuality.

Journal: *Educational and Psychological Measurement,* Spring 1972, *32*(1), 147–154.

Related Research: Strodtbeck, F. (1958). Family interaction, values and achievement. In D. McClelland et al. (Eds.), *Talent and society.* Princeton, NJ: Van Nostrand, 135–194.

● ● ●

986

Test Name: STRODTBECK PLANFULNESS SCALE

Purpose: To assess a subject's values with respect to planfulness.

Validity: Correlation with number of organizations was .213 ($p < .01$); correlation with impulsiveness was .277 ($p < .001$); correlation with fatalism was .412 ($p < .001$).

Author: Friis, R., and Knox, A.

Article: A validity study of scales to measure need achievement, need affiliation, impulsiveness, and intellectuality.

Journal: *Educational and Psychological Measurement,* Spring 1972, *32*(1), 147–154.

Related Research: Strodtbeck, F. (1958). Family interaction, values and achievement. In D. McClelland et al. (Eds.), *Talent and society* (pp. 135–194). Princeton, NJ: Van Nostrand.

● ● ●

987

Test Name: STRODTBECK THOUGHTFULNESS SCALE

Purpose: To assess a subject's values with respect to thoughtfulness.

Validity: Correlation with Borgotta intellectual interest scale was .255 ($p < .001$); correlation with Strodtbeck fatalism scale was .412 ($p < .001$).

Author: Friis, R., and Knox, A.

Article: A validity study of scales to measure need achievement, need affiliation, impulsiveness and intellectuality.

Journal: *Educational and Psychological Measurement,* Spring 1972, *32*(1), 147–154.

Related Research: Strodtbeck, F. (1958). Family interaction, values and achievement. In D. McClelland et al. (Eds.), *Talent and society.* Princeton, NJ: Van Nostrand, 135–194.

● ● ●

988

Test Name: TWENTY STATEMENTS TEST

Purpose: To "measure salience of religious identification for self concept."

Number of Items: 20

Validity: Correlation with 11 scales of religious commitment ranged .172 to .48, median about .4.

Author: Johnson, W.

Article: The religious crusade: Revival or ritual.

Journal: *American Journal of Sociology,* March 1971, *76*(5), 873–890.

● ● ●

989

Test Name: VALUE INVENTORY

Purpose: To assess values.

Format: Includes five factors: other orientations, achievement (controlled), competitive achievement, individualism, detachment. Norms are available.

Author: Goldman, R.

Article: Psychosocial development in cross-cultural perspective: A new look at an old issue.

Journal: *Developmental*

Psychology, November 1971, *5*(3), 411–419.

Related Research: Wolins, M. (1969). Group care friend or foe. *Social Work, 14,* 35–53.

■ ■ ■

990

Test Name: VALUES CONCERNING DISADVANTAGED PUPILS QUESTIONNAIRE

Purpose: To measure the values of teachers concerning disadvantaged pupils and the values of principles concerning disadvantaged pupils as perceived by their teachers.

Number of Items: 42

Format: In the form of a Likert scale consisting of 5 points with numerical values assigned to each point.

Reliability: Kuder-Richardson formula 20 for establishing internal consistency yielded correlation coefficients of .929 for values of teachers and .922 for values of principals.

Author: Gies, F. J., and Leonard, B. C.

Article: Value consensus concerning disadvantaged pupils in inner city elementary schools.

Journal: *Educational Leadership,* December 1970, *30*(3), 254–256.

Related Research: Gies, F. J. (1970). *Values concerning disadvantaged pupils in differing organizational climates.*

Unpublished doctoral dissertation, University of Missouri.

■ ■ ■

991

Test Name: VALUES SENTENCE COMPLETION TEST

Purpose: To assess prescriptive or proscriptive value orientation.

Number of Items: 28

Format: 14 items were fillers.

Reliability: Interrater reliability was .98; split-half reliability for prescription scores was .64.

Author: McKinney, J.

Article: The development of values—Prescriptive or proscriptive?

Journal: *Human Development,* 1971, *14*(1), 71–80.

CHAPTER 23
Vocational Evaluation

992

Test Name: ACADEMIC ASSISTANT EVALUATION INSTRUMENT

Purpose: To evaluate services of undergraduates as academic advisers.

Number of Items: 14

Format: Statements such as "My academic assistant was available to me when I needed him" were responded to as satisfactory/not satisfactory.

Author: Upcraft, M.

Article: Undergraduate students as academic adviser.

Journal: *Personnel and Guidance Journal,* June 1971, *49*(10), 827–831.

• • •

993

Test Name: ADJECTIVE CHECK LIST FOR CAMPUS HELP GIVERS

Purpose: To discriminate student views of counselors, advisers, and psychiatrists.

Number of Items: 100 adjectives.

Format: Student checked how well the adjective described the role of the three "help givers" on a 5-point scale.

Validity: 41 of the 100 items discriminated among mean ratings of three help givers.

Author: Strong, S., et al.

Article: College students' views of campus help givers: Counselors, advisers, and psychiatrists.

Journal: *Journal of Counseling Psychology,* May 1971, *18*(2), 234–238.

• • •

994

Test Name: ADVISING SATISFACTION SCALE

Purpose: To measure adviser characteristics.

Number of Items: 14

Format: Includes seven characteristics related to successful academic advising. Responses are made on a 5-point scale from strongly agree to strongly disagree.

Author: Murry, J. P.

Article: The comparative effectiveness of student-to-student and faculty advising programs.

Journal: *Journal of College Student Personnel,* November 1972, *13*(6), 562–566.

Related Research: Rosenberg, G. L. (1969). A study of undergraduate academic advising in a university setting. Unpublished doctoral dissertation, the University of Iowa.

• • •

995

Test Name: AID MEASURE

Purpose: To assess therapist technique and record patient expectations of therapist.

Format: Two clusters of scores: one, patients who expect a relationship with the therapist, the other, patients who expect detachment.

Validity: Correlations with a self disclosure measure were low (.10, .08) and nonsignificant.

Author: Lieberman, L., and Begley, C.

Article: Studies of the patient version of the AID: Internal–external control, interactive style, self disclosure.

Journal: *Psychological Reports,* April 1972, *30*(2), 493–494.

Related Research: Begley, C., & Lieberman, L. (1970). Patient expectations of therapists' techniques. *Journal of Clinical Psychology, 26,* 112–116.

• • •

996

Test Name: BEGINNING SUPERVISOR'S PROBLEMS QUESTIONNAIRE

Purpose: To identify problems of the beginning supervisor.

Number of Items: 30

Format: Subjects rate each problem as 0 (*little or no difficulty*), 1 (*average difficulty*), or 2 (*much difficulty*). Some items are presented.

Reliability: .93

Author: Burstiner, I.

Article: Problems of the beginning supervisor.

Journal: *Education,* April-May 1972, *92*(4), 69–71.

• • •

997

Test Name: BRYAN'S STUDENT OPINION QUESTIONNAIRE— REVISED

Purpose: To measure student perception of teacher performance.

Author: Bultman, J. E.

Article: Concerted effort can change the teacher image.

Journal: *Journal of Experimental Education*, Summer 1972, *40*(4), 43–45.

Related Research: Bryan, R. C. (1968). *Some observations concerning written student reactions to high school teachers.* Annual report of the student reaction center, Western Michigan University, Kalamazoo.

■ ■ ■

998

Test Name: CLIENT PERSONAL REACTION QUESTIONNAIRE

Purpose: To assess client's reaction to the interview.

Format: True–false, all verbs in the past tense.

Author: Murphy, K., and Strong, S.

Article: Some effects of similarity self-disclosure.

Journal: *Journal of Counseling Psychology*, March 1972, *19*(2), 121–124.

Related Research: Ashby, J. D., et al. (1957). Effects on clients of reflective and a leading type of therapy. *Psychological Monographs, 71*(24, Whole No. 452).

■ ■ ■

999

Test Name: COUNSELOR EVALUATION INVENTORY

Purpose: To measure client attitudes toward the counseling experience.

Number of Items: 21

Format: Includes three factors: counselor comfort, client

satisfaction, and counseling climate.

Author: Brown, D. B., et al.

Article: Attitudes of Black junior college students toward counseling services.

Journal: *Journal of College Student Personnel*, September 1972, *13*(5), 421–424.

Related Research: Linden, J. D., et al. (1965). Development and evaluation of an inventory for rating counseling. *Personnel and Guidance Journal, 44*, 267–276.

Pfeifer, H. (1971). Client perceptions of counselors with and without a practicum. *Counselor Education and Supervision*, September, *11*(1), 49–55.

■ ■ ■

1000

Test Name: COUNSELING EVALUATION QUESTIONNAIRE

Purpose: To determine the counselee's acceptance or rejection of the student-to-student approach to counseling.

Number of Items: 60

Format: Responses were made on a 5-point scale ranging from *strongly agree* to *strongly disagree*.

Author: Brown, W. F., et al.

Article: Effectiveness of student-to-student counseling on the academic adjustment of potential college dropouts.

Journal: *Journal of Educational Psychology*, August 1971, *62*(4), 285–289.

■ ■ ■

1001

Test Name: COUNSELOR EFFECTIVENESS SCALE

Purpose: To provide a system by which judges could rate samples of counseling behavior.

Number of Items: 33

Format: Behavioral and feeling items used by three judges to rate two selected four-minute segments of video tapes.

Reliability: Between Judge 1 and 2, reliability was .46 (significant); 1 and 3, .31 (*ns*); 2 and 3, .30 (*ns*).

Author: Ward, G., et al.

Article: An attempt to measure and facilitate counselor effectiveness.

Journal: *Counselor Education and Supervision*, March 1972, *11*(3), 179–186.

■ ■ ■

1002

Test Name: COUNSELOR EFFECTIVENESS SCALE

Purpose: To assess counseling effectiveness.

Number of Items: 33

Format: Semantic differential, with 33 adjective continuums.

Author: Guttman, M., and Haase, R.

Article: Effect of experimentally induced sets of high and low "expertness" during brief vocational counseling.

Journal: *Counselor Education and Supervision*, March 1972, *11*(3), 171–178.

Related Research: Ivey, A., et al. (1967). *The counselor effectiveness scale.* Unpublished manuscript, Colorado State University.

■ ■ ■

1003

Test Name: COUNSELOR PRACTICUM EVALUATION FORM

Purpose: To evaluate counselor trainee in five areas.

Format: Nine-point scale rating counseling relationships; professional responsibilities, interest and effort; interpersonal relations with staff; overall competence.

Author: Eberlein, L., and Park, J.

Article: Self concept, ideal self concept, congruence, and rated effectiveness of counselor trainees.

Journal: *Counselor Education and Supervision,* Winter 1971, *10*(2), 126–132.

■ ■ ■

1004

Test Name: COUNSELOR SELECTION INSTRUMENT

Purpose: To select candidates for school counselor positions.

Format: Consists of an interview schedule, rating forms (1–5 scale) for personal characteristics, graduate education, experience, and "other" as well as provision for recording special interests or qualifications.

Author: Salim, M., et al.

Article: Counselor education: A critical event in program management and development.

Journal: *Counselor Education and Supervision,* Summer 1971, *10*(4), 337–342.

■ ■ ■

1005

Test Name: DIAGNOSTIC FORCED CHOICE SCALE FOR FIRST LINE SUPERVISORS

Purpose: To evaluate supervisory training needs.

Number of Items: 390

Format: Completed by managers, the forced choice scale included 12 factors (personal compliance, job knowledge, direction for group performance, rewarding performance, company loyalty, etc.).

Reliability: Split-half reliabilities

ranged .49 to .85 for various factors.

Author: Roach, D.

Article: Diagnostic forced choice scale for first line supervisors.

Journal: *Personnel Journal,* March 1971, *50*(3), 226–230, 236.

■ ■ ■

1006

Test Name: DUNCAN RESIDENCE HALL COUNSELOR EVALUATION SCALE

Purpose: To permit evaluation of residence hall counselors.

Format: A forced-choice questionnaire in which items are presented in groups of three, all of which are weighted as equally desirable socially but not equally discriminating between effective and ineffective counselors.

Validity: Students' evaluation with head resident's evaluation, rs = .47 and .61.

Author: Wyrick, T. J., and Mitchell, K. M.

Article: Relationship between residence assistants' empathy and warmth and their effectiveness.

Journal: *Journal of College Student Personnel,* January 1971, *12*(1), 36–40.

Related Research: Duncan, J. P. (1967). A rating scale for student evaluation of residence hall counselors. *Personnel and Guidance Journal, 45,* 452–454.

■ ■ ■

1007

Test Name: EMPLOYEE PERFORMANCE EVALUATION BY SUPERVISOR FORM

Purpose: To permit the supervisor to evaluate employee performance.

Format: Includes subjective information on specific duties;

performance of the assigned duties; personal observations on appearance, attitude, and aptitude; and an overall rating of the subject as compared with others in similar functions. The rating is based on a 4-point scale where 1 is *below average* and 4 is *superior.*

Author: Apostal, R. A., and Doherty, C. P.

Article: Effects of positive and routine job assignments on academic performance.

Journal: *Journal of College Student Personnel,* May 1972, *13*(3), 270–272.

■ ■ ■

1008

Test Name: EMPLOYEE PERFORMANCE SELF-EVALUATION

Purpose: To measure the subject's opinion of his job performance.

Format: Includes a sequence of questions about the job assignment, the relationship of the job to the academic program, and a rating of overall job performance. A 4-point scale is used where 1 is *below average* and 4 is *superior.*

Author: Apostal, R. A., and Doherty, C. P.

Article: Effects of positive and routine job assignments on academic performance.

Journal: *Journal of College Student Personnel,* May 1972, *13*(3), 270–272.

■ ■ ■

1009

Test Name: FACULTY COMPETENCE RATING SCALE

Purpose: To judge faculty performance using either junior or senior colleagues as judges.

Number of Items: 20

Format: Variables included willingness to use research tools, keeps current in related fields, and so forth.

Author: Paul, R., and Schooler, R.

Article: Generation conflict in academia.

Journal: *Personnel Journal,* January 1971, *50*(1), 22–27.

■ ■ ■

1010

Test Name: FOLLOW-UP ON COUNSELING SUGGESTIONS QUESTIONNAIRE

Purpose: To determine whether students actually followed up on suggestions given by their counselors.

Format: Counselor prepared a set of two to three recommendations; interview of student followed up several months later.

Reliability: Inter-judge agreement (97%) on whether action or no action was taken.

Author: Atkinson, D. R.

Article: Effect of selected behavior modification techniques on student-initiated action.

Journal: *Journal of Counseling Psychology,* September 1971, *18*(5), 395–400.

■ ■ ■

1011

Test Name: FOREMAN JOB RESPONSIBILITY QUESTIONNAIRE

Purpose: To assess job responsibilities of foreman.

Format: Includes areas such as: employee relations, training and supervision, tools–equipment, production schedule, and so forth.

Author: Muendel, H.

Article: Divisionalizing a line

organization: A challenge to the traditional foreman training concept.

Journal: *Personnel Journal,* January 1971, *50*(1), 14–21.

■ ■ ■

1012

Test Name: FOREMAN SURVEY FORM

Purpose: To assess foreman perception of his job.

Number of Items: 294

Format: Four sections: general background, first experiences as a new supervisor, preparation for supervision, present job, and preparation for future responsibilities.

Author: Schappe, R.

Article: The production foreman today—His needs and difficulties.

Journal: *Personnel Journal,* July 1972, *51*(7), 489–494.

■ ■ ■

1013

Test Name: GROUP ORAL PERFORMANCE TEST

Purpose: To screen candidates for an employment interviewer position.

Number of Items: Nine short answer questions.

Format: A fabricated problem is given for applicant to discuss and client is asked to discuss problems in the situation and show how they would be handled. In addition, nine short answer questions are used.

Author: None given.

Article: As you were saying—The group oral performance test.

Journal: *Personnel Journal,* June 1971, *50*(6), 486–487.

1014

Test Name: INSTRUCTOR EVALUATION QUESTIONNAIRE

Purpose: To obtain information from students about instructors who have made them think.

Number of Items: 27

Format: Includes three areas: selected instructors who made students think and characteristics of these men and women; qualities of the instructor that students felt triggered their thought processes; the total number of instructors in contact with the students, and how many of these made students think beyond the facts and data level. The items are presented.

Author: Walsh, G. V.

Article: One in five made us think.

Journal: *Improving College and University Teaching,* Summer 1972, *20*(3), 153–155.

■ ■ ■

1015

Test Name: INSTRUMENT FOR THE OBSERVATION OF TEACHING ACTIVITIES— INTERVIEW SCALES

Purpose: To evaluate teacher competency in various areas as derived from information secured through the medium of an interview between the teacher and the school administrator.

Number of Items: 9

Reliability: .62 to .96.

Author: Owens, M. S.

Article: Evaluation of teaching competence by three groups of educators.

Journal: *Journal of Experimental Education,* Winter 1971, *40*(3), 77–82.

Related Research: National IOTA Council. (1970). *The role of the*

teacher in society. Tempe: Arizona State University, The College of Education.

■ ■ ■

1016

Test Name: JOB PERFORMANCE APPRAISAL CHECKLIST

Purpose: To evaluate employee job performance.

Format: For one function (working with outside groups) there were 28 activities to be rated, on a 0–50 scale.

Author: Brumback, G.

Article: Consolidating job descriptions, performance appraisals, and manpower reports.

Journal: *Personnel Journal,* 1971, *50*(8), 604–610.

■ ■ ■

1017

Test Name: PERSONAL HISTORY QUESTIONNAIRE

Purpose: To identify effective supervisors.

Number of Items: 101

Format: Categories of multiple choice items included education, early family life, marital history, and so forth.

Validity: Ten items surviving a double cross validation predicted effectiveness with a validity coefficient of .47.

Author: Penfield, R.

Article: Identifying effective supervisors.

Journal: *Personnel Journal,* March 1971, *50*(3), 209–212.

■ ■ ■

1018

Test Name: PRE-EMPLOYMENT INQUIRY QUIZ

Purpose: To assess knowledge of

employment interviewer with respect to federal and state employment laws.

Number of Items: 19

Author: Minter, R.

Article: Human rights laws and pre-employment inquiries.

Journal: *Personnel Journal,* June 1972, *51*(6), 431–433.

■ ■ ■

1019

Test Name: RESIDENCE COUNSELOR JOB PERFORMANCE RATING FORM

Purpose: To rate job performance of residence hall counselors.

Number of Items: 23

Format: Includes four sections: interest in position, supervisory ability, relationships with others, and personal characteristics; also a total score. For each item the rater checks one of the following: improvement needed, satisfactory, improving, or excellent.

Reliability: From .69 to .93.

Author: Biggs, D. A.

Article: Selecting residence counselors—Job viewpoints and interpersonal attitudes.

Journal: *Journal of College Student Personnel,* March 1971, *12*(2), 111–115.

■ ■ ■

1020

Test Name: RESIDENCE COUNSELOR SURVEY

Purpose: To assess student opinions about residence counselors.

Number of Items: 60

Format: Section 1: 23 topics for discussion with a competent counselor. Section 2: 15 bipolar

evaluative adjectives formed a semantic differential for evaluating the concept "Residence Counselor." Section 3: three items to measure satisfaction with residence counselor. Section 4: 19 items using a 5-point scale for students to describe their present residence counselors' job behaviors and personal qualities. Excerpts of many of the items are presented.

Author: Biggs, D. A.

Article: Student evaluation of residence hall counselors.

Journal: *Journal of Educational Research,* March 1972, *65*(7), 305–308.

■ ■ ■

1021

Test Name: STUDENT COUNSELOR RATING SCALE

Purpose: To evaluate a student counselor in a supervised counseling experience.

Number of Items: 27

Format: Yields three scores: counseling, supervision, total; 7-point Likert scale.

Reliability: Split-half .95 (corrected). Counseling and supervisory scores correlated .86. Test–retest (4 weeks) reliability was .94.

Author: Myrick, R., and Kelly, F.

Article: A scale for evaluating practicum students in counseling and supervision.

Journal: *Counselor Education and Supervision,* Summer 1971, *10*(4), 330–336.

■ ■ ■

1022

Test Name: STUDENT-OPINION QUESTIONNAIRE

Purpose: To secure student

reactions as the basis for helping teachers.

Number of Items: 10

Format: Students answer questions pertaining to 10 characteristics of their teacher. All items are included in the article.

Author: Dalton, E. L.

Article: Pupil selection of teachers.

Journal: *Educational Leadership,* February 1971, *28*(5), 476–479.

Related Research: Bryan, R. C. (1959). *Twelve teachers and their effects on students* (Faculty Contributions, Series 4, No. 4, pp. 8–9). Kalamazoo: Western Michigan University, School of Graduate Studies.

■ ■ ■

1023

Test Name: SUPERVISORY PERFORMANCE RATING INSTRUMENT

Purpose: To evaluate supervisory job performance.

Format: Scale included 10 dimensions (job knowledge, dependability, job attitude, initiative, judgment and organization, ability to teach, communication, safety, leadership skills, interpersonal relationships).

Validity: Correlations of 10 dimensions with overall performance ranged .547 to .818.

Author: Sabet-shargi, Z., and Davis, D.

Article: Development of supervisory performance evaluation.

Journal: *Personnel Journal,* April 1971, *50*(4), 306–309.

■ ■ ■

1024

Test Name: SURVEY OF STUDENT OPINION OF TEACHING

Purpose: To permit students to assess the instructor and the course.

Number of Items: 15

Format: Ten items refer to instructor characteristics and five items refer to characteristics of the course.

Author: Miller, M. T.

Article: Instructor attitudes toward, and their use of, student ratings of teachers.

Journal: *Journal of Educational Psychology,* June 1971, *62*(3), 235–239.

Related Research: Stuit, D. B., & Ebel, R. L. (1952). Instructor ratings at a large state university. *College and University,* 247–254.

■ ■ ■

1025

Test Name: TEACHER COMPETENCE RATING SCALES

Purpose: To measure teaching competence.

Number of Items: 23

Format: The following ratings are used for each scale: 1 (*unsatisfactory*), 2 (*satisfactory*), 3 (*good*), 4 (*excellent*).

Author: Cook, M. A., and Richards, H. C.

Article: Dimensions of principal and supervisor ratings of teacher behavior.

Journal: *Journal of Experimental Education,* Winter 1972, *41*(2), 11–14.

■ ■ ■

1026

Test Name: TEACHER IMAGE QUESTIONNAIRE

Purpose: To measure student

perceptions of teacher effectiveness.

Number of Items: 12

Time Required: 10 to 15 minutes.

Format: Student responds to each question on a 5-point scale from poor to excellent. Sample items are presented.

Validity: Interitem correlations range from .32 to .85.

Author: Coats, W. D., et al.

Article: Student perceptions of teachers—A factor analytic study.

Journal: *Journal of Educational Research,* April 1972, *65*(8), 357–360.

■ ■ ■

1027

Test Name: TEACHER PERFORMANCE EVALUATION SCALE

Purpose: To measure specific behaviors of persons engaged in teaching.

Number of Items: 42

Format: Includes six categories of items: personality traits, warmth of teacher behavior, general classroom atmosphere, lesson usefulness, teacher interest in pupils, and teacher interest in student achievement. Each item is rated on an 8-point scale (0–7). Examples are presented.

Validity: Interitem correlation of .60 or better.

Author: Jensen, L. C., and Young, J. I.

Article: Effect of televised simulated instruction on subsequent teaching.

Journal: *Journal of Educational Psychology,* August 1972, *63*(4), 368–373.

Related Research: Sinha, P. B. (1962). *A teacher evaluation instrument for secondary schools* *in India.* Unpublished dissertation, Brigham Young University.

■ ■ ■

1028

Test Name: TEACHER RATING QUESTIONNAIRE

Purpose: To permit students to rate their teacher.

Format: Contained three tasks: (a) a rating of the instructor's overall teaching ability on a 5-point rating scale and nine ratings of specific behaviors on a 5-point frequency scale; (b) a rating of the desirability of each frequency point on the nine items; and (c) a background questionnaire asking the student's age, sex, previous quarter's grade in psychology, and so forth. Samples are presented.

Author: Andrews, O. E.

Article: Student evaluations of teacher behaviors as estimations of real-ideal discrepancies: A critique of teacher rating methods.

Journal: *Journal of Educational Psychology,* April 1971, *62*(2), 104–107.

■ ■ ■

1029

Test Name: TEACHING ASSESSMENT BLANK

Purpose: To enable college students to assess their class experiences. Evaluation is limited to the instructor's teaching ability.

Format: Includes four factors: quality of instructor's presentations, evaluation process and student instructor interactions, degree to which students were stimulated and motivated by instructors, and clarity of tests. All items are presented.

Validity: Correlations between factor scores and subscale scores range from .62 to .85.

Author: Holmes, D. S.

Article: The Teaching Assessment Blank: A form for the student assessment of college instructors.

Journal: *Journal of Experimental Education,* Spring 1971, *39*(3), 34–38.

Related Research: Holmes, D. S. (1972). Effects of grades and disconfirmed grade expectancies on students' evaluations of their instructor. *Journal of Educational Psychology,* April, *63*(2), 130–133.

■ ■ ■

1030

Test Name: TEACHING EFFECTIVENESS SCALE

Purpose: To measure self-perception of effectiveness of elementary and secondary teachers.

Number of Items: Two lists of 35 items utilized.

Time Required: 15 minutes.

Format: Eleven-step scale presented to teachers to rate themselves.

Reliability: Test–retest reliabilities were .81, .92, and .90.

Author: Chiu, L.

Article: Structured self-anchoring scale for study of perceptions of teaching effectiveness.

Journal: *Perceptual and Motor Skills,* October 1972, *35*(2), 367–370.

■ ■ ■

1031

Test Name: TEST OF TEACHER JUDGMENT OF WRITTEN COMPOSITION

Purpose: To measure teacher judgment in the evaluation of written composition.

Number of Items: Five.

Format: Raters are asked to rank

the five essays from best to worst. Forms A and B.

Reliability: .79, .84 and .96 to .98.

Author: Whalen, T. E.

Article: A validation of the Smith test for measuring teacher judgment of written composition.

Journal: *Education,* November–December 1972, *93*(1), 172–175.

Related Research: Smith, V. H. (1969). Measuring teacher judgment in the evaluation of written composition. *Research in the Teaching of English, 3*(2), 181–195.

■ ■ ■

1032

Test Name: UNIVERSITY OF WASHINGTON SURVEY OF STUDENT OPINION OF TEACHING

Purpose: To permit student evaluation of the instructor.

Number of Items: 20

Format: Two groups of 10 items. Sixteen of the items involve a 5-point rating scale from 1 (*outstanding*) to 5 (*of less value*). Most items are presented.

Validity: Correlations of individual items with total score for the first 10 items ranged from .41 to .86. Correlations between the two parts were .39, .42, and .19. Correlation of the first 10 items with course grades was .43, .65; and correlation of the second 10 items with course grades, *r*s = .35, .25, and .04.

Author: Shaver, J. P., and Richards, H. E.

Article: Open-closed mindedness and an inquiry-oriented social studies methods course.

Journal: *Journal of Educational Research,* October 1971, *65*(2), 85–93.

Related Research: Guthrie, E. R.

(1954). *The evaluation of teaching: A progress report.* Seattle: University of Washington.

■ ■ ■

1033

Test Name: VOCATIONAL ADJUSTMENT RATING SCALE FOR THE RETARDED

Purpose: To assess how well a person actually performs and behaves in all types of work settings.

Number of Items: 52

Format: Five parts to scale: work ability, work habits, withdrawn behavior, aggressive behavior, bizarre behavior. Scale rated by immediate work supervisor on 5-point scale.

Reliability: Test–retest (2 weeks) ranged from .75 to .93. Split-half reliability was .97.

Validity: Correlation with supervisor's independent classification ranged .59 to .97; significant differences were found between five independently rated criterion groups. Predictive validity: correlations with employer ratings .07 to .42 with two negative correlations (.22, .07). Construct validity: low correlations with intelligence.

Author: Song, R., and Song, A. Y.

Article: Development of a vocational adjustment rating scale for the retarded.

Journal: *Journal of Counseling Psychology,* March 1971, *18*(2), 173–176.

■ ■ ■

1034

Test Name: WORK DEPENDENCE SCALE

Purpose: To assess extent with which a worker depends upon direction and guidance from a superior.

Number of Items: 8

Format: Four-categories of response (*strongly agree* to *strongly disagree*).

Reliability: Split-half (Spearman Brown) reliability was .95.

Validity: Correlation with emotional dependence score was .28 ($p > .05$).

Author: Shivdasani, H.

Article: Construct of dependence need: Bi-dimensional dependence proneness in work organization.

Journal: *Psychological Reports,* August 1971, *29*(1), 282.

Directory of Unpublished

Experimental Mental Measures

VOLUME 3

BERT A. GOLDMAN, EDD

Dean, Academic Advising and Professor of Education
University of North Carolina at Greensboro

JOHN CHRISTIAN BUSCH, EDD

Associate Professor of Education
University of North Carolina at Greensboro

Contents

A cumulative subject index to Volumes 1 through 3 appears at the end of this book.

...

Preface

From the Original Printing of Volume 3, 1982

Purpose: This *Directory of Unpublished Experimental Mental Measures* marks the third in a series of publications designed to fill a need for reference tools in behavioral and social science research. The authors recognized the need for the publication of a directory to experimental test instruments, i.e., tests that are not currently marketed commercially. It is intended that this reference primarily serves to provide researchers with ready access to sources of recently developed experimental measurement devices. The authors did not evaluate the instruments, however it is anticipated that the directory may stimulate further use of these experimental instruments by providing researchers with relatively easy access to such information. In essence this directory is a reference to recently developed, nonstandardized, experimental mental measures without evaluation. The directory is not intended to provide all necessary information for the researcher contemplating the use of a particular instrument, rather it should serve as a reference point to enable the reader to identify potentially useful measures and other sources from which this information can be obtained.

Development: Forty-six relevant professional journals available to the authors were examined. The following list includes those journals which, in the judgment of the authors, contained research involving instruments of value to researchers in education, psychology, and sociology. The list is similar to that of Volume 2 with the exception that it deletes one nonrelevant journal and includes five additional journals which were found to contain relevant information. In general, foreign journals were not surveyed for use in this directory, however, one exception is the British journal, *Occupational Psychology*. Measures identified in dissertations were excluded as a matter of expediency and because the microfilm abstracts contain minimal information.

American Educational Research Journal
American Journal of Economics and Sociology
American Journal of Psychology
American Journal of Sociology
American Sociologist
American Vocational Journal
Behavioral Science
California Journal of Educational Research
Child Development
Colorado Journal of Educational Research
Counseling Psychologist
Counselor Education and Supervision
Developmental Psychology
Education
Educational and Psychological Measurement
Educational Leadership
Elementary School Guidance and Counseling
Gifted Child Quarterly
Human Development

Improving College and University Teaching
International Journal of Comparative Sociology
Journal of Applied Psychology
Journal of College Student Personnel
Journal of Counseling Psychology
Journal of Creative Behavior
Journal of Education
Journal of Educational Measurement
Journal of Educational Psychology
Journal of Educational Research
Journal of Experimental Education
Journal of General Education
Journal of Personality Assessment
Journal of Reading
Journal of School Psychology
Measurement and Evaluation in Guidance
Occupational Psychology
Peabody Journal of Education
Perceptual and Motor Skills
Personnel and Guidance Journal
Personnel Journal
Phi Delta Kappan
Psychological Reports
Reading Research Quarterly
Social Education
Sociology and Social Research
Sociology of Education

This volume incorporates a change in procedure. Volume 2 reviewed the two year period from 1971 to 1972. This directory lists all tests described in the 1973 issues of the previously cited journals. We trust that the currently completed reviews for 1974–76 will soon be published. An attempt was made to omit commercially published standardized tests, task-type activities such as memory word lists used in serial learning research and achievement tests developed for a single, isolated course of study. The reader should not assume that the instruments described herein form a representative sample of the universe of unpublished experimental measures.

Organization: Another change in Vol. 3 consists of deleting the category "Interest" and incorporating a new category "Vocational Interest". Following is a brief description of each of the twenty-three categories under which the authors grouped the mental measures of Volume 3:

Achievement: Measure learning and/or comprehension in specific areas. Also include tests of memory and tests of drug knowledge.
Adjustment—Educational: Measure academic satisfaction. Also include tests of school anxiety.
Adjustment—Psychological: Evaluate conditions and levels of adjustment along the psychological dimension including, for example, tests of mood, fear of death, anxiety, depression, etc.
Adjustment—Social: Evaluate aspects of interactions with others. Also include tests of alienation, conformity, need for social approval, social desirability, and instruments for assessing interpersonal attraction and sensitivity.

Aptitude: Predict success in given activities.

Attitude: Measure reaction to a variety of experiences and objects.

Behavior: Measure general and specific types of activities such as classroom behavior and drug use behavior.

Communication: Evaluate information exchange. Also include tests of self disclosure and counselor/client interaction.

Concept Meaning: Test one's understanding of words and other concepts. Also include tests of conceptual structure, style, and information
processing.

Creativity: Measure ability to reorganize data or information into unique configurations. Also include tests of divergent thinking.

Development: Measure emerging characteristics, primarily for preschool ages. Also include tests of cognitive and moral development.

Family: Measure intrafamily relations. Also include tests of marital satisfaction, nurturance, parental interest, and warmth.

Institutional Information: Evaluate institutions and their functioning.

Motivation: Measure goal strength. Also include measures of curiosity.

Perception: Determine how one sees self and other objects. Also include tests dealing with empathy, imagery, locus of control, self concept, and time.

Personality: Measure general personal attributes. Also include biographical information and defense mechanisms.

Preference: Identify choices. Also include tests of preference for objects, taste preference, and sex role preference.

Problem-Solving and Reasoning: General ability to reason through a number of alternative solutions, to generate such solutions to problems. etc.

Status: Identify a hierarchy of acceptability.

Trait Measurement: Identify and evaluate unitary traits. Also include tests of anger, anxiety, authoritarianism, blame, and cheating.

Values: Measure worth one ascribes to an object or activity. Include tests of moral, philosophical, political, and religious values.

Vocational Evaluation: Evaluate a person for a specific position.

Vocational Interest: Measure interest in specific occupations and vocations as well as interest in general categories of activity.

The choice of the category under which each test was grouped was determined by the purpose of the test and/or its apparent content. The authors attempted to include any of the following facts regarding each test, however, in many cases only a few of these facts were provided in the journal article:

Test Name
Purpose
Description
>   *Number of items*
>   *Time required*
>   *Format*
Statistics
>   *Reliability* (In most cases the particular design used to assess consistency is specified)
>   *Validity* (Includes correlation with other tests, group difference information, which help to define the characteristic being measured by the test.)

Source

    Author

    Title

    Journal, including date of publication, volume and page number

Related Research

    Information identifying publications related to the source.

    In instances where additional information may be found in Volume 1 and/or 2 of the *Directory of Unpublished Experimental Mental Measures,* the reader is referred to D.U.E.M.M. with specific reference following.

    Further, the reader is alerted to the fact that the numbers within the Index refer to test numbers rather than to page numbers as was the case with Volume 1. As a convenience to the reader, the authors have incorporated the indices from both previous volumes in this Index and in so doing they converted all page numbers to test numbers. Thus, numbers 1 through 339 refer to tests of Volume 1, numbers 340 through 1034 refer to tests of Volume 2, numbers 1035 through 1595 refer to tests of Volume 3.

    The authors express their appreciation to Ms. Jody Taylor for typing the manuscript.

Bert Arthur Goldman
John Christian Busch

CHAPTER 1
Achievement

1035

Test Name: ASSOCIATIVE VERBAL ENCODING

Purpose: To obtain a measure of associative verbal encoding.

Number of Items: 120

Time Required: Approximately 30 minutes.

Format: Two forms were constructed.

Reliability: Coefficients of reliability were greater than .90.

Author: Mickelson, N. I.

Article: Associative verbal encoding (a/v/e): A measure of language performance and its relationship to reading achievement (abstract).

Journal: *Reading Abstract Quarterly,* 1973–74, *9*(2), 227–231.

1036

Test Name: AUDITORY BLENDING TEST

Purpose: To assess auditory blending skills.

Number of Items: 46

Format: Includes two subtests: syllables to words and phonemes to words.

Validity: Each part was correlated with reading achievement: syllables to words = .61; phonemes to words = .62.

Author: Weintraub, S., et al.

Article: Summary of investigations relating to reading July 1, 1972, to June 30, 1973.

Journal: *Reading Research Quarterly,* 1973–74, *9*(3), 307–308.

Related Research: Hardy, M., et al. (1973). Auditory segmentation and auditory blending in relation to beginning reading. *The Alberta Journal of Educational Research, 19,* 144–158.

1037

Test Name: AUDITORY SEGMENTATION TEST

Purpose: To assess auditory segmentation skills.

Number of Items: 45

Format: Includes three subtests: sentences into words, words into syllables, words into phonemes.

Validity: Correlation of each part with reading achievement: sentences into words, .15; words into syllables, .36; words into phonemes, .26.

Author: Weintraub, S., et al.

Article: Summary of investigations relating to reading, July 1, 1972, to June 30, 1973.

Journal: *Reading Research Quarterly,* 1973–74, *9*(3), 307–308.

Related Research: Hardy, M., et al. (1973). Auditory segmentation and auditory blending in relation to beginning reading. *The Alberta Journal of Educational Research, 19,* 144–158.

1038

Test Name: BASIC OCCUPATIONAL LITERACY TEST

Purpose: To measure arithmetic and reading skills of the disadvantaged.

Time Required: 2.5 hours.

Format: Designed for use in counseling and personal development.

Author: Van Doren, R. (Ed.).

Article: Manpower, human assessment and the disadvantaged.

Journal: *American Vocational Journal,* January 1973, *48*(1), 86–100.

1039

Test Name: BASIC READING RATE SCALE

Purpose: To measure the rate at which individuals can read very easy reading material.

Format: Categorizes readers into four types: beginning, good, better, best.

Author: Carver, R. P.

Article: Understanding, information processing, and learning from prose materials.

Journal: *Journal of Educational Psychology,* February 1973, *64*(1), 76–84.

Related Research: Carver, R. P., & Darby, C. A., Jr. *Analysis of the chunked reading test.* Unpublished manuscript. (Available from American

Institutes for Research, 8555 Sixteenth Street, Silver Spring, Maryland 20910).

• • •

1040

Test Name: COGNITIVE VOCATIONAL MATURITY TESTS

Purpose: To measure career knowledges and abilities within six areas of the cognitive domain of vocational maturity: fields of work, job selection, work conditions, education required, attributes required, duties.

Number of Items: 120

Reliability: Kuder-Richardson formula values were .67 to .91.

Validity: Correlations with the California Test of Mental Maturity were .53 to .69.

Author: Westbrook, B. W., and Mastie, M. M.

Article: Three measures of vocational maturity: A beginning to know about.

Journal: *Measurement and Evaluation in Guidance,* April 1973, *6*(1), 8–16.

Related Research: Westbrook, B. W., & Parry-Hill, J. W., Jr. (1973). The measurement of cognitive vocational maturity. *Journal of Vocational Behavior, 3*(3), 239–252.

• • •

1041

Test Name: DISCRIMINATION TEST

Purpose: To measure discrimination ability of 3- to 5-year-olds.

Number of Items: 5

Format: Discrimination arrays were presented to the subject with instructions to point out the

geometric shape that was the same as the model.

Author: Rand, C. W.

Article: Copy in drawing: The importance of adequate visual analysis versus the ability to utilize drawing rules.

Journal: *Child Development,* March 1973, *44*(1), 47–53.

• • •

1042

Test Name: DRUG KNOWLEDGE TEST

Purpose: To measure any changes in level of students' knowledge regarding the various drugs of abuse.

Number of Items: 41

Author: Swisher, J. D., et al.

Article: Four approaches to drug abuse prevention among college students.

Journal: *Journal of College Student Personnel,* May 1973, *14*(3), 231–235.

• • •

1043

Test Name: EARLY ELEMENTARY SCHOOL CHILDREN RATING SCALE

Purpose: To provide teacher rating on four areas of academic achievement of pupils: reading achievement, quantitative achievement, verbal achievement, listening achievement.

Number of Items: 4

Format: Rated on 9-point scale.

Reliability: For children grades K-3 with Cronbach's alpha: .92, .95, .97, .92.

Validity: For children grades K-3, correlation with Otis Lennon: .72, .58, .64, .56.

Author: Thomas, J. R., and Chissom, B. S.

Article: Relationship between teacher ratings and objective tests of aptitude for early elementary school children.

Journal: *Measurement and Evaluation in Guidance,* April 1973, *6*(1), 54–56.

• • •

1044

Test Name: ELEMENTARY GRADES ANTHROPOLOGY ACHIEVEMENT TESTS

Purpose: To assess effects of an anthropology curriculum for grades 3 and 6.

Number of Items: 15 (grade 3); 10 (grade 6).

Reliability: Kuder-Richardson formula 20: Grade 3 = .78.; Grade 6 = .81.

Author: Clawson, E., and Barnes, B.

Article: The effects of organizers on the learning of structural anthropology materials in the elementary grades.

Journal: *Journal of Experimental Education,* Fall 1973, *42*(1), 11–15.

• • •

1045

Test Name: FORCED VOWEL SELECTION TEST

Purpose: To measure the extent to which children are able to select the letter that best represents a particular sound.

Number of Items: 23

Format: Subject must select either an *a*, an *e*, or an *i* to fit a particular word.

Author: Rystrom, R.

Article: Perceptions of vowel letter-sound relationships by first grade children.

Journal: *Reading Research Quarterly,* 1973–74, *9*(2), 170–185.

. . .

1046

Test Name: IMITATION AND COMPREHENSION ENGLISH TEST

Purpose: To measure imitation and comprehension of four omissions of Black nonstandard English dialect from standard English.

Number of Items: 16

Format: Items based on four Black nonstandard English transformations: omission of the possessive *'s*; omission of the past ending *-ed*; omission of the critical phrase markers; and omission of the third person singular marker *-s*. All items were presented.

Validity: Correlations with the Raven Coloured Progressive Matrices Test ranged from –.27 to .64.

Author: Hall, V. C., et al.

Article: Ability of children from four subcultures and two grade levels to imitate and comprehend crucial aspects of standard English: A test of the different language explanation.

Journal: *Journal of Educational Psychology,* April 1973, *64*(2), 147–158.

. . .

1047

Test Name: INDEPENDENCE OF WORK HABITS TEST

Purpose: To measure the ability to meet course objectives with minimal reliance on outside resources.

Number of Items: 40

Time Required: 12–15 minutes.

Reliability: Test–retest reliability was .88; split half reliability was .72.

Validity: The point-biserial correlation was .48 (scored on test with category: those who finished course requirements, those not).

Author: Pare, R., and Butzow, J.

Article: The reliability and predictive validity of a test of independence of work habits.

Journal: *Educational and Psychological Measurement,* Winter 1973, *33*(4), 963–965.

. . .

1048

Test Name: KENNEDY INSTITUTE PHONICS TEST

Purpose: To measure reading subskills.

Number of Items: 300

Format: Includes 15 subtests; criterion referenced test; items within each subtest contain words graduated in difficulty from low to high.

Reliability: Kuder-Richardson formula 21 reliability coefficients ranged from .20 to .91 for subtests and .98 for total score.

Validity: Correlations of some subtests with the Gates-MacGinitie Reading Test ranged from .37 to .83.

Author: Guthrie, J. T.

Article: Models of reading and reading disability.

Journal: *Journal of Educational Psychology,* August 1973, *65*(1), 9–18.

. . .

1049

Test Name: KNOWLEDGE OF FLANDERS' INTERACTION ANALYSIS SYSTEM ACHIEVEMENT TEST

Purpose: To assess knowledge of the Flanders System.

Format: Maximum score, 75 points.

Author: Walker, J.

Article: Gifted teacher know thyself.

Journal: *Gifted Child Quarterly,* Winter 1973, *17*(4), 288–292.

. . .

1050

Test Name: KNOWLEDGE OF INFANT DEVELOPMENT SCALE

Purpose: To measure knowledge of concepts and terminology in early childhood development.

Number of Items: 42

Format: Multiple choice short statements requiring a response of *agree, disagree,* or *not sure.* The scale assumes the appearance of an opinionaire rather than a test and may be administered under this guise to subjects who present special problems in formal testing.

Reliability: Kuder-Richardson formula 20 was .81.

Author: Dusewicz, R. A.

Article: A scale for assessing knowledge of child development.

Journal: *Education,* February–March 1973, *93*(3), 252–253.

. . .

1051

Test Name: LETTER DISCRIMINATION TEST

Purpose: To assess how adequately kindergarten pupils discriminate between correct and incorrect letter forms.

Number of Items: 12

Format: All but one item contained one correct alternative; one contained two. One point awarded for every correctly circled letter.

Author: Hirsch, E., and Niedermeyer, F. C.

Article: The effects of tracing prompts and discrimination training on kindergarten handwriting performance.

Journal: *Journal of Educational Research,* October 1973, *67*(2), 81–86.

■ ■ ■

1052

Test Name: LETTER FORMATION TEST

Purpose: To assess letter formation ability of kindergarten pupils.

Number of Items: 24

Format: Subject copies upper and lower-case letters that include horizontal and/or vertical strokes, slanted and straight line strokes, curved strokes, and curved with straight line strokes. A 5-point rating scale of legibility is used.

Reliability: Interjudge reliability coefficient was .89.

Author: Hirsch, E., and Niedermeyer, F. C.

Article: The effects of tracing prompts and discrimination training on kindergarten handwriting performance.

Journal: *Journal of Educational Research,* October 1973, *67*(2), 81–86.

■ ■ ■

1053

Test Name: NOVEL MATURITY SCALE

Purpose: To assess a student's reading maturity.

Number of Items: 22

Format: Includes a list of common themes in fiction. Student checks each theme that appears in the novel read. Format and items are presented.

Validity: Correlation with Diagnostic Reading Test was .51; with socioeconomic status, *r* = .39; with reading skill (socioeconomic status partialled out), *r* = .36.

Author: Reich, C.

Article: A scale to assess reading maturity.

Journal: *Journal of Reading,* December 1973, *17*(3), 220–223.

■ ■ ■

1054

Test Name: PEARSON-MADDI SIMILES PERFORMANCE INVENTORY-REVISED

Purpose: To measure ability to learn simile endings.

Number of Items: 30

Format: 30 cards with a simile stem on each to be matched with one of five possible stem endings.

Author: Nakamura, C. Y., and Finck, D.

Article: Effect of social or task orientation and evaluative or nonevaluative situations on performance.

Journal: *Child Development,* March 1973, *44*(1), 83–93.

Related Research: Pearson, P. H., & Maddi, S. R. (1966). The similes preference inventory: Development of a structured measure of the tendency toward variety. *Journal of Consulting Psychology, 30,* 301–308.

■ ■ ■

1055

Test Name: READING COMPREHENSION TEST

Purpose: To measure reading comprehension based on Piaget's developmental construct of intelligence.

Number of Items: 32

Format: Multiple-choice test based on four paragraphs representing classificatory–additive, classificatory–multiplicative, serial–additive, and serial–multiplicative.

Reliability: Internal consistency reliability coefficients were .736 for grade 3 and .837 for grade 6.

Author: Kretschmer, J. C.

Article: Measuring reading comprehension (abstract).

Journal: *Reading Research Quarterly,* 1973–74, *9*(2), 224–226.

■ ■ ■

1056

Test Name: REPRODUCTIVE KNOWLEDGE SCALE

Purpose: To ascertain respondents' knowledge about reproduction.

Format: Respondent interviewed about knowledge in eight areas of reproduction.

Validity: Costa Rican women in legal marital unions achieved significantly higher reproductive knowledge scores than those in consensual unions.

Author: Michielutte, R., et al.

Article: Consensual and legal marital unions in Costa Rica.

Journal: *International Journal of Comparative Sociology,* March–June 1973, *14*(1–2), 119–128.

■ ■ ■

1057

Test Name: SCERC INFORMATION TEST IN REHABILITATION COUNSELING

Purpose: To measure subject matter knowledge in rehabilitation counseling.

Number of Items: 300

Format: 30 subtests, each with 10 items.

Reliability: Split-half corrected reliability was .98.

Author: Richardson, B., and Obermann, C.

Article: Relationship of rehabilitation counselor characteristics to supervisor's ratings.

Journal: *Counselor Education and Supervision,* December 1973, *13*(2), 94–104.

Related Research: Richardson, B. (1969). *The prediction of rehabilitation counselor effectiveness.* Unpublished doctoral dissertation, University of Iowa.

■ ■ ■

1058

Test Name: SLANG TEST

Purpose: To assess counselors' understanding of nonstandard Black English.

Author: Grantham, R.

Article: Effects of counselor sex, race and language style in Black students in initial interviews.

Journal: *Journal of Counseling Psychology,* November 1973, *20*(6), 553–559.

Related Research: Grantham, R. (1969). *Slang test.* Unpublished manuscript, State University of New York at Buffalo.

■ ■ ■

1059

Test Name: SMITH TEST FOR MEASURING TEACHER JUDGMENT OF WRITTEN COMPOSITION

Purpose: To measure teacher judgment in evaluating written composition.

Number of Items: 5

Format: Forms A and B: each contain five short essays taken from the Sequential Tests of Educational Progress, Essay Test, and other samples of student writing. Raters rank the 10 essays from best to worst.

Reliability: Correlations ranged from .84 to .98.

Author: Whalen, T. E.

Article: A validation of the Smith Test for Measuring Teacher Judgment of Written Composition.

Journal: *Education,* November–December 1973, *94*(2), 160–161.

■ ■ ■

1060

Test Name: SOCIAL STUDIES INFORMATION TEST

Purpose: To measure factual knowledge about community life and organization.

Number of Items: 23

Time Required: 15 minutes.

Format: Items measure knowledge about specific occupations, transportation and communication systems, social institutions, and the physical environment. Responses are scored on a 6-point scale.

Author: McKinney, J. D., and Golden, L.

Article: Social studies dramatic play with elementary school children.

Journal: *Journal of Educational Research,* December 1973, *67*(4), 172–176.

■ ■ ■

1061

Test Name: SPATIAL TEST

Purpose: To measure child's ability to conserve spatial

representations, transform spatial displays, and distinguish horizontal and vertical concepts.

Format: The test is on a green T-shaped board mounted vertically that can be rotated on its axis. A detailed description with diagram is presented.

Validity: With WISC Block Design, $r = -.08$; WISC Object Assembly, $r = .26$; Bender Gestalt, $r = .33$; Piagetian Tasks, $r = .31$; Pintner-Cunningham, $r = .17$.

Author: Duncan, B., and Eliot, J.

Article: Some variables affecting children's spatial conservation.

Journal: *Child Development,* December 1973, *44*(4), 828–830.

Related Research: Kershner, J. R. (1971). Conservation of multiple space relations by children: Effects of perception and representation. *Journal of Learning Disabilities, 4,* 316–321.

■ ■ ■

1062

Test Name: SPELLING-SOUND TRANSLATION TEST

Purpose: To measure letter-sound translation ability.

Number of Items: 20

Format: Synthetic words presented one at a time on flash cards. Subjects respond by reading the word aloud.

Validity: Correlations with Gates-MacGinitie reading comprehension scores ranged from .77 to .63.

Author: Venezky, R. L., and Johnson, D.

Article: Development of two letter-sound patterns in grades one through three.

Journal: *Journal of Educational Psychology,* February 1973, *64*(1), 109–115.

1063

Test Name: TEACHER RATING SCALE

Purpose: To permit teachers to assess the performance of children in early elementary grades.

Format: Permits assessment of four areas of academic achievement: reading, quantitative, verbal, listening. Children are rated in each area on a 9-point scale.

Reliability: .92 to .97.

Validity: Otis-Lennon Mental Ability Test Elementary I level ranged from .56 to .72.

Author: Thomas, J. R., and Chissom, B. S.

Article: Relationship between teacher ratings and objective tests of aptitude for elementary school children.

Journal: *Measurement and Evaluation in Guidance,* April 1973, *6*(1), 54–56.

■ ■ ■

1064

Test Name: TEST-WISENESS INSTRUMENT

Purpose: To measure the ability to use characteristics of a test to obtain a high score.

Number of Items: 16

Format: Multiple choice items measuring four test-wiseness behaviors using the stem to choose proper option, eliminating options known to be wrong, options that imply correctness of each other, and options that include specific determiners.

Reliability: Kuder-Richardson formula 20 values for 4 test-wiseness behaviors were –.11, –.05, .20, and .07 for Chinese students.

Validity: Intercorrelations of test-wiseness behaviors ranged from –.02 to .17.

Author: Lo, M., and Slakter, M.

Article: Risk taking and test wiseness of Chinese students.

Journal: *Journal of Experimental Education,* Winter 1973, *42*(2), 56–59.

Related Research: Millman, J., et al. (1965). An analysis of test wiseness. *Educational and Psychological Measurement, 25,* 707–726.

■ ■ ■

1065

Test Name: VERBAL ANALOGY TEST

Purpose: To provide verbal analogy test applicable to low socioeconomic status groups.

Number of Items: 30

Format: 4 items used antonyms, 24 used synonyms, 2 used word form.

Author: Ace, M. C., and Davis, R. V.

Article: Item structure as a determinant of item difficulty in verbal analogies.

Journal: *Educational and Psychological Measurement,* Spring 1973, *33*(1), 143–149.

■ ■ ■

1066

Test Name: VISUAL AND AUDITORY MEMORY TESTS

Purpose: To measure visual and auditory memory.

Number of Items: 20

Format: Visual memory: two words are placed before subjects for 10 seconds. If these can be repeated in order after they are removed, 3 words are next presented, and so on. Auditory test utilizes the same words and procedure except the examiner presents the words orally.

Reliability: Test–retest reliability was .561 for visual memory, .657 for auditory memory.

Author: Weintraub, S., et al.

Article: Summary of investigations relating to reading, July 1, 1972, to June 30, 1973.

Journal: *Reading Research Quarterly,* 1973–74, *9*(3), 287–288.

Related Research: Lilly, M. S., & Kelleher, J. (1973). Modality strengths and aptitude-treatment interaction. *The Journal of Special Education, 7,* 5–13.

CHAPTER 2
Adjustment—Educational

1067

Test Name: ADJUSTMENT SEMANTIC DIFFERENTIAL

Purpose: To measure adjustment.

Number of Items: 11 concepts.

Format: Each concept is judged on 18 bipolar adjective scales. Concepts include myself, my mother, my father, school pupils, school teachers, top of the class, the person I would like to be, pleasant and good things, unpleasant and bad things, school, examinations. The 18 scales include: sweet–sour, glad–sad, fast–slow, good–bad, wet–dry, hard–soft, weak–strong, tall–small, thick–thin, long–short, first–last, before–behind, inside–outside, light–dark, active–passive, below–above, warm–cool, poor–rich.

Author: Naylor, F. D., and Gaudry, E.

Article: The relationship of adjustment, anxiety, and intelligence to mathematics performance.

Journal: *Journal of Educational Research,* May–June 1973, *66*(9), 413–417.

· · ·

1068

Test Name: EDUCATIONAL SET SCALE

Purpose: To divide subjects into conceptually set factually set learners.

Author: Brinkman, E. H.

Article: Personality correlates of educational set in the classroom.

Journal: *Journal of Educational Research,* January 1973, *66*(5), 221–223.

Related Research: Siegel, L., & Siegel, L. C. (1965). Educational set: A determinant of acquisition. *Journal of Educational Psychology, 56,* 1–12.

· · ·

1069

Test Name: MCQUARY-TRUAX UNDERACHIEVEMENT SCALE

Purpose: To identify underachievers.

Number of Items: 24

Format: True–false; modification of the Minnesota Multiphasic Personality Inventory.

Validity: Significantly differentiated between low and high achievers (college), $p < .001$.

Author: Felton, G.

Article: Use of the MMPI Underachievement Scale as an aid in counseling academic low achievers in college.

Journal: *Psychological Reports,* 1973, *32*(1), 151–157.

Related Research: McQuary, J., & Truax, W. (1955). An underachievement scale. *Journal of Educational Research, 48,* 393–399.

· · ·

1070

Test Name: SCHOOL ACCEPTANCE SCALE

Purpose: To measure school acceptance.

Number of Items: 20

Format: Likert format.

Author: Chabassol, D. J.

Article: The measurement of some aspects of structure in adolescence.

Journal: *Journal of Educational Research,* February 1973, *66*(6), 247–250.

· · ·

1071

Test Name: STUDENT OPINION POLL II

Purpose: To provide a general measure of student satisfaction and dissatisfaction with school.

Number of Items: 47

Format: Multiple choice; one point awarded for each answer indicating greatest degree of satisfaction; scores range from 0 to 47.

Validity: With reading levels, $r = -.022$; grade point level, $r = .156$; IQ, $r = -.010$.

Author: Beelick, D. B.

Article: Sources of student satisfaction and dissatisfaction.

Journal: *Journal of Educational Research,* September 1973, *67*(1), 19–22, 28.

Related Research: Getzels, J. W., & Jackson, P. W. (1962). *Creativity and intelligence.* New York: Wiley.

1072

Test Name: STUDY STRATEGY QUESTIONNAIRE

Purpose: To determine which study techniques, goals, and self-evaluations students use.

Number of Items: 64

Format: Each item answered on a 5-point scale: 1 = *strongly agree*, 5 = *strongly disagree*.

Author: Goldman, R. D., and Warren, R.

Article: Discriminant analysis of study strategies connected with college grade success in different major fields.

Journal: *Journal of Educational Measurement*, Spring 1973, *10*(1), 39–47.

■ ■ ■

1073

Test Name: STUDY TECHNIQUES QUESTIONNAIRE

Purpose: To reflect study strategies connected with college grade success.

Format: Seven subscales: clerical diligence, academic savvy, mnemonics, planfulness, formal thinking, note-taking, transformation, and application. All items are answered on a 5-point scale of agreement–disagreement. Examples are provided.

Validity: Canonical correlation coefficient between ability and strategy measure was .40.

Author: Goldman, R. D., and Hudson, D. J.

Article: A multivariate analysis of academic abilities and strategies for successful and unsuccessful college students in different major fields.

Journal: *Journal of Educational Psychology,* December 1973, *65*(3), 364–370.

Related Research: Goldman, R., & Warren, R. (1973). Discriminant analysis of study strategies connected with college grade success in different major fields. *Journal of Educational Measurement, 10,* 39–47.

■ ■ ■

1074

Test Name: SUINN TEST ANXIETY BEHAVIOR SCALE

Purpose: To identify and measure changes in test anxiety.

Number of Items: 50

Format: Behavioral situations are presented that may arouse different levels of test anxiety; subjects rate each item from 1, *not at all,* to 5, *very much,* based on how much anxiety the situation typically evokes. High scores indicate high levels of test anxiety.

Author: Suinn, R. M., et al.

Article: Automated short-term desensitization.

Journal: *Journal of College Student Personnel,* November 1973, *14*(6), 471–476.

Related Research: Suinn, R. (1969). The STABS, a measure of test anxiety for behavior therapy: Normative data. *Behaviour Research and Therapy, 7,* 335–340.

■ ■ ■

1075

Test Name: TEST ANXIETY QUESTIONNAIRE

Purpose: To measure test anxiety.

Validity: California F scale correlation was .016.

Author: Sales, S., and Friend, K.

Article: Success and failure as determinants of level of authoritarianism.

Journal: *Behavioral Science,* May 1973, *18*(3), 163–172.

Related Research: Cowen, J. (1957). *Test anxiety in high school students and its relationship to performance on group tests.* Unpublished doctoral dissertation, Harvard University, School of Education.

■ ■ ■

1076

Test Name: TEST ANXIETY SCALE FOR CHILDREN

Purpose: To measure anxiety for children.

Number of Items: 30

Time Required: Approximately 25 minutes.

Format: A test booklet with each item on a separate page. The subject answers each item by circling either *yes* or *no.* Four factors are identified: test anxiety, remote school concern, poor self-evaluation, somatic signs of anxiety.

Author: Rhine, W. R., and Spaner, S. D.

Article: A comparison of the factor structure of the Test Anxiety Scale for Children among lower- and middle-class children.

Journal: *Developmental Psychology,* November 1973, *9*(3), 421–423.

■ ■ ■

1077

Test Name: TEST OF RISK-TAKING ON OBJECTIVE EXAMINATIONS

Purpose: To measure the effect of risk-taking on test scores.

Number of Items: 5

Format: Five nonsense synonym–antonym vocabulary items embedded in five other legitimate items.

Reliability: Kuder-Richardson formula 20 = .88 (Chinese students).

Author: Lo, M., and Slakter, M.

Article: Risk taking and test wiseness of Chinese students.

Journal: *Journal of Experimental Education,* Winter 1973, *42*(2), 56–59.

Related Research: Slakter, M. (1969). Quality of risk taking on objective examinations. *Educational and Psychological Measurement, 4,* 31–43.

...

CHAPTER 3
Adjustment—Psychological

1078

Test Name: ANOMIE SCALE

Purpose: To measure individual anomie.

Number of Items: 5

Format: Scores from 0 to 5.

Author: Cryns, A. G., and Finn, J. D.

Article: A multivariate analysis of some attitudinal and ideological correlates of student activism.

Journal: *Sociology of Education,* Winter 1973, *46*(1), 127–142.

Related Research: Srole, L. (1956). Social integration and certain corollaries: An exploratory study. *American Sociological Review, 21,* 709–716.
See also *D.U.E.M.M., 2,* 1978: 424.

...

1079

Test Name: BRIEF PSYCHIATRIC RATING SCALE

Purpose: To provide psychiatric (clinical) evaluation.

Format: 18 scales including somatic concern, tension, disorientation.

Reliability: Variety of reliability data are offered including simulation studies.

Author: Flemenbaum, A., and Zimmermann, R.

Article: Inter- and intrarater reliability of the Brief Psychiatric Rating Scale.

Journal: *Psychological Reports,* June 1973, *32*(3), 783–792.

Related Research: Overall, J., & Gotham, D. (1962). The brief psychiatric rating scale. *Psychological Reports, 10,* 799–812.
See also *D.U.E.M.M., 2,* 1978: 405.

...

1080

Test Name: CLIENT ASSESSMENT QUESTIONNAIRE

Purpose: To assess self reported severity of problems in 10 problem areas.

Number of Items: 10

Format: Subjects report severity of problem on a 7-point scale and list specific behaviors following each question. Problem areas included physical complaints, financial status, family life, and so forth.

Reliability: Interrater reliability ranged from .92 to .98.

Validity: Correlation between clients' perception of change following therapy and therapists' estimate was .10 (*ns*); correlation with independent judge was .54 (*p* < .001).

Author: Horenstein, D., et al.

Article: Clients', therapists', and judges' evaluation of psychotherapy.

Journal: *Journal of Counseling Psychology,* March 1973, *20*(2), 149–153.

...

1081

Test Name: FEAR OF DEATH SCALE

Purpose: To measure "conscious fantasy, and below the level of awareness reactions to one's own death, frequency of death thoughts, and perception of life after death" (p. 933).

Number of Items: 6

Format: Questions varied from open-ended to measures patterned after the Word Association Test.

Reliability: Coefficients of agreement of raters ranged from .88 to .90.

Validity: No significant differences between normal and mentally ill patients.

Author: Feifel, H., and Hermann, L.

Article: Fear of death in the mentally ill.

Journal: *Psychological Reports,* December 1973, *33*(3), 931–938.

...

1082

Test Name: KAHN PROBLEM CHECKLIST

Purpose: To assess the presence or absence of clinical symptoms indicative of emotional disturbance.

Format: Two factors: apathy–withdrawal and anger–defiance.

Author: Kohn, M., and Rosman, B. L.

Article: Cognitive functioning in five-year old boys as related to social-emotional and background-demographic variables.

Journal: *Developmental*

Psychology, March 1973, *8*(2), 277–294.

Related Research: Kohn, M., & Rosman, B. L. (1972). A social competence scale and symptom checklist for the preschool child: Factor dimensions, their cross-instrument generality, and longitudinal persistence. *Developmental Psychology, 6*, 430–444.

■ ■ ■

1083

Test Name: MOOD SCALE

Purpose: To self-assess mood.

Number of Items: 7 scales.

Format: Scales tapped receptivity toward world, personal freedom, harmony, sociability, impulse expression, energy, and elation.

Validity: Correlations of certain mood scales with type of defense mechanisms used.

Author: Clum, G., and Clum, J.

Article: Choice of defense mechanisms and their relationship to mood level.

Journal: *Psychological Reports,* April 1973, *32*(2), 507–510.

Related Research: Wessman, A., & Ricks, D. (1966). *Mood and personality.* New York: Holt, Rinehart & Winston.

■ ■ ■

1084

Test Name: PHILLIP'S SYMPTOM CHECKLIST

Purpose: To classify patients as process or reactive schizophrenics.

Format: Ratings by psychologists utilized; scores ranged from 0 to 1.00.

Author: Royer, F., and Janowitch, L.

Article: Performance of process and reactive schizophrenics on a

symbol-digit substitution task.

Journal: *Perceptual and Motor Skills,* August 1973, *37*(1), 63–70.

Related Research: Zigler, E., & Phillips, L. (1962). Social competence and the process-reactive distinction in psychopathology. *Journal of Abnormal and Social Psychology, 65*, 215–222.

■ ■ ■

1085

Test Name: PICTURE INTERPRETATION TASK

Purpose: To assess coping strategies.

Number of Items: 15 pictures

Format: Each picture was shown with increasing clarity on six trials; the subject was asked to interpret what was going on.

Reliability: Interrater reliability was 93.7% agreement.

Validity: Normal subjects shifted more than schizophrenic subjects across repeated trials.

Author: Kaufman, G.

Article: Capacity to handle unassimilable material: Coping strategies of schizophrenics and normals.

Journal: *Journal of Personality Assessment,* 1973, *37*(6), 519–526.

■ ■ ■

1086

Test Name: SUBJECTIVE STRESS SCALE

Purpose: To assess subjective stress in research and clinical setting.

Format: Subjects indicate which of 14 adjectives describes their feelings.

Author: Neufeld, R.

Article: Semantic dimensionality of

the subjective stress scale.

Journal: *Psychological Reports,* December 1973, *33*(3), 885–886.

Related Research: Kerle, R., & Bialek, A. (1958, February). *The construction, validation and application of a subjective stress scale* (Staff Memorandum). U.S. Army Leadership Human Research Unit, Presidio of Monterey.

■ ■ ■

1087

Test Name: SUICIDE CONTEMPLATION MEASURE

Purpose: To assess extent that individuals have contemplated suicide.

Format: Subjects write a short essay; grouped by reader as having or not having contemplated suicide.

Validity: No significant difference in Rotter Locus of Control scores between those contemplating and those not contemplating suicide.

Author: Lambley, P., and Silbowitz, M.

Article: Rotter's internal–external scale and prediction of suicide contemplators among students.

Journal: *Psychological Reports,* October 1973, *33*(2), 585–586.

■ ■ ■

1088

Test Name: SUICIDE QUESTIONNAIRE

Purpose: To assess suicidal and depressive thoughts in college students.

Number of Items: 10

Format: Fixed format and open-ended questions.

Validity: Relationships of items to locus of control, social desirability, and test anxiety measures were not significant.

Author: Murray, D.

Article: Suicidal and depressive feelings among college students.

Journal: *Psychological Reports,* August 1973, *33*(1), 175–181.

■ ■ ■

1089

Test Name: ZUNG DEPRESSION INVENTORY

Purpose: To self-report depression.

Number of Items: 20

Format: Originally designed for adults; also used with adolescents (Ivanoff, 1973).

Validity: Correlations with Lubin and Martin scales; Ivanoff (1973) found significant differences between students with adjustment problems and control students: Pre- and post-treatment change in Zung and change in Death Anxiety correlated .37 (*p* < .05; Templer, 1974).

Author: Yenney, E.

Article: Correlation between two standardized tests of depression.

Journal: *Psychological Reports,* June 1973, *32*(3), 840.

Related Research: Ivanoff, J., et al. (1973, April). Use of the Zung in identifying potential student adjustment problems.

Psychological Reports, 32(2), 489–490.

Lubin, B. (1967). *Manual for the Depression Adjective Checklist.* San Diego, CA: Psychological and Industrial Testing Service.

Martin, W. (1971). *Manual for the Martin S-D Inventory.* Jacksonville, IL: Psychologists and Educators Press.

Templer, D., et al. (1974). Alleviation of high death anxiety with symptomatic treatment of depression. *Psychological Reports,* August, *35*(1), 216.

Zung, W. (1995). A self-rating depression scale. *Archives of General Psychiatry, 1,* 63–70.

CHAPTER 4
Adjustment—Social

1090

Test Name: ALIENATION SCALE

Purpose: To measure alienation.

Number of Items: 38

Format: Likert items with five possible responses from *strongly agree* through *undecided* to *strongly disagree*.

Validity: Correlations with two factors of bureaucracy: $r = -.12$ for status maintenance; $r = .19$ for behavior control.

Author: Anderson, B. D.

Article: School bureaucratization and alienation from high school.

Journal: *Sociology of Education,* Summer 1973, *46*(3), 315–334.

· · ·

1091

Test Name: ANOMIE SCALE

Purpose: To measure general alienation.

Number of Items: 44

Format: True–false.

Reliability: Internal consistency was .96; Short form (26 items) correlation with full length ranged from .65 to .83.

Validity: Significant difference in alienation found between those who were counseled and those not counseled.

Author: Galassi, J., and Galassi, M.

Article: Alienation in college students: A comparison of counseling seekers and nonseekers.

Journal: *Journal of Counseling Psychology,* January 1973, *20*(1), 44–49.

Related Research: Lowe, C., & Damankos, F. (1965). The measurement of anomie in a psychiatric population. *Newsletter for Research in Psychology, 7,* 19–21.

· · ·

1092

Test Name: CULTURAL ALIENATION AND CULTURAL COMMITMENT SCALES

Purpose: To assess cultural alienation.

Number of Items: 20

Format: High scorers on scales tend to reject middle class values.

Validity: Correlation ranged from .16 to .59 with other scales measuring alienation. Counseled versus noncounseled subjects differed on this scale.

Author: Galassi, J., and Galassi, M.

Article: Alienation in college students: A comparison of counseling seekers and nonseekers.

Journal: *Journal of Counseling Psychology,* January 1973, *20*(1), 44–49.

Related Research: Keniston, K. (1965). *Alienation scales.* Unpublished report, New Haven, CT: Yale University Medical School.

Keniston, K. (1965). *The uncommitted: Alienated youths in American society.* New York: Harcourt, Brace & World.

· · ·

1093

Test Name: DEAN ALIENATION SCALE

Purpose: To assess powerlessness, normlessness, and isolation.

Author: Burbach, H., and Thompson, M.

Article: Note on alienation, race and college attrition.

Journal: *Psychological Reports,* August 1973, *33*(1), 273–274.

Related Research: Dean, D. G. (1961). Alienation: Its meaning and measurement. *American Sociological Review, 26,* 753–758.

See *D.U.E.M.M., 2,* 1978: 437.

· · ·

1094

Test Name: DIFFICULTY IN AMERICA SCALE

Purpose: To measure relative deprivation during a foreign student's stay in the United States.

Format: Guttman scale including items on language problems, special favors to foreign students, anxiety about getting a job back home, and the danger of Americanization.

Author: Davis, F. J.

Article: Problems of development in Turkey as seen by Turks returned home from study in American universities.

Journal: *Sociology and Social*

Research, July 1973, *57*(4), 429–442.

• • •

1095

Test Name: ENVIRONMENTAL FORCE UNIT (EFU) OBSERVATIONAL SYSTEM

Purpose: To assess the attempt by an agent in the environment to cope with another person's behavior.

Format: Observations made on 15 randomly selected students; Conflict and non-conflict EFUs recorded.

Reliability: Agreement between two coders ranged from .86 to 1.

Author: Innes, R.

Article: Environmental forces in open and closed classroom settings.

Journal: *Journal of Experimental Education,* Summer 1973, *41*(4), 38–42.

Related Research: Schoggen, P. (1963). Environmental forces in the everyday lives of children. In R. Barker (Ed.), *The stream of behavior* (pp. 42–69). New York: Appleton-Century-Crofts.

• • •

1096

Test Name: FEFFER ROLE TAKING TEST

Purpose: To assess social intelligence.

Format: Subject is presented a Thematic Apperception Test-like picture and asked to tell a story, then to retell the story as the central character in the picture. Scoring criteria assess ability to retell from the character's perspective.

Reliability: Interrater reliability was .89 (rank order; Feffer, 1959).

Validity: Consistent increases with

age in children aged 6 to 13 years (Feffer & Gourevitch, 1960).

Author: Walker, R., and Foley, T.

Article: Social intelligence: Its history and measurement.

Journal: *Psychological Reports,* December 1973, *33*(3), 839–864.

Related Research: Feffer, M. (1959). The cognitive implications of role taking behavior. *Journal of Personality, 27,* 152–168.

Feffer, M., & Gourevitch, V. (1960). Cognitive aspects of role taking in children. *Journal of Personality, 28,* 383–396.

See *D.U.E.M.M. 2,* 1978, 579.

• • •

1097

Test Name: FRIENDSHIP ANALYSIS SCALE

Purpose: To permit an analysis of the importance of concepts of friend and friendship.

Number of Items: 26

Format: Subjects rate 26 items pertaining to friend and friendship according to their importance on a 5-point Likert scale ranging from *essential* to *not at all important.* The items are presented.

Author: Loeb, R.

Article: Disengagement, activity, or maturity?

Journal: *Sociology and Social Research,* April 1973, *57*(3), 367–382.

• • •

1098

Test Name: GENERAL SOCIAL ALIENATION SCALE

Purpose: To measure general social alienation.

Reliability: Internal consistency was .70.

Author: Biggs, D. A., and Barnhart, W. J.

Article: Opinions and attitudes of urban citizens concerning a campus disturbance and campus dissent.

Journal: *Journal of College Student Personnel,* November 1973, *14*(6), 521–526.

Related Research: Srole, L. (1956). Social integration and certain collaries: An explanatory study. *American Sociological Review, 21,* 709–716.

• • •

1099

Test Name: GILLILAND-BURKE MEASURE OF SOCIAL INTELLIGENCE

Purpose: To assess social intelligence.

Author: Walker, R., and Foley, J.

Article: Social intelligence: Its history and measurement.

Journal: *Psychological Reports,* December 1973, *33*(3), 839–864.

Related Research: Gilliland, A., & Burke, R. (1926). A measurement of sociability. *Journal of Applied Psychology, 10,* 315–326.

• • •

1100

Test Name: HOGAN EMPATHY SCALE

Purpose: To measure social intelligence.

Number of Items: 64

Format: Self-report.

Author: Walker, R., and Foley, J.

Article: Social intelligence: Its history and measurement.

Journal: *Psychological Reports,* December 1973, *33*(3), 839–864.

Related Research: Hogan, R. (1969). Development of an empathy scale. *Journal of Consulting and Clinical Psychology, 33,* 307–316.

■ ■ ■

1101

Test Name: HYPOTHETICAL SITUATION QUESTIONNAIRE

Purpose: To measure social orientation, task orientation, and self-assurance on tasks.

Number of Items: 18

Format: Three subscales of six items each. Items are hypothetical academic school situations followed by the question, "What would you do if you were the child in that situation?"

Reliability: Test–retest reliability ranged from .60 to .83.

Author: Nakamura, C. Y., and Finck, D.

Article: Effect of social or task orientation and evaluative or nonevaluative situations on performance.

Journal: *Child Development,* March 1973, *44*(1), 83–93.

■ ■ ■

1102

Test Name: INTERPERSONAL RELATIONSHIP RATING SCALE

Purpose: To measure attitudes and behaviors in individuals' relationships with others and how they see themselves.

Number of Items: 24

Format: Items are 7-point numerical rating scales; high ratings are positive and low ratings are negative. This is a self-administered paper-and-pencil inventory. Most items are presented.

Reliability: Test–retest coefficients ranged from .29 to .78 (1 week interval); test–retest coefficients ranged from .14 to .70 (6-week interval). Spearman rank order correlations between average profiles: test–retest coefficient of .83 for 1-week interval; .85 for 6-week interval.

Author: Hipple, J. L.

Article: Personal growth outcomes due to human relations training experiences.

Journal: *College Student Personnel,* March 1973, *14*(2), 156–164.

Related Research: Hipple, J. L. (1970). *Effects of differential human relations laboratory training designs on the interpersonal behavior of college students.* Unpublished doctoral dissertation, University of Iowa.

■ ■ ■

1103

Test Name: MANIFEST ALIENATION MEASURE

Purpose: To measure level of alienation.

Number of Items: 20

Format: Likert scales are based on conceptualization of alienation as a "syndrome consisting of feelings of pessimism, cynicism, distrust, apathy, and emotional distance" (Gould, 1969, pp. 43–44).

Author: Tolor, A.

Article: Evaluation of perceived teacher effectiveness.

Journal: *Journal of Educational Psychology,* February 1973, *64*(1), 98–104.

Related Research: Gould, L. J. (1964). *The alienation syndrome: Psychological correlates and behavior consequences.* Doctoral dissertation, University of Connecticut. (University

Microfilms No. 66–848)

Gould, L. J. (1969). Conformity and marginality: Two faces of alienation. *Journal of Social Issues, 25,* 39–63.

■ ■ ■

1104

Test Name: OHIO SOCIAL ACCEPTANCE SCALE

Purpose: To assess the general nature of children's social relations with their peers; may be used to identify socially neglected or rejected individuals.

Format: Six-point continuum to measure the extent to which pre-adolescents accept their peers. The six degrees of social distance include three accepting, one noncommital, and two rejective. Scale descriptions are provided.

Author: Lorber, N. M.

Article: Measuring the character of children's peer relations using the Ohio Social Acceptance Scale.

Journal: *California Journal of Educational Research,* March 1973, *24*(2), 71–77.

Related Research: Raths, L. (1943). Identifying the social acceptance of children. *Educational Research Bulletin, 22,* 72–74.

■ ■ ■

1105

Test Name: PERSONAL COMPETENCE INVENTORY

Purpose: To obtain degree of pupils' acceptance or rejection by classmates and measure perception of self to peers, teacher, and school tasks.

Format: Two tests of affective perceptions: Peer Acceptance Index (PAI) and Self Perceptions Index (SPI). PAI: each pupil is rated on a 5-point scale by each classmate. Score is a composite of classmates' ratings. A classroom average indicates the degree of socialization among pupils. SPI: ten items in each of three areas of pupils' perceptions: pupil–pupil interaction effectiveness; pupil–teacher interaction effectiveness; effectiveness in study habits and school tasks. Sample items are presented.

Author: Brown, J. A., and MacDougall, M. A.

Article: The impact of teacher consultation on the self perception of elementary school children.

Journal: *Education,* April–May 1973, *93*(4), 339–345.

Related Research: *Virginia Educational Needs Assessment Study.* The Bureau of Educational Research, University of Virginia, and the Virginia State Department of Education, under provisions of Title III, Public Law 89–110.

Rist, R. C. (1970). Student social class and teacher expectations: The self-fulfilling prophecy in ghetto education. *Harvard Educational Review, 40,* 3.

- - -

1106

Test Name: PERSONAL, HOME, SOCIAL, FORMAL RELATIONS QUESTIONNAIRE

Purpose: To assess general adjustment.

Format: Questions regarding subject's relation to self, home, social situations, and formal situations.

Author: Broekmann, N., and Moller, A.

Article: Preferred seating position and distance in various situations.

Journal: *Journal of Counseling Psychology,* November 1973, *20*(6), 504–508.

Related Research: Human Sciences

Research Council. (1968). *Personal, Home, Social, Formal Relations Questionnaire.* Pretoria, South Africa: Author.

- - -

1107

Test Name: PERSONAL SPACE MEASURE

Purpose: To assess the chosen, comfortable distance between a subject and others.

Number of Items: 24 scores

Format: Performance task: Subject adjusts drawn profiles of individuals "as close as is comfortable for you in most social situations."

Reliability: 24 test–retest reliabilities ranged from .51 to .91; most were satisfactory.

Validity: Correlations with two criteria were .16 ($p < .05$) and .41 ($p < .01$). These criteria involved measurement of the actual physical distance the subject used.

Author: Pedersen, D.

Article: Development of a personal space measure.

Journal: *Psychological Reports,* April 1973, *32*(2), 527–535.

- - -

1108

Test Name: PETERSON PROBLEM CHECKLIST

Purpose: To measure elementary school social-emotional functioning.

Format: Checklist measuring two dimensions of pathology: Factor I, personality problems; Factor II, conduct problems.

Validity: Schaefer Classroom Behavior Inventory Factor I, $r = .64$; Factor II, $r = .76$.

Author: Kohn, M., and Rosman, B. L.

Article: Cross-situational and longitudinal stability of social-emotional functioning in young children.

Journal: *Child Development,* December 1973, *44*(4), 721–729.

Related Research: Peterson, D. R. (1960). The age generality of personality factors derived from ratings. *Educational and Psychological Measurement, 20,* 461–474.

- - -

1109

Test Name: SOCIAL EGOCENTRISM INSTRUMENT

Purpose: To measure social egocentrism.

Number of Items: 10

Format: Ten cartoon sequences and a 5-point scoring system reflecting different levels of potential egocentric intrusion.

Reliability: Spearman-Brown split-half reliability coefficient was .92.

Author: Chandler, M. J.

Article: Egocentrism and antisocial behavior: The assessment and training of social perspective-taking skills.

Journal: *Developmental Psychology,* November 1973, *9*(3), 326–332.

Related Research: Flavell, J. H., et al. (1968). *The development of role-taking and communication skills in children.* New York: Wiley.

- - -

1110

Test Name: SOCIAL ISOLATION SCALE

Purpose: To measure interpersonal alienation.

Number of Items: 9

Format: Items are rated on a 5-point scale; high scores are associated with feelings of aloneness and separation.

Reliability: Split-half (corrected) reliability was .83.

Validity: Counseled and noncounseled subjects scored differently on the scale.

Author: Galassi, J., and Galassi, M.

Article: Alienation in college students: A comparison of counseling seekers and non-seekers.

Journal: *Journal of Counseling Psychology,* January 1973, *20*(1), 44–49.

Related Research: Dean, D. (1960). Alienation and political apathy. *Social Forces, 38,* 185–189.

● ● ●

1111

Test Name: SOCIALIZATION SCALE

Purpose: To assess socialization in schizophrenic patients.

Number of Items: 45

Format: Rated by psychiatric nurses.

Reliability: Interjudge reliability, $r = .87$.

Author: Ravensborg, M.

Article: A taxonomy of objectives for socialization.

Journal: *Psychological Reports,* June 1973, *32*(3), 921–922.

● ● ●

1112

Test Name: SOCIAL POWER QUESTIONNAIRE

Purpose: To assess five bases of social power.

Number of Items: 80

Format: Questions dealt with the following bases of social power with fellow workers and supervisors: expertness, legitimacy, positive sanctions, negative sanctions, and attractions.

Validity: Factor analysis resulted in 11 factors accounting for 47% of the variance; factors and loadings are given in the article.

Author: Galinsky, M., et al.

Article: Distinctiveness of bases of social power.

Journal: *Psychological Reports,* December 1973, *33*(3), 727–730.

● ● ●

1113

Test Name: SOCIAL RESPONSIBILITY SCALE

Purpose: To assess a person's traditional social responsibility and orientation toward helping others.

Author: Poorkaj, H., and Bockelman, C.

Article: The impact of community volunteers on delinquency prevention.

Journal: *Sociology and Social Research,* April 1973, *57*(3), 335–341.

Related Research: Berkowitz, L., & Lutterman, K. (1968). The traditionally socially responsible personality. *Public Opinion Quarterly, 32,* 169–185.

● ● ●

1114

Test Name: TEST OF SOCIAL INFERENCE

Purpose: To assess retardate interpretation of social cues.

Number of Items: 35

Time Required: 20–45 minutes.

Format: This is an individual test using pictorial presentation; the subject is asked to tell "what picture is about."

Reliability: Interscorer reliability was in the .90s (Edmonson et al. 1971), test–retest (1 week) reliability was .84 (Edmonson et al. 1971).

Validity: Correlation with IQ ranged from .27 to .61 (median = .46); a wide review of validity data is available in the article.

Author: DeJung, J., et al.

Article: Test of social inference for retarded adolescents: Measuring social-cue perception.

Journal: *Psychological Reports,* April 1973, *32*(2), 603–618.

Related Research: Edmonson, B., et al. (1971). *Social inference training of retarded adolescents and the Test of Social Inference* (Revised Project Report VRA Project No. RD-1388P). Eugene: University of Oregon.

● ● ●

1115

Test Name: VISUAL JUDGMENT SCALE

Purpose: To assess extent of social yielding to group norm.

Format: Two forms: Subject is asked to make a judgment regarding which of two cubes is larger than the other. The test is administered in a group in which certain subjects' responses are manipulated.

Validity: There was significantly greater yielding to group in primary grades than intermediate grades; girls yielded more than boys.

Author: Pasternack, T.

Article: Qualitative differences in development of yielding behavior by elementary school children.

Journal: *Psychological Reports,* June 1973, *32*(3), 883–896.

■ ■ ■

1116

Test Name: WORK RELATIONS QUESTIONNAIRE

Purpose: To determine employee work relations.

Number of Items: 18

Format: Two major areas: human organizational elements and human behavioral elements. Structured questions with five multiple-choice answers.

Author: Newport, M. G., and Duncan, W. J.

Article: Employees and supervisors: Four cases in point.

Journal: *Personnel Journal,* July 1973, *52*(7), 619–625.

Related Research: Brianas, J. G. (1970, November). Between employees and supervisors: Three cases in point. *Personnel Journal, 49*(10), 892–899.

CHAPTER 5
Aptitude

1117

Test Name: DRAW A DOG SCALE

Purpose: To assess intelligence.

Number of Items: 41

Format: Subjects are asked to draw a picture of a dog.

Reliability: Test–retest reliability was .76 (2 months). Interrater reliability was .91.

Validity: Correlation with Harris DAM was .54.

Author: Levinson, B., and Mezei, H.

Article: The draw a dog scale.

Journal: *Perceptual and Motor Skills,* February 1973, *36*(1), 19–22.

. . .

1118

Test Name: JOHNSON-KENNEY SCREENING READINESS TEST

Purpose: To identify learning problems in first graders.

Number of Items: 10 subtests.

Time Required: Two 1-hour sessions.

Format: Subtests are described in the article and include number of concepts, visual motor coordination, symbol recognition, and so forth.

Validity: Correlation with teacher rating of child's progress (satisfactory/unsatisfactory) at end of year was .66 ($p < .01$) in the first study; point biserial correlation was .65 ($p < .001$) in the second study.

Author: Seitz, F., et al.

Article: Detection of learning difficulties in first grade: Preliminary analysis of the Johnson-Kenney screening readiness test.

Journal: *Psychological Reports,* August 1973, *33*(1), 219–225.

Related Research: Johnson, R., & Kenney, R. *Johnson-Kenney Screening Readiness Test.* San Rafael, CA: 1970.

. . .

1119

Test Name: MMPI WOMEN'S SCHOLASTIC PERSONALITY SCALE

Purpose: To predict scholastic potential in women.

Number of Items: 68

Format: MMPI items from the standardized test differentiating a criterion (National Merit) group from a comparison group.

Validity: Significant differences between criterion groups in scale performance were found.

Author: Clopton, J., and Neuringer, C.

Article: An MMPI scale to measure scholastic personality in women.

Journal: *Perceptual and Motor Skills,* December 1973, *37*(3), 963–966.

. . .

1120

Test Name: OWENS BIOGRAPHICAL INVENTORY

Purpose: To predict college grade point average (GPA) using biographical data.

Number of Items: 389

Format: Multiple choice with responses arranged to form a continuum.

Reliability: Halpin (1972) median stability was .60 over 2 years.

Validity: There were moderate to low correlations between biographical inventory (BI) scores and GPA; in a multiple correlation, the BI Factor for academic achievement was selected first ($rs= .45$ and .41 for men and women, respectively).

Author: Payne, D. A., et al.

Article: Application of a biographical data inventory to estimate college achievement.

Journal: *Measurement and Evaluation in Guidance,* 1973, *6*(3), 152–156.

Related Research: Halpin, W. G. (1972). *A study of the life histories and creative abilities of potential teachers.* Unpublished doctoral dissertation, University of Georgia.

Owens, W. (1969). *The UGA Biographical Questionnaire.* Unpublished biographical inventory. University of Georgia.

Schoenfeldt, L. F. (1970, March). *Life experiences as a moderator in the prediction of educational criteria.* Paper presented at the meeting of the American Educational Research Association, Minneapolis, MN.

1121

Test Name: READING READINESS BATTERY

Purpose: To assess reading readiness of school beginners.

Format: Includes 13 subtests measuring four general areas: concept of the reading task, perceptual ability, linguistic competence, cognitive functioning.

Reliability: For the 13 subtests, r ranged from .50 to .95.

Author: Weintraub, S., et al.

Article: Summary of investigations relating to reading July 1, 1972, to June 30, 1973.

Journal: *Reading Research Quarterly*, 1973–74, *9*(3), 431–432.

Related Research: Evanechko, P., et al. (1973). An investigation of the reading readiness domain. *Research in the Teaching of English*, *7*, 61–78.

CHAPTER 6
Attitude

1122

Test Name: ALCOHOL, CIGARETTES, AND COFFEE ATTITUDE SCALES

Purpose: To identify attitudes toward alcohol, cigarettes, and coffee.

Number of Items: 60

Format: Basically the same 20 items are repeated with reference to alcohol, cigarettes, and coffee. Subjects expressed agreement or disagreement on a 7-point bipolar scale. Items for alcohol are presented.

Author: Perry, A.

Article: The effect of heredity on attitudes toward alcohol, cigarettes, and coffee.

Journal: *Journal of Applied Psychology,* October 1973, *58*(2), 275–277.

· · ·

1123

Test Name: ANTISEXISM MEASURE

Purpose: To assess equalitarianism.

Validity: Correlation with Scholastic Aptitude Test Verbal was .38, $p < .01$, for Math, $r = .31$, $p < .05$.

Author: Joesting, J., and Joesting, R.

Article: Equalitarianism and Scholastic Aptitude Test scores for college women.

Journal: *Psychological Reports,* April 1973, *32*(2), 664.

Related Research: Joesting, J., & Joesting, R. (1972). Attitudes about sex roles, sex and marital status of antiwar demonstrators. *Psychological Reports, 31,* 413–414.

· · ·

1124

Test Name: ATTITUDE OF THE GIFTED TOWARD THE GIFTED QUESTIONNAIRE

Purpose: To examine self-perception of gifted children.

Number of Items: 20

Format: Incomplete sentences.

Author: Wittek, M.

Article: Reflections of the gifted by the gifted on the gifted.

Journal: *Gifted Child Quarterly,* Winter 1973, *17*(4), 250–253.

· · ·

1125

Test Name: ATTITUDE SURVEY

Purpose: To measure attitudes toward censorship, firearm registration, and so forth.

Number of Items: 15

Format: Subject indicated agreement/disagreement on a 6-step scale.

Author: Good, L., et al.

Article: Similarity of attitude and attraction to a community.

Journal: *Psychological Reports,* June 1973, *32*(3), 975–981.

Related Research: Byrne, D. (1971). *The attraction paradigm.* New York: Academic Press.

1126

Test Name: ATTITUDES TOWARD THE ACADEMIC ENVIRONMENT QUESTIONNAIRE

Purpose: To measure student attitudes toward tests, study, academic competition, and potential reform.

Number of Items: 107

Format: Each statement was answered on a 5-point scale, from 1, *strong agreement,* to 5, *strong disagreement.*

Reliability: .75 to .82.

Author: Priest, R. F.

Article: Effects of social background on attitudes toward the academic environment.

Journal: *Journal of College Student Personnel,* May 1973, *14*(3), 265–268.

Related Research: Fishbein, M., & Raven, B. H. (1962). The AB Scales: An operational definition of belief and attitude. *Human Relations, 15,* 35–44.

Ostrom, T. M. (1969). The relationship between the affective behavioral and cognitive components of attitude. *Journal of Experimental and Social Psychology, 12,* 120–126.

Priest, R. F. (1969, June). *Attitudes to competitive grading in college as a function of aspiration anxiety and grades.* Paper presented at the Western Psychological Association Meeting, Vancouver, British Columbia, Canada.

1127

Test Name: ATTITUDES TOWARD APPLIED PSYCHOLOGY SCALES

Purpose: To assess the magnitude and direction of attitudes toward industrial psychology and psychological testing.

Number of Items: 96

Format: Two forms: Thurstone and Likert design.

Reliability: Thurstone: split-half reliabilities corrected by the Spearman-Brown formula were .81 and .84. Likert: Kuder-Richardson formula 20 reliability estimates were .92 and .95.

Author: Rhoads, R. F., and Landy, F. J.

Article: Measurement of attitudes of industrial work groups toward psychology and testing.

Journal: *Journal of Applied Psychology,* October 1973, *58*(2), 197–201.

● ● ●

1128

Test Name: ATTITUDES TOWARD BIRTH CONTROL SCALE

Purpose: To assess Costa Rican women's positive–negative attitudes toward birth control.

Number of Items: 4

Format: Scores ranged from 0 (negative) to 16 (positive).

Validity: No significant difference between attitudes of women who had legal marriages and those in consensual unions.

Author: Michielutte, R., et al.

Article: Consensual and legal marital unions in Costa Rica.

Journal: *International Journal of Comparative Sociology,* May–June 1973, *14*(1–2), 119–128.

1129

Test Name: ATTITUDE TOWARD CHANGE SCALE

Purpose: To measure attitude to change in managerial practices in general.

Number of Items: 9

Format: Items rated on Likert scales.

Validity: For Managerial status, $r = -.08$; Education, $r = .24$; Age, $r = -.36$; Discontent scale, $r = .09$; Confidence scale, $r = .28$; Extraversion, $r = .10$; Neuroticism, $r = .08$.

Author: Kirton, M. J., and Mulligan, G.

Article: Correlates of managers' attitudes toward change.

Journal: *Journal of Applied Psychology,* August 1973, *58*(1), 101–107.

Related Research: Trumbo, D. A. (1961). Individual and group correlates of attitudes to work-related change. *Journal of Applied Psychology, 45,* 338–344.

● ● ●

1130

Test Name: ATTITUDES TOWARD DRUG USAGE AND DRUG EDUCATION QUESTIONNAIRE

Purpose: To identify attitudes of public school teachers toward drug usage and drug education.

Format: Part I: drug usage; Part II: drug education.

Author: Penn, J. R., and Erekson, C. F.

Article: What do teachers really know about drugs?

Journal: *Education,* April–May 1973, *93*(4), 353–356.

Related Research: Mason, R., & Holloway, R. (1970). *An analysis of student attitudes toward drug*

usage in university affiliated residence halls, cooperatives, fraternities, and sororities at Oregon State University (Research Bulletin: Center for Research on Student Life and Development). Oregon State University.

● ● ●

1131

Test Name: ATTITUDES TOWARD LEGALIZED ABORTION SCALE

Purpose: To assess attitudes toward legalized abortion.

Author: Corenblum, B.

Article: Locus of control, latitude of acceptance and attitudes toward abortion.

Journal: *Psychological Reports,* June 1973, *32*(3), 753–754.

Related Research: Acknowledgment for scale is given to Dr. J. McCroskey.

● ● ●

1132

Test Name: ATTITUDES TOWARD MARIJUANA SCALE

Purpose: To measure attitudes toward the legalization of marijuana.

Number of Items: 16

Format: All items are presented.

Author: Albrecht, S. L.

Article: Verbal attitudes and significant others expectations as predictors of marijuana use.

Journal: *Sociology and Social Research,* January 1973, *57*(2), 196–207.

● ● ●

1133

Test Name: ATTITUDES TOWARD MARIJUANA QUESTIONNAIRE

Purpose: To assess college

students' attitude toward marijuana.

Number of Items: 18

Format: 8 demographic and 10 Likert scale attitude questions related to ethnic, social, legal aspects of use of the drug.

Author: Martino, E., and Truss, C.

Article: Drug use and attitudes toward social and legal aspects of marijuana in a large metropolitan university.

Journal: *Journal of Counseling Psychology*, March 1973, *20*(2), 120–126.

• • •

1134

Test Name: ATTITUDES TOWARD MARRIED PROFESSIONAL WOMEN SCALE

Purpose: To assess attitudes toward women serving in a dual role.

Format: Personal History Data and six items with which the respondent agrees or disagrees.

Validity: Sex of respondent correlated significantly with 3/6 items (women were more positive than men).

Author: Etaugh, C.

Article: Attitudes of professionals toward the married professional woman.

Journal: *Psychological Reports,* June 1973, *32*, 775–780.

Related Research: Kaley, M. (1971). Attitudes toward the dual role of the married professional woman. *American Psychologist, 26*, 301–306.

• • •

1135

Test Name: ATTITUDES TOWARD NATIONALITIES

Purpose: To assess flexibility of attitude toward nationalities.

Format: Subjects asked preference among seven nationalities of roommate (Chinese, English, French, German, Greek, Italian, Russian); rankings were requested.

Author: Berger, L., et al.

Article: An attitude survey of college freshmen and seniors: Preference toward seven nationalities.

Journal: *Psychological Reports,* December 1973, *33*(3), 837–838.

• • •

1136

Test Name: ATTITUDES TOWARD SCHOOL MEASURE

Purpose: To assess elementary school children's attitudes.

Number of Items: 30

Format: Items from three sources listed below.

Author: Hicks, J., et al.

Article: Attitudes toward school as related to non-grading and intelligence.

Journal: *Psychological Reports,* December 1973, *33*(3), 739–742.

Related Research: Conner, H. (1971). *An attitude scale to determine the attitude of public school students toward school.* Raleigh: Department of Public Instruction in cooperation with the North Carolina State University, Department of Food Science.

Shaw, M., & Wright, J. (1967). *Scales for the measurement of attitudes.* New York: McGraw Hill.

Zeligs, R. (1966). Children's favorable attitudes toward home and school. *Journal of Educational Research, 60,* 13–21.

1137

Test Name: ATTITUDES TOWARD SEEKING PROFESSIONAL PSYCHOLOGICAL HELP SCALE

Purpose: To measure recognition of personal need for professional psychological help; tolerance of the stigma associated with psychiatric help; interpersonal openness regarding one's problems; confidence in the mental health professional.

Number of Items: 29

Format: Fixed-alternative, four alternative items, questionnaire. High score (87) indicates a positive orientation toward seeking help.

Reliability: $r = .83$.

Author: Wolkon, G. H., et al.

Article: Race and social class as factors in the orientation toward psychotherapy.

Journal: *Journal of Counseling Psychology,* July 1973, *20*(4), 312–316.

Related Research: Fischer, E. H., & Turner, J. L. (1970). Orientation to seeking professional help: Development and research utility of an attitude scale. *Journal of Consulting and Clinical Psychology, 35,* 79–90.

• • •

1138

Test Name: ATTITUDES TOWARD SOCIAL STUDIES TEST

Purpose: To determine attitude toward social studies instruction and cooperative situations.

Format: Subjects indicate by circling 1, 2, 3, or 4 (*strongly agree* to *strongly disagree*) whether they favored or did not favor specific evaluative statements concerning cooperative and competitive social studies environments. Examples are given.

Reliability: Pearson product-moment correlations were .71 and .72.

Author: Wheeler, R., and Ryan, F. L.

Article: Effects of cooperative and competitive classroom environments on the attitudes and achievement of elementary school students engaged in social studies inquiry activities.

Journal: *Journal of Educational Psychology,* December 1973, *65*(3), 402–407.

■ ■ ■

1139

Test Name: ATTITUDES TOWARD SUPERNATURAL PHENOMENA SCALE

Purpose: To assess attitudes toward witchcraft, extrasensory perception, and so forth.

Number of Items: 32

Format: Likert format (7-point scale).

Author: Scheidt, R.

Article: Belief in supernatural phenomena and locus of control.

Journal: *Psychological Reports,* June 1973, *32*(3), 1159–1162.

■ ■ ■

1140

Test Name: ATTITUDES TOWARD TEACHING AS A CAREER SCALE

Purpose: To measure attitude toward teaching as a career.

Number of Items: 11

Format: Likert scale with four items stated in an unfavorable direction and seven in a favorable direction.

Reliability: Corrected split-half *r* =

.71; test–retest *r* = .79.

Author: Shaw, M. E., et al.

Article: Team teaching: A source of support for teacher attitudes toward teaching.

Journal: *Education,* February–March 1973, *93*(3), 295–300.

Related Research: Merwin, J. C., & DiVesta, F. L. (1959). A study of need theory and career choice. *Journal of Counseling Psychology, 6,* 302–308.

■ ■ ■

1141

Test Name: ATTITUDES TOWARD YOUTH SCALE

Purpose: To determine parents' degree of agreement with statements about youth.

Reliability: *r* = .76.

Author: Winkworth, J. M., et al.

Article: Intervention programs designed to improve communications between parents and students.

Journal: *Journal of College Student Personnel,* May 1973, *14*(3), 206–215.

■ ■ ■

1142

Test Name: AVIATION AND FLYING ATTITUDE QUESTIONNAIRE

Purpose: To identify attitudes toward aviation and flying.

Number of Items: 50

Format: Responses to each item on a 7-point bipolar scale ranging from *strongly agree* to *strongly disagree.* Fourteen factors are identified. Some items are presented.

Author: Perry, A., and Friedman, S. T.

Article: Dimensional analysis of

attitudes toward commercial flying.

Journal: *Journal of Applied Psychology,* December 1973, *58*(3), 388–390.

■ ■ ■

1143

Test Name: BLACK–WHITE INTERACTIONS ATTITUDE SCALE

Purpose: To identify Black–White attitudes toward advisability.

Number of Items: 50

Format: Each item is a situation involving Blacks interacting with Whites. Subjects respond on a 7-point scale from *extremely advisable* to *extremely inadvisable.* A few examples are presented.

Author: Wenckowski, C.

Article: Black–White attitudes toward advisability of opposite race interactions.

Journal: *Journal of College Student Personnel,* July 1973, *14*(4), 303–308.

■ ■ ■

1144

Test Name: BOGARDUS SOCIAL DISTANCE SCALE—MODIFIED

Purpose: To measure social distance.

Format: Includes the following races: Chinese, Japanese, Korean, Caucasian, Filipino, Negro, mixed.

Author: Kinloch, G. C.

Article: Race, socio-economic status, and social distance in Hawaii.

Journal: *Sociology and Social Research,* January 1973, *57*(2), 156–167.

Related Research: Smith, M. W. (1970). Measuring ethnocentrism in Hilo, Hawaii: A social distance scale. *Sociology and Social Research, 54,* 220–236.

∎ ∎ ∎

1145

Test Name: BREHEM AND BLACK DRUG ATTITUDE SCALE

Purpose: To measure student attitudes toward drugs.

Format: Five factors (three correlated highly with drug usage).

Author: Webster, W.

Article: Trends in reported drug usage among public school children.

Journal: *Journal of Experimental Education,* Winter 1973, *42*(2), 80–86.

Related Research: Brehem, M., & Black, K. (1968). Self image and attitude toward drugs. *Journal of Personality, 36,* 299–310.

∎ ∎ ∎

1146

Test Name: BUYS' SCALE OF ATTITUDE TOWARD CONTEMPORARY SOCIAL ISSUES

Purpose: To assess attitudes toward contemporary issues.

Format: Seven scales used: family roles, societal values, college attitudes, overt anti-Black attitudes, religious conservatism, anti-ecology alert.

Reliability: Reliability coefficients, and homogeneity ratios reported for each scale without indicating the specific method.

Author: Buys, C., and Schmidt, M.

Article: Student–father attitudes toward contemporary social issues: Replication with a matched sample.

Journal: *Psychological Reports,*

August 1973, *33*(1), 271–272.

Related Research: Buys, C. (1972). Student–father attitudes toward contemporary social issues. *Psychological Reports, 31,* 699–706.

∎ ∎ ∎

1147

Test Name: CATEGORIES TEST

Purpose: To measure attitude of White children toward Black children.

Author: Litcher, J.

Article: Use of pictures of multi-ethnic interaction to change attitudes of White elementary school students toward Blacks.

Journal: *Psychological Reports,* October 1973, *33*(2), 367–372.

Related Research: Horowitz, L., & Horowitz, R. (1938). Development of social attitudes in children. *Sociometry, 1,* 301–339.

∎ ∎ ∎

1148

Test Name: CHILD-REARING QUESTIONNAIRE

Purpose: To identify parental child-rearing attitudes.

Number of Items: 16

Format: Includes items involving disciplinary, indulgent, rejecting, and protective attitudes. A 5-point Likert scale is used.

Author: Willerman, L., and Plomin, R.

Article: Activity level in children and their parents.

Journal: *Child Development,* December 1973, *44*(4), 854–858.

Related Research: Pumroy, D. K. (1966). Maryland Parent Attitude Survey: A research instrument with social desirability controlled.

Journal of Psychology, 64, 73–78.

∎ ∎ ∎

1149

Test Name: CHILD REPORT: SCHOOL ATTITUDE SCALE

Purpose: To assess positive or negative attitude toward facets of the school situation, including classroom learning, school work, and school in general.

Reliability: Hoyt reliability coefficient was .84.

Validity: Point biserial correlation coefficients indicated item validity ranging from .73 to .88.

Author: Bennett, R. V.

Article: Curricular organizing strategies, classroom interaction patterns, and pupil affect.

Journal: *Journal of Educational Research,* May–June 1973, *66*(9), 387–393.

Related Research: Wisconsin teacher education project. (1963). University of Wisconsin—Madison.

∎ ∎ ∎

1150

Test Name: CLARK DOLL TEST

Purpose: To measure attitude of White children toward Black children.

Author: Litcher, J.

Article: Use of pictures of multi-ethnic interaction to change attitudes of White elementary school students toward Blacks.

Journal: *Psychological Reports,* October 1973, *33*(2), 367–372.

Related Research: Gregor, A., & McPherson, D. (1968). Racial attitudes among White and Negro children in a deep-South standard metropolitan area. *Journal of Social Psychology, 68,* 95–106.

1151

Test Name: COLLEGE PRESS AND ATTITUDE SCALES

Purpose: To measure a variety of students' attitudes and perceived characteristics of peers and teachers.

Number of Items: 33

Format: Items were rated on Likert scales. Factor analysis indicated eight factors were included.

Reliability: The 1-month reliability estimates ranged from .71 to .94.

Author: Thistlethwaite, D. L.

Article: Accentuation of differences in values and exposures to major fields of study.

Journal: *Journal of Educational Psychology,* December 1973, *65*(3), 279–293.

Related Research: Thistlethwaite, D. L. (1969). Some ecological effects of entering a field of study. *Journal of Educational Psychology, 60,* 284–293.

Robinson, J. P., et al. (1968). *Measures of political attitudes.* Ann Arbor, MI: Institute for Social Research.

■ ■ ■

1152

Test Name: CONCERN FOR ENVIRONMENTAL RIGHTS SCALE

Purpose: To measure attitudes toward environmental issues.

Number of Items: 8

Format: Items are answered either *agree, disagree,* or *undecided.*

Reliability: Internal consistency ranged from .34 to .58; average of split-half reliabilities was .76; interitem correlations ranged from .15 to .65.

Author: Dunlap, R. E., et al.

Article: Concern for environmental

rights among college students.

Journal: *The American Journal of Economics and Sociology,* January 1973, *32*(1), 45–60.

■ ■ ■

1153

Test Name: CROSS-CULTURAL ATTITUDE BEHAVIOR SCALE

Purpose: To measure attitudes of Blacks and Whites.

Number of Items: 14 items for each of seven scales.

Format: Attitude content areas: characteristics—personal, education, housing, jobs, law and order, political activism, war and military. Also a composite 14-item scale (two items from each of seven scales).

Reliability: Hoyt ranged from .70 to .90 for scales.

Author: Hamersma, R., et al.

Article: Construction of a Guttman facet designed cross-cultural attitude–behavior scale toward racial-ethnic interaction.

Journal: *Educational and Psychological Measurement,* Autumn 1973, *33*(3), 565–576.

■ ■ ■

1154

Test Name: DIRECT COMPARISON TEST

Purpose: To determine stereotype of White children toward Blacks.

Author: Litcher, J.

Article: Use of pictures of multi-ethnic interaction to change attitudes of White elementary school students toward Blacks.

Journal: *Psychological Reports,* October 1973, *33*(2), 367–372.

Related Research: Blake, R., & Dennis, W. (1943). The development of stereotypes concerning the Negro. *Journal of*

Abnormal and Social Psychology, 38, 525–531.

■ ■ ■

1155

Test Name: DRUG ATTITUDE QUESTIONNAIRE

Purpose: To ascertain attitudes toward the personal use of drugs.

Number of Items: 14

Format: Responses to each item were indicated on a 5-point scale from *agree* to *disagree.* Scores range from 14 for conservative, anti-drug attitude to 70 for liberal, pro-drug attitude.

Reliability: Split-half reliabilities were .84 and .87.

Author: Hoffman, A. M., and Warner, R. W., Jr.

Article: A comparison of college students' and parents' attitudes toward the abuse of drugs.

Journal: *Journal of College Student Personnel,* September 1973, *14*(5), 430–433.

Related Research: Horan, J. J. (1972). *A reliability study of the drug education evaluation scale.* Unpublished paper, Pennsylvania State University.

■ ■ ■

1156

Test Name: EMPLOYEE ATTITUDE SURVEY

Purpose: To determine employee attitudes.

Number of Items: 98

Format: Each item answered by checking one of five response categories from *very satisfied* to *very dissatisfied.* Includes 17 factors.

Author: Roach, D. E., and Davis, R. R.

Article: Stability of the structure of employee attitudes: An empirical test of factor invariance.

Journal: *Journal of Applied Psychology,* October 1973, *58*(2), 181–185.

Related Research: Roach, D. E. (1958). Dimensions of employee morale. *Personnel Psychology, 11,* 419–431.

■ ■ ■

1157

Test Name: EROTICISM SCALE

Purpose: To assess reaction to erotic literature.

Format: Items were rated on a 15-point Likert scale from *mildly sexually stimulating* to *very sexually stimulating.*

Validity: No sex differences in response to hard core pornography were found.

Author: Englar, R., and Walker, C.

Article: Male and female reactions to erotic literature.

Journal: *Psychological Reports,* April 1973, *32*(2), 481–482.

■ ■ ■

1158

Test Name: GRUEN TRADITIONAL AMERICAN IDEOLOGY SCALE

Purpose: To assess attitude toward upward mobility.

Number of Items: 41

Format: Example of items: "given the proper start and the proper education, almost every person can reach the goals he sets for himself."

Validity: Internal locus of control individuals scored higher on the scale than externals ($p < .005$).

Author: Fink, H., and Hjelle, L.

Article: Internal vs external control and ideology.

Journal: *Psychological Reports,* December 1973, *33*(3), 967–974.

Related Research: Gruen, W. (1966). Composition and some correlates of the American culture. *Psychological Reports, 18,* 483–486.

■ ■ ■

1159

Test Name: INVENTORY OF FACULTY ATTITUDES

Purpose: To take a current reading of the existing attitudes of community college faculties toward low-ability and inadequately prepared students.

Number of Items: 25

Format: Responses indicated on a 5-point scale from *strongly agree* to *strongly disagree.* 12 of the more descriptive attitude statements are presented.

Author: Spickelmier, D. O.

Article: Community college faculty attitudes toward educationally disadvantaged students.

Journal: *California Journal of Educational Research,* September 1973, *24*(4), 169–174.

■ ■ ■

1160

Test Name: JUNIOR HIGH SCHOOL DESEGREGATION QUESTIONNAIRE

Purpose: To determine changes in student attitudes and feelings toward each other and the desegregated schools.

Number of Items: 19

Format: Each item answered on a 4-point scale. Sample items are presented.

Author: Sachdeva, D.

Article: A measurement of changes in inter-racial student attitudes in desegregated schools.

Journal: *Journal of Educational Research,* May–June 1973, *66*(9), 418–422.

■ ■ ■

1161

Test Name: MARRIAGE AND FAMILY QUESTIONNAIRE

Purpose: To determine marriage and family attitudinal orientations of college students.

Number of Items: 15

Format: For each item respondent checks either *agree, disagree,* or *undecided.* Qualifying comments can be made.

Reliability: Alpha coefficient was .92.

Author: Whatley, A. E., and Appel, V. H.

Article: Convergence of attitudes among college students.

Journal: *Journal of College Student Personnel,* November 1973, *14*(6), 511–516.

■ ■ ■

1162

Test Name: MECHANIZATION SCALE

Purpose: To measure attitude toward technology.

Number of Items: 40

Format: Five scales (eight items each) measuring global attitude, mechanical curiosity, preference for handmade goods, spiritual benefits of technology, human vitalism.

Reliability: Reliability coefficient ranged from .40 to .79 for 5 scales.

Validity: Intercorrelation subscales ranged from .03 to .45.

Author: Goldman, R., et al.

Article: Sex differences in the relationships of attitudes toward technology to choice of field of study.

Journal: *Journal of Counseling Psychology*, September 1973, *20*(5), 412–418.

Related Research: Goldman, R., et al. (1973). Dimensions of attitude toward technology. *Journal of Applied Psychology, 57*, 184–187.

■ ■ ■

1163

Test Name: MICHIGAN STUDENT QUESTIONNAIRE

Purpose: To measure student attitudes.

Number of Items: 60

Format: Includes four areas: teacher attractiveness, fairness of rewards and punishments, teacher competence, interest in school work. Responses are marked on a 4-point scale ranging from *strongly agree* to *strongly disagree*; higher score represented more positive attitudes and perceptions. Examples are provided.

Reliability: Test–retest correlation ranged from .88 to .96.

Validity: Correlations with teacher behaviors ranged from −.52 to .62.

Author: Rosenshine, B.

Article: Teacher behavior and student attitudes revisited.

Journal: *Journal of Educational Psychology*, October 1973, *65*(2), 177–180.

■ ■ ■

1164

Test Name: MODERNITY SCALE

Purpose: To assess modernity attitudes and information in Brazilian children.

Number of Items: 15 (modernity); 5 (information).

Format: Items and basic descriptive statistics are given.

Reliability: Kuder-Richardson formula 20: .570 (modernity) .460

(information); Test–retest reliability was .754 (5 months).

Author: Holsinger, D.

Article: The elementary school as modernizer: A Brazilian study.

Journal: *International Journal of Comparative Sociology*, September–December 1973, *14*(3–4), 180–202.

■ ■ ■

1165

Test Name: MODERNITY SCALE

Purpose: To measure modernity in Tunisian adolescents.

Number of Items: 29

Format: Items are given: 10 subscales are identified.

Reliability: Kuder-Richardson formula 20 for 10 subscales ranged from .68 to .88 with majority from .70 to .79.

Author: Sack, R.

Article: The impact of education on individual modernity in Tunisia.

Journal: *International Journal of Comparative Sociology*, September–December 1973, *14*(3–4), 245–272.

■ ■ ■

1166

Test Name: MOVIES ATTITUDE SCALE

Purpose: To measure attitude toward movies.

Number of Items: 40

Format: Subject agrees or disagrees with each item.

Author: Landy, F. I., and Bates, F.

Article: The noneffect of three variables on mail survey response rate.

Journal: *Journal of Applied Psychology*, August 1973, *58*(1), 147–148.

Related Research: Thurstone, L. L. (1930). A scale for measuring attitude toward the movies. *Journal of Educational Research, 22*, 89–94.

■ ■ ■

1167

Test Name: OPINIONNAIRE ON ATTITUDES TOWARD EDUCATION

Purpose: To measure teachers' attitudes toward child-centered practices as contrasted with subject-matter centeredness.

Number of Items: 50

Format: Likert scale with half of the items stated in a favorable and half in an unfavorable direction concerning child-centered educational practices.

Reliability: Corrected split-half reliability was .82.

Author: Shaw, M. E., et al.

Article: Team teaching: A source of support for teacher attitudes toward teaching.

Journal: *Education*, February–March 1973, *93*(3), 295–300.

Related Research: Lindgren, H. C., & Patton, G. M. (1958). Attitudes of high school and other teachers toward children and current educational methodology. *California Journal of Educational Research, 9*, 80–85.

■ ■ ■

1168

Test Name: PEER EVALUATION AND PREFERENCE TEST

Purpose: To measure attitude of White children toward Black children.

Author: Litcher, J.

Article: Use of pictures of multi-ethnic interaction to change attitudes of White elementary school students toward Blacks.

Journal: *Psychological Reports,* October 1973, *33*(2), 367–372.

Related Research: Koslin, S., et al. (1969). *The effect of race on peer evaluation and preference in primary grade children: An exploratory study.* Princeton, NJ: Educational Testing Service.

■ ■ ■

1169

Test Name: PERSONNEL MANAGERS' ATTITUDES SCALE

Purpose: To measure personnel managers' attitudes toward college placement offices, private employment agencies, interviewing, and related recruiting topics.

Number of Items: 16

Format: Responses to each item on a 5-point scale: 2 (*strongly agree*), 1 (*agree*), 0 (*undecided*), –1 (*disagree*), and –2 (*strongly disagree*).

Author: Dennis, T. L., and Gustafson, D. P.

Article: College campuses vs. employment agencies as sources of manpower.

Journal: *Personnel Journal,* August 1973, *52*(8), 720–724.

■ ■ ■

1170

Test Name: PHARISAIC VIRTUE SCALE

Purpose: To measure self-righteous attitudes.

Format: Variation of the MMPI.

Validity: Correlation with locus of control scale, –356 ($p < .01$).

Author: Powell, A., and Gable, P.

Article: Adult locus of control and self-righteous attitude.

Journal: *Psychological Reports,* 1973, *32*(1), 302.

Related Research: Cook, W., & Medley, D. (1954). Proposed hostility and pharisaic virtue scales for the MMPI. *Journal of Applied Psychology, 38,* 414–418.

■ ■ ■

1171

Test Name: PHYSICAL ACTIVITY ATTITUDE INVENTORY

Purpose: To assess attitude toward physical activity.

Format: 5 categories of ratings: *strongly agree, agree, undecided, disagree, strongly disagree.*

Author: Dowell, L.

Article: Attitudes of parents of athletes and non-athletes toward physical activity.

Journal: *Psychological Reports,* June 1973, *32*(3), 813–814.

Related Research: Wear, C. (1951). The evaluation of attitudes toward physical education as an activity course. *Research Quarterly, 22,* 114–126.

■ ■ ■

1172

Test Name: POLITICAL ATTITUDE QUESTIONNAIRE

Purpose: To assess attitude toward various political issues.

Number of Items: 28

Format: Questionnaire included both demographic and political attitude data: political outlook, hawk–dove, law and order, integration–segregation.

Validity: Wallace supporters were more conservative than Humphrey supporters.

Author: Rawls, J., et al.

Article: Comparisons of Wallace, Nixon and Humphrey supporters along certain demographic, attitudinal and value system dimensions.

Journal: *Psychological Reports,* 1973, *32*(1), 35–39.

■ ■ ■

1173

Test Name: PORTER TEST OF COUNSELOR ATTITUDES

Purpose: To measure counselors' attitudes.

Format: Scales: understanding, supportive, probing, interpretive, evaluative.

Author: Rochester, D.

Article: Counseling attitudes of American and Welsh counselor education students.

Journal: *Counselor Education and Supervision,* September 1973, *13*(1), 41–45.

Related Research: Hopile, W. (1955). The measurement of counselor attitudes. *Journal of Counseling Psychology, 2,* 212–216.

■ ■ ■

1174

Test Name: PREJUDICE MEASURE

Purpose: To measure prejudicial attitudes of pre-school children.

Format: Subjects were asked six questions (e.g., "which one of these children is good [naughty]") and were presented four pictures, two of which were Black and two White; responses were scored 1–5.

Author: Fulcher, D., and Perry, D.

Article: Cooperation and competition in inter-ethnic evaluation in preschool children.

Journal: *Psychological Reports,* 1973, *33*(3), 795–800.

Related Research: Horowitz, E. (1936). The development of attitude toward the Negro. *Archives of Psychology, 194.*

1175

Test Name: PRIMARY PUPILS' READING ATTITUDE INVENTORY

Purpose: To assess attitude toward reading.

Number of Items: 30

Format: Paired comparison of two pictures, one showing a child reading and the other engaged in a favorite recreational activity.

Reliability: Hoyt Total Test: Grade 1, .785, .774; Grade 3, .865, .850.

Validity: Very little change in attitude over summer vacation; multiple correlation of two achievement measures with attitude scores was .203.

Author: Askov, E., and Fishbach, T.

Article: An investigation of primary pupils' attitudes toward reading.

Journal: *Journal of Experimental Education*, Spring 1973, *41*(3), 1–7.

Related Research: Askov, E. (1972). *Assessment of attitudes toward reading in primary pupils* (Technical Report No. 206). Madison: University of Wisconsin—Madison, Wisconsin Research and Development Center for Cognitive Learning.

■ ■ ■

1176

Test Name: PROJECTIVE PREJUDICE TEST

Purpose: To measure degree of prejudice.

Number of Items: 24

Format: Each multiple choice item scored 0, 1, or 2 depending on degree of prejudice. Total range of scores is 0 to 48 with the higher score for greater degree of prejudice.

Reliability: Split-half reliability was .70.

Author: Katz, P. A.

Article: Stimulus predifferentiation and modification of children's racial attitudes.

Journal: *Child Development*, June 1973, *44*(2), 232–237.

■ ■ ■

1177

Test Name: *PSYCHOLOGY TODAY* WOMAN AND MAN SCALE

Purpose: To assess equalitarianism.

Format: Form A and Form B.

Validity: Correlation with Scholastic Aptitude Test Verbal, .16, .20; Math, .20, .12.

Author: Joesting, J., and Joesting, R.

Article: Equalitarianism and Scholastic Aptitude Test scores for college women.

Journal: *Psychological Reports*, April 1973, *32*(2), 664.

Related Research: Tavris, C. (1971). Woman and man—A *Psychology Today* questionnaire. *Psychology Today, 4*, 82–88.

■ ■ ■

1178

Test Name: RELIGIOUS ATTITUDE SCALE

Purpose: To assess religious attitude.

Format: Three scores provided: attitude toward religion, attitude toward church, and combined score.

Validity: No significant prediction of religious attitude from the High School Personality Questionnaire.

Author: Barton, K.

Article: Personality variables as predictors of attitudes toward science and religion.

Journal: *Psychological Reports*, February 1973, *32*(1), 223–228.

Related Research: Hyde, K. (1965). *Religious learning in adolescence*. London: Oliver and Boyd.

■ ■ ■

1179

Test Name: SCHOOL SENTIMENT INDEX

Purpose: To measure student attitudes toward school.

Number of Items: 82

Format: Students self-report by indicating either *strong agreement*, *agreement*, *disagreement*, or *strong disagreement* to each item. Includes five aspects of attitude toward school: teacher, learning, school structure and climate, peer, and general. Examples of each are provided.

Author: Funkand, A. K., et al.

Article: Evaluation of an ethnic studies course taught at Mineral County High School.

Journal: *Education*, November–December 1973, *94*(2), 162–167.

■ ■ ■

1180

Test Name: SEMANTIC DIFFERENTIAL

Purpose: To probe subjects' attitudes toward other national groups.

Format: Eight scales each presenting four steps along a continuum between two bipolar adjectives. Factor analysis produced two factors: evaluative and similarity.

Reliability: Hoyt's analysis of variance, $r = .89$ on all eight scales; evaluative factor, $r = .83$, similarity factor, $r = .48$.

Author: Berg, M., and Wolleat, P.

Article: A comparison of the effects of information and the effects of contact on children's attitudes toward other national groups.

Journal: *California Journal of Educational Research,* November 1973, *24*(5), 200–208.

Related Research: Osgood, C. E., et al. (1957). *The measurement of meaning.* Chicago: University of Illinois Press.

■ ■ ■

1181

Test Name: SEMANTIC DIFFERENTIAL

Purpose: To reflect attitudes toward schools, children, and the aide role.

Number of Items: 10

Format: Nine 7-point evaluative scales reflecting attitudes toward elementary school, teacher, school principal, mental health workers, mental health, children, emotionally disturbed children, slow-learning children, myself, homemaking.

Author: Dorr, D., et al.

Article: Changes in nonprofessional mental health workers' response preference and attitudes as a function of training and supervised field experience.

Journal: *Journal of School Psychology,* Summer 1973, *11*(2), 118–122.

■ ■ ■

1182

Test Name: SHOP AND LABORATORY INVENTORY

Purpose: To assess student's attitude toward a specific period of instruction completed, that is, hour, day, or week.

Format: Negative (unfavorable) and positive (favorable)

instructionally related statements, randomly ordered and placed on forms with a 5-point scale from *strongly agree* to *strongly disagree.*

Reliability: Kuder-Richardson formula 20 coefficient was .92.

Author: Wentling, T. L.

Article: Mastery versus nonmastery instruction with varying test item feedback treatments.

Journal: *Journal of Educational Psychology,* August 1973, *65*(1), 50–58.

Related Research: Finch, C. R. (1969). An instrument to assess student attitude toward instruction. *Journal of Educational Measurement, 6,* 257–258.

■ ■ ■

1183

Test Name: "SHOW ME" TEST

Purpose: To measure attitude of White students toward Blacks.

Author: Litcher, J.

Article: Use of pictures of multi-ethnic interaction to change attitudes of White elementary school students toward Blacks.

Journal: *Psychological Reports,* October 1973, *33*(2), 367–372.

Related Research: Horowitz, L., & Horowitz, R. (1938). Development of social attitudes in children. *Sociometry, 1,* 301–339.

■ ■ ■

1184

Test Name: SOCIAL DISTANCE INDEX

Purpose: To assess children's ethnic attitudes.

Format: Scores from 0 to 18 with the higher score associated with greater prejudice.

Reliability: Split-half reliability was .72.

Author: Katz, P. A.

Article: Stimulus predifferentiation and modification of children's racial attitudes.

Journal: *Child Development,* June 1973, *44*(2), 232–237.

■ ■ ■

1185

Test Name: SOCIAL DISTANCE QUESTIONNAIRE

Purpose: To measure social distance.

Format: Six-point Bogardus scale with 11 categories of racial, ethnic, and nationality groups.

Author: Ames, R. G., et al.

Article: Inquiries into the criteria for evaluating others.

Journal: *Sociology and Social Research,* April 1973, *57*(3), 307–314.

■ ■ ■

1186

Test Name: STEREOTYPE MEASURE

Purpose: To assess stereotype beliefs held by liberals and conservatives.

Number of Items: 171

Time Required: 20 minutes.

Format: Adjective checklist: subject checked off adjectives thought to apply to conservatives and liberals and provided a self-rating of political orientation on a 5-point scale.

Author: Udolf, R.

Article: Liberal and conservative political stereotypes in terms of belief response hierarchies.

Journal: *Psychological Reports,* 1973, *32*(1), 275–284.

1187

Test Name: STRECKLER ATTITUDE TOWARD NEGRO SCALE

Purpose: To assess prejudice.

Validity: Correlation with Adorno E Scale was .98.

Author: Montgomery, R., and Enzie, R.

Article: Predicting behavior in a social influence-situation from attitude-scale measures of prejudice.

Journal: *Psychological Reports,* 1973, *32*(1), 235–240.

Related Research: Streckler, G. (1957). Authoritarian ideology in Negro college students. *Journal of Abnormal and Social Psychology, 54,* 396–399.

• • •

1188

Test Name: STUDENT ATTITUDE QUESTIONNAIRE

Purpose: To measure students' attitudes toward the establishment, drugs, cheating, sex, personal appearance, academic freedom, politics, religion.

Number of Items: 35

Reliability: Split-half reliability corrected for attenuation was .74 for political statements, .76 for religious statements.

Author: Clouse, B.

Article: Attitudes of college students as a function of sex, politics, and religion.

Journal: *Journal of College Student Personnel,* May 1973, *14*(3), 260–264.

• • •

1189

Test Name: STUDENT QUESTIONNAIRE

Purpose: To identify demographic and attitudinal information of college students.

Format: Section 1: questions on students' socioeconomic variables at the time of their high school graduation; Sections 2 and 3: 33 items on academic, social, vocational, or intellectual activities rated on a Likert scale from 1 (*never*) to 5 (*always*). Several items are presented.

Author: Paulson, D. L., Jr., and Stahmann, R. F.

Article: High risk students who graduated: A follow-up study.

Journal: *Journal of College Student Personnel,* March 1973, *14*(2), 149–152.

• • •

1190

Test Name: STUDENT'S ATTITUDES TOWARD WOMEN'S INCREASED PARTICIPATION IN SOCIAL, ECONOMIC, AND POLITICAL SPHERES QUESTIONNAIRE

Purpose: To assess students' attitudes toward women's increased participation in fields typically considered male.

Number of Items: 20

Format: *Yes–no* responses to each question. All items are presented.

Author: Greenberg, S. B.

Article: Attitudes of elementary and secondary students toward increased social, economic, and political participation by women.

Journal: *Journal of Educational Research,* December 1973, *67*(4), 147–148.

• • •

1191

Test Name: SUBSTANCE ABUSE SCALES

Purpose: To assess attitude toward abusers of various substances such as alcohol, LSD.

Number of Items: 60

Format: Six scales: drug users, alcoholics, marijuana users, LSD users, amphetamine users, barbiturate users.

Reliability: Kuder-Richardson formula 20: .659 (alcoholic scale); .757 (amphetamine scale); others: range from .794 to .852.

Validity: Significant association between scales and drug use.

Author: Monroe, J., and English, G.

Article: Ascription of favorable and unfavorable attributes to substance abusers by college age males.

Journal: *Psychological Reports,* June 1973, *32*(3), 875–882.

• • •

1192

Test Name: SUICIDE SEMANTIC DIFFERENTIAL

Purpose: To assess social attitudes toward suicide.

Format: Four concepts (males who committed suicide, males who attempted suicide, females who committed suicide, females who attempted suicide) are rated on social desirability, meek goodness, dependable goodness, dynamic goodness, moral evaluative, social evaluative, potency, activity, and masculinity. Scale scored on 1 to 9 range.

Author: Linehan, M.

Article: Suicide and attempted suicide: Study of perceived sex differences.

Journal: *Perceptual and Motor Skills,* August 1973, *37*(1), 31–34.

• • •

1193

Test Name: SURVEY OF ATTITUDE

Purpose: To assess attitude of parents and students toward a variety of issues.

Number of Items: 18

Format: Respondent checks one of six statements about bussing to attain racial integration, importance of college education, censorship of movies, marijuana legalization, government surveillance.

Author: Good, L., et al.

Article: Assumed attitude similarity and perceived intra-familial communication and understanding.

Journal: *Psychological Reports,* 1973, *32*(1), 3–11.

Related Research: Byrne, D. (1971). *The attraction paradigm.* New York: Academic Press.

■ ■ ■

1194

Test Name: SURVEY OF ATTITUDES

Purpose: To assess attitude of college students toward a variety of subjects (e.g., drinking, science fiction, women in today's society).

Number of Items: 14

Format: Subjects check one of six statements that most closely agrees with their position.

Author: Good, K., and Good, L.

Article: Attitude similarity and attraction to an instructor.

Journal: *Psychological Reports,* August 1973, *33*(1), 335–337.

■ ■ ■

1195

Test Name: TEACHER– ADMINISTRATOR QUESTIONNAIRE

Purpose: To assess attitudes related to five factors influencing the extent of involvement in

projects to improve instruction.

Number of Items: 29

Format: Positive and negative Likert items involving five factors. Four response categories range from *strongly agree* to *strongly disagree.* Examples of each factor are presented.

Reliability: Kuder-Richardson formula-20 Internal Consistency correlations range from .63 to .89 for factors and .87 for total.

Author: Kerr, R. D., et al.

Article: Teacher and administrator attitudes and extent of school involvement in Title III projects.

Journal: *Educational Leadership,* April 1973, *30*(7), 644–648.

■ ■ ■

1196

Test Name: TEACHER ATTITUDE INSTRUMENT

Purpose: To assess teachers' attitude toward the classroom.

Number of Items: 25

Format: Five-point Likert scale (SA to SD); items adapted from MTAI.

Reliability: Test–retest reliability was .76.

Author: Zevin, J.

Article: Training teachers in inquiry.

Journal: *Social Education,* April 1973, *37*(4), 310–316.

■ ■ ■

1197

Test Name: U.S. DEFENSE POLICIES AND POLITICAL PROTEST QUESTIONNAIRE

Purpose: To assess attitude toward defense policy and political protest.

Number of Items: 10

Format: Likert format.

Validity: Attitude change followed participation in the 1969 Washington moratorium protest march.

Author: Abrams, L.

Article: Commitment via public protest as a determinant of attitudes concerning U.S. defense policy and political dissent.

Journal: *Psychological Reports,* 1973, *32*(1), 251–254.

■ ■ ■

1198

Test Name: VERBAL CHECKLIST

Purpose: To assess attitude toward Whites and Blacks.

Number of Items: 48

Format: Figure drawings of Black and White boys; subject ascribed characteristics to one of the drawings.

Author: Lerner, R., and Karson, M.

Article: Racial stereotypes of early adolescent White children.

Journal: *Psychological Reports,* April 1973, *32*(2), 381–382.

Related Research: Lerner, R., & Korn, S. (1972). The development of body-build stereotypes in males. *Child Development, 43,* 908–920.

■ ■ ■

1199

Test Name: WALTHER WORK-RELEVANT ATTITUDES INVENTORY

Purpose: To identify factors related to work adjustment and satisfaction.

Number of Items: 26

Time Required: 10–15 minutes.

Format: Designed for program

evaluation and planning with the disadvantaged.

Author: VanDoren, R. (Ed.).

Article: Manpower, human assessment and the disadvantaged.

Journal: *American Vocational Journal,* January 1973, *48*(1), 86–100.

■ ■ ■

1200

Test Name: WOMEN'S LIBERATION QUESTIONNAIRE

Purpose: To assess attitudes toward the principles of women's rights and the role of women in modern American society.

Number of Items: 20

Format: Statements rated on 6-point Likert scale ranging from *strongly agree* to *strongly disagree.* A few items are presented.

Reliability: Spearman-Brown split half reliability was .82.

Author: Miller, T. W.

Article: Male self-esteem and attitudes toward women's roles.

Journal: *Journal of College Student Personnel,* September 1973, *14*(5), 402–406.

Related Research: Bove, M., & Miller, T. (1970). *Women's Liberation Questionnaire.* Unpublished senior project, Rosary Hill College, Buffalo, NY.

■ ■ ■

1201

Test Name: WORLD-MINDED ATTITUDES SCALE

Purpose: To measure world-minded attitudes.

Author: Berg, M., and Wolleat, P.

Article: A comparison of the effects of information and the effect of contact on children's attitudes toward other national groups.

Journal: *California Journal of Educational Research,* November 1973, *24*(5), 200–208.

Related Research: Sampson, D. L., & Smith, H. (1957). A scale to measure world-minded attitudes. *Journal of Social Psychology, 45,* 99–105.

1202

Test Name: YOUTH CORRECTIONAL CENTER QUESTIONNAIRE

Purpose: To measure specific attitudes of youths in a correctional center.

Number of Items: 37

Format: Includes six scales: coercive power, cooperative attitude, cooperative norm, work values of the elite, work values of subject, and leadership. Some examples are presented.

Reliability: Cronbach's alphas ranged from .59 to .84 (*N* = 97).

Validity: Homogeneity ratios ranged from .19 to .57 (*N* = 97).

Author: Bigelow, D. A., and Driscoll, R. H.

Article: Effect of minimizing coercion on the rehabilitation of prisoners.

Journal: *Journal of Applied Psychology,* 1973, *57*(1), 10–14.

CHAPTER 7
Behavior

1203

Test Name: ACTIVITY LEVEL QUESTIONNAIRE

Purpose: To provide a means of qualifying activity level and estimating the effectiveness of drug treatment for hyperactivity.

Number of Items: 32

Format: Items rated on a 3-point scale from *none* (0 points) to *yes–very much* (2 points) for a number of different situations.

Author: Willerman, L., and Plomin, R.

Article: Activity level in children and their parents.

Journal: *Child Development,* December 1973, *44*(4), 854–858.

Related Research: Werry, J. S. (1970). Hyperactivity. In C. G. Costello (Ed.), *Symptoms of psychopathology.* New York: Wiley, 397–417.

Willerman, L. (1973). Activity level and hyperactivity in twins. *Child Development, 44,* 288–293.

■ ■ ■

1204

Test Name: AGE OF INITIAL DRUG USE QUESTIONNAIRE

Purpose: To determine age at which certain drugs were first used.

Number of Items: 14

Format: Fourteen drugs are listed: respondent records age at which each drug was taken.

Author: Baer, D., and Corroda, J.

Article: Age of initial drug use and

subsequent preference for other drugs.

Journal: *Psychological Reports,* June 1973, *23*(3), 963.

■ ■ ■

1205

Test Name: AUTOMATED PATIENT BEHAVIOR CHECKLIST

Purpose: To evaluate psychiatric patient status on a day-to-day basis.

Number of Items: 47

Format: Each item includes a key word and an explicit behaviorally oriented definition. There are five alternative response categories: unable to rate the behavior, patient did not display this behavior, behavior minimally observed, behavior definitely observed, behavior observed in a severe degree. Includes four factors: acting out, depression-withdrawal, degree of disturbance, adaptation to the ward. Items are presented.

Author: Morgan, D. W., et al.

Article: An automated patient behavior checklist.

Journal: *Journal of Applied Psychology,* December 1973, *58*(3), 393–396.

■ ■ ■

1206

Test Name: BEHAVIORAL MATURITY SCALE

Purpose: To describe academic behaviors.

Number of Items: 6

Format: Teacher rating of students' interest in reading, persistence, and so forth. Items were rated on a 1–5 scale.

Validity: Correlations for total Academic Factor Score with teacher grades were .67, .60, .60 (Kim et al., 1968).

Author: Skovholt, T., et al.

Article: Birth order and academic behavior in first grade.

Journal: *Psychological Reports,* April 1973, *32*(2), 395–398.

Related Research: Kim, Y., et al. (1968). Social maturity, achievement, and basic ability. *Educational and Psychological Measurement, 28,* 535–543.

■ ■ ■

1207

Test Name: BEHAVIORAL OBSERVATION SYSTEM

Purpose: To assess behaviors of children watching "Sesame Street" on television.

Format: Video tapes were analyzed for a variety of behaviors, including attention, modeling, amusement, body movement, various verbalizations: behavior categories were determined from viewing tapes rather than from a priori categories.

Author: Sproull, N.

Article: Visual attention, modeling behaviors, and other verbal and non verbal meta-communication of pre-kindergarten children viewing Sesame Street.

Journal: *American Educational*

Research Journal, Spring 1973, *10*(2), 101–114.

. . .

1208

Test Name: CINCINNATI AUTONOMY TEST BATTERY (CATB)

Purpose: To assess curiosity, exploratory behavior, and innovative behavior.

Author: Feitelson, D., and Ross, G.

Article: The neglected factor—play.

Journal: *Human Development,* 1973, *16*(3), 202–223.

Related Research: Banta, T. (1968). *Tests for the evaluation of early childhood education: The Cincinnati Autonomy Test Battery (CATB).* Unpublished manuscript, University of Cincinnati.

. . .

1209

Test Name: COGNITIVE COMPONENTS SYSTEM

Purpose: Differentiates content behaviors of teachers and students into association, description, conceptual, generalization, and explanation levels.

Format: Data expressed as percentages of total units of cognitive behavior in each category.

Reliability: Estimates of stability from interclass correlations ranged from .16 to .80.

Author: Emmer, E. T., and Peck, R. F.

Article: Dimensions of classroom behavior.

Journal: *Journal of Educational Psychology,* April 1973, *64*(2), 223–240.

Related Research: Emmer, E. T., & Albrecht, I. D. (1970). *The*

cognitive components system manual. Austin: University of Texas, Research and Development Center for Teacher Education.

. . .

1210

Test Name: COLLEGE STUDENT DRUG USE QUESTIONNAIRE

Purpose: To determine drug abuse and attitudes toward drugs.

Number of Items: 112

Time Required: 20 minutes.

Format: Multiple choice items of three general types: classification, biographical information, drug abuse and attitudes toward drugs. A sample item is presented.

Author: Strimbu, J. L., et al.

Article: Sex differences in college student drug use.

Journal: *Journal of College Student Personnel,* November 1973, *14*(6), 507–510.

Related Research: Schoenfeldt, L. F. (1970, March). *Life experience as a moderator in the prediction of educational criteria.* Paper presented at the meeting of the American Educational Research Association, Minneapolis, MN.

Louria, D. B. (1968). *The drug scene.* New York: McGraw-Hill.

. . .

1211

Test Name: COPING ANALYSIS SCHEDULE FOR EDUCATIONAL SETTINGS

Purpose: Codes individual student behaviors including negative attention-getting, passive aggression, self-directed activity, attentiveness, observation, cooperative behavior.

Format: For observation of individual students; data expressed as a percentage of the total time spent in each category.

Reliability: Estimates of stability from interclass correlations ranged from .10 to .71.

Author: Emmer, E. T., and Peck, R. F.

Article: Dimensions of classroom behavior.

Journal: *Journal of Educational Psychology,* April 1973, *64*(2), 223–240.

Related Research: Spaulding, R. L. (1970). *Classroom behavior analysis and treatment.* San Jose State College.

. . .

1212

Test Name: DELAY TOLERANCE INVENTORY

Purpose: To select subjects with high and low tolerance for delay.

Number of Items: 41

Validity: No significant difference between low and high tolerance groups on aggression following an actual delay.

Author: Buss, A.

Article: Delay of frustration and aggression.

Journal: *Psychological Reports,* June 1973, *32*(3), 1074.

. . .

1213

Test Name: DELINQUENCY QUESTIONNAIRE

Purpose: To assess extent of delinquent behavior among adolescent Swiss boys.

Number of Items: 23

Format: Each item represented a violation of Swiss law; subject responded regarding extent of violation (*never, once or twice, three or four, five or more violations*).

Validity: Very few significant relationships between social class and self-reported delinquency.

Author: Casparis, J., and Vaz, E.

Article: Social class and self-reported delinquent acts among Swiss boys.

Journal: *International Journal of Comparative Sociology.* March–June 1973, *14*(1–2) 47–58.

• • •

1214

Test Name: DRUG INVOLVEMENT SCALE

Purpose: To obtain measures of extent of drug involvement.

Format: Ratings from 1 (*no involvement*) to 7 (*heavy involvement*).

Reliability: Interrater reliability based on clinician application of scales to 100 case studies was .97.

Validity: Correlations were reported with four drug ratings obtained from four other scales: Marijuana Stage Scale, $r = .80$; Marijuana Frequency Scale, $r = .46$; Pharmacological Rating, $r = .04$, Drug Number Scale, $r = .90$ (all $p < .001$).

Author: Kahn, M., and Holroyd, K.

Article: Comparability of drug abuse rating scales.

Journal: *Psychological Reports,* December 1973, *33*(3), 699–702.

Related Research: Holroyd, K., & Kahn, M. (1971). *Behavioral and personality dimensions related to undergraduate drug use.* Paper presented to the meeting of the Southeastern Psychological Association, Miami, FL.

• • •

1215

Test Name: DRUG NUMBER SCALE

Purpose: To assess extent of drug use.

Format: Based on the number of illicit drugs used.

Validity: Correlation with Drug Involvement Scale was .90 ($p < .001$).

Author: Kahn, M., and Holroyd, K.

Article: Comparability of drug abuse rating scales.

Journal: *Psychological Reports,* December 1973, *33*(3), 699–702.

• • •

1216

Test Name: FRUSTRATION MEASURE

Purpose: To assess response to frustration by parents and children.

Format: Semi-projective technique: subjects were presented a picture and description of a frustrating situation and their reaction (aggression, dependency, withdrawal) was recorded; there were adult and child forms.

Validity: Significant differences between parents who were and were not aggressive, dependent, withdrawing were found in children's aggression, dependence, and withdrawal.

Author: Sethi, R.

Article: Parent–child similarity in choice of responses to frustrating situations.

Journal: *Psychological Reports,* June 1973, *32*(3), 1227–1233.

Related Research: Revelle, C. (1963). *Generalization of frustration reactions following exposure to models.* Unpublished master's thesis, Stanford University.

• • •

1217

Test Name: FULLER AFFECTIVE INTERACTION RECORDS (FAIR)

Purpose: To provide categories for describing interpersonal affective teacher and pupil behaviors and for denoting content and procedure.

Format: Categories include: criticizes, delves, manages, owns up, values, nurtures, confirms. Equal numbers of teacher and student behaviors. Data expressed as percentages of time observed in each category.

Reliability: Estimates of stability from intraclass correlations ranged from .15 to .83.

Author: Emmer, E. T., and Peck, R. F.

Article: Dimensions of classroom behavior.

Journal: *Journal of Educational Psychology,* April 1973, *64*(2), 223–240.

Related Research: Fuller, F. F. (1970). *FAIR system manual.* Austin: University of Texas, Research and Development Center for Teacher Education.

• • •

1218

Test Name: GAMES INVENTORY SCALES

Purpose: To measure play patterns in normal and gender-deviant boys.

Number of Items: 64

Format: Four scales: feminine, preschool games; masculine, nonathletic games; athletic games: all items in scales 1–3. All items are presented.

Reliability: Kuder-Richardson formula 20 values were .85, .74, .83, and .72 for Scales 1–3 and the composite. Coefficients theta for scales 1–3 were .97, .94, .93.

Validity: Correlations between the scales of the Games Inventory and the factors of the Gender Behavior Inventory for Boys ranged from

−.43 to .41. Correlations between the Games Inventory Scales and clinicians' rankings ranged from −.65 to .66.

Author: Bates, J. E., and Bentler, P. M.

Article: Play activities of normal and effeminate boys.

Journal: *Developmental Psychology*, July 1973, *9*(1), 20–27.

• • •

1219

Test Name: GENDER BEHAVIOR INVENTORY FOR BOYS

Purpose: To differentiate normal and effeminate boys.

Format: Four factors: effeminacy, extraversion, behavior disturbance, mother orientation, and neatness.

Validity: Correlations between the scales of the Games Inventory and the factors of the Gender Behavior Inventory for Boys ranged from −.43 to .41.

Author: Bates, J. E., and Bentler, P. M.

Article: Play activities of normal and effeminate boys.

Journal: *Developmental Psychology*, July 1973, *9*(1), 20–27.

• • •

1220

Test Name: HEALTH HABITS SCALE

Purpose: To assess students' current involvement with drugs, motivation for using drugs, the circumstances in which they abuse drugs, and sources of drugs.

Number of Items: 35

Author: Swisher, J. D., et al.

Article: Four approaches to drug abuse prevention among college students.

Journal: *Journal of College Student Personnel*, May 1973, *14*(3), 231–235.

• • •

1221

Test Name: INTERPERSONAL AGGRESSION SCALE

Purpose: To measure delinquent involvement in interpersonal aggression.

Number of Items: 8

Format: Respondents indicate the extent (from *none to one* to *more than ten times*) since the beginning of high school that they have committed certain acts of interpersonal aggression. All items are presented.

Reliability: Coefficients of reproducibility were .89 and .94.

Validity: Bivariate correlations with delinquent peer associations and delinquent involvement, .32; with delinquent attitudes and delinquent involvement, .14; with delinquent attitudes and delinquent peer associations, .50.

Author: Liska, A. E.

Article: Causal structures underlying the relationship between delinquent involvement and delinquent peers.

Journal: *Sociology and Social Research*, October 1973, *58*(1), 23–36.

Related Research: Arnold, W. R. (1965). Continuities in research: Scaling delinquent behavior, *Social problems, 13,* 59–65.

• • •

1222

Test Name: MARIJUANA FREQUENCY SCALE

Purpose: To assess number of times marijuana is used per week.

Validity: Correlation with Drug Involvement Scale was .64 (*p* <

.001). Correlation with Marijuana Stage Scale was .85 (*p* < .001).

Author: Kahn, M., and Holroyd, K.

Article: Comparability of drug abuse rating scales.

Journal: *Psychological Reports,* December 1973, *33*(3), 699–702.

• • •

1223

Test Name: MARIJUANA STAGE SCALE

Purpose: To rate degree of involvement with marijuana over several stages.

Format: Five-point scale: rates degree of involvement over stages– initial, casual, occasional, regular.

Validity: Correlation with Marijuana Frequency Scale was .85 (*p* < .001).

Author: Kahn, M., and Holroyd. K.

Article: Comparability of drug abuse rating scales.

Journal: *Psychological Reports,* December 1973, *33*(3), 699–702.

Related Research: Sadava, S. (1972). Stages of college drug use: A methodological contribution to cross sectional study. *Journal of Consulting and Clinical Psychology, 38,* 298.

• • •

1224

Test Name: OBJECT CLASSIFICATION TEST

Purpose: To assess overinclusive thinking in schizophrenic patients.

Validity: With Lovibond Object Sorting Test, rho was .60.

Author: Prior, M.

Article: Overinclusions in chronic schizophrenia.

Journal: *Psychological Reports,* April 1973, *32*(2), 426.

Related Research: Payne, R. (1962). An object classification test as a measure of overinclusive thinking in schizophrenic patients. *British Journal of Social and Clinical Psychology, 1,* 213–221.

■ ■ ■

1225

Test Name: OPPOSITIONALITY SCALE

Purpose: To assess extent of oppositional behavior.

Format: Semantic differential type. Subjects were rated by supervisor on six separate scales, each 1–7.

Validity: Correlations with Rorschach Whitespace scores were .46 and .53 (*p* < .01).

Author: Stein, M.

Article: An empirical validation of the relation between Rorschach Whitespace and oppositionality.

Journal: *Perceptual and Motor Skills,* October 1973, *37*(2), 375–381.

■ ■ ■

1226

Test Name: PATHOLOGICAL BEHAVIOR RATING SCALE

Purpose: To assess "sick" behavior in a mental hospital.

Format: Observational system: recorded, in 30-s intervals, any behavior that would be inappropriate outside of the hospital.

Reliability: Correlation between two observers was .98.

Author: Dana, R., and Barling, P.

Article: Structured treatment environments and pathological behaviors.

Journal: *Psychological Reports,* June 1973, *32*(3), 991–994.

1227

Test Name: PERCEPTION OF CLASSROOM BEHAVIOR SCALE

Purpose: To permit students to indicate the frequency with which various kinds of classroom behavior had occurred during the semester.

Number of Items: 25

Format: Included five factors: teacher skill, student involvement, teacher support, negative affect, teacher control. Responses were recorded on a 5-point scale from 5 (*almost always occurred*) to 1 (*almost never occurred*).

Validity: Product–moment correlations with traits ranged from –.63 to .80.

Author: Costin, F., and Grush, J. E.

Article: Personality correlates of teacher–student behavior in the college classroom.

Journal: *Journal of Educational Psychology,* August 1973, *65*(1), 35–44.

Related Research: Costin, F. (1968). A graduate course in the teaching of psychology: Description and evaluation. *Journal of Teacher Education, 19,* 425–432.

Costin, F. (1971). An empirical test of the "teacher-centered" dichotomy. *Journal of Educational Psychology, 62,* 410–412.

■ ■ ■

1228

Test Name: PHARMACOLOGICAL RATING SCALE

Purpose: To provide information on types of drug use.

Format: Four-point classification system (*no use, cannabis use,*

hallucinogen use, and *opiate use*).

Validity: Correlation with Drug Involvement Scale was .70 (*p* < .001).

Author: Kahn, M., and Holroyd, K.

Article: Comparability of drug abuse rating scales.

Journal: *Psychological Reports,* December 1973, *33*(3), 699–702.

■ ■ ■

1229

Test Name: PICTURE TEST OF FRUSTRATION RESPONSE

Purpose: To assess response to frustration in preschool children.

Time Required: 15 minutes.

Format: Cartoon format for 18 picture sets presented with verbal comment by the examiner.

Reliability: Internal reliabilities for total sample were .58, .75, and .43 for aggression, prosocial, and avoidance variables, respectively.

Validity: Correlations with teacher global ratings were not impressive; moderate to low correlations with mother rating.

Author: VonDracek, F., et al.

Article: A non-verbal technique for assessing frustration responses in pre-school children.

Journal: *Journal of Personality Assessment,* 1973, *37*(4), 355–362.

■ ■ ■

1230

Test Name: POST-HOSPITAL BEHAVIOR QUESTIONNAIRE

Purpose: To measure changes in children's behavior after hospitalization.

Number of Items: 27

Format: Mother responds to each item using one of five response alternatives.

Author: Vernon, D.T.A.

Article: Use of modeling to modify children's responses to a natural, potentially stressful situation.

Journal: *Journal of Applied Psychology,* December 1973, *58*(3), 351–356.

Related Research: Vernon, D.T.A., et al. (1966). Changes in children's behavior after hospitalization. *American Journal of the Diseases of Children, 3,* 581–593.

■ ■ ■

1231

Test Name: POWER USAGE CHECKLIST

Purpose: To evaluate power use by supervisors.

Number of Items: 27

Format: Checklist including four categories of power usage, one category reflecting the supervisor's attempt to get help from others in dealing with the subordinate, and an item for those supervisors who did nothing about the problem subordinate. All items presented.

Author: Kipnis, D., et al.

Article: Effects of emotional arousal on the use of supervised coercion with Black and union employees.

Journal: *Journal of Applied Psychology,* February 1973, *57*(1), 38–43.

■ ■ ■

1232

Test Name: PROBLEM-ATTACK BEHAVIOR INVENTORY

Purpose: To gather behavior descriptions of high school principals from their teachers.

Number of Items: 15

Format: Responses are made on a 7-point frequency scale. Includes two dimensions: problem-

recognition behavior and group participation behavior. Examples are presented.

Validity: Correlation coefficient with Learning Climate Inventory was .703.

Author: Hoyle, J. R.

Article: Are open-space high schools more open?

Journal: *Journal of Educational Research,* December 1973, *67*(4), 153–156.

Related Research: Randall, R. S. (1964). *The development and testing of an instrument to describe problem-attack behavior of high school principals.* Unpublished doctoral dissertation, University of Texas, Austin.

■ ■ ■

1233

Test Name: QUESTIONNAIRE OF RESPONSE TO CERTAIN AUDITORY STIMULI

Purpose: To assess experience of having "teeth set on edge," for example, by the sound of a shovel on concrete.

Number of Items: 7

Format: Open-ended questionnaire.

Author: Delin, P., and Winefield, A.

Article: On having the teeth set on edge: Preliminary inquiry.

Journal: *Psychological Reports,* October 1973, *33*(2), 379–382.

■ ■ ■

1234

Test Name: RETTIG BEHAVIOR PREDICTION SCALE

Purpose: To measure risk-taking.

Number of Items: 16

Format: Involves questions on some unethical behaviors.

Author: Chapko, M.

Article: Self-other discrepancy in ethical risk taking.

Journal: *Psychological Reports,* June 1973, *32*(3), 706.

Related Research: Rettig, S. (1966). Group discussion and predicted ethical risk taking. *Journal of Personality and Social Psychology, 3,* 629–633.

■ ■ ■

1235

Test Name: RHEINGOLD SOCIAL RESPONSIVENESS SCALE

Purpose: To assess social responsiveness in babies.

Format: Observational rating on "immediacy and extent of socially positive and socially negative behaviors ... in four standardized situations" (p. 401).

Author: Beckwith, L.

Article: Relationship between infants' social behavior and their mothers' behavior.

Journal: *Child Development,* June 1972, *43*(2), 397–411.

Related Research: Rheingold, H. (1956). The modification of social responsiveness in institutional babies. *Monographs of the Society for Research in Child Development, 21*(Serial No. 63).

■ ■ ■

1236

Test Name: ROLE-TAKING TEST

Purpose: To measure children's role-taking ability.

Format: An experimenter presents a seven-picture cartoon sequence suggesting an obvious story, which the child tells. A second experimenter enters, three pictures are removed, which now suggests a different story, and the child pretends to take the first experimenter's place and tells the story to the second experimenter.

Author: Hollos, M., and Cowan, P. A.

Article: Social isolation and cognitive development: Logical operations and role-taking abilities in three Norwegian social settings.

Journal: *Child Development,* September 1973, *44*(3), 630–641.

Related Research: Flavell, J. H. (1968). *The development of role-taking and communication skills in children.* New York: Wiley.

■ ■ ■

1237

Test Name: SCHAEFER CLASSROOM BEHAVIOR INVENTORY

Purpose: To measure preschool social-emotional functioning.

Format: Includes three factors: extraversion–introversion; adjustment–maladjustment; high–low task orientation.

Reliability: Interrater correlations were .50 (Kohn & Rosman, 1973).

Validity: With Peterson Problem Checklist Factor I, $r = .64$; with Factor II, $r = .76$.

Author: Kohn, M., and Rosman, B. L.

Article: Cross-situational and longitudinal stability of social-emotional functioning in young children.

Journal: *Child Development,* December 1973, *44*(4), 721–727.

Related Research: Kohn, M., & Rosman, B. L. (1973). Cognitive functioning in five-year-old boys as related to social-emotional and background-demographic variables. *Developmental Psychology, 8,* 277–294.

Kohn, M., & Rosman, B. L. (1974). Social-emotional, cognitive, and demographic

determinants of poor school achievement: Implication for a strategy of intervention. *Journal of Educational Psychology, 66,* 267–276.

Schaefer, E. S., et al. (1965). *Development of a classroom behavior checklist and factor analysis of children's school behavior in the U.S. and the Netherlands.* Unpublished manuscript.

Schaefer, E. S., & Aaronson, M. R. (1966). *Classroom behavior inventory: Preschool to primary.* Unpublished manuscript.

■ ■ ■

1238

Test Name: SCHOOL BEHAVIOR PROFILE

Purpose: To measure behavior adjustment.

Format: Classroom teacher rates child's in behavior five areas: general characteristics, language and thought, intrapersonal behavior, interpersonal behavior, problem behavior.

Author: Dietrich, C.

Article: An experimental analysis of perceptual motor approaches to learning problems.

Journal: *Education,* April–May 1973, *93*(4), 381–392.

■ ■ ■

1239

Test Name: SICK ROLE QUESTIONNAIRE

Purpose: To assess tendency to adopt the "sick role" as an adaptative response.

Number of Items: 3

Format: Four alternatives to each item: subjects were given a hypothetical situation and were asked whether they would seek medical assistance.

Validity: Significant differences were found between first-born (greater tendency to play role) and later-born subjects.

Author: Franklin, B.

Article: Birth order and tendency to "adopt the sick role."

Journal: *Psychological Reports,* October 1973, *33*(2), 437–438.

Related Research: Mechanic, D., & Volkart, E. (1961). Stress, illness behavior and the sick role. *American Sociological Review, 26,* 51–58.

■ ■ ■

1240

Test Name: STUDENT BEHAVIOR OBSERVATION INSTRUMENT

Purpose: To assess extent of peer tutoring in a classroom.

Format: Time sampling was used; subject behavior was classified in one of six categories (categories were defined).

Reliability: There was 80% to 85% agreement.

Author: DeVries, D., and Edwards, K.

Article: Learning games and student teams: Their effects on classroom process.

Journal: *American Educational Research Journal,* Fall 1973, *10*(4), 307–318.

■ ■ ■

1241

Test Name: SUPERVISORY BEHAVIOR DESCRIPTION QUESTIONNAIRE

Purpose: To measure the dimensions of consideration and initiating structure.

Number of Items: 48

Format: Each item was responded to on a 5-point scale: *always,* *often, occasionally, seldom, never.* All items are presented.

Reliability: Split-half reliability for "consideration" was .92 and for "structure," .87.

Author: Tscheulin, D.

Article: Leader behavior measurement in German industry.

Journal: *Journal of Applied Psychology,* February 1973, *57*(1), 28–31.

Related Research: Fleishman, E. A. (1951). *Relationship between supervisory behavior and leadership climate.* Columbus: Ohio State University Personnel Research Board.

Fleishman, E. A. (1953). The description of supervisory behavior. *Journal of Applied Psychology, 37,* 1–6.

■ ■ ■

1242

Test Name: TEST BEHAVIOR INVENTORY

Purpose: To assess preschool test behavior.

Number of Items: 26

Format: Includes two factors: confident-friendly versus anxious-withdrawn; attentive-cooperative versus distractible-disruptive. All items are presented.

Author: Kohn, M., and Rosman, B. L.

Article: Cross-situational and longitudinal stability of social-emotional functioning in young children.

Journal: *Child Development,* December 1973, *44*(4), 721–727.

■ ■ ■

1243

Test Name: TEST OF FANTASY

Purpose: To assess fantasy.

Format: Subjects are shown a 2.5 minute film of geometric figures and asked to fantasize about what happened in the film.

Validity: Correlation with a "regression in the service of the ego" measure was .321 ($p < .01$).

Author: Maini, S.

Article: Personality and cognitive differences between an original and non-original group.

Journal: *Perceptual and Motor Skills,* October 1973, *37*(2), 555–563.

Related Research: Heider, F., & Simmel, M. (1944). An experimental study of apparent behavior. *American Journal of Psychology, 57,* 243–259.

■ ■ ■

1244

Test Name: THEFT SCALE

Purpose: To measure delinquent involvement in theft.

Number of Items: 5

Format: Respondents are asked to indicate the extent (from 0 or 1 to more than 10 times) since the beginning of high school that they have committed certain acts of theft. All items are presented.

Reliability: Coefficients of reproducibility were .94 and .93.

Validity: For delinquent peer associations and delinquent involvement, $r = .20$; delinquent attitudes and delinquent involvement, $r = .26$; delinquent attitudes and delinquent peer associations, $r = .09$.

Author: Liska, A. E.

Article: Causal structures underlying the relationship between delinquent involvement and delinquent peers.

Journal: *Sociology and Social*

Research, October 1973, *58*(1), 23–36.

Related Research: Dentler, A. R., & Monroe, L. J. (1961). Social correlates of early adolescent theft. *American Sociological Review, 26,* 733–743.

■ ■ ■

1245

Test Name: VANDALISM SCALE

Purpose: To measure delinquent involvement in vandalism.

Number of Items: 8

Format: Respondents indicate the extent (from 0 or 1, to more than 10 times) since the beginning of high school that they have committed certain acts of vandalism. All items are presented.

Reliability: Coefficients of reproducibility were .91 and .92.

Validity: For delinquent peer associations and delinquent involvement, $r = .22$; delinquent attitudes and delinquent involvement, $r = .05$; delinquent attitudes and delinquent peer associations, $r = .38$.

Author: Liska, A. E.

Article: Causal structures underlying the relationship between delinquent involvement and delinquent peers.

Journal: *Sociology and Social Research,* October 1973, *58*(1), 23–36.

Related Research: Arnold, W. R. (1965). Continuities in research; scaling delinquent behavior. *Social Problems, 13,* 59–65.

■ ■ ■

1246

Test Name: WORK REQUIREMENTS RATING SCALE

Purpose: To identify the importance of vocationally related behavior.

Number of Items: 47

Format: Questionnaire for use with the disadvantaged.

Author: Van Doren, R. (Ed.).

Article: Manpower, human assessment and the disadvantaged.

Journal: *American Vocational Journal,* January 1973, *48*(1), 86–100.

...

CHAPTER 8
Communication

1247

Test Name: ARBITRATION PROCEDURE QUESTIONNAIRE

Purpose: To obtain information regarding the arbitration procedure as perceived by respondents.

Number of Items: 7

Format: Responses are yes–no or multiple-choice; all items are presented.

Author: Glasser, J.

Article: An analysis of the arbitration procedure.

Journal: *Personnel Journal*, November 1973, *52*(11), 970–976.

...

1248

Test Name: BLUMBERG SUPERVISOR INTERACTION SYSTEM

Purpose: To measure supervisor-teacher interaction.

Format: 10 categories of supervisor behavior, 5 of teacher behavior recorded from videotaped interaction.

Author: Douglass, J., and Pfeiffer, J.

Article: Changes of supervisor behavior in a microteaching practicum.

Journal: *Journal of Experimental Education*, Winter 1973, *42*(2), 36–41.

Related Research: Blumberg, A. *System for analyzing supervisor teacher interaction.* Unpublished manuscript. Philadelphia, PA: Temple University.

...

1249

Test Name: CARKHUFF'S DISCRIMINATION INDEXES

Purpose: To determine measures of discrimination ability.

Author: Emener, W. G., Jr.

Article: A practicum laboratory training experience.

Journal: *Counselor Education and Supervision*, March 1973, *12*(3), 213–220.

Related Research: Carkhuff, R. R. (1969). *Helping and human relations: 1. Selection and training.* New York: Holt, Rinehart & Winston.

...

1250

Test Name: DEFENSIVE-NONDEFENSIVE COMMUNICATION BEHAVIOR RATING SCALE

Purpose: To distinguish between defensive and non-defensive communication behavior.

Format: 7-point Likert scale used by raters of videotape.

Reliability: Interrater reliability was .94.

Author: Guttman, M.

Article: Reduction of the defensive behavior of counselor trainees during counseling supervision.

Journal: *Counselor Education and Supervision*, June 1973, *12*(4), 294–299.

Related Research: Gibb, J. (1961). Defensive communication. *Journal of Communication, 11*, 141–148.

...

1251

Test Name: DYADIC SYSTEM

Purpose: To code the interchange or contact between teacher and student.

Format: Variables describing the interchange between teacher and student are determined by a sequential coding procedure.

Reliability: Estimates of stability from interclass correlations ranged from .13 to .66.

Author: Emmer, E. T., and Peck, R. F.

Article: Dimensions of classroom behavior.

Journal: *Journal of Educational Psychology*, April 1973, *64*(2), 223–240.

Related Research: Brophy, J. E., & Good, T. L. (1970). Teacher–child dyadic interaction: A manual for coding classroom behavior. Austin: University of Texas, Research and Development Center for Teacher Education.

...

1252

Test Name: FELDSTEIN AFFECT JUDGMENT TEST

Purpose: To measure sensitivity to affective expression.

Number of Items: 32

Format: Tape recorded neutral passage read to convey affective tone (anger, nervousness, etc.). Accuracy based on congruence of subjects' judgment to actors' intention.

Validity: With Embedded Figures Test, $r = .29$; Rod and Frame, $r = -.39$ ($p < .05$); EFT and RFT, $r = .40$ ($p < .05$).

Author: Wolitzky, D.

Article: Cognitive controls and person perception.

Journal: *Perceptual and Motor Skills*, April 1973, *36*(2), 619–623.

Related Research: Feldstein, S. (1964). Vocal patterning of emotional expression. In J. H. Masserman (Ed.), *Science and Psychoanalysis, VII*. New York: Grune & Stratton, 193–208.

■ ■ ■

1253

Test Name: FIELD INTERACTION SCALE

Purpose: To measure interaction between counselor and client.

Format: Listing of observable behaviors exhibited by counselors: Includes 14 items regarding behaviors of counselors toward client; open and close interview, clarifying and exploring, offering assistance, and so forth.

Reliability: Two judges, $r = .81$.

Author: Field, T.

Article: Sex and status of models.

Journal: *Journal of Experimental Education*, Winter 1973, *42*(2), 42–47.

■ ■ ■

1254

Test Name: GROUP THERAPIST ORIENTATION SCALE

Purpose: To assess group leaders' opinions on appropriateness of therapist self-disclosure.

Number of Items: 20

Format: Items are rated on a Likert scale.

Author: Dies, R. R.

Article: Group therapist self-disclosure: An evaluation by clients.

Journal: *Journal of Counseling Psychology*, July 1973, *20*(4), 344–348.

Related Research: Dies, R. R. (1972). Group therapist self-disclosure: Development and validation of a scale [summary]. *Proceedings of the 80th Annual Convention of the American Psychological Association, 7*, 369–370.

■ ■ ■

1255

Test Name: INSTRUCTOR COGNITIVE OPERATION INDEX

Purpose: To examine a teacher's total verbal pattern.

Format: Includes 12 categories: expository modes of instruction—stating, explaining, interpreting, defining, opining, justifying; and examinatory modes of instruction—information, comprehension, application, analysis, synthesis, judgment.

Author: Hogg, J. H.

Article: Development of verbal behavior through cognitive awareness training.

Journal: *Journal of Educational Research*, September 1973, *67*(1), 9–12.

Related Research: Searles, J. E. (1970). Verbal styles of teachers in a Latin American Society. *Pennsylvania State University Studies: Vol. 30. Institute for the Arts and Humanistic Studies*. University Park: Pennsylvania State University.

1256

Test Name: INTERPERSONAL RELATIONSHIP RATING SCALE

Purpose: Designed to test for outcomes in growth experiences and to measure attitudes and/or behaviors in individuals' relationships with others and self-perception.

Number of Items: 24

Format: 7-point numerical rating scale.

Author: Arbes, B. H., and Hubbell, R. N.

Article: Packaged impact: A structured communication skills workshop.

Journal: *Journal of Counseling Psychology*, July 1973, *20*(4), 332–337.

Related Research: Hipple, J. L. (1971). *Effects of differential human relations training designs on interpersonal behavior of college students*. Unpublished doctoral dissertation, University of Iowa.

Hipple, J. L. (1972). Interpersonal relationship rating scale. In J. W. Pfeiffer & J. E. Jones (Eds.), *The annual handbook of group facilitators*. Iowa City: University Associates Press.

■ ■ ■

1257

Test Name: INTIMACY AND EYE CONTACT SCALES

Purpose: To assess perceived intimacy and amount of eye contact.

Number of Items: 54

Time Required: 10 seconds per item.

Format: Subjects view 54 slides and rate each in perceived intimacy and eye contact on Likert scales ranging from 1 (*very intimate*) to 7 (*very aloof*) and 1 (*very direct eye contact*) to 7 (*no eye contact whatsoever*).

Author: Scherer, S., and Schiff, M.

Article: Perceived intimacy, physical distance and eye contact.

Journal: *Perceptual and Motor Skills,* June 1973, *36*(3), 835–841.

■ ■ ■

1258

Test Name: JOURARD'S SELF-DISCLOSURE SCALE

Purpose: To measure the degree of self-disclosure by testing self-aspects regarding attitudes and opinions, tastes and interests, work or studies, money, personality, and body.

Number of Items: 18

Author: Wolken, G. H., et al.

Article: Race and social class as factors in the orientation toward psychotherapy.

Journal: *Journal of Counseling Psychology,* July 1973, *20*(4), 312–316.

Related Research: Jourard, S. M., & Lasakow, P. (1958). Some factors in self-disclosure. *Journal of Abnormal and Social Psychology, 56,* 91–98.

■ ■ ■

1259

Test Name: KOLB-BOYATZIS FEEDBACK ANALYSIS FORM

Purpose: To provide feedback from person to person in a counseling practicum.

Format: Subjects indicate who gave most feedback, three pieces of feedback that were most meaningful, and who gave each bit of feedback. Feedback is described in dimensions including positive–negative, strong–weak.

Author: Graves, W., and Graves, L.

Article: Analysis of feedback among group practicum members.

Journal: *Counselor Education and Supervision,* December 1973, *13*(2), 111–116.

Related Research: Kolb, D., & Boyatzis, R. (1970). On the dynamics of helping relationships. *Journal of Applied Behavioral Science, 6,* 267–290.

■ ■ ■

1260

Test Name: PICTURE TEST OF SEXUAL THOUGHTS

Purpose: To assess the ability to express sexual thoughts.

Number of Items: 16

Format: Subject was shown pictures and asked to write a story under two instructional conditions: dramatic and sexy.

Validity: "Sexier" stories were told when given instruction to do so, and when "sexier" pictures were shown.

Author: Routh, D., et al.

Article: Measuring the ability to express sexual thoughts.

Journal: *Journal of Personality Assessment,* 1973, *37*(4), 342–350.

■ ■ ■

1261

Test Name: RECIPROCAL CATEGORY SYSTEM

Purpose: To assess teacher–student classroom verbal interaction.

Format: Modifies and expands the number of categories in Flanders' original instrument and provides a student verbal behavior category for each teacher behavior category.

Validity: Product–moment

correlations between the Purdue Teacher Opinionaire Factors and Seven Reciprocal Category System Variables ranged from –.46 through .00 to .47.

Author: Greenwood, G. E., and Soar, R. S.

Article: Some relationships between teacher morale and teacher behavior.

Journal: *Journal of Educational Psychology,* February 1973, *64*(1), 105–108.

Related Research: Ober, R. L., et al. (1968, February). *The development of a reciprocal category system for assessing teacher–student classroom verbal interaction.* Paper presented at the Annual Meeting of the American Educational Research Association, Chicago.

■ ■ ■

1262

Test Name: RELATIONSHIP INVENTORY

Purpose: To measure both the therapist's and client's perception of the degree to which empathic understanding, unconditional positive regard, and congruence are present in the relationship.

Number of Items: 64

Format: A total of 48 points with even distribution of negative and positive points possible in each of four areas.

Author: Massey, S. R.

Article: Becoming an effective counselor–researcher: A lesson to be learned.

Journal: *Colorado Journal of Educational Research,* Winter 1973, *12*(2), 4–5.

Related Research: Barrett-Lennard, G. T. *Relationship inventory.* Waterloo, Ontario, Canada: University of Waterloo,

Department of Psychology.

Barrett-Lennard, G. T. (1962). Dimensions of therapist response as causal factors in therapeutic change. *Psychological Monographs, 76,* 562.

Lin, T. (1973). Counseling relationships as a function of counselor's self confidence. *Journal of Counseling Psychology, 20,* 293–297.

McWhirter, J. (1973). Two measures of the facilitative condition: A correlation study. *Journal of Counseling Psychology, 20,* 317–320.

Sorenson, A. G. (1967). *Toward an instructional model for counseling* (Occasional Report No. 6). Los Angeles: University of California, Center for the Study of Evaluation of Instruction Program.

Ziemelis, A. (1974). Effects of client preference and expectancy upon the initial interview. *Journal of Counseling Psychology, 21,* 23–30.

■ ■ ■

1263

Test Name: SELF-DISCLOSURE MEASURE

Purpose: To assess degree of willingness for self-disclosure.

Number of Items: 10

Format: Subjects rate extent of disclosure (*none* to *honesty in detail*) to stranger, acquaintance, best friend; half of itches were high intimacy, half low intimacy.

Validity: Subjects reported self as more disclosing than their peers.

Author: Higbee, K.

Article: Group influence on self disclosure.

Journal: *Psychological Reports,* June 1973, *32*(3), 903–909.

1264

Test Name: SELF-DISCLOSURE QUESTIONNAIRE

Purpose: To measure the extent to which individuals disclose themselves to different target persons.

Format: Yields six scores, includes disclosure in the areas of studies, personality, and body.

Reliability: Odd–even correlation was .94; test–retest correlation was .71 (6-week intervals).

Author: Hipple, J. L.

Article: Personal growth outcomes due to human relations training experience.

Journal: *Journal of College Student Personnel,* March 1973, *14*(2), 156–164.

Related Research: Jourard, S. M. (1964). *The transparent self.* Princeton, NJ: Van Nostrand.

Sote, G., & Good, L. (1974). Similarity of self disclosure and interpersonal attraction. *Psychological Reports, 34,* 491–494.

■ ■ ■

1265

Test Name: SELF-DISCLOSURE QUESTIONNAIRE

Purpose: To measure the amount of personal information disclosed to another.

Number of Items: 60

Format: Each item (important areas in person's life) rated on 1–6 scale for amount of information disclosed to a specified person.

Validity: Correlation between amount of information subject reported and amount a friend reported he received was .63; correlation between subjects' amount of information to friend and friends' amount to subject was .61; correlation between amount to friend and amount from friend was .95.

Author: Panyard, C.

Article: Self disclosure between friends: A validity study.

Journal: *Journal of Counseling Psychology,* January 1973, *20*(1), 66–68.

Related Research: Jourard, S., & Lasakow, P. (1958). Some factors in self disclosure. *Journal of Abnormal and Social Psychology, 56,* 91–98.

■ ■ ■

1266

Test Name: TEACHER–PUPIL QUESTION INVENTORY— REVISED

Purpose: Permits teacher to categorize teacher–pupil questions from 5 minute segments of the class or the entire lesson.

Format: Teacher tapes the lesson and categorizes the questions using the Inventory.

Author: Tinsley, D. C.

Article: Use of questions.

Journal: *Educational Leadership,* May 1973, *30*(8), 710–713.

Related Research: Hunkins, F. P. (1972). *Questioning strategies and techniques.* Boston: Allyn and Bacon.

■ ■ ■

1267

Test Name: TEACHER–PUPIL RESPONSE INVENTORY

Purpose: Permits the teacher to categorize pupil responses.

Format: Teacher tapes the lesson, then uses Inventory to categorize the responses.

Author: Tinsley, D.C.

Article: Use of questions.

Journal: *Educational Leadership,* May 1973, *30*(8), 710–713.

■ ■ ■

1268

Test Name: TRUAX-CARKHUFF RELATIONSHIP QUESTIONNAIRE—SHORT FORM

Purpose: To measure five characteristics that facilitate counseling: accurate empathy, nonpossessive warmth, genuineness, intensity and intimacy of interpersonal contact, and concreteness.

Number of Items: 34

Reliability: Internal consistency was .92.

Validity: Moderate to high concurrent validity with Barrett-Lennard and Sorenson scales.

Author: Lin, T.

Article: Revision and validation of the Truax-Carkhuff relationship questionnaire.

Journal: *Measurement and Evaluation in Guidance,* July 1973, *6*(2), 82–86.

CHAPTER 9
Concept Meaning

1269

Test Name:
ANTHROPOLOGICAL
CONCEPT ATTAINMENT TEST

Purpose: To indicate the level of conceptual understanding of selected anthropological concepts.

Number of Items: 20

Format: Multiple choice items consisting of four pictures: three illustrate a particular concept, one is irrelevant.

Reliability: Odd-even split half reliability was .83.

Author: Ryan, F. L., and Bushyager, D.

Article: An analysis of the conceptual understanding of first grade students involved in a study of anthropology.

Journal: *California Journal of Educational Research*, May 1973, *24*(3), 120–128.

. . .

1270

Test Name: BALDWIN PICTURE-STORY MEASURE OF KINDNESS CONCEPT

Purpose: To assess the acquisition of the understanding of kindness as a concept.

Format: 10 pairs of stories with line drawing illustrations, depicting interactions between two children.

Author: Brown, A. M., et al.

Article: Baldwin's kindness concept measure as related to children's cognition and

temperament: A twin study.

Journal: *Child Development*, March 1973, *44*(1), 193–195.

Related Research: Baldwin, C. P., & Baldwin, A. L. (1970). Children's judgments of kindness. *Child Development, 41*, 29–47.

. . .

1271

Test Name: CATEGORY WIDTH QUESTIONNAIRE

Purpose: To assess the aspect of cognitive functioning called category width.

Number of Items: 20

Format: Multiple choice; subject is asked to estimate extremes, for example, the width of windows; higher scores are associated with broader categorizers.

Validity: Correlated .329 ($p < .05$) with miss rate on an auditory discrimination task for male subjects.

Author: Rogers, R.

Article: Category width and decision making in perception.

Journal: *Perceptual and Motor Skills*, October 1973, *37*(2), 647–652.

Related Research: Donnelly, J. H., et al. (1973). The relationship between consumers category width and trial of new products. *Journal of Applied Psychology, 53*, 335–338.

Pettigrew, T. (1958). Measurement and correlates of category width as a cognitive variable. *Journal of*

Personality, 26, 532–544.

. . .

1272

Test Name: CONCEPTUAL STYLE TEST

Purpose: To measure differences in the aspects of stimuli that children initially select for cognitive processing.

Number of Items: 19

Format: Children are asked to pick out two pictures that are alike or go together in some way from a picture of a triad of familiar objects and to state the reason for their grouping.

Author: Stanes, D.

Article: Analytic responses to conceptual style test as a function of instruction.

Journal: *Child Development*, June 1973, *44*(2), 289–301.

Related Research: Kagan, J., et al. (1963). Psychological significance of styles of conceptualization. *Monographs of the Society for Research in Child Development, 28*, 73–112.

. . .

1273

Test Name: OBJECT SORTING TEST

Purpose: To assess conceptual differentiation.

Reliability: Test–retest reliability was .60.

Author: Gardner, R.

Article: Reliability of group test

scores for cognitive control and intellectual abilities over a one year period.

Journal: *Perceptual and Motor Skills,* June 1973, *36*(3), 753–754.

Related Research: Gardner, R., & Lohrenz, L. (1969). Some old and new group tests of cognitive controls and intellectual abilities. *Perceptual and Motor Skills, 29,* 935–950.

● ● ●

1274

Test Name: OBSCENE WORD SEMANTIC DIFFERENTIAL

Purpose: To obtain evaluative meaning of taboo words.

Number of Items: 20 concepts

Validity: Differences between religious, excretory, and sexual words.

Author: Baudhuin, E.

Article: Obscene language and evaluative response: An empirical study.

Journal: *Psychological Reports,* April 1973, *32*(2), 399–402.

● ● ●

1275

Test Name: ORAL P/S LANGUAGE INVENTORY

Purpose: To identify oral responses to word stimuli.

Number of Items: 30

Format: Subjects provide associations; responses are classified as either paradigmatic or syntagmatic.

Author: Weintraub, S., et al.

Article: Summary of investigations related to reading, July 1, 1972, to June 30, 1973.

Journal: *Reading Research Quarterly,* 1973–74, *9*(3), 309.

Related Research: Bickley, R. T.,

et al. (1971). Oral language responses and reading performance in the intermediate grades. In F. P. Greene (Ed.), *Reading: The right to participate. Twentieth Yearbook of the National Reading Conference* (pp. 11–13).

● ● ●

1276

Test Name: SEMANTIC CONSENSUS INDEX (SCI)

Purpose: To measure extent of word meaning.

Format: Subjects give four associations to a stimulus word; homogeneity of responses assessed by SCI.

Validity: Predicted that reaction time would be faster for high SCI words because they would have fewer competing responses. Index did predict response latency ($p <$ .01).

Author: Kanungo, R.

Article: Effects of semantic consensus index on associative response strength.

Journal: *Psychological Reports,* August 1973, *33*(1), 239–249.

● ● ●

1277

Test Name: STUDENT SOCIAL WORKER SEMANTIC DIFFERENTIAL

Purpose: To assess meaning of social work-related concepts to graduate students.

Format: Consists of five concepts— social caseworkers, social group worker, research social worker, social worker, and me-as-student—rated on nine bipolar adjective scales (evaluative, potency, activity).

Validity: No significant difference between student and instructor rating, suggesting that students are

similar in attitude to professionals.

Author: Greenwald, S., and Linn, M.

Article: Graduate students' semantic judgments of practice methods both before and after their first academic year in social work.

Journal: *Psychological Reports,* April 1973, *32*(2), 491–496.

● ● ●

1278

Test Name: SUNDBERG TEST OF IMPLIED MEANING

Purpose: To assess subjects' ability to perceive implied meaning in statements.

Number of Items: 38

Format: Three typed statements are read to express an implied meaning; subject must recognize intended meaning.

Reliability: Test–retest reliability ranged from .83 to .89.

Validity: With RFT, $r = -.64$ ($p <$ .001); EFT, $r = .53$ ($p < .01$); combined, $r = .69$ ($p < .001$).

Author: Wolitzky, D.

Article: Cognitive controls and person perception.

Journal: *Perceptual and Motor Skills,* April 1973, *36*(2), 619–623.

Related Research: Sundberg, N. (1964). *A method for studying sensitivity to implied meaning.* Paper read at the meeting of the American Psychological Association, Los Angeles.

● ● ●

1279

Test Name: TUCKMAN TOPICAL INVENTORY

Purpose: To measure cognitive complexity.

Number of Items: 72

Format: Subjects choose statements closest to their world view.

Author: Corenblum, B.

Article: Locus of control, latitude of acceptance and attitudes toward abortion.

Journal: *Psychological Reports,* June 1973, *32*(3), 753–754.

Related Research: Tuckman, B. (1966). Interpersonal probing and revealing systems of integrative complexity. *Journal of Personality and Social Psychology, 3,* 655–664.

CHAPTER 10
Creativity

1280

Test Name: CREATIVITY QUESTIONNAIRE

Purpose: To identify creative persons.

Number of Items: 22

Format: Yes–no responses are requested to questions including, "Do you engage in any social activities?" "Can you use tools skillfully?" All items are presented.

Validity: Two sets of mutually exclusive groups (inventor/analyst; creator/other) based on self-reported behavior. Of 44 chi square tests on items; only 14 significant differences found.

Author: Bergum, B.

Article: Selection of specialized creators.

Journal: *Psychological Reports,* October 1973, *33*(2), 635–639.

● ● ●

1281

Test Name: ONOMATOPOEIA AND IMAGES

Purpose: To test verbal originality.

Format: Onomatopoeic stimuli in a repeated presentation format:

fixed interval between the presentation of each word.

Author: Khatena, J.

Article: Imagination imagery of children and the production of analogy.

Journal: *The Gifted Child Quarterly,* Summer 1973, *17*(2), 98–102.

Related Research: Khatena, J. (1969). Onomatopoeia and images: Preliminary validity study of a test of originality. *Perceptual and Motor Skills, 28,* 235–238.

● ● ●

1282

Test Name: SOCIAL STUDIES IMPLICATIONS TEST

Purpose: To measure productive and imaginative thinking in relation to social relationships and community organization.

Number of Items: 3

Time Required: 10–20 minutes.

Format: Items are individually administered and responses recorded on tape. Test yields a fluency score based on total number of relevant responses summed over the three questions and a flexibility score based upon

the number of different response categories used in each question. Descriptions of the items are presented.

Author: McKinney, J. D., and Golden, L.

Article: Social studies dramatic play with elementary school children.

Journal: *Journal of Educational Research,* December 1973, *67*(4), 172–176.

● ● ●

1283

Test Name: TORRENCE CHECKLIST OF CREATIVE POSITIVES

Purpose: To select, guide, and encourage disadvantaged gifted children.

Number of Items: 12 parts with varying subsections.

Format: Checklist based on observation of children.

Author: Torrence, E.

Article: Non-test indicators of creative talent among disadvantaged children.

Journal: *Gifted Child Quarterly,* Spring 1973, *17*(1), 3–9.

CHAPTER 11
Development

1284

Test Name: BRAZELTON CAMBRIDGE NEWBORN SCALES

Purpose: To test neurological and developmental status in newborns.

Author: Scarr, S., and Williams, M.

Article: The effects of early stimulation on low-birth-weight infants.

Journal: *Child Development,* March 1973, *44*(1), 94–101.

Related Research: Horowitz, F. D., et al. (1971, April). *Newborn and four week retest on a normative population using the Brazelton Newborn Assessment Procedure.* Paper presented at the Biennial Meeting of the Society for Research in Child Development, Minneapolis, MN.

Scarr, S., & Williams, M. (1971, April). *The assessment of neonatal and later status in low-birth-weight infants.* Paper presented at the Biennial Meeting of the Society for Research in Child Development, Minneapolis, MN.

• • •

1285

Test Name: GENDER BEHAVIOR INVENTORY FOR BOYS

Purpose: To measure extreme ranges of childhood gender development.

Number of Items: 173

Format: Four factors: feminine

behavior, extraversion, behavior disturbance, mother's boy. An 8-point scale scores 43 items and a 5-point scale scores 130 items. Many items are presented.

Author: Bates, J. E., et al.

Article: Measurement of deviant gender development in boys.

Journal: *Child Development,* September 1973, *44*(3), 591–598.

• • •

1286

Test Name: IDENTITY ACHIEVEMENT SCALE

Purpose: To assess achievement of identity within an Eriksonian theory of development.

Validity: Correlation with Yeasaying Scale, –.34 ($p < .01$; Couch & Keniston, 1960); with Eysenck's Neuroticism Scale, –.32 ($p < .01$).

Author: Simmons, D.

Article: Further psychometric correlates of the identity achievement scale.

Journal: *Psychological Reports,* June 1973, *32*(3), 1042.

Related Research: Couch, A., & Keniston, K. (1960). Yea sayers and nay sayers: Agreement response set as a personality variable. *Journal of Abnormal and Social Psychology, 60,* 151–174.

Simmons, D. (1970). Development of an objective measure of identity achievement status. *Journal of Projective Techniques and*

Personality Assessment, 34, 241–244.

• • •

1287

Test Name: INFANT PSYCHOLOGICAL DEVELOPMENT SCALE

Purpose: To measure aspects of cognitive functioning.

Format: Includes seven scales: schemata, means, causality, object, space, gestural and vocal imitation.

Validity: Predictive validities over 8 months: for 14 and 18 months, correlations ranged from .01 to .55; for 18 and 22 months, correlations ranged from .09 to .42; for 14 and 22 months, correlations ranged from .00 to .56. Correlations with the Bayley Mental and Motor Scales ranged from –.14 to .44 at 14 months; from –.33 to .64 at 18 months; and from –.19 to .54 at 22 months.

Author: King, W. L., and Seegmiller, B.

Article: Performance of 14- to 22-month-old Black, first born male infants on two tests of cognitive development: The Bayley Scales and the Infant Psychological Development Scales.

Journal: *Developmental Psychology,* May 1973, *8*(3), 317–326.

Related Research: Uzgiris, I. C., & Hunt, J. M. (1966). *An instrument for assessing infant psychological development.* Unpublished manuscript. Urbana: University of

Illinois Psychological Development Laboratory.

■ ■ ■

1288

Test Name: LIFE HISTORY QUESTIONNAIRE

Purpose: To assess experience and behavior during a subject's first 19 years.

Number of Items: 32

Format: 12 questions are answered 19 times, once each year; 20 questions are answered only in appropriate years. Types of questions are provided.

Author: Helmreich, R., et al.

Article: The life history questionnaire as a predictor of performance in Navy Diver Training.

Journal: *Journal of Applied Psychology,* April 1973, *57*(2), 148–153.

Related Research: Radluff, R., & Helmreich, R. (1972). The life history questionnaire. *JSAS Catalog of Selected Documents, 2,* 13.

■ ■ ■

1289

Test Name: SAPIR DEVELOPMENTAL SCALE-C

Purpose: To identify kindergarten children with developmental lags in perceptual-motor, bodily schema, and/or language development.

Validity: With Frostig Test of Visual Perception, *r* = .45; New State Reading Readiness Test, *r* = .66; Total Stanford Achievement Test, *r* = .64; Subtests of Scholastic Aptitude Tests from .30 (vocabulary) to .71 (spelling).

Author: Weintraub, et al.

Article: Summary of investigations

relating to reading July 1, 1972, to June 30, 1973.

Journal: *Reading Research Quarterly,* 1973–74, *9*(3), 346–347.

Related Research: Sapir, S. G., & Wilson, B. (1972). A developmental scale to assist in the prevention of learning disability. In J. F. Reid (Ed.), *Reading: Problems and practices* (pp. 380–386). London: Ward Lock.

■ ■ ■

1290

Test Name: SCHEDULE OF RECENT EXPERIENCE

Purpose: To quantify psychological magnitude of a cluster of life changes over a given period.

Number of Items: 42

Format: Areas of change assessed: personal, family, community, social, religious, economic, occupational, residential, health; for periods 0–6 months, 6 months–1 year, 1–2 years, 2–3 years before answering questionnaire.

Validity: Low but significant (about one-half) correlations with subscales of Profile of Mood State Instrument. Clinard and Golden (1973) report correlations with 16 self-report criteria (e.g., grade point, tardy to class); four were significant: personal illness (.41), promotions (.34), raises (.29), number of previous jobs (.35).

Author: Constantini, A., et al.

Article: Personality and mood correlates of schedule of recent experiences scores.

Journal: *Psychological Reports,* June 1973, *32*(3), 1143–1150.

Related Research: Clinard, J., & Golden, S. (1973). Life change events as related to self report academic and job performance.

Psychological Reports, 33, 391–394.

Constantini, A., et al. (1974). The Life Change Inventory: A device quantifying psychological magnitude of changes experienced by college students. *Psychological Reports, 34,* 991–1000.

Holmes, T., & Rahe, R. (1967). The social readjustment rating scale. *Journal of Psychosomatic Research, 11,* 213–218.

■ ■ ■

1291

Test Name: VOCATIONAL DEVELOPMENT INVENTORY

Purpose: To measure the dispositional factor in vocational maturity. Includes five attitudinal variables: involvement in vocational choice; orientation toward problem of vocational choice; independence in decision making; preference for factors in vocational choice; conceptions of vocational choice.

Number of Items: 100

Time Required: 15–20 minutes.

Format: Form I: Likert format; Form II: true–false; Form III: 50 true–false items.

Reliability: Internal consistency ranged from .60 to .84. Test–retest reliability was .71.

Author: Westbrook, B. W., and Mastie, M. M.

Article: Three measures of vocational maturity: A beginning to know about.

Journal: *Measurement & Evaluation in Guidance,* April 1973, *6*(1), 8–16.

Related Research: Crites, J. O. (1965). Measurement of vocational maturity in adolescence: I. Attitude Test of the Vocational Development Inventory.

Psychological Monographs, 72, 595.

• • •

1292

Test Name: ZYGOSITY QUESTIONNAIRE

Purpose: To determine zygosity.

Format: Mothers respond to questions.

Validity: Test was 93% accurate in estimating correct zygosity.

Author: Willerman, L.

Article: Activity level and hyperactivity in twins.

Journal: *Child Development,* June 1973, *44*(2), 288–293.

Related Research: Nichols, R. C., & Bilbro, J. (1966). The diagnosis of twin zygosity. *Acta Genetica, 16,* 265–275.

...

CHAPTER 12
Family

1293

Test Name: ACTIVITY REACTION INVENTORY

Purpose: To determine what parents would do if their child engaged in certain student activities.

Format: Four scales: school, personal, independence, behavior. Five alternative responses, from *take disciplinary action* to *do nothing at all.*

Reliability: Ranged from .59–.76.

Author: Winkworth, J. M., et al.

Article: Intervention programs designed to improve communication between parents and students.

Journal: *Journal of College Student Personnel,* May 1973, *14*(3), 206–215.

...

1294

Test Name: COGNITIVE HOME ENVIRONMENT SCALE

Purpose: To identify child-rearing practices.

Number of Items: 25

Format: Each item scored from 1 to 7, 7 being the highest rating. Example: "How many years of schooling do you expect your child to receive?"

Author: Radin, N.

Article: Observed paternal behaviors as antecedents of intellectual functioning in young boys.

Journal: *Developmental*

Psychology, May 1973, *8*(3), 369–376.

Related Research: Radin, N., & Sonquist, H. (1968, March 12). *The Gale preschool program: Final report.* Ypsilanti, MI: Ypsilanti Public Schools.

...

1295

Test Name: DISCUSSION TOPIC SURVEY

Purpose: To determine what parents talk about with their children.

Format: Six scales: world affairs, abstract sharing, experience sharing, problem sharing, sex and marriage, controversial behavior.

Reliability: Ranged from .53 to .85.

Author: Winkworth, J. M., et al.

Article: Intervention programs designed to improve communication between parents and students.

Journal: *Journal of College Student Personnel,* May 1973, *14*(3), 206–215.

...

1296

Test Name: FAMILY RELATIONS INVENTORY

Purpose: To assess parental acceptance, avoidance, or concentration as a familial interpersonal orientation (based on Roe's theory).

Number of Items: 202

Format: True–false; distributed on

six scales: acceptance, avoidance, concentration, each by father and mother.

Author: Medvene, A.

Article: Early parent child interactions of education–vocational and emotional–social clients.

Journal: *Journal of Counseling Psychology,* January 1973, *20*(1), 94–96.

Reliability: Berdie, R. (1964). Comment. *Journal of Counseling Psychology, 11,* 3–12.

Brunkan, R., & Crites, J. O. (1964). An inventory to measure the parental attitude variables in Roe's theory of vocational choice. *Journal of Counseling Psychology, 11,* 3–12.

...

1297

Test Name: FREQUENCY OF DISCUSSION CHECKLIST

Purpose: To determine parents' frequency of discussion of certain topics with their son or daughter just before the child left for college.

Format: Five discussion scales: academic, vocational, social, independence, communication.

Reliability: Ranged from .50 to .74.

Author: Winkworth, J. M., et al.

Article: Intervention programs designed to improve communication between parents and students.

Journal: *Journal of College*

Student Personnel, May 1973, *14*(3), 206–215.

* * *

1298

Test Name: HOME ENVIRONMENTAL FORCES SCHEDULE

Purpose: To measure intensity of learning environment in the home and cumulative nature of learning environment.

Number of Items: 188

Time Required: Approximately 2 hours.

Format: Semistructured home interview schedule to elicit responses from both mothers and fathers, with a 6-point rating scale for each item. Includes eight environmental press areas.

Reliability: Internal consistency alpha reliabilities for the 8 press areas ranged from .66 to .95.

Author: Walberg, H. J., and Marjoribanks, K.

Article: Differential mental abilities and home environment: A canonical analysis.

Journal: *Developmental Psychology,* November 1973, *9*(3), 363–368.

Related Research: Marjoribanks, K. (1972). Ethnic and learning patterns: A replication and an explanation. *Sociology, 6,* 417–431.

* * *

1299

Test Name: MARITAL ADJUSTMENT TEST

Purpose: To assess perceived marital success.

Number of Items: 15

Reliability: Correlation between husband and wife of graduate student couples was .20 ($p < .05$).

Validity: Correlation between shared personal constructs and marital satisfaction was nonsignificant.

Author: Weigel, R., et al.

Article: Congruence of spouses' personal constructs and reported marital success: Pitfalls in instrumentation.

Journal: *Psychological Reports,* August 1973, *33*(1), 212–214.

Related Research: Locke, H., & Wallace, K. (1959). Short marital-adjustment and prediction tests: Their reliability and validity. *Marriage and Family Living, 21,* 251–255.

* * *

1300

Test Name: MOTHER'S INTERACTION INDEX

Purpose: To assess mothers' interaction.

Format: Includes avoidance index, chatter index, and mothers' views on use of toys. High score indicates a disposition to encourage the child to interact with home environment on a verbal–cognitive level.

Author: Jones, P. A.

Article: Home environment and the development verbal ability.

Journal: *Child Development,* September 1973, *43*(3), 1081–1086.

* * *

1301

Test Name: PARENTAL DOMINANCE SCALE

Purpose: To assess perceived dominance by parents.

Number of Items: 5

Format: Multiple choice.

Author: Medvene, A.

Article: Early parent child interactions of educational–vocational and emotional–social client.

Journal: *Journal of Counseling Psychology,* January 1973, *20*(1), 94–96.

Related Research: Roe, A., & Siegelman, M. (1964). *The origin of interests.* Washington, DC: American Personnel and Guidance Association.

* * *

1302

Test Name: PARENTAL EXPECTATIONS SURVEY

Purpose: To determine what parents think the chances are that their freshman son or daughter will do certain things.

Format: Five expectation scales: academics, vocational, social, independence, communication.

Reliability: Ranged from .34 to .67.

Author: Winkworth, J. M., et al.

Article: Intervention programs designed to improve communication between parents and students.

Journal: *Journal of College Student Personnel,* May 1973, *14*(3), 206–215.

* * *

1303

Test Name: PARENT RATING SCALE

Purpose: To evaluate mother–daughter and father–daughter relationships.

Number of Items: 61

Format: Part 1: subjects indicate statements most descriptive of each parent's attitude toward them as they were growing up; Part 2: subject indicates what each parent actually did to implement attitudes toward achievement and the display of affection in the parent–child relationship.

Author: Grebow, H.

Article: The relationship of some parental variables to achievement and values in college women.

Journal: *Journal of Educational Research,* January 1973, *66*(5), 203–209.

Related Research: Bronfenbrenner, U. (1961). Some familial antecedents of responsibility and leadership in adolescents. In L. Petrullo & B. M. Bass (Eds.), *Leadership and interpersonal behavior.* New York: Holt, Rinehart & Winston.

Crandall, V., et al. (1964). Parent's attitudes and behaviors and grade school children's academic achievement. *Journal of Genetic Psychology, 104,* 53–66.

■ ■ ■

1304

Test Name: PERCEIVED PARENTING QUESTIONNAIRE

Purpose: To measure nine child-rearing behaviors.

Number of Items: 21

Format: Behaviors: nurturance, instrumental companionship, principled discipline, predictability of standards, protectiveness, physical punishment, achievement

pressure, deprivation of privileges, and affective punishment. Two forms: paternal behaviors and maternal behaviors.

Author: Levenson, H.

Article: Perceived parental antecedents of internal, powerful others, and chance locus of control orientation.

Journal: *Developmental Psychology,* September 1973, *9*(2) 260–265.

Related Research: Devereux, E. C., et al. (1969). Child-rearing in England and the United States: A cross-national comparison. *Journal of Marriage and Family, 31,* 257–270.

MacDonald, A. P. (1971). Internal-external locus of control: Parental antecedents. *Journal of Consulting and Clinical Psychology, 37,* 141–147.

■ ■ ■

1305

Test Name: SHARED PERSONAL CONSTRUCTS

Purpose: To assess degree of congruence between spouses in personal constructs.

Number of Items: 40

Format: Each item consisted of bipolar adjectives (e.g., calm–quick tempered); subject chose 10 "most meaningful" and 10 "least meaningful" in other people.

Degree of congruence was number of items both spouses agreed upon.

Validity: Correlation with measure of marital satisfaction was nonsignificant.

Author: Weigel, R., et al.

Article: Congruence of spouses' personal constructs and reported marital success.

Journal: *Psychological Reports,* August 1973, *33*(1), 212–214.

■ ■ ■

1306

Test Name: WIVES' PROBLEM SCALE

Purpose: To assess wives' problems regarding their responsibility attribution, interpersonal attraction, and understanding.

Format: Nine stories in booklet; subjects rate nine questions on 7-point scale; questions include: was wife responsible for problem, she deserves help, she is adjusted, I would like her.

Author: Phares, E., and Wilson, K.

Article: Source and type of wives' problems as related to responsibility attribution, interpersonal attraction, and understanding.

Journal: *Psychological Reports,* June 1973, *32*(3), 923–930.

CHAPTER 13
Institutional Information

1307

Test Name: ADMINISTRATOR IMAGE QUESTIONNAIRE

Purpose: To identify perceived and ideal behavior of school superintendents.

Number of Items: 23

Format: Subjects respond to each item on a 5-point scale. All items are presented.

Author: Bartz, D. E.

Article: Changes in superintendents' perceived behaviors following feedback from principals and school board members.

Journal: *Journal of Educational Research,* December 1973, *67*(4), 157–160.

. . .

1308

Test Name: BANK SWITCHING QUESTIONNAIRE

Purpose: To determine the behavioral intention to switch banks.

Number of Items: 13

Format: Subjects respond to each item with *Y* (if it describes their feelings or experience), *N* (if it does not describe them), or *?* (undecided).

Author: Shneider, B.

Article: The perception of organizational climate: The customer's view.

Journal: *Journal of Applied Psychology,* June 1973, *57*(3), 248–256.

1309

Test Name: BUREAUCRACY SCALE

Purpose: To identify bureaucratic structure of the school.

Format: Likert items with five possible responses from *strongly agree* through *undecided* to *strongly disagree.* Includes two factors: behavior control and status maintenance.

Validity: Correlations with alienation were reported: $r = -.12$ (status maintenance); $r = .19$ (behavior control).

Author: Anderson, B. D.

Article: School bureaucratization and alienation from high school.

Journal: *Sociology of Education,* Summer 1973, *46*(3), 315–334.

. . .

1310

Test Name: CHARACTERISTICS OF A TREATMENT ENVIRONMENT INSTRUMENT

Purpose: To assess five characteristics of a treatment environment.

Format: Observational system rates on five scales: staff activity, socioemotional freedom, patient self management, behavior modification, instrumental freedom.

Author: Dana, R., and Barling, P.

Article: Structured treatment environments and pathological behaviors.

Journal: *Psychological Reports,*

June 1973, *32*(3), 991–994.

Related Research: Jackson, J. (1964). Toward the comparative study of mental hospitals: Characteristics of the hospital environment. In A. Wessen (Ed.), *The psychiatric hospital as a social system* (35–87). Springfield, IL: Charles C Thomas.

. . .

1311

Test Name: COLLEGE CHARACTERISTIC INDEX

Purpose: To identify intellectual and nonintellectual attributes of campus environments.

Number of Items: 300

Format: Thirty scales of 10 true–false items. Scales are combined into 11 environmental factors defining both an intellectual and nonintellectual, psychological environment.

Author: Donato, D. J.

Article: Junior college transfers and a university environment.

Journal: *Journal of College Student Personnel,* May 1973, *14*(3), 254–259.

Related Research: Pace, C. R., & Stern, G. G. (1958). An approach to the measurement of psychological characteristics of college environments. *Journal of Educational Psychology,* *49,* 269–277.

. . .

1312

Test Name: COMMUNITY JUDGMENT SCALE

Purpose: To assess attitude toward a community.

Number of Items: 6

Format: Items were rated on 7-point scales: community's friendliness to newcomers, morality, sense of well-being, community responsibility, how well they liked and would enjoy living in the community.

Author: Good, L., et al.

Article: Similarity of attitude and attraction to a community.

Journal: *Psychological Reports,* June 1973, *32*(3), 975–981.

• • •

1313

Test Name: COUNSELING CENTER QUESTIONNAIRE

Purpose: To determine students' image of the counseling center.

Number of Items: 53

Time Required: 40 minutes.

Format: Multiple choice questions on students' perceptions of the counseling center.

Author: King, P. T., et al.

Article: A counseling center studies itself.

Journal: *Journal of College Student Personnel,* July 1973, *14*(4), 338–344.

• • •

1314

Test Name: CURRICULUM DEVELOPMENT CRITERIA

Purpose: To provide criteria for the development of curriculum.

Number of Items: 24

Format: Each criterion was included because it was crucial, functional, and observable. All are presented.

Author: Wickert, J. J.

Article: Criteria for curriculum development.

Journal: *Educational Leadership,* January 1973, *30*(4), 339–342.

• • •

1315

Test Name: DISABLED STUDENT FACILITIES QUESTIONNAIRE

Purpose: To determine the degree to which colleges are prepared to meet the needs of disabled students.

Number of Items: 21

Format: Includes the following areas: admission and orientation, wheelchair disabled, blind, auditorily disabled, and systemic-neurological disabled. Some items are presented.

Author: Stilwell, W. E., and Schulker, S.

Article: Facilities available to disabled higher education students.

Journal: *Journal of College Student Personnel,* September 1973, *14*(5), 419–424.

• • •

1316

Test Name: ELEMENTARY SCHOOL ENVIRONMENT SURVEY

Purpose: To measure specific dimensions of elementary school environments.

Number of Items: 40

Format: Includes six environmental dimensions: alienation, humanism, autonomy, morale, opportunism, resources. Two forms: A and B.

Author: Sadker, D.

Article: Dimensions of the elementary school environment: A factor analytic study.

Journal: *Journal of Educational Research,* July–August 1973, *66*(10), 441–442.

• • •

1317

Test Name: EVALUATION OF FIELD PRACTICE SUPERVISION

Purpose: To permit counselor trainees to evaluate their field practice assignment.

Number of Items: 31

Format: 29 items rated from 1 (*low*) to 9 (*high*) and two open-ended items asking how supervisors had been most helpful and for suggestions as to how they would be more helpful.

Author: Nelson, R. C., and Segrist, A. E.

Article: Implementing the on-site supervision model.

Journal: *Counselor Education and Supervision,* March 1973, *12*(3), 206–212.

• • •

1318

Test Name: IMPORTANCE QUESTIONNAIRE

Purpose: To identify importance of job conditions and opportunities of the disadvantaged.

Number of Items: 20

Format: Subject rates each item on an importance scale.

Author: Van Doren, R. (Ed.).

Article: Manpower, human assessment and the disadvantaged.

Journal: *American Vocational Journal,* January 1973, *48*(1), 86–100.

• • •

1319

Test Name: INSERVICE EDUCATION PROGRAMS EVALUATION INSTRUMENTS

Purpose: To evaluate many facets of in-service programs for teachers.

Number of Items: 19

Format: Includes rating scale and open-ended items for evaluation of inservice workshops. All items are presented.

Author: Means, D.

Article: Evaluation in-service education programs.

Journal: *Education,* February–March 1973, *93*(3), 292–294.

• • •

1320

Test Name: INVASION OF PRIVACY QUESTIONNAIRE

Purpose: To measure the degree to which job applicants think their privacy is being invaded.

Number of Items: 66

Format: Includes five factors: family background and influences, personal history data, interests and values, financial management data, social adjustment.

Validity: Correlation of cluster scores with Guilford-Zimmerman Temperament Survey ranged from −.11 to .24 (*N* = 352). Correlation of cluster scores with Edwards Personal Preference Schedule ranged from −.10 to .16 (*N* = 352).

Author: Rosenbaum, B. L.

Article: Attitude toward invasion of privacy in the personnel selection process and job applicant demographic and personality correlates.

Journal: *Journal of Applied Psychology,* December 1973, *58*(3), 333–338.

• • •

1321

Test Name: JOB DESCRIPTIVE INDEX

Purpose: To provide a job description.

Format: Subjects indicate those adjectives from a checklist that describe five principal dimensions of their job: work itself, supervisor, pay, promotion, co-workers.

Author: Herman, J. B., and Hulin, C. L.

Article: Managerial satisfactions and organizational roles: An investigation of Porter's need deficiency scales.

Journal: *Journal of Applied Psychology,* April 1973, *57*(2), 118–124.

Related Research: Smith, P. C., et al. (1969). *The measurement of satisfaction in work and retirement.* Chicago: Rand McNally.

• • •

1322

Test Name: JOB INVOLVEMENT SCALE–SHORT FORM

Purpose: To measure work involvement.

Reliability: Split-half reliability estimated at .73.

Author: Runyon, K. E.

Article: Some interactions between personality variables and management styles.

Journal: *Journal of Applied Psychology,* June 1973, *57*(3), 288–294.

Related Research: Lodahl, T., & Kejner, M. (1965). The definition and measure of job involvement. *Journal of Applied Psychology, 49,* 24–33.

• • •

1323

Test Name: LEARNING CLIMATE INVENTORY

Purpose: To analyze the learning climate and leader behavior in open-space and traditional elementary schools.

Number of Items: 20

Format: Teachers respond on a 7-point frequency scale. Each dimension has a minimum value of 1 and a maximum value of 7. A mean is computed for each dimension. Optimum score is 128 because of two negative items scored in reverse. Sample items are presented.

Validity: With the Problem-Attack Behavior Inventory, correlation coefficient was .703.

Author: Hoyle, J. R.

Article: Are open-space high schools more open?

Journal: *Journal of Educational Research,* December 1973, *67*(4), 153–156.

Related Research: Preston, R. L. (1972). *A comparative analysis of leader behavior and its relationship to climate in open-space and traditional schools.* Doctoral dissertation, Miami University, Oxford, Ohio.

• • •

1324

Test Name: LEARNING ENVIRONMENT INVENTORY

Purpose: To describe the classroom environment.

Format: 14 scales.

Author: DeVries, D., and Edwards, K.

Article: Learning games and student teams: Their effects on classroom process.

Journal: *American Educational Research Journal,* Fall 1973, *10*(4), 307–318.

Related Research: Walberg, H., & Anderson, G. (1968). Classroom climate and individual learning.

Journal of Educational Psychology, 59, 414–419.

■ ■ ■

1325

Test Name: LEARNING MATERIALS QUESTIONNAIRE

Purpose: To evaluate textbooks and other learning materials. Includes criteria for evaluating the treatment of minority groups and women in these materials.

Number of Items: 20

Format: Yes–no questions. All items are presented.

Author: Rosenberg, M.

Article: Evaluate your textbooks for racism, sexism!

Journal: *Educational Leadership.* November 1973, *31*(2), 107–109.

■ ■ ■

1326

Test Name: MIDDLE SCHOOL QUESTIONNAIRE

Purpose: To provide guidelines for evaluating whether existing or proposed programs provide for middle school students.

Number of Items: 16

Format: Yes–no questions. All items are presented.

Author: Georgiady, N. P., and Romano, L. G.

Article: Do you have a middle school?

Journal: *Educational Leadership,* December 1973, *31*(3), 238–241.

■ ■ ■

1327

Test Name: MODERNITY MEASURE

Purpose: To assess the extent of modernity in various cultures.

Number of Items: 17

Format: All items are presented.

Validity: Six factors derived from a factor analysis: intrafamily orientations, urban experience, religiosity, general information, reproductive orientation.

Author: Portes, A.

Article: The factorial structure of modernity: Empirical replications and a critique.

Journal: *American Journal of Sociology,* July 1973, *79*(1), 15–44.

■ ■ ■

1328

Test Name: MODULAR-FLEXIBLE SCHEDULE QUESTIONNAIRE

Purpose: To identify problems experienced in the implementation of a modular-flexible schedule.

Number of Items: 99

Format: Types of items included pupil personnel, teacher personnel, administration, public relations, and school plant. Examples are provided.

Author: Sturges, A. W., and Mrdjenovich, D.

Article: Anticipated and experienced problems in implementing a flexible-modular schedule.

Journal: *Journal of Educational Research,* February 1973, *66*(6), 269–273.

■ ■ ■

1329

Test Name: NEED ASSESSMENT QUESTIONNAIRE

Purpose: To determine the need students have for a course.

Number of Items: 7

Format: Five items are answered either *yes* or *no.* Two are open-ended. All items are presented.

Author: Mohan, M.

Article: Is there a need for a course in creativity in teacher education?

Journal: *The Journal of Creative Behavior,* 1973, *7*(3), 175–186.

■ ■ ■

1330

Test Name: ORGANIZATIONAL HEALTH DESCRIPTION QUESTIONNAIRE

Purpose: To measure the organizational health of a school.

Format: Includes five factors: decision making, interpersonal relationships, innovativeness, autonomy, school-community relations.

Author: Kimpston, R. D., and Sonnabend, L. C.

Article: Organizational health: A requisite for innovation.

Journal: *Educational Leadership,* March 1973, *30*(6), 543–547.

■ ■ ■

1331

Test Name: ORGANIZATIONAL RESEARCH EVALUATION SCALES

Purpose: To evaluate psychological research within organizations.

Number of Items: 20

Format: Items are rated on a 7-point scale. All items are included.

Author: Warr, P. B.

Article: Better working lives: A symposium. A university psychologist's view.

Journal: *Occupational Psychology,* 1973, *47*(1, 2), 15–22.

■ ■ ■

1332

Test Name: ORGANIZATIONAL STRUCTURE MEASURE

Purpose: To measure "structural characteristics of complex organizations."

Format: Two sets of measures: institutional (documents and informants) and survey (questionnaires and interviews).

Validity: Some convergent validity: correlations are reported.

Author: Pennings, J.

Article: Measures of organizational structure: A methodological note.

Journal: *American Journal of Sociology,* November 1973, *79*(3), 686–704.

■ ■ ■

1333

Test Name: PROFILES OF ORGANIZATIONAL CHARACTERISTICS

Purpose: To examine various styles of management within types of organizations.

Format: Range of styles from "no trust in subordinates" to "confidence in subordinates": staff responded to questionnaire.

Author: Moy, J., and Hales, L.

Article: Management styles and leadership behavior within a residence life program.

Journal: *Journal of Experimental Education,* Fall 1973, *42*(1), 33–36.

Related Research: Likert, R. (1967). *The human organization: Its management and value.* New York: McGraw Hill.

1334

Test Name: READING CONSULTANT RESPONSIBILITIES QUESTIONNAIRE

Purpose: To determine preferences for reading consultant responsibilities.

Number of Items: 42

Format: Respondent rates each item on a 5-point scale: *very important, important, undecided, not too important, unimportant.* Respondent also indicates teaching or administrative responsibilities. All items are presented.

Author: Hesse, K. D., et al.

Article: Content teachers consider the role of the reading consultant.

Journal: *Journal of Reading,* December 1973, *17*(3), 210–215.

■ ■ ■

1335

Test Name: STUDENT PERCEPTION OF ACADEMIC CLIMATE

Purpose: To assess perception of academic climate by college students.

Number of Items: 34

Time Required: 20 minutes.

Format: Students responded to statements on an "agreement" (*strongly agree* to *strongly disagree*) and an "importance" scale (*very great* to *very little*). Dimensions include degree requirements, course work,

examinations, physical facilities, faculty competency, and faculty interest in students.

Author: Saitta, W., et al.

Article: Measuring student perception of academic climate: Implications for improved validity.

Journal: *Educational and Psychological Measurement,* Summer 1973, *33*(2), 485–490.

■ ■ ■

1336

Test Name: WARMAN'S COUNSELING APPROPRIATENESS CHECKLIST

Purpose: To assess the appropriateness of certain student problems for treatment in a counseling center.

Number of Items: 66

Format: Ratings made on a 1 (*definitely inappropriate*) to 5 (*most appropriate*) scale; three factors found: college routine, vocational choice, adjustment to self and others.

Author: Gelso, C., and McKenzie, J.

Article: Effect of information on students' perceptions of counseling and their willingness to seek help.

Journal: *Journal of Counseling Psychology,* September 1973, *20*(5), 406–411.

Related Research: Warman, R. (1961). The counseling role of college university counseling centers. *Journal of Counseling Psychology, 8,* 231–238.

...
CHAPTER 14
Motivation

1337

Test Name: ACADEMIC ACHIEVEMENT SCALE

Purpose: To reflect interests in scientific and intellectual endeavors versus interests in sales, business, and skilled trade activities.

Format: Developed for the male form of the Strong Vocational Interest Blank.

Author: Higgins, P. S., and Rossmann, J. E.

Article: Student characteristics preferred by the faculty at a liberal arts college.

Journal: *Journal of College Student Personnel,* May 1973, *14*(3), 225–230.

...

1338

Test Name: ACHIEVEMENT MOTIVATION MEASURE

Purpose: To tap the direction of behavior (approach or avoidance) exhibited in achievement contexts; the kind of affect (hope or fear) associated with achievement situations, and the degree of risk (intermediate, easy, or difficult odds) preferred.

Number of Items: 34

Format: Self-report items rated from +3 (*very strong agreement*) to –3 (*very strong disagreement*). A sample item is presented.

Reliability: 10-week stability estimate was .78.

Validity: Validity with repression–sensitization was –.23.

Author: Farley, F. H., and Mealiea, W. L., Jr.

Article: Motivation and the recall of completed and incompleted achievement items.

Journal: *Journal of Educational Research,* March 1973, *66*(7), 302–306.

Related Research: Weiner, B., et al. (1968). Achievement motivation and the recall of incompleted and completed exam questions. *Journal of Educational Psychology, 59,* 181–185.

...

1339

Test Name: ACTIVITIES INDEX

Purpose: To measure psychological needs.

Number of Items: 30

Author: Nielsen, R. P.

Article: Communicating with and motivating high fatalists.

Journal: *American Journal of Economics and Sociology,* October 1973, *32*(4), 337–350.

Related Research: Stern, G. (1970). *People in context.* New York: Wiley.

...

1340

Test Name: CUE INTERPRETATIONS TEST

Purpose: To assess need for achievement.

Format: Subjects are given four written statements and asked to write an imaginative story; stories are scored for need for achievement.

Reliability: Interrater reliability was .90.

Author: Wish, P., and Hasazi, J.

Article: Motivational determinants of curricular choice in college males.

Journal: *Journal of Counseling Psychology,* March 1973, *20*(2), 127–131.

Related Research: Horner, M. (1968). *Sex differences in achievement motivation and performance in competitive and non-competitive situations.* Unpublished doctoral dissertation, University of Michigan.

...

1341

Test Name: EDUCATIONAL WORK COMPONENTS STUDY QUESTIONNAIRE

Purpose: A selection device to measure motivation to work.

Number of Items: 55

Format: Self report form; 5–choice Likert items; six factors: potential for personal challenge, competitiveness, desirability, tolerance for work pressure, conservative security, willingness to seek reward, surround concern.

Reliability: Cronbach's alpha ranged from .73 to .83.

Author: Miskel, C., and Heller, I.

Article: The educational work components study: An adapted set of measures for work motivation.

Journal: *Journal of Experimental*

Education, Fall 1973, *42*(1), 45–50.

Related Research: Borgatta, E., et al. (1968). The work components study: A revised set of measures of work motivation. *Multivariate Behavioral Research, 3,* 403–414.

• • •

1342

Test Name: HOSTILE PRESS MOTIVATION INSTRUMENT

Purpose: To measure fear of failure motive.

Format: Four TAT slides (father–son, boy in checkered shirt, man at mirror, man in barren office) shown in group conditions: subject responses scored by standard format.

Reliability: Interscorer reliability was .92.

Validity: Significant differences ($p < .05$, one trial) between protestors and nonprotestors.

Author: Teevan, R., and Stamps, L.

Article: A motivational correlate of Viet Nam protest group members.

Journal: *Psychological Reports,* 1973, *33*(3), 777–778.

Related Research: Birney, R., et al. (1969). *Fear of failure.* New York: Van Nostrand.

Hancock, J., & Teevan, R. (1964). Fear of failure and risk taking behavior. *Journal of Personality, 32,* 200–209.

• • •

1343

Test Name: INDEPENDENCE NEED QUESTIONNAIRE

Purpose: To measure need for independence.

Number of Items: 16

Reliability: Test–retest reliability

of a shortened form (8 items) was .61.

Author: Wexley, K. N., et al.

Article: Subordinate personality as a moderator of the effects of participation in three types of appraisal interviews.

Journal: *Journal of Applied Psychology,* August 1973, *58*(1), 54–59.

Related Research: Vroom, V. H. (1959). Some personality determinants of the effects of participation. *Journal of Abnormal and Social Psychology, 59,* 322–327.

• • •

1344

Test Name: INDIK WORK MOTIVATION SCALES

Purpose: To identify work motivation of the disadvantaged.

Time Required: 15 minutes.

Format: Individual, oral interview-type questionnaire with Likert and multiple choice completion items. Scales include: motive to work and to avoid work, expectancy to work and to avoid work, incentive to work and to avoid work.

Author: Van Doren, R. (Ed.).

Article: Manpower, human assessment and the disadvantaged.

Journal: *American Vocational Journal,* January 1973, *48*(1), 86–100.

• • •

1345

Test Name: IOWA PICTURE INTERPRETATION TEST

Purpose: To measure m-achievement.

Author: Herbert, S., and Sassenrath, J.

Article: Achieve, motivation, test anxiety, achievement conditions,

and performance in programmed learning.

Journal: *California Journal of Educational Research,* January 1973, *24*(1), 12–22.

Related Research: Hedlund, J. L. (1953). *Construction and evaluation of an objective test of achievement imagery.* Doctoral dissertation, State University of Iowa.

• • •

1346

Test Name: JOB ATTITUDE QUESTIONNAIRE

Purpose: To measure all but the lowest (physiological) Maslow need categories plus non-Maslow category of autonomy.

Number of Items: 16

Format: Items include security, social, esteem, autonomy, self-actualization, and noncategorized (pay, amount of pressure, and feelings of being informed). Responses are given on a 7-point scale.

Author: Wade, M.

Article: Personnel research.

Journal: *Personnel Journal,* October 1973, *52*(10), 919–920, 926.

Related Research: Waters, L. K., & Roach, D. (1973). A factor analysis of need-fulfillment items designed to measure Maslow need categories. *Personnel Psychology, 26,* 185–190.

• • •

1347

Test Name: LYNN ACHIEVEMENT MOTIVATION QUESTIONNAIRE

Purpose: To discriminate levels of achievement motivation among entrepreneurs, managers, and other occupational categories.

Number of Items: 8

Format: Subjects answer each question *yes* or *no.* All items are presented.

Author: Hines, G. H.

Article: Achievement motivation, occupations, and labor turnover in New Zealand.

Journal: *Journal of Applied Psychology*, December 1973, *58*(3), 313–317.

Related Research: Lynn, R. (1969). An achievement motivation questionnaire. *British Journal of Psychology*, *60*, 529–534.

. . .

1348

Test Name: MANAGERS NEED SATISFACTION QUESTIONNAIRE

Purpose: To measure the need satisfaction of managers.

Number of Items: 8

Format: Subjects respond to each item on a 7-point scale by indicating how much of each characteristic or quality is presently connected with their job and how much they feel should be connected with their job. All items are presented.

Validity: Correlations of each item with absenteeism ranged from .24 to .53.

Author: Hrebiniak, L. G., and Roteman, M. R.

Article: A study of the relationship between need satisfaction and absenteeism among managerial personnel.

Journal: *Journal of Applied Psychology*, December 1973, *58*(3), 381–383.

Related Research: Porter, L. W. (1961). A study of perceived job satisfaction in bottom and middle management jobs. *Journal of*

Applied Psychology, 45, 1–10.

. . .

1349

Test Name: MARRIED STUDENTS COUNSELING NEEDS QUESTIONNAIRE

Purpose: To identify counseling needs of married students.

Format: Part 1 included items sampling degree of concern expressed on a 5-point scale in 13 areas dealing with marital adjustment difficulties. Scale points were *not at all, slightly, somewhat, moderately, considerably.* Part 2 elicited *yes, no,* or *not sure* responses to items concerning familiarity with and use of the counseling center and desire to initiate counseling in one of the areas in Part I.

Author: Graff, R. W, and Horne, A. M.

Article: Counseling needs of married students.

Journal: *Journal of College Student Personnel,* September 1973, *14*(5), 438–442.

. . .

1350

Test Name: MEHRABIAN ACHIEVEMENT SCALE

Purpose: To distinguish high achievers who have a stronger motive to achieve than to avoid failure from low achievers who have a stronger motive to avoid failure than to achieve.

Format: Separate male and female scales of achievement.

Author: Brinkmann, F. H.

Article: Personality correlates of educational set in the classroom.

Journal: *Journal of Educational Research,* January 1973, *66*(5), 221–223.

Related Research: Mehrabian, A.

(1968). Male and female scales of the tendency to achieve. *Educational and Psychological Measurement, 28,* 493–502.

See *D.U.E.M.M., 2,* 1978: 728.

. . .

1351

Test Name: MOTIVATION CHECK-SHEET

Purpose: To provide an indication of motivation.

Number of Items: 40

Format: Items are scored *right* or *wrong* and total *right* is recorded. *Right* is defined as "in the direction of the overachiever." All items are presented.

Validity: Correlation with grade point average for females is .28 and .35 for males.

Author: Packwood, W. T.

Article: Motivation and junior college achievement.

Journal: *Journal of Educational Research,* March 1973, *66*(7), 299–301.

Related Research: Taylor, R. G. Personality traits and discrepant achievement: A review. *Journal of Counseling Psychology,* 1964, *11,* 76–82.

. . .

1352

Test Name: MOTIVATION TO AVOID APPEARING INCOMPETENT SCALE

Purpose: To assess motivation to "save face."

Number of Items: 36

Format: True–false scale; all items given in article.

Reliability: Initial form Kuder-Richardson formula 20 was .88; Final form Kuder-Richardson formula 20 was .89.

Author: Good, L., and Good, K.

Article: An objective measure of the motive to avoid appearing incompetent.

Journal: *Psychological Reports,* June 1973, *32*(3), 1075–1078.

• • •

1353

Test Name: NEED-FOR-ACHIEVEMENT SCALE

Purpose: To measure achievement motivation.

Number of Items: 42

Format: Seven items are embedded in the instrument, which is scored on a 5-point scale from 1 (*rejecting or negative attitude*) to 5 (*accepting or positive attitude*).

Reliability: Reliability estimates among judges' ratings ranged from correlations of .81 to .96.

Author: Ashbaugh, J. A.

Article: Persistence and the disadvantaged college student.

Journal: *Journal of Educational Research,* October 1973, *67*(2), 64–66.

Related Research: Irvin, E. S. (1967). Sentence-completion responses and scholastic success or failure. *Journal of Counseling Psychology, 14,* 269–271.

• • •

1354

Test Name: ORGANIZATIONAL NEED SATISFACTION SCALES

Purpose: To measure the extent of organizational need satisfaction.

Number of Items: 65

Format: Eight multiquestion Likert scales: goal attainment, power, funds, staff and facilities, space, integration, academic freedom, pattern maintenance, and tension reduction. Examples are provided.

Reliability: Kuder-Richardson

formula 20 for subscales ranged from .68 to .91.

Author: Bess, J. L.

Article: Patterns of satisfaction of organizational prerequisites and personal needs in university academic departments.

Journal: *Sociology of Education,* Winter 1973, *46*(1), 99–114.

Related Research: Bess, J. L. (1971). *Patterns of satisfaction of organizational prerequisites and personal needs in university departments of high and low quality.* Doctoral dissertation, University of California, Berkeley.

• • •

1355

Test Name: PERCEIVED NEED-DEFICIENCY SCALE

Purpose: To measure need-deficiency according to the Maslow Theory.

Number of Items: 13

Format: One example provided.

Reliability: Test–retest correlation was .80.

Author: Giandomenico, L. L.

Article: Teacher needs, militancy, and the scope of collective bargaining.

Journal: *Journal of Educational Research,* February 1973, *66*(6), 257–259.

Related Research: Porter, L. W. (1961). A study of perceived need satisfaction in bottom and middle management jobs. *Journal of Applied Psychology, 45,* 1–10.

• • •

1356

Test Name: PERSONAL NEED SCALES

Purpose: To measure degree of personal satisfaction.

Number of Items: 20

Format: Includes: safety–security, affiliation, autonomy, ego, self-fulfillment.

Reliability: Kuder-Richardson formula 20 for subscales ranged from .71 to .84. Examples are presented.

Author: Bess, J. L.

Article: Patterns of satisfaction of organizational prerequisites and personal needs in university academic departments.

Journal: *Sociology of Education,* Winter, 1973, *46*(1), 99–114.

Related Research: Bess, J. L. (1971). *Patterns of satisfaction of organizational prerequisites and personal needs in university departments of high and low quality.* Doctoral dissertation, University of California, Berkeley.

• • •

1357

Test Name: PORTER NEED SATISFACTION QUESTIONNAIRE

Purpose: To assess organizational needs or motivation.

Number of Items: 13

Format: Five need areas were rated on a 7-point scale, in two parts: "How much is there now?" and "How much should there be?" Two scores were subtracted.

Validity: Relationship of scales to rated importance of job characteristics: All correlations with "should be" responses were significant but moderate.

Author: Waters, L., and Roach, D.

Article: Relation between importance ratings and two parts of the Porter Need Satisfaction Questionnaire.

Journal: *Psychological Reports,* 1973, *32*(1), 59–62.

Related Research: Herman, J., & Holin, C. (1973). Managerial satisfaction and organizational roles: An investigation of Porter's need deficiency scales. *Journal of Applied Psychology, 57*, 118–124.

Porter, L. (1961). A study of perceived need satisfaction in bottom and middle management jobs. *Journal of Applied Psychology, 45*, 1–10.

. . .

1358

Test Name: PRECOUNSELING GOAL CHECKLIST

Purpose: To identify goals to be attained through counseling.

Number of Items: 38

Format: Subjects check goals of concern to them that they wish the counselor to help them attain. A few items are presented.

Author: Thompson, A., and Miller, A.

Article: A criterion system for measuring outcomes of counseling.

Journal: *Journal of College Student Personnel*, November 1973, *14*(6), 483–489.

Related Research: Miller, A., & Thompson, A. (1973). Factor structure of a goal checklist for clients. *Psychological Reports, 32,* 497–498.

. . .

1359

Test Name: SELF–PEER NEED RATING

Purpose: To rate self and peers on seven needs defined in Edwards Personal Preference Schedule (EPPS).

Format: Self and others are rated on each need on a 7-point scale; abasement, dominance, aggression, succorance, deference, autonomy, nurturance.

Reliability: Peer average ratings, intraclass, were .77, .86, .51, .92, .62, .87, and .80.

Validity: Self-ratings with EPPS ranged from .22 to .57; peer ratings with EPPS ranged from –.24 to .45.

Author: Markey, V.

Article: Psychological need relationships in dyadic attraction and rejection.

Journal: *Psychological Reports,* 1973, *32*(1), 111–123.

. . .

1360

Test Name: SENTENCE COMPLETION TEST OF SAFETY AND ESTEEM MOTIVES

Purpose: To assess Maslow's safety and esteem motives.

Number of Items: Not reported.

Format: Sentence completion.

Reliability: Interjudge reliability ranged from .66 to .85 with means of .78 and .73 for safety and esteem scores.

Validity: Subjects classified as safety and esteem-oriented on the SCT were significantly different in Minnesota Multiphasic Personality Inventory scores for manifest anxiety, dominance, dependency.

Author: Wilson, J., and Aronoff, J.

Article: A sentence completion test assessing safety and esteem motives.

Journal: *Journal of Personality Assessment*, 1973, *37*(4), 351–354.

Related Research: Aronoff, J. (1972). *A manual to score safety, love and belongingness and esteem motives.* Unpublished Technical Report.

. . .

1361

Test Name: SPEED AND PERSISTENCE TEST

Purpose: To assess motivation and understanding of instructions.

Number of Items: 300

Time Required: 3 minutes.

Format: Subject is instructed to make a mark in 300 squares as quickly as possible; two 1.5 minute periods.

Author: Jensen, A.

Article: Level I and Level II abilities in three ethnic groups.

Journal: *American Educational Research Journal*, Fall 1973, *10*(4), 263–276.

Related Research: Jensen, A. (1974). The effect of race of examiner on the mental test scores of White and Black pupils. *Journal of Educational Measurement, 11*, 1–14.

. . .

1362

Test Name: SUCCESS AVOIDANCE MEASURE

Purpose: To assess motivation to avoid success.

Number of Items: 29

Format: True–false.

Reliability: Kuder-Richardson formula 20 was .81.

Validity: Females scored significantly higher ($p < .01$) in motivation to avoid success than males.

Author: Good, L., and Good, K.

Article: An objective measure of the motive to avoid success.

Journal: *Psychological Reports,* December 1973, *33*(3), 1009–1010.

. . .

1363

Test Name: TEACHERS PROFESSIONAL AMBITION INDEX

Purpose: To measure teachers' professional ambition.

Format: Content centers on colleague leadership based on high levels of professional skill. Each item has five Likert responses. Some items are presented.

Validity: Intercorrelation of items ranged from .31 to .52.

Author: Cohen, E. G.

Article: Open-space schools: The opportunity to become ambitious.

Journal: *Sociology of Education,* Spring 1973, *46*(2), 143–161.

• • •

1364

Test Name: TEACHERS' VERTICAL AMBITION INDEX

Purpose: To measure teachers' interest in promotion into administrative ranks.

Format: Items concern lack of promotion opportunities in school hierarchy. They reflect a desire for upward occupational mobility. Each item has five Likert responses. Some items are presented.

Author: Cohen, E. G.

Article: Open-space schools: The opportunity to become ambitious.

Journal: *Sociology of Education,* Spring 1973, *46*(2), 143–161.

• • •

1365

Test Name: THERAPY GOAL CHECKLIST

Purpose: To assess patients' goals for therapy.

Format: Test consists of a 43–item list checked by patients on social and family relations and self-improvement.

Validity: Four factors (principal components) identified: Social Personal Security, Vocational Emotional, Academic Skills, Marital–Close Relationships.

Author: Miller, A., and Thompson, A.

Article: Factor structure of a goal-checklist for clients.

Journal: *Psychological Reports,* April 1973, *32*(2), 497–498.

Related Research: Request Document NAPS-02018 from Microfiche Publications, 305 E. 46th St., New York, New York 10017 ($1.50 for microfiche copy of instrument).

• • •

1366

Test Name: WORK MOTIVATION SCALES

Purpose: To measure work motivation of engineers.

Number of Items: 7

Format: Each item or dimension has scaled behavioral incidents as reference points along a 9-point scale. Raters select a point on the continuum that best describes them.

Validity: Correlations with supervisor and engineer ratings ($N = 202$) ranged from .08 to .79.

Author: Williams, W. E., and Seiler, D. A.

Article: Relationship between measures of effort and job performance.

Journal: *Journal of Applied Psychology,* February 1973, *57*(1), 49–54.

Related Research: Landy, J. L., & Guion, R. M. (1970). Development of scales for the measurement of work motivation. *Organizational Behavior and Human Performance, 5,* 93–103.

···

CHAPTER 15
Perception

···

1367

Test Name: ACADEMIC ACHIEVEMENT ACCOUNTABILITY SCALE

Purpose: To measure a subject's feeling of personal accountability for performance outcome.

Number of Items: 15

Format: Forced-choice.

Reliability: Kuder-Richardson formula 20 estimates of .63 and .65.

Author: Clifford, M. M.

Article: How learning and liking are related—A clue.

Journal: *Journal of Educational Psychology,* April 1973, *64*(2), 183–186.

Related Research: Clifford, M. M., & Cleary, T. A. (1972). The relationship between children's academic performance and achievement accountability. *Child Development, 43,* 647–655.

···

1368

Test Name: ACADEMIC INTERNAL–EXTERNAL (I-E) CONTROL SCALE

Purpose: To assess locus of control in college situations.

Number of Items: 20

Format: Based on Intellectual Achievement Responsibility Scale.

Validity: Correlation with Rotter I-E was −.18 ($p < .05$); correlation with measure of debilitating test anxiety was −.25 ($p < .05$).

Author: Procuik, T., and Breen, L.

Article: Internal external control, test anxiety and academic achievement: Additional data.

Journal: *Psychological Reports,* October 1973, *33*(2), 563–566.

···

1369

Test Name: ADJECTIVE GENERATION TECHNIQUE

Purpose: To describe self.

Format: Subject is asked to generate spontaneously five adjectives to describe self.

Reliability: Test–retest (4 weeks) reliability was .74 ($p < .001$).

Validity: Correlation with self-regard scale of Personal Orientation Inventory was .53 ($p < .01$).

Author: Potkay, C., and Allen, B.

Article: The adjective generation technique: An alternative to adjective checklists.

Journal: *Psychological Reports,* April 1973, *32*(2), 457–458.

Related Research: Allen, B. (1971). Implications of social research for racism. *Psychological Reports, 29,* 883–891.

···

1370

Test Name: ANALYTIC EMPATHY SCALE

Purpose: To assess empathic understanding.

Format: Four actor clients rated concepts on a bipolar summative scale (1–7) with respect to self, ideal self, best friend, ideal employer, ideal teacher. After watching 10 minute video tape subjects were asked to predict actors' ratings. Discrepancy between actual and predicted score was computed.

Author: Leung, P.

Article: Comparative effects of training in external and internal concentration on two counseling behaviors.

Journal: *Journal of Counseling Psychology,* May 1973, *20*(3), 227–234.

Related Research: Kelly, G. (1965). *The psychology of personal constructs.* New York: Norton.

···

1371

Test Name: ATTITUDES TOWARD COOPERATION TEST

Purpose: To measure perception of the cooperative–competitive learning environment.

Format: Subjects indicate by circling 1, 2, 3, or 4 (*never, sometimes, most of the time, always*) the frequency with which cooperative and competitive events occur in their classroom. Examples are given.

Reliability: Test–retest product–moment correlation was .89.

Author: Wheeler, R., and Ryan, F. L.

Article: Effects of cooperative and competitive classroom environnents on the attitudes and achievements of elementary school students engaged in social studies inquiring activities.

Journal: *Journal of Educational Psychology,* December 1973, *65*(3), 402–407.

▪ ▪ ▪

1372

Test Name: ATTRIBUTE RATING SCALE

Purpose: To assess perception and perception of counselor by client.

Format: Subject rated self or counselor on: openness, maturity, acceptance, sensitivity, masculinity. Forms had five Likert scales with 6 divisions (*extremely* to *not at all*).

Author: Baldwin, B.

Article: Generalization of self-discrepant information as a function of defensive style.

Journal: *Journal of Counseling Psychology,* May 1973, *20*(3), 235–239.

▪ ▪ ▪

1373

Test Name: ATTRIBUTION OF SUCCESS OR FAILURE SCALE

Purpose: To determine whether subjects attributed their performance on a task as due to themselves (internal) or to other factors (external).

Number of Items: 8

Format: Subjects rank eight statements explaining the basis of their performance.

Validity: Correlation with Text Anxiety Questionnaire was –.162 (*ns*). Correlation with F Scale was .328 (*ns*).

Author: Sales, S., and Friend, K.

Article: Success and failure as determinants of levels of authoritarianism.

Journal: *Behavioral Science,* May 1973, *18*(3), 163–172.

Related Research: Doris, J., & Sarason, S. (1955). Test anxiety and blame assignment in a failure situation. *Journal of Abnormal and Social Psychology, 50,* 335–338.

▪ ▪ ▪

1374

Test Name: AUDITORY ANALYSIS TEST

Purpose: To assess children's ability to analyze components of the sound of words.

Number of Items: 40

Format: Child is asked to say a word, then to repeat it with a specific sound omitted; testing is discontinued after four successive errors.

Validity: Rosner and Simon (1970) reported that 30 to 70% of the variance of reading scores of first through sixth grade children has been accounted for. Correlations with Stanford Achievement World Meaning (.49); Paragraph Meaning (.47); Spelling (.48) tests were reported.

Author: Rosner, J.

Article: Language arts and arithmetic achievement, and specifically related perceptual skills.

Journal: *American Educational Research Journal,* Winter 1973, *10*(1), 59–68.

Related Research: Rosner, J., & Simon, D. (1970). *The auditory analysis test: An initial report.* Pittsburgh, PA: University of Pittsburgh, Learning Research and Development Center.

▪ ▪ ▪

1375

Test Name: BETT'S VIVIDNESS OF IMAGERY SCALE

Purpose: To measure vividness of imagery.

Format: Seven modalities and a total score; modalities were visual, auditory, tactile, kinesthetic, gustatory, olfactory, and organic.

Reliability: Test–retest (total score, 6–week interval) reliability was .91.

Author: Evans, I., and Kamemoto, W.

Article: Reliability of the short form of Bett's Questionnaire on Mental Imagery: Replication.

Journal: *Psychological Reports,* August 1973, *33*(1), 281–282.

See *D.U.E.M.M., 2,* 1978: 753.

▪ ▪ ▪

1376

Test Name: BLEDSOE SELF CONCEPT SCALE

Purpose: To assess self concept.

Number of Items: 30

Format: 30 adjectives to which subject responds: "… I am nearly always … about half the time … or just now and then …"

Validity: Sex differences on certain adjectives may have been due to an association of "feminine" items with "positive" attributes.

Author: Bledsoe, J.

Article: Sex differences in self concept: Fact or artifact?

Journal: Psychological Reports, June 1973, *32*(3), 1253–1254.

Related Research: Bledsoe, J. C. (1964). Self concepts of children and their intelligence, achievement, interests, and anxiety. *Journal of Individual Psychology, 20,* 55–58.

▪ ▪ ▪

1377

Test Name: BRESKIN RIGIDITY TEST

Purpose: To assess perceptual rigidity.

Number of Items: 15

Format: Subject is asked to select pairs of figures; the rigid person presumably chooses the pair that best fit together.

Validity: Marijuana users were significantly ($p < .01$) lower in rigidity than nonusers.

Author: Simon, W., et al.

Article: Marijuana use and a measure of perceptual rigidity.

Journal: *Psychological Reports,* August 1973, *33*(1), 122.

Related Research: Breskin, S. (1968). Measurement of rigidity, a non-verbal test. *Perceptual and Motor Skills, 27,* 1203–1206.

See *D.U.E.M.M., 2,* 1978: 917.

• • •

1378

Test Name: CHABASSOL ADOLESCENT STRUCTURE INVENTORY

Purpose: To measure the extent to which the adolescent wants information and direction from an adult and the degree to which the adolescent perceives such structure.

Format: Two subscales: "Wants structure" and "has structure."

Author: Chabassol, D. J.

Article: The measurement of some aspects of structure in adolescents.

Journal: *Journal of Educational Research,* February 1973, *66*(6), 247–250.

Related Research: Chabassol, D. J. (1971). A scale for the evaluation of structure needs and perceptions in adolescence. *Journal of Experimental Education, 40,* 12–16.

See *D.U.E.M.M., 2,* 1978: 760.

1379

Test Name: CLARITY OF SELF CONCEPT SEMANTIC DIFFERENTIAL

Purpose: To measure clarity of self-concept.

Format: Concept "myself" rated on 13 bipolar adjective pair scales; subject indicated degree of certainty of response to scales.

Reliability: Coefficient of internal consistency was greater than .80 in all cases.

Validity: Correlation with locus of control was .32 ($p < .01$).

Author: Organ, D.

Article: Locus of control and clarity of self concept.

Journal: *Perceptual and Motor Skills,* August 1973, *37*(1), 100–102.

Related Research: Pervin, L., & Lilly, R. (1967). Social desirability and self-ideal self ratings on the Semantic Differential. *Educational and Psychological Measurement, 27,* 845–853.

• • •

1380

Test Name: CLASS ACTIVITIES QUESTIONNAIRE

Purpose: To obtain students' perception of prevailing patterns of cognitive and affective emphasis.

Number of Items: 23

Format: Students agree or disagree on a 4-point scale to statements describing tasks and other activities characterizing their class.

Author: Walberg, H. J., et al.

Article: Grade level, cognition, and affect: A cross-section of classroom perceptions.

Journal: *Journal of Educational*

Psychology, April 1973, *64*(2), 142–146.

Related Research: Steele, J., et al. (1971). An instrument for assessing instructional climate through low-inference student judgments. *American Educational Research Journal, 8,* 447–466.

• • •

1381

Test Name: CONCEPT-SPECIFIC ANXIETY SCALE

Purpose: To measure affective response to the concept of "the self."

Format: 15 scales with a semantic differential format.

Author: Cole, C., et al.

Article: Effects of verbal interaction conditions on self concept discrimination and anxiety.

Journal: *Journal of Counseling Psychology,* September 1973, *20*(5), 431–436.

Related Research: Cole, C., et al. (1969). Measurement of stimulus-specific anxiety. *Psychological Reports, 25,* 49–50.

• • •

1382

Test Name: COUNSELOR EXPECTANCY TEST

Purpose: To assess extent that clients expect counselors to make vocational choices for them.

Number of Items: 6

Format: Same style as statements on Rotter I-E Scale.

Author: Ullrich, M.

Article: Several measures of expectancy of vocational counseling.

Journal: *Psychological Reports,* August 1973, *33*(1), 299–304.

1383

Test Name: CRANDALL LOCUS OF CONTROL INSTRUMENT

Purpose: To measure students' feelings of control over reinforcements they receive in math.

Number of Items: 10

Format: Five negatively expressed and five positively expressed items are included.

Reliability: Internal consistency coefficients of .29 and .35.

Author: Smith, I. D.

Article: Impact of computer-assisted instruction on student attitudes.

Journal: *Journal of Educational Psychology,* June 1973, *64*(3), 366–373.

Related Research: Crandall, V. C., et al. (1965). Children's beliefs in their own control of reinforcements in intellectual academic achievement situations. *Child Development, 36,* 91–111.

See *D.U.E.M.M., 2,* 1978: 786.

∎ ∎ ∎

1384

Test Name: DRIVING MOTION PICTURE TEST

Purpose: To assess the characteristics of perceptually handicapped children.

Number of Items: 12

Format: Individual and group forms; subject watches toy truck move through model town, then must retrace route on a photograph, from a different orientation.

Reliability: Kuder-Richardson formula 20 values were .83 (individual) and .74 to .86 (group).

Validity: Correlation with Iowa Reading Scores was .09 to .49.

Author: McDaniel, E.

Article: Ten motion picture tests of perceptual abilities.

Journal: *Perceptual and Motor Skills,* June 1973, *36*(3), 755–759.

∎ ∎ ∎

1385

Test Name: DYMOND RATING TESTS

Purpose: To measure empathy and insight.

Format: Forms A and B; subjects rated on six characteristics (e.g., superior–inferior); 5-point scale; discrepancy scores used to rate empathy. Insight score was based on consistency of scores.

Validity: Correlation with abstract intelligence ranged from .02 to .17 (Lindgren & Robinson, 1953).

Author: Walker, R., and Foley, J.

Article: Social intelligence: Its history and measurement.

Journal: *Psychological Reports,* December 1973, *33,* 839–864.

Related Research: Dymond, R. F. (1949). A scale for measurement of empathic ability. *Journal of Consulting Psychology, 13,* 127–133.

Lindgren, H., & Robinson, J. (1953). An evaluation of Dymond's test of insight and empathy. *Journal of Consulting Psychology, 17,* 172–176.

∎ ∎ ∎

1386

Test Name: EMBEDDED FIGURES MOTION PICTURE TEST

Purpose: To assess characteristics of perceptually handicapped children.

Number of Items: 18

Format: Group and individual forms: after seeing a geometric figure the subject must choose one of four designs holding the initial stimulus.

Reliability: Kuder-Richardson formula 20 values were .73 (individual forms) and .28 to .61 (group forms).

Validity: Correlations with Iowa Reading Scores were .28 to .58.

Author: McDaniel, E.

Article: Ten motion picture tests of perceptual abilities.

Journal: *Perceptual and Motor Skills,* June 1973, *36*(3), 755–759.

∎ ∎ ∎

1387

Test Name: EMPATHY SCALE

Purpose: To assess ability to enter into another's life.

Number of Items: 11

Format: Items were rated on a Likert scale.

Author: Freehill, M. F.

Article: Intelligence, empathy and methodologic bias about teaching the gifted.

Journal: *The Gifted Child Quarterly,* Winter 1973, *18*(4), 247–248.

Related Research: Sherman, S. E., & Stotland, E. (1973). *Development of scales to measure tendencies to empathize in empathy, fantasy, and help* (E. Matthews et al., Eds.). Unpublished manuscript, University of Washington, Seattle.

∎ ∎ ∎

1388

Test Name: FIGURAL MEMORY SPAN MOTION PICTURE TEST

Purpose: To assess the characteristics of the perceptually handicapped child.

Number of Items: 18

Format: Subjects must arrange two designs in the same order as presented to them; the test has group and individual forms.

Reliability: Kuder-Richardson formula 20 values were .50 (individual form) and −.06 to .47 (group form).

Validity: Correlations with Iowa Reading Scores ranged from .18 to .33.

Author: McDaniel, E.

Article: Ten motion picture tests of perceptual abilities.

Journal: *Perceptual and Motor Skills,* June 1973, *36*(3), 755–759.

• • •

1389

Test Name: FLORIDA KEY TEST

Purpose: To assess student self concepts as learners.

Number of Items: 18

Format: Filled out by teacher; four dimensions: relating, asserting, investing, coping.

Reliability: Split-half reliability ranged from .62 to .96 for teachers.

Validity: Validity with the Coopersmith Scale was .14.

Author: Purkey, W., et al.

Article: The Florida Key: A scale to infer learners' self concept.

Journal: *Educational and Psychological Measurement,* Winter 1973, *33*(4), 979–984.

• • •

1390

Test Name: FORM IDENTIFICATION: MOTION PICTURE TEST

Purpose: To assess characteristics of perceptually handicapped children.

Number of Items: 18

Format: Group and individual forms: Subject shown designs in motion picture and must choose the same from four alternatives.

Reliability: Kuder-Richardson formula 20 values were .32 (individual form) and .23 to .56 (group form).

Validity: Correlations with Iowa Reading scores ranged from −.16 to .37.

Author: McDaniel, E.

Article: Ten motion picture tests of perceptual abilities.

Journal: *Perceptual and Motor Skills,* June 1973, *36*(3), 755–759.

• • •

1391

Test Name: GIBSON SCRIBBLES TEST

Purpose: To measure subject's ability to perceive critical distinctive features.

Validity: Correlation with Moral Judgement Maturity was −.39 (*p* < .01).

Author: Arbuthnot, J.

Article: Relationships between maturity of moral judgement and measures of cognitive abilities.

Journal: *Psychological Reports,* December 1973, *33*(3), 945–946.

Related Research: Gibson, E. (1969). *Principles of perceptual learning and development.* New York: Appleton-Century-Crofts.

• • •

1392

Test Name: GROUP JUDGMENT SCALE

Purpose: To assess perception by subject of how a group would work together (modified version of

Byrne Interpersonal Judgment Scale).

Number of Items: 6

Format: Each item had seven choices (e.g., *below* to *above average*) regarding group productivity, morale, belongingness, efficiency, personal feelings, enjoyment of working together.

Reliability: Split half reliability on four of the scales was .77 (corrected).

Author: Good, L., and Nelson, D.

Article: Effects of person–group and intragroup attitude similarity on perceived group attractiveness and cohesiveness: II.

Journal: *Psychological Reports,* October 1973, *33*(3), 551–560.

• • •

1393

Test Name: GRUEN-KORTE-STEPHENS INTERNAL–EXTERNAL SCALE

Purpose: To assess locus of control orientation.

Reliability: Test–retest (10 days) reliability was .83.

Validity: Internal boys imitated externals' behavior more than external boys when the given behavior was instrumental to the task at hand but less when the behavior was not instrumental.

Author: Bottinelli, S., and Weizmann, F.

Article: Task independence and locus of control orientation in children.

Journal: *Journal of Personality Assessment,* 1973, *37*(4), 375–381.

Related Research: Asher, J., et al. (1971). *Final Report: The development of new measures in elementary school children* (U.S. Office of Education, Contract No.

OEC-0-70-4952). Washington, DC: U.S. Office of Education.

• • •

1394

Test Name: HOW I FEEL ABOUT MYSELF INVENTORY

Purpose: To measure self-concept.

Number of Items: 100

Format: Multidimensional inventory includes 10 behavior categories: physical abilities, mental abilities, social relations with peers of the opposite sex, social relationships with peers of the same sex, social relations with parents, social relations with teachers, work habits, personality-social virtues, personality-happy qualities, school subjects. *Yes, no, not sure* were the possible answers.

Author: Grant, C. A.

Article: Black studies materials do make a difference.

Journal: *Journal of Educational Research,* May–June 1973, *66*(3), 400–404.

• • •

1395

Test Name: HOW I SEE MYSELF SCALE

Purpose: To measure students' concepts of their academic and social ability when rating themselves compared with classmates.

Number of Items: 8

Format: Items include: reading, social studies, spelling, arithmetic, art, sports, making friends, getting along with classmates.

Reliability: Test–retest correlation of .74.

Validity: Correlations between selected battery scores and corresponding achievement test results ranged from –.12 to .59

and for total scores, *r*s = .50 and .65.

Author: Busk, P. L., et al.

Article: Effects of schools' racial composition on the self-concept of Black and White students.

Journal: *Journal of Educational Research,* October 1973, *67*(2), 57–63.

Related Research: Sears, P. S. (1940). Levels of aspiration in academically successful and unsuccessful children. *Journal of Abnormal and Social Psychology, 35,* 498–536.

• • •

1396

Test Name: I-E SCALE

Purpose: To measure sense of control over one's environment.

Number of Items: 29 forced-choice items.

Format: Subjects choose the statement for each item that is more true for them. The higher the score, the more external the person's orientation. Scores range from 0 to 23.

Reliability: Test–retest reliability ranged from .55 to .83. Internal consistency coefficients ranged from .63 to .79.

Author: Gozali, H., et al.

Article: Relationship between the internal–external control construct and achievement.

Journal: *Journal of Educational Psychology,* February 1973, *64*(1), 9–14.

Related Research: Rotter, J. B. (1966). Generalized expectancies for internal versus external control of reinforcement. *Psychological Monographs, 80,* 609.

See *D.U.E.M.M., 2,* 1978, 818.

1397

Test Name: IMAGINARY COMPANION QUESTIONNAIRE

Purpose: To provide specific data about the home setting and play activities of preschool children.

Format: Two parts: Part I has six topics, Part II has nine.

Author: Manosevitz, M., et al.

Article: Individual and family correlates of imaginary companions in preschool children.

Journal: *Developmental Psychology,* January 1973, *8*(1), 72–79.

• • •

1398

Test Name: INDEX OF ADJUSTMENT AND VALUES

Purpose: To measure global self-concepts.

Reliability: Test–retest reliability was .92.

Author: Fretz, B. R., and Engle, D. A.

Article: Changes in self-concept as a function of academic test results.

Journal: *Journal of Educational Research,* January 1973, *66*(5), 227–229.

Related Research: Bills, R. E., et al. (1951). An index of adjustment and values. *Journal of Consulting Psychology, 15,* 257–261.

• • •

1399

Test Name: INTERNAL–EXTERNAL CONTROL PROVERBS TEST

Purpose: To assess locus of control in university students.

Number of Items: 25

Time Required: Less than 30 minutes.

Format: Subjects rated proverbs on a 6-point scale from *strongly agree* to *strongly disagree*.

Validity: Principal axis method yielded nine factors (Internality, Conformity, Action Now, Chance, Time is Ripe, Verticality, Pragmatism, Initiative, Appropriateness); items and loadings are given in article. Factor scores were correlated with Rotter Locus of Control scores with 5/9 significant; all correlations low.

Author: Friedman, S., and Manaster, B.

Article: Internal–external control: Studies through the use of proverbs.

Journal: *Psychological Reports,* October 1973, *33*(2), 611–615.

■ ■ ■

1400

Test Name: INVENTORY OF TEMPORAL EXPERIENCES

Purpose: To measure the meaning of time experiences.

Number of Items: 171 original, 111 retained on basis of theoretical relevance.

Format: Paper-and-pencil format yielded four scores: human, animal, vital, and physical time.

Reliability: $N = 223$ college students, corrected split-half reliability coefficients were .78, .80, .88, and .82.

Validity: Intercorrelation of four scores resulted in four significant correlations: –.23, .31, –.18, –.58, and .27; article also reports relation of time scores to adjective checklist items and the Omnibus Personality Inventory.

Author: Yonge, G.

Article: Time experiences as measures of personality.

Journal: *Measurement and*

Evaluation in Guidance, 1973, *5*(4), 475–482.

■ ■ ■

1401

Test Name: JAMES I-E SCALE

Purpose: To assess locus of control.

Validity: Significant differences between "internals" and "externals" in academic achievement.

Author: Foster, J., and Gade, E.

Article: Locus of control, consistency of vocational interest patterns, and academic achievement.

Journal: *Journal of Counseling Psychology,* May 1973, *20*(3), 290–292.

Related Research: James, W. (1963). *The I-E Scale–scoring directions.* Grand Forks: University of North Dakota, Department of Psychology.

■ ■ ■

1402

Test Name: JANIS AND FIELD FEELINGS OF INADEQUACY SCALE

Purpose: To assess self-esteem.

Validity: Correlation with locus of control was –.29 ($p < .001$) for male subjects, –.20 ($p < .01$) for female subjects.

Author: Ryckman, R., and Sherman, M.

Article: Relationship between self-esteem and internal–external control for men and women.

Journal: *Psychological Reports,* June 1973, *32*(3), 1106.

Related Research: Janis, I., & Field, P. (1969). Sex differences and personality factors related to persuasibility. In I. Janis & C. Hovland (Eds.), *Personality and*

persuasibility. New Haven: Yale University Press.

■ ■ ■

1403

Test Name: JEWISH-AMERICAN IDENTITY SCALE

Purpose: To measure dimensions of Jewish-American identity.

Number of Items: 20 (some of the items are given)

Format: 7-point scale.

Reliability: Cronbach's alpha ranged from .72 to .88 for Jewish identity and from .84 to .89 for American identity on four samples.

Validity: Factor analysis resulted in two factors: each differentiated the American identity and Jewish identity factors.

Author: Zak, I.

Article: Dimensions of Jewish-American identity.

Journal: *Psychological Reports,* December 1973, *33*(3), 891–900.

Related Research: Herman, S. (1970). *Israelis and Jews: The continuity of identity.* New York: Random House.

Hofman, J., & Zak, I. (1969). Interpersonal contact and attitude change in a cross-cultural situation. *Journal of Social Psychology, 78,* 165–171.

■ ■ ■

1404

Test Name: JOB CONDITIONS QUESTIONNAIRE

Purpose: To identify perceptions of the work environment.

Format: Eight-page questionnaire designed for the disadvantaged.

Author: VanDoren, R. (Ed.).

Article: Manpower, human assessment and the disadvantaged.

Journal: *American Vocational Journal,* January 1973, *48*(1), 86–100.

● ● ●

1405

Test Name: LEVENSON INTERNAL, POWERFUL OTHERS, AND CHANCE SCALES

Purpose: To measure expectations of internality, control by powerful others, and control by chance forces.

Number of Items: 24

Format: Likert format of eight items for each of three scales. Possible range on each scale is from 0 to 48.

Author: Levenson, H.

Article: Perceived parental antecedents of internal, powerful others, and chance locus of control orientations.

Journal: *Developmental Psychology,* September 1973, *9*(2), 268–274.

● ● ●

1406

Test Name: LEVENSON LOCUS OF CONTROL SCALE

Purpose: To assess internality and externality.

Format: Three subscales: personal, powerful others, chance.

Validity: Correlations of three subscales with the Dogmatism Scale were .34 (*p* < .01), .49 (*p* < .001), and .34 (*p* < .01) for college women.

Author: Sherman, M., et al.

Article: Replication of the relationship between dogmatism and locus of control.

Journal: *Psychological Reports,* December 1973, *33*(3), 749–750.

Related Research: Levenson, H.

(1972). *Distractions within the concept of internal–external control: Development of a new scale.* Paper presented at the 80th Meeting of the American Psychological Association, Honolulu, Hawaii.

● ● ●

1407

Test Name: LIKERT PROFILE OF A SCHOOL PRINCIPAL QUESTIONNAIRE

Purpose: To identify principals' perception of style of administration.

Number of Items: 38

Format: Six categories: leadership, motivation, communication, interaction influence, decision making, performance goals. Scores for each item range from 0 to 20 (exploitative–authoritative to participative group).

Author: Culler, B., et al.

Article: Administrative behavior and student dissatisfaction: A possible relationship.

Journal: *Peabody Journal of Education,* January 1973, *50*(2), 155–163.

● ● ●

1408

Test Name: LIKERT PROFILE OF A SCHOOL TEACHER QUESTIONNAIRE

Purpose: To identify teachers' perception of style of administration.

Number of Items: 31

Format: Six categories: leadership, motivation, communication, interaction influence, decision making, performance goals. Scores for each item range from 0 to 20 (exploitative–authoritative to participative group).

Author: Cullers, B., et al.

Article: Administrative behavior and student dissatisfaction: A possible relationship.

Journal: *Peabody Journal of Education,* January 1973, *50*(2), 155–163.

● ● ●

1409

Test Name: MATHEMATICS SELF-CONCEPT SCALE

Purpose: To measure self-perception with respect to mathematics.

Number of Items: 10

Format: Subject responds on 5-point scale from *strongly agree* to *strongly disagree.*

Validity: With School Sentiment Index, *r* = .48 (*p* < .01); with Prescriptive Math Inventory, *r* = .48 (*p* < .01); with CTBS (Pretest in Math), *r* = .47 (*p* < .01).

Author: Holly, K., et al.

Article: The relationship of an experimental form of the mathematics self concept scale to cognitive and noncognitive variable for a sample of seventh grade pupils in a middle class southern California community.

Journal: *Educational and Psychological Measurement,* Summer 1973, *33*(2), 505–508.

● ● ●

1410

Test Name: MICHILL ADJECTIVE RATING SCALE

Purpose: To assess rating of self and others.

Number of Items: 48

Format: Self and others are rated on 48 adjectives (including ambitious and determined) on 5-point rating scales. Four independent factors: Unhappiness, Extraversion, Self Assertiveness, Productive Persistence.

Reliability: Ranged from .78 to .90.

Author: Quereshi, M., and Widlak, F.

Article: Students perception of a college teacher as a function of their sex and achievement level.

Journal: *Journal of Experimental Education,* Spring 1973, *41*(3), 53–57.

Related Research: Quereshi, M. (1970). The development of the Michill Adjective Rating Scale (MARS). *Journal of Clinical Psychology, 26,* 192–196.

• • •

1411

Test Name: MOVING SLOT MOTION PICTURE TEST

Purpose: To assess characteristics of perceptually handicapped children.

Number of Items: 16

Format: Subject is exposed to small portions of a moving design and must identify from four alternatives; group and individual forms.

Reliability: Kuder-Richardson formula 20 values were .40 (individual form) and .65 to –.14 (group form).

Validity: Correlation with Iowa Reading Scores ranged from .24 to .34.

Author: McDaniel, E.

Article: Ten motion picture tests for perceptual abilities.

Journal: *Perceptual and Motor Skills,* June 1973, *36*(3), 755–759.

• • •

1412

Test Name: MULTIPLE CHOICE BENDER TEST

Purpose: To provide an index of level of visual discrimination and

to familiarize children with the crucial aspects of the Bender designs.

Format: Child matches the Bender figure standard from four choices including three variations representative of errors scored by the Koppitz system.

Author: Isaac, B. K.

Article: Perceptual-motor development of first graders as related to class, race, intelligence, visual discrimination, and motivation.

Journal: *Journal of School Psychology,* March 1973, *11*(1), 47–56.

• • •

1413

Test Name: NOWICKI-STRICKLAND LOCUS OF CONTROL SCALE FOR ADULTS

Purpose: To assess locus of control.

Number of Items: 40

Format: Yes–no response. Sample items: "Do you believe it is better to be smarter than lucky?"

Validity: Correlation with 16 Adjective Checklist Scales: 6/16 were significant, ranging from .25 to .46 for 36 undergraduate men and women.

Author: Duke, M., and Nowicki, S.

Article: Personality correlates of the Nowicki-Strickland Locus of Control Scale for Adults.

Journal: *Psychological Reports,* August 1973, *33*(1), 267–270.

Related Research: See *D.U.E.M.M., 2,* 1978: 799.

• • •

1414

Test Name: PERCEPTUAL TEST BATTERY

Purpose: To explore children's

auditory and visual perceptual processing abilities.

Format: Four auditory subscales: discrimination, memory for words, memory for sentences, for number sequences; two visual subscales: form discrimination, form memory.

Author: Weintraub, S., et al.

Article: Summary of investigations related to reading July 1, 1972, to June 30, 1973.

Journal: *Reading Research Quarterly,* 1973–74, *9*(3), 429–430.

Related Research: Truraids, D., et al. (1972, April). A perceptual test battery: Development and standardization. *The Elementary School Journal, 72,* 351–361.

• • •

1415

Test Name: PERSONAL EFFICACY SCALE

Purpose: To assess perception of personal control.

Validity: Correlation with Rokeach Dogmatism Scale was –.309 ($p < $ .01; undergraduate students).

Author: Franklin, B.

Article: Dogmatism and personal efficacy.

Journal: *Psychological Reports,* October 1973, *33*(2), 594.

Related Research: Gurin, C. (1968). *Inner city Negro youth in a job training project: A study of factors related to attrition and job success.* Washington, DC: U.S. Department of Labor.

• • •

1416

Test Name: POSTTREATMENT QUESTIONNAIRE

Purpose: To determine extent of

subject's awareness of contingencies of reinforcement after treatment.

Format: In addition to awareness items, scaled questions regarding: effectiveness of feedback, importance of success, need for Experimenter's approval, importance of task success, task difficulty, pleasantness of experimenters.

Author: Weisenberg, M.

Article: Informative and affective feedback: Implications for interviewing.

Journal: *Psychological Reports,* October 1973, *33*(2), 527–534.

• • •

1417

Test Name: PSYCHOLOGICAL DIFFERENTIATION INVENTORY

Purpose: To assess degree of differentiation.

Number of Items: 50

Format: Four-point items. Five subscales: embeddedness, ego functioning, social awareness, controls and defenses, body image, global score.

Validity: Correlations with RFT were all nonsignificant.

Author: Gaines, L., and Miller, L.

Article: Measures of psychological differentiation: Rod and Frame Test and the Psychological Differentiation Inventory.

Journal: *Perceptual and Motor Skills,* August 1973, *37*(1), 146.

Related Research: Evans, F. (1969). *The psychological differentiation inventory: A questionnaire measure of field dependence.* Paper read at the meeting of the Eastern Psychological Association, Philadelphia, PA.

1418

Test Name: RAWLS' PERSONAL SPACE MEASURE

Purpose: To assess individual personal space.

Format: Drawing of a standing man is presented to the subjects who draw a circle around it to show how far away they prefer individuals to stand in a social situation. Score is the distance from the figure to the circle.

Validity: Correlation with scale measuring body accessibility was low but significant.

Author: Pedersen, D.

Article: Self disclosure, body accessibility and personal space.

Journal: *Psychological Reports,* December 1973, *33*(3), 975–980.

Related Research: Rawls, J., et al. (1968). *A comparison of personal space measures* (Report of NASA Grant NGR-44–009–008). Fort Worth: Texas Christian University, Institute of Behavioral Research.

• • •

1419

Test Name: RESPONDENT'S PSYCHOLOGICAL PARTICIPATION SCALE

Purpose: To measure the extent to which individuals feel that they influence joint decisions made with superiors.

Number of Items: 6

Author: House, R. J., and Kerr, S.

Article: Organizational independence, leader behavior, and managerial practices: A replicated study.

Journal: *Journal of Applied Psychology,* October 1973, *58*(2), 173–180.

Related Research: Vroom, V. H. (1960). *Some personality*

determinants of the effects of participation. Englewood Cliffs, NJ: Prentice-Hall.

• • •

1420

Test Name: RICKS-EPLEY-WESSMAN TEMPORAL EXPERIENCE QUESTIONNAIRE

Purpose: To study different ways in which people experience and use time in their daily activity.

Number of Items: 201

Format: Items are rated *agree* or *disagree.*

Author: Wessman, A. E.

Article: Personality and the subjective experience of time.

Journal: *Journal of Personality Assessment,* April 1973, *37*(2), 103–114.

• • •

1421

Test Name: RINGEL TEST OF ORAL FORM DISCRIMINATION

Purpose: To measure oral kinesthetic sensitivity.

Number of Items: 55

Format: The subject indicates whether two successively presented forms are the same or different. Each item is paired with every other item and with itself. Includes geometric configuration of triangles, rectangles, ovals, and biconcaves. Pictures of the forms are presented.

Validity: Correlations with: Wepman Auditory Discrimination Test–Form I, $r = .57$; Templin Test of Auditory Discrimination, $r = .70$; Auditory Sequential Memory, $r = .44$; Flynn Syllable Blending Test, $r = .97$; Monroe Diagnostic Reading Examination, $r = .47$; Auditory Closure, $r = .52$.

Author: Larsen, S. C., and Hudson, F. G.

Article: Oral kinesthetic sensitivity and the perception of speech.

Journal: *Child Development*, December 1973, *44*(4), 845–848.

Related Research: Ringel, R., et al. (1970). Some relations between orosensory discrimination and articulatory aspects of speech production. *Journal of Speech and Hearing Disorders, 35*, 1–11.

• • •

1422

Test Name: SALIENCE ASSESSMENT TASK

Purpose: To assess salience.

Number of Items: 12

Format: Modified method of triads involving the dimensions of form, color, number, and position. Each item provides a choice between two pairs of cards, one with identical values from one dimension, the other with identical values from a second dimension. Subjects are instructed to choose the pair of cards most alike.

Author: Odom, R. D., and Corbin, D. W.

Article: Perceptual salience and children's multi-dimensional problem solving.

Journal: *Child Development*, September 1973, *44*(3), 425–432.

Related Research: Odom, R. D., & Guzman, R. D. (1972). Development of hierarchies of dimensional salience. *Developmental Psychology, 6,* 271–287.

• • •

1423

Test Name: SCREENING TEST OF AUDITORY PERCEPTUAL SKILLS

Purpose: To identify auditory

perceptual skills of kindergarten and first grade pupils.

Number of Items: 42

Format: Four subtests: auditory memory, auditory discrimination, auditory blending, and auditory-visual integration.

Reliability: Kuder-Richardson formula 20 reliabilities: Total scores were .67, .80, and .92. Subtests ranged from .24 to .95.

Author: Weintraub, S.

Article: Summary of investigations relating to reading, July 1, 1972, to June 30, 1973.

Journal: *Reading Research Quarterly*, 1973–74, *9*(3), 306.

Related Research: McNinch, G., et al. (1972). Auditory perceptual testing of young children. *Journal of Reading Behavior, 4,* 120–128.

• • •

1424

Test Name: SEARS' SELF-CONCEPT INVENTORY

Purpose: To measure aspects of a student's self.

Number of Items: 32

Format: Test consists of a 5-point rating scale in which students compare themselves with other students of their age on items such as "understanding something new." Includes seven scales: physical ability, attractive appearance, convergent mental ability (general), social relations, social virtues, school subjects, and math.

Reliability: Internal consistency coefficients ranged from .59 to .93.

Author: Smith, I. D.

Article: Impact of computer-assisted instruction on student attitudes.

Journal: *Journal of Educational*

Psychology, June 1973, *64*(3), 366–372.

Related Research: Sears, P. S. (1964). Self-concept in the service of educational goals. *California Journal for Instructional Improvement, 7,* 3–17.

• • •

1425

Test Name: SELF-ACCEPTANCE SCALE

Purpose: To assess relative presence or lack of self-acceptance.

Number of Items: 36

Format: Items are rated on a 5-point scale.

Reliability: Split-half reliability was .89 (corrected).

Validity: Counseled compared with noncounseled students were significantly different in response to scale.

Author: Galassi, J., and Galassi, M.

Article: Alienation in college students: A comparison of counseling seekers and non-seekers.

Journal: *Journal of Counseling Psychology*, January 1973, *20*(1), 44–49.

Related Research: Berger, E. (1952). The relation between expressed acceptance of self and expressed acceptance of others. *Journal of Abnormal and Social Psychology, 47,* 778–782.

• • •

1426

Test Name: SELF AS COUNSELOR, IDEAL COUNSELOR, OTHER COUNSELOR, SEMANTIC DIFFERENTIAL INSTRUMENT

Purpose: To measure congruence of self-perception as counselor and perception of the ideal counselor.

Number of Items: 10 pairs of bipolar adjectives.

Format: Adjectives were chosen to be desirable and undesirable to a counselor, for example, *flexible–rigid*.

Author: Redfering, D.

Article: Changes in the perception of the counselor: Self, Ideal Self, and Self As Judged by Peers.

Journal: *Counselor Education and Supervision,* June 1973, *12*(4), 289–293.

• • •

1427

Test Name: SELF-ASSURANCE SCALE

Purpose: To measure extent to which individuals perceive themselves as effective in dealing with problems confronting them.

Number of Items: 31

Format: Forced-choice adjective pairs.

Author: Gavin, J. F.

Article: Self-esteem as moderator of the relationship between expectancies and job performance.

Journal: *Journal of Applied Psychology,* August 1973, *58*(1), 83–88.

Related Research: Ghiselli, E. E. (1971). *Explorations in managerial talent.* Pacific Palisades, CA: Goodyear.

• • •

1428

Test Name: SELF-CONCEPT OF ABILITY INSTRUMENT

Purpose: To ascertain individual's perceptions of ability to succeed in academic pursuits and how these perceptions are related to actual accomplishments.

Number of Items: 8

Format: Multiple-choice.

Author: Ponzo, Z., and Strowig, R. W.

Article: Relations among sex-role identity and selected intellectual and non-intellectual factors for high school freshman and seniors.

Journal: *Journal of Educational Research,* November 1973, *67*(3), 137–141.

Related Research: Brookover, W. B., et al. (1962). *Self-concept of ability and school achievement.* East Lansing: Michigan State University, Office of Research and Publications.

See *D.U.E.M.M., 2,* 1978: 823.

• • •

1429

Test Name: SELF-CONCEPT OF ABILITY QUESTIONNAIRE

Purpose: To determine a student's overall self-concept of ability.

Number of Items: 8

Format: Five-choice items coded from 5 to 1; positive self-concept alternatives receive higher values.

Validity: Correlations with selected achievement test results ranged from –.19 to .60.

Author: Busk, P. L., et al.

Article: Effects of schools' racial composition on the self-concept of Black and White students.

Journal: *Journal of Educational Research,* October 1973, *67*(2), 57–63.

• • •

1430

Test Name: SELF-CONCEPT SEMANTIC DIFFERENTIAL

Purpose: To study the connotative structure of self-concepts.

Number of Items: 21

Format: Test includes 21 adjective pairs and 7-point semantic differential scales to rate the concept "My characteristic self (yourself as you most often feel about yourself)." All items are presented.

Author: Monge, R. H.

Article: Developmental trends in factors of adolescent self-concept.

Journal: *Developmental Psychology,* May 1973, *8*(3), 382–393.

Related Research: Smith, P. A. (1962). A comparison of three sets of rotated factor analytic solutions of self-concept data. *Journal of Abnormal and Social Psychology, 64,* 326–333.

• • •

1431

Test Name: SELF DISCRIMINATION SEMANTIC DIFFERENTIAL INSTRUMENT

Purpose: To obtain a measure of self-discrimination.

Number of Items: 20 bipolar adjective pairs

Format: Adjective pairs are loaded on the evaluative factor; 7-point scale.

Author: Cole, C., et al.

Article: Effects of verbal interaction conditions of self-concept discrimination and anxiety.

Journal: *Journal of Counseling Psychology,* September 1973, *20*(5), 431–436.

• • •

1432

Test Name: SELF-EXPECTATIONS INSTRUMENT

Purpose: To measure adolescents' concepts of how they believe they should behave.

Number of Items: 39

Format: Subjects choose from the same four alternatives of how they believe they should behave, for each item.

Author: Ponzo, Z., and Strowig, R. W.

Article: Relations among sex-role identity and selected intellectual and non-intellectual factors for high school freshman and seniors.

Journal: *Journal of Educational Research,* November 1973, *67*(3), 137–141.

Related Research: Binder, D. (1965). *Relationships among self-expectations, self-concept, and academic achievement.* Unpublished doctoral dissertation, University of Wisconsin.

• • •

1433

Test Name: SPATIAL ORIENTATION OF OBJECTS, MOTION PICTURE TEST

Purpose: To assess characteristics of perceptually handicapped children.

Number of Items: 16

Format: Group and individual forms; children required to duplicate movement on screen using blocks.

Reliability: Kuder-Richardson formula 20 values were .76 (individual form) and .40 to .81 (group form).

Validity: Correlations with Iowa Reading Scores ranged from .21 to .65.

Author: McDaniel, E.

Article: Ten motion picture tests of perceptual abilities.

Journal: *Perceptual and Motor Skills,* June 1973, *36*(3), 755–759.

1434

Test Name: STEPHENS-DELYS REINFORCEMENT CONTINGENCY INTERVIEW

Purpose: To measure locus-of-control expectancies.

Number of Items: 40

Format: Free-response structured interview. Each question gives the occurrence of a social reinforcement (or cue associated with reinforcement) and asks child to provide contingency for that reinforcement, for example, "What makes Mother smile?"

Reliability: Interrater reliability was .98.

Author: Stephens, M. W., and Delys, P.

Article: External control expectancies among disadvantaged children at preschool age.

Journal: *Child Development,* September 1973, *44*(3), 670–674.

Related Research: Delys, P. (1971). *Individual and socioeconomic group differences in locus of control expectancies among preschool populations.* Unpublished master's thesis, Purdue University.

Stephens, M., & Delys, P. (1973). A locus of control measure for pre-school children. *Developmental Psychology, 9,* 55–65.

• • •

1435

Test Name: SUCCESSIVE FIGURES MOTION PICTURE TEST

Purpose: To assess characteristics of perceptually handicapped children.

Number of Items: 18

Format: Subject must organize separately presented lines into a geometric figure; individual and group forms.

Reliability: Kuder-Richardson

formula 20 values were .67 (individual form) and .31 to .77 (group form).

Validity: Correlations with Iowa Reading Scores were .14 to .39.

Author: McDaniel, E.

Article: Ten motion picture tests of perceptual abilities.

Journal: *Perceptual and Motor Skills,* June 1973, *36*(3), 755–759.

• • •

1436

Test Name: TEMPORAL MEMORY SPAN I–MOTION PICTURE TEST

Purpose: To assess characteristics of perceptually handicapped children.

Number of Items: 18

Format: Child must rename common items in same order as presented on the screen; group and individual forms.

Reliability: Kuder-Richardson formula 20 values were .62 (individual form) and .48 – .77 (group form).

Validity: Correlations with Iowa Reading Scores ranged from –.24 to .43.

Author: McDaniel, E.

Article: Ten motion picture tests of perceptual abilities.

Journal: *Perceptual and Motor Skills,* June 1973, *36*(3), 755–759.

• • •

1437

Test Name: TEMPORAL MEMORY SPAN II–MOTION PICTURE TEST

Purpose: To assess characteristics of perceptually handicapped children.

Number of Items: 18

Format: Subject must recall the order of presentation of two to six designs; individual and group form.

Reliability: Kuder-Richardson formula 20 values were .66 (individual form) and −.09 to .57 (group form).

Validity: Correlations with Iowa Reading Scores ranged from .25 to .27.

Author: McDaniel, E.

Article: Ten motion picture tests of perceptual abilities.

Journal: *Perceptual and Motor Skills,* June 1973, *36*(3), 755–759.

■ ■ ■

1438

Test Name: TRUAX RATING SCALES

Purpose: To measure empathy, warmth, genuineness.

Format: Interview scored by trained judges.

Author: McWhirter, J. J.

Article: Two measures of the facilative conditions: A correlation study.

Journal: *Journal of Counseling Psychology,* July 1973, *20*(4), 317–320.

Related Research: Truax, C. B., & Carkhuff, R. R. (1967). *Toward effective counseling and psychotherapy: Training and practice.* Chicago: Aldine.

■ ■ ■

1439

Test Name: TWENTY STATEMENTS TEST

Purpose: To assess self-attitude.

Number of Items: 20

Time Required: 6–8 minutes.

Format: Subjects were asked to give 20 responses to "Who am I?"

Validity: Under short (8 minutes) time limits, correlation of number of responses with intelligence was .23 ($p < .01$); with increased time (12 minutes) correlation was nonsignificant.

Author: Nudelman, A.

Article: Bias in the Twenty Statements Test: Administration time, incomplete protocols and intelligence.

Journal: *Psychological Reports,* October 1973, *33*(2), 524–526.

Related Research: Kuhn, M., & McPartland, T. (1954). An empirical investigation of self attitudes. *American Sociological Review, 19,* 68–76.

Lubin, B., et al. (1974). Factor structure of psychological assessment at a community mental health center. *Journal of Psychological Reports, 35,* 455–460.

■ ■ ■

1440

Test Name: UNIVERSITY ENVIRONMENT PERCEPTIONS SCALE

Purpose: To obtain perceptions of the university environment from students and student personnel workers.

Number of Items: 41

Format: Four scales: academic, community, awareness, personnel services. Responses are made on a 5-point Likert scale from 1 (*strongly agree*) to 5 (*strongly disagree*). Some items are presented.

Reliability: 3–week interval Pearson product–moment coefficient of .71.

Author: Noeth, R. J., and Dye, H. A.

Article: Perceptions of a university environment: Students and

student personnel workers.

Journal: *Journal of College Student Personnel,* November 1973, *14*(6), 527–531.

■ ■ ■

1441

Test Name: VISUAL ANALYSIS TEST

Purpose: Subject must analyze elements of a geometric design, relate these elements, and apply rules in reproducing the design.

Number of Items: 27 tasks.

Format: Subject copies geometric designs (represented in a matrix of dots) into a blank matrix of dots; designs vary in complexity.

Reliability: Interrater reliability was .98. Test–retest reliability was .83 (no time interval given; Rosner, 1971).

Validity: Correlation with Stanford Arithmetic Computations was .50 and with Arithmetic Concepts was .48.

Author: Rosner, J.

Article: Language arts and arithmetic achievement, and specifically related perceptual skills.

Journal: *American Educational Research Journal,* Winter 1973, *10*(1), 59–68.

Related Research: Rosner, J. (1971). *The Visual Analysis Test: An initial report.* Pittsburgh: University of Pittsburgh, Learning Research and Development Center.

■ ■ ■

1442

Test Name: VISUAL DISCRIMINATION INVENTORY

Purpose: To measure visual cognition.

Format: Two factors: position in

space and closure.

Author: Kohn, M., and Rosman, B. L.

Article: Cognitive functioning in five-year-old boys as related to social-emotional and background-demographic variables.

Journal: *Developmental Psychology,* March 1973, *8*(2), 277–294.

Related Research: Lombard, A., & Stern, C. (1967, September). *An instrument to measure visual discrimination of young children.* Paper presented at the meeting of the American Psychological Association, Washington, DC.

1443

Test Name: VISUAL PERSPECTIVES TEST

Purpose: To measure child's perceptual egocentrism.

Format: Test includes a three-dimensional display of buildings mounted on a square of wood, photographs taken from each of the four sides, and a doll with a camera rotated around the three sides of the display not directly faced by the child. The child is to pick out the picture the doll would have taken. Three egocentric answers receive a score of 1, two egocentric answers receive a score of 2.

Author: Hollos, M., and Cowan, P. A.

Article: Social isolation and cognitive development: Logical operations and role-taking abilities in three Norwegian social settings.

Journal: *Child Development,* September 1973, *44*(3), 630–641.

Related Research: Piaget, J., & Inhelder, B. (1956). *The child's conception of space.* London: Routledge & Kegan Paul.

CHAPTER 16
Personality

1444

Test Name:
AUTOBIOGRAPHICAL DATA
BOOKLET-B

Purpose: To assess various
biographical factors.

Number of Items: 389

Format: Yields scores on 15
independent biographical factors
for women and 13 for men.

Validity: Multiple correlations of
Biographical Factors with college
grade point average and
educational psychology grades,
respectively, were .38 and .37 ($p <$
.01) for women.

Author: Halpin, G., et al.

Article: Biographical factors
related to academic achievement.

Journal: *Psychological Reports,*
August 1973, *33*(1), 321–322.

Related Research: Owens, W.
(1968). *Autobiographical Data
Booklet B.* Unpublished
biographical inventory, University
of Georgia.

Scott, O., et al. (1974).
Relationships between students'
perceptions of college instruction
and selected students'
characteristics. *Perceptual and
Motor Skills, 39,* 855–860.

• • •

1445

Test Name: BIOGRAPHICAL
INFORMATION BLANK

Purpose: To identify biographical
information for job placement of
the disadvantaged.

Format: Fourth grade reading
level.

Author: Van Doren, R. (Ed).

Article: Manpower, human
assessment and the disadvantaged.

Journal: *American Vocational
Journal,* January 1973, *48*(1), 86–
100.

• • •

1446

Test Name: BIOGRAPHICAL
QUESTIONNAIRE

Purpose: To secure biographical
information.

Number of Items: 63

Author: Smith, M. G., and Fruth,
M. J.

Article: The second change transfer
student.

Journal: *Journal of Educational
Research,* March 1973, *66*(7),
307–308.

• • •

1447

Test Name: DESCRIPTIVE
INDEX

Purpose: To provide descriptions
of men in general, women in
general, and successful middle
managers.

Number of Items: 92

Format: Three forms: men in
general, women in general,
successful middle managers.
Ratings are made on a scale from 1
(*not characteristic*) to 5
(*characteristic*).

Author: Wade, M.

Article: Personnel research.

Journal: *Personnel Journal,*
September 1973, *52*(9), 829–831.

Related Research: Schein, V. E.
(1973). The relationship between
sex role stereotypes and requisite
management characteristics.
*Journal of Applied Psychology,
57,* 95–100.

• • •

1448

Test Name: IOWA PICTURE
INTERPRETATION TEST

Purpose: To assess personality.

Time Required: 60 seconds per
slide.

Format: Multiple-choice version of
the Thematic Apperception Test: a
picture is presented as a slide;
subjects rank four statements
according to their own perception.

Author: Malatesha, R., and
Fakouri, M.

Article: Relationship between
achievement imagery index,
perceptual coding task and
intelligence.

Journal: *Perceptual & Motor
Skills,* June 1973, *36*(3), 803–806.

Related Research: Hurley, J.
(1955). The Iowa Picture
Interpretation Test: A multiple
choice variation of the TAT.
*Journal of Consulting Psychology,
19,* 372–376.

• • •

1449

Test Name: PSYCHOLOGICAL
EFFECTIVENESS SCALE

Purpose: To self-rate personality.

Reliability: Coefficient alpha was .91 (81 men, 55 women, urban college students).

Author: Poe, C.

Article: Internal consistency of a psychological effectiveness scale.

Journal: *Psychological Reports,* October 1973, *33*(2), 466.

Related Research: Copies of the Scale are available from author, Psychology Service, Veterans Administration Center, Hampton, Virginia 23667.

• • •

1450

Test Name: PUZZLE FORM OF THE CHILDREN'S APPERCEPTION TEST (CAT)

Purpose: A projective personality test.

Number of Items: CAT cards

Format: Set of CAT cards cut into interlocking jigsaw puzzle pieces with a frame; individually administered.

Reliability: Interrater reliabilities

were 90 and 89% on two occasions.

Validity: The puzzle form resulted in more "perceptive" and "apperceptive" responses than the standard form.

Author: Hoar, M., and Faust, W.

Article: The Children's Apperception Test: Puzzle and regular form.

Journal: *Journal of Personality Assessment,* 1973, *37*(3), 244–247.

• • •

1451

Test Name: SEMANTIC DIFFERENTIAL PERSONALITY MEASURE

Purpose: To measure individual personality factors.

Number of Items: Nine concepts each with four bipolar adjectives for evaluation, potency, and activity

Format: Study 1 concepts were myself, student, failure, ambition, persistency, excuses, career, accomplishment, success competition. Study 2 concepts

were six value areas of a scale of values and myself.

Author: Everett, A.

Article: Personality assessment at the individual level using the semantic differential.

Journal: *Educational and Psychological Measurement,* Winter 1973, *33*(4), 837–844.

• • •

1452

Test Name: SOCIAL ACCESS QUESTIONNAIRE

Purpose: To measure personality and personal history of the disadvantaged.

Number of Items: 89

Time Required: 30 minutes.

Format: Six personality factors and personal history using multiple choice and agree–disagree items.

Author: Van Doren, R. (Ed.).

Article: Manpower, human assessment and the disadvantaged.

Journal: *American Vocational Journal,* January 1973, *48*(1), 86–100.

CHAPTER 17
Preference

1453

Test Name: ATTITUDE TOWARD SUBJECT–WEIGHTED OR CONVENTIONAL MULTIPLE CHOICE TESTS

Purpose: To assess student preference for multiple choice items taken conventionally or in which students could weight responses.

Number of Items: 7

Format: Range of scores was 0 to 4.

Author: Krauft, C., and Beggs, D.

Article: Test taking procedure, risk taking, and multiple choice test scores.

Journal: *Journal of Experimental Education,* Summer 1973, *41*(4), 74–77.

...

1454

Test Name: COMMUNITY ORGANIZATIONAL SCALE

Purpose: To determine interest and participation in community organization.

Number of Items: 12

Format: Test included three subcategories of questions: children's belonging to, wanting to join, and participation in community organizations.

Author: Poorkaj, H., and Bockelman, C.

Article: The impact of community volunteers on delinquency prevention.

Journal: *Sociology and Social*

Research, April 1973, *57*(3), 335–341.

...

1455

Test Name: FOURTH GRADE READING PREFERENCE QUESTIONNAIRE

Purpose: To study reading preferences for 10 categories of books.

Number of Items: 45

Format: Each of 10 statements was paired with each of the other nine statements and presented as a forced-choice question. Each of the 10 statements was presented with a sample pairing.

Reliability: Test–retest coefficients ranged from .60 to .86.

Author: Chiu, L. H.

Article: Reading preference of fourth grade children related to sex and reading ability.

Journal: *Journal of Educational Research,* April 1973, *66*(8), 369–373.

...

1456

Test Name: HUMOR TEST

Purpose: To measure children's preference for humor.

Number of Items: 5

Format: Subject is given an incomplete drawing and asked to choose between two alternatives to complete the drawing: one nonsensical, the other hostile–aggressive.

Validity: Significant ($p < .05$)

preference for hostile–aggressive drawings, with values greater for 4 year olds than for 5 year olds and for boys than for girls.

Author: King, P., and King, J.

Article: A children's humor test.

Journal: *Psychological Reports,* October 1973, *33*(2), 632.

Related Research: Request Document NAPS-02181, Micro-fiche Publications, 305 E. 46th St., New York, New York 10017 ($1.50).

...

1457

Test Name: JUDGMENT ANALYSIS

Purpose: To assess policies used in judging the beauty of paintings.

Format: Judges rated 19 paintings for beauty on a 1 to 7 scale and noted 11 characteristics including colorful, realism, depth.

Validity: It was reported that five different judgment policies were used.

Author: Holmes, G., and Zedeck, S.

Article: Judgment analysis for assessing paintings.

Journal: *Journal of Experimental Education,* Summer 1973, *41*(4), 26–30.

...

1458

Test Name: LEAST PREFERRED CO-WORKER QUESTIONNAIRE

Purpose: To measure esteem for least preferred co-worker.

Number of Items: 16

Format: Respondents are asked to think of everyone with whom they have ever worked and then to describe the person with whom they could work least well on a series of bipolar scales. Some examples are given.

Author: Fox, W. M., et al.

Article: Dimensional analysis of the least preferred co-worker scales.

Journal: *Journal of Applied Psychology,* April 1973, *57*(2), 192–194.

Related Research: Fiedler, F. E. (1967). *A theory of leadership effectiveness.* New York: McGraw-Hill.

• • •

1459

Test Name: RACIAL PREFERENCE INSTRUMENT

Purpose: To assess racial preference of kindergarten children.

Format: Semantic differential type instrument; subjects asked to rate 8 photos (Black and White) on four bipolar adjective pairs.

Reliability: Split-half reliability was .72 (Hohn & Swartz, 1971).

Author: Hohn, R.

Article: Perceptual training and its effect on racial preferences of kindergarten children.

Journal: *Psychological Reports,* April 1973, *32*(2), 435–441.

Related Research: Hohn, R., & Swartz, M. (1971). The assessment and facilitation of attitudes toward others in young children. *Kansas Studies in Education, 21,* 1–19.

• • •

1460

Test Name: READING PREFERENCE QUESTIONNAIRE

Purpose: To determine the reading preferences of fourth grade children.

Number of Items: 45

Format: A paired comparison method for 10 categories of books included in the questionnaire.

Reliability: Test–retest reliability ranged from .33 to .94.

Author: Chiu, L. H.

Article: Reading preferences of fourth grade children related to sex and reading ability.

Journal: *Journal of Education Research,* April 1973, *66*(8), 369–373.

• • •

1461

Test Name: ROLE CONSISTENCY MEASURE

Purpose: To measure sex role identification.

Format: "20 self descriptive adjectives and descriptions of eight interpersonal situations (p. 1135)."

Author: Morris, G., and Zoerner, C.

Article: Interaction of anxiety and sex role identification characteristics in American male sex role behavior.

Journal: *Psychological Reports,* June 1973, *32*(3), 1135–1142.

Related Research: Heilbron, A. (1964).Conformity to masculinity-femininity stereotypes and ego identity in adolescents. *Psychological Reports, 19,* 351–357.

• • •

1462

Test Name: SITUATIONAL RESPONSE TEST

Purpose: To measure preference for response styles in working with ineffectively functioning children.

Number of Items: 10

Format: Each item: description of an interaction between an aide and a young child followed by four response options reflecting control, nurturance, understanding, rejection. Subject ranks choices in order of preference.

Author: Dorr, D., et al.

Article: Changes in nonprofessional mental health workers' response preference and attitudes as a function of training and supervised field experiences.

Journal: *Journal of School Psychology,* Summer 1973, *11*(2), 118–122.

• • •

1463

Test Name: SKIN COLOR PREFERENCE

Purpose: To assess preference for skin color among Blacks.

Format: Part 1: subjects choose a real (like own) and ideal face from 11 faces varying in skin color; Part 2: subjects are shown five cards, each contains 10 Caucasian and 10 others ranging from light to dark complexion. Subjects choose 5 people who fit a given description (e.g., "Which five have never committed a criminal act?").

Validity: No preference among adult subjects for dark or light skin colors. Younger males attributed more positive characteristics to darker skin.

Author: Hamm, N., et al.

Article: Preference for Black skin among Negro males.

Journal: *Psychological Reports,* June 1973, *32*(3), 1171–1175.

1464

Test Name: STYLES OF
CATEGORIZATION TEST

Purpose: To measure children's
categorizing style preferences.

Number of Items: 80

Format: 20 sets of four pictures
(three choice items and a
standard) depicting familiar
human, animal, and object
content. Subjects select one of the
choice pictures that goes with or is
like the standard and states
reasons for the selection.

Reliability: 98% agreement.

Author: Davis, A. J., and
Lange, G.

Article: Parent–child
communication and the
development of categorization
styles in preschool children.

Journal: *Child Development,*
September 1973, *44*(3), 624–629.

CHAPTER 18
Problem Solving and Reasoning

1465

Test Name: ADAPTED MODIFIED ROLE REPERTORY TEST

Purpose: To assess cognitive complexity.

Format: Adapted for use in the classroom with elementary subjects. Subjects rate significant self and significant others (mother, teacher, etc.) on 6-point Likert scales.

Reliability: Test–retest reliability was .82 ($p < .05$) for third graders.

Validity: Modified and Adapted Form administered to two groups of college students: $r = .51$ ($p < .05$) and .55 ($p < .05$) between the two forms.

Author: Vacc, N., and Vacc, N.

Article: An adaptation for children of the modified role repertory test—a measure of cognitive complexity.

Journal: *Psychological Reports,* December 1973, *33*(3), 771–776.

Related Research: Bieri, J. (1955). Cognitive complexity–Simplicity and predictive behavior. *Journal of Abnormal and Social Psychology, 51,* 163–168.

1466

Test Name: CHILD-STUDY TEAM CONFLICT QUESTIONNAIRE

Purpose: To explore perceived and desired methods of resolving disagreements regarding classification decisions among child-study team members.

Number of Items: 36

Format: Items include demographic information about the respondent, the possible resolutions of reaching classification decisions with one item for a write-in possibility, and situations in which the team must make a decision on classification with two alternatives. Items are presented.

Author: Hyman, I., et al.

Article: Patterns of interprofessional conflict resolution on school child study teams.

Journal: *Journal of School Psychology,* Fall 1973, *2*(3), 187–195.

1467

Test Name: FAMILIARIZATION MATRIX TEST

Purpose: To familiarize the subject with strategies for solving the Raven Coloured Progressive Matrices (RCPM).

Number of Items: 12

Format: Each item similar to those in the RCPM; a matrix with the lower right piece missing and detractors presented below. Examples are presented.

Author: Turner, R. R., et al.

Article: Effects of familiarization feedback on the performance of lower-class and middle-class kindergarteners on the Raven Coloured Progressive Matrices.

Journal: *Journal of Educational Psychology,* December 1973, *65*(3), 356–363.

1468

Test Name: PURDUE ELEMENTARY PROBLEM-SOLVING INVENTORY

Purpose: To measure problem-solving ability.

Validity: For 2nd, 4th, and 6th graders, with measure of logical thinking, $r = .45$ to .51; Concept formation, $r = .31$ to .40; IQ measures, $r = .40$ to .46; Reading, $r = .38$ to .52; Arithmetic problems, $r = .29$ to .39; Perceptual tests, $r = .40$ to .54.

Author: Houtz, J., et al.

Article: Relationship of problem solving to other cognitive variables.

Journal: *Psychological Reports,* October 1973, *33*(3), 389–390.

Related Research: Feldhusen, J., et al. (1972). Development of the Purdue Elementary Problem Solving Inventory. *Psychological Reports, 31,* 891–901.

See *D.U.E.M.M., 2,* 1978: 894.

1469

Test Name: TRAIL MAKING TEST

Purpose: To assess brain damage.

Validity: Part A: correlations with Wechsler-Bellevue Test, Full Scale IQ were –.50 (brain-damaged subjects) and −.38 (non-brain-damaged subjects). Part B: correlations with Bellevue Test Full Scale IQ were −.57 (brain damaged subjects) and −.49 (non-brain damaged subjects). All $ps <$ .01.

Author: Boll, T., and Reitan, R.

Article: Effect of age on performance of the trail making test.

Journal: *Perceptual and Motor Skills,* June 1973, *36*(3), 691–694.

CHAPTER 19
Status

1470

Test Name: DUNCAN OCCUPATIONAL STATUS SCALE-MODIFIED

Purpose: To code occupational status of the family wagearner.

Format: Occupations are grouped in quintiles.

Author: Larkin, R. W.

Article: Research notes: Contextual influence on teacher leadership styles.

Journal: *Sociology of Education,* Fall 1973, *46*(4), 471–479.

Related Research: Duncan, O. D. (1961). A socio-economic index for all occupations. In A. Reiss, Jr., et al. (Eds.), *Occupations and social status.* New York: The Free Press.

1471

Test Name: HOLLINGSHEAD'S TWO FACTOR INDEX

Purpose: To classify subjects according to socioeconomic level.

Format: Occupational and educational level of the head of household used as indices of socioeconomic status; broken down into five classes.

Author: Mensing, P.M., and Traxler, A. J.

Article: Social class differences in free recall of categorized and uncategorized lists of Black children.

Journal: *Journal of Educational Psychology,* December 1973, *65*(3), 378–382.

Related Research: Hollingshead,

A. B. (1957). *Two factor index of social position.* Unpublished report, New Haven, CT.

See *D.U.E.M.M., 2,* 1978: 898.

1472

Test Name: HOME INDEX

Purpose: To measure socioeconomic status.

Number of Items: 24

Author: Wientraub, S., et al.

Article: Summary of investigations relating to reading July 1, 1972, to June 30, 1073.

Journal: *Reading Research Quarterly,* 1973–74, *9*(3), 360–361.

1473

Test Name: HOME INDEX SCALE

Purpose: To determine socioeconomic status.

Author: Means, G. H., et al.

Article: Task persistence as a function of verbal reinforcement and socio-economic status.

Journal: *California Journal of Educational Research,* January 1973, *24*(1), 5–11.

Related Research: Gough, H. G. (1949). A short social status inventory. *Journal of Educational Psychology, 40,* 52–56.

1474

Test Name: INDEX OF SOCIAL POSITION REVISED

Purpose: To measure social class.

Format: Seven positions, from 1, *higher executives of large concerns, proprietors, and major professionals* to 7, *unskilled employees.*

Author: Frease, D. E.

Article: Delinquency, social class, and the schools.

Journal: *Sociology and Social Research,* July 1973, *57*(4), 443–459.

1475

Test Name: KAUFMAN'S SCALE OF STATUS CONCERN

Purpose: To measure concern with prestige and social standing.

Number of Items: 10

Reliability: Guttman Coefficient of Reproducibility was .86; Minimum Marginal Reproducibility was .75.

Validity: Kendalls Tau with socioeconomic status was $-.31$ ($p < .00001$), with age it was .23 ($p < .0001$).

Author: Owens, W.

Article: The less they have, the more they want: Reexamination of concern with status.

Journal: *Psychological Reports,* December 1973, *33*(3), 828–830.

Related Research: Kaufman, W. (1957). Status, authoritarianism and anti-semitism. *American Journal of Sociology, 62,* 379–382.

CHAPTER 20
Trait Measurement

1476

Test Name: AGGRESSION-POTENTIAL MEASURE

Purpose: To elicit verbal estimates of subjects' responses to a wide range of hypothetical interpersonal conflict situations.

Number of Items: 6

Format: Descriptions of real-life situations found, in interviews with children aged 4 to 16 years, to be irritating and moderately likely to elicit aggression from them. Each is accompanied by four types of responses. The subjects' scores are average frequency with which they choose physical aggression from the six items.

Author: Collins, W. A.

Article: Effect of temporal separation between motivation, aggression, and consequences: A developmental study.

Journal: *Developmental Psychology*, March 1973, *8*(2), 215–221.

Related Research: Leifer, A., & Roberts, D. (1972). Children's responses to television violence. In J. Murray et al. (Eds.), *Television and social behavior* (Vol. 2). Washington, DC: U.S. Government Printing Office.

. . .

1477

Test Name: BRESKIN NONVERBAL RIGIDITY TEST

Purpose: To assess rigidity.

Number of Items: 15

Format: Subject expresses preference between pairs of figures that differ in their similarity.

Validity: With Gestalt measure of "Stimulus Free," $r = -.286$ ($p < .05$); with dogmatism, $r = .05$ (Primavera & Higgins, 1973); with Mach IV Test, $r = -.04$.

Author: Maini, S.

Article: Personality and cognitive differences between an original and non-original group.

Journal: *Perceptual and Motor Skills*, October 1973, *37*(2), 555–563.

Related Research: Breskin, S. (1968). Measurement of rigidity, a non-verbal test. *Perceptual and Motor Skills, 27*, 1203–1206.

See *D.U.E.M.M., 2*, 1978: 917.

Primavera, L., & Higgins, M. (1973). Nonverbal rigidity and its relationship to dogmatism and Machiavellianism. *Perceptual and Motor Skills, 36*, 356–358.

. . .

1478

Test Name: CHILDREN'S MANIFEST ANXIETY SCALE

Purpose: To assess anxiety.

Number of Items: 42 and 11 item lie scale.

Format: Yes–no response format.

Reliability: Kuder-Richardson formula was .86 (Kitano, 1960).

Test–retest reliability (Ziv & Luz, 1973) was .77 ($p < .001$), anxiety scale (See Finch et al., 1974).

Validity: Significant differences in anxiety between fourth and sixth graders.

Author: Bledsoe, J.

Article: Sex and grade differences in children's manifest anxiety.

Journal: *Psychological Reports*, 1973, *32*(1), 285–286.

Related Research: Castaneda, A., et al. (1956). The children's form of the manifest anxiety scale. *Child Development, 27*, 317–326.

Finch, A., et al. (1974). Children's manifest anxiety scale: Reliability with emotionally disturbed children. *Psychological Reports, 34*, 658.

Kitano, H. (1960). The validity of the children's manifest anxiety scale and the modified revised California Inventory. *Child Development, 31*, 67–72.

Merryman, E. (1974). The effects of manifest anxiety on the reading achievement of fifth grade students. *Journal of Experimental Education, 42*, 36–41.

Ziv, A., & Luz, M. (1973). Manifest anxiety in children of different sociometric levels. *Human Development, 16*, 224–232.

. . .

1479

Test Name: COGNITIVE PREFERENCE INVENTORY

Purpose: To assess cognitive style.

Number of Items: 19

Format: Each page has drawings of three common objects. The subject marks two items that "belong together." Responses are categorized as analytic–descriptive, inferential–categorical, or relational.

Validity: Relationship (for boys) between cognitive style and science achievement level.

Author: Ogunyemi, E.

Article: Cognitive styles and student science achievement in Nigeria.

Journal: *Journal of Experimental Education,* Fall 1973, *42*(1), 59–63.

Related Research: Kagan, J., & Moss, H. (1963). Psychological significance of styles of conceptualization. In J. Wright & J. Kagan (Eds.), Basic cognitive processes in children. *Monograph of the Society for Research in Child Development, 28,* 73–112.

● ● ●

1480

Test Name: COMMUNICATIVE EGOCENTRISM SCALE

Purpose: To measure communicative egocentrism.

Number of Items: 10

Format: A low communicative-egocentrism score indicates a high degree of egocentricity.

Reliability: Test–retest ranged from .85 to .95; Interobserver reliability ranged from .82 to .98.

Author: Rubin, K. H.

Article: Egocentrism in childhood: A unitary construct?

Journal: *Child Development,* March 1973, *44*(1), 102–110.

Related Research: Glucksberg, S., & Krauss, R. M. (1967). What do people say after they have learned how to talk? Studies of the development of referential communication. *Merrill-Palmer Quarterly, 13,* 309–316.

1481

Test Name: COMPLEXITY SELF-DESCRIPTION SCALE

Purpose: To measure conceptual complexity.

Format: Various scales yielding score for general complexity: hierarchic complexity, flexible complexity, differentiation flexibility, openness, simplicity. Detailed description of scales given in article.

Author: Russell, G., and Sandilands, M.

Article: Some correlates of conceptual complexity.

Journal: *Psychological Reports,* October 1973, *33*(2), 587–593.

Related Research: Driver, M., & Streufert, S. (1967). *Complexity self-description scales.* Unpublished report, Purdue University.

Kagan, J. (1966). Developmental studies on reflection and analysis. In A. Kidd & J. Rivoire (Eds.), *Perceptual and conceptual development in children.* New York: International Universities Press.

● ● ●

1482

Test Name: DESCRIPTIVE INDEX

Purpose: To describe sex role stereotypes and characteristics of successful middle managers.

Number of Items: 92

Format: Descriptive terms and adjectives rated on a 5-point scale from 1 (*not characteristic*) to 5 (*characteristic*) with a neutral rating of 3 (*neither characteristic nor uncharacteristic*). Three forms were developed (men, women, managers).

Author: Schein, V. E.

Article: The relationship between sex role stereotypes and requisite management characteristics.

Journal: *Journal of Applied Psychology,* April 1973, *57*(2), 95–100.

● ● ●

1483

Test Name: DOGMATISM SCALE, FORM E

Purpose: To measure dogmatism.

Number of Items: 40

Format: 12 subscales with a range of scores from 40 through 280. Separate subscale scores are provided.

Author: Cryns, A. G., and Finn, J. D.

Article: A multivariate analysis of some attitudinal and ideological correlates of student activism.

Journal: *Sociology of Education,* Winter 1973, *46*(1), 127–142.

Related Research: Rokeach, M. (1960). *The open and closed mind.* New York: Basic Books.

See *D.U.E.M.M., 2,* 1978: 953.

● ● ●

1484

Test Name: EXNER SELF FOCUS SENTENCE COMPLETION

Purpose: To measure egocentricity as a response style.

Number of Items: 30

Format: Forced-choice sentence completion test yielding six scores.

Reliability: Three studies were conducted on interrater reliability: most coefficients are in mid .80s to .90s.

Validity: Psychiatric patients rated as "improved" changed significantly in five of the six scores; difference in self-viewing in a mirror was not significant.

Author: Exner, J.

Article: The self focus sentence completion: A study of egocentricity.

Journal: *Journal of Personality Assessment*, 1973, *37*(5), 437–456.

• • •

1485

Test Name: FLAVELL SPATIAL EGOCENTRISM SCALE

Purpose: To measure spatial egocentrism.

Format: Total number of points was 18. The higher the score, the less spatially egocentric the child.

Reliability: Test–retest reliability ranged from .85 to .95. Interobserver reliability ranged from .82 to .98.

Author: Rubin, K. H.

Article: Egocentrism in childhood: A unitary construct?

Journal: *Child Development*, March 1973, *44*(1), 102–110.

Related Research: Flavell, J., et al. (1968). *The development of role taking and communication skills in children*. New York: Wiley.

• • •

1486

Test Name: GOUGH-SANFORD RIGIDITY SCALE

Purpose: To assess rigidity–flexibility.

Format: Scores ranged from 0 to 18.

Validity: Liberal arts upperclassmen were significantly less rigid than business and education upperclassmen.

Author: Margavio, A., and Floyd, H.

Article: Rigidity and choice of college among university students.

Journal: *Psychological Reports*,

June 1973, *32*(3), 821–822.

• • •

1487

Test Name: HEALTH-ENGENDERINGNESS SCALE

Purpose: To assess the health-engenderingness of resident assistants.

Number of Items: 11

Format: Respondents rate the target person on each item on a 6-point scale from 1 (*never displays this characteristic*) to 6 (*always displays this characteristic*).

Author: Newton, M., and Krauss, H. H.

Article: The health-engenderingness of resident assistants as related to student achievement and adjustment.

Journal: *Journal of College Student Personnel*, July 1973, *14*(4), 321–325.

Related Research: Alsobrook, J. M. (1962). *A study of health-engendering people in a campus community*. Unpublished doctoral dissertation, University of Florida.

• • •

1488

Test Name: HOSPITAL PROJECTIVE TEST

Purpose: To measure children's fear or anxiety during hospitalization.

Format: A series of hospital scenes in which the central child's face is left blank. Subjects select happy or sad face that they feel is appropriate to the action.

Author: Vernon, D. T. A.

Article: Use of modeling to modify children's responses to a natural, potentially stressful situation.

Journal: *Journal of Applied Psychology*, December 1973, *58*(3), 351–356.

Reliability: Dorkey, M., & Amen, E. W. (1947). A continuation study of anxiety reactions in young children by means of a projective technique. *Genetic Psychology Monographs, 35*, 139–183.

• • •

1489

Test Name: INTERPERSONAL STYLE INVENTORY

Purpose: To assess an individual's interpersonal trait variables.

Number of Items: 257

Format: 257 true–false statements in 14 scales.

Validity: Construct validity evidence from four sources, including correlates with the 16 PF (Cattell) and Eysenck personality inventory. Values ranged from .49 to .71.

Author: Lorr, M., and Youniss, R. P.

Article: An inventory of interpersonal style.

Journal: *Journal of Personality Assessment*, April 1973, *37*(2), 165–173.

• • •

1490

Test Name: KANSAS REFLECTION–IMPULSIVITY SCALE

Purpose: To determine reflective–impulsive classification of preschool children.

Number of Items: 10

Time Required: Approximately 10 minutes.

Format: Based on the Matching Familiar Figures test; requires less difficult discriminations and consists of much grosser feature differences. There are also five warm-up items.

Author: Siegel, A. W., et al.

Article: Recognition memory in reflective and impulsive preschool children.

Journal: *Child Development,* September 1973, *44*(3), 651–656.

• • •

1491

Test Name: KOHLBERG DEVELOPMENT HIERARCHY OF PRIVATE SPEECH FORMS

Purpose: To measure cognitive egocentrism.

Format: Includes seven categories.

Reliability: Test–retest ranged from .85 to .95; interobserver reliability ranged from .82 to .98.

Author: Rubin, H. K.

Article: Egocentrism in childhood: A unitary construct?

Journal: *Child Development,* March 1973, *44*(1), 102–110.

Related Research: Kohlberg, L., et al. (1968). Private speech: Four studies and a review of theories. *Child Development, 39,* 692–736.

• • •

1492

Test Name: MACH IV SCALE

Purpose: To measure the degree to which subjects manipulate their environment.

Validity: Correlation with Dogmatism Scale was .22 ($p < .05$).

Author: Primavera, L., and Higgins, M.

Article: Non-verbal rigidity and its relationships to dogmatism and Machiavellianism.

Journal: *Perceptual and Motor Skills,* April 1973, *36*(2), 356–358.

Related Research: Christie, R., & Geis, F. (1970). *Studies in Machiavellianism.* New York: Academic Press.

1493

Test Name: MANIFEST ANXIETY SCALE— CHILDREN'S FORM

Purpose: To assess anxiety in school-age children.

Number of Items: 53

Format: 42 anxiety items and 11 items to identify subject's tendency to falsify responses. Index of anxiety is the sum of the 42 items answered *yes.*

Validity: With Criterion Phrase Test, rs = −.37, −.39, −.40; with State Trait Anxiety, $r = .27$ (A state $p < .05$) and $r = .54$ (A + Trait, $p < .005$; Finch & Nelson, 1974).

Author: Amble, B.

Article: The effects of anxiety on the perception of word phrases.

Journal: *Journal of School Psychology,* March 1973, *11*(1), 21–25.

Related Research: Castaneda, A., et al. (1956). The children's form of the manifest anxiety scale. *Child Development, 27,* 317–326.

Finch, A., & Nelson, W. (1974). Locus of control and anxiety in emotionally disturbed children. *Psychological Reports, 35,* 469–470.

• • •

1494

Test Name: MATCHING FAMILIAR FIGURES TEST— REVISED

Purpose: To measure impulsivity– reflectivity.

Number of Items: 10

Format: Items are held in a ring binder. Child points to the picture on the page of variants that exactly matches the stimulus picture. Latency to the first response is recorded to the half-

second and total number of errors is recorded for each item.

Author: Erickson, L., and Otto, W.

Article: Effect of intra-list similarity and impulsivity– reflectivity on kindergarten children's word recognition performance.

Journal: *Journal of Educational Research,* July–August 1973, *66*(10), 466–470.

Related Research: Kagan, J. (1965). Reflection–impulsivity and reading ability in primary grade children. *Child Development, 36,* 609–628.

See *D.U.E.M.M., 2,* 1978: 942.

• • •

1495

Test Name: MILITANCY SCALE

Purpose: To measure militancy among public school teachers.

Number of Items: 14

Format: The greater the score, the more militant the respondent's attitude; responses are scored on a Likert scale ranging from *strongly disagree* to *strongly agree.* An example is provided.

Reliability: Split-half reliability was .82.

Author: Giandomenico, L. L.

Article: Teacher needs, militancy, and the scope of collective bargaining.

Journal: *Journal of Educational Research,* February 1973, *66*(6), 257–259.

• • •

1496

Test Name: MOOD ADJECTIVE CHECKLIST

Purpose: To measure anxiety level.

Number of Items: 25

Format: 24 adjectives and an open-ended response. Responses were assigned points as follows: 4 (*definitely*), 3 (*slightly*), 2 (*can't decide*), 1 (*definitely not*).

Author: Mandelson, L. R.

Article: Test performance on a verbal learning task as a function of anxiety-arousing testing instructions.

Journal: *Journal of Educational Research*, September 1973, *63*(1), 37–40.

Related Research: Nowlis, V., & Green, R. F. (1965). *Research program on mood and attitude change* (Research Project No. NR 171–342, Contract No. NR–668 12). Rochester, NY: University of Rochester.

■ ■ ■

1497

Test Name: O'DONOVAN TRUST SCALE

Purpose: To measure trust of others and of self.

Validity: Correlation of Coopersmith Self Esteem and trust of self was .50 (*p* < .05) for boys and .27 (*ns*) for girls.

Author: Smith, R., et al.

Article: Correlations between trust, self esteem, sociometric choice and internal–external control.

Journal: *Psychological Reports,* June 1973, *32*(3), 739–743.

Related Research: Tedeschi, J., et al. (1969). Trust and the prisoners' dilemma game. *Journal of Social Psychology, 79,* 43–50.

■ ■ ■

1498

Test Name: PARAGRAPH COMPLETION TEST (PCT)

Purpose: To assess cognitive style: how a person receives, processes,

and holds various interpersonal stimuli.

Number of Items: 5

Time Required: 2 minutes.

Format: Subject completes five incomplete sentences in 2-minute intervals. For example, "When someone disagrees with me...."

Reliability: Interrater reliability was .75.

Validity: High scores on PCT expressed higher degrees of empathy in a counseling analogue.

Author: Heck, E., and Davis, C.

Article: Differential expression of empathy in a counseling analogue.

Journal: *Journal of Counseling Psychology,* March 1973, *20*(2), 101–104.

Related Research: Hunt, D., & Kingsley, R., et al. (1967). *Conceptual level scoring from paragraph completions in adolescents.* Unpublished manuscript, Syracuse University.

■ ■ ■

1499

Test Name: PARAGRAPH COMPLETION TEST

Purpose: To assess conceptual complexity.

Validity: Correlation with Interpersonal Topical Inventory was –.18 (*p* < .025); the correlation with 7 scales and Complexity Self Description Scale ranged from –.01 to .23 (5/7 significant at .025 level).

Author: Russell, G., and Sandilands, M.

Article: Some correlates of conceptual complexity.

Journal: *Psychological Reports,* October 1973, *33*(2), 587–593.

Related Research: Schroeder, H., et al. (1967). *Human information processing.* New York: Holt, Rinehart & Winston.

■ ■ ■

1500

Test Name: PENSACOLA Z SCALE

Purpose: To measure authoritarianism.

Number of Items: 66

Format: Forced choice; measured four traits: dependency, hostility, rigidity, anxiety.

Validity: Correlation with California F was .4 (Jones, 1957).

Author: Martoccia, C.

Article: Authoritarianism and party switching in 1972.

Journal: *Perceptual and Motor Skills,* December 1973, *37*(3), 694.

Related Research: Jones, M. (1957). The Pensacola Z Survey: A study in the measurement of authoritarian tendency. *Psychological Monographs, 71* (452).

■ ■ ■

1501

Test Name: REACTION INVENTORY

Purpose: To measure anger.

Number of Items: 76

Format: Self-descriptive instrument.

Author: Evans, D., and Hearn, M.

Article: Anger and systematic desensitization: A follow-up.

Journal: *Psychological Reports,* April 1973, *32*(2), 569–570.

Related Research: Evans, D., & Stangeland, M. (1971). The development of the reaction inventory to measure anger. *Psychological Reports, 29,* 412–414.

See *D.U.E.M.M., 2,* 1978: 950.

• • •

1502

Test Name: REPRESSION–SENSITIZATION TENDENCIES SCALE

Purpose: To measure individual differences in repressing–sensitizing tendencies.

Number of Items: 127

Format: True–false self-report.

Reliability: Corrected split-half estimate was .94; test–retest estimate over 3 months was .82.

Validity: Correlation with achievement motivation was –.23.

Author: Farley, F. H., and Mealiea, W. L., Jr.

Article: Motivation and the recall of completed and incomplete achievement items.

Journal: *Journal of Educational Research,* March 1973, *66*(7), 302–306.

Related Research: Byrne, D. Repression-sensitization as a dimension of personality. In B. A. Maher (Ed.), *Progress in experimental personality research.* New York: Academic Press, 1964, 169–220.

See *D.U.E.M.M., 2,* 1978: 951.

• • •

1503

Test Name: ROLE-TAKING EGOCENTRISM SCALE

Purpose: To trace the child's growing understanding of the recursive nature of thought.

Number of Items: 12 drawings.

Format: Includes four developmental categories of recursive thought. Items are scored 1 point if correct or 0 if incorrect. The higher the score the less egocentric the child with regard to role-taking.

Reliability: Test–retest reliability was .85 to .95. Interobserver reliability was .82 to .98.

Author: Rubin, K. H.

Article: Egocentrism in childhood: A unitary construct?

Journal: *Child Development,* March 1973, *44*(1), 102–110.

Related Research: Miller, P. H., et al. (1970). Thinking about people thinking about people thinking about ... A study of social cognitive development. *Child Development, 41,* 613–623.

• • •

1504

Test Name: ROTTER INTERPERSONAL TRUST SCALE

Purpose: To assess degree of trust put in an individual or a group.

Number of Items: 40 (15 filler items).

Format: Declarative statements, for example, "Parents and teachers are likely to say what they believe..."

Validity: Scale significantly ($p <$ .01) differentiated between groups of normals and paranoid schizophrenics; did not differentiate between levels of social class (Sawyer, 1973).

Author: Pasewark, R., et al.

Article: Validity of Rotter's Interpersonal Trust Scale: A study of paranoid schizophrenics.

Journal: *Psychological Reports,* June 1973, *32*(3), 982.

Related Research: Roller, J. (1967). A new scale for the measurement of interpersonal trust. *Journal of Personality, 35,* 651–665.

Sawyer, R., et al. (1973). Relationship of Rotter's interpersonal trust scale and social class. *Psychological Reports, 32,* 989–990.

See *D.U.E.M.M., 2,* 1978: 954.

• • •

1505

Test Name: RYDELL-ROSEN TOLERANCE OF AMBIGUITY SCALE

Purpose: To assess tolerance for ambiguity.

Validity: Members of a women's liberation group were significantly more tolerant of ambiguity than nonmember women.

Author: Pawlicki, R., and Almquist, C.

Article: Authoritarianism, locus of control, and tolerance of ambiguity as reflected in membership and nonmembership in a women's liberation group.

Journal: *Psychological Reports,* June 1973, *32*(3), 1331–1337.

Related Research: MacDonald, A. (1970). Revised scale for ambiguity tolerance: Reliability and validity. *Psychological Reports, 26,* 791–798.

See *D.U.E.M.M., 2,* 1978: 955.

• • •

1506

Test Name: STEIN PHYSIOGNOMIC CUE TEST

Purpose: To assess physiognomic reactivity; a cognitive control measure.

Reliability: Test–retest coefficients were .68 and .74.

Author: Gardner, R.

Article: Reliability of group test scores for cognitive controls and intellectual abilities over a one year period.

Journal: *Perceptual and Motor Skills,* June 1973, *36*(3), 753–754.

Related Research: Rosett, H., et al. (1967). Standardization and construct validity of the Physiognomic Cue Test. *Perceptual and Motor Skills, 24,* 403–420.

■ ■ ■

1507

Test Name: TEACHER LEADERSHIP STYLE SCALE

Purpose: To assess each teacher's leadership style.

Number of Items: 14

Format: Students respond to each item on a Guttman scale. Includes three dimensions of leadership: task orientation, power orientation, expressive orientation. All items are presented.

Reliability: Coefficients of reproducibility were .91, .93, and .94. Coefficients of scalability were .64, .73, and .75.

Validity: Correlations with community socioeconomic status were −.13, .05, and .20. Correlations with community size were .19, .12, and −.09.

Author: Larkin, R. W.

Article: Research notes: Contextual influences on teacher leadership styles.

Journal: *Sociology of Education,* Fall 1973, *46*(4), 471–479.

■ ■ ■

1508

Test Name: TOLERANCE OF BUREAUCRATIC STRUCTURE SCALE

Purpose: To measure disadvantaged persons' tolerance for bureaucratic structure.

Number of Items: 43

Format: Job placement scale containing a 4-point Likert scale format.

Author: Van Doren, R. (Ed).

Article: Manpower, human assessment and the disadvantaged.

Journal: *American Vocational Journal,* January 1973, *48*(1), 86–100.

■ ■ ■

1509

Test Name: TUCKMAN'S INTERPERSONAL TOPICAL INVENTORY

Purpose: To measure conceptual complexity.

Validity: For university students the correlation with the Paragraph Completion Test measure of conceptual complexity was −.18 ($p < .025$).

Author: Russell, G., and Sandilands, M.

Article: Some correlates of conceptual complexity.

Journal: *Psychological Reports,* October 1973, *33*(2), 587–593.

Related Research: Tuckman, B. (1966). Integrative complexity: Its measurement and relation to creativity. *Educational and Psychological Measurement, 26,* 369–383.

■ ■ ■

1510

Test Name: ZAKS-WALTERS SCALE OF AGGRESSION

Purpose: To assess behavioral aggression.

Number of Items: 12

Format: MMPI-type instrument.

Validity: Biserial correlation with Yuker Attitude Toward the Disabled Scale was .34 ($p < .05$).

Author: Evans, J.

Article: Attitude toward the disabled and aggression.

Journal: *Perceptual and Motor Skills,* December 1973, *37*(3), 834.

Related Research: Zaks, M., & Walters, R. (1959). First steps in the construction of a scale for the measurement of aggression. *Journal of Psychology, 47,* 199–208.

CHAPTER 21
Values

1511

Test Name: ARE YOU SOMEONE WHO?

Purpose: To provide a strategy to allow subjects to consider more thoughtfully what they value, what they want of life, and what type of person they are.

Number of Items: 20

Format: Questions answered *yes, no,* or *maybe.*

Author: Simon, S., and Massey, S.

Article: Value clarification.

Journal: *Educational Leadership,* May 1973, *30*(8), 738–739.

Related Research: Simon, S., et al. (1972). *Value clarification: A handbook of practical strategies for teachers and students.* New York: Hart.

...

1512

Test Name: CHANEY SHORT FORM VOCATIONAL VALUES INVENTORY

Purpose: To assess vocational values.

Number of Items: 42

Format: Measures: altruism, control, job freedom, money, prestige, security, self-realization.

Author: Cooker, P.

Article: Vocational values of children in grades four, five and six.

Journal: *Elementary School Guidance and Counseling,* December 1973, *8*(2), 112–118.

Related Research: Chaney, R. (1968). *Vocational values of children as they relate to economic community, grade level, sex and parental occupational level.* Unpublished doctoral dissertation, Ohio University.

...

1513

Test Name: CHILDREN'S CONSERVATISM SCALE

Purpose: To assess the social attitude of conservatism.

Number of Items: 50

Format: Subjects reply to whether they believe in 50 issues (e.g., Sunday school).

Reliability: Split-half reliability was .89 (Insel & Wilson, 1971).

Author: Nias, D.

Article: The structuring of social attitudes in children.

Journal: *Child Development,* March 1973, *43*(1), 211–219.

Related Research: Insel, P., & Wilson, G. (1971). Measuring social attitudes in children. *British Journal of Social and Clinical Psychology, 10,* 84–86.

...

1514

Test Name: HOOD RELIGIOUS EXPERIENCE EPISODES MEASURE

Purpose: To assess intensity of religious experience.

Format: 15 descriptions of religious experiences are presented to subject, who rates (on a 5-point scale) the similarity of his or her personal experience to descriptions. Single summed and averaged score obtained.

Validity: Correlation with the Harvard Measure of hypnotic susceptibility was .36 ($p < .01$).

Author: Hood, R.

Article: Hypnotic susceptibility and reported religious experience.

Journal: *Psychological Reports,* October 1973, *33*(2), 549–550.

Related Research: Hood, R. (1972). Normative and motivational determinants of reported religious experience in two Baptist samples. *Review of Religious Experience, 13,* 192–196.

...

1515

Test Name: INTELLECTUALISM-PRAGMATISM SCALE

Purpose: To measure development of intellectual versus pragmatic attitude.

Number of Items: 30

Format: Likert instrument answered by marking one of three categories of agreement or disagreement. Scoring ranges from +3 to –3 on each item.

Validity: SCAT correlations were .12, .14, and .24. High School Rank correlations were –.01, –.04, .05, and .10. Minnesota Teacher Attitude Inventory correlations were .11, .18, .19, and .28. Graduation GPA correlations were .03, .20, and .28.

Author: Burton, R. L., and Polmantier, P. C.

Article: Intellectual attitude development of students in a teacher education program.

Journal: *Journal of College Student Personnel,* July 1973, *14*(4), 352–354.

Related Research: Block, J. R., & Yuker, H. E. (1965). Correlates of an intellectual orientation among college students. In *Proceedings of the 73rd Annual Convention of the American Psychological Association* (pp. 315–316). Washington, DC: American Psychological Association.

■ ■ ■

1516

Test Name: IRRATIONAL BELIEFS TEST (IBT)

Purpose: A test of commonly held irrational beliefs.

Number of Items: 100

Format: Subject rates agreement–disagreement with each item on a 5-point scale.

Reliability: Test–retest reliability was .88.

Validity: Validity was supported through predicted changed IBT scores before and after treatment, differentiating unlike groups, and correlations reported with several other measures.

Author: Trexler, L. D., and Karst, T. O.

Article: Further validation for a new measure of irrational cognitions.

Journal: *Journal of Personality Assessment,* April 1973, *37*(2), 150–155.

■ ■ ■

1517

Test Name: MACHIAVELLIANISM SCALE

Purpose: To measure machiavellianism.

Number of Items: 10

Format: Positively stated items producing score range from 10 to 70.

Author: Cryns, A. G., and Finn, J. D.

Article: A multivariate analysis of some attitudinal and ideological correlates of student activism.

Journal: *Sociology of Education,* Winter 1973, *46*(1), 127–142.

Related Research: Christie, R., & Geis, F. (1970). *Studies in Machiavellianism.* New York: Academic Press.

■ ■ ■

1518

Test Name: McCLOSKY CONSERVATISM SCALE

Purpose: To assess general political philosophy of conservatism.

Number of Items: 11

Validity: External locus of control subjects scored higher on the conservatism scale than internal subjects ($p < .005$).

Author: Fink, H., and Hjelle, L.

Article: Internal vs external control and ideology.

Journal: *Psychological Reports,* December 1973, *33*(3), 967–974.

Related Research: McClosky, H. (1958). Conservatism and personality. *American Political Science Review, 52,* 27–45.

■ ■ ■

1519

Test Name: MORAL JUDGMENT MEASURE

Purpose: To measure moral judgment.

Number of Items: 6

Format: Includes three "authority vs altruism" and three "peer vs altruism" situations read to the subject. All six stories present a conflict between two legitimate alternatives. Subjects' solution was scored on a 5-point scale with total score ranging from 6 to 30.

Validity: With egocentrism, $r = .59$; mental age, $r = .42$.

Author: Rubin, K. H., and Schneider, F. W.

Article: The relationship between moral judgment, egocentrism, and altruistic behavior.

Journal: *Child Development,* September 1973, *44*(3), 661–665.

Related Research: Lee, L. C. (1971). The concomitant development of cognitive and moral modes of thought: A test of selected deductions from Piaget's theory. *Genetic Psychology Monographs, 83,* 93–146.

■ ■ ■

1520

Test Name: NEW LEFT SCALE

Purpose: To assess political belief (leftist orientation).

Number of Items: 28

Format: Examples of items are given.

Validity: Significant ($p < .02$) differences between external and internal locus of control subjects.

Author: Fink, H., and Hjelle, L.

Article: Internal–external control and ideology.

Journal: *Psychological Reports,* December 1973, *33*(3), 967–974.

Related Research: Christie, R., et al. (1969). The new left and its ideology: An exploratory study. *Proceedings of the 77th Annual Convention of the American Psychological Association, 4,* 293–294.

1521

Test Name: PERSONAL VALUES INVENTORY

Purpose: To assess personal values.

Format: Eight orientations: affiliative–romantic, status–security, intellectual–humanist, family values, rugged individualist, undemanding–passive, boy scout, Don Juan.

Author: Gorlow, L., and Black, H.

Article: Values and behavior in the natural world.

Journal: *Psychological Reports,* June, 1973, *32*(3), 920.

• • •

1522

Test Name: PHILOSOPHIES OF HUMAN NATURE SCALE

Purpose: To measure beliefs about human nature.

Number of Items: 84

Format: Likert attitude inventory includes six dimensions of human nature: trustworthiness or untrustworthiness, strength of will and rationality versus external locus of control and irrationality, altruism versus selfishness, independence versus conformity to group pressure, complexity versus simplicity, and variability versus similarity.

Reliability: Split-half coefficients for men ranged from .61 to .91; for women, from .60 to .92. Test–retest (3-month interval) reliabilities were .74; higher for each subscale, except complexity, .52.

Author: Wilkinson, L. D., and Hood, W. D.

Article: Student responses to the Philosophies of Human Nature Scale.

Journal: *Journal of College Student Personnel,* September 1973, *14*(5), 434–437.

Related Research: Wrightsman, L. S., Jr. (1964). Measurement of philosophies of human nature. *Psychological Reports, 14,* 743–751.

See *D.U.E.M.M., 2,* 1978: 980.

• • •

1523

Test Name: PUPIL CONTROL IDEOLOGY FORM

Purpose: To measure teachers' pupil control orientation.

Number of Items: 20

Format: Items represent facets of school life. Subjects respond on a 5-point, Likert scale from 5 (*strongly agree*) to 1 (*strongly disagree*). The higher the total score, the more authoritarian the pupil control orientation; the lower the score, the more humanistic the pupil control orientation.

Reliability: Stability coefficient was .86.

Author: Halpin, G., et al.

Article: Are creative teachers more humanistic in their pupil control ideologies?

Journal: *Journal of Creative Behavior,* 1973, *7*(4), 282–286.

Related Research: Willower, D. J., et al. (1967). *The school and pupil control ideology* (The Pennsylvania State University Studies, No. 24). University Park: Pennsylvania State University.

• • •

1524

Test Name: QUESTIONNAIRE OF AMERICAN VALUES BY 2000 A.D.

Purpose: To measure prediction of future American values.

Number of Items: 17

Format: Each item elicits an opinion of probable change in emphasis on a 5-point scale from 1 (*greatly increased emphasis*) to 5 (*greatly decreased emphasis*).

Author: Welty, G.

Article: Some problems of selecting Delphi experts for educational planning and forecasting exercises.

Journal: *California Journal of Educational Research,* May 1973, *24*(3), 129–134.

Related Research: Rescher, N. (1969). A questionnaire study of American values by 2000 A.D. In K. Baier & N. Rescher (Eds.), *Values and the future free press* (pp. 136–137, 141, 146).

• • •

1525

Test Name: RELIGIOSITY QUESTIONNAIRE

Purpose: To identify religious affiliation, practices, beliefs, instruction, and training of university faculty.

Format: Questions about past and present religious affiliation, church attendance and other religious practices, nature of religious beliefs, reasons for change (if any) in religiosity, religious instruction and training, parents' and spouse's religiosity, academic specialty, and the relationship between religious orientation and professional work. Some items are presented.

Author: Thalheimer, F.

Article: Religiosity and secularization in the academic professions.

Journal: *Sociology of Education,* Spring 1973, *46*(2), 183–202.

1526

Test Name: ROKEACH SELF-REPORT SCALE–REVISED

Purpose: To measure relative importance of other-centered values.

Number of Items: 12

Format: Four statements are considered self-centered values, four are neutral, and four are other-centered.

Reliability: Test–retest reliability was .83.

Author: Dlugokinski, E., and Firestone, I. J.

Article: Congruence among four methods of measuring other-centeredness.

Journal: *Child Development*, June 1973, *44*(2), 304–308.

■ ■ ■

1527

Test Name: SOCIAL ATTITUDE SCALE

Purpose: To measure along a liberalism–conservatism dimension.

Number of Items: 44

Format: Likert style (two forms).

Validity: With external–internal scale, $r = -.24$ ($p < .01$); Alienation, $r = -.35$ ($p < .01$); Status Concern, $r = .49$ ($p < .01$).

Author: Rambo, W.

Article: Validation of a scale measuring liberal–conservative attitudes.

Journal: *Perceptual and Motor Skills*, February 1973, *36*(1), 103–106.

Related Research: Rambo, W. (1972). The measurement of broad spectrum social attitudes: Liberalism–conservativism. *Perceptual and Motor Skills, 35*, 463–477.

1528

Test Name: SOCIAL VALUES TEST

Purpose: To indicate adherence to statements of values and beliefs.

Number of Items: 40

Format: Likert with 10 relatively independent value dimensions: Public aid versus private effort, social protection versus social retribution, pluralism versus homogeneity, secularism versus religiosity, social causation versus individual autonomy, positive satisfaction versus struggle-denial, innovation-change versus traditionalism, self-determinism versus fatalism, personal freedom versus social controls, personal goals versus maintenance groups.

Author: Franks, D. D., et al.

Article: Differential exposure to courses in two majors and differences in students' value responses.

Journal: *Sociology of Education*, Summer 1973, *46*(3), 361–369.

Related Research: Meyer, H. S. (1962). *Social values test.* Unpublished manuscript, University of Michigan, School of Social Work and Department of Sociology.

■ ■ ■

1529

Test Name: SPECIFIC VALUE SCALE

Purpose: To assess human values, activities, and feelings.

Number of Items: 107

Format: Forced-choice.

Validity: Factor analysis identified one general and 23 primary factors.

Author: Mason, R.

Article: Creativity to sexual values as factors of importance, frequency, and feeling ratings.

Journal: *Journal of Personality Assessment,* 1973, *37*(3), 267–275.

■ ■ ■

1530

Test Name: STUDENT ATTITUDE SCALE—REVISED

Purpose: To measure intellectual and woman's role values.

Number of Items: 69

Format: True–false items comprising two subscales. (Copies are available from the author on request.)

Validity: Correlation between scales was −.446.

Author: Grebow, H.

Article: The relationship of some parental variables to achievement and values in college women.

Journal: *Journal of Educational Research,* January 1973, *66*(5), 203–209.

Related Research: French, E., & Lesser, G. (1964). Some characteristics of the achievement motive in women. *Journal of Abnormal and Social Psychology, 68*, 119–138.

■ ■ ■

1531

Test Name: SURVEY OF WORK VALUES

Purpose: To identify work values of disadvantaged applicants.

Number of Items: 54

Format: Six subscales: pride in work, job involvement, activity preference, attitude toward earnings, social status of job, upward striving. Subjects indicate that they *agree* or *disagree* with each statement.

Reliability: Test–retest reliabilities ranged from .68 to .76.

Author: Goodale, J. G.

Article: Effects of personal background and training on work values of the hard-core unemployed.

Journal: *Journal of Applied Psychology,* February 1973, *57*(1), 1–9.

Related Research: Wollack, S., et al. (1971). The development of the Survey of Work Values. *Journal of Applied Psychology, 55,* 331–338.

■ ■ ■

1532

Test Name: SURVEY OF WORK VALUES

Purpose: To survey employees' work values.

Format: Six subscales: attitude toward earnings, activity preference, pride in work, job involvement, upward striving, social status of job.

Author: Wade, M.

Article: Personnel research.

Journal: *Personnel Journal,* June 1973, *52*(6), 489–491.

1533

Test Name: VALUE CLARIFICATION QUESTIONNAIRE

Purpose: To permit discovery of one's own values.

Number of Items: 20

Format: Questions begin "Are you someone who … ?" All items are presented.

Author: Simon, S., and Massey, S.

Article: Value clarification.

Journal: *Educational Leadership,* May 1973, *30*(8), 738–739.

■ ■ ■

1534

Test Name: VALENCE OF JOB OUTCOMES-Q-SORT

Purpose: To measure the valence of job outcomes.

Number of Items: 13

Format: Subject places each of 13 job outcomes in one of five *a priori* categories based on the importance of each outcome to the subject.

Author: Jorgenson, D. O., et al.

Article: Effects of the manipulation of a performance-reward contingency on behavior in a simulated work setting.

Journal: *Journal of Applied Psychology,* June 1973, *57*(3), 271–280.

■ ■ ■

1535

Test Name: VALUE INTEREST DYNAMICS INSTRUMENT

Purpose: To measure value interest, change–nonchange orientations.

Number of Items: 80

Format: Four groups of cliche-type items: value, interest, change, nonchange. Responses from 1 *(strongly disagree)* to 4 (*did not answer*) to 7 (*strongly agree*). Examples are provided.

Author: Clagett, A. F.

Article: Role adjustment modes of public school teachers.

Journal: *Journal of Educational Research,* September 1973, *67*(1), 29–33.

Related Research: Clagett, A. F. (1968). *Public school teachers' modes of role adjustment to change.* Unpublished doctoral dissertation, Louisiana State University.

CHAPTER 22
Vocational Evaluation

1536

Test Name: APPRAISAL SCHEME SCALE

Purpose: To measure managers' confidence, discontent, and appraisal attitude.

Number of Items: 17

Format: Includes three factors of confidence, discontent, appraisal attitude. All items are presented.

Validity: With Managerial status, $r = -.42$; Confidence scale, $r = .49$; Education, $r = .07$; Extraversion, $r = .06$; Age, $r = .39$; Neuroticism, $r = -.02$; Discontent scale, $r = -.02$; Change scale, $r = .31$.

Author: Kirton, M. J., and Mulligan, G.

Article: Correlates of managers' attitudes toward change.

Journal: *Journal of Applied Psychology*, August 1973, *58*(1), 101–107.

• • •

1537

Test Name: BANK TELLER JOB PERFORMANCE AND EFFECTIVENESS SCALE

Purpose: To rate job performance and overall effectiveness of bank tellers.

Number of Items: 6

Format: Includes five job factors and an overall effectiveness rating.

Reliability: Interrater reliabilities for two raters corrected by Spearman-Brown ranged from .69 to .83.

Author: Bass, A. R., and Turner, J. N.

Article: Ethnic group difference in relationships among criteria of job performance.

Journal: *Journal of Applied Psychology*, April 1973, *57*(2), 101–109.

• • •

1538

Test Name: BARRETT-LENNARD RELATIONSHIP INVENTORY

Purpose: To assess the dimensions of congruence, empathic understanding, unconditionality of regard, and level of regard.

Author: Boller, J. D., and Boller, J. D.

Article: Sensitivity training and the school teacher: An experiment in favorable publicity.

Journal: *Journal of Educational Research*, March 1973, *66*(7), 309–312.

Related Research: Barrett-Lennard, G. T. (1962). Dimensions of therapist response as causal factors in therapeutic change. *Psychological Monographs*, *76*(No. 562).

See *D.U.E.M.M.*, *2*, 1978: 309.

• • •

1539

Test Name: CLASSROOM ENVIRONMENT SCALE—FORM D

Purpose: To assess nine dimensions of the classroom.

Number of Items: 90

Format: Dimensions: Involvement, affiliation, support, task orientation, competition, order and organization, rule clarity, teacher control, innovation. Examples of each dimension are provided.

Reliability: Internal consistency coefficient ranged from .67 to .86.

Author: Trickett, E. J., and Moos, R. H.

Article: Social environment of junior high and high school classrooms.

Journal: *Journal of Educational Psychology*, August 1973, *65*(1), 98–102.

• • •

1540

Test Name: COLLEGE COURSE EVALUATION FORM

Purpose: To enable college students to evaluate their courses.

Number of Items: 20

Format: Subject responds to each item on a 5-interval rating scale. Two forms: one permits evaluation of college courses in general, the other permits the evaluation of a particular course.

Author: Jandt, F. E.

Article: A new method of student evaluation of teaching.

Journal: *Improving College and University Teaching*, Winter 1973, *21*(1), 15–16.

• • •

1541

Test Name: COLLEGE TEACHER-DESCRIPTION SCALES

Purpose: To provide colleagues with an instrument for judging others' teaching effectiveness.

Number of Items: 113

Format: Items are grouped under the following five scales, each answered *yes* or *no*: research activity and recognition, participation in the academic community, intellectual breadth, relation with students, concern for teaching.

Reliability: Ranged from .71 to .86.

Author: Wilson, R. C., et al.

Article: Characteristics of effective college teachers as perceived by their colleagues.

Journal: *Journal of Educational Measurement,* Spring 1973, *10*(1), 31–37.

Related Research: Request National Auxiliary Publications Service, Document 01963. ASIS National Auxiliary Publications Services, Inc., 909 Third Avenue, New York, NY 10022.

■ ■ ■

1542

Test Name: COLLEGE TEACHING EFFECTIVENESS QUESTIONNAIRE

Purpose: To assess some of the characteristics ascribed to colleagues regarded as effective teachers.

Number of Items: 113

Format: Subjects answer *yes* or *no* to a series of statements applied to the best teacher they know.

Reliability: Reliabilities ranged from .71 to .86, mode = .76.

Validity: Factor analysis resulted in 5 dimensions. Scales correlated relatively low with each other. Research activity and recognition scale was related to academic rank

and discipline of teachers considered effective.

Author: Wilson, R., et al.

Article: Characteristics of effective college teachers as perceived by their colleagues.

Journal: *Journal of Educational Measurement,* 1973, *10*(1), 31–37.

■ ■ ■

1543

Test Name: COUNSELING SKILLS RATING SCALE

Purpose: To assess various counselor behaviors.

Author: Burck, H., et al.

Article: Teaching a course in counseling theories and practice: Description and evaluation.

Journal: *Counselor Education and Supervision,* March 1973, *12*(3), 162–171.

Related Research: Myrick, R., & Kelly, D. (1971, March). *A scale for evaluating particular students in counseling and supervision.* Paper presented at the American Personnel and Guidance Association Convention, Atlantic City.

Ravsten, L. (1968). *Counselor trait scale.* Unpublished form, Brigham Young University.

■ ■ ■

1544

Test Name: COUNSELOR PREFERENCE SURVEY

Purpose: To rate the extent of counselors' understanding and care for a client.

Time Required: 40 minutes to rate six counselors.

Format: Rater listens to a counselor's recorded response to a hypothetical client and rates it on a 5-point scale; also ratings of

counselors on a 4-point perceived helpfulness scale.

Reliability: Coefficient of concordance used; researchers reported that 72% were significant, no coefficient was given.

Author: Dilley, J., and Bowers, I.

Article: A long distance approach to evaluating counselor communication.

Journal: *Counselor Education and Supervision,* March 1973, *12*(3), 178–183.

■ ■ ■

1545

Test Name: COUNSELOR SOCIAL REINFORCEMENT AND PERSUASION SCALES

Purpose: To assess the extent of positive reinforcement by a counselor and client behavior and the amount of counselor conviction and client agreement.

Format: 3-minute segments of taped interviews were analyzed and rated by three trained observers for each of the two scales.

Reliability: Rate–rerate reliabilities were .71, .72, and .84 for persuasion and .74, .82, and .85 for social reinforcement.

Validity: Counselors differentially trained to reinforce socially or to persuade performed differently on the two scales.

Author: Packwood, V., et al.

Article: Validation of counselor social reinforcement and persuasion scales.

Journal: *Journal of Counseling Psychology,* September 1973, *20*(5), 491–492.

Related Research: Packwood, W., & Parker, C. (1973). A method for rating counselor social reinforcement and persuasion. *Journal of Counseling Psychology,* 20, 38–43.

▪ ▪ ▪

1546

Test Name: COURSE AND INSTRUCTOR QUESTIONNAIRE

Purpose: To permit students to evaluate courses and instructors.

Number of Items: 48

Format: Responses recorded on a scale from 4 (*most favorable*) to 1 (*least favorable*). Five factors included: general course attitude, attitude toward examinations, attitude toward method, instructor/student rapport, attitude toward work load. Most of the items are presented.

Author: Finkbeiner, C. T., et al.

Article: Course and instructor evaluation.

Journal: *Journal of Educational Psychology,* April 1973, 64(2), 159–163.

▪ ▪ ▪

1547

Test Name: COURSE EVALUATION INVENTORY

Purpose: To permit college students to evaluate their instructors and courses.

Number of Items: 58

Format: True–false responses; all items are presented.

Reliability: Spearman-Brown estimates varied from .80 to .99.

Validity: Predictive validity varied from .50 to .83.

Author: Hoyt, D. P.

Article: Identifying effective instructional procedures.

Journal: *Improving College and University Teaching,* Winter 1973, 21(1), 73–76.

1548

Test Name: FACULTY EVALUATION INSTRUMENT

Purpose: To evaluate college faculty members.

Number of Items: 15

Format: Ratings are made on observable behavior.

Validity: Four primary factors identified: teacher presentation, work load, grading procedure, teacher accessibility; loadings for each item are reported.

Author: Frey, P.

Article: Comparative judgment scaling of student course ratings.

Journal: *American Educational Research Journal,* Spring 1973, 10(2), 149–154.

▪ ▪ ▪

1549

Test Name: FIREMAN LEADERSHIP PROFILES

Purpose: To identify leadership qualities of firemen.

Number of Items: 15

Format: Includes three variables of five items each: human relations, technical skills, administrative skills.

Author: Keelan, J. A., et al.

Article: Leadership policies as perceived by firemen.

Journal: *Colorado Journal of Educational Research,* Winter 1973, 12(2), 20–23.

▪ ▪ ▪

1550

Test Name: INSTRUCTOR EVALUATION SCALE

Purpose: To provide instructor assessment.

Number of Items: 6

Format: 7-point scales regarding

instructor: open-mindedness, ease and relaxed attitude, stimulation, competence, liked as a person, desirability as an instructor.

Author: Good, K., and Good, L.

Article: Attitude similarity and attraction to an instructor.

Journal: *Psychological Reports,* August 1973, 33(1), 335–337.

▪ ▪ ▪

1551

Test Name: INVENTORY OF TEACHING FACTORS

Purpose: To evaluate college classroom teaching effectiveness.

Number on items: 50.

Format: Includes 47 multiple-choice and three write-in items; items pertained to the behavior of teachers in and out of the classroom, methods of teaching, classroom atmosphere, general relationships between students and teachers, and the identification of significant events or factors in student–teacher relationships that led to crucial effects of students' creative development.

Author: Chambers, J. A.

Article: College teachers: Their effect on creativity of students.

Journal: *Journal of Educational Psychology,* December 1973, 65(3), 326–334.

Related Research: Ronan, W. W. (1971). *Development of an instrument to evaluate college classroom teaching effectiveness* (U.S. Office of Education Project 1–D–0–45, Grant OEG–4–71–0067). Atlanta: Georgia Institute of Technology.

▪ ▪ ▪

1552

Test Name: JOB DESCRIPTION INDEX

Purpose: To determine satisfaction

with immediate supervision.

Author: Falcione, R. L.

Article: The relationship of supervisor credibility to subordinate satisfaction.

Journal: *Personnel Journal,* September 1973, *52*(9), 800–803.

Related Research: Smith, P. C., et al. (1969). *The measurement of work and retirement.* Chicago: Rand McNally.

• • •

1553

Test Name: JOB PERFORMANCE QUESTIONNAIRE

Purpose: To measure job performance.

Number of Items: 5

Format: Supervisors evaluate employees' performance relative to other persons who have done or are now doing the same work.

Author: Prybil, L. D.

Article: Job satisfaction in relation to job performance and occupational level.

Journal: *Personnel Journal,* February 1973, *52*(2), 94–100.

• • •

1554

Test Name: LEADER HIERARCHICAL INFLUENCE SCALE

Purpose: To measure upward influence of leaders with respect to personnel management of their subordinates and participation in policy decisions.

Number of Items: 7

Author: House, R. J., and Kerr, S.

Article: Organizational independence, leader behavior, and managerial practices: A replicated study.

Journal: *Journal of Applied Psychology,* October 1973, *58*(2), 173–180.

Related Research: Comrey, A. L., et al. (1954). *Factors influencing organizational effectiveness.* Los Angeles: University of Southern California Bookstore.

• • •

1555

Test Name: LEADER TECHNICAL COMPETENCE SCALE

Purpose: To measure the degree to which the superior is perceived as capable of providing advice on technical or specialized problems.

Number of Items: 6

Author: House, R. J., and Kerr, S.

Article: Organizational independence, leader behavior, and managerial practices: A replicated study.

Journal: *Journal of Applied Psychology,* October 1973, *58*(2), 173–180.

Related Research: Comrey, A. L., et al. (1954). *Factors influencing organizational effectiveness.* Los Angeles: University of Southern California Bookstore.

• • •

1556

Test Name: PERCEIVED SUPERVISOR CREDIBILITY SEMANTIC DIFFERENTIAL

Purpose: To determine perceived supervisor credibility.

Number of Items: 24

Format: A semantic differential employing bipolar adjectives.

Author: Falcione, R. L.

Article: The relationship of supervisor credibility to subordinate satisfaction.

Journal: *Personnel Journal,*

September 1973, *52*(9), 800–803.

Related Research: Berlo, D. K., et al. (1969–1970). Evaluating the acceptability of message sources. *Public Opinion Quarterly, 33,* 563–576.

• • •

1557

Test Name: PERFORMANCE RATING SCALES

Purpose: To measure performance of engineers.

Number of Items: 5

Format: Scaled behavioral incidents were used as reference points for ratings on each dimension.

Validity: Correlations with supervisor and engineer ratings ($N = 202$) ranged from .37 to .86.

Author: Williams, W. E., and Seiler, D. A.

Article: Relationship between measures of effort and job performance.

Journal: *Journal of Applied Psychology,* February 1973, *57*(1), 49–54.

• • •

1558

Test Name: PRINCIPALS' INTERVIEW GUIDE

Purpose: To evaluate principals' administrative performance.

Format: Includes five critical tasks of administration: involving people, making policy, determining role, setting goals, appraising programs.

Author: McLoughlin, W. P.

Article: A comparison of the administrative leadership of principals in graded and nongraded elementary schools.

Journal: *Educational Leadership,* February 1973, *30*(5), 450–456.

1559

Test Name: RATING SCALE OF COUNSELOR EFFECTIVENESS

Purpose: To rate the effectiveness of a counselor's performance.

Number of Items: 25

Format: The scale of items is a semantic differential, available in parallel forms with Likert scaling. Each item has seven discrete steps between the positive and negative counselor trait.

Reliability: Reliability was .37 by Kendall's Coefficient of Concordance.

Author: Altmann, H. A.

Article: Effects of empathy, warmth, and genuineness in the initial counseling interview.

Journal: *Counselor Education and Supervision,* March 1973, *12*(3), 225–235.

Related Research: Ivey, A. E. (1968). *Development and initial evaluation of a scale to measure counselor effectiveness.* Unpublished report, University of Massachusetts.

Ivey, A. E., et al. (1968). Microcounseling and attending behavior: An approach to pre-practicum counselor training. *Journal of Counseling Psychology Monograph, 15,* 1–12.

■ ■ ■

1560

Test Name: RETAIL STORE DEPARTMENT MANAGER RATING SCALE

Purpose: To provide a performance rating scale of retail store department managers.

Number of Items: 9

Format: Each of nine scales rated on a 9-point scale. Items are presented.

Reliability: Correlations were 87 and .68.

Author: Campbell, J. P., et al.

Article: The development and evaluation of behaviorally based rating scales.

Journal: *Journal of Applied Psychology,* February 1973, *57*(1), 15–22.

■ ■ ■

1561

Test Name: SCERC SUPERVISORY RATING BLANK

Purpose: To assess rehabilitation counselor effectiveness.

Format: Six criteria: getting along with co-workers, managing time and case load, communicating oral and written ideas, using community and professional resources, initiative regarding professional knowledge and skill, total rating.

Reliability: Intraclass correlations ranged from .50 to 1.00.

Validity: Intercorrelation of five dimensions ranged from .35 to .54.

Author: Richardson, B., and Obermann, C.

Article: Relationship of rehabilitation counselor characteristics to supervisors' ratings.

Journal: *Counselor Education and Supervision,* December 1973, *13*(2), 94–104.

■ ■ ■

1562

Test Name: STUDENT EVALUATION FORM

Purpose: To permit college students to evaluate their courses.

Number of Items: 16

Format: Entire questionnaire is presented.

Author: Bridger, J. A.

Article: Teacher evaluation with a computerized student opinionnaire.

Journal: *Improving College and University Teaching,* Winter, 1973, *21*(1), 43–45.

■ ■ ■

1563

Test Name: STUDENT EVALUATION QUESTIONNAIRE

Purpose: To permit students to judge efffective teaching.

Number of Items: 18

Format: Four items request demographic data; 11 items provide a 7-choice attitude rating scale from 1 (*poor*) to 5 (*excellent*), 6 (*nonapplicable*), 7 (*no response*); three items assess instructor attitude to student, overall instructor rating, and fairness of the questionnaire.

Author: Bromley, A., et al.

Article: Evaluation is vital and integral.

Journal: *Improving College and University Teaching,* Winter 1973, *21*(1), 49–50.

■ ■ ■

1564

Test Name: STUDENT EVALUATION QUESTIONNAIRE

Purpose: To permit college students to evaluate teaching.

Number of Items: 18

Format: Includes six factors: skill, overload, structure, feedback, group interaction, rapport.

Author: Simpkins, W. S., et al.

Article: Teacher differences as perceived by students.

Journal: *Improving College and*

University Teaching, Winter 1973, *21*(1), 64–66.

Related Research: Isaacson, R. L., et al. (1964). Dimensions of student evaluation of teaching. *Journal of Educational Psychology, 55,* 344–351.

● ● ●

1565

Test Name: STUDENT OPINION QUESTIONNAIRE

Purpose: To describe aspects of the instructor's behavior.

Format: Describes instructor's availability to students, use of class time, clarity of assignments, stimulation of interests, and so forth. Also includes an overall evaluation of the course and the instructor. Responses are recorded on a 5-point scale.

Author: Braunstein, D. N., and Benston, G. J.

Article: Student and department chairman views of the performance of university professors.

Journal: *Journal of Applied Psychology,* October 1973, *58*(2), 244–249.

● ● ●

1566

Test Name: SUPERVISORY RATING FORM

Purpose: To measure job performance.

Format: Includes 10 dimensions measured on a 9-point scale: quality of work, quantity of work, attendance, cooperation with co-workers, willingness to work, attitude toward the company, punctuality, common sense, ability to follow instructions, overall job performance.

Author: Wade, M.

Article: Personnel research.

Journal: *Personnel Journal,* March 1973, *52*(3), 223–229.

Related Research: Greenhaus, J. H., & Gavin, J. F. (1972). The relationship between expectancies and job behavior for White and Black employees. *Personnel Psychology, 25,* 449–455.

● ● ●

1567

Test Name: TEACHER COMPETENCY SCALE

Purpose: To identify specific teacher competencies necessary for effective teaching.

Number of Items: 12

Time Required: 30 minutes.

Format: Observation within classroom three times per year rating each of 12 items on 1 to 5 scale; points are defined behaviorally.

Author: Resnick, N., and Reinert, H.

Article: Competency based teacher evaluation.

Journal: *Colorado Journal of Educational Research,* Fall 1973, *13*(1), 19–21.

● ● ●

1568

Test Name: TEACHER EFFECTIVENESS QUESTIONNAIRE

Purpose: To identify characteristics that high school students felt made a teacher effective in the classroom.

Number of Items: 100

Format: Likert scaling; several items are presented.

Author: Tollefson, N.

Article: Selected student variables and perceived teacher effectiveness.

Journal: *Education,* September–

October 1973, *94*(1), 30–35.

● ● ●

1569

Test Name: TEACHING EVALUATION QUESTIONNAIRE

Purpose: To evaluate specific behavioral characteristics of faculty members that might reasonably change during the semester.

Number of Items: 23

Format: Items include overall evaluation of the course and the instructor, giving consideration to student backgrounds, giving feedback, providing schedules of course events, stating expectations, showing enthusiasm, making clear assignments, stimulating thinking, conveying information clearly. Responses included 5-point Likert scaling and multiple choice with various numbers of alternatives.

Reliability: Median Product–Moment correlations between midterm and final ratings were .85 for the control group and .88 for the experimental group.

Author: Braunstein, D. N., et al.

Article: Feedback expectancy and shifts in student ratings of college faculty.

Journal: *Journal of Applied Psychology,* October 1973, *58*(2), 254–258.

Related Research: McKeachie, W. J. (1969). Student ratings of faculty. *AAUP Bulletin, 55,* 439–444.

● ● ●

1570

Test Name: TEACHER RATING SCALE

Purpose: To permit college students to evaluate teaching.

Number of Items: 49

Format: 7-point rating scale from 1 (*highest*) to 7 (*lowest*). All items are presented.

Author: Wyeth, E.

Article: A rating scale for instructors.

Journal: *Improving College and University Teaching,* Winter 1973, *21*(1), 71–72.

■ ■ ■

1571

Test Name: TEACHING STYLE QUESTIONNAIRE

Purpose: To evaluate teaching practices.

Number of Items: 33

Format: True–false items deal with examinations, classroom procedures, instructor/student interaction, assignments, instructor attitudes.

Author: Baird, L. L.

Article: Teaching styles: An exploratory study of dimensions and effects.

Journal: *Journal of Educational Psychology,* February 1973, *64*(1), 15–21.

■ ■ ■

1572

Test Name: THE ADVISOR

Purpose: To evaluate courses.

Number of Items: 34

Format: Four subscales: overall evaluation of course, instructor, quiz or discussion, laboratory or language laboratory.

Validity: Correlation with subscales of the Illinois Course Evaluation Questionnaire ranged from .44 to .58.

Author: Aleamoni, L. M., and Yimer, M.

Article: An investigation of the relationship between colleague rating, student rating, research productivity, and academic rank in rating instructional effectiveness.

Journal: *Journal of Educational Psychology,* June 1973, *64*(3), 274–277.

■ ■ ■

1573

Test Name: WORK PERFORMANCE MEASURE

Purpose: To evaluate work performance.

Number of Items: 9

Format: Supervisor responds to each item on a 9-point scale; item scores are summed to obtain a total performance score.

Reliability: Kuder-Richardson formula 20 for men was .85 and for women was .95.

Author: Gavin, J. F.

Article: Self-esteem as a moderator of the relationship between expectancies and job performance.

Journal: *Journal of Applied Psychology,* August 1973, *58*(1), 83–88.

CHAPTER 23
Vocational Interest

1574

Test Name: ACADEMIC VOCATIONAL INVOLVEMENT SCALE

Purpose: To test vocational choice.

Number of Items: 156

Format: Semantic differential format; items rated on 40 bipolar adjective scales. There were three factors: Valuing, Striving, and Enjoying.

Validity: Differentiates between intellectually oriented and socially oriented categories.

Author: Butzow, J., and Williams, C.

Article: The content and construct validation of the academic–vocational involvement scale.

Journal: *Educational and Psychological Measurement,* Summer 1973, *33*(2), 495–498.

● ● ●

1575

Test Name: BRAYFIELD-ROTHE INDEX

Purpose: To measure overall job satisfaction.

Number of Items: 18

Author: O'Reilly, C. A., and Roberts, K. H.

Article: Job satisfaction among Whites and non-Whites: A cross-cultural approach.

Journal: *Journal of Applied Psychology,* June 1973, *57*(3), 295–299.

Related Research: Brayfield, A., & Rothe, H. (1951). An index of job

satisfaction. *Journal of Applied Psychology, 35,* 307–311.

● ● ●

1576

Test Name: CAREER ORIENTATION SCALE

Purpose: To investigate career orientation.

Number of Items: 7

Format: Each item involves a 5-point scale of disagreement–agreement. Includes two factors: job involvement and job importance.

Author: Wade, M.

Article: Personnel research.

Journal: *Personnel Journal,* November 1973, *52*(11), 999–1000.

Related Research: Gannon, M. J., & Hendrickson, D. H. (1973). Career orientation and job satisfaction among working wives. *Journal of Applied Psychology, 57,* 339–340.

● ● ●

1577

Test Name: EMPLOYMENT SATISFACTION QUESTIONNAIRE

Purpose: To identify job satisfaction of the disadvantaged.

Number of Items: 20

Format: Subject rates each item on a satisfaction scale.

Author: Van Doren, R. (Ed.).

Article: Manpower, human assessment and the disadvantaged.

Journal: *American Vocational Journal,* January 1973, *48*(1), 86–100.

● ● ●

1578

Test Name: GM FACES SCALE

Purpose: To measure overall job satisfaction.

Format: A projective rather than a descriptive technique.

Validity: Correlations with Job Description Index ranged from −.04 to .73.

Author: O'Reilly, C. A., III., and Roberts, K. H.

Article: Job satisfaction among Whites and non-Whites: A cross-cultural approach.

Journal: *Journal of Applied Psychology,* June 1973, *57*(3), 295–299.

Related Research: Kumin, T. (1955). The construction of a new type of attitude measure. *Personnel Psychology, 8,* 65–77.

● ● ●

1579

Test Name: HARREN VOCATIONAL DECISION CHECKLIST

Purpose: To assess vocational decision making.

Author: Smith, R., and Evans, J.

Article: Comparison of experimental group guidance and individual counseling as facilitators of vocational development.

Journal: *Journal of Counseling*

Psychology, May 1973, *20*(3), 202–208.

Related Research: Harren, V. (1964). *A study of the vocational decision making process among college males.* Unpublished doctoral dissertation, University of Texas.

▪ ▪ ▪

1580

Test Name: INVENTORY OF RELIGIOUS ACTIVITIES AND INTERESTS

Purpose: To measure interest in performing activities found in 10 role segments of the occupation of clergyman.

Format: Scores for counselor, administrator, teacher, scholar, evangelist, spiritual guide, preacher, reformer, priest, musician.

Author: Webb, S.

Article: Convergent–discriminant validity of a role oriented interest inventory.

Journal: *Educational and Psychological Measurement,* Summer 1973, *33*(2), 441–451.

▪ ▪ ▪

1581

Test Name: JOB DESCRIPTION INDEX

Purpose: To assess job satisfaction.

Format: Measures satisfaction with work, co-workers, supervision, pay, promotion opportunities.

Validity: Correlation with Leadership Behavior Description Questionnaire scales "Consideration" and "Initiating Structure" was .57 (*p* < .01); correlations with GM Faces Scale ranged from –.04 to .73 (O'Reilly & Roberts, 1973); correlations with Porter Need Satisfaction (Total) ranged from –.36 to –.60 (Wade, 1973).

Author: Distefano, M., and Pryer, M.

Article: Comparisons of leader and subordinate descriptions of leadership behavior.

Journal: *Perceptual and Motor Skills,* December 1973, *37*(3), 714.

Related Research: Imparato, N. (1972). Relationship between Porter's Need Satisfaction Questionnaire and the Job Description Index. *Journal of Applied Psychology, 56,* 397–405.

O'Reilly, C., & Roberts, K. (1973). Job satisfaction among Whites and non-Whites: A cross cultural approach. *Journal of Applied Psychology, 57,* 295–299.

Smith, P., et al. (1969). *The measurement of satisfaction in work and retirement.* Chicago: Rand McNally.

Wade, M. (1973). Personnel research. *Personnel Journal, 52,* 227–229.

▪ ▪ ▪

1582

Test Name: JOB SATISFACTION INDEX

Purpose: To measure job satisfaction.

Number of Items: 5

Format: Includes questions on satisfaction with present teaching job, choice of teaching as an occupation, and likelihood of accepting a job outside of education. Each item has five Likert responses.

Validity: Inter-item correlation coefficients ranged from .18 to .63.

Author: Cohen, E. G.

Article: Open-space schools: The opportunity to become ambitious.

Journal: *Sociology of Education,* Spring 1973, *46*(2), 143–161.

Related Research: Meyer, J., et al. (1971). The impact of the open-space school upon teacher influence and autonomy: The effects of an organizational innovation (Technical Report No. 21). Stanford, CA: Stanford Center for Research and Development in Teaching.

▪ ▪ ▪

1583

Test Name: JOB SATISFACTION MEASURE

Purpose: To measure extrinsic and intrinsic variables in job satisfaction.

Number of Items: 14

Format: Items are rated on a 5-point scale.

Author: Waters, L., et al.

Article: Further correlational analysis of five versions of two factor theory of job satisfaction.

Journal: *Psychological Reports,* June 1973, *32*(3), 1127–1130.

Related Research: Friedlander, F. (1963). Underlying sources of job satisfaction. *Journal of Applied Psychology, 47,* 246–250.

▪ ▪ ▪

1584

Test Name: JOB SATISFACTION QUESTIONNAIRE

Purpose: To measure job satisfaction.

Format: Includes 12 job satisfaction factors as well as overall job satisfaction. Subject rates various aspects of current job using 7-point graphic rating scale.

Author: Hines, G. H.

Article: Cross-cultural differences in two-factor motivation theory.

Journal: *Journal of Applied Psychology,* December 1973, *58*(3), 375–377.

Related Research: Halpern, G. (1966). Relative contributions of motivator and hygiene factors to overall job satisfaction. *Journal of Applied Psychology, 50,* 198–200.

■ ■ ■

1585

Test Name: JOB SATISFACTION QUESTIONNAIRE

Purpose: To measure job satisfaction.

Number of Items: 100

Format: Includes 10 job factors. Subject responds to each item by agreeing, disagreeing, or remaining neutral. Sample items are presented.

Reliability: Split-half reliability was .81.

Author: Spillane, R.

Article: Intrinsic and extrinsic job satisfaction and labour turnover. A questionnaire study of Australian managers.

Journal: *Occupational Psychology,* 1973, *47*(1 & 2), 71–74.

Related Research: Myers, M. S. (1964). Who are your motivated workers? *Harvard Business Review, 42,* 73–88.

Myers, M. S. (1970). *Every employee a manager: More meaningful work through job enrichment.* New York: McGraw-Hill.

■ ■ ■

1586

Test Name: JOB SATISFACTION SCALE

Purpose: To measure job satisfaction.

Number of Items: 10

Format: The first 9 items require response to one of five alternatives ranging from *highly satisfied* to *highly dissatisfied.* Tenth item requires the respondent to indicate

overall job satisfaction on a summary scale.

Reliability: Test–retest reliability coefficient was .94. Split-half reliability coefficients were .90 and .93.

Author: Greene, C. N.

Article: Causal connections among managers' merit pay, job satisfaction, and performance.

Journal: *Journal of Applied Psychology,* August 1973, *58*(1), 95–100.

Related Research: Bullock, R. P. (1952). *Social factors related to job satisfaction.* Columbus: Ohio State University, Bureau of Business Research.

■ ■ ■

1587

Test Name: NEW YORK UNIVERSITY OCCUPATIONAL CHOICE QUESTIONNAIRE

Purpose: To assess self-evaluation in vocational development.

Format: Subjects are asked to identify occupation they would like to hold, those who have influenced them, and so forth.

Author: Pallone, N., et al.

Article: Further data on key influencers of occupational expectation among minority youth.

Journal: *Journal of Counseling Psychology,* September 1973, *5,* 484–486.

Related Research: Pallone, N., et al. (1970). *Project aspiration search: An evaluation.* New York: New York University, Center for Field Research, School of Education.

■ ■ ■

1588

Test Name: PORTER MANAGEMENT POSITION QUESTIONNAIRE—MODIFIED

Purpose: To measure job satisfaction.

Format: Includes six job characteristics.

Author: Prybil, L. D.

Article: Job satisfaction in relation to job performance and occupational level.

Journal: *Personnel Journal,* February 1973, *52*(2), 94–100.

■ ■ ■

1589

Test Name: PORTER NEED SATISFACTION QUESTIONNAIRE

Purpose: To measure job satisfaction.

Format: Includes five need areas: security, social, esteem, autonomy, self-actualization. The respondent rates on a 7-point scale how much of an opportunity there is for prestige, personal growth, and so forth.

Validity: Correlations of total score with subscales of the Job Descriptive Index ranged from −.36 to −.60.

Author: Wade, M.

Article: Personnel research.

Journal: *Personnel Journal,* March 1973, *52*(3), 227–229.

Related Research: Imparato, N. (1972). Relationship between Porter's Need Satisfaction Questionnaire and the Job Descriptive Index. *Journal of Applied Psychology, 56,* 397–405.

■ ■ ■

1590

Test Name: REALISM OF VOCATIONAL PLANS SCALE

Purpose: To assess whether the vocational plans expressed by high school students were realistic.

Format: Questionnaires

administered to assess vocational plans; judges used other background data to assess the realism of the choices on a 1 to 5 scale.

Reliability: Interjudge reliabilities were .76, .78, and .77.

Author: Hanson, J., and Sander, D.

Article: Differential effects of individual and group counseling on realism of vocational choice.

Journal: *Journal of Counseling Psychology*, November 1973, *20*(6), 541–544.

• • •

1591

Test Name: SELF-ESTIMATE QUESTIONNAIRE

Purpose: To index 10 vocational interest measures and 15 work volume measures.

Number of Items: 25

Format: Questionnaire with responses scored on a 5-point scale ranging from *unimportant* to *very important.*

Author: Tierney, R. J., and Herman, A.

Article: Self-estimate ability in adolescence.

Journal: *Journal of Counseling Psychology*, July 1973, *20*(4), 298–302.

Related Research: O'Hara, R. P. Vocational self-concepts and high school achievement. *Vocational Guidance Quarterly*, 1966, *14*, 106–112.

Tierney, R. J. (1971). *Self-estimate ability in relation to interests and work values in adolescence.* Unpublished master's thesis, University of Calgary.

• • •

1592

Test Name: SURVEY OF EMPLOYEE OPINIONS

Purpose: To measure job satisfaction and effort-reward expectancies.

Number of Items: 65

Format: Includes 53 job satisfaction items and 12 work rewards, rated on a 3-point scale.

Author: Wade, M.

Article: Personnel research.

Journal: *Personnel Journal,* March 1973, *52*(3), 223–229.

Related Research: Greenhaus, J. H., & Gavin, J. F. (1972). The relationship between expectancies and job behavior for White and Black employees. *Personnel Psychology, 25,* 449–455.

• • •

1593

Test Name: TEACHING IN URBAN SCHOOLS QUESTIONNAIRE

Purpose: To identify perceptions of the attributes most essential for teachers' success in their school.

Format: Includes the general range of problems related to job satisfaction and dissatisfaction in the urban schools.

Author: Eubanks, E. E.

Article: A study of teachers' perceptions of essential teacher attributes in de facto segregated high schools.

Journal: *Education*, April–May 1973, *93*(4), 373–378.

• • •

1594

Test Name: VOCATIONAL CHOICE SCALE

Purpose: To assess certainty and satisfaction with vocational choice.

Number of Items: 2

Format: Items were rated on 11-point scales ranging from *uncertain* to *certain* and *dissatisfied* to *satisfied.*

Validity: There were significant differences in certainty ratings between counseled and noncounseled groups; no differences were found in satisfaction.

Author: Ullrich, M.

Article: Several measures of expectancy of vocational counseling.

Journal: *Psychological Reports*, August 1973, *33*(1), 299–304.

Related Research: Hoyt, D. P. (1955). An evaluation of group and individual programs in vocational guidance. *Journal of Applied Psychology, 39*, 26–30.

• • •

1595

Test Name: WORKER OPINION SURVEY

Purpose: To measure job satisfaction.

Number of Items: 48

Format: Includes six sub-scales. Each item is answered *yes, no,* or *not sure.* All items are presented.

Reliability: Internal reliability coefficient for subscales calculated by the Kuder-Richardson formula ranged from .71 to .86 for males and females combined.

Validity: Correlations of subscales with a global measure of job satisfaction ranged from .13 to .50 and for the total score with the global measure was .59.

Author: Cross, D.

Article: The worker opinion survey: A measure of shop-floor satisfaction.

Journal: *Occupational Psychology,* 1973, *47*(3 & 4), 193–208.

Author Index

All numbers refer to test numbers for Volume 3. Volumes 1 and 2 did not include an author index.

Cook, W., 1170
Cooker, P., 1512
Corbin, D. W., 1422
Corenblum, B., 1131, 1279
Corroda, J., 1204
Costin, F., 1227
Couch, A., 1286
Cowan, P. A., 1236, 1443
Cowen, J., 1075
Crandall, V., 1303, 1383
Crites, J. O., 1291, 1296
Cross, D., 1595
Cryns, A. G., 1078, 1483, 1517
Cullers, B., 1407, 1408

• • •

Damankos, F., 1091
Dana, R., 1226, 1310
Darby, C. A., 1039
Davis, A. J., 1464
Davis, C., 1498
Davis, F. J., 1094
Davis, R. R., 1156
Davis, R. V., 1065
Dean, D., 1093, 1110
DeJung, J., 1114
Delin, P., 1233
Delys, P., 1434
Dennis, T. L., 1169
Dennis, W., 1154
Dentler, A. R., 1244
Devereux, E. C., 1304
DeVries, D., 1240, 1324
Dies, R. R., 1254
Dietrich, C., 1238
Dilley, J., 1544
Distefano, M., 1581
DiVesta, F. L., 1140
Dlugokinski, E., 1526
Donato, D. J., 1311
Donnelly, J. H., 1271
Doris, J., 1373
Dorkey, M., 1488
Dorr, D., 1181, 1462
Douglass, J., 1248
Dowell, L., 1171
Driscoll, R. H., 1202
Driver, M., 1481
Duke, M., 1413
Duncan, B., 1061
Duncan, O. D., 1470
Duncan, W. J., 1116
Dunlap, R. E., 1152
Dusewicz, R. A., 1050
Dye, H. A., 1440

• • •

Edmonson, B., 1114
Edwards, K., 1240, 1324
Eliot, J., 1061
Emener, W. G., 1249
Emmer, E. T., 1209, 1211, 1217, 1251
Englar, R., 1157
Engle, D. A., 1398
English, C., 1191
Enzie, R., 1187
Erekson, C. F., 1130
Erickson, L., 1494
Etaugh, C., 1134
Eubanks, E. E., 1594
Evanechko, P., 1121
Evans, D., 1501
Evans, F., 1417
Evans, I., 1375
Evans, J., 1510, 1579
Everett, A., 1451
Exner, J., 1484

• • •

Fakouri, M., 1448
Falcione, R. L., 1552, 1556
Farley, F. H., 1338, 1502
Faust, W., 1450
Feffer, M., 1096
Feifel, H., 1081
Feitelson, D., 1208
Feldhusen, J., 1468
Feldstein, S., 1252
Felton, G., 1069
Fiedler, F. E., 1458
Field, P., 1402
Field, T., 1253
Finch, A., 1478, 1493
Finch, C. R., 1182
Finck, D., 1054, 1101
Fink, H., 1158, 1518, 1520
Finkbeiner, C. T., 1546
Finn, J. D., 1078, 1483, 1517
Firestone, I. J., 1526
Fishbach, T., 1175
Fishbein, M., 1126
Fisher, E. H., 1137
Flavell, J. H., 1109, 1236, 1485
Fleishman, E, A., 1241
Flemenbaum, A., 1079
Floyd, H., 1486
Foley, J., 1099, 1385
Foley, T., 1096, 1100
Foster, J., 1401
Fox, W. M., 1458

Franklin, B., 1239, 1415
Franks, D. D., 1528
Frease, D. E., 1474
Freehill, M. F., 1387
French, E., 1530
Fretz, B. R., 1398
Frey, P., 1548
Friedlander, F., 1583
Friedman, S., 1399
Friedman, S. T., 1142
Friend, K., 1075, 1373
Fruth, M. J., 1446
Fulcher, D., 1174
Fuller, F. F., 1217
Funkand, A. K., 1179

• • •

Gable, P., 1170
Gade, E., 1401
Gaines, L., 1417
Galassi, J., 1091, 1092, 1110, 1425
Galassi, M., 1091, 1092, 1110, 1425
Galinsky, M., 1112
Gannon, M. J., 1576
Gardner, R., 1273, 1506
Gaudry, E., 1067
Gavin, J. F., 1427, 1566, 1573, 1592
Geis, F., 1492, 1517
Gelso, C., 1336
Georgiady, N. P., 1326
Getzels, J. W., 1071
Ghiselli, E. E., 1427
Giandomenico, L. L., 1355, 1495
Gibb, J., 1250
Gibson, E., 1391
Gilliland, A., 1099
Glasser, J., 1247
Glucksberg, S., 1480
Golden, L., 1060, 1282
Golden, S., 1290
Goldman, R., 1162
Goldman, R. D., 1072, 1073
Good, K., 1194, 1352, 1362, 1550
Good, L., 1125, 1193, 1194, 1264, 1312, 1352, 1362, 1392, 1550
Good, T. L., 1251
Goodale, J. G., 1531
Gorham, D., 1079
Gorlow, L., 1521
Gough, H. G., 1473
Gould, L. J., 1103
Gourevitch, V., 1096
Gozali, H., 1396

Krauft, C., 1453
Krauss, H. H., 1487
Krauss, R. M., 1480
Kretschmer, J. C., 1055
Kuhn, M., 1439
Kumin, T., 1578

• • •

Lambley, P., 1087
Landy, F. I., 1166
Landy, F. J., 1127
Landy, J. L., 1366
Lange, G., 1464
Larkin, R. W., 1470, 1507
Larsen, S. C., 1421
Lasakow, P., 1258, 1265
Lee, L. C., 1519
Leifer, A., 1476
Lerner, R., 1198
Lesser, G., 1530
Leung, P., 1370
Levenson, H., 1304, 1405, 1406
Levinson, B., 1117
Likert, R., 1333
Lilly, M. S., 1066
Lilly, R., 1379
Lin, T., 1262, 1268
Lindgren, H., 1385
Lindgren, H. C., 1167
Linehan, M., 1192
Linn, M., 1277
Liska, A. E., 1221, 1244, 1245
Litcher, J., 1147, 1150, 1154, 1168, 1183
Lo, M., 1064, 1077
Locke, H., 1299
Lodahl, T., 1322
Loeb, R., 1097
Lohrenz, L., 1273
Lombard, A., 1442
Lorber, N. M., 1104,
Lorr, M., 1489
Louria, D. B., 1210
Lowe, C., 1091
Lubin, B., 1089, 1439
Luz, M., 1478
Lynn, R., 1347

• • •

MacDonald, A., 1505
MacDonald, A. P., 1304
MacDougall, M. A., 1105
Maddi, S. R., 1054
Maini, S., 1243, 1477
Malatesha, R., 1448
Manaster, B., 1399

Mandelson, L. R., 1496
Manosevitz, M., 1397
Margavio, A., 1486
Marjoribanks, K., 1298
Markey, V., 1359
Martin, W., 1089
Martino, E., 1133
Martoccia, C., 1500
Mason, R., 1130, 1529
Massey, S., 1511, 1533
Massey, S. R., 1262
Mastie, M. M., 1040, 1291
McClosky, H., 1518
McDaniel, E., 1384, 1386, 1388, 1390, 1411, 1433, 1435—1437
McKeachie, W. J., 1569
McKenzie, J., 1336
McKinney, J. D., 1060, 1282
McLoughlin, W. P., 1558
McNinch, G., 1423
McPartland, T., 1439
McPherson, D., 1150
McQuary, J., 1069
McWhirter, J., 1262, 1438
Mealiea, W. L., 1338, 1502
Means, D., 1319
Means, G. H., 1473
Mechanic, D., 1239
Medley, D., 1170
Medvene, A., 1296, 1301
Mehrabian, A., 1350
Mensing, P. M., 1471
Merryman, E., 1478
Merwin, J. C., 1140
Meyer, H. S., 1428
Meyer, J., 1582
Mezei, H., 1117
Michielutte, R., 1056, 1128
Mickelson, N. I., 1035
Miller, A., 1358, 1365
Miller, L., 1417
Miller, P. H., 1503
Miller, T. W., 1200
Millman, J., 1064
Miskel, C., 1341
Mohan, M., 1329
Moller, A., 1106
Monge, R. H., 1430
Monroe, J., 1191
Monroe, L. J., 1244
Montgomery, R., 1187
Moos, R. H., 1539
Morgan, D. W., 1205
Morris, G., 1461
Moss, H., 1479
Moy, J., 1333

Mrdjenovich, D., 1328
Mulligan, G., 1129, 1536
Murray, D., 1088
Myers, M. S., 1585
Myrick, R., 1543

• • •

Nakamura, C. Y., 1054, 1101
Naylor, F. D., 1067
Nelson, D., 1392
Nelson, R. C., 1317
Nelson, W., 1493
Neufeld, R., 1086
Neuringer, C., 1119
Newport, M. G., 1116
Newton, M., 1487
Nias, D., 1513
Nichols, R. C., 1292
Niedermeyer, F. C., 1051, 1052
Nielsen, R. P., 1339
Noeth, R. J., 1440
Nowicki, S., 1413
Nowlis, V., 1496
Nudelman, A., 1439

• • •

Ober, R. L., 1261
Obermann, C., 1057, 1561
Odom, R. D., 1422
Ogunyemi, E., 1479
O'Hara, R. P., 1591
O'Reilly, C., 1575, 1578, 1581
Organ, D., 1379
Osgood, C. E., 1180
Ostrom, T. M., 1126
Otto, W., 1494
Overall, J., 1079
Owens, W., 1120, 1444, 1475

• • •

Pace, C. R., 1311
Packwood, V., 1545
Packwood, W. T., 1351
Pallone, N., 1587
Panyard, C., 1265
Pare, R., 1047
Parker, C. A., 1545
Parry-Hill, J. W., 1040
Pasewark, K. R., 1504
Pasternack, T., 1115
Patton, G. M., 1167
Paulson, D. L., 1189
Pawlicki, R., 1505
Payne, D. A., 1120
Payne, R., 1224
Pearson, P. H., 1054

Subject Index

All numbers refer to test numbers. Numbers 1 through 339 refer to entries of Volume 1, numbers 340 through 1034 refer to entries of Volume 2, and numbers 1035 through 1595 refer to entries of Volume 3